PROFESSIONAL
MICROSOFT® SQL SERVER® 2016
REPORTING SERVICES AND MOBIL

INTRODUCTION xxix

▶ **PART I** **GETTING STARTED**
CHAPTER 1 Introducing Reporting Services. 3
CHAPTER 2 What's New in SQL Server 2016 Reporting Services? 23
CHAPTER 3 Reporting Services Installation and Architecture. 39

▶ **PART II** **BASIC REPORT DESIGN**
CHAPTER 4 Report Layout and Formatting 87
CHAPTER 5 Data Access and Query Basics 113
CHAPTER 6 Grouping and Totals 139

▶ **PART III** **ADVANCED AND ANALYTIC REPORTING**
CHAPTER 7 Advanced Report Design. 175
CHAPTER 8 Graphical Report Design 221
CHAPTER 9 Advanced Queries and Parameters 251
CHAPTER 10 Reporting with Analysis Services 277
CHAPTER 11 SSAS Reporting Advanced Techniques. 311
CHAPTER 12 Expressions and Actions 365

▶ **PART IV** **SOLUTION PATTERNS**
CHAPTER 13 Report Projects and Consolidation 397
CHAPTER 14 Report Solutions, Patterns, and Recipes. 429

▶ **PART V** **REPORTING SERVICES CUSTOM PROGRAMMING**
CHAPTER 15 Integrating Reports into Custom Applications. 461
CHAPTER 16 Extending Reporting Services. 521

▶ PART VI   MOBILE REPORT SOLUTIONS

CHAPTER 17   Introducing Reporting Services Mobile Reports 575

CHAPTER 18   Implementing a Mobile Report with
Design-First Development 593

CHAPTER 19   Mobile Report Design Patterns. 623

CHAPTER 20   Advanced Mobile Report Solutions 653

▶ PART VII   ADMINISTERING REPORTING SERVICES

CHAPTER 21   Content Management 679

CHAPTER 22   Server Administration 715

INDEX 753

PROFESSIONAL

Microsoft® SQL Server® 2016 Reporting Services and Mobile Reports

Paul Turley

wrox™

A Wiley Brand

Microsoft® SQL Server® 2016 Reporting Services and Mobile Reports

Published by
John Wiley & Sons, Inc.
10475 Crosspoint Boulevard
Indianapolis, IN 46256
www.wiley.com

Copyright © 2017 by John Wiley & Sons, Inc., Indianapolis, Indiana

Published simultaneously in Canada

ISBN: 978-1-119-25835-3
ISBN: 978-1-119-25838-4 (ebk)
ISBN: 978-1-119-25836-0 (ebk)

Manufactured in the United States of America

10 9 8 7 6 5 4 3 2 1

Limit of Liability/Disclaimer of Warranty: The publisher and the author make no representations or warranties with respect to the accuracy or completeness of the contents of this work and specifically disclaim all warranties, including without limitation warranties of fitness for a particular purpose. No warranty may be created or extended by sales or promotional materials. The advice and strategies contained herein may not be suitable for every situation. This work is sold with the understanding that the publisher is not engaged in rendering legal, accounting, or other professional services. If professional assistance is required, the services of a competent professional person should be sought. Neither the publisher nor the author shall be liable for damages arising herefrom. The fact that an organization or Web site is referred to in this work as a citation and/or a potential source of further information does not mean that the author or the publisher endorses the information the organization or Web site may provide or recommendations it may make. Further, readers should be aware that Internet Web sites listed in this work may have changed or disappeared between when this work was written and when it is read.

For general information on our other products and services please contact our Customer Care Department within the United States at (877) 762-2974, outside the United States at (317) 572-3993 or fax (317) 572-4002.

Wiley publishes in a variety of print and electronic formats and by print-on-demand. Some material included with standard print versions of this book may not be included in e-books or in print-on-demand. If this book refers to media such as a CD or DVD that is not included in the version you purchased, you may download this material at http://booksupport.wiley.com. For more information about Wiley products, visit www.wiley.com.

Library of Congress Control Number: 2016954844

Trademarks: Wiley, the Wiley logo, Wrox, the Wrox logo, Programmer to Programmer, and related trade dress are trademarks or registered trademarks of John Wiley & Sons, Inc. and/or its affiliates, in the United States and other countries, and may not be used without written permission. Microsoft and SQL Server are registered trademarks of Microsoft Corporation. All other trademarks are the property of their respective owners. John Wiley & Sons, Inc., is not associated with any product or vendor mentioned in this book.

This book is dedicated to my wonderful wife, Sherri. You are beautiful in so many ways and I love you. Thank you for managing the household and the business, and helping me preserve a thread of sanity while writing this book. You raised four great kids who are now adults; and one overgrown kid who refuses to grow up. Thank you for your word-smithing skills, managing figure files, and correcting my run-on sentences.

ABOUT THE AUTHOR

PAUL TURLEY is Principal Consultant for Intelligent Business, a Mentor with SolidQ, and a Microsoft Data Platform MVP. He consults, writes, speaks, teaches, and blogs about business intelligence and reporting solutions. He works with many organizations to model data, and visualize and deliver critical information to make informed business decisions using the Microsoft data platform and business analytics tools. He is a Director of the Oregon SQL PASS chapter and user group, and the author and lead author of 15 publications. He holds several certifications including MCSE for the Data Platform and BI. He posts and can be contacted through his blog at `SqlServerBiBlog.com`.

ABOUT THE TECHNICAL EDITOR

NIGEL PETER SAMMY is a Microsoft Data Platform Most Valuable Professional (MVP) with over 15 years of technical experience including 12 years of database and SQL Server experience. He currently works at SoftwareONE as a Senior Data Platform Engineer where his responsibilities include consulting, solution design and implementation, hands-on training, and pre-sales. Besides working at SoftwareONE, he is also a Lecturer at the School of Business and Computer Science (SBCS) where he teaches the Microsoft Certified Solutions Associate (MCSA): SQL Server certification as well as other BSc courses for the University of London and University of Greenwich.

Nigel previously worked at Microsoft as an Account Technology Strategist (ATS) where he was responsible for providing pre-sales technical/architectural support for over 200 agencies in both the commercial and public sectors. As an ATS he delivered technical presentations and proofs of concept using SQL Server, Azure, Power BI, and Office 365. Nigel was also a Data Platform Architect (DPA) at SolidQ, a global provider of advanced consulting, mentoring, and education solutions for the Microsoft Data, Business Intelligence, Collaboration, and Development platforms. Microsoft and SolidQ have given him at least five years' working experience with large international companies.

He has progressed through other roles in his career including Application Developer, Analyst, Database Administrator, Database Developer, Project Manager, Architect, Team Lead, and Manager. In 2010, Nigel co-founded the Trinidad and Tobago SQL Server User Group (TTSSUG), a volunteer, independent, non-profit organization providing a community for Microsoft SQL Server professionals, hobbyists, and enthusiasts. Nigel is a co-author of Microsoft's SQL Server 2012 Upgrade Technical Guide and a technical editor of Wrox's *Professional Microsoft SQL Server 2012 Reporting Services* book. For the last eight years he has been presenting on data platform topics for conferences locally and internationally. When he gets extra time, he blogs at `www.nigelpsammy.com`.

CREDITS

SENIOR ACQUISITIONS EDITOR
Kenyon Brown

PROJECT EDITOR
Tom Dinse

TECHNICAL EDITOR
Nigel Peter Sammy

PRODUCTION EDITOR
Athiyappan Lalith Kumar

COPY EDITOR
Kimberly A. Cofer

**MANAGER OF CONTENT DEVELOPMENT
& ASSEMBLY**
Mary Beth Wakefield

PRODUCTION MANAGER
Kathleen Wisor

MARKETING MANAGER
Carrie Sherrill

**PROFESSIONAL TECHNOLOGY & STRATEGY
DIRECTOR**
Barry Pruett

BUSINESS MANAGER
Amy Knies

EXECUTIVE EDITOR
Jim Minatel

PROJECT COORDINATOR, COVER
Brent Savage

PROOFREADER
Nancy Bell

INDEXER
Nancy Guenther

COVER DESIGNER
Wiley

COVER IMAGE
© afby71/iStockphoto

ACKNOWLEDGMENTS

My endless appreciation and gratitude goes to the co-authors and contributors of the four previous editions of this book series over the past 13 years. As technical reviewer, Nigel Sammy worked tirelessly to test and research the 2016 product as it was readied for release, and to make sure we were current, complete, and accurate. This product continues to be a moving target, and Nigel went far above and beyond any reasonable expectation.

I appreciate my 2012 edition co-authors who helped refresh and update material for the new product version. Thanks go to Grant Paisley, Thiago Silva, and Robert Bruckner for your revisions and direction. Tom Dinse, thank you for your patience and persistence through this hardscrabble effort. Riccardo Muti and Chris Finlan from the product team, thanks for sewing the monster together and once again giving him life. Seriously, thanks for the direct product team access and on-going support for this set of marvelous tools.

CONTENTS

INTRODUCTION   *xxix*

PART I: GETTING STARTED

CHAPTER 1: INTRODUCING REPORTING SERVICES   3

Who Uses Reporting Services?   4
    Information Workers and Data Analysts   5
    Information Consumers   6
    Business Managers and Leaders   6
    Software Developers   6
    System Administrators   7
Dashboards, Reports, and Applications   7
    Application Integration   7
    Business Intelligence and Analytics Solutions   10
    Mobile Reports and KPIs   11
Report Tool Choices   14
    Simple Report Design   15
    IT-Designed Reports   16
    User-Designed Reports   16
    Server-Based Reports   17
    Report Data Sources   18
    Enterprise Scale   19
Optimizing Performance   19
    Performance   20
Summary   20

CHAPTER 2: WHAT'S NEW IN SQL SERVER 2016 REPORTING SERVICES?   23

Report Builder and Designer Enhancements   25
Modern Browser Rendering   26
Parameter Layout Control   26
Updated RDL Specification   27
Mobile Reports   28
KPIs   30
Native Printing Control   31

PowerPoint Rendering 31
Integrated and Improved Web Portal 31
New Charts and Visual Enhancements 32
Standardized, Modern Browser Rendering 33
Power BI Dashboard Pinning 33
Summary 36

**CHAPTER 3: REPORTING SERVICES INSTALLATION
AND ARCHITECTURE** 39

What's Changed in SQL Server 2016? 41
The Basic Installation 41
Installing Reporting Services 42
Installing the Reporting Services Samples, Exercises,
and SQL Server Databases 56
The Enterprise Deployment 57
SQL Server Editions 58
Default and Named Instances 58
Topology 60
Modes 61
Installation Options 61
The Reporting Life Cycle 63
Authoring 63
Management 63
Delivery 64
Reporting Services Tools 64
Report Builder 64
Web Portal 64
SharePoint Libraries and Web Parts 64
Reporting Services Configuration Manager 65
SQL Server Management Applications 65
Command-Line Utilities 65
HTML Viewer 66
Report Viewer Control 66
Reporting Services Web Service 67
Reporting Services Windows Service 68
HTTP.SYS and the HTTP Listener 69
The Security Sublayer 69
Web Portal and the Web Service 70
Core Processing 71
Service Management 71
WMI and the RPC Interface 72

Reporting Services Processors and Extensions	73
The Report Processor	74
Data Processing Extensions	75
Report Items	76
Rendering Extensions	77
The Scheduling and Delivery Processor	80
Delivery Extensions	80
Reporting Services Application Databases	80
ReportServer	80
ReportServerTempDB	82
Summary	82

PART II: BASIC REPORT DESIGN

CHAPTER 4: REPORT LAYOUT AND FORMATTING   **87**

Using Report Design Tools	88
Understanding Report Data Building Blocks	89
Data Sources	89
Datasets	90
Data Regions	90
Report Items	93
Samples and Exercises	93
Preparing the Report Data	96
Designing the Report Layout	100
Reviewing the Report	104
Setting Formatting Properties	105
Validating Report Design and Grouping Data	108
Summary	112

CHAPTER 5: DATA ACCESS AND QUERY BASICS   **113**

Database Essentials	114
Relational Database Concepts	114
What's a Sequel?	114
Data Source Management	115
Embedded and Shared Data Sources	115
Datasets and Fields	119
Embedded and Shared Datasets	120
Exercises	120
Authoring a Query with SQL Server Management Studio	120
Add the Query to the Report Dataset	124

Design the Report Body 128
Enhance the Parameter 131
Using Multiple Parameter Values 134
Summary 138

CHAPTER 6: GROUPING AND TOTALS 139

SQL Server Data Tools 140
Getting Started 140
Getting Started with Sample Reports Projects 144
Report Groups 150
Adding Totals to a Table or Matrix Report 153
Expression Basics 154
Introducing Aggregate Functions and Totals 155
Sorting 155
Exercise 158
Design the Dataset Query 158
Design and Lay Out a Table Report 160
Add Summary Totals and Drill-Down 163
Aggregate Detail Row Summaries 167
Create Parameter List 168
Summary 171

PART III: ADVANCED AND ANALYTIC REPORTING

CHAPTER 7: ADVANCED REPORT DESIGN 175

Pagination and Flow Control 176
Headers and Footers 178
Tablix Headers and Detail Cells 182
Designing the Page Headers 182
Composite Reports and Embedded Content 187
Unlocking the Textbox 187
Padding and Indenting 188
Embedded Formatting 189
Designing Master/Detail Reports 195
Repeating Data Regions: Table, Matrix, and List 196
Groups and Dataset Scope 200
More Aggregate Functions and Totals 200
Designing Subreports 203
Federating Data with a Subreport 205

Navigating Reports 208
Creating a Document Map 209
Exercises 210
Exercise 1: Create a Report Template 210
Exercise 2: Create a Report from the Template
with Dynamic Expressions 215
Summary 219

CHAPTER 8: GRAPHICAL REPORT DESIGN 221

Visual Design Principles 222
Keep Charts Simple 222
Properties, Oh My! 223
The Fashion of Visualization 223
Visual Storytelling 224
Perspective and Skewing 224
Chart Types 225
Chart Type Summary 225
Column and Stacked Charts 228
Area and Line Charts 229
Pie and Doughnut Charts 229
Bubble and Stock Charts 233
New Chart Types 233
The Anatomy of a Chart 235
Multiple Series, Axes, and Areas 237
Exercises 240
Exercise 1: Creating and Styling a Simple Chart 240
Exercise 2: Creating a Multi-series Chart 245
Useful Properties and Settings 248
Summary 249

CHAPTER 9: ADVANCED QUERIES AND PARAMETERS 251

T-SQL Queries and Parameters 252
Parameter Lists and Multi-select 252
Cascading Parameters 257
Arranging Parameters in the Parameter Bar 259
Managing Long Parameter Lists 259
All Value Selection 261
Handling Conditional Logic 264
MDX Queries and Parameters 266
Single-Valued Parameter 270

Multi-Valued Parameter 270
Date Value Ranges 271
Summary 275

CHAPTER 10: REPORTING WITH ANALYSIS SERVICES 277

Analysis Services for Reporting 278
Using Reporting Services with Analysis Services Data 279
Working with Multidimensional Expression Language 280
MDX: Simple or Complex? 280
Building Queries with the MDX Query Designer 281
Modifying an MDX Query 293
Adding Nonadditive Measures 302
When to Use the Aggregate Function 304
MDX Properties and Cube Formatting 305
Drill-Through Reports 307
Parameter Safety Precautions 308
Best Practices and Provisions 308
Summary 309

CHAPTER 11: SSAS REPORTING ADVANCED TECHNIQUES 311

Building a Dynamic Cube Browser with SSRS 312
Cube Dynamic Rows 312
Cube Dynamic Rows Anatomy 313
Cube Dynamic Rows Summary 322
Cube Dynamic Rows Expanded 324
MDX Query Modifications 324
Design Surface Modifications 325
Cube Restricting Rows 326
Designing the Report 326
Cube Metadata 332
Designing the Report 332
Adding Other Cube Metadata 336
Cube Browser 342
Anatomy of the Reports 342
Behind the Scenes 346
Final Thoughts 362
Summary 364

CHAPTER 12: EXPRESSIONS AND ACTIONS 365

Basic Expressions Recap 365
Using the Expression Builder 367

Calculated Fields 369
Conditional Expressions 371
The IIF() Function 372
Using Custom Code 375
    Using Custom Code in a Report 376
    Links and Drill-Through Reports 378
Reporting on Recursive Relationships 381
Actions and Report Navigation 385
Summary 392

PART IV: SOLUTION PATTERNS

CHAPTER 13: REPORT PROJECTS AND CONSOLIDATION 397

SSDT Solutions and Projects 398
    Project Structure and Development Phases 399
    Shared Datasets and Data Sources 401
    Key Success Factors 402
    Report Specifications 403
    Report Template 406
Version Control 407
    Setting Up Version Control 408
    Getting the Latest Version 408
    Viewing a Report's History 409
    Restoring a Previous Version of a Report 409
    Setting Check-out and Check-in Policies 409
    Applying Labels 409
Synchronizing Content 409
    Deploying an Individual Report 410
    Deploying a Suite of Reports 410
    Checking for Build Errors 410
    Excluding a Report from a Deployment 410
Managing Server Content 410
    Checking the Deployment Location 411
    Managing Content in Native Mode 412
    Managing Content in SharePoint 413
Report Builder and Self-Service Reporting Strategies 414
Report Builder and Semantic Model History 415
Planning a Self-Service Reporting Environment 416
    You Need a Plan 416
    Design Approaches and Usage Scenarios 416
    Define Ownership 417
    Data Governance 418

Data Source Access and Security	419
User Education	419
Data Source and Query Options	421
User Report Migration Strategies	**425**
Review	425
Consolidate	426
Design	426
Test	426
Maintain	426
Summary	**427**

CHAPTER 14: REPORT SOLUTIONS, PATTERNS, AND RECIPES	**429**
Super Reports	**430**
Working with the Strengths and Limitations of the Reporting Services Architecture	431
Seeking the Excel Export Holy Grail	431
Report Recipes: Building on Basic Skills	**435**
Dashboard Solution Data Sources and Datasets	436
KPI Scorecard	437
Gauges	441
Interactive Sparkline and Chart	443
Thumbnail Map with Drill-Through Navigation	450
Summary	**456**

PART V: REPORTING SERVICES CUSTOM PROGRAMMING

CHAPTER 15: INTEGRATING REPORTS INTO CUSTOM APPLICATIONS	**461**
URL Access	**462**
URL Syntax	463
Accessing Reporting Services Objects	463
Reporting Services URL Parameters	469
Passing Report Information Through the URL	474
Programmatic Rendering	**477**
Common Scenarios	478
Rendering Through Windows	479
Rendering to the Web	502
Using the ReportViewer Control	**509**
Embedding a Server-Side Report in a Windows Application	512
Summary	**519**

CHAPTER 16: EXTENDING REPORTING SERVICES — 521

Extension Through Interfaces — 524
  What Is an Interface? — 524
  Interface Language Differences — 524
  A Detailed Look at Data Processing Extensions — 527
Creating a Custom Data Processing Extension — 529
  The Scenario — 530
  Creating and Setting Up the Project — 530
  Creating the DataSetConnection Object — 533
  Creating the DataSetParameter Class — 542
  Implementing IDataParameter — 543
  Creating the DataSetParameterCollection Class — 545
  Creating the DataSetCommand Class — 547
  Creating the DataSetDataReader Object — 562
  Installing the DataSetDataProcessing Extension — 566
  Testing DataSetDataExtension — 569
Summary — 572

PART VI: MOBILE REPORT SOLUTIONS

CHAPTER 17: INTRODUCING REPORTING SERVICES MOBILE REPORTS — 575

The Mobile Report Experience and Business Case — 576
  Report Drill-Through Navigation — 579
  When to Use Mobile Reports — 579
Connection and Dataset Design Basics — 581
Introducing Mobile Report Publisher — 581
  Layout View — 582
  Data View — 582
  Dashboard Settings — 583
  Preview — 583
Visual Control Categories — 584
  Navigators — 585
Summary — 592

CHAPTER 18: IMPLEMENTING A MOBILE REPORT WITH DESIGN-FIRST DEVELOPMENT — 593

Design-First Mobile Report Development Exercise — 593
  Add Visual Controls — 598
  Preview the Mobile Report — 601

Add Data to the Report 602
Apply Mobile Layouts and Color Styling 613
Test the Completed Mobile Report from the Server 616
Summary 620

CHAPTER 19: MOBILE REPORT DESIGN PATTERNS 623

Key Performance Indicators 623
The Thing About KPIs 630
You Need Goals 630
Time-Series Calculations and Time Grain 631
Creating a Time-Series Mobile Report 632
Lay Out the Report Using Design-First Report Development 633
Add Data and Set Control Data Properties 635
Set Color Palette and Mobile Device Layouts 642
Server Access and Live Mobile Connectivity 647
Summary 650

CHAPTER 20: ADVANCED MOBILE REPORT SOLUTIONS 653

Designing a Chart Data Grid Mobile Report 653
Exercise: Chart Data Grid 654
Exercise: Adding a Drill-Through Mobile Report 662
Exercise: Adding a Drill-Through Paginated Report 666
Getting Serious with Maps 671
Summary 676

PART VII: ADMINISTERING REPORTING SERVICES

CHAPTER 21: CONTENT MANAGEMENT 679

Using Web Portal 680
Content Management Activities 683
Folders 684
Shared Data Sources 685
Reports 688
Report Resources 694
Shared Schedules 695
Site and Content Security 696
Site Security 697
Item-Level Security 697
Site Branding 707

Content Management Automation	**710**
The RS Utility	710
Reporting Services Scripts	713
Summary	**714**

CHAPTER 22: SERVER ADMINISTRATION | **715**

Security	716
Account Management	717
System-Level Roles	721
Surface Area Management	723
Backup and Recovery	724
Application Databases	725
Encryption Keys	727
Configuration Files	730
Other Items	730
Monitoring	731
Setup Logs	731
Windows Application Event Logs	731
Trace Logs	732
Execution Logs	735
Performance Counters	736
Server Management Reports	741
Configuration	742
Memory Management	742
URL Reservations	743
E-mail Delivery	745
Rendering Extensions	747
My Reports	749
Summary	751

INDEX | *753*

FOREWORD

Riccardo Muti
Group Program Manager, SQL Server Reporting Services
Microsoft

On a mild Seattle day in 2010, I headed to the Microsoft campus to start my new job working on the SQL Server Reporting Services product. Once there, I learned that my computer would take a few more days to arrive. What was I supposed to do for a few days without a computer? My manager handed me a book and said, "Read this." That book was *Microsoft SQL Server Reporting Services Recipes for Designing Expert Reports* by Paul Turley and Robert Bruckner. For those few days, I could do nothing but get to know my teammates and pore over that book. By the time my laptop arrived, I was primed to put everything I'd studied into practice. It's no exaggeration, then, to say that I've been learning Reporting Services from Paul's books since my first day on the Reporting Services team at Microsoft.

Long after I'd received my laptop, I kept that book on my desk, referring to it often as I worked to deepen my report design expertise. Whether I was trying to figure out the best way to design a multi-lingual report or to pass a multi-value parameter into a stored procedure, one of the many recipes in that book held the answer. Many people have turned investments in learning Reporting Services into rewarding careers, in no small part with the help of Paul's many books on the topic, which expertly guide readers on a journey from foundational knowledge to the most advanced techniques. *Professional Microsoft SQL Server 2016 Reporting Services and Mobile Reports* carries on that tradition. A must-read for novices and experts alike, it covers everything from setting up a report server to designing sophisticated reports to crafting enterprise solutions to optimizing for today's mobile devices.

Last year, after a few years working on other parts of Microsoft's Business Intelligence offering, I had the opportunity to rejoin the Reporting Services team and revitalize the product that hadn't been updated in a few years. A year of a team's hard work later, SQL Server 2016 Reporting Services, the product of an ambitious overhaul, offers a modern enterprise reporting platform, including a nifty mobile dashboard solution. What has powered the widespread adoption of Reporting Services goes beyond the product itself to the community that has flourished around it, thanks in large part to leaders such as Paul. In reading this book, you're participating in that community and learning from a master. If you'd asked me where to start learning Reporting Services, I would've handed you none other than this book. Enjoy!

FOREWORD

Christopher Finlan
Senior Program Manager
SQL Server Reporting Services

"So, is Reporting Services dead?"

That question, and my non-answer, was usually the extent of my conversations with my Microsoft customers when it came to SQL Server Reporting Services. You see, prior to joining the product team, I was part of the pre-sales team at Microsoft. My entire job was to get customers excited about the latest tools and products we had in the Microsoft Business Intelligence Suite. This meant we were generally avoiding the topic of SQL Server Reporting Services, which looked dated and hadn't seen much added to it in the last few years. Instead, I was either talking about Power BI or about a little-known Microsoft partner called Datazen, which had these amazing mobile dashboards that looked beautiful on every device you consumed them on.

Fast forward to today, and much has changed in these last 12–18 months. Nowadays, customers can't get enough information about what's new in SQL Server Reporting Services. In fact, it's often the first thing customers want to talk about when it comes to Microsoft Business Intelligence. The SQL Server 2016 release saw the product transformed, bringing a modern look and feel along with all the mobile capabilities previously available in the standalone Datazen product. Combine this with the planned improvements already communicated on the Microsoft BI roadmap, and it's an incredibly exciting time to be a part of the Reporting Services product group. Just seeing our customer's excitement at what's been delivered and what's still to come is incredibly gratifying to all of us.

But this same excitement also brings with it an entirely new set of challenges—many of you reading this book may never have touched Reporting Services before for the reasons mentioned earlier. Now that you've seen what you have available as part of your SQL Server investment, you're looking to unlock it and don't know where to start. Or perhaps you've used SSRS in the past, but want to dive into creating mobile reports and KPIs for the first time. Regardless of why you are here now, be glad you are. There are few people better equipped to navigate you through what you can accomplish with Reporting Services than the author of this book, Paul Turley.

For over a decade, Paul's books on SQL Server Reporting Services have become "the SSRS bible" for thousands of SQL Server report developers every day. His writing style makes it easy for anyone to understand the wide-ranging topics he covers, from report design to server administration. There's even a copy of one of his books in our team room. I know this because I've picked it up and used it on more than one occasion. And I'm looking forward to adding this version to our collection, as you all have already.

Thanks to Paul and all of you for being a part of the Reporting Services community, and enjoy the book!

INTRODUCTION

FOURTEEN YEARS! I had to say that out loud just to make sure it was right... yes; fourteen years. That is how long it has been since I began using Reporting Services to create reports and reporting solutions.

Consulting clients, conference attendees, and students often ask which of all the BI or reporting tools they should use for their business reporting needs. I have used several other Microsoft products including SQL Server, Analysis Services, Integration Services, SharePoint, Access, Excel, and Power BI, but Reporting Services is the tool I keep coming back to because it does so much.

My peers and I have been tracking this product through every version since it was released in 2003; since that time, we have produced six Wrox Press books on Reporting Services. I have worked closely with the Microsoft product team leadership, and the product developers who continue to innovate and move it forward. I have learned to use SSRS correctly, and, on occasion, incorrectly; benefiting from some tough lessons about what it can and can't do along the way. My goal is to share this experience with you, in addition to the best practices we have developed over the years.

WHO THIS BOOK IS FOR

This book is written to meet the needs of a broad audience, and includes specific solutions for report designers, developers, administrators, and business professionals. My goal for this book is to be a comprehensive guide and valuable reference. It is written for the novice report designer as well as the expert interested in learning to use advanced functionality.

WHAT THIS BOOK COVERS

This book is divided into seven parts.

Part I: Getting Started

This part covers what Reporting Services is and how it is used. The three chapters in this part of the book will help you understand the capabilities of Reporting Services and the reporting platform. You will get to know the server platform and the report design tools used to create KPIs, paginated reports, and mobile reports. You will learn what's new in SQL Server 2016 Reporting Services.

Chapter 1 covers Reporting Services use cases, using and creating dashboards, creating reports, and building integrated applications. We discuss how to choose the right reporting tool based on the business need, as well as optimizing report performance.

Chapter 2 is all about what is new in SSRS 2016. You learn about report designer enhancements, modern browser rendering, and parameter layout management. We introduce mobile reports and KPIs, new printing and rendering options, the new report web portal, and Power BI dashboard pinning and integration.

In **Chapter 3** you learn about how to install Reporting Services and understand the server architecture. We discuss what has changed in the SQL Server 2016 architecture, and how to install and set up a report server. You will understand how to build an enterprise report server deployment, and how to use tools to manage the reporting lifecycle and leverage Reporting Services extensions.

Part II: Basic Report Design

These chapters include hands-on exercises that step through the process of building reports, queries, and the solutions that are discussed in each chapter. Finished copies of all the reports and exercises are provided for your reference. These chapters lead you through the building blocks that are fundamental to all report designs. You learn the mechanics behind data regions, groups, report items, page breaks, tables, matrices, and charts.

Chapter 4 covers report layout and formatting. You learn to use datasets, data regions, and other report data building blocks. You'll design report layouts using tables and matrices, and set grouping and formatting properties using expressions.

Chapter 5 teaches database query essentials. You learn to understand relational database principles and concepts and data source management, and you build simple and complex datasets using the query design tools. We will perform query authoring using the Report Builder query designer, SSDT report designer, and SQL Server Management Studio. You will become proficient using single- and multi-select parameters in queries.

Chapter 6 introduces SQL Server Data Tools for Visual Studio. You build more advanced reports in your chapter exercises using the graphical query designer and hand-written queries with parameters and complex query logic. You will understand query groups in table joins and the report dataflow, and understand report groups and expressions used for complex grouping, sorting, and visibility.

Part III: Advanced and Analytic Reporting

These chapters deal with advanced and more complex reporting scenarios. You build on your grouping and expression skills, incorporating more advanced queries with parameters, expressions, and programming logic.

Chapter 7 is about advanced report design. You will manage pagination and report page headers and footers. You will use conditional logic for text formatting and layout properties, embedded HTML text and styling, master/detail reports, subreports, and document maps.

In **Chapter 8**, you learn about graphical report design principles and standards. We review both standard and advanced chart types and design approaches, and we dive deep into more complex charting features, creating multi-series and multiple area charts. Also, you learn to use KPI indicators, sparklines, and data bars.

Chapter 9 is all about advanced queries and parameters. You learn more about T-SQL queries and parameters, and MDX queries and parameters.

In **Chapter 10** you use SQL Server Analysis Services as a data source for reports working with Multidimensional Expressions (MDX). You learn to build queries with the MDX query designer and learn to handwrite MDX with parameters.

Chapter 11 is a complex example of a reporting solution that leverages the power of the MDX language and Analysis Services. In this cube browser solution, we use reports to enumerate and prompt the user for parameter selections and then dynamically navigate an entire cube structure. This example showcases some very useful, complex report navigation and design techniques.

In **Chapter 12** you learn about interactions and report navigation. We revisit the expressions used to implement conditional logic. You learn to use common functions such as IIF and SWITCH in decision-based expressions and custom code, and you learn reporting techniques using recursive relationships and actions to navigate between reports.

Part IV: Solution Patterns

If you use Visual Studio with integrated version control and work with teams to build solutions, this part of the book is for you. You learn to manage report projects alongside other report and solution developers using formal project methodologies.

Chapter 13 is about report projects and report consolidation. You learn to apply SSDT solution patterns, understand how to work with report specifications and requirements, and work within project development phases. You will create report templates and manage reports within projects and solutions. You will also learn to plan self-service reporting solutions and how to support non-technical report designers who use Report Builder to create their own reports within a managed environment.

In **Chapter 14** you learn about report solutions, patterns, and recipes. You will combine multiple report components into super reports and business dashboards. You will design a KPI scorecard, an interactive sparkline report with a drill-through chart, and a map report with drill-through navigation.

Part 5: Reporting Services Custom Programming

In this part, you learn how to integrate Reporting Services into custom applications and to use reports outside of the web portal environment using URL access and web service calls.

Chapter 15 is about integrating reports into custom applications. You'll use URL access and web services to render reports, build a custom Windows form or web form application to enter parameters, and render reports in your own custom interface. You will see how to create a custom-made input interface for Reporting Services reports.

In **Chapter 16** you learn to extend Reporting Services and leverage extensibility options. We begin by discussing the reasons for extending SQL Server Reporting Services and creating custom extensions. Often, these options are complex and specific to the business needs outside of standard reporting scenarios. You will learn how each type of Reporting Services extension can be used to provide custom rendering, security, data access, and delivery of reports.

Part VI: Mobile Report Solutions

This section of the book introduces new mobile reporting capabilities introduced in SQL Server 2016. You learn to use Mobile Report Publisher and the new mobile reporting platform to deliver reports specifically designed for tablets, smart phones, and other mobile devices. We start with basic mobile report design approaches and techniques. You will learn to use each of the visual controls, navigators and selectors, report navigation, and styling options.

Chapter 17 introduces Reporting Services Mobile Reports. You'll learn to use the Mobile Report Publisher to consume shared datasets and deliver interactive information for a mobile device. You'll also learn the basic building blocks and how the components within each of the visual control categories are used for navigation and visualization.

In **Chapter 18** you implement a mobile report using design-first development. Using the designer to add visual controls to your mobile report, simulated data is automatically generated to demonstrate visual control interactivity and report navigation. You will learn techniques for fast prototyping and effective user requirement gathering sessions. You will learn to use Time navigators, selectors, number gauges, and charts. You will apply layouts for different device types and color styling, and then deploy and test a complete mobile report.

Chapter 19 introduces mobile report design patterns for advanced reporting scenarios. You will use controls to create mobile reports for time-series, segmentation, performance, and geographic visualization and interaction. You will configure server access and publish reports that may be used from the web and on different mobile devices.

Chapter 20 covers Advanced Mobile Report solutions. We introduce the chart data grid visual control, and learn to correlate multiple datasets in the control. You learn to use dataset and query parameters in mobile reports, drill-through to a mobile report with dataset parameters, and drill-through to a paginated report with dataset parameters. Additionally, you learn to use map visuals, add custom maps, and manage map shapes for geographic reporting.

Part VII: Administering Reporting Services

These chapters will help you manage content and perform server administration, configuration, troubleshooting, and maintenance.

Chapter 21 is all about report server content management. You learn to use the web portal as an administration tool where you will perform content management activities, which include security administration, as well as data source, shared dataset, and report optimization. You learn to manage and enforce security access to folders and reports for groups and individual users.

In **Chapter 22** you learn about account management and system-level rules, implement surface area management, plan for backup in disaster recovery, manage application databases, manage encryption keys, and learn to use configuration files. You learn to perform auditing and logging of the report server; and use performance counters and server management reports. You also learn proper memory and resource management for your report servers, and configure URL reservations, administer e-mail delivery, and manage custom extensions on servers.

WHAT YOU NEED TO USE THIS BOOK

The hardware and software requirements for designing and running SQL Server 2016 and Reporting Services are such that they will run on newest business grade computers. Custom programming examples require that you install any edition of Visual Studio 2015 or newer. The requirements for SQL Server 2016 specified by Microsoft may be found online in the MSDN library located at: http://msdn.microsoft.com/en-us/library/ms143506.aspx.

➤ The Developer Edition of SQL Server 2016 is available for free with a Visual Studio Dev Essentials account, available at: www.visualstudio.com/dev-essentials. You can also download SQL Server 2016 Developer or Enterprise Edition, and Visual Studio if you have an MSDN subscription.

➤ Report design examples that use paginated Reporting Services reports will work with any edition of SQL Server 2016 and will run on a computer meeting the minimum computer requirements. Mobile Reports and KPIs require SQL Server 2016 Developer or Enterprise Edition.

➤ Chapters 9, 10, and 11 require an installation of SQL Server Analysis Services in multidimensional storage mode. This is an optional part of the SQL Server setup.

➤ Examples of custom programming performed outside of the report designer will require a separate installation of Visual Studio 2015 or later. This includes the material in Chapters 15 and 16.

➤ The sample databases used in the examples and exercises are available to download from www.wrox.com along with the sample projects for this book. Additional resources may be available.

➤ The complete source code for the samples is available for download from this book's web site at www.wrox.com. For programming examples, versions are available in both Visual Basic .NET and C#.

CONVENTIONS

To help you get the most from the text and keep track of what's happening, we've used a number of conventions throughout the book.

> **WARNING** *Boxes like this one hold important, not-to-be-forgotten information that is directly relevant to the surrounding text.*

> **NOTE** *Notes, tips, hints, tricks, and asides to the current discussion are offset and placed in italics like this.*

As for styles in the text:

- ➤ We *italicize* new terms and important words when we introduce them.
- ➤ We show keyboard strokes like this: Ctrl+A.
- ➤ We show file names, URLs, and code within the text like so: `persistence.properties`.

For code:

```
We use a monofont type for code examples.
We use bold to emphasize code that is of particular importance in
the current context.
```

SAMPLE REPORTS AND PROJECTS

Sample reports, Visual Studio projects, and completed copies of all the report files produced by following the chapter exercises are provided in the files that accompany the book. All of the samples and completed exercise files are available for download at `www.wrox.com`. Once at the site, search for this book's ISBN (978-1-119-25835-3), then simply click the Download Code link on the book's detail page to obtain all the sample files for the book.

Once you download the file archive, just extract it with Windows File Manager or your favorite compression tool.

> **NOTE** *You can go to the main Wrox code download page at* `http://www.wrox.com/dynamic/books/download.aspx` *to see the code available for all Wrox books.*

ERRATA

We make every effort to ensure that there are no errors in the text or in the code. However, no one is perfect, and mistakes do occur. If you find an error in one of our books, such as a spelling mistake or a faulty piece of code, we would be very grateful for your feedback. By sending in errata, you may save another reader hours of frustration and at the same time you will be helping us provide even higher quality information.

To find the errata page for this book, go to `http://www.wrox.com` and locate the title using the Search box or one of the title lists. Then, on the book details page, click the Book Errata link. On this page you can view all errata that have been submitted for this book and posted by Wrox editors. A complete book list including links to each book's errata is also available at `www.wrox.com/misc-pages/booklist.shtml`.

If you don't spot "your" error on the Book Errata page, go to `www.wrox.com/contact/techsupport.shtml` and complete the form there to send us the error you have found. We'll check the information and, if appropriate, post a message to the book's errata page and fix the problem in subsequent editions of the book.

P2P.WROX.COM

For author and peer discussion, join the P2P forums at p2p.wrox.com. The forums are a web-based system for you to post messages relating to Wrox books and related technologies and interact with other readers and technology users. The forums offer a subscription feature to e-mail you topics of interest of your choosing when new posts are made to the forums. Wrox authors, editors, other industry experts, and your fellow readers are present on these forums.

At http://p2p.wrox.com you will find a number of different forums that will help you not only as you read this book, but also as you develop your own applications. To join the forums, just follow these steps:

1. Go to p2p.wrox.com and click the Register link.

2. Read the terms of use and click Agree.

3. Complete the required information to join as well as any optional information you wish to provide and click Submit.

4. You will receive an e-mail with information describing how to verify your account and complete the joining process.

> **NOTE** *You can read messages in the forums without joining P2P but in order to post your own messages, you must join.*

Once you join, you can post new messages and respond to messages other users post. You can read messages at any time on the web. If you would like to have new messages from a particular forum e-mailed to you, click the Subscribe to This Forum icon by the forum name in the forum listing.

For more information about how to use the Wrox P2P, be sure to read the P2P FAQs for answers to questions about how the forum software works as well as many common questions specific to P2P and Wrox books. To read the FAQs, click the FAQ link on any P2P page.

PART I
Getting Started

What exactly is SQL Server Reporting Services? How is it used and what are its capabilities and boundaries? Is it a product, a part of SQL Server, or a development platform? The three chapters in Part 1 will get you started with understanding the capabilities of Reporting Services at a high level. You will become acquainted with the entire SSRS platform, the components it encompasses, and their capabilities.

You'll learn about the new features introduced in SQL Server 2016: the new web portal, key performance indicators, and mobile reports. Chapter 2 introduces several key integrations with the Microsoft business analytics platform and advanced visualizations. You'll also see how to install and configure Reporting Services tools and the server so you can get up and running.

▶ **CHAPTER 1:** Introducing Reporting Services

▶ **CHAPTER 2:** What's New in SQL Server 2016 Reporting Services

▶ **CHAPTER 3:** Reporting Services Installation and Architecture

1

Introducing Reporting Services

WHAT'S IN THIS CHAPTER?

➤ Identifying who uses Reporting Services

➤ Using dashboards, reports, and applications

➤ Understanding application integration

➤ Using Business Intelligence (BI) reporting

➤ Using mobile reports and KPIs

➤ Choosing a report tool

➤ Optimizing report performance

Welcome to SQL Server 2016 Reporting Services. This chapter provides an overview that includes a high-level introduction featuring not only concepts and capabilities of this powerful reporting tool, but also of the Microsoft data analysis platform. Reporting Services embodies a rich history as a rock-solid reporting tool. Although many features have been part of the product for more than 12 years, some features are new, have changed, or were introduced in later versions.

This is the fifth edition of this book. Reporting Services was officially released in early 2004. Since that time, I gained assistance from trusted and experienced colleagues who contributed to previous book editions, and this edition draws upon that foundation of expertise. In areas where the product has matured and evolved forward, I share advanced capabilities and patterns for solving new business problems. The book includes material and techniques using the new or existing features more effectively.

As a Microsoft Data Platform MVP, a specialist, and a respected contractor for Microsoft, I spend considerable time working with different organizations to design reporting solutions. For many years, I frequently have had the opportunity to work alongside the Reporting Services product team. Through leadership changes, product development cycles, and industry trends, the development team has maintained a relevant and durable reporting product that focuses on the needs of the modern business. As you continue to read, you will learn to appreciate the depth of this product.

In 2003, a few months before the product was released, I started using pre-release versions of Reporting Services. At the time, I was doing web development and database work, and found Reporting Services to be a perfect fit for the reports I needed to add to a web application. Since then, SQL Server Reporting Services (SSRS) has grown to become the de facto industry standard reporting tool. SSRS provides a foundation upon which you can construct complete report, scorecard, dashboard, and mobile solutions for business users. Today, it does everything from simple ad hoc data reporting to delivering enterprise-ready, integrated reporting into business portals and custom applications. In 2016, the product expanded beyond classic "paginated reports" to add mobile reporting, key performance indicators (KPIs), and integration with cloud-based and on-premises dashboard and self-service analytic tools.

The information technology (IT) group for a large financial services company wanted to make sure that they were using the best reporting tool on the market. My team was assigned to evaluate every major reporting product and give them an unbiased analysis. We worked with the client to identify about 50 points of evaluation criteria. Then I contacted the major vendors, installed evaluation copies, explored features, and spoke with other customers and with those who specialized in using these various products. It really helped the team see the industry from a broad perspective, and resulted in a valuable learning experience. There are some respectable products on the market, and all have their strengths, but I can honestly say that Microsoft has a unique and special platform.

WHO USES REPORTING SERVICES?

The various titles given to someone who creates reports in different organizations is an interesting topic. An observation I have made over the years and in different work environments is the perception of this role. In some places, people who write reports are called *report developers*. In some environments, application developers assign the name *report users* to people creating reports.

Business users fit into a few categories when you consider how they use reports. Some are *report consumers* only. They're content to use reports that have been written and published for them. Others prefer to create their own reports without becoming mired in the intricacies of programming code and complex database queries. Maybe they just want to browse information to look for trends and to understand how the business is measuring up against their goals. In recent years, a new generation of *data consumers* has changed the landscape of self-service reporting and business data analytics. These are the data scientists and the data analysts who collect, wrangle, sculpt, model, and explore data using analytic reporting tools like Power BI and advanced add-ins for Excel.

Traditional roles have changed. New reporting and analytic tools have matured to accommodate the business climate. Not long ago, a typical IT group at most large organizations had three common roles: system administrators, application developers, and project managers. Where does the report designer fit in the organization? People who design business reports often don't come from a common pool of IT professionals. In fact, many people who spend the majority of their time creating reports are part of the business community and are not hard-core computer geeks.

If you're a business-type person, you probably don't care about integrating your reports into custom applications and websites, or about writing complex programming logic. Some of us live for that. What you may care about is giving your savvy business users the capability to easily visualize important key metrics to see what products are performing well in their sales territories. Maybe you want to enable business leaders to access important metrics and performance indicators on mobile devices.

Over the years, I've taken inventory of the people who consider themselves report designers. They generally fall into one of two camps: business-focused or technology-focused. There has been a significant shift toward more accessible reporting tools for those who have less technical roles in their organization. The following roles represent the majority and describe some of the trends noted as the industry continues to change.

Information Workers and Data Analysts

People in this role have strong computer skills, but do not spend their time writing code and using programming tools. Their primary interest is exploring information and finding answers, rather than designing complex reports. If you're an *information worker* (IW), you need easy-to-use tools to browse data and create simple reports quickly, and with less technical expertise. IWs typically create a report to answer a specific question or address a particular need, and then they may discard the report or save it to a personal area for reuse. They tend to create a separate report for each task, and may or may not share these reports with others who have similar needs. This is by far the fastest-growing group of report tool users in the industry.

A rapidly growing subset of the IW community is the *self-service analyst*. This persona not only has an aptitude for working with data and analytic tools, but also understands a particular field of business and what the data means in business terms. This subset may have specialized skills in a discipline of science or statistics. Data analysts usually have a mind for numbers and perhaps an artistic propensity for graphical presentation and storytelling with data.

An interesting transition has occurred in more progressive business environments, but has not yet happened in more traditional places. Whereas Excel has long been the primary data analysis tool, forward-thinking business data analysts are adopting tools like Power Pivot, Power BI, and Tableau Desktop to curate, deeply analyze, and visualize data to dredge out insights and valuable opportunities in order to take action. The only thing they need from IT is to give them access to reliable data so they can analyze it themselves. This new generation of analysts insists that they have access to data and permission to use their own tools to manage their areas of the business. The former generation of leadership insists that the IT and report "developers" export their spreadsheet-like reports into Excel so that the data can be manipulated and spreadsheet functions (full of calculation formulas that reference worksheets, and that do more calculations) can be performed to make it all line up and balance.

Spreadsheets and spreadsheet-style reports are the heart and soul of many financial organizations for good reason. However, some people experience a world outside the traditional, two-dimensional view, and break the routine to see things a different way.

Report Builder was designed for advanced report users and business-centric report designers. The capabilities are nearly identical to SQL Server Data Tools (SSDT) for Visual Studio, but it is simple and streamlined for the advanced user, rather than the developer.

Information Consumers

In the traditional user role of a user who runs or receives reports (perhaps through a portal or by e-mail), *information consumers* simply view information. Individuals within this group may be occasional report users and business workers, or consumers who use reports to perform a specific task, rather than interacting with data.

This role will always exist. But just as people are becoming more experienced and proficient with analytic tools, many consumers are also becoming occasional IWs and business data analysts.

> **TIP** *A common temptation for the experienced report developer (present company included) is to try to convince users that they need advanced report features. Be cautious about selling users on "cool" tricks and capabilities they may not need in their reports.*

In light of many different reporting scenarios, it is important to acknowledge and serve the needs of users who simply need to run or print reports. Making that experience as convenient and trouble-free as possible can make a huge impact on streamlining a business.

Business Managers and Leaders

If you are a *business manager*, you are interested primarily in your own domain of the business. Managers need reports to support specific processes, to address their analytical needs, and to help them make informed decisions. Like IWs, they have little interest in the implementation details or technology used to make it work. As IWs, managers may create their own reports to analyze the productivity of their team or area of responsibility.

Managers tend to view reporting from one of two different perspectives:

➤ They may need (or prefer to use) operational reports prepared for them that they can simply run and view results in a static, predictable format.

➤ They may extract data to a format suitable for analysis and manipulation (such as into an Excel workbook, or a tool they can use to further analyze and visualize results).

Mobile reporting solutions enable line managers, traveling business leaders, and IWs to access information on touch-optimized mobile devices. These reports are best suited for scenarios with key metrics and aggregated results, rather than multi-page, detail reports.

Software Developers

To achieve advanced reporting features, *software developers* write queries and custom programming code to process business rules and give reports conditional formatting and behavior. Developers typically feel right at home with the report design environment because it is similar to familiar programming tools. However, report design is not the same as application development. Designing a report can be faster and easier in some ways than developing software. Advanced report design can involve writing code and even developing custom components. Reporting Services offers several opportunities to integrate reports into custom-developed software solutions.

Developers and serious report designers will typically prefer to use developer-centric tools for report design such as SSDT for Visual Studio.

System Administrators

If you are a *system administrator*, you are typically concerned with the setup and ongoing maintenance of servers and the infrastructure to keep reporting solutions available and working. Administrators typically spend their time and energy managing security and optimizing the system for efficiency. Reporting Services has an administrative component that is especially important in large-scale implementations.

In smaller organizations, the same person may play the role of system administrator, developer, and report designer. Reports can be created to help monitor system usage and maintenance statistics to make a system administrator's job easier.

DASHBOARDS, REPORTS, AND APPLICATIONS

What exactly is the difference between a report, a dashboard, and a scorecard? It depends on a few factors, but there is some overlap between these concepts.

Quite a few years ago, a shift developed from client-based processing toward applications that ran on servers. Web technologies have proven to be an effective way to make systems available to a large number of people. Like a web application, browser-based reports do not always offer the same tactile and responsive user experience as a client application. Now, with the advent of smart mobile devices and applications, the climate has shifted once again from client, to server, and then to a balance of client/server technologies that support both connected and disconnected user experiences.

When Reporting Services was first released, it was available only as a server-based solution, with reports delivered almost exclusively through the web browser—and this is primarily how SSRS reports are used today. However, the capabilities do not stop there. Reporting Services lets you run reports in a variety of modes and applications. If we have learned anything from decades of computer system evolution, it is that centralized server-based solutions and client-side applications each offer unique advantages and trade-offs in terms of features, capabilities, interactive user experience, and scalability. Having the capability to operate in a disconnected mode offers tremendous advantages over purely server-side, connected systems.

Application Integration

You can integrate reports into applications in such a way that users may not be able to tell the difference between the report content and the application interface. With a little bit of programming code, reporting features can be extended to look and act much like applications. Many intranet sites run on web portals, rather than custom-programmed websites, and Reporting Services naturally plays well in practically any web portal environment.

If you are a report designer with simple needs, the good news is that using Reporting Services to design simple reports is, well, simple. If you are a software developer and you intend to use this powerful framework to explore the vast reaches of this impressive technology, welcome to the wonderful world of creative custom reporting.

After years of experience with this product, I have learned an important lesson on this topic. They say that to a hammer, everything looks like a nail. Likewise, to a programmer, a lot of challenges may look like an opportunity to write program code. That may be the right solution under certain conditions. But often, the most effective solution is to simply use a feature already baked into the product—and implement that feature as it was designed to work. I often have this conversation with programmers after they have spent hours writing a complicated solution to a simple problem.

Not to single out the programmers (who are generally a pretty smart bunch), the same concept applies to practitioners of any single discipline. The point is that different tools and technologies solve different problems, and sometimes it's important to look outside of one's discipline to gain a fresh perspective and ensure that you're using the right tool for the job.

User Interaction

Hyperlinks and application shortcuts can easily be added to documents and custom applications. Much of the standard report-viewing environment may be controlled using parameters passed to the report in the URL. Reports may be designed to prompt users for parameter values used to filter data and to modify the report format and output. Report elements such as text labels, column headers, and chart data points can be used to navigate to different report sections and new reports. Because navigation links may be data-driven and dynamically created based on program logic, report links may also be used to navigate into business applications.

Rather than cramming all the details into one report, a summary report or dashboard presents high-level information and key metrics. As shown in Figure 1-1, users can click a chart or summary value to navigate to a detail report in the context of the selected item, revealing more details and relevant facts. Using report navigation actions, drill-down, and other interactive features, reports may be orchestrated into complete solutions that enable a data exploration experience.

Techniques can be used to incorporate reports into a web application in a variety of ways:

➤ Hyperlinking to navigate the web browser window to a report

➤ Hyperlinking to open reports in a separate web browser window, with control over report display and browser features

➤ Embedding reports into a page using a frame, inline frame (`<iframe>` tag), or `ReportViewer` web control

➤ Programmatically writing reports to files available for download from a website

➤ Using a web part to embed reports into a SharePoint Web portal

➤ Fully integrating the report server in SharePoint Integration mode

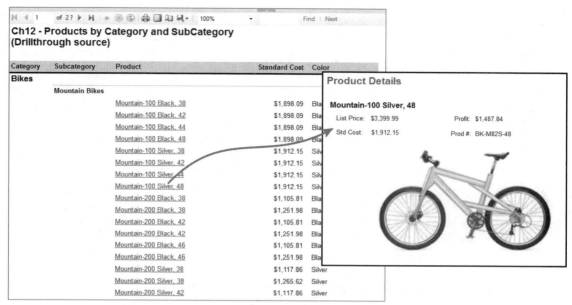

FIGURE 1-1: Using navigation links.

> **NOTE** *When compared with custom-developed solutions, Reporting Services provides useful functionality and business value for relatively little investment. Be mindful that Reporting Services provides the means to extend its capabilities through custom programming, but the cost (in terms of time and effort) may be considerably higher, and, in some cases, may be more restrictive than using custom programming components.*

Numerous creative ways exist to integrate reports into a web or desktop application. These techniques range from simple (for example, requiring a little HTML script) to complex, custom methods. And, if it is not enough to be able to embed reports into custom web pages, it is possible to use custom program code to embed additional content into reports.

The Reporting Services `ReportViewer` control can be used to view server-based reports in a form. These reports are managed on the report server and maintain all the security settings and configuration options defined by an administrator. Queries and data access are still performed on the server. The other option is to embed these reports directly into the client-side application. The Windows Forms `ReportViewer` controls can act as a lightweight report-rendering engine, meaning that reports built into a custom application can run independently from the report server.

SharePoint Integration

Reporting Services has native integration with Microsoft SharePoint Server and it works quite well. SharePoint is an abundant platform for document collaboration, as well as for managing document workflows and approval processes. At the same time, it is complex to administer and manage.

I have learned some valuable lessons about using Reporting Services with SharePoint. If you had asked me eight years ago about whether to include SharePoint in your reporting and business intelligence (BI) platform, I would have likely echoed Microsoft's recommendation to use SharePoint as the backbone for most solutions. Today, I am more cautious with my recommendations and ask more questions. SharePoint can be expensive, as well as complicated to set up and support. It adds processing overhead, which can affect performance and hardware requirements.

If your organization has invested in SharePoint on-premises and you are enjoying business value from the many services and capabilities that the platform offers, adding Reporting Services may be a natural fit for you. I have worked with several large organizations to fold SSRS, along with SQL Server Analysis Services (SSAS), Power Pivot, and Office into their SharePoint platform to build integrated business reporting and analytic solutions with great benefit.

Business Intelligence and Analytics Solutions

Once upon a time, reports were little more than transaction records printed on paper, also called *ledgers*, *journals*, and *lists*. As the need for more useful information arose, so did the sophistication of reporting. Today, reports serve as more than a method to dump data records to the printed page. Users need to gain insight and knowledge about their business. Dynamic reports allow users to interact and investigate trends in their business environments, rather than just view static transaction lists. It is important to realize that, as the sophistication of the business user grows, the complexity of the data and the reporting medium also increases. Sophisticated analytics uses a historical perspective to look into the future. Using accurate and reliable data from the past and present, as well as appropriate reporting models, allows analysts to forecast and predict trends and future activities.

A BI solution is the foundation upon which a capable business reporting platform can be constructed. Depending on your needs and business environment, this may simply entail designing a new database. Just because you need to analyze business data doesn't necessarily mean that you need to build a full-scale BI solution. However, if you need to aggregate large volumes of data to analyze business performance with key metrics and trends, relational databases designed for transaction processing may not effectively serve this purpose. Understanding these core concepts and investing in BI before report design will often reduce costs and enable you to create an enduring reporting platform for your business users and leaders. Most BI solutions integrate data from multiple sources to measure business success and trends. Consequently, this often requires a data warehouse, data mart, and/or semantic data model, as well as data extract, transform, and load (ETL) processes. Recent enhancements to the SQL Server database engine (such as in-memory column store indexes) may improve performance without radical database redesign.

Using modern analytic modeling tools, smaller-scale BI solutions can be created with a comparatively moderate investment. Complex analysis solutions often require tabular or multidimensional data structures created with SSAS. Microsoft developed the SSAS multidimensional database technology, often called *online analytical processing (OLAP)*. This uses cubes and dimensions storing data in a pre-grouped and pre-aggregated format on disk. The data is quickly available for reporting and browsing.

In SQL Server 2012, Microsoft released a "tabular," in-memory implementation of Analysis Services that has matured significantly in 2016. Tabular and multidimensional semantic models each offer unique strengths for efficient analytic reporting. In many cases, tabular models are easier to design, more efficient, and faster for reporting and analysis. But multidimensional SSAS includes complex and mature features. Both flavors of Analysis Services can be queried from SSRS reports using the MDX query language.

Past editions of Microsoft platform tools required an investment in SharePoint Server to fully implement BI solutions. SharePoint (either online or on-premises) still serves an important purpose today, but it is not a requirement to do BI right.

To say that the scope of a reporting or BI solution is relative to the size of a business would be a gross generalization. In some cases, small businesses manage large data volumes, and sometimes big organizations have simple needs. The point is that as your data grows, so does the need to store, manage, and analyze it in the best way.

A BI solution enables business leaders to use the right tools to proactively make informed decisions about their business. Sophisticated reporting and analytics allow IWs and leaders to look beyond the history of their business data. By examining the past and present, you can spot trends and patterns. You can use reliable business analytics to forecast future trends, to plan for improved business processes, and make informed decisions.

Yesterday's static reporting applications have given way to BI solutions. BI is more than the capability to "go get" data. It involves mechanisms that put high-level intelligence in front of leaders in the form of self-service report tools, dashboards, and business scorecards. It proactively alerts users when important events occur and when thresholds are exceeded.

At first, a simple reporting application may use data from a data source or two, but eventually reports may be based on multiple data sources. Sustainable BI solutions are designed around consistent and reliable data sources engineered specifically for reporting. Data is transformed from multiple sources into a central repository using data transformation packages. Data may then be processed into a semantic model (multidimensional cube, or tabular model). Reports may use a relational data warehouse, data mart, or semantic model. A variety of reports can be created to support business leaders and the important decisions and processes. These decision-support reports may take on many different forms, such as charts, detail summaries, dynamic drill-down and drill-through reports, dashboards, and business scorecards.

Mobile Reports and KPIs

Mobile device reporting is a completely different paradigm from traditional desktop reporting, with the goal being to present important information in a simple and touch-friendly medium.

All report types, paginated reports, and KPIs are managed and accessed through a new web portal. The web portal (shown in Figure 1-2) can be accessed in a web browser and on mobile devices using the Power BI mobile app.

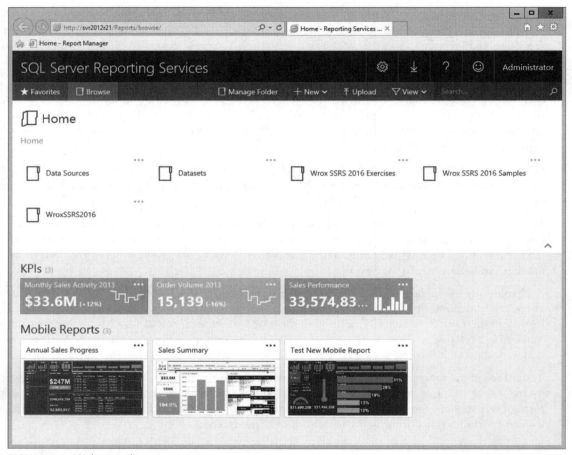

FIGURE 1-2: Web portal.

Figure 1-3 shows the Web portal in the Power BI app for the iPhone.

The mobile reporting addition to SQL Server 2016 Reporting Services is a new and unique capability. It is different for a couple of reasons. Using a fresh perspective, the feature was developed by another organization and was designed to provide a different user experience than conventional SSRS reports. Mobile reports are simple with focus on the user experience. They can be easy to design, but require some data and query preparation.

Mobile reports are designed using the Mobile Report Publisher, a standalone tool connecting results from predefined datasets. Reports are styled using a color palette theme, and individual layouts are applied to a report for desktop, tablet, and phone devices. After a report is published to the report server, alongside other Reporting Services content, users can connect with their mobile devices.

Using a freely available app installed from the device provider's application store, users interact with offline data. The offline report cache is synchronized on-demand, or at scheduled intervals using shared datasets. These are part of the standard Reporting Services server architecture.

FIGURE 1-3: Web portal on iPhone.

Mobile reports are optimized for use on mobile devices using the Power BI mobile app for each mobile device platform and form factor. The appropriate app for a user's device is downloaded and installed from the Windows, Android, or Apple App Store. Figure 1-4 shows a mobile report optimized for Portrait layout in the iPad app.

KPIs are a standard feature of the new web portal. They also get data through SSRS shared datasets. After datasets are prepared, KPI design is very simple and performed through a web interface. Key metrics are visualized using color, text, and bold graphics to indicate metric status comparing it to a target or goal, as well as trends using simple sparklines and chart visuals.

FIGURE 1-4: Mobile report on iPad.

REPORT TOOL CHOICES

The universe expands. Software vendors add more applications to their collections much faster than they sunset the old ones. Likewise, Microsoft continues to add applications and features without distinct use case boundaries between them. As a result, if there were two different options before, now there are three or four—and it is up to us to decide which choice is best for our needs. Like it or not, this is the nature of the technology-saturated world in which we live and work. I spend much of my time giving advice about the pros and cons—advantages and feature gaps—between different reporting tools. Throughout this book, this topic is addressed, best practices are called out, and proven design patterns are described as learned from various projects and field experience.

The majority of new Reporting Services implementations for most organizations use the de facto web-based web portal interface, or are integrated into a company SharePoint site. Other options to integrate reports into custom applications or web pages may be used to meet specific business needs, but are less common. In reality, reports can be integrated into a variety of custom solutions with relative ease. Here are some software solutions that might incorporate reports:

➤   Out-of-the-box, server-based reporting features, using reports created by report designers and deployed to a central web server.

➤   Reports integrated into web applications using URL links to open in a web browser window.

➤   Reports integrated into SharePoint Services applications using SharePoint web parts.

➤   Custom-built application features that render reports using programming code. Reports can be displayed within a desktop or web application, or may be saved to a file for later viewing.

➤   Interactive data visualizations using the Power View visualization tool for data exposed through a tabular semantic model.

Simple Report Design

If you need to create common report types to summarize or output information contained in a database, Reporting Services offers some great tools that make this easy to do. For example, suppose you have a record of customers and the products they have purchased. You want to produce a list of customers that contains the number of transactions and the total amount the customers have spent. You can use Report Builder to produce a simple table report that includes this information. If you want to compare the sales for each customer, day-to-day, over a period of time, you can generate a line chart report to view the sales trend. The point is that common report types can be easy to create with tools and features that do not require users to know a lot about complicated things like programming, writing queries, and building expressions.

Managing a fully scaled corporate BI solution can be complex and expensive. Fortunately, all the components of a working solution can be scaled down to a single server if necessary. Small and midscale reporting solutions may use a single, multipurpose database serving as an operational data store and a reporting data structure. As the solution matures, the eventual separation of these databases is almost inevitable. A small-scale data mart, populated from operational databases at regular intervals, will provide a simpler data source for reporting that doesn't compete with users and applications for system resources.

Simple reports are easy to design and deploy for short-term use. With a little planning and discipline, you can design reports to meet future requirements. Properly designed, your reports can include advanced features that meet simple needs now, and more sophisticated needs in the future.

IT-Designed Reports

Reporting Services was first designed and optimized for programmers and application developers who were accustomed to using Visual Studio. The report project design add-in for Visual Studio, originally called Business Intelligence Development Studio (BIDS), is now called SQL Server Data Tools (SSDT). Advanced capabilities are accessible using a variety of tools familiar to application developers. Like other Visual Studio solutions, report definition files can be managed as a single deployment unit to publish reports and related objects to the appropriate folders on a report server.

Likewise, in application development projects, reports, data sources, shared datasets, and all other design elements can be managed with integrated version control in the SSDT environment. Developers can use Microsoft Team Foundation Server, GitHub, or other source code management systems to collaborate as a team and recover from file loss.

User-Designed Reports

The industry's quest to create the perfect easy-to-use BI tool has produced many different products, each with its own unique capabilities. Under the Reporting Services umbrella, two self-service reporting tools serve different needs. The current incarnation of Report Builder is based on the mature report definition architecture. Report Builder reports can span the spectrum from simple to complex, with many design options.

Report Builder creates reports that are entirely cross-compatible with SSDT, and that can be enhanced with advanced features. Incremental product improvements over the past few versions have made out-of-the-box report design even easier. Users can design their own queries, or simply use data source and dataset objects that have been prepared for them by corporate IT so that they can drag and drop items or use simple design wizards to produce reports. In Report Builder, each report is managed as a single document that can be deployed directly to a folder on the report server or in the SharePoint document library. The version number has been dropped from the Report Builder name; now it is simply differentiated from previous versions by the version of SQL Server that installs it.

Table 1-1 summarizes the report design tools available in the current product.

TABLE 1-1: Report Designer and Visualization Options

REPORT DESIGNER	BACKGROUND
SQL Server Data Tools (SSDT)	This implementation of the Visual Studio shell is typically used by IT professionals to design reports with a project and team focus. It currently uses the Visual Studio 2010 shell.
Report Builder	Successor to previous tools introduced in 2005 and 2008, Report Builder has had incremental improvements in 2012, 2014, and 2016.

REPORT DESIGNER	BACKGROUND
Mobile Report Publisher	This is a new addition to the 2016 product. Mobile reports are designed separately from paginated reports and deployed to the common report server. Reports may be viewed on most any mobile device (phone or tablet) using the Power BI mobile app or Datazen mobile app. These reports can also be viewed in the web browser through the web portal.
Web portal KPI Designer	KPI tiles (with sparkline trend and thumbnail comparison charts) are designed in a web interface using the web portal. Data for each KPI element uses dataset queries stored in report server folders.

Server-Based Reports

Reports can run on either a report server, or in a standalone application on the client computer. It is important to note that Reporting Services is designed and optimized for server-based reporting first. The client-side option (called *Local Mode*) is possible with some custom programming, and takes a little more effort and expertise to implement. For the remainder of this chapter, the discussion is limited to server-based reporting.

> **NOTE** *Local Mode reports use a special report definition file with an* RDLC *extension. These reports run within a Windows or Web form control that is deployed with the hosting application. Some programming code is necessary and they are typically best used for low data volume applications.*

It is important to understand the difference between SQL Server Reporting Services and a desktop reporting tool such as Microsoft Access. Reporting Services is not an application you would typically install on any desktop computer; rather, it is designed for business use. It requires Microsoft SQL Server, a serious business-class relational database management tool and typically runs on a dedicated server. Likewise, reports may be integrated into SharePoint Services to be managed, secured, and administered alongside other shared corporate documents and assets. At the same time, Reporting Services can be used in a simple standalone deployment with relatively little administrative overhead.

Reporting Services is scalable and adaptable for use by a handful, as well as thousands, of users, for reporting on large sets of data stored in a variety of database platforms. Just because Reporting Services is a business-sized product does not mean that reports need to be complicated or difficult to design.

Report users need to be connected to a network, or perhaps to the Internet, with connectivity to the report server. When a report is selected for viewing from a folder on the report server or the

SharePoint library, it is displayed as a web page in the user's web browser. Optionally, the same report can be displayed in a number of different formats, including Word, Excel, PowerPoint, and Adobe PDF, or as a PNG, JPEG, GIF, or TIFF image. Reports can be saved to files in these and other formats for offline viewing. Reports can also be scheduled for automatic delivery by the report server by e-mail, or can be saved to files. These features are standard and require only simple configuration settings and minor user interaction.

Report Data Sources

Every report has at least one data source and query or reference to the entities that return data values, called a *dataset*. Operational data stores are often the most complex databases. Some packaged systems have databases with thousands of tables. As the dependence on databases and data-driven computer systems increases, most organizations cross a threshold in three areas:

➤ The complexity of each database grows to accommodate more complex processes.

➤ The volume of the data increases.

➤ The number of different databases increases to handle different business data that management needs.

> **NOTE** *I have used Reporting Services to connect to many different data sources, including products outside the Microsoft product portfolio. Although SSRS can connect effectively to sources like Oracle, Teradata, IBM DB2, SyBase, MySQL, PostgreSQL, XML files, and SharePoint lists, sometimes it is easier to transform data into SQL Server so that you can connect trouble-free. The optimal choice will depend primarily on the complexity of the data.*

Aside from sheer complexity, it is not uncommon for midsized companies to store terabytes of data. Storage space is fairly inexpensive when compared with equally capable systems a few years ago. There may be great value in tracking orders, shipments, calls, cases, and customers, but all this data adds up over time. Recording all this activity means you have a lot of data on hand for reporting. Putting data into a database is the easy part. Getting intelligent, useful information back out—now there is the challenge!

Finally, different systems are used to manage the same types of data in different ways. For example, a customer relationship management system tracks sales leads and potential customers for a marketing organization differently than an order management system does to support the sales team. In each of these two systems, you may track something called a "customer," but in these systems, the definition may vary. Perhaps a "customer" may represent a consumer, contact, or company in one system, and a lead, vendor, or reseller in another system. Larger companies may have similar records duplicated across other systems such as enterprise resource planning, human resources management, benefits, vendor management, accounting, and payables and receivables systems.

At some point, most solution designers conclude that to obtain valuable reporting metrics from all these operational data sources, they will have to be consolidated into a central, simplified data store specifically designed to support business reporting requirements. A *data warehouse system* is a central data store used to standardize the data extracted from these complex and specialized data sources. It typically makes use of the same relational database technologies used to house the operational data stores, but it does so in a protected, read-only environment to keep reporting simple and straightforward.

Modest data aggregation can be performed on large sets of data from a data warehouse. In contrast, deep analysis requires special data storage technology, as well as a more capable mathematical and statistical reporting engine.

Enterprise Scale

Delivering reports to many users requires a scalable reporting environment. Reporting Services processes queries and then renders reports on the report server. Because it uses industry-standard Windows services, shared server-based components, and HTTP web services, all the processing occurs in an efficient and secure environment. Standard data-source connection providers for SQL Server and other enterprise-class databases promote efficient use of server resources. In simple terms, many users can run reports at the same time while consuming minimal server resources. To serve more users, report servers may be scaled out using load balancing and distributed server farms.

The Reporting Services report server exposes its functionality in the same way that a standard ASP.NET website is hosted for users. Reports can be accessed from anywhere within or outside of the corporate firewall, and are still available only to selected users. In SharePoint integrated mode, reports are available to users through document libraries and are secured and managed within the SharePoint server environment. In Native or nonintegrated server mode, reports are managed and accessed through the web portal web interface installed with Reporting Services. Reports can also be exposed in custom-developed web applications using practically any set of web technologies or development tools.

OPTIMIZING PERFORMANCE

Often, system performance is one of the most significant drivers of an effective BI solution. As an organization's reporting needs become more sophisticated and the data's complexity and volume increase, the cost is usually measured first in performance. Queries take longer to run and compete for resources on the report and database servers. In this case, IT professionals typically react by recognizing the value of and need for a simplified database. Whether this is to be a truly enterprise-ready data warehouse, a departmental data mart, or a simple "reporting structure," the basic concept is usually the same—simplify the database design to focus on reporting requirements.

As mentioned, some performance and advanced analytical requirements may drive the solution's maturity to include OLAP cubes. This does not necessarily mean all the reports designed against other data sources must be updated. A variety of reports may work just fine with an operational data source or relational data warehouse. But other, more sophisticated reports require specialized data sources (such as OLAP cubes) to perform well.

Reports may be delivered in a variety of ways (not just when a user navigates to a report in real time). Reports may be automatically rendered to the server cache so that they open quickly and don't burden data sources. They may be delivered via e-mail and to file shares on a regular schedule. Using data-driven subscriptions, reports may be "broadcast" to a large audience during off-hours. Each user may receive a copy of the report rendered in a different format or with data filtered differently. Throughout this book, you learn to plan for, manage, and configure these features.

You also learn how to optimize, back up, and recover the Report Server database, web service, and Windows service. You learn how to use the management utilities, configuration files, and logs to customize the server environment and prevent and diagnose problems.

Performance

While on a consulting assignment, I developed complex financial formula reports using the original database structure as the report data source. The T-SQL queries were complex and difficult to debug. The client was thrilled when one of the more complicated reports took 45 minutes to run instead of the 90 minutes it took before we "optimized" the query. After transforming the same data into a simplified data mart structure, it took less than 3 minutes to run the same report. With an OLAP cube in Analysis Services, the same report ran in just a few seconds. Needless to say, the "acceptable" 45-minute report rendering time was no longer acceptable after the users found out that they could run the same report in a few seconds! Although this makes for a good story, the fact is that today people expect results quickly.

Users typically have little concern for the complexity of a database solution or the technology used to deliver data. They simply need results fast, and that's usually what they expect. The task is left for us to architect solutions to deliver results and perform calculations and metrics from large volumes of business data. Optimal performance is achievable using several innovative features of the SQL Server reporting architecture. Examples include in-memory storage and column store indexing, in-memory tabular and multidimensional semantic modeling, report instance caching, and report page-level rendering. Mobile reports can also use client-side data cache to optimize report performance and provide off-line viewing.

SUMMARY

Your role as a report designer or solution developer will determine how deep you need to immerse yourself into the complexities of Reporting Services. The needs of report users vary from simple to complex, and the time and energy you invest could vary from hours to months, depending on the solution scope.

Some users need to simply run or print reports. Others need or want to be more self-sufficient—either designing reports by themselves, or using self-service tools to perform design and data exploration.

Business Intelligence (BI) reporting solutions include dashboards, scorecards, KPIs, and interactive mobile reports that enable business information workers and business leaders to get insights from data. These solutions often use data modeling technologies like SSAS with visual reports and BI tools. Mobile reports allow users to interact with business data on their mobile devices, tablets, and smartphones on every device platform. Comparatively, mobile reports allow users to operate with disconnected data on touch-enabled devices.

Reports are integrated into applications and custom solutions using web service components, page frames, and form controls. Reporting Services integrates with applications and enterprise solutions using a variety of options. The spectrum of integration options is vast. Your solutions may be very simple using "out of the box" features or tightly integrated with SharePoint, custom applications, Power BI, and the entire Microsoft reporting ecosystem.

If you are new to SSRS, start small and learn the platform. With a little experience, you will figure out which features to use to meet your business and user needs. If you have been using earlier versions SSRS for a while, I will show you how the product has grown and demonstrate new patterns in a best practice.

Chapter 2 introduces you to the new web portal for report navigation and management. You'll learn about several significant report rendering enhancements and modernized features.

2

What's New in SQL Server 2016 Reporting Services?

WHAT'S IN THIS CHAPTER

➤ Report designer enhancements

➤ Modern browser rendering

➤ Parameter layout management

➤ Introducing Mobile Reports and KPIs

➤ New printing and rendering options

➤ The new web portal

➤ Power BI dashboard pinning and integration

The enhancements to Reporting Services in SQL Server 2016 range from subtle to significant. Several notable enhancements expand the reporting platform and help round out the Microsoft Business Intelligence (BI) product tool belt. Chapter 2 contains no hands-on exercises so there is nothing to download and no exercises for this chapter. We will introduce the hands-on exercises and samples in the Chapter 3. Just sit back and learn about how Reporting Services is improved and enhanced; in some ways, it is the same or similar to the past few versions.

Before you learn about several new features introduced in Reporting Services for SQL Server 2016, take a look at the quick history lesson shown in Figure 2-1 that highlights the origins of the product.

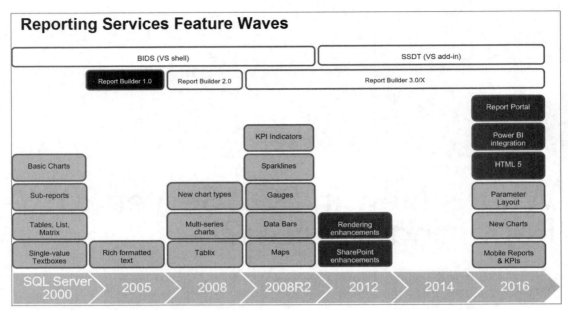

FIGURE 2-1: Evolution of Reporting Services.

Reporting Services was released as an add-in tool for SQL Server 2000 in early 2004. At the time, the feature set was light when compared to the product today, but the foundational architecture hasn't changed significantly. Essential features included basic charts, sub-report data regions, and single-value textboxes.

The second release in 2005 added a self-service report authoring tool called Report Builder (later named Report Builder 1.0) that was paired with a semantic modeling tool in the designer. The original modeling and ad hoc report tool has since been deprecated, but it inspired more capable replacement technologies like Power Pivot and the later generations of Report Builder. Not to be confused with the original Report Builder tool, Report Builder 2.0 and 3.0 produce report definition files compatible with the report project tools that are integrated with Visual Studio, originally called Business Intelligence Development Studio (BIDS).

Several improved and progressively more powerful features appeared in later product versions. SQL Server 2008 R2 introduced many advanced visual elements such as gauges, sparklines, data bars, key performance indicators (KPI), and maps. After the introduction of so many new features, the only minor improvements in SQL Server 2012 and 2014 were a noticeable change to the feature cadence as product development resources were redirected to emerging products like Power Pivot, Power View, and then Power BI.

In 2015, under new leadership and restructured product teams, Microsoft reaffirmed its commitment to Reporting Services as a core feature of the Microsoft reporting and BI platform. The product now emerges from a period at rest to another wave of aggressive development and improvements. Many of the core features remain the same, and the design experience is relatively unchanged. But as discussed in this chapter, several new improvements are driving new momentum.

REPORT BUILDER AND DESIGNER ENHANCEMENTS

The report design experience for standard "paginated" reports hasn't really changed much over the past few product versions, but there have been incremental improvements. Report Builder is restyled to conform to Microsoft Office 2016 standards. The installation process for Report Builder changes to an "evergreen" application. This means that Microsoft maintains updates for frequent download, rather than the old "ClickOnce" installation from your on-premises server. Similar to prior versions, users can elect to install Report Builder from the web portal menu.

Report Builder has been updated with a modern look-and-feel, simple and sleek, as shown in Figure 2-2. Changes are mostly cosmetic, while the fundamental features are the same.

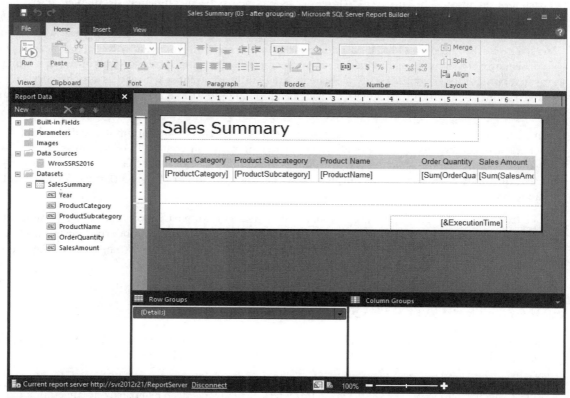

FIGURE 2-2: Report Builder's new look.

The Visual Studio–integrated Report Designer is now part of SQL Server Data Tools (SSDT), a downloadable add-in for Visual Studio. Although the tool set hasn't changed significantly, there are some subtle changes to the way SSDT is installed and the way updates are delivered. First of all, confusion about the name "SSDT" is dispelled because the former "SSDT" (the previous-version add-in for database projects) and "SSDT for BI" (the previous-version add-in for SQL Server Integration Services, SQL Server Analysis Services, and SQL Server Reporting Services projects) are now a combined package, simply called SSDT (which also includes a project template for SQL Server database projects). Secondly, you can simply download and install a version of SSDT that will work with the current version of Visual Studio or a few versions back. If Visual Studio is not installed on the computer, the SSDT setup package installs the Visual Studio shell. The SSDT add-in will be updated frequently, and you will have the option to install updates on-demand from within Visual Studio.

MODERN BROWSER RENDERING

One of the most significant product improvements in 2016 may be one of the least apparent under casual observation. The entire HTML rendering engine has been completely overhauled across the platform. The web portal, used to navigate and manage report content, and the actual report content are rendered to modern HTML5 standards, which are supported by all modern web browsers. The shift to modern HTML output means that web content produced by Reporting Services is consistently consumable on any device, regardless of the operating system or web browser, so long as it supports modern standards. The benefits are readily apparent when reports simply work on smartphones of any type, on tablets, as well as laptop and desktop machines, regardless of the brand or operating system.

In earlier versions of Reporting Services, report output consistency was attempted with multiple version and browser logic in the rendering code to emit different content HTML for different browsers and versions, which quickly resulted in a patchwork of branched code and logic. By contrast, the modern rendering code outputs one lightweight stream of HTML5 that works across all modern devices.

The trade-off is that some backward compatibility is sacrificed, particularly with older versions of Internet Explorer (IE). Potentially, the most adverse effect of this shift to modern web standards is that users on older computers with an outdated operating system will need to upgrade to the latest available version of IE or their preferred web browser.

PARAMETER LAYOUT CONTROL

Have you ever had to explain to a user or project stakeholder that the parameter prompts are inflexible and that you have little control over how and where they are placed?

You will have improved control over parameter formatting and placement. Since the inception of Reporting Services about 12 years ago, parameters have always been arbitrarily arranged in a narrow bar at the top of the browser window, from left-to-right, and then top-down. Figure 2-3 shows that the Report Designer has a grid to manage the placement of parameters, in the parameter bar, in any configuration, within definable rows and columns.

The new parameter bar applies SSRS deployments in Native mode, but does not change the way parameters are rendered in SharePoint integrated mode.

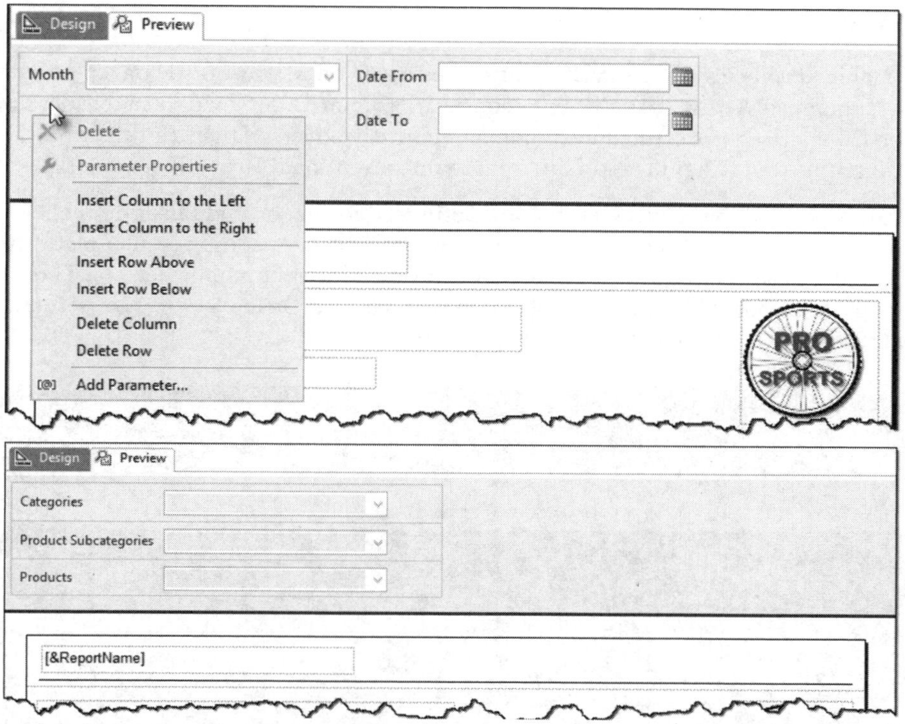

FIGURE 2-3: Report Designer grid.

UPDATED RDL SPECIFICATION

As with previous Reporting Services upgrades, the RDL has been revised in 2016. Figure 2-4 shows two code snippets from the Visual Studio XML viewer with the RDL namespace header and the `ReportParametersLayout` element near the end of the RDL file. Note that the `xmns` attribute version for the `reportdefinition` namespace is `2016/01`.

When SSDT for SQL Server 2016 is used to deploy reports to an earlier version report server, the Report Designer provides backward version compatibility by removing this metadata from the report definition file when the project is built. The versioned RDL file is written to the configuration output sub-folder under the project `bin` folder (the `bin\debug` folder by default), and then this file is deployed to the report server.

```
<Report
xmlns:rd="http://schemas.microsoft.com/SQLSer
ver/reporting/reportdesigner"
xmlns:cl="http://schemas.microsoft.com/sqlser
ver/reporting/2010/01/componentdefinition"
xmlns="http://schemas.microsoft.com/sqlserver
/reporting/2016/01/reportdefinition">

<ReportParametersLayout>
  <GridLayoutDefinition>
    <NumberOfColumns>1</NumberOfColumns>
    <NumberOfRows>3</NumberOfRows>
    <CellDefinitions>
      <CellDefinition>
    ...
```

FIGURE 2-4: RDL file snippet

MOBILE REPORTS

The addition of mobile dashboards to the SSRS platform is based on Microsoft's Datazen product acquisition from ComponentArt in 2015. Mobile reports are primarily designed to enable data interactivity in dashboard-style reports created by a mobile report developer. Managing this expectation is important because this tool is significantly different than conventional Reporting Services.

Mobile reports can be viewed in the browser, but are optimized for phone and tablet devices through native, installed applications running on all the major mobile operating system platforms. Figures 2-5 and 2-6 demonstrate the same mobile report on two different mobile devices. They are not a replacement for high-fidelity paginated reports created with Reporting Services, or self-service analytics in Power BI. They serve an entirely different purpose.

FIGURE 2-5: Mobile report on tablet.

FIGURE 2-6: Mobile report on phone.

At first, the mobile dashboard experience may seem to be a simple drop-in of the Datazen product. But, it is apparent that some integration with the SSRS architecture has already taken place, and more adaptations are likely on the horizon. The first notable difference is the Datazen server is entirely replaced by the SQL Server report server, and queries are now managed as SSRS shared datasets.

The SQL Server Mobile Report Publisher is a separate download that can be obtained by simply choosing the Mobile Report option from the web portal menu. In 2015, I wrote a series of articles for *SQL Server Pro Magazine* about how to create a mobile dashboard solution with Datazen. Datazen is still available as a standalone product—free to SQL Server Enterprise customers—but any future enhancements are likely to only take place in the new integrated platform. The article series is available here: http://sqlmag.com/business-intelligence/getting-started-datazen-microsoft-s-new-mobile-dashboard-platform. The essential design experience for mobile reports is nearly the same as I described in that series, but a few details change with the new integration. Microsoft Senior Program Manager Chris Finlan provides a complete step-by-step tutorial in his post titled "How to create Mobile Reports and KPI's in SQL Server Reporting Services 2016 – An end-to-end walkthrough."

KPIs

New KPIs integrated with the web portal are also based on the Datazen product acquisition. These KPI visuals are created and managed entirely within the portal. In addition to the standard traffic-light style comparison of actual versus target values, KPIs can include a trend line or segment chart.

The KPI shown in Figure 2-7 is driven by data from one or more shared datasets that were created in the SSDT Report Designer. For ease and simplicity, any value of the KPI can be entered manually through the design page.

FIGURE 2-7: KPI from SSDT Report Designer dataset.

Although they are visualized in the web portal, KPIs are delivered to mobile devices through the Power BI mobile applications currently on every popular device platform.

NATIVE PRINTING CONTROL

The previous printing capability in SSRS relied on an ActiveX control that was only supported on Windows desktops and in certain web browsers. Even in tightly controlled Windows server environments, system administrators would rescind ActiveX support and disallow report printing from the server. The modern printing solution uses the PDF renderer to produce printable output, and then the Adobe document viewer to perform the actual printing.

POWERPOINT RENDERING

Users have had the option to export and render report content to Excel for several versions of SSRS. Output to Word was added in SQL Server 2008, and then both of these rendering options were improved and updated in the 2008 R2 version. Now, a third Office application format will be supported with the introduction of PowerPoint document rendering.

Most report items and data regions are converted to individual image objects in the resulting PowerPoint sides with one side generated per report page. Additional slides are created based on the report content size and layout. Textboxes are created for titles and report text, which support some report actions and textbox properties.

INTEGRATED AND IMPROVED WEB PORTAL

A new web portal web interface is introduced to replace the Report Manager. Like Report Manager, the portal is an ASP.NET web application used to access, run and manage reports in the web browser. The new portal has a look-and-feel we are accustomed to seeing in other modern apps from Microsoft these days; with responsive design for constancy on different device form factors. Web portal will be the home for mobile reports, KPIs, and paginated reports—the new name for RDL reports authored with Reporting Services. In the future, we may see support for additional content types. Figure 2-8 shows the Content menu in the web portal with options to selectively show different types of reports and folders.

Web portal supports in all modern web browsers by emitting responsive HTML5 with adaptations for mobile devices and screen orientations.

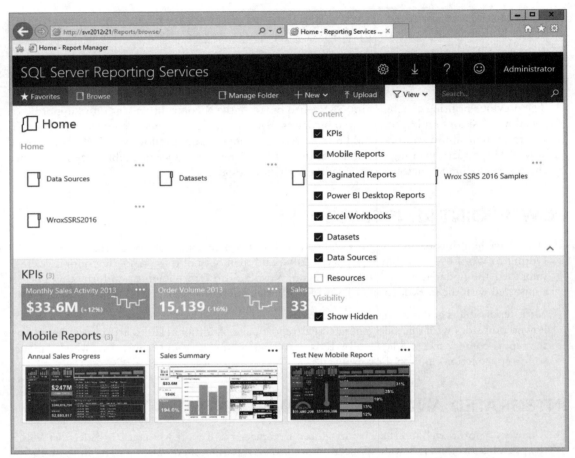

FIGURE 2-8: Content menu in the web portal.

NEW CHARTS AND VISUAL ENHANCEMENTS

With the addition of two new chart types, visualization improvements are inched forward in Reporting Services. The new Sunburst and Treemap charts shown in Figure 2-9 apply multi-level field groups visualized in both color and visual boundaries.

Although the core chart and gauge components are largely unchanged, the default styling properties have been modernized in the new product version. New and updated report visuals are likely to be an area of focus for future Reporting Services enhancements, given the success of self-service BI tools like Power BI. The design interface is identical to existing chart types, and the only real difference is that groups of rows are visualized in these unique formats. The Sunburst chart is also capable of consuming unbalanced hierarchies with slices generated for different levels only where data points exist.

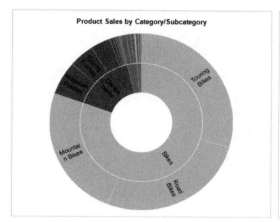

FIGURE 2-9: Two new chart types.

STANDARDIZED, MODERN BROWSER RENDERING

At first, you may not notice significant changes from previous versions, but the HTML renderer has been completely overhauled and updated. Now, reports are rendered to HTML 5 standards, whereby they should consistently maintain the same appearance and behavior in all modern browsers that support the HTML 5 standard such as Microsoft Edge, IE 11, and newer versions of Google Chrome, Safari, and Firefox. This change is a welcome improvement, which should clear up many problems with inconsistent and quirky report layouts while using different web browsers and devices. By the same token, the change means there is no specific backward-compatibility for outdated browsers; consequently, reports that may have worked (or partially worked) in an old version of Internet Explorer may no longer work until the user upgrades.

POWER BI DASHBOARD PINNING

For organizations that have invested in the Power BI cloud service, the Power BI integration feature allows users to pin graphical SSRS report visuals to their online dashboards. In order to use this feature, an administrator must register the report server with an existing Power BI subscription, and a report user must have access to the Power BI subscription.

The Reporting Services Configuration Manager (shown in Figure 2-10) includes a new page to manage Power BI Integration. This is where you register the report server instance with the Power BI subscription.

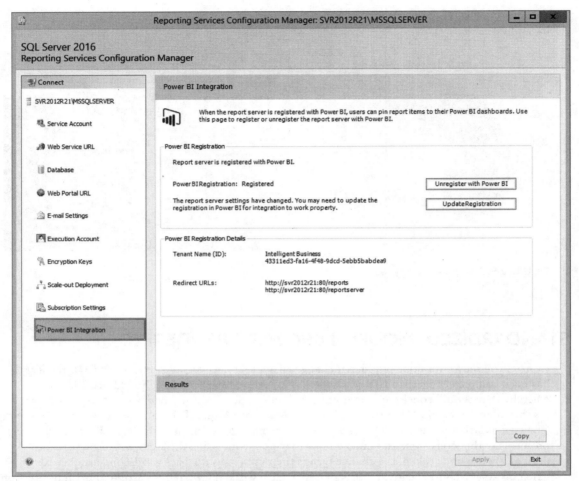

FIGURE 2-10: Reporting Services Configuration Manager.

When a report with "pinnable" items (such as images, charts, and gauges) is viewed in web portal, the Power BI icon is displayed on the toolbar (as shown in Figure 2-11).

FIGURE 2-11: Power BI pinning added to report toolbar.

Figure 2-12 shows that "pinnable" items are highlighted in web portal. When a visual is selected, you are prompted to select a Power BI dashboard and the refresh frequency. This schedules an Agent job on the report server to push updated visuals to the dashboard at the selected frequency.

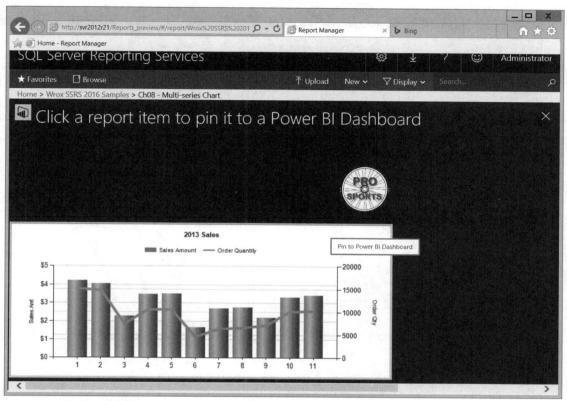

FIGURE 2-12: "Pinnable" items highlighted in web portal.

The "Select frequency of updates" option (in Figure 2-13) utilizes the SSRS subscription architecture by scheduling a SQL Server Agent job on the database server with the report server catalog. The Agent job re-queries the report data, and then a report server component refreshes the Power BI dashboard tile with an updated report visual.

Pinned report visuals appear on the dashboard alongside the Power BI report and Excel visuals, as shown in Figure 2-14. Clicking one of these visuals will drill-through to the report back on the on-premises report server. This gives users a seamless navigation experience between cloud-hosted Power BI content and selected report visual elements on your own report server.

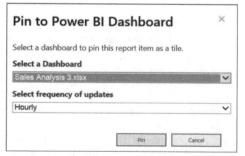

FIGURE 2-13: Power BI dashboard and update frequency.

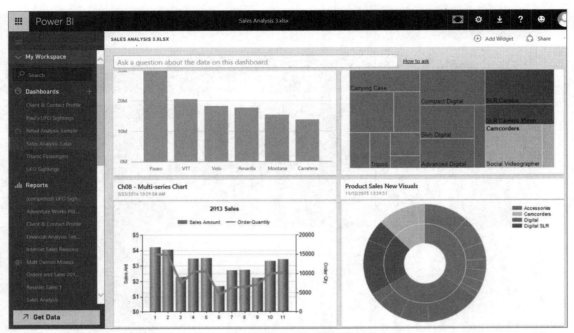

FIGURE 2-14: Pinned report visuals appearing on the dashboard alongside the Power BI visuals.

The integrated Power BI experience is a big step forward in providing a completely integrated IT-hosted and self-service reporting, BI and analytics solution.

SUMMARY

As the components of Microsoft's reporting platform continue to cross-pollinate, additional integration will be delivered through the web portal for desktop users and on device-specific applications for mobile users.

Report Builder continues to be the SSRS power user's tool for creating reports the way Office users create and update documents. The Visual Studio–based SQL Server Data Tools (SSDT) is engineered for the developer and serious report designer. It now includes database project and BI add-ins in a single "evergreen" package for multiple versions of Visual Studio that can be maintained and updated independently from SQL Server. The SSDT designer produces RDL reports for SQL Server 2016, and will produce backward-compatible reports through the project build and deployment process.

Mobile reports and KPIs are a new addition to the Reporting Services family. These are simple by design, responsive, interactive, and optimized to run on native mobile applications installed from the device-specific app store. Mobile reports are integrated with the Reporting Services portal, using shared datasets developed in SSDT.

Several enhancements to the SSRS core functionality include native web browser print support, PowerPoint rendering, and new chart visuals. Probably the most significant (although the least obvious) improvement is that the underlying rendering of all reports and the web portal interface is fully compatible with all modern web browsers, applying HTML5 standards and responsive design. This means that the entire report experience can be had on a user's device and browser of choice.

Chapter 3 addresses the requirements and steps to install and configure SQL Server Reporting Services and the dependent components. We discuss building a basic development environment and enterprise server deployments. You'll learn about the report server architecture, which will help you gain a comprehensive understanding of the features and capabilities of Reporting Services.

3

Reporting Services Installation and Architecture

WHAT'S IN THIS CHAPTER?

➤ What's changed in SQL Server 2016?

➤ Installing a report server

➤ Building an enterprise deployment

➤ Using tools to manage the reporting life cycle

➤ Exploring report server architecture

➤ Leveraging reporting services extensions

To use the examples and work through the exercises in this book, you need a report server and administrative rights to access it. Unless you have a server set up for this purpose, I recommend that you install a local instance of SQL Server on a machine that you manage. Your learning machine can be on your local computer, a local virtual machine, or a virtual server hosted in a cloud service like Windows Azure. I recommend that you install the Developer Edition of SQL Server 2016 on Windows 8 Professional or higher, or Windows Server 2012 or higher.

> **TIP** *If you are just getting started or you are new to Reporting Services, some of the technical information in this chapter may not be relevant or necessary at this stage in your experience. To get up-and-running quickly, follow the steps in "Installing Reporting Services" section of this chapter and then follow the section titled "Installing the Reporting Services Samples, Exercises, and SQL Server Databases." To use the chapter samples and exercises, you should install Reporting Services in native mode and install Analysis Services in multidimensional mode.*

You need the SQL Server database engine and Reporting Services for the majority of the book samples and exercises. For some of the optional and specialized topics later in the book, you need to run Analysis Service in multidimensional mode and a full version of Visual Studio 2015 or newer, with Visual Basic or C# language support.

> **TIP** *The Developer Edition is essentially the same is the Enterprise Edition of SQL Server, priced and scaled-down for desktop use. The Standard Edition is sufficient for most business purposes but lacks a few enterprise features we discuss in later sections.*

You could get by with as little as 4 GB of memory but I recommend that you have at least 8 GB. You should install the 64-bit version of SQL Server on a 64-bit operating system.

> **NOTE** *It is possible to install SQL Server on older and less-capable equipment with some additional upgrades. If you are working on a computer that doesn't meet these recommended specifications, check the product system require-ments for more details:* https://msdn.microsoft.com/en-us/library/ms143506(v=sql.130).aspx. *Keep in mind that the minimum documented requirements are sufficient for the software to load and services to run, before you start working with data.*

The topics of SQL Server setup and server architecture are kind of a chicken-and-egg thing. On one hand, it's helpful to understand all the product nuances sufficiently to appreciate what all the options mean. On the other hand, I would like to give you enough guidance to get started without unnecessary details. This chapter guides you through a basic installation of SQL Server 2016 Reporting Services, and reviews some important considerations for an enterprise deployment.

Although the basic installation may not cover some of the choices critical in an enterprise deployment, a development instance provides an environment in which features and the installation process itself can be explored. Such an environment is ideal for performing the exercises and tutorials in this book.

You explore how features in Reporting Services are implemented and exposed. This information is foundational for both administrators and developers. Subsequent chapters build off concepts explored here.

The reporting life cycle gives you the context within which Reporting Services is employed. You explore the various applications and utilities associated with Reporting Services.

Following this, you dig a little deeper into Reporting Services itself by examining the architecture of the Reporting Services Windows service, its components, and supporting databases. By the end of the chapter, you will have a solid understanding of how all these pieces come together to deliver Reporting Services' functionality.

This chapter covers the following topics:

- Basic installation
- Enterprise deployment considerations
- Reporting life cycle
- Reporting Services tools
- Reporting Services Windows service
- Reporting Services processors and extensions
- Reporting Services application databases

WHAT'S CHANGED IN SQL SERVER 2016?

If you have been using previous versions of Reporting Services, I will save you some time by summarizing a few minor changes to the installation experience. The changes are brief so it is easy to keep this simple. In previous versions of SQL Server, you would normally include the Client Tools options from the Feature Selection page on the Setup Wizard. This would install SQL Server Management Studio and the Visual Studio project designer add-ins (called Business Intelligence Development Studio or SQL Server Data Tools, depending on the product version) from the SQL Server installation media.

The SSMS and SSDT client tools are now managed as separate downloads so they can be updated frequently and integrated with multiple versions of Visual Studio. The new web portal replaces the Report Manager web interface for Reporting Services. Although the portal has a different visual presentation, installation and configuration is really no different. You'll just see a different report user interface after you finish the installation. Several new components and enhancements have been added to the Reporting Services feature set that do not affect the standard installation experience when compared to prior versions.

THE BASIC INSTALLATION

To understand the installation of Reporting Services, it is important to have some knowledge of its components. In SQL Server 2016, Reporting Services offers two modes:

- Native mode
- SharePoint Integrated mode

At its core, Reporting Services is a Windows service that relies on a pair of databases hosted by an instance of the SQL Server Database Engine. Note that in SharePoint Integrated mode, Reporting Services in SQL Server 2016 runs as a SharePoint shared service. This chapter is focused primarily on Reporting Services Native mode installations.

Interaction with the Reporting Services service is provided through applications such as web portal or the SharePoint Add-in, and other applications such as the SQL Server Data Tools. These applications, the SSRS service, and the report catalog databases are introduced in this chapter.

With the basic installation of Native mode, server-side and client-side components are installed on a single system. The Reporting Services databases are also installed to a local instance of the SQL Server Database Engine. With no dependencies on other systems, the basic installation is often referred to as a standalone installation.

SQL Server Developer Edition is a good choice for evaluation, development and testing environments. In addition to providing access to the full suite of Reporting Services features at no licensing cost, Developer edition supports a wider range of operating systems than other production-ready versions of SQL Server. The operating systems supported include Windows Server 2012, various editions of Windows 8 and, of course, new versions of Windows.

> **TIP** *As I mentioned at the beginning of the chapter, a practical development machine configuration should have significantly more horsepower than the stated minimum requirements. As a baseline, the virtual machine I have is configured to run all the book samples with optimal performance, has two processor cores assigned, and is configured to use dynamic memory, which typically uses 5–8 GB of RAM.*

The minimum system requirements include 1 GB of memory. The basic installation also requires at least 6 GB of free storage space and additional space for the system updates and SQL Server samples. SQL Server 2016 is supported in virtual machine environments running on the Hyper-V role.

Installing Reporting Services

Before performing the Reporting Services installation, it's a good idea to be certain your system is up-to-date with the latest service packs and Windows updates. You also need to be a member of the local Administrators group on the system on which you intend to perform the installation or be prepared to run the setup application using the credentials of an account that is a member of the local Administrators group.

> **TIP** *In the examples, I am installing SQL Server 2016 Developer Edition, which is what I recommend if you are setting up a development or evaluation machine with a local instance of SQL Server and Reporting Services. These instructions also apply to Standard and Enterprise Editions, although there may be subtle differences in the setup experience. SQL Server Developer Edition is available for free through the Visual Studio Dev Essentials program. To sign up and download software, go to* `https://www.visualstudio.com/en-us/products/visual-studio-dev-essentials-vs.aspx`.

To start the installation, access the installation media for SQL Server 2016 You can run setup from a DVD, mount an ISO file as a logical DVD drive, or use a folder or file share. Figure 3-1 shows the SQL Server setup DVD image mounted as a logical drive. It is important that the media be accessed from the system on which you intend to install the Reporting Services software. Start the setup application by launching SETUP.EXE, located at the root of the installation media.

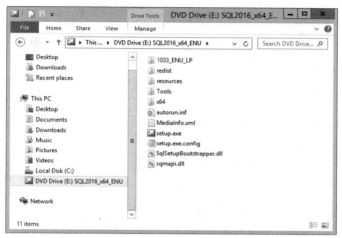

FIGURE 3-1: SQL Server setup DVD image mounted as a logical drive.

First the setup application checks your system for the Microsoft .NET Framework 3.5 SP1 and Windows Installer. If these are not present, the setup application initiates their installation. If either the .NET Framework or Windows Installer is installed by the setup application, your system may require a reboot. Upon restart, you need to relaunch the SQL Server 2016 setup application.

The setup application displays the SQL Server Installation Center, as shown in Figure 3-2. The Installation Center is divided into several pages, each providing access to documentation and tools supporting various aspects of the installation process.

For the purposes of the basic installation, proceed to the Installation page by clicking the appropriate link on the left side of the Installation Center form. On the Installation page, shown in Figure 3-3, select the option "New SQL Server stand-alone installation or add features to an existing installation." This launches the SQL Server Setup Wizard.

The first step the SQL Server Setup Wizard performs is to compare your system against a set of "setup support" rules. These rules determine whether the system configuration prerequisites for installation are met. When the analysis is complete, the wizard shows summary information. If violations are present, you see the list of rules, identifying which ones require attention. If there are no violations, you can click the Show Details button to see this list, which is shown in Figure 3-4.

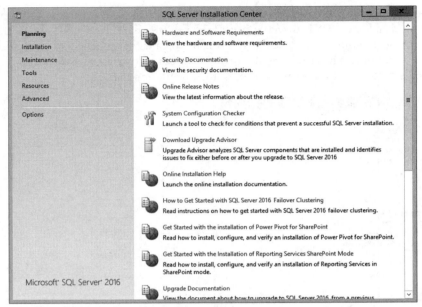

FIGURE 3-2: SQL Server Installation Center.

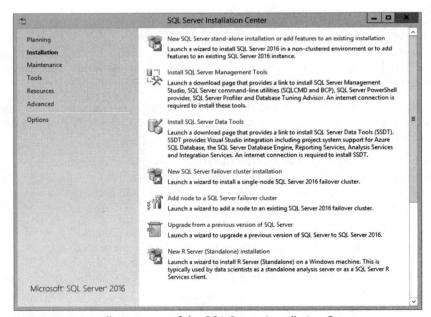

FIGURE 3-3: Installation page of the SQL Server Installation Center.

Clicking the "View detailed report" link on the Global Rules page opens a new window with a detailed report containing recommendations for addressing any warnings or violations, as shown in Figure 3-5. After reviewing this report, you can close this window.

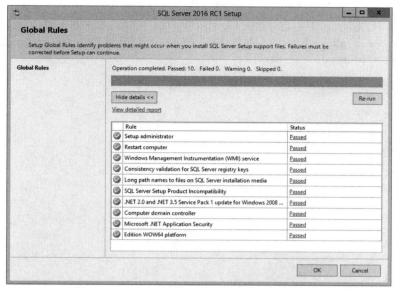

FIGURE 3-4: Setup Support Rules page.

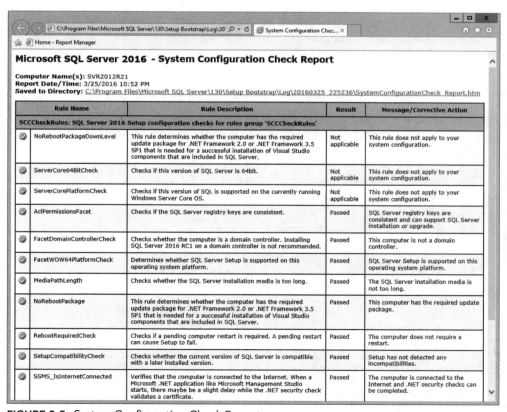

FIGURE 3-5: System Configuration Check Report.

On the Global Rules page of the SQL Server Setup Wizard, click the OK button to go to the Product Key page, shown in Figure 3-6. You can select one of the free editions of SQL Server or enter a product key for one of the other editions. Select the Evaluation edition or enter the product key of the Developer edition to proceed.

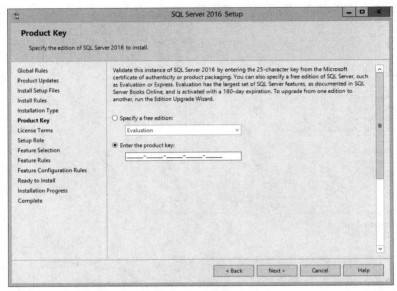

FIGURE 3-6: Product Key page.

Click the Next button to proceed to the License Terms page, shown in Figure 3-7.

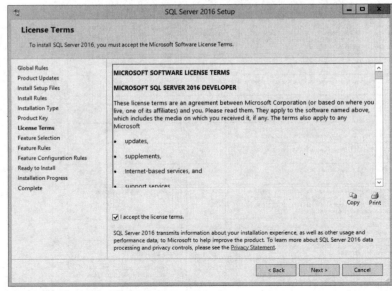

FIGURE 3-7: License Terms page.

> **NOTE** *This is the point where I'm supposed to advise you to carefully read the terms of the product license before you agree to them. Please read the fine print if you feel so inclined.*

To continue with the installation, check the box labeled "I accept the license terms." This agreement allows high-level information about hardware and SQL Server component usage to be sent to Microsoft to help improve the product. You can read the privacy statement by clicking the hyperlink. Examples of feature usage are whether Reporting Services or other services are installed, and the operating system of the host computer.

> **NOTE** *Having worked with the SQL Server product teams at Microsoft over the years, I can tell you that any usage and telemetry information is gathered and sent to Microsoft only with a customer's permission. This information is used to make product improvements and to prioritize feature development.*

The usage data collection is very small and not granular. It does not count how often a feature area is used, just whether it is used at all.

Click the Next button to go to the Install Setup Files page, shown in Figure 3-8. This page informs you that files will be installed for the purposes of the setup process. When this process is complete, the wizard proceeds to the next page.

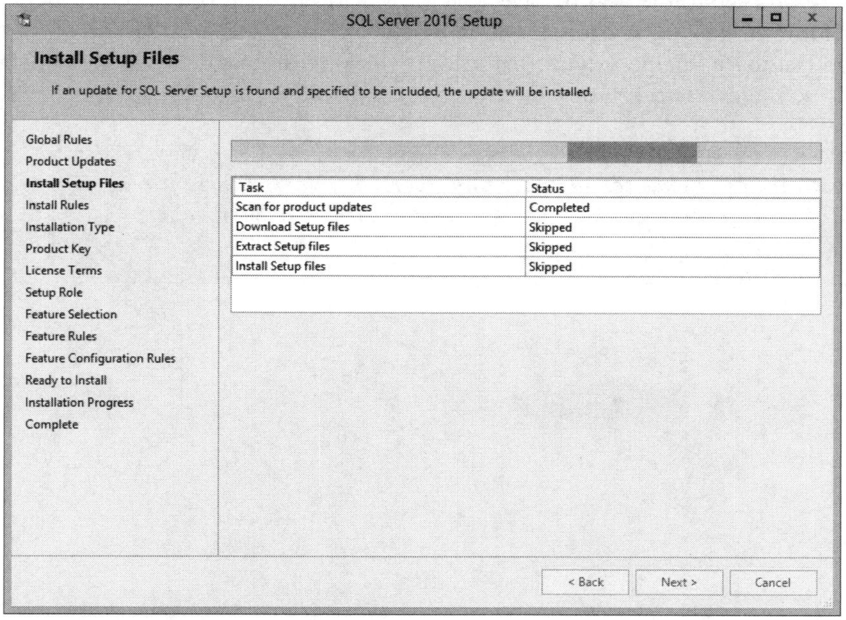

FIGURE 3-8: Install Setup Files page.

Click the Next button to proceed to the Setup Role page, within which you select a SQL Server Feature Installation, as shown in Figure 3-9.

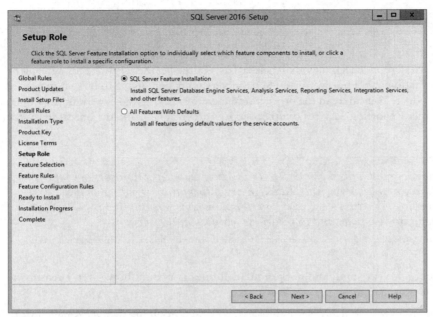

FIGURE 3-9: Selecting a SQL Server Feature Installation.

Click the Next button to proceed to the Feature Selection page, within which you select the SQL Server products and features to install, as shown in Figure 3-10. For the basic installation, select the Reporting Services and Database Engine Services features. If you want to install other components, such as Analysis Services, you can select these as well.

> **TIP** *To support all of the chapter samples and exercises, particularly for Chapters 9, 10, and 11, choose the option to install Analysis Services in Multidimensional mode.*

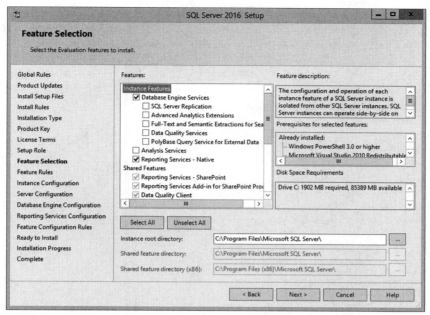

FIGURE 3-10: Selecting products and features to install.

The Feature Selection page also allows you to modify the path to which shared components will be installed. For the basic installation, typically this is left at the default location. If you have a compelling reason to change this location, click the button next to the displayed path, and select an appropriate alternative location.

> **TIP** *The difference between default and named instances are explained in "The Enterprise Deployment" section later in this chapter. For simplicity, if you are installing SQL Server and Reporting Services for the first time on a nonproduction server for development and learning, install a default instance.*

Click the Next button to go to the Instance Configuration page, shown in Figure 3-11. Here you identify the instance name for the Database Engine and Reporting Services instances selected on the previous page. Other SQL Server instances that are already installed on the system are listed in the bottom half of the page. If a default instance is not already installed, you can choose to perform this installation to a default instance; otherwise, you need to provide an appropriate instance name.

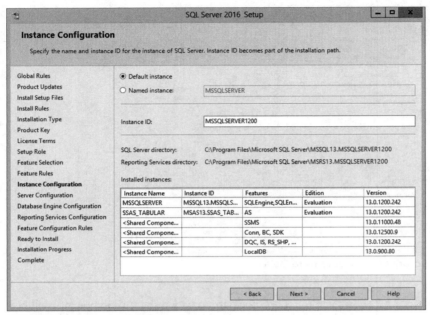

FIGURE 3-11: Instance Configuration page.

When naming an instance, it's important to keep in mind that the name is not case-sensitive and must be unique on the system. The name must also be no longer than 16 characters and may include letters, numbers, underscores (_), and the dollar sign ($). The first character must be a letter, and the instance name must not be one of the 174 setup reserved words listed in Books Online. In addition, it is recommended that the instance name not be one of the 235 ODBC reserved words, also listed in Books Online.

> **NOTE** *The Instance Configuration page also allows you to enter an installation ID other than the instance name. The instance ID is used to identify installation directories and registry keys for the SQL Server instance. In general, you should not alter the instance ID without a compelling reason to do so.*

Click the Next button to proceed to the Disk Space Requirements page. Here you can review the amount of space consumed by the various components of the installation.

You will have the option to change service accounts and collation settings. On the Service Accounts tab in the Server Configuration page, shown in Figure 3-12, select the service account to be used for each service. For the local development installation, it is generally recommended that you accept the defaults and use the local service or (generated) network service accounts for the Database Engine and Reporting Services Windows service. You can change the service accounts later, after the installation.

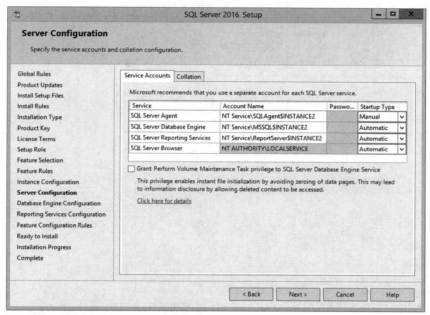

FIGURE 3-12: Server Configuration page.

You can typically skip the Collation page because the default selection is determined by the locale configured with the local operating system. As with other options, it is generally recommended that you not alter the collation unless you have a compelling reason to do so.

Click the Next button to proceed to the Database Engine Configuration page. This page allows you to configure the instance of the SQL Server Database Engine you are installing with Reporting Services. It is divided into four tabs: Server Configuration, Data Directories, FILESTREAM, and TempDB.

On the Server Configuration tab, shown in Figure 3-13, click the Add Current User button so that you will be set up as an administrator of the Database Engine instance. Leave all other options on this tab as they are, unless you have a compelling reason to change them.

On the Data Directories tab, you can alter various paths used by the Database Engine instance. Again, unless you have a compelling reason to make changes, leave the settings as they are configured by default. You won't be using the FILESTREAM feature for the book samples so you can leave the default setting unless you plan to use the feature for other reasons.

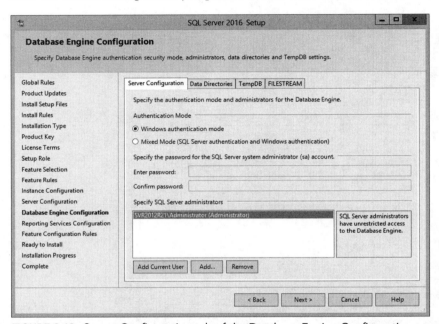

FIGURE 3-13: Server Configuration tab of the Database Engine Configuration page.

> **NOTE** *For simple development purposes, you can accept the default TempDB options. In a true production server, the configuration options on this page are crucial for achieving good performance for production workloads. The right settings will depend on several factors including data storage, number of processor cores, and memory. For example, among many recommended practices, configuring one file per CPU core will improve concurrency and query times.*

Click the Next button to go to the Reporting Services Configuration page, shown in Figure 3-14. On this page, you can select different Reporting Services installation options. The various options are discussed in the second half of this chapter. For most basic installations, you should select the "Install and configure" option under Reporting Services Native Mode. The remaining instructions assume that you have selected this option.

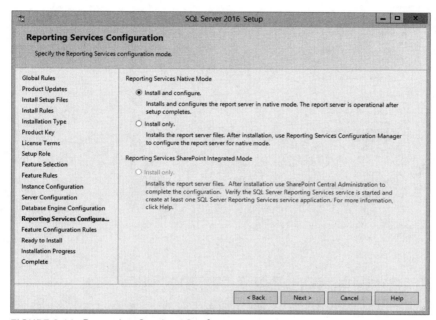

FIGURE 3-14: Reporting Services Configuration page.

Click the Next button to go to the Feature Configuration Rules page. These rules check that everything is in order before proceeding with the installation given the options you have selected. As before, the "View detailed report" link opens a separate report.

Click the Next button to go to the Ready to Install page, shown in Figure 3-15. Carefully review the options you have selected. If you will be repeating this installation on other systems, consider copying the path of the INI file listed at the bottom of the page.

Click the Install button to start the software installation. The installation process can take quite a bit of time to complete. During this time, an Installation Progress page appears, as shown in Figure 3-16. Upon completion, a summary of the installation process is presented.

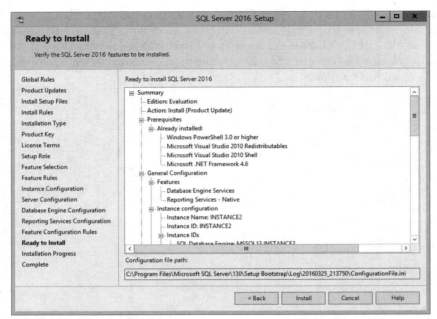

FIGURE 3-15: Ready to Install page.

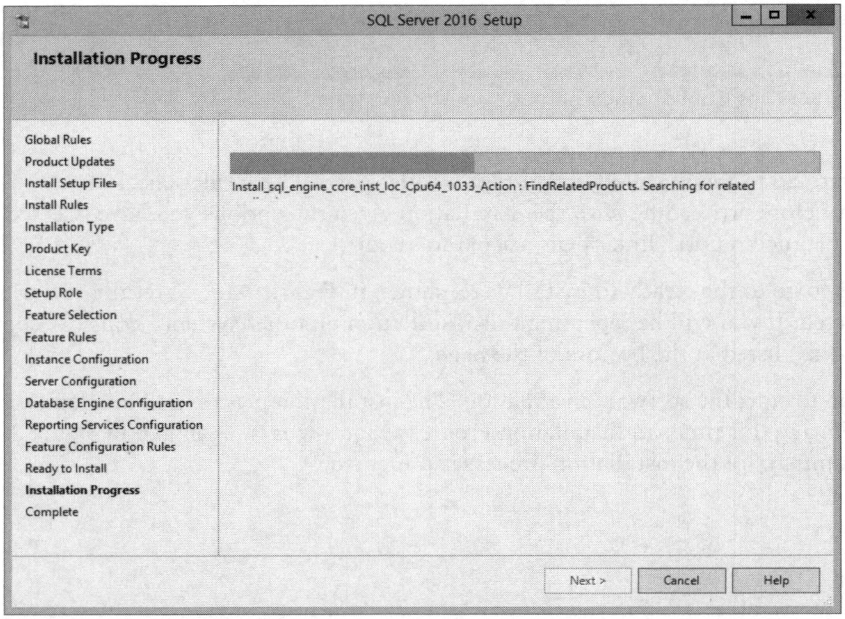

FIGURE 3-16: Installation Progress page.

Click the Close button to complete the wizard and return to the Installation Center. You can now close the Installation Center.

With the installation completed, your final step should be to verify the installation. Open Internet Explorer, and enter one of the following URLs:

➤ If you installed a default instance on the local computer, enter `http://localhost/reports`.

➤ If you installed a named instance, enter `http://localhost/reports_instancename`, with the appropriate substitution. If you installed on a different machine, substitute the server name for localhost.

The URL may take a while to completely resolve upon this first use, but it should take you to the web portal, shown in Figure 3-17.

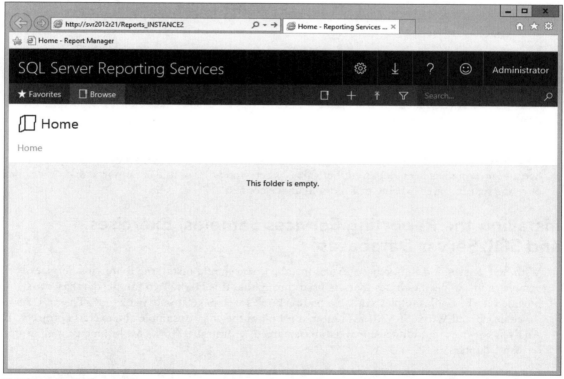

FIGURE 3-17: Web portal.

You can also navigate directly to the report server by replacing "Reports" with "ReportServer" in the address as you see in Figure 3-18.

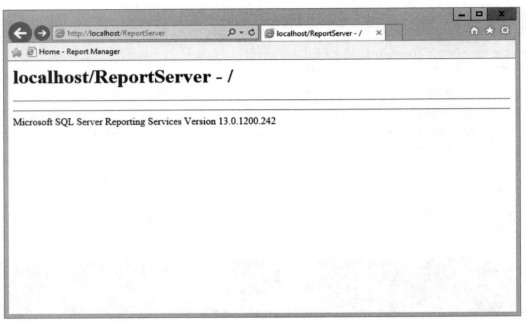

FIGURE 3-18: Navigating directly to the report server.

Of course, there is no content visible in the web portal or in the browser view of the report server because nothing has been deployed, but this is where you will see folders, reports, and other items once the report server is being utilized to manage content.

Installing the Reporting Services Samples, Exercises, and SQL Server Databases

With SQL Server and Reporting Services installed, you should install the Reporting Services samples and sample databases that are used throughout this book. Two sample databases are included in the book samples available on this book's web page at www.wrox.com. The SQL Server database named WroxSSRS2016 is required for all of the chapter sample and exercise projects. The Analysis Services multidimensional database named "Adventure Works Multidimensional" is used only in Chapters 9, 10, and 11.

> **NOTE** *Both of the provided sample databases are prepared specifically for the report samples and chapter exercises in the book. The WroxSSRS2016 database includes data and database objects built from the Adventure Works Cycles data warehouse database from Microsoft, that have been simplified and adapted for reporting purposes. Don't try to use other sample databases in place of these.*

Verify that the SQL Server Database Engine, Reporting Services, and SQL Server Analysis Services are running.

The downloaded files from the book sample site include these three files:

➤   `WroxSSRS2016 Projects.zip`

➤   `WroxSSRS2016.bak`

➤   `Adventure Works Multidimensional.abf`

Setup is quite simple:

1.   Extract the contents of the `WroxSSRS2016 Projects.zip` archive file to your C: drive or a location of your choice. When completed, you should have a folder named WroxSSRS2016. The contents of this folder contains all of the sample and exercise projects used throughout the book.

2.   Use SQL Server Management Studio to restore the WroxSSRS2016 database to your SQL Server instance. Using the default restore option in SSMS will restore the database to the default location with all the capabilities needed. Additional information about restoring a database from SSMS can be found at: `https://msdn.microsoft.com/en-us/library/ ms177429.aspx`.

3.   Restoring the Analysis Services sample databases is recommended and is required for the samples and exercises for Chapters 9, 10, and 11. Use SQL Server Management Studio to restore the Adventure Works Multidimensional database to your SQL Server Analysis Services instance. Additional information about restoring an Analysis Services database can be found at: `https://msdn.microsoft.com/en-us/library/ms188098.aspx`.

THE ENTERPRISE DEPLOYMENT

The basic installation sidesteps many of the considerations important to an enterprise deployment of Reporting Services. As you have seen, default selections are fine for a basic or local development setup but when planning for how Reporting Services will be installed, configured, and distributed within your enterprise environment, you should carefully consider the topics covered in the rest of this section:

➤   SQL Server editions

➤   Named instances

➤   Topology

➤   Modes

➤   Installation options

➤   Command-line installation

➤   Scripting and automating

SQL Server Editions

SQL Server 2016 comes in several editions, the following of which include Reporting Services:

➤ Enterprise

➤ Standard

➤ Developer

➤ Web

➤ Express

Enterprise, Standard, and Web editions are the only editions supported in a production environment. The Enterprise edition provides access to the full set of features available with Reporting Services. The Standard and Web editions provide access to a reduced feature set. They cost less than the Enterprise edition, and may be more appropriate for smaller installations.

The Developer edition provides access to the same features available through the Enterprise edition. The Developer edition is free and is intended for development, evaluation, and testing environments only.

The Web edition supports a reduced feature set, even more so than the Standard edition, and reduced capacity as may be appropriate for small-scale or web-based deployments.

Finally, the Express edition is a highly restricted edition of SQL Server with limited support for Reporting Services. This edition is freely available, but its limitations make it unlikely to be used for anything other than highly specialized needs.

Default and Named Instances

Instance planning is an essential part of SQL Server deployment. A SQL Server instance is a virtually self-contained, separate installation of SQL Server encompassing any combination of services. Separate instances isolate database servers and other services for security and administration purposes. Each instance can be used as a sandbox for testing and deployment build planning.

The components within an instance run as separately managed services that share some system resources. Each instance can have any combination of services. For example, one instance might include the SQL Server relational engine and Analysis Services and another instance might include the relational engine and Reporting Services.

Figure 3-19 shows the filesystem folders created by multiple instances of SQL Server. Each folder is prefixed with the abbreviated service name and postfixed with the instance name. Additional folders with SQL Server version numbers are created for backward version compatibility. In this example, SQL Server was installed three different times. The default instance is named MSSQLSERVER, which includes all the relational engine and Reporting Services. An instance named SSAS_ TABULAR includes Analysis Services. Another instance named INSTANCE2 includes the relational engine and Reporting Services. The two Reporting Services instances are indicated in Figure 3-19.

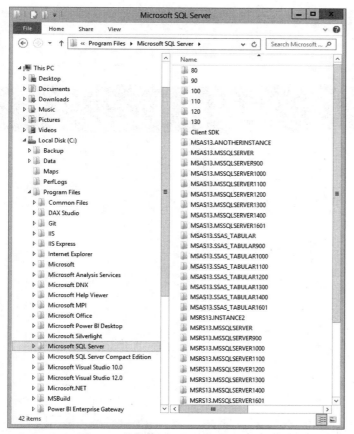

FIGURE 3-19: The two Reporting Services instances.

More than one instance of Reporting Services can be installed on a single server. Each instance runs independently of the others and may be a different version and/or edition of SQL Server. Each has its own Windows service, its own code base, and its own pair of Reporting Services databases with which it interacts. These databases may be housed on separate SQL Server Database Engine instances or on a shared instance, so long as each database is assigned a unique name.

To distinguish between the Reporting Services instances on a server, each is assigned a name, unique on that system. This is called the *instance name*, and an instance with a name assigned to it is called a *named instance*. In addition to named instances, one instance on a given server may be assigned no instance name. This is called the *default instance*. When only one instance is installed to a server, it is often a default instance. Figure 3-20 demonstrates how instance names are translated to a web address for the web portal. In this example a web browser is open to the default instance web portal and another browser window is open to the INSTANCE2 web portal.

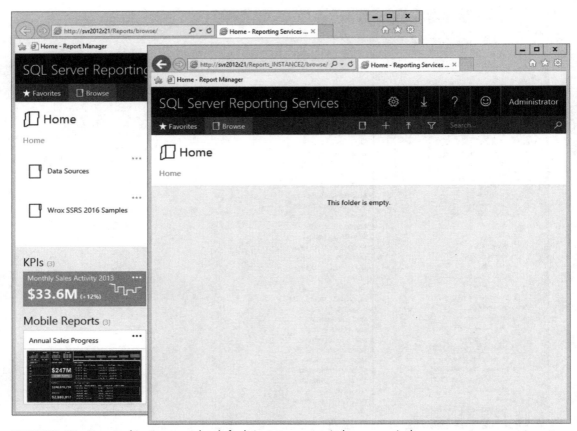

FIGURE 3-20: A named instance and a default instance open in browser windows.

Multiple instances on a single server, whether all named or a combination of named instances and a default instance, can be practical for supporting the migration of a Reporting Services instance from SQL Server 2008 or SQL Server 2008 R2 to SQL Server 2016 when server hardware is limited. Multiple instances can also be a convenient way to minimize the licensing requirements associated with a deployment. That said, historically it has been recommended that a single Reporting Services instance, whether named or default, should be deployed to a production server for the optimal allocation of resources and overall stability.

Topology

Topology refers to how Reporting Services components are distributed among servers while presenting users with unified access to the service's features. The emphasis is on the Reporting Services Windows service and the Reporting Services databases, as opposed to the client tools. Reporting Services provides support for two generalized topologies: standard and scale-outs.

In a standard topology, the Reporting Services Windows service is installed on a system. It interacts with a pair of Reporting Services databases hosted locally or remotely and dedicated for use by this one instance of Reporting Services. The basic installation performed at the beginning of this chapter is an example of a standard topology.

With a scale-out topology, in Native mode, multiple instances of the Reporting Services Windows service are installed across various servers. In SharePoint Integrated mode, the Reporting Services service runs as a shared service on multiple nodes of the SharePoint farm.

In both types of scale-out topologies, these Reporting Services instances share a pair of Reporting Services databases. By sharing these databases, each server (called a *node*) hosting the Reporting Services service has access to the same content and security configuration as the other nodes within the scale-out topology. If load-balancing hardware or software is available on the network, some or all of the nodes in the topology can be presented to end users as a single resource, but with greater and more flexible capacity than is available through a standard deployment. Other nodes within the scale-out topology can be configured to be dedicated to scheduled processing, removing this burden from other nodes in the environment.

As you are deciding between a standard and scale-out topology, it is important to note that scale-outs are supported with only the Enterprise edition of the product. Setting up the scale-out requires additional configuration following the standard installation.

Finally, if you are considering a scale-out topology in pursuit of higher availability, you might want to consider implementing the Reporting Services databases on a failover cluster. It's important to keep in mind that although the SQL Server Database Engine supports failover clustering, and Reporting Services can interact with databases hosted on a cluster, the Reporting Services service itself does not have any clustering capabilities.

Modes

Reporting Services runs in one of two modes: Native or SharePoint Integrated. In Native mode, Reporting Services manages its content using its own internal, or "native," functionality.

Reporting Services deployments using Enterprise, Developer or Standard editions can run in SharePoint Integrated mode. In this mode, content management is handled through SharePoint. Native content management is performed in the Reporting Services web portal.

SharePoint Integrated mode is an option for organizations that want to leverage SharePoint as their enterprise content-management solution and alerting for reports. However, Integrated mode has some limitations, such as the lack of support for linked reports.

For organizations that want to run Reporting Services in Native mode but still want to display Reporting Services content through SharePoint, the Reporting Services web parts provide an alternative to SharePoint Integrated mode.

Installation Options

During installation, you are presented with three Reporting Services configuration options. You can install Reporting Services in Native mode using a default configuration, in SharePoint Integrated mode also using a default configuration, or in a minimally configured mode called a *files only* installation.

The Native with default configuration option is available only if you are installing Reporting Services and the Database Engine as part of the same installation process. These installation options leave Reporting Services in an operational state following the completion of the setup process, although not all Reporting Services features (such as the unattended execution account and e-mail delivery) are configured upon completion. If you are installing Reporting Services using SharePoint Integrated mode, there are two administrative components to the installation and configuration effort. The integrated report server component is simply installed from the SQL Server Installation Center. That part is easy. After that, the remaining configuration is performed in SharePoint Central Admin. The SharePoint farm and services configuration is beyond the scope of this book.

> **NOTE** *I've elected not to cover SharePoint services configuration in this book for a few important reasons. In the previous edition, for SSRS 2012, we did include the basic setup and configuration for SharePoint 2013 Enterprise Server. There is much to consider when building and configuring a SharePoint farm that we simply cannot do justice to within the context of a Reporting Service book. In particular, configuring security and data sources can be quite complex, with several different options. When this chapter was written, SharePoint 2016 was in early preview edition and the Reporting Services integration was still in flux, with integration improvements planned.*

For enterprise deployments, "Reporting Services – Native" installation is the option most frequently used. With the install-only option, the server components are installed but not configured. Following installation, you are required to use the Reporting Services Configuration tool to configure the Reporting Services databases and URLs for the Reporting Services web service and Report Manager before the service can be made operational.

> **TIP** *If you do not have a specific requirement to support Reporting Services running in SharePoint integrated mode, I recommend that you use the Native mode option. It is simpler, easier to support, and will typically perform better. Just to be clear, Reporting Services does work in SharePoint integrated mode and there are advantages if you have an existing SharePoint environment, but the configuration can be quite complex.*

THE REPORTING LIFE CYCLE

The reporting life cycle is often described as consisting of three phases. A report is designed and developed in the authoring phase, made accessible to end users in the management phase, and placed in the hands of end users in the delivery phase.

Authoring

The *authoring phase* of the reporting life cycle starts with gathering requirements through formal and informal processes. These requirements then drive the design of queries that provide data for the report. Data is integrated with charts, tables, matrices, or other presentation elements to form the basic report. Formatting and layout adjustments are then applied to produce a draft report that is validated for accuracy and consistency with the requirements before being published to a centralized management system in preparation for end-user consumption.

Report authoring is handled by two general categories of workers:

End-user authors develop reports as a secondary part of their job. These folks typically belong to the non-IT part of an organization and tend to require less technical, more user-friendly report authoring tools. These tools present data in a manner that is easy to interpret and incorporate into the report design. They make report layout and formatting a relatively simple or even automatic task.

Reporting specialists focus on report development as a primary part of their job. These folks often reside within the IT department. Reporting specialists demand precise control over query and report design. Their authoring tools tend to be more technical, providing access to the complete array of features available through the reporting system.

Of course, not every report author falls neatly into one of these groups. The end-user author and the reporting specialist represent two ends of a spectrum, with many authors leaning toward one end or the other. A variety of report development tools are needed to address the full range of needs along this spectrum.

Management

In the *management phase* of the reporting life cycle, published reports are organized, secured, and configured for end-user access. Resources employed by multiple reports and specialized features, such as subscription delivery and caching, are configured. These activities are collectively referred to as *content management* and are often handled to some degree by both authors and administrators.

The report management system itself requires configuration and ongoing maintenance to ensure its continued operation. System management activities are often the exclusive domain of administrators.

Delivery

After it is deployed and configured, a report is ready for end-user consumption in the *delivery phase* of the reporting life cycle. End users may view reports on demand or may request that reports be delivered to them on a predefined schedule. These are called the *pull* and *push* methods of report delivery, respectively. The key to successful report delivery is flexibility.

REPORTING SERVICES TOOLS

Reporting Services supports the full reporting life cycle using two different report authoring tools for paginated reports and a modern desktop authoring tool for mobile reports.

Report Designer exposes the full range of available report-development features, giving report specialists precise control over their reports. The application is accessible through the SQL Server Data Tools (SSDT), which is a collection of specialized designers available through Visual Studio. SSDT is installed as a separate download and integrates with existing installations of Visual Studio 2012 and newer. The new SSDT is an "evergreen" application, which means that it will be updated frequently and will continue to work with newer versions of Visual Studio.

Report Designer is divided into two tabs: Design and Preview. Each of these tabs provides access to interfaces supporting query development, report layout and formatting, and validation. Wizards and dialogs accessible through Report Designer provide support for the development of highly customized, sophisticated reports. In the following chapters, you will gain deep exposure to these features.

Report Builder

Report Builder is a report designer with capabilities similar to those in the SSDT Report Designer, but it has more of a Microsoft Office look and feel. Rather than an end-to-end solution development platform like SSDT, Report Builder is a single document-centric report design tool created with the self-service report user in mind. It is available as a standalone download, which is initiated for a user upon first use from the web portal web interface.

Web Portal

The modern replacement for the previous Report Manager web interface, *web portal* is a content-management and report presentation tool that provides access to reports and other items through an intuitive, folder-based navigational structure. It is securable, easy to navigate, and allows users to customize their experience using favorites and familiar content browsing techniques.

It is important to note that web portal is available only with Reporting Services instances running in Native mode. For instances running in SharePoint Integrated mode, content management and report display functionality are provided through SharePoint.

SharePoint Libraries and Web Parts

For Reporting Services instances running in SharePoint Integrated mode, reports and other Reporting Services items are presented as part of standard SharePoint libraries and are managed as SharePoint content. The Report Viewer web part, installed during the setup of SharePoint integration, allows reports from instances in this mode to be presented through SharePoint.

Access to Reporting Services content through SharePoint is not the exclusive domain of instances running in SharePoint Integrated mode. Native-mode instances can also present content using an older version of Reporting Services SharePoint 2.0 web parts. The Report Explorer 2.0 and Report Viewer 2.0 web parts allow reports from Native-mode instances to be displayed within a SharePoint site.

Reporting Services Configuration Manager

The Reporting Services Configuration Manager lets you access system-critical settings. In addition, the tool provides support for certain administrative tasks, such as creating the Reporting Services application database and backing up and restoring encryption keys. Chapter 22 covers these tasks and the use of the Reporting Services Configuration Manager to perform them.

SQL Server Management Applications

Because Reporting Services is a member of the SQL Server product suite, it is supported through the standard SQL Server management applications. SQL Server Management Studio allows you to perform several administrative tasks, including managing shared schedules and roles. Configuration of the Reporting Services Windows service is supported through the SQL Server Configuration Manager, although some of this functionality is redundant with the Reporting Services Configuration Manager.

Command-Line Utilities

To assist with the automation of management tasks, Reporting Services comes with a series of command-line utilities. Table 3-1 describes each utility and its default location.

TABLE 3-1: Command-Line Utilities

UTILITY	DESCRIPTION	DEFAULT LOCATION
Rs.exe	Executes VB.NET scripts, automating administrative tasks. This tool may be used with Reporting Services installations not running in SharePoint Integrated mode.	\<drive>:\Program Files\ Microsoft SQL Server\110\ Tools\Binn\rs.exe
Rsconfig.exe	Modifies connection information for the Reporting Services database and sets the default execution account used by Reporting Services to connect to data sources when no credentials are provided.	\<drive>:\Program Files\ Microsoft SQL Server\110\ Tools\Binn\rsconfig.exe
Rskeymgmt.exe	Manages the encryption keys used by Reporting Services. It is also used to join a Reporting Services installation with another Reporting Services installation to form a "scale-out" deployment.	\<drive>:\Program Files\ Microsoft SQL Server\110\ Tools\Binn\rskeymgmt.exe

> **NOTE** *At the time of this writing, there is an effort underway to create a comprehensive set of PowerShell CmdLets for Reporting Services, with an interim project that currently exists in GitHub. Since there is a good chance this location will change by the time you read this, I'll direct you to a post on my blog where I'm tracking the progress of this effort. The post may be found here:* `https://sqlserverbiblog.wordpress.com/2016/07/29/reporting-services-2016-powershell-cmdlets/`.

HTML Viewer

Reporting Services delivers web content to HTML5-compliant browsers to provide several interactive features, including a toolbar, document maps, fixed table headers, and table sorting. Collectively, these script-based features are called the *HTML Viewer*.

To ensure compatibility with the HTML Viewer, it is recommended that you use the latest version of Internet Explorer, Edge Browser, or Google Chrome. Prior versions of Reporting Services had issues with web browsers other than newer versions of Internet Explorer but most popular modern browsers are now supported. Web browsers can be used to view Reporting Services reports rendered to HTML, such as Firefox, Chrome, and Safari. Refer to Books Online for details on which features are supported by which browsers.

Report Viewer Control

The *Report Viewer control* lets you display Reporting Services reports within custom applications. The Report Viewer control is actually two controls—one for use in web applications, and the other for Windows Forms applications. Each supports the same functionality.

> **NOTE** *Don't confuse the Report Viewer control with the SharePoint Report Viewer web part and the Report Viewer 2.0 web part used to support the display of Reporting Services content within SharePoint.*

The Report Viewer control runs in one of two modes. In the default Remote Processing mode, reports are rendered by a Reporting Services instance and displayed through the control. This is the preferred mode, because the full feature set of Reporting Services is available, and the processing power of the Reporting Services server can be employed.

In situations in which a Reporting Services server is unavailable or data must be retrieved directly through the client system, the Report Viewer control can be run in Local Processing mode. In this mode, the application retrieves data and couples it with the report definition to produce a rendered report on the host system without the support of a Reporting Services server. Not all Reporting Services features are available when the control is executed in Local Processing mode.

Integrating reports with custom applications through the Report Viewer control is covered in detail in Chapter 15.

Reporting Services Web Service

To support specialized application integration needs, Reporting Services offers a web service through which reports can be both managed and delivered. As described in Table 3-2, the web service has several endpoints that provide access to various programmatic classes.

TABLE 3-2: Web Service Endpoints

ENDPOINT	DESCRIPTION
ReportExecution2005	Provides programmatic access to Reporting Services report processing and rendering functionality. Available in both Native and SharePoint Integrated modes, although different URLs are used.
ReportService2010	Provides programmatic access to Reporting Services report management functionality. Available in both Native and SharePoint Integrated modes.
ReportService Authentication	Provides support for user authentication when Reporting Services runs in SharePoint Integrated mode and SharePoint is configured for forms authentication.

A special feature of the Reporting Services web service is *URL access*, in which a rendered report is retrieved through a relatively simple call to a URL. Parameters and rendering options are supplied in the URL's query string to affect the resulting report.

Subscriptions

Subscriptions allow you to put reports into the hands of your users based on a predefined schedule or following an event, such as the update of data. Reporting Services supports two types of subscriptions:

Standard subscriptions render a report in a specific format with predefined parameter values and deliver them to a single, preset location. This type of subscription meets the needs of many report consumers, giving them sufficient freedom to determine how, when, and where they will view reports.

Data-driven subscriptions support even more flexibility, and are better suited for managing delivery of reports to a large number of users with varying needs. These subscriptions are established with a reference to a custom relational table holding a record for each report recipient. Each record in the table may specify rendering and delivery options as well as report parameter values. Through data-driven subscriptions, a single subscription can be tailored to the specific needs of many individual consumers.

By default, subscription delivery is limited to e-mail transmittal or file share drop-off. Additional delivery options are supported through the integration of custom delivery extensions, as discussed in Chapter 16.

REPORTING SERVICES WINDOWS SERVICE

The preceding section looked at the applications through which authors, administrators, and end users interact with Reporting Services. This section covers the basic architecture of the Reporting Services service itself.

In Native mode, the service is a Windows service. For SharePoint Integrated mode, SQL Server 2012 introduced deeper integration with SharePoint than previous product versions; the service runs as a shared service directly as part of SharePoint.

Interaction with the service takes place through HTTP and WMI interfaces. The HTTP interfaces provide access to the core report management and delivery functionality of Reporting Services, and the WMI interface provides direct access to service management functionality in Native mode. SharePoint integrated mode in SSRS 2016 integrates its service configuration directly into the SharePoint configuration pages. External configuration files and application databases support the service. Figure 3-21 shows these interfaces and features.

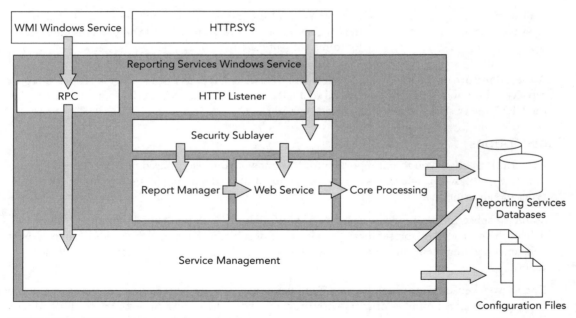

FIGURE 3-21: SSRS services and dependencies.

The following sections explore these aspects of the Reporting Services Windows service:

➤ HTTP.SYS and the HTTP Listener

➤ The security sublayer

> ➤ Web portal and the web service
> ➤ Core processing
> ➤ Service management
> ➤ Configuration files
> ➤ WMI and the RPC interface

HTTP.SYS and the HTTP Listener

When an HTTP request is sent to the Reporting Services server in Native mode, the request is first received by the server operating system through the HTTP.SYS driver. HTTP.SYS is responsible for managing a connection with the requestor and routing HTTP communications to the appropriate application on the server.

URL reservations recorded in the Registry by Reporting Services provide the instructions HTTP .SYS requires to route communications to Reporting Services. The HTTP Listener feature of the Reporting Services Windows service receives the rerouted requests from HTTP.SYS and engages either the Web portal or the web service application it hosts.

Reporting Services in Native mode does not use Internet Information Server (IIS), Microsoft's web server. This simplifies the installation and management requirements for Reporting Services.

Although Reporting Services does not depend on or interact with IIS, you can still run IIS on the Reporting Services server if you have some other need for it. So long as URL reservations recorded by the two do not conflict, both Reporting Services and IIS can even communicate over the same TCP ports.

> **NOTE** *The one exception is that IIS 5.1 and Reporting Services cannot share TCP ports on 32-bit Windows XP. If you have this configuration, you need to alter the URL reservations to use different TCP port numbers. You can alter the Reporting Services reservations using the Reporting Services Configuration Manager, as described in Chapter 22.*

The Security Sublayer

As requests are received, the HTTP Listener hands them over to the Reporting Services security sublayer. The sublayer is responsible for determining the requestor's identity and then determining if the user has the required rights for the request to be fulfilled. These steps are called *authentication* and *authorization*.

Reporting Services in SharePoint Integrated mode plugs into the SharePoint site authentication mechanisms.

The Reporting Services security sublayer is implemented through a component called a *security extension*. The extension handles the mechanics of authentication and authorization and exposes a standard set of interfaces for Reporting Services to call. Various security extensions can be used with Reporting Services, but Reporting Services deployment can be configured to use only one at a time.

Reporting Services in Native mode comes preconfigured with the Windows-integrated security extension. This extension authenticates users based on their Windows credentials and supports four mechanisms for exchanging credentials, called *authentication types*:

Kerberos is the preferred mechanism for authentication if the feature is supported within the domain. Kerberos is highly secure. If delegation and impersonation are enabled, Kerberos can be used to allow Reporting Services to impersonate the end user when querying an external data source.

NT Lan Manager (NTLM) employs a challenge-response mechanism to authenticate end users. This is a secure but limited method of authentication in that impersonation and delegation are not supported.

The Negotiate authentication type is the default authentication type of the Windows Integrated Security extension. With this authentication type, Kerberos is used if available. Otherwise, NTLM is used.

Basic authentication is the least secure of the authentication types. With Basic authentication, user credentials are passed between the client and Reporting Services in plaintext. If you are using Basic authentication, you should consider implementing a Secure Sockets Layer (SSL) certificate to encrypt your HTTP communications.

Regardless of whether the default or a custom security extension is used, as soon as identity is established, the user's rights to perform a requested action must be verified. (Closer to the actual sequence of events, the user is authenticated, and the request is passed directly or indirectly to the web service, which then calls back to the security extension for authorization.) Like many other Microsoft products, authorization in Reporting Services is based on role assignments. As roles are created, the rights to perform system- and item-level tasks are assigned to a role. Users are then made members of a role, providing the linkage required to determine whether a user is authorized to perform a requested task.

Web Portal and the Web Service

All requests sent via HTTP are targeted to the web portal or web service applications. The functionality of these applications is outlined in the "Reporting Services Tools" section earlier in this chapter.

What's important in the context of this discussion is to understand that both ASP.NET applications—web portal and the Reporting Services web service—are hosted from within the

Reporting Services Windows service (with no dependencies on IIS, as discussed a moment ago). Both operate in their own application domains. This allows the Windows service to manage these as independent applications (despite web portal's functional dependency on the web service). The benefit is that problems within an application domain can be isolated. The Windows service can respond by starting a new instance of the application domain while dissolving the problem instance of the application domain.

Core Processing

Reporting Services' core processing features—scheduling, subscription management, delivery, and report processing—are performed by a collection of components hosted within the Reporting Services service. Although not based on ASP.NET, these components are managed as a separate application domain within the service. The "Reporting Services Processors and Extensions" section later in this chapter explores these components in more detail.

Service Management

Much goes on within Reporting Services. To ensure that resources are available and the service is working properly, a collection of internal service management features is implemented. Although not truly a single entity, these can be thought of collectively as a service management sublayer.

One critical feature of the sublayer is application domain management. As mentioned, web portal, the web service, and core processing features are hosted within the Reporting Services Windows service as three separate application domains. Occasionally, problems within these arise. The service management sublayer's application-domain management feature monitors for these problems and recycles the affected application domains. This helps ensure the overall stability of the Reporting Services Windows service.

Another critical feature of this sublayer is memory management. Report processing can be memory-intensive. The Reporting Services service monitors memory pressure and responds, if needed, by temporarily moving portions of large requests out of memory to disk, while small requests proceed unaffected. Much of this is achieved through dynamic memory allocation and the use of disk caching in memory-constrained situations. The Reporting Services memory management model is outlined in Chapter 22.

Configuration Files

Reporting Services' internal and external features are controlled by collections of parameters recorded in configuration files. *Configuration files* are XML documents that follow a prescribed structure containing information governing the behavior of various components of the Reporting Services Windows service. Table 3-4 lists the most critical of these configuration files.

TABLE 3-4: SSRS CONFIGURATION FILES

CONFIGURATION FILE	DESCRIPTION	DEFAULT LOCATION
`ReportingServicesService.exe.config`	Contains settings affecting tracing and logging by the Reporting Services Windows service.	`<drive>:\Program Files\ Microsoft SQL Server\ MSRS13.<instancename>\Reporting Services\ReportServer\Bin`
`RSReportServer.config`	Contains settings affecting numerous aspects of Reporting Services. This is the primary configuration file for Reporting Services functionality.	`<drive>:\Program Files\ Microsoft SQL Server\ MSRS13.<instancename>\Reporting Services\ReportServer`
`RSSrvPolicy.config`	Contains settings regulating code access security policies for the Reporting Services extensions.	`<drive>:\Program Files\ Microsoft SQL Server\ MSRS13.<instancename>\Reporting Services\ReportServer`
`RSMgrPolicy.config`	Contains settings regulating code access security policies for web portal.	`<drive>:\Program Files\ Microsoft SQL Server\ MSRS13.<instancename>\Reporting Services\ReportManager`

WMI and the RPC Interface

Microsoft's Windows Management Instrumentation (WMI) technology lets you consistently manage devices and applications running on Windows platforms. The Reporting Services Windows service exposes itself to WMI by registering two classes with the local WMI Windows service. These classes expose properties and methods that the WMI service makes available to administrative applications.

The first of the two classes registered by Reporting Services, `MSReportServer_Instance`, provides basic information about the Reporting Services installation, including edition, version, and mode.

The second class, `MSReportServer_ConfigurationSetting`, provides access to many of the settings in the `RSReportServer.config` configuration file and exposes a host of methods supporting critical administrative tasks. Administrative interfaces such as the Reporting Services Configuration tool leverage this provider for their functionality.

> **NOTE** *Developers can also take advantage of these and other WMI interfaces. The chief difficulty is making sense of the namespace organization within WMI. The WMI Code Creator utility, available from the Microsoft website, is an excellent tool for exploring the WMI namespaces and the properties and methods exposed through each.*

A remote procedure call (RPC) interface provided by the Reporting Services service acts as a bridge between the WMI and Reporting Services Windows service. Through this bridge, calls against the registered classes received by the WMI service are relayed to Reporting Services.

REPORTING SERVICES PROCESSORS AND EXTENSIONS

In the "Reporting Services Tools" section of this chapter, you looked inside the Reporting Services Windows service. The service's core processing features were introduced as an application domain whose functionality is provided through a collection of components. You now explore those components to gain a deeper understanding of just how Reporting Services delivers its primary functionality and where that functionality can be extended.

Before jumping into the specific components, you should be aware of the difference between extensions and processors. *Processors* are the coordinators and facilitators in Reporting Services' component architecture. They call the extensions as needed and provide mechanisms for data exchange between them (see Figure 3-22). Although configuration settings may alter their behavior, processors cannot be extended through custom code.

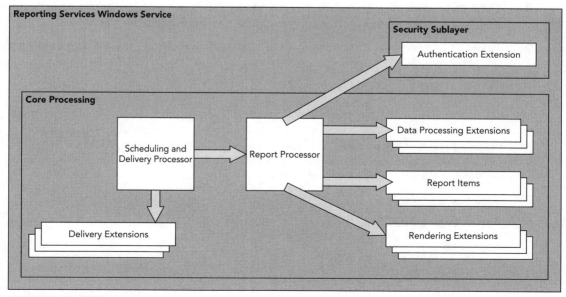

FIGURE 3-22: SSRS core processing.

Extensions are components registered with Reporting Services to provide specific functionality. They expose standardized interfaces, which provide the mechanism by which Reporting Services engages them.

With these concepts in mind, let's now take a look at the following:

- ➤ The Report Processor
- ➤ Data processing extensions
- ➤ Report items
- ➤ Rendering extensions
- ➤ The Scheduling and Delivery Processor
- ➤ Delivery extensions

The security extension was discussed in the earlier section "The Security Sublayer."

The Report Processor

The Report Processor combines data and layout instructions to produce a report. Following the arrival of a request for a report, the processor does the following:

1. Calls the security extension to authorize the request
2. Retrieves the report definition from the Reporting Services database
3. Communicates data retrieval instructions in the report definition to the data processing extensions
4. Combines data returned from the data processing extensions with layout instructions, using report processing extensions if needed to produce an intermediate format report
5. Passes the intermediate format report to the appropriate rendering extension to produce the final report
6. Returns the final report to the requestor

End users can't view the intermediate format report, but it can be rendered to any of the formats supported by Reporting Services. To reduce the time and resource expense of producing a final report, the intermediate format report can be stored (cached) for reuse. This provides a way to skip Steps 2, 3, and 4, allowing a report to be returned with less time and resource consumption. Reporting Services supports three forms of caching:

- ➤ Report session caching
- ➤ Report execution caching
- ➤ Snapshots

Report Session Caching

When an end user connects to Reporting Services, a session is established. Requests from an end user are made within the context of a specific session until that session expires.

During a session, users often request that the same report be rendered multiple times, possibly in differing formats. Reporting Services anticipates this by storing the intermediate format report in its Session cache. The cached copy is recorded with Session identifiers so that when an end user repeats a request for a report as part of his or her session, the cached copy can be leveraged. This feature of Reporting Services, known as *report session caching*, is always enabled.

If you change report parameter selections and those parameter values are used in dataset queries, an additional cache for the changed datasets is created in the report session.

Report Execution Caching

Why tie cached reports to a session? Why not make them available to all users requesting the same report? The reason has to do with security.

Reports are populated by data retrieved from external data sources. Connections to those data sources are established using credentials. The credentials used depend on the report's configuration or the shared data source it uses.

If data is retrieved using the requestor's credentials, the report may contain data appropriate only to that specific user. The intermediate report contains this data so that if it is cached and made available to another requestor, that user may be exposed to data that he or she otherwise should not see.

For this reason, only reports that do not use the requestor's credentials to retrieve data from external data sources can be configured for report execution caching. With report execution caching, the intermediate report generated from a report request is cached for some period of time and is used to render reports for other users until the cached copy expires.

Snapshots

With both report session and report execution caching, the end user requests a report, and the Report Processor checks for a cached copy. If none exists, the Report Processor must assemble the intermediate format report, store it in a cache for subsequent requests, and then render the requested final report. Later requests may take advantage of the cached copy, but the first request does not have this option. This can lead to an inconsistent end-user experience.

To address this issue, snapshots are scheduled to populate the cache before an end-user request. Snapshots are recorded in the same intermediate format and have the same security requirements as report execution caching.

Data Processing Extensions

As mentioned, the Report Processor reads data retrieval instructions from the report definition, but hands over the work of establishing connections and retrieving data from external sources to the data processing extensions. These extensions expose a data reader interface back to the Report Processor, allowing data to flow through them to the Report Processor and into the intermediate report.

Multiple data source extensions can be in use on the Report Server and even employed from within a single report. Reporting Services includes several data extensions, providing support for the following data sources:

- ➤ Microsoft SQL Server
- ➤ Microsoft SQL Server Analysis Services
- ➤ OLE DB data sources
- ➤ ODBC data sources
- ➤ Oracle
- ➤ XML data sources
- ➤ SAP NetWeaver BI
- ➤ Hyperion Essbase
- ➤ Teradata

It's important to note that the SAP NetWeaver BI, Hyperion Essbase, and Teradata extensions require the separate installation of client components or .NET data providers. If you need to use these data processing extensions, refer to Books Online for details on how to make these fully operational.

If access to other data sources is required, you can implement a custom data processing extension and register it with Reporting Services. Alternatively, you may be able to use a standard .NET or OLE DB data provider to obtain the data access you require. As mentioned a moment ago, data processing extensions expose a standard data reader interface. This interface is based on .NET specifications, which are themselves not that far removed from interfaces exposed by some OLE DB providers. As a result, many .NET and OLE DB data providers can be registered and used by Reporting Services in place of a formal data processing extension. Books Online provides details on the registration of data providers for use with Reporting Services.

Report Items

The Report Processor can generate tables, matrices, charts, and various other report items. These standard report items meet the needs of most report authors. Still, sometimes other report items are required. In these situations, additional report items can be registered with Reporting Services.

Typically these report items, such as barcode and chart controls, are purchased from third-party vendors. Custom report items can be developed as well. Report items, whether purchased or custom, consist of both design and runtime components that must be registered with the Report Designer and Reporting Services, respectively. Both expose standard interfaces allowing the Report Designer or the Report Processor to interact with them appropriately.

Rendering Extensions

After the intermediate format report has been generated (or retrieved from cache) by the Report Processor, it is delivered to a rendering extension for translation to the end-user requested format. Reporting Services comes with a standard set of rendering extensions, as described in Table 3-5. Each supports one or more report formats. Custom rendering extensions are also supported, although Microsoft does not encourage their development. Custom rendering extensions typically involve a large development cost.

TABLE 3-5: Included SSRS rendering extensions

RENDERING EXTENSION	FORMATS SUPPORTED
HTML	HTML5 (default)
	HTML4.0
	MHTML
CSV	Excel-optimized CSV (default)
	CSV-compliant CSV
XML	XML
Image	TIFF (default)
	BMP
	EMF
	GIF
	JPEG
	PNG
	WMF
PDF	PDF 1.3
Excel	Excel (XLSX)
Word	Word (DOCX)
PowerPoint	PowerPoint (PPTX)
Atom	Produces an Atom data feed metadata descriptor file (ATOMSVC)

Parameters affecting how each rendering extension generates the final report are known as *device information settings*. Default settings for each rendering extension can be set in the `rsreportserver.config` file. These can be overridden as part of a specific request to deliver the report in the precise format required.

It is important to note that the Report Processor does not simply hand over the intermediate format report to a rendering extension. Instead, the processor engages the rendering extension, which, in return, accesses the intermediate report through the Rendering Object Model (ROM) exposed by the Report Processor.

The ROM has retained the same basic structure since the release of Reporting Services 2008 and has many benefits. The most significant of these is improved consistency between online and print versions of a report and reduced memory consumption during rendering.

The HTML-Rendering Extension

HTML is highly accessible and the principal format for interactive reports. For these reasons, HTML 5 is now the default rendering format for Reporting Services reports. The HTML rendering experience introduced in SQL Server 2016 is a significant improvement over previous version HTML renderings, which primarily targeted Microsoft Internet Explorer. As the HTML standards have superseded individual vender browser specifications, HTML 5 will render consistently in all modern browsers and with limited support for older web browsers.

The CSV-Rendering Extension

The *comma-separated values (CSV)-rendering extension* renders the data portion of a report to a comma-delimited flat-file format accessible by spreadsheets and other applications.

The CSV-rendering extension operates in two modes. In the default, Excel-optimized mode, each data region of the report is rendered as a separate block of comma-delimited values. In CSV-compliant mode, the extension produces a single, uniform block of data accessible to a wider range of applications.

The XML-Rendering Extension

XML is another format commonly used to render reports. The *XML-rendering extension* incorporates both data and layout information in the XML it generates. One of the most powerful features of the XML-rendering extension is its ability to accept an XSLT document. XSLT documents provide instructions for converting XML to other text-based formats. These formats may include HTML, CSV, XML, or a custom file format. The Reporting Services team recommends that you attempt to leverage the XML-rendering format with XSLT for specialized rendering needs before you attempt to implement a custom rendering extension.

The Image-Rendering Extension

Through the *image-rendering extension*, reports are published to one of seven image formats. Tagged Image File Format (TIFF) is the default. TIFF is widely used for storing document images. Many fax programs use TIFF as their transfer standard, and many organizations use it for document archives. The image renderer also supports image output for BMP, GIF, JPG, PNG, and EMF image files.

The PDF-Rendering Extension

Reporting Services comes with a rendering extension for Adobe's Portable Document Format (PDF). PDF is one of the most popular formats for document sharing over the Internet. It produces clean, easy-to-read documents with exceptional printing capabilities. In addition, PDF documents are not easily altered.

Although they are not as interactive as an HTML report with the HTML Viewer, PDFs do support document maps. This functionality enables the creation of a table of contents-like feature, which is invaluable with large reports. Windows 10 native PDF support or Adobe Reader 8.0 or higher is required for viewing the PDF documents produced by Reporting Services. The Adobe Reader is available for free download from the Adobe website.

When possible, the PDF rendering extension embeds the subset of each font that is needed to display the report in the PDF file. Fonts that are used in the report must be installed on the report server. When the report server generates a report in PDF format, it uses the information stored in the font referenced by the report to create character mappings within the PDF file. If the referenced font is not installed on the report server, the resulting PDF file might not contain the correct mappings and might not display correctly when viewed.

The Excel-Rendering Extension

Rendering reports to Excel is another option that Reporting Services supports. Rendering to Excel is highly useful if the end user needs to perform additional analysis on the data.

Reporting Services in SQL Server 2016 by default produces Excel Office Open XML format (XLSX). The original Excel renderer producing BIFF8-based format for Excel 97 and above is still available, but it is hidden in `rsReportServer.config` by default.

Not all report elements translate well to Excel. Rectangles, subreports, the report body, and data regions are rendered as a range of Excel cells. Textboxes, images, and charts must be rendered within one Excel cell, which might be merged, depending on the layout of the rest of the report.

It is a good idea to review your reports rendered to this format prior to publication to end users if Excel rendering is a critical requirement. Reporting Services Books Online provides details on how each report feature is handled when rendered to Excel.

The Word-Rendering Extension

This extension renders reports in Microsoft Word format with many of the same features and limitations as rendering in PDF. Unlike PDF, the Word format allows reports to be more easily edited by the end user following rendering.

Reporting Services in SQL Server 2016 by default produces Word Office Open XML format (DOCX). The original Word renderer producing Word 97 format is still available, but it is hidden in `rsReportServer.config` by default.

The PowerPoint-Rendering Extension

The PowerPoint-rendering extension is introduced in SQL Server 2016. It converts report page content into sides in a PowerPoint presentation deck using the PowerPoint Office Open XML (PPTX) format. All visual report elements and data regions are converted to image shapes. Chart titles and text are rendered as textboxes.

The Scheduling and Delivery Processor

The Scheduling and Delivery Processor's primary function is to send requests for subscribed reports to the Report Processor, accept the returned report, and engage the delivery extensions for subscription delivery. The processor also generates snapshots.

The processor works by periodically reviewing the contents of tables within one of the Reporting Services application databases. These tables are populated through on-demand events, through programmatic execution of the Reporting Services web service's `FireEvent` method, or through schedules configured through Reporting Services. Schedules themselves are jobs created by Reporting Services but executed by the SQL Server SQL Agent Windows service. Reporting Services handles the details of setting up and configuring these jobs when you create a schedule, but the use of schedules creates a dependency on this additional Windows service.

Delivery Extensions

The Scheduling and Delivery Processor calls the delivery extensions to send reports to subscribers. Reporting Services comes with delivery extensions for e-mail and file share delivery. If running in SharePoint Integrated mode, Reporting Services also supports the SharePoint delivery extension for delivery of content to a SharePoint site.

As with other extensions discussed in this chapter, custom delivery extensions can be assembled and registered for use by Reporting Services. Books Online provides sample code for a custom delivery extension, sending reports directly to a printer.

REPORTING SERVICES APPLICATION DATABASES

Reporting Services includes two application databases with the default names: ReportServer and ReportServerTempDB. These databases store report definitions, snapshots, cache, security information, and much more. Although it is strongly recommended that you not directly access these databases and modify data, it is important to understand their basic structure and role within the Reporting Services architecture.

> **NOTE** *When run in SharePoint Integrated mode, Reporting Services stores content and settings in the SharePoint content and configuration databases. These databases are the domain of the SharePoint application and therefore are not discussed here. As with the Reporting Services databases, it is recommended that you not directly access those databases.*

ReportServer

The ReportServer database is the main store for data in Reporting Services. It contains all report definitions, report models, data sources, schedules, security information, and snapshots. Because of this, it is critical that the database be backed up regularly.

Table 3-6 lists some of the tables and their related functions.

TABLE 3-6: ReportServer database tables

FUNCTIONAL AREA	TABLE NAME	WHAT IT CONTAINS
Resources	Catalog	Report definitions, folder locations, and data source information
	DataSource	Individual data source information
Security	Users	Username and security ID (SID) information for authorized users
	Policies	A list of references to different security policies
	PolicyUserRole	An association of users/groups, roles, and policies
	Roles	A list of defined roles and the tasks they can perform
Snapshots	SnapshotData	Information used to run an individual snapshot, including query parameters and snapshot dependencies
	ChunkData	The report snapshots
	History	A reference between stored snapshots and the date they were captured
Scheduling	Schedule	Information for different report execution and subscription delivery schedules
	ReportSchedule	An association between a given report, its execution schedule, and the action to take
	Subscriptions	A list of individual subscriptions, including the owner, parameters, and delivery extension
	Notifications	Subscription notification information such as date processed, last run time, and delivery extension
	Event	Temporary storage location for event notifications
	ActiveSubscriptions	Subscription success/failure information
	RunningJobs	The currently executing scheduled processes
Administration	ConfigurationInfo	Reporting Services configuration information, which should be administered through prescribed interfaces and not by directly editing this table's data
	Keys	A list of public and private keys for data encryption
	ExecutionLogStorage	A list of reports that have been executed and critical metadata about the event

ReportServerTempDB

The ReportServerTempDB database stores temporary Reporting Services information. This includes both session and cache data.

Reporting Services do not function properly without the ReportServerTempDB database. Still, there is no need to back up the database, because all data within it is temporary. If the database is lost, you can simply rebuild it.

Table 3-7 lists some of the tables and their related functions.

TABLE 3-7: ReportServerTempDB database tables

TABLE NAME	DESCRIPTION
ChunkData	Stores report definition and data for session cached reports and cached instances
ExecutionCache	Stores execution information, including time-out for cached instances
PersistedStream	Stores session-level rendered output for an individual user
SessionData	Persists individual user session-level information, including report paths and time-outs for given session information
SessionLock	Temporary storage to handle locking of session data
SnapshotData	Stores a temporary snapshot

SUMMARY

The purpose of this chapter was to help you get a basic installation of Reporting Services in Native mode up and running so that you can explore the product as you progress through this book with the sample databases, project files, and chapter exercises.

This chapter also toured the Reporting Services Native mode architecture. Through this chapter, you explored the following:

➤ The reporting life cycle as a three-phase process. Reports are authored by end users and reporting specialists, managed as part of a centralized reporting system, and ultimately delivered to end users through various means.

➤ The numerous applications provided by Reporting Services in support of the reporting life cycle. These include but are not limited to Report Builder, SSDT Report Designer, Report Web Portal, the Reporting Services Configuration tool, HTML Viewer, the Reporting Services web service, and subscriptions.

➤ The structure of the Windows service as well as the components (processors, extensions, and databases) the service uses to provide its functionality.

The knowledge you have obtained in this chapter will provide a solid foundation for you to get started with a working report server and report design environment. You are now prepared to begin authoring reports and to learn the intricacies of advanced report design.

In Part 2, beginning with Chapter 4, we get back to basics—literally—and start designing basic reports. Chapters 4, 5, and 6 introduce the fundamental building blocks of report design so you can understand the essentials and develop necessary skills. You'll start with basic layout and formatting, progress to data access and query basics, and then learn to perform grouping and totals.

PART II
Basic Report Design

With the topic of report design essentials having been introduced in four previous editions of this book, as well as the topic being included in four previous versions of Reporting Services over the past 12 years, I've had several opportunities to approach the "right" way to teach report design. Keeping things simple and on point is the method I chose for this book. As you work with this product, the recognizable theme is that there are different ways to design reports and solve problems that might get you to the same or a similar outcome. Rather than enumerating every option, I'll recommend what I believe could be considered the best approach and avoids getting lost in the details (which, by the way, is pretty easy to do with this product).

Occasionally, you may be given a little history behind why one option is a better choice than another, but there's no need to waste your time by explaining how to use ineffective techniques when there is a better way. For example, when creating a new report, you are often presented with the Report Wizard. It's cute, and may serve to hand-hold a complete novice if he or she had no earthly idea of what they were doing. Instead, a better approach might be to skip the Report Wizard, learn to design your reports your way, and take ownership of your splendid work. I am pleased you chose this book; I have put forth my best to give you as much value as possible.

Each chapter in this part concludes with a hands-on exercise that steps you through building the reports, queries, and solutions discussed in the chapter. Finished versions are also provided for those who have less patience or who are accustomed to buying the *Cliff's Notes* the night before a college final exam.

Part 4 includes three chapters that will lead you through the building blocks of essential report design. Chapter 4 introduces report layout and formatting. In that chapter you will learn the mechanics behind Reporting Services and how reports are constructed using datasets, data regions, and report items. Chapter 5 will teach you query design basics. You will learn how to use shared and embedded data sources and how datasets process queries and parameters to filter a set of data for presentation. Finally, Chapter 6 will introduce the essential concept of groups, which are used throughout report design to collect data rows for aggregation, summaries, and totals. You will discover how expressions are used to craft field values and parameters for grouping, filtering, and many other property values to customize a user's reporting experience.

▶ **CHAPTER 4:** Report Layout and Formatting

▶ **CHAPTER 5:** Data Access and Query Basics

▶ **CHAPTER 6:** Grouping and Totals

Report Layout and Formatting

WHAT'S IN THIS CHAPTER

- ➤ Using report design tools
- ➤ Using report data building blocks
- ➤ Preparing the report data
- ➤ Designing the report layout
- ➤ Setting formatting properties
- ➤ Validating report design and grouping data

In this chapter, you learn about the essential building blocks for all reports, along with the design patterns for the most common report types. I'll start by explaining the fundamental components of standard reports, followed by three exercises to step you through the process to create them. You learn to do the following:

- ➤ Create an embedded data source
- ➤ Define a dataset query
- ➤ Design a simple table report
- ➤ Add a detail group and multi-level row groups
- ➤ Design a simple matrix report with a column group
- ➤ Design a report with a list data region

Report design is both a science and an art. It is a science because there are definitely standard and repeatable methods for designing common report types. Like other forms of science, report design can be a methodical and sometimes tedious process of repeating the same steps and tasks with a very predictable outcome in each report you create. Comparatively, report design is also an art because good reports have elements of composition and style. Experienced report designers learn to use color, font and styling choices, graphic elements, as well as shading and white space to create balance and attractive presentations. The trick is finding the right balance between the methodical science and expressive art of report design.

USING REPORT DESIGN TOOLS

Two different tools are used to design reports. These include a standalone design tool called Report Builder that enables you to design and deploy reports one-at-a-time, just as you would edit a document with Microsoft Word or Excel. The second tool, The Visual Studio Report Designer, is part of the SQL Server Data Tools that install with the SQL Server 2016 client tools. This tool is optimized for developers and project teams to create and manage multiple reports in a coordinated IT solution. Most of the skills learned with one tool will transfer to the other.

Figure 4-1 shows the Report Builder with different areas of the designer.

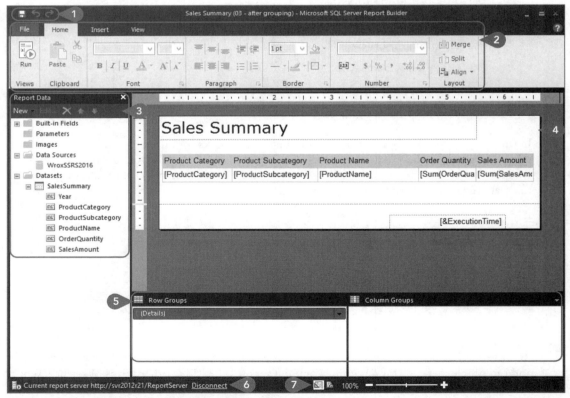

FIGURE 4-1: Report Builder with different areas of the designer.

Following is brief description of each numbered callout:

1. Quick Access toolbar

Similar to modern Office applications, shortcuts to popular commands are available here.

2. Tabs and Ribbon area

All of the Report Builder commands are accessed from the File, Home, Insert, or View ribbons. Commands are arranged in groups with titles along the bottom of the ribbon, such as "Font," "Paragraph," "Border," "Number," and "Layout."

3. Report Data pane

This provides access to data, built-in fields, and other items used in the report design. This is where you create and manage parameters, images, data sources, and datasets.

4. Report design canvas

This is the area where you design your report. Use the Insert ribbon to add data regions and report items to the canvas, and then interact with these items to complete the report design.

5. Row groups and Column groups

For a selected data region, this is where you add or modify groups used to consolidate and aggregate detail records.

6. Report server connection information

When Report Builder is launched from web portal, a connection is maintained to the report server. When connected, changes to the report are saved to the server rather than to the local filesystem.

7. Design, Run, and Zoom controls

The Design and Run icons have the same function as the Design/Run toggle icon on the Home ribbon. Report Builder offers a zoom feature, while the SQL Server Data Tools Report Designer does not have this capability. There are some additional window panes and features not shown by default. These options can be enabled on the View ribbon. These are discussed in more detail in later chapters.

UNDERSTANDING REPORT DATA BUILDING BLOCKS

Reports are made up of some basic components, which are shown in Figure 4-2. In this introductory chapter, I'll cover these concepts just enough so that you can get started and see how the essential mechanics of a report work. You'll learn more in the next few chapters.

Data Sources

You will learn more about both data sources and datasets in Chapter 5, "Database Query Basics," when the discussion spotlights working with databases and designing queries. Every report will have at least one data source and one or more datasets.

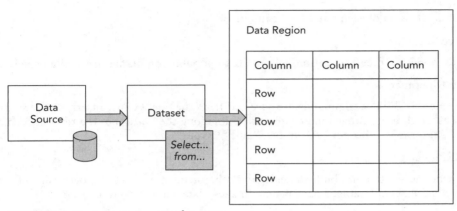

FIGURE 4-2: Basic components of reports.

A *data source* is a simple object that contains information needed to connect to a data source (usually a database). For a relational database product like Microsoft SQL Server, the data source contains the address and information needed to connect to a database server and a specific database. It includes information about how the report should authenticate when it connects and runs queries.

A data source can either be embedded into each report, or a single data source can be shared among multiple reports so that the connection information can be maintained in one place. If the report administrator were to update the shared data source with the address of a new production server, every report would suddenly query the new server. Generally speaking, using shared data sources is considered a good practice, but some notable exceptions are addressed in Chapter 5. For now, let's keep this simple.

Datasets

A *dataset* is the report object that handles the actual data and fields to populate a report region. Datasets are more than just a container for report queries because they also manage all the field metadata and the parameters used for filtering data. Some advanced dataset properties also allow the data to be filtered and manipulated before the data gets to the report data region.

Data Regions

The best way to begin to understand *data regions* and report items is to take a look at the Insert ribbon in Report Builder, as shown in Figure 4-3.

FIGURE 4-3: Report Builder Insert ribbon.

Three different data region components act as containers for report items. The Table, Matrix, and List data regions provide different grouping and layout options. The purpose of a data region is to repeat a region of data-bound report items based on detail data rows or a group of data field values.

Table

In its simplest form, a *table* is a grid with a detail row having one cell or column per field from the associated dataset. When the report is rendered, the detail row is repeated once per row returned by the dataset query. Again, that's the simple version. Optionally, the detail row can be grouped by any field or combination of fields. This causes the data to be summarized for unique values in the grouped field(s). Further, multiple groups and associated header and/or footer rows can be added to the table to form a hierarchy of grouped values. Imagine sales orders grouped by year and then month with headings and totals for each group. Then for each month, each order date is displayed as a detail row.

The table report in Figure 4-4 shows orders grouped by Product Category, Product Subcategory, and then by Product Name. All of the subcategories with the Accessories category are summed into a group total.

Sales Summary

Product Category	Product Subcategory	Product Name	Order Quantity	Sales Amount
Accessories	Bike Racks	Hitch Rack- 4-Bike	2,838	$197,736.16
	Bottles and Cages	Water Bottle- 30 oz.	2,571	$7,476.60
	Cleaners	Bike Wash- Dissolver	2,411	$11,188.37
	Helmets	Sport-100 Helmet, Black	4,447	$87,915.37
		Sport-100 Helmet, Blue	4,618	$91,052.87
		Sport-100 Helmet, Red	4,036	$79,744.70
	Hydration Packs	Hydration Pack- 70 oz.	2,028	$65,518.75
	Locks	Cable Lock	1,086	$16,225.22
	Pumps	Minipump	1,130	$13,514.69
	Tires and Tubes	Patch Kit/8 Patches	674	$925.21
	Total		**25,839**	**$571,297.93**
Bikes	Mountain Bikes	Mountain-100 Black, 38	633	$1,174,622.74
		Mountain-100 Black, 42	589	$1,102,848.18
		Mountain-100 Black, 44	618	$1,163,352.98
		Mountain-100 Black, 48	559	$1,041,901.60
		Mountain-100 Silver, 38	584	$1,094,669.28
		Mountain-100 Silver, 42	551	$1,043,695.27

FIGURE 4-4: Simple multi-level table report.

Matrix

A *matrix* is a variation of a table where data is grouped by columns as well as rows. A couple of key differences between a table and matrix are that matrix reports typically don't include detail cells (in the same way that a table would include detail rows) because values at the lowest level are a summary of both row and column groups. Another differentiator is that, because of the expanding column groups, matrix reports are often not confined to a printed page. There are exceptions, but matrix reports are intended to be flexible by design.

Figure 4-5 shows a matrix report with repeated columns for each year, followed by a column group total. If one more year of data was present in the results, the matrix would be two more columns wide.

Sales Summary

Product Category	Product Subcategory	Product Name	2012		2013		Total	
			Order Quantity	Sales Amount	Order Quantity	Sales Amount	Order Quantity	Sales Amount
Accessories	Bike Racks	Hitch Rack- 4-Bike	221.0	$14,905.27	2,617.0	$182,830.88	**2,838.0**	**$197,736.16**
	Bottles and Cages	Water Bottle- 30 oz.	235.0	$645.77	2,336.0	$6,830.84	**2,571.0**	**$7,476.60**
	Cleaners	Bike Wash- Dissolver	227.0	$1,016.99	2,184.0	$10,171.38	**2,411.0**	**$11,188.37**
	Helmets	Sport-100 Helmet, Black	1,706.0	$32,548.37	1,988.0	$40,952.52	**3,694.0**	**$73,500.89**
		Sport-100 Helmet, Blue	1,796.0	$34,247.28	1,984.0	$40,794.24	**3,780.0**	**$75,041.53**
		Sport-100 Helmet, Red	1,553.0	$29,549.86	1,757.0	$36,356.98	**3,310.0**	**$65,906.85**
	Hydration Packs	Hydration Pack- 70 oz.	168.0	$5,367.40	1,860.0	$60,151.35	**2,028.0**	**$65,518.75**
	Locks	Cable Lock	979.0	$14,637.60			**979.0**	**$14,637.60**
	Pumps	Minipump	1,008.0	$12,073.53			**1,008.0**	**$12,073.53**
	Tires and Tubes	Patch Kit/8 Patches	84.0	$115.42	590.0	$809.79	**674.0**	**$925.21**
	Total							
Bikes	Mountain Bikes	Mountain-200 Black, 38	1,177.0	$1,454,407.26	1,135.0	$1,549,274.31	**2,312.0**	**$3,003,681.57**
		Mountain-200 Black, 42	1,089.0	$1,344,786.04	879.0	$1,201,528.02	**1,968.0**	**$2,546,314.06**
		Mountain-200 Black, 46	733.0	$905,310.42	687.0	$943,601.66	**1,420.0**	**$1,848,912.09**

FIGURE 4-5: Matrix report.

List

Data regions can contain report items and other data regions. The *list* is a flexible container for data-bound report items and other data regions that can be positioned anywhere within the rectangular list area. As a data region, it's really just a rectangular container bound to a dataset and grouped on a field value.

The example in Figure 4-6 shows a design view of a list grouped by the Year field, containing a textbox showing the year alongside a simplified copy of the table from the earlier example.

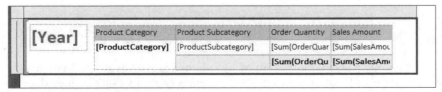

FIGURE 4-6: List in design view.

In Figure 4-7, you see the resulting report. Note that the year textbox and the table are completely independent as far as size and position, but the data in each instance of the table is filtered only for the corresponding year.

Sales Summary

2010

Product Category	Product Subcategory	Order Quantity	Sales Amount
Accessories	Helmets	84	$1,695.67
		84	**$1,695.67**
Bikes	Mountain Bikes	117	$237,464.30
	Road Bikes	338	$215,767.50
		455	**$453,231.80**
Clothing	Caps	40	$207.46
	Jerseys	84	$2,422.59
	Socks	43	$245.10
		167	**$2,875.15**
Components	Mountain Frames	13	$9,633.66
	Road Frames	101	$21,892.30
		114	**$31,525.96**

2011

Product Category	Product Subcategory	Order Quantity	Sales Amount
Accessories	Helmets	2,233	$42,568.01
	Locks	107	$1,587.62
	Pumps	122	$1,441.16
		2,462	**$45,596.79**
Bikes	Mountain Bikes	5,135	$9,044,828.37

FIGURE 4-7: List report preview.

Report Items

A *report item* is the simplest object used in report design. Some report items (such as a textbox or image) can be bound to a dataset field, while others (such as a line or rectangle) are used for display or formatting purposes.

When Reporting Services was being created, the early documentation referred to objects like textboxes, images, lines, and rectangles as "controls" because they were similar to the objects used by application developers to add visual elements to a form. Although the concepts are very similar, reports and custom-developed applications are different. This category of objects was given the name "report items" so it wouldn't be confused with controls used in other types of Visual Studio projects. Sticking with textboxes for now, other report items are examined in later chapters.

SAMPLES AND EXERCISES

Now it's your turn to apply the concepts you just learned. This section includes exercises to familiarize you with basic report design using Report Builder. You need SQL Server 2016 installed with Reporting Services in native mode. The detailed instructions were provided in Chapter 3,

"Installing and Configuring SSRS." Be sure to restore the `WroxSSRS2016` database provided with the book, and download exercise files.

To get started, you must be sure that you are on the same page as the discussion so that you may follow along.

1. Start by opening your web browser and navigating to the web portal. If you installed Reporting Services with SQL Server 2016 using all default settings, the path will be `HTTP://LocalHost/Reports`.

> **TIP** *The report server name is established when you installed or configured Reporting Services. If the report server was installed as part of a default instance of SQL Server, the web portal address will be* `HTTP://servername/ Reports`; *or you can use* `HTTP://LocalHost/Reports` *on the same computer. Other configuration settings can affect the report server address, such as installing a named instance or using an alternate port number or host header in the URL reservation. For example, if a named instance was installed, the address would be* `HTTP://servername/Reports$instancename`. *You can always find the address on the Web Portal URL page of the Reporting Services Configuration Manager.*

2. Click the Browse icon in the web portal menu bar to navigate to the Home folder.

3. Click the "+" icon and choose Folder from the menu.

4. Enter the new folder name, WroxSSRS2016, and click the Create button as shown in Figure 4-8.

5. Click the new folder icon to navigate to the WroxSSRS2016 folder, as shown in Figure 4-9.

   This switches back to the earlier view of the web portal.

6. Click the Report Builder icon on the toolbar and wait for the Report Builder to run.

> **NOTE** *You are given the option to download and install the current version of Report Builder. This is quick and easy to install. Once the installation is completed, Report Builder will open automatically in the future. Once the application is installed, clicking the Report Builder button in the future launches the application.*

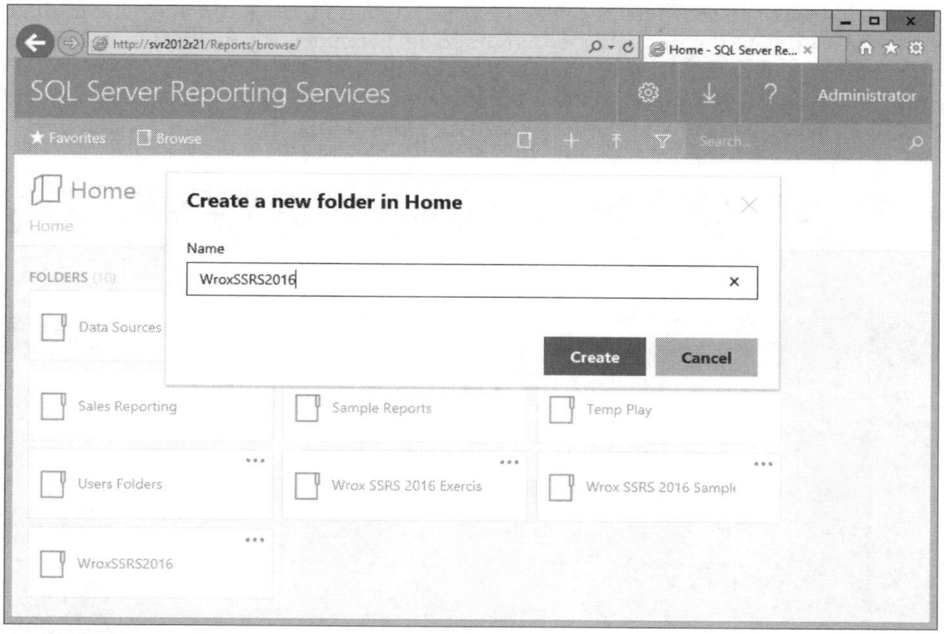

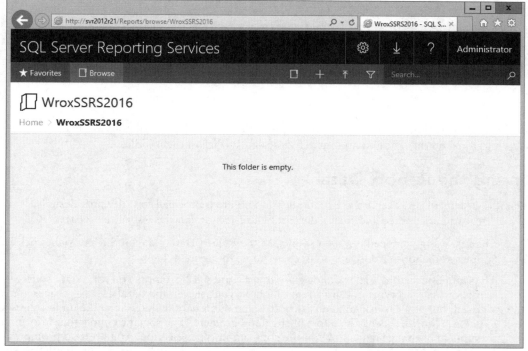

FIGURE 4-8: Creating a new folder.

FIGURE 4-9: A new empty folder.

Report Builder opens to the Getting Started page shown in Figure 4-10. The wizard dialogs may help you automate the first few steps and may be beneficial if you haven't created a certain report style before. However, you will quickly graduate beyond the wizards, and I am not going to use them so that you can become more familiar with the basic and essential building blocks used in nearly all reports. Just trust me on this.

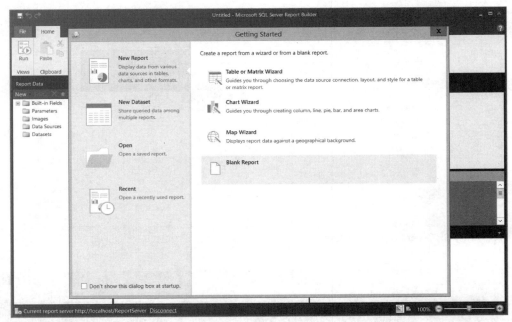

FIGURE 4-10: Getting Started page.

7. Click the X in the upper-right corner to make the Getting Started page vaporize.

Report Builder is laid out a lot like an Office application with tabs and ribbons along the top, objects and tools on the left, and an interactive design surface in the middle.

Preparing the Report Data

The first few steps in this exercise are fundamental and are performed for all report designs. You will create a data source and then a dataset before you design the rest of the report.

1. The first thing you need is a data source. In the Report Data pane on the left, right-click Data Sources and choose Add Data Source, as shown in Figure 4-11.

The Data Source Properties dialog shown in Figure 4-12 prompts you for a data source name, connection type, and information about your server and database. No spaces are allowed, but you can use mixed case with some punctuation characters like underscores and hyphens. Consider using the name of the database here. The specific connection information prompts may change depending on the connection type selection. You are also prompted to use a shared or embedded connection, which is discussed in Chapter 5. For simplicity, you will use an embedded connection in this report.

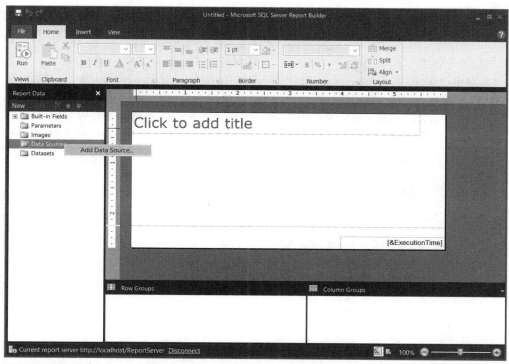

FIGURE 4-11: Selecting Add Data Source in the Report Data pane.

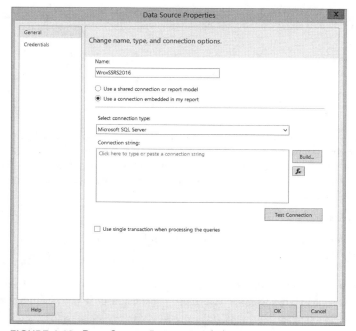

FIGURE 4-12: Data Source Properties dialog.

2. Enter the name **WroxSSRS2016**.

3. Choose "Use a connection embedded in my report."

4. For the connection type, choose or verify that Microsoft SQL Server is selected.

5. Click the Build... button to create the connection string.

    This opens the Connection Properties dialog shown in Figure 4-13, and prompts you for information about your SQL Server. Because you're using a local instance of SQL Server, you will connect to the SQL Server service on your development machine. In a production environment, you would enter the server name. If you are connecting to a named instance of SQL Server, the name would be entered as **SERVERNAME\INSTANCENAME**.

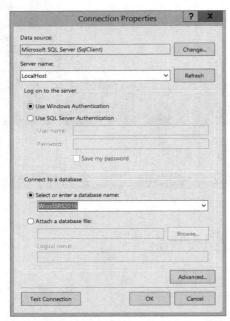

FIGURE 4-13: Connection Properties dialog.

Note that in a large production environment when you know the server and instance names, avoid using the Server name drop-down list, which causes the SQL Server Browser service to search the entire network for servers, and can be time-consuming. When a default instance of SQL Server is installed locally, for convenience, you can use the aliases LocalHost or (local) in place of the server name.

6. Enter **LocalHost** for the server name.

7. Leave the "Log on to the server" option set to Use Windows Authentication.

8. Under "Connect to a database," drop down the list and select the WroxSSRS2016 database.

9. You can test the connection before saving changes. This is a good time to consider whether the person designing this report has rights to read data from the database. If your Windows

username or a Windows group you are a member of was used to create a login with read permission granted to the necessary tables, you should be good to go.

Note that the selections you made on the Connection Properties dialog resulted in building the following connection string:

```
Data Source=LocalHost; Initial Catalog=WroxSSRS2016
```

10. Click OK to close and save changes.

11. Right-click the Datasets folder and choose Add Dataset…, as shown in Figure 4-14. The Dataset Properties dialog opens.

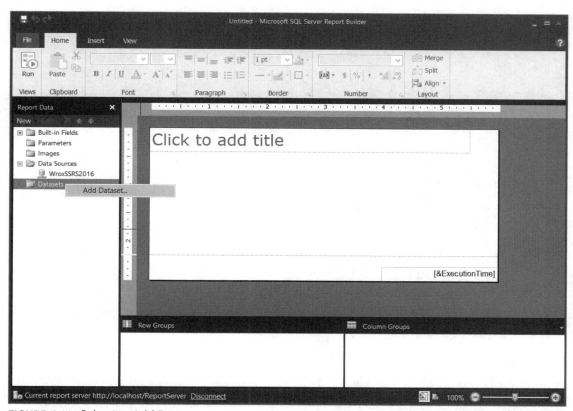

FIGURE 4-14: Selecting Add Dataset.

12. In the Name box, enter **SalesSummary**.

13. Select the data source you created.

14. Click the Query Designer… button. The Report Builder Query Designer dialog shown in Figure 4-15 opens.

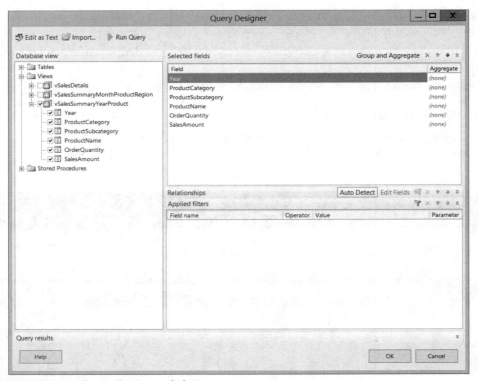

FIGURE 4-15: Query Designer dialog.

15. In the Database view pane on the left, expand the Views folder and check the box next to the view named vSalesSummaryYearProduct.

16. Click the OK button to accept the query.

Figure 4-16 shows the resulting dataset created by the Query Designer, the data source and T-SQL query script.

17. Click the OK button to close the Dataset Properties dialog.

Designing the Report Layout

A table is one of the most fundamental yet useful data regions you will use in report design. This exercise uses a simple table with five columns for fields. Totals, headers, and footers are covered in the subsequent chapters, but for now, you will define a detail group to consolidate the dataset rows for each product.

Take a look at the dataset in the Report Data pane to the left and notice that a list of fields was added, as shown in Figure 4-17.

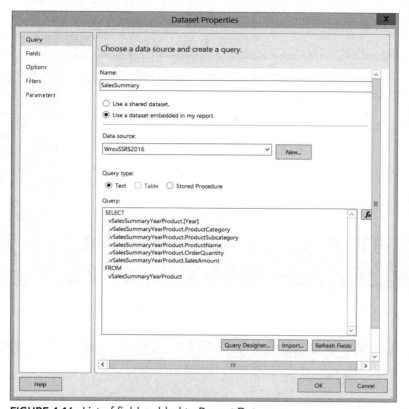

FIGURE 4-16: List of fields added to Report Data pane.

Now that the data source and dataset are in place, you can begin working on the rest of the report.

1. Place the cursor in the report title and type a name for the report such as **Sales Summary**.

2. Select the Insert tab at the top of the Report Builder window to show the Insert ribbon.

3. Click the down arrow below the Table icon in the Data Regions group to show the menu options.

4. Select Insert Table from the drop-down menu, as shown in Figure 4-17. The mouse pointer changes to indicate that you can insert a table on the report canvas.

5. Move the mouse pointer to the upper-left area of the blank report canvas, under the report title textbox, and then click to place the table, as shown in Figure 4-18.

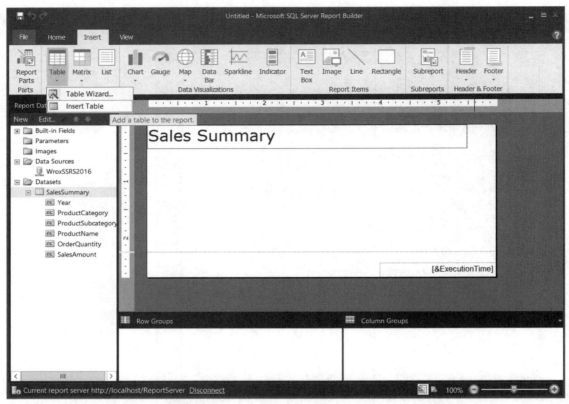

FIGURE 4-17: Selecting the Insert Table option.

A new table is added to the report.

You have two different ways to add fields to a new table. You can either drag-and-drop fields from the dataset in the Report Data pane, or use the field selection list in the detail cells of the table. In this exercise, you will use the second method.

With a little experience, you will become accustomed to how tables behave in the designer. Until then, it is easy to fumble a bit. When a table isn't selected, clicking once on any cell will show a set of gray boxes above each column and to the left of each row. These are called column and row *selectors* or *selection handles*. If a cell is selected, a heavy border is displayed around that cell. Click in the cell but not on the text to select a cell. If you click once more, the cursor is placed within the textbox contained in the selected cell. Click on a different cell to deselect the textbox.

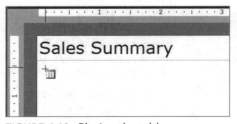

FIGURE 4-18: Placing the table.

6. Hover the mouse pointer over the first detail cell (left of the cell labeled Data) to show the field selection icon in the right corner of that cell.

7. Click the icon to drop down the field list and select the ProductCategory field, as shown in Figure 4-19.

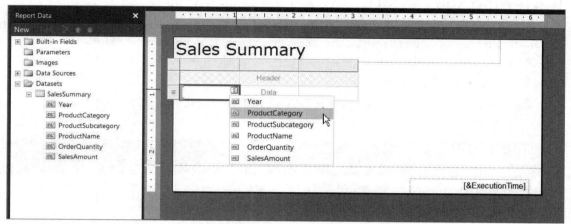

FIGURE 4-19: Selecting the ProductCategory field.

8. Move one cell to the right and select the ProductSubcategory field.

9. Move to the next cell and select the ProductName field.

10. Right-click the gray column selection handle over the third column and choose Insert Column ⇨ Right, as shown in Figure 4-20.

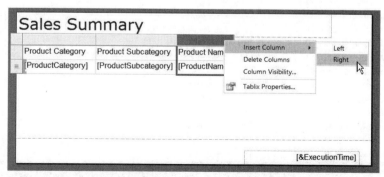

FIGURE 4-20: Inserting columns.

11. Repeat the last step so that there are five columns in all.

12. Use the field list to add the OrderQuantity and SalesAmount fields to the last two columns.

With the table selected, hovering over the line separating the column headers will show a horizontal double arrow point indicating the option to resize the columns.

13. Resize each of the columns so the heading labels are visible on one line.

Reviewing the Report

Take a look at your work so far. You can toggle between Design and Run views to preview how the report will look when it runs with data. These options are found both on the Home ribbon and on the right side of the status bar at the bottom of the Report Builder.

1. Select the Home ribbon tab.

2. The leftmost icon on the Home ribbon is titled Run, as shown in Figure 4-21. Click this icon to preview the report.

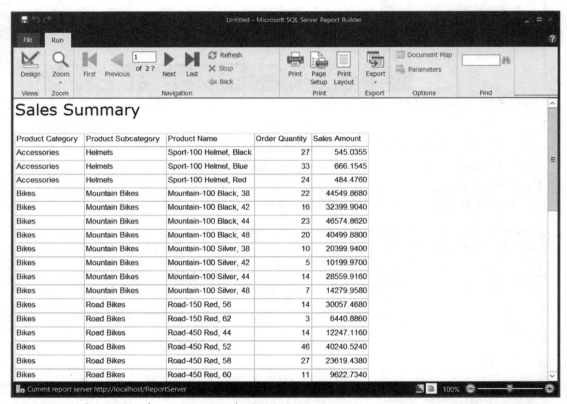

FIGURE 4-21: Previewing the report using the Run icon.

Setting Formatting Properties

You will notice that the table looks very plain and that the Sales Amount values aren't formatted as currency, so you should fix that.

1. Ensure that the Home ribbon tab is selected.

2. Click anywhere in the table to show the column and row selectors.

3. Click the gray row selector to the left of the table heading row. It is to the immediate left of the top cell labeled Product Category. Clicking this gray handle selects the table heading row.

4. In the Border ribbon group, use the drop-down arrow next to the paint bucket icon to change the background color of the cells in the header row.

5. Select Light Gray for the background color, as shown in Figure 4-22.

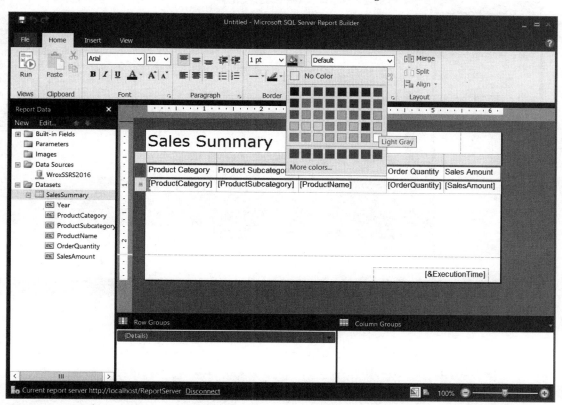

FIGURE 4-22: Selecting the background color.

6. Ensure that the table is still selected.

7. Click the gray column selector above the Sales Amount column. Doing this selects the column so that you can set properties for the cells in that column.

8. Click the dollar sign icon in the Number group on the Home ribbon to set the format of this column to currency, as shown in Figure 4-23.

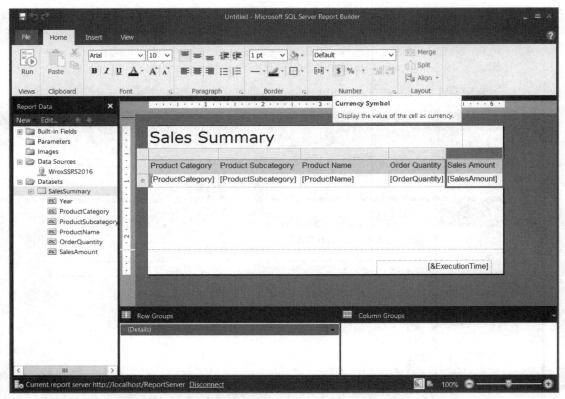

FIGURE 4-23: Formatting the column for currency.

> **NOTE** *Specific formatting features, such as regional and fixed formats, are covered in Chapter 8, "Graphical and Advanced Report Design."*

9. Let's preview the report again to see the formatting changes. Click the Run icon on the Home ribbon once again to preview the report, as shown in Figure 4-24.

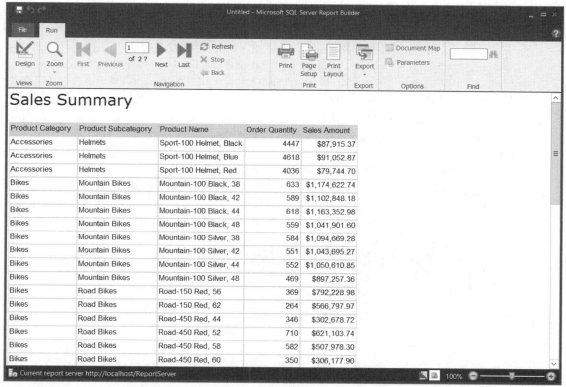

FIGURE 4-24: Previewing the report.

10. You need to do something really important now—and this is something you should get in the habit of doing often. Do you see that the title bar in Report Builder says "Untitled"? That means this report hasn't been saved. All the work you've done up to this point is just sitting in memory and not stored on your computer. If a volcano erupted, an asteroid fell from space, or your cat jumped on your keyboard, you'd lose your work. Let's fix that. Up on the Quick Access toolbar you'll see the universal symbol for saving your work—the floppy disk (because everyone knows what a floppy disk is these days). Click the floppy disk icon on the Quick Access toolbar.

11. When prompted, enter "Sales Summary" for the name for your report.

Since you opened Report Builder from the web portal, the report is saved to the report server rather than the filesystem.

Congratulations! You've created a table report showing a summary of product orders. At this point you could call the report done and move on but, as Columbo always said, there is one more thing…

Validating Report Design and Grouping Data

I do a lot of demos for consulting clients and at conferences. The thing about a demo is that it's usually prepared and practiced so you never see the little flaws. I won't do that to you. This report has a potential flaw that should be addressed. Recall that you used a view named vSalesSummary-YearProduct for the report dataset. This view summarizes all the sales orders and returns one row for every unique combination of Year, Product Category, Subcategory, and Product.

I purposely didn't include the Year field in the report to demonstrate this common scenario. How much data is displayed in the report? If you look at the page count in the report toolbar, it doesn't actually tell you. See where it says "1 of 2?"... Reporting Service doesn't actually know how many pages there are because it has only rendered two pages so far.

1. On the Run ribbon, click the Last icon in the Navigation group. This navigates to the last page of the report. In order to do this, Reporting Services must figure out the pagination. As you can see in Figure 4-25, there are 14 pages (give or take... there are a few variables).

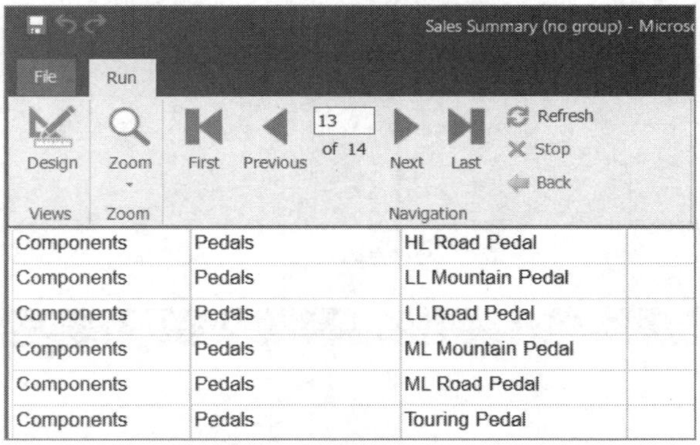

FIGURE 4-25: Revealing the total number of pages.

2. Take a close look at the values in the first three columns and you'll see some of the product names repeated. Why? Because each row actually represents the product sales for one year. Unless you want to add the Year column or filter data for only one year, this would be confusing.

3. Switch back to design view by clicking the Design icon on the far left of the ribbon.

4. Click on any cell in the table.

5. At the bottom of the designer window, under Row Groups, you'll see one row labeled (Details). On the right side of this row, you'll see a drop-down arrow.

6. Click the down arrow to show the menu.

7. Select Group Properties... from the drop-down menu, as shown in Figure 4-26.

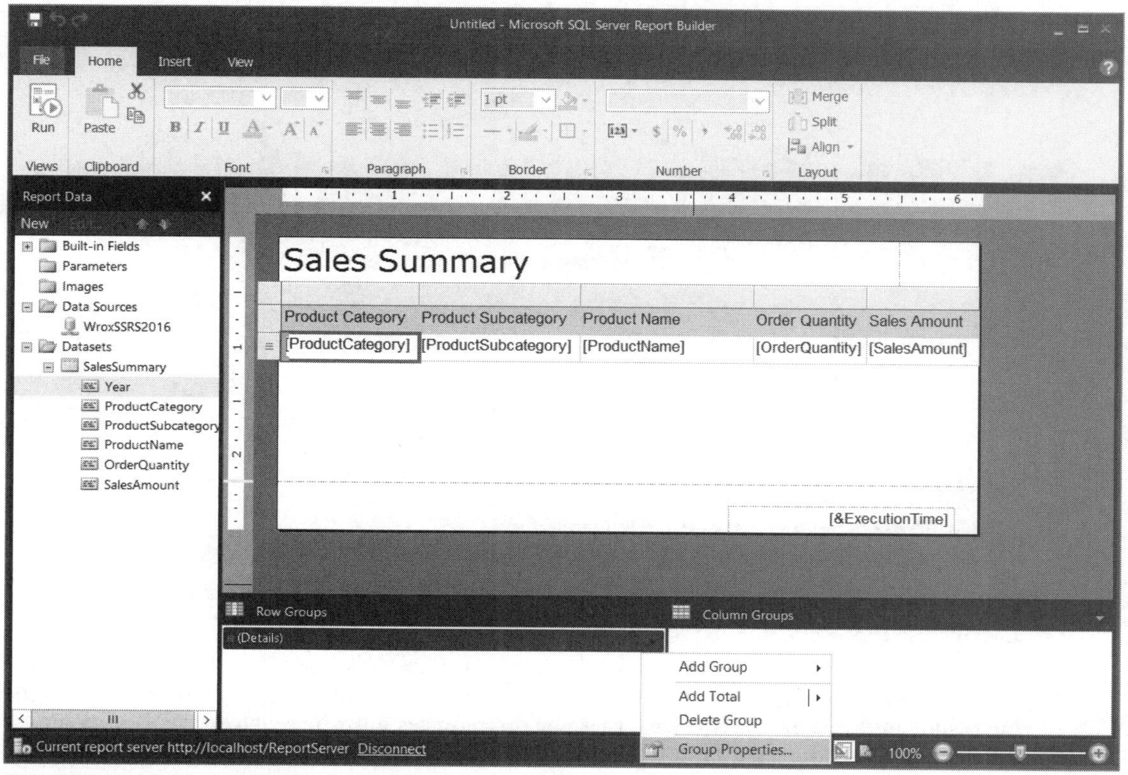

FIGURE 4-26: Selecting Group Properties.

The Group Properties dialog has seven pages that you can access using the page list on the left side. You'll learn more about using groups and these advanced features in Chapter 6, "Grouping and Expressions." Your objective is to consolidate the duplicate product rows.

8. Under "Group expressions," click the Add button to add a new group expression.

> **NOTE** *Even though you're only selecting a field for grouping, this does, in fact, create an expression. In this simple example, it's just a field reference.*

9. Drop down the fields list and select [ProductName], as shown in Figure 4-27.

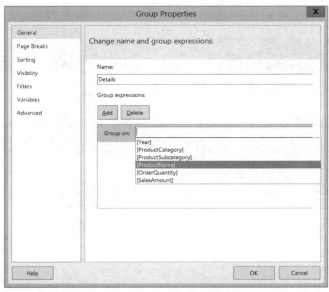

FIGURE 4-27: Selecting the [ProductName] field.

10. Click the OK button to accept this change.

Earlier when you selected the `OrderQuantity` and `SalesAmounts` fields for the last two columns, expressions were created that just referred to field value. Now that a row might include multiple grouped values, these field references must be replaced with expressions that aggregate multiple values. All you need to do is re-select the fields (as you did before), and the `SUM` function will be added to the field expression.

11. Hover the mouse pointer over the detail cell in the Order Quantity column to show the field list icon.

12. Click the field icon to show the field list and select [OrderQuantity], as shown in Figure 4-28.

> **NOTE** *There is a subtle but important behavior to look for when selecting a field in this way. Note that when you selected the OrderQuantity field in the detail row, the cell displays [OrderQuantity], but when the same field is selected in a grouped cell, the cell displays [Sum(OrderQuantity)] to indicate that the grouped values will be aggregated.*

13. Repeat the same steps to select the [SalesAmount] field in the Sales Amount column.

14. Click the Save icon. (Remember, this is a good habit, so do it often.)

15. Click the Run button to preview the report.

16. Use the navigation buttons to go to the last page again, as shown in Figure 4-29.

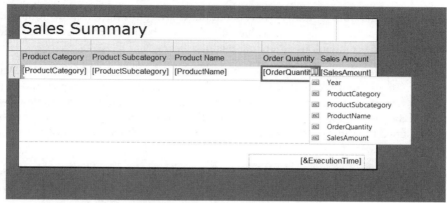

FIGURE 4-28: Selecting the [OrderQuantity] field.

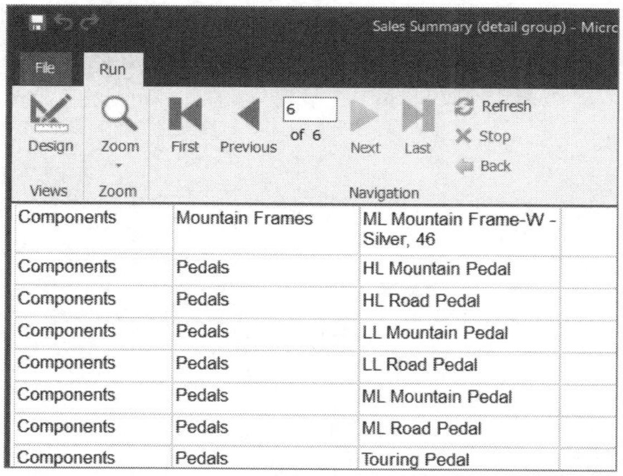

FIGURE 4-29: Jumping to the last page of the report.

With records grouped by product, you should see the total page numbers reduced because you no longer have one row per unique year and product. Each row now shows the total product sales for all years.

17. Close Report Builder.

18. Return to the web browser window you used to launch Report Builder.

19. Refresh the web browser. You should see the new report in the web portal.

20. Click to open the report in the browser.

You've done it! The new report is deployed to the report server. It includes sales orders for all years grouped by product.

SUMMARY

Effective reporting is all about simplicity. If you can put useful information in front of a user so that it answers important questions, that adds value and improves business. Even a simple table report like this one can provide tremendous value to a business user.

You used Report Builder to author your first report. Later you will use the SQL Server Data Tools Report Designer (an add-in for Visual Studio) to apply the same design techniques and build on these skills. You started with an embedded SQL Server data source and used a simple view to define a dataset to feed data to a table data region. Because the dataset returned rows for every year and product, you grouped the table on the `ProductName` field to consolidate the detail rows and aggregate the numeric values.

The skills you learned in this chapter will help as you progress to more complex designs. The chapters that follow will expand these concepts and introduce some new ones as you move to the next level.

5

Data Access and Query Basics

WHAT'S IN THIS CHAPTER

➤ Database and query essentials

➤ Understanding relational database principles and concepts

➤ Data source management

➤ Datasets and using query design tools

➤ Query authoring using the Report Builder query designer

➤ Query authoring with SQL Server Management Studio

➤ Using single and multi-select parameters

Data source queries are the foundation of reporting and writing effective queries and are essential to design. If your reports use the SQL Server relational engine, or SQL Server Analysis Services for data sources, you may prefer to use a familiar and more-sophisticated query design tool like SQL Server Management Studio (SSMS). By contrast, the report designer includes useful but simplified query tools. Many other data sources are supported with more rudimentary query design options, as well. This chapter addresses T-SQL query design for SQL Server.

> **NOTE** *If you are new to the T-SQL language and are designing reports for SQL Server, pick up a copy of* Microsoft SQL Server 2012 T-SQL Fundamentals *(Microsoft Press: Redmond, WA, 2012) by Itzik Ben-Gan.*

Reporting Services strives to reach two audiences—namely, a broad spectrum of users who can be grouped into two camps. The first is the business user needing to create simple reports easily, and the second is the experienced developer or database professional who needs to create sophisticated reports using complex queries and intricate program logic. History has proven that meeting both needs is not an easy balance. As a result, there are two report design tools and myriad features addressing the needs of the novice, as well as the advanced report designers. Report Builder is right-sized for business users, making it an ideal choice for those who will use database objects that have been prepared for them by their corporate IT staff. You will continue to use Report Builder and then you will also use SQL Server Management Studio for T-SQL query design with the SQL Server relational database engine.

DATABASE ESSENTIALS

You have learned that using Report Builder to get data from a database view is pretty simple. The Query Designer in Report Builder is relatively simple, but it lacks some of the sophistication available in the SQL Server Data Tools (SSDT) Report Designer. If you have the luxury of encapsulating query logic into database objects like views and stored procedures, in theory, you should not need to embed complex queries in your reports. That may be true in a perfect world, where you have permission to create objects, or your database administrator is actively involved in report projects and creating views and stored procedures for you, but that's not always practical.

SSDT Report Designer leverages query design tools that get installed with the SQL Server client tools. These tools give more advanced users a great deal of functionality and capabilities that are usually appropriate for application developers and IT professionals. As an IT professional and ten-ured report designer, I often prefer to use Report Builder in many cases. If I need to build complex queries, I step out of Report Builder and use the SQL Server Management Studio (SSMS) query design tools. For me, this is the best of both worlds. Whether using Report Builder or SSDT to create reports, SSMS is a superior query authoring experience.

Relational Database Concepts

Have you heard of the five-minute university? You would have to be as old as I am to remember this classic comedy routine from Don Novello (the entertainer known as Father Guido Sarducci) says that after four years of college, after you've finished studying and passing all the exams, all you're going to remember years later can be taught in five minutes. That's probably a stretch of the truth, but the basics can be quite simple. So, what follows is the five-minute course on T-SQL.

What's a Sequel?

This is a true story. Back in the early days of database technology, as the products and languages used today were in their infancy, the math geniuses at IBM were pioneering relational data-base principles and the rules of normal form. That part of history, and the design patterns that ensued, is sacred ground that few would ever challenge. Several development teams and companies followed, all with their own database products modeled after the same founding ideas and language constructs.

The Battle of the SQL Acronym

One early incarnation of the relational database was actually named "SEQUEL," which stood for *Select English QUEry Language.* It was one of many attempts to create a memorable phonetic contraction. The word "English" fell out of favor because there were those with other persuasions in the community, and the driving concept was that the language had "Structure" and not so much the ability to just "Select" things. By committee and community consensus, the official language became known as SQL, which stood for "Structured Query Language." People with slightly different product alignments or even "religious" persuasions about their toolset will often butcher the name. Pronouncing SQL correctly is a little bit like the traditional pronunciation of some U.S. cities like Louisville, Kentucky (pronounced *"Lew-A-Vul"*), Aloha, Oregon (pronounced *"Ah-Low-Uh"*) or New Orleans (let's not even try). Likewise (and just to be clear), the language for Microsoft's database product is SQL pronounced "See-Kwel," not "Es-Kew-El," and not "Em Es Es Kew El."

The Battle of the Brand

There are quite a few dialects of SQL used with various database products. Some have MySQL (pronounced "My See-Kwel") and others have PL/SQL (pronounced "Pee-El See-Kwel") and others just have plain-old SQL. But we have T-SQL. Why T-SQL? End-to-end, the purpose of the SQL data-manipulation language is to execute database commands and manage transactional integrity by ensuring that all database operations are consistent, reliable, and durable. The term "Transaction" reaffirms SQL Server's commitment to enforcing transactional integrity, and, thus, the product name was eventually shortened to T-SQL.

DATA SOURCE MANAGEMENT

A *data source* contains the connection information for a dataset. Data sources can be created for a specific report dataset, or can be shared among different reports. Because most reports get data from a common data source, it often makes sense to create a shared data source. Using shared data sources has a few advantages. Even if you don't have several reports that need to share a central data source, it takes no additional effort to create a shared data source. This may be advantageous in this case because the data source is managed separately from each report and can be easily updated if necessary. Then, as you add new reports, the shared data source will already be established and deployed to the report server.

Embedded and Shared Data Sources

Data sources can be embedded into each report or deployed to the report server as a shared object. The latter option has the advantage of giving you or your report server administrator one place to manage connection information for several reports. Using shared connections is generally a recommended practice, especially in a large-scale environment. SQL Server Data Tools is introduced in Chapter 6, "Grouping and Expressions," and that's the tool you will use to define shared data sources. A shared data source can also be created directly on the server using the web portal, but you can only consume a shared data source created this way using Report Builder.

Query Design Tools

For SQL Server data sources, you have some Query Designer options to choose from. The best choice will depend on the complexity of your needs and the tool you're accustomed to using.

The Report Designer add-in for Visual Studio (called SSDT) relies on shared components installed with the SQL Server client tools. If you're a developer with prior SQL Server experience and you know your way around the T-SQL query language, you'll probably prefer to use SSMS or the query tool in SSDT Report Designer. If you are using Report Builder and have not installed the SQL Server client tools, you will not have access to the SSMS query designer. If you are planning to design complex queries, it would be advisable to install and learn to use SSMS.

Experienced report developers often choose Report Builder over SSDT for simple report design work, but may not be big fans of the Report Builder Query Designer. This is primarily because they are more accustomed to using SSMS and prefer to hand-write T-SQL queries. In the example that follows, you'll see that the Query Designer actually generates pretty decent SQL script, so, in the end, it really comes down to using the method you are most comfortable with, as long as it meets your needs.

Using the Report Builder Query Designer

This section gets you started with the most basic query tool. You use SSMS to author a similar query in the exercise that follows. Let's start with the Report Builder designer to give you experience using both tools. First, create a data source. In the same manner you created a dataset in Chapter 4, "Report Layout and Formatting," choose the option to create a new embedded dataset, select the data source, and then click the Query Designer... button.

The Query Designer displays all of the objects in the database. Adding columns from multiple tables to the query output is a matter of expanding each table and checking the box next to each column. Columns are added to the query in the order you select them. Three sections on the right ("Selected fields," Relationships, and "Applied filters") can each be expanded and collapsed using the chevron (double arrow) icon on the right side of the section toolbar.

Unless you need the query to return every detail row, it is always a good idea to group the results by the non-measure columns and then aggregate the numeric measure columns. For example, Figure 5-1 shows that the MonthNumber, Year, Country, OrderQuantity, and SalesAmount columns have been selected. The last two columns are *numeric measures*, which means that if you group results by the first three columns, you must aggregate these column values. This is easy to do. First, note that the MonthNumber column has been selected before the Year column (done so for demonstration purposes). Before grouping, the columns should be listed in logical order, so you use the up and down arrows next to "Group and Aggregate" to set the column order of the first three columns to Year, MonthNumber, and then Country.

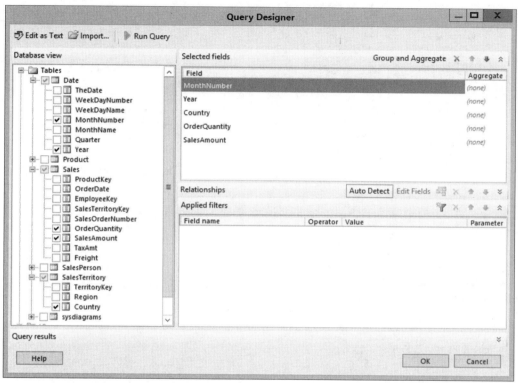

FIGURE 5-1: Selecting columns in Query Designer.

In the Aggregate column of the "Selected fields" list, choose "Group by" for the first three columns and choose "Sum" for the two numeric measures. Because the selected tables are related to each other in the database, using the Auto Detect feature should add corresponding joins using the appropriate key columns. Figure 5-2 shows that this feature is enabled by default. You should always double-check to ensure sure that the right tables and columns are used to join the tables.

You can add, remove, and modify joins between tables by expanding the Relationships section. Add filters and parameters using the "Applied filters" section. In Figure 5-3, the Year column has been added. After dropping down the Value list, 2013 was entered for the filter value. By checking the Parameter check box, this adds a report parameter using the field name.

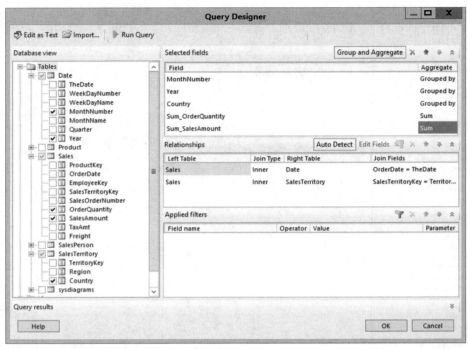

FIGURE 5-2: Using the Auto Detect feature.

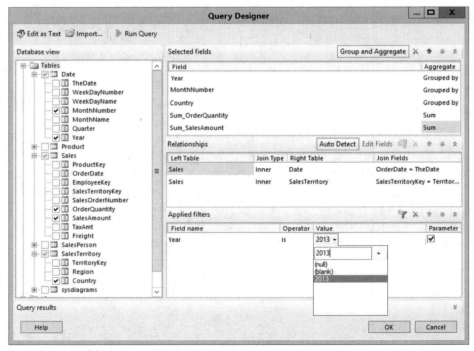

FIGURE 5-3: Adding a report parameter.

The Query Designer generates a T-SQL query that can be viewed using the "Edit as Text" button, as shown in Figure 5-4.

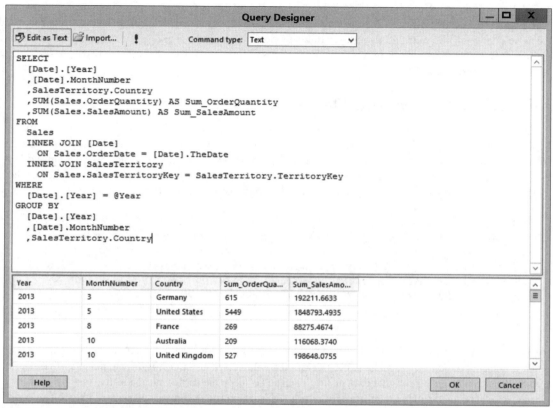

FIGURE 5-4: Generating a T-SQL query.

The resulting T-SQL query is quite well-written. The script is efficient, well-formatted, and easy to read. In the future, you may use the graphical designer to generate this query, switch to the text view, and just hand-write the query script here, or write the query in SSMS and then copy-and-paste the resulting query script into this view. My preference is the latter and that's the technique you will use in the exercise later in this chapter.

DATASETS AND FIELDS

A query or command statement that produces a set of report data is called a *dataset*. There is more to a dataset than just a query, though. It's actually a fairly sophisticated object used to centrally manage all of the data and metadata associated with the query. A dataset is essentially the glue that maps report parameters to query parameters, columns returned by the query to fields used in the report, and optional filtering expressions that are applied after the data is returned by the query. In simple reports, all these objects are just created by the designer and may be of little concern. In more advanced reports, the dataset can provide complex capabilities to manipulate and manage dynamic report data.

For the purposes of this chapter's exercise, you write a T-SQL query using a single query parameter. The query designer will map the query parameter to a report parameter, and the columns returned by the query will be mapped to dataset fields to populate a matrix data region. Later, when learning about advanced report designs, you will use expressions to map the parameters through the dataset and apply conditional filter logic.

Embedded and Shared Datasets

Like data sources, datasets can be contained entirely within a report design, or they can be published to the report server as a shared object to be used in multiple reports. This is a powerful feature for creating efficient reporting solutions. Shared datasets are designed just like an embedded dataset, using the SSDT or Report Builder query designers, but rather than residing within each report, shared datasets are deployed and stored as named objects on the report server.

> **NOTE** *I wasn't a fan of shared datasets after I started using them when the feature was introduced a few versions back. It wasn't until I learned how to embrace the caching behavior (and turn it off in some cases) that I began to have a good experience with shared datasets. Now that this is a requirement for Mobile Reports, learning to use this feature is a necessity.*

One advantage of using shared datasets is that they cache result sets in such a way that when the same query is executed with the same parameter values (within a configurable period of time), cached results from a previous execution are used to improve performance and conserve server resources. The trade-off is that users may not see data changes that have occurred since the previous query execution. Now, this is all configurable on the report server but you need to be mindful of these settings and the caching behavior.

In Chapters 17 through 20 you will use shared datasets for mobile report designs. Since Mobile Reports don't support embedded datasets like paginated reports, you must design and deploy shared datasets before consuming data in the report.

Exercises

The following hands-on exercises will guide you through the query authoring steps in SSMS, creating a dataset in the Report Designer, and building a simple report. You will enhance the query and report design using a parameter to filter data and then employ a multi-value parameter.

Authoring a Query with SQL Server Management Studio

This exercise introduces SSMS as a query authoring tool, used in conjunction with the Report Designer, to build T-SQL queries and report datasets.

1. Open SQL Server Management Studio from the SQL Server 2016 program group. The "Connect to Server" dialog opens and prompts you for the server type and connection information.

2. Ensure that the Server type is set to Database Engine and enter the Server name, as shown in Figure 5-5.

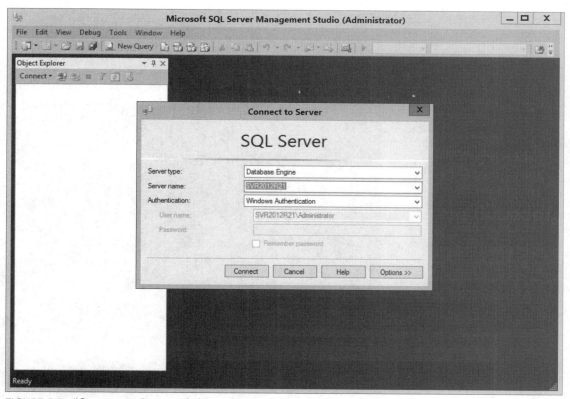

FIGURE 5-5: "Connect to Server" dialog.

This will be the same server connection information you used in the Chapter 4 exercise. Because you're using a local instance of SQL Server, you will connect to the SQL Server service on your development machine. Enter the server name if the connection is not local, and if you are connecting to a named instance of SQL Server, the name is entered as SERVERNAME\INSTANCENAME.

3. Click the Connect button to open the connection. On the left side of the screen, SSMS displays the Object Explorer, which contains all of the objects on the database server organized in a hierarchical tree view. Every object (or node) in this list can be expanded to show all of the related objects. There are literally thousands of objects within this tree, most of which are of little concern to you. Those that are important include servers, databases, tables, and columns. Later, you'll also be concerned with views and stored procedures.

> **TIP** *If you don't see the Object Explorer on the left side of the SSMS window, it may have been closed in a previous session. You can show the Object Explorer by pressing F8 or by choosing Object Explorer from the View menu.*

4. Expand the Databases node.

5. Right-click the WroxSSRS2016 database, as shown in Figure 5-6.

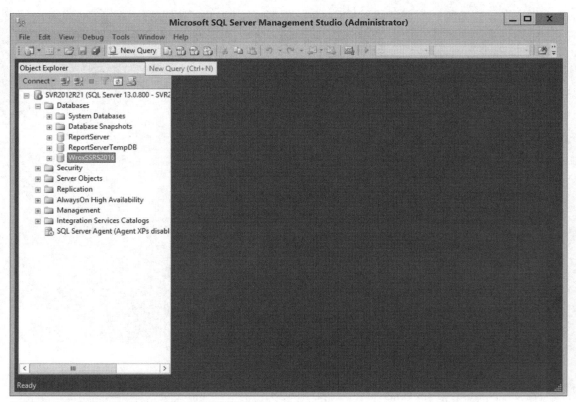

FIGURE 5-6: Right-clicking the WroxSSRS2016 database.

6. On the toolbar, click the New Query button.

7. Expand the WroxSSRS2016 database.

Showing the Tables and Columns can assist your query design effort by giving you a list of objects for reference.

8. Expand Tables.

9. For each of the following tables, expand the Columns folder.

> **NOTE** *As you enter the following query into the query window, you can drag and drop objects from the Object Explorer, or just type into the query window. Don't be concerned with extra brackets or object prefixes that are added for proper object referencing.*

10. Enter this text into the query window:

```
SELECT
        YEAR(s.OrderDate) AS OrderYear,
        MONTH(s.OrderDate) AS OrderMonth,
        t.Country,
        s.SalesAmount
FROM
        [dbo].[Sales] AS s
              INNER JOIN [dbo].[SalesTerritory] AS t
              ON s.SalesTerritoryKey = t.TerritoryKey
WHERE
        YEAR(s.OrderDate) = 2013
;
```

11. Click the Execute button on the toolbar to see the results displayed in the grid below.

12. Note the row count in the status bar in the bottom right. The query returns more than 28,000 rows. This is because this query returns every transaction in 2013. With the objective to report summary information for each year, month, and country, you can group the query and consolidate the results. Two changes are needed.

13. Add the GROUP BY clause to the end of the query. This includes the same expressions as those in the SELECT column list without the column aliases (AS...). Any column that is not in the GROUP BY column list must be aggregated. In this query, that is only the SalesAmount column.

14. Modify the SalesAmount column expression to use the SUM function and add the alias AS SalesAmountSum.

15. Verify that your changes to the query match the following:

```
SELECT
        YEAR(s.OrderDate) AS OrderYear,
        MONTH(s.OrderDate) AS OrderMonth,
        t.Country,
        SUM(s.SalesAmount) AS SalesAmountSum
FROM
        [dbo].[Sales] AS s
              INNER JOIN [dbo].[SalesTerritory] AS t
              ON s.SalesTerritoryKey = t.TerritoryKey
WHERE
        YEAR(s.OrderDate) = 2013
GROUP BY
        YEAR(s.OrderDate),
```

```
      MONTH(s.OrderDate),
      t.Country
;
```

16. Execute the query again. Note the row count in the status bar. The query returns only 66 rows this time.

17. Select and copy the query text to the clipboard.

Add the Query to the Report Dataset

Now that you've authored a query in SSMS, you will add it to a new report designed using Report Builder.

1. In web portal, add a new Paginated report using Report Builder just as you did in the Chapter 4 exercise and create an embedded data source to the WroxSSRS2016 database.

2. Enter the text **Sales Summary by Country** in the title textbox at the top of the report body.

3. Create a new embedded dataset named **SalesSummaryCountry**.

4. Select the data source, as shown in Figure 5-7.

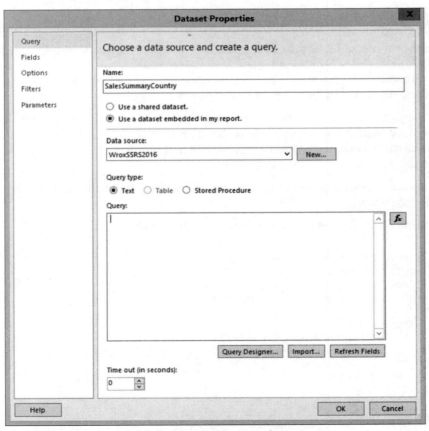

FIGURE 5-7: Selecting the SalesSummaryCountry dataset.

5. Click the Query Designer... button.

6. Click the "Edit as text" button on the Query Designer dialog.

7. Paste the query you copied from SSMS into the Query Designer window, as shown in Figure 5-8.

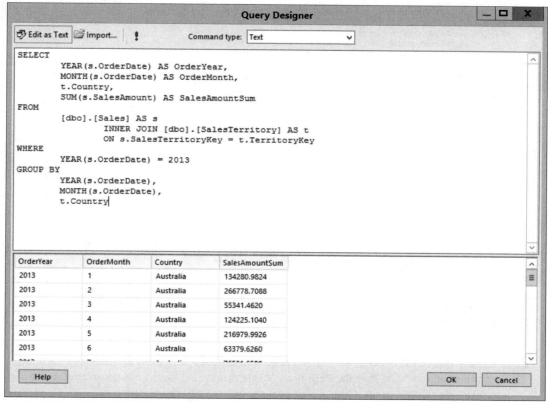

FIGURE 5-8: Pasting the query copied from SSMS.

8. Add the Year parameter by changing the text 2013 to @Year.

9. Click the red exclamation icon on the toolbar to execute the query. This will cause the Query Designer to add a parameter to the report and dataset definition. The Define Query Parameters dialog opens.

10. Enter the year 2013 for the Parameter Value, as shown in Figure 5-9, and click the OK button.

11. Click OK in the Query Designer window to accept the query changes and close the window. Figure 5-10 sows the Parameter Properties window with the query added.

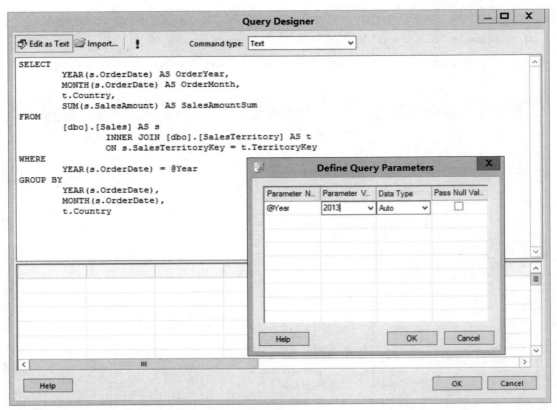

FIGURE 5-9: Entering the year for the Parameter Value.

12. On the Dataset Properties dialog, select the Parameters page from the list on the left side of the window. Note that the Parameter Value box on the right side doesn't reference a parameter. This is because the report parameter hasn't been created yet.

13. Click the OK button on the Dataset Properties window.

14. In the Report Data window on the left, double-click the new dataset to re-open the Dataset Properties window.

15. Select the Parameters page again. Note that a report parameter has been added, as shown in Figure 5-10.

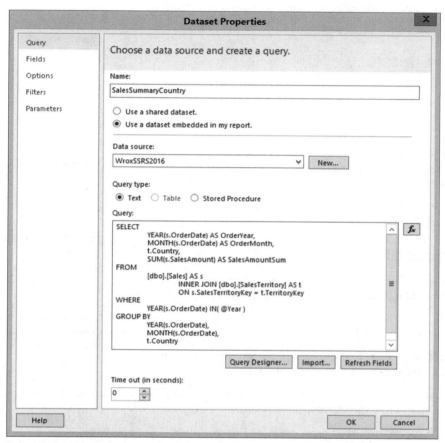

FIGURE 5-10: Dataset Properties with query.

> **NOTE** *Although these two objects have the same name, there is a difference between a* query parameter *and a* report parameter. *Note that the Parameter Name is the query parameter you had typed into the query text, as shown in Figure 5-11. The "Parameter value" actually refers to a corresponding report parameter that the designer just generated. This shows that the report parameter sends its value to the query parameter when the query executes.*

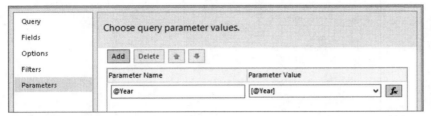

FIGURE 5-11: "Parameter value" referring to a report parameter.

16. In the Report Data pane on the left side of the Report Builder, expand the Parameters node in the tree to see the Year parameter.

17. Note the four fields belonging to the dataset, as shown in Figure 5-12.

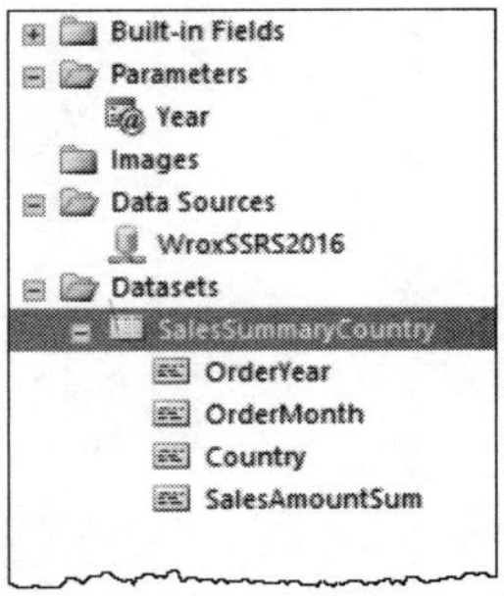

Design the Report Body

The purpose of this exercise is to develop skills with datasets and query design. With that objective in mind, you will create a simple report to view the dataset results.

FIGURE 5-12: Four fields belonging to the dataset.

1. Select the Insert ribbon tab.

2. Click the down arrow below the Matrix button on the ribbon. Select Insert Matrix..., as shown in Figure 5-13.

3. Drop the matrix into the report body as you did with the table in the exercise in Chapter 4, near the top just below the title textbox, as shown in Figure 5-14.

4. The matrix displays three field drop zones labeled Columns, Rows, and Data.

5. Drag and drop the OrderYear field into the Rows cell.

6. Drag and drop the Country field into the Columns cell.

7. Drag and drop the SalesAmountSum field into the Data cell.

8. Drag the OrderMonth field to the same cell as the OrderYear, but don't release the mouse button yet. Hover over this cell and note the position of the heavy "I-beam" cursor on the edge of the cell.

9. Move the pointer to the right so this cursor is on the right edge of the row header cell where you dropped the OrderYear field.

10. When the cursor is in the right position (on the right edge of the cell), release the mouse button to create a second row group after the OrderYear.

> **NOTE** *You can use the Undo and Redo buttons in the Quick Access toolbar if you need to rewind and repeat a step.*

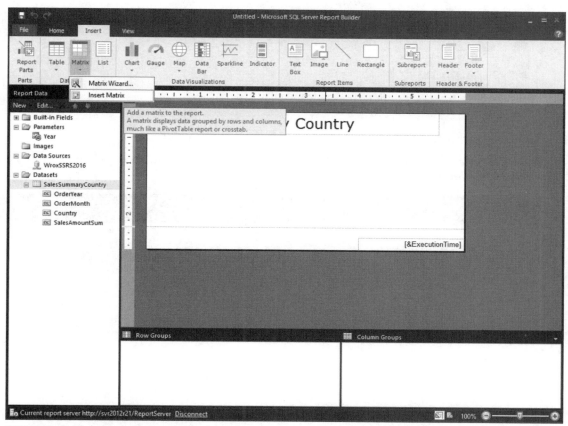

FIGURE 5-13: Selecting the Insert Matrix option.

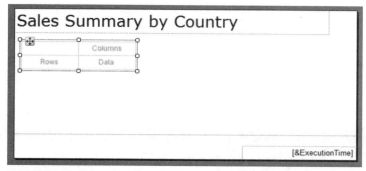

FIGURE 5-14: Dropping the matrix into the report body.

11. Select the Data cell that displays [SUM(SalesAmountSum)], as shown in Figure 5-15. Use the Number group on the Home ribbon to set the format to currency.

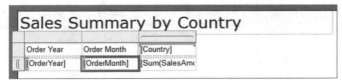

FIGURE 5-15: Selecting the [SUM(SalesAmountSum)] data cell.

12. Click the Run icon on the Home ribbon to preview the report.

13. Enter **2013** for the Year parameter as shown in Figure 5-16, and then click the View Report icon on the right.

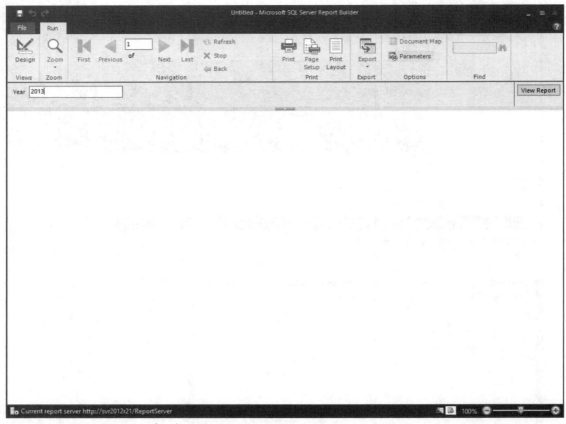

FIGURE 5-16: Entering 2013 for the Year parameter.

> **NOTE** *You can also just press the Enter key to run the report. The report runs with the provided parameter value.*

You should notice the difference between the table style report you created in the exercise in Chapter 4 and this matrix report where the Country field values are repeated across columns, as shown in Figure 5-17.

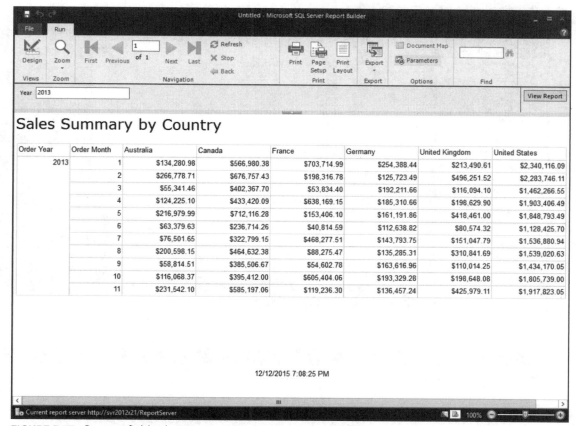

FIGURE 5-17: Country field values repeated across columns.

Enhance the Parameter

The point of this exercise is to demonstrate and experiment with parameters and query options, and not to dress up the report so much.

So far, you have a parameter that allows you to type a single year value into a textbox and run the report query with one value for the filter. This is effective, but it is not very sexy. Let's take it up a half notch.

1. Switch to design view and in the Report Data pane on the left of the Report Builder window, double-click or right-click to open the Report Parameter Properties dialog. You'll add on a sequence of features one step at a time.

2. Change the data type from Text to Integer, as shown in Figure 5-18.

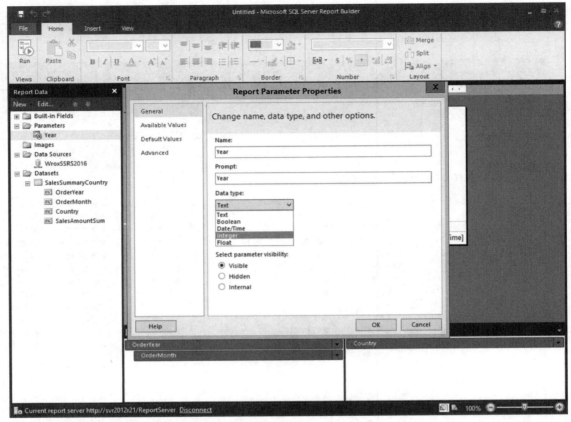

FIGURE 5-18: Report Parameter Properties dialog.

> **NOTE** *Parameters are generally very forgiving about the data type until you need to use them in certain expressions like a multi-value parameter list.*

3. On the second page of the Report Parameter Properties dialog, select the Available Values page.

4. Change the option to "Specify values."

5. Click the Add button three times to add three pairs of Label and Value boxes.

6. Enter the years 2011, 2012, and 2013, each twice (once for the Label and once for the Value), so it looks like Figure 5-19.

7. Change to the Default Value page.

8. On this page, choose "Specify values."

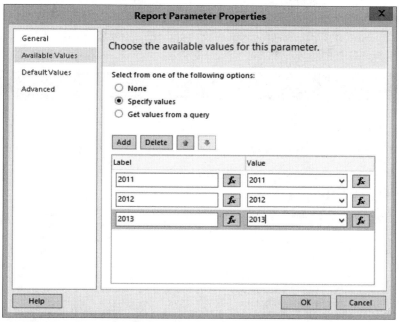

FIGURE 5-19: Entering report parameters.

9. Click the Add button and then type the text 2013 into the box to provide this as a default value for the parameter, as shown in Figure 5-20.

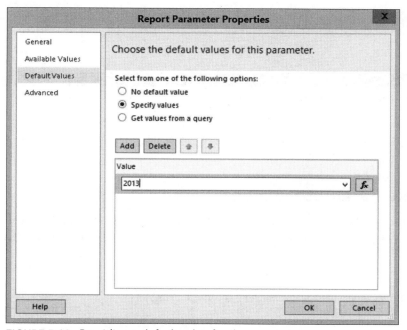

FIGURE 5-20: Providing a default value for the parameter.

10. Click OK to save and close the window.

11. Click the Run button to preview the report with the query results for the default year 2013, as shown in Figure 5-21.

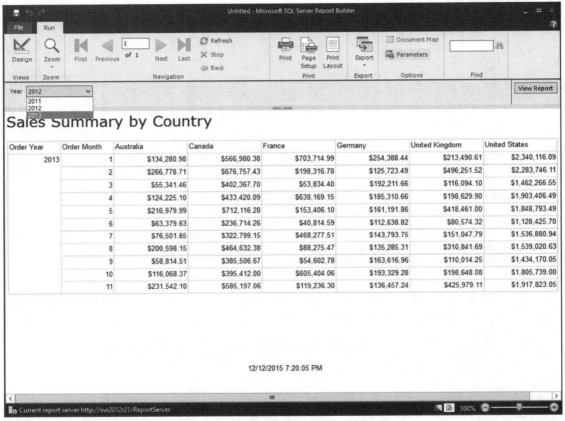

FIGURE 5-21: Report with the new parameter value.

12. Use the Year parameter list to select a different year, and then press Enter to run the report with the new parameter value.

Using Multiple Parameter Values

Multi-value parameters allow users to select any combination of items from the value list. The dataset converts the array of selected values in the report parameter to a comma-separated list in the query parameter, which can be used to filter records in the query.

1. Switch back to design view.

2. In the Report Data pane on the left, expand the Parameters.

3. Double-click the `Year` parameter and open the Report Parameter Properties dialog, as shown in Figure 5-22.

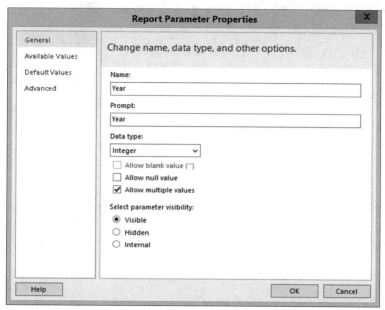

FIGURE 5-22: Report Parameter Properties dialog.

4. Check the box labeled "Allow multiple values."

5. Click OK to save and close the window.

6. Right-click the `SalesSummaryCountry` dataset and choose Dataset Properties. This opens the Dataset Properties dialog.

Rather than opening the Query Designer, you can make simple query changes right here on the Query page.

7. In the WHERE clause of the query, change the text `= @Year` shown in Figure 5-23 to `IN( @Year )`.

> **NOTE** *The T-SQL* IN *function accepts a comma-separated list of values. Because the* YEAR *function, used in the query to convert the* OrderDate *column to a year value, is a numeric value, the* Year *parameter must also be numeric. A numeric multi-value parameter is converted to a list of comma-separated values without quotes around each value, which is the appropriate format to use in this query.*

8. Click the OK button to accept the change and close the Dataset Properties window.

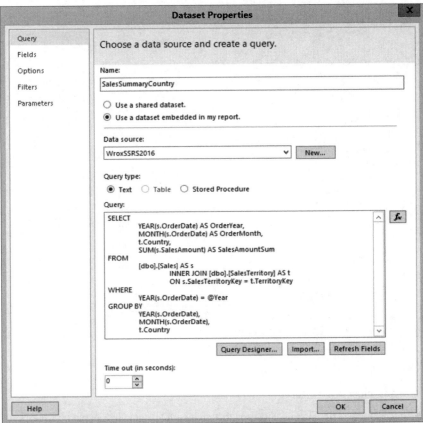

FIGURE 5-23: Changing the WHERE clause of the query.

9. Run the report again.

10. Drop down the Year parameter list and you'll see that each year is preceded by a check box.

11. Note the behavior of the (Select All) box in the first row of the list.

12. Check the values 2012 and 2013, as shown in Figure 5-24.

13. Click the Save icon to ensure that changes have been save to the report.

14. Press Enter to run the report. Notice that both of the selected years are displayed in the row group headers in the left-most column of the report.

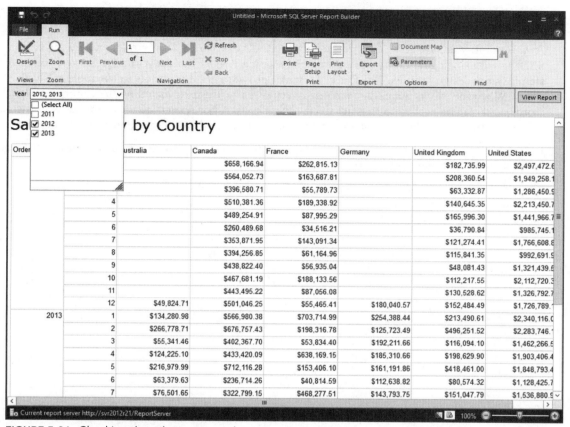

FIGURE 5-24: Checking the values 2012 and 2013.

> **NOTE** *Try running the report without having a parameter value selected. Since the Year parameter is required, you can see that the report doesn't run. This is a good reminder to either set a default parameter value or at least guide users to make parameter selections before running a report.*

This is a simple report with a single parameter. You'll likely be creating reports with more complex queries and multiple parameters, but the same patterns apply, and you'll be able to use these skills in real production reports.

SUMMARY

At this point, you have some experience with the tools to create a dataset query and apply basic filtering with single and multi-select parameters. Using Report Builder with SQL Server, you have simple query design options. The Query Designer provides graphical tools to assemble a T-SQL query. When the tool is done, the resulting query is really just text, including the commands, keywords, and clauses needed to instruct the database engine. For serious queries, you know how to use SSMS and then paste the working query into the designer, add parameters, and build your report.

In Chapter 6, you use the SSDT Query Designer, and then learn how to expand on these techniques to create more complex and functional reports.

Grouping and Totals

WHAT'S IN THIS CHAPTER

➤ Introducing SQL Server Data Tools for Visual Studio

➤ Sample reports projects and exercises

➤ Using the graphical Query Designer

➤ Understanding query groups and table joins

➤ Understanding report data flow

➤ Understanding report groups

➤ Grasping expression basics

➤ Utilizing group sorting and visibility

This chapter introduces and explains one of the most fundamental and essential concepts in SSRS report design. All of the data regions—tables, matrices, lists, and visual controls like charts—rely on groups. You will get started with the sample report project in SSDT that contains several completed examples. You will learn the differences between grouping and aggregating rows in queries and performing grouping on datasets within a report region. We explain the flow of data through the report along with the opportunities to filter, group, and aggregate values at multiple points along this path. You will add groups and related header tiles and footer totals to groups in a table and then a matrix. Then you'll see how multiple groups for hierarchies of grouped results make for effective reporting.

Another important topic, essential to effective report design, is the use of expressions to define groups and properties. We introduce aggregate functions and aggregate scope, which will be expanded in Chapter 7. Finally, you will learn to design a table report with multi-level drill-down navigation so users can explore details within summary groups as needed.

SQL SERVER DATA TOOLS

So far, you have been working with Report Builder, the simplest of the two report design tools. Before moving into the next report design topic, you should become familiar with the other report designer: SQL Server Data Tools (SSDT) for Visual Studio. This report tool was created primarily with the IT professional in mind. An earlier version of the Visual Studio report design tool was once called Business Intelligence Development Studio (BIDS).

Honestly, most of the report design features in both Report Builder and SSDT are the same. Conversely, subtle differences and some capabilities in SSDT don't exist in Report Builder. The tool you choose to use to accomplish your day-to-day report design work will likely depend on your organizational role and the complexity of the report design solutions. Before making a final decision, you should learn to use both tools, and then decide which one is right for you and your project.

> **NOTE** *After several years of experience, I have changed my approach to teaching people to use both design tools. Even so, it is continually a quandary for instructors and authors to develop the best instructional method. In classes, and in previous editions of this book, I gave instructions using one tool, and then call-out some of the differences along the way. Because there are so many subtle differences, this approach can confuse new users. Consequently, if you really want to learn serious report design, educate yourself on both tools, one at a time; and then make your choice.*

Getting Started

Before you get started using SSDT, decide where you prefer to store the project files. As you'll see when you create a new project, the default project file path is in your Windows `Documents` library. If you are new to Visual Studio, I recommend you use the default project path for this quick introductory walkthrough. I like to keep mine in a folder named Projects in my OneDrive, or in a folder named `Projects` right off the root of the main storage drive. Whatever your choice, decide now, and create a folder named `Projects` in your preferred storage location.

The following numbered steps are not a complete exercise, but rather a few simple instructions to help you create a new project. The project and report names you use in this little practice run are not critical so just use some names that make sense to you. You will quickly move on and not use this project and report in future exercises.

1. The first thing is to open SQL Server Data Tools 2015. Depending on your version of Windows, either use the SQL Server 2016 program group, or just type the name of the program until you see it in the search results.

TIP *Because SQL Server Data Tools now installs as a separate setup package from the link provided in the SQL Server Installation Center, it may not appear under the SQL Server 2016 program group. This may change over time with subsequent version upgrades, or if you had upgraded from a previous version of SQL Server. On my Windows 2012 development server, which has a fresh install, SQL Server Data Tools 2015 shows up in the Apps list under the letter "S."*

2. Run SQL Server Data Tools 2015.

NOTE *Running Visual Studio 2015 is exactly the same as running SQL Server Data Tools 2015. Keep in mind that Visual Studio 2015 was the current version of Visual Studio at the time of publication. Newer versions of Visual Studio will work with appropriate updates to the SSDT add-in.*

3. After the Visual Studio shell opens, from the File menu, choose New ⇨ Project….

4. The New Project dialog opens. From the Templates pane on the left, expand Business Intelligence and choose Reporting Services, as shown in Figure 6-1.

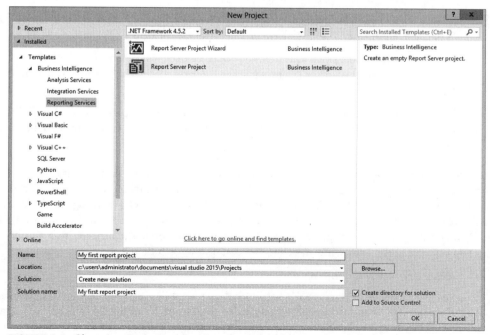

FIGURE 6-1: Choosing Reporting Services from the New Project dialog.

5. Within the project templates list in the middle of the dialog, select Report Server Project.

6. At the bottom of the window, Enter the name for the project as `My first report project`.

> **NOTE** *This should be a short name including spaces and descriptive text, which will create a folder and file names. I usually use a name that briefly describes the purpose of the project and that I will recognize later. The project name I just recommended is only to get you started and give you some experience with new project setup. As I mentioned earlier, you will soon leave this project behind and then open an existing project I have prepared for you.*

7. Note the default project folder path. If you prefer, use the Browse button to navigate to a `Projects` folder you created earlier to complete the path in the Location box.

The Solution name will be the same as the Project name unless you change it. In larger, full-scale solutions that include multiple projects, you might name the solution something like `Sales Analysis Solution` with a report project name `Sales Analysis Reports`. This allows you to add related projects. In this example, an Integration Services project named `Sales Analysis ETL` may be added to the solution, and then a database project named `Sales Analysis Data Warehouse` and an Analysis Service project name `Sales Analysis Data Model`. The solution could be placed under version control using Team Foundation Services (TFS), thus enabling a team of developers to collaborate and share these project files.

8. If the project won't be managed as part of a larger solution, just leave the names the same. When you're finished making changes, click the OK button.

9. With a report project open and the Solution Explorer visible on the right-side of the SSDT/Visual Studio main window, right-click the Reports folder and choose Add ⇨ Existing Item....

10. From the Add New dialog, select Report and then give the report file a name. This should normally be a friendly name with spaces and mixed case. When you're ready, click the Add button.

When the Report Designer opens, notice there are different window panes containing controls and properties docked to both sides of the main window. These are labeled in Figure 6-2, and the key that follows explains the labels. The four tool windows used for reports design include, on the left, the Report Data and Toolbox windows arranged as tabs, and, on the right, the Solution Explorer and Properties windows arranged as docked windows, one above the other with a sliding separation bar. You will see additional windows that you can ignore or hide if you prefer.

1. *Report Formatting toolbars*

Set properties for the currently selected object or objects in the Report Designer when in Design view. Standard properties include Font Name, Font Size, Weight, Italic, Underline, Foreground color, Background color, Alignment, List styles, and Indentation.

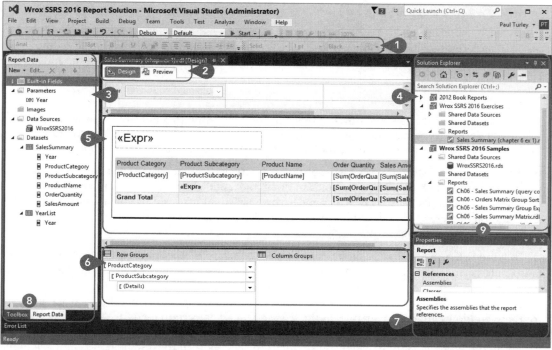

FIGURE 6-2: Window panes in Report Designer.

2. *Report Designer view selection tabs*

Switch between Design and Preview.

3. *Report Data window*

The Toolbox window is also displayed in this area. Switch windows using the selection tabs at the bottom of the window pane.

4. *Solution Explorer window*

Navigate the solution, projects, and project files. Right-click to set project properties, add new items, and perform actions.

5. *Report Designer window*

This is the main design canvas used to design reports and set properties for data regions and report items.

6. *Grouping window*

Add, remove, and set properties for row and column groups.

7. *Properties window*

Displays and manages all properties for the selected object or group of selected objects.

8.   *Tabbed documents selection*

In the default view, windows in this pane are selected using these tabs. The Report Data and Toolbox are used for report design, and other windows are available. Windows can be added with the View menu. Use the window pane toolbar to hide, move, pin, and auto-hide windows.

9.   *Sliding window separator*

In the default view, windows in this pane are docked with a movable separator bar. The Solution Explorer and Properties windows are used for report design and solution management. Use the window pane toolbar to hide, move, pin, and auto-hide windows.

The best way to get started with Visual Studio is to create a test project and spend some time familiarizing yourself with the interface. You can dock, hide, and show windows so that you have what you need at your fingertips, as well as remove the ones you don't need. If you are new to Visual Studio, don't go crazy moving things around and closing windows until you are familiar with these tools enough to set things back.

Each window has a familiar pushpin icon that will either "pin" the window in place, or allow it to auto-hide when the mouse moves away from it. Use the auto-hide feature and resize tool windows rather than closing windows you'll need again. If you close or hide a window using the right-click menu or drop-down arrow in the window header, you can get it back using the View menu. Some of these windows are only available on the View menu when certain items are selected in the design interface. For example, if you were to close the Report Data window, the option to display it again is listed on the View menu only when you set focus to the report in the designer.

In the next section you will be using a sample solution that contains a set of existing projects provided for you. If prompted to save your changes to this new project, answer "Yes," but you're not actually going to use that project any more.

Getting Started with Sample Reports Projects

As mentioned in Chapter 3, copies of all the reports used throughout the book are provided on this book's website at www.wrox.com. These are organized into two projects contained in a Visual Studio solution in the folders you extract with the book download sample files.

1.   On the File menu, select Open ⇨ Project / Solution....

2.   Use the Open File dialog to navigate to the location where you extracted the book sample files. Locate and open the folder named Wrox SSRS 2016 Report Solution.

3.   Open the file named Wrox SSRS 2016 Report Solution.sln. SSDT opens with the solution and related projects listed in the Object Explorer on the right side of the report design interface. Figure 6-3 shows SSDT open with a report open in the Design window.

The solution contains multiple projects. Use the Solution Explorer window on the right side of the main window to expand and collapse each project in order to access the files it contains. Reports and shared data sources are also added in Solution Explorer.

Generally, you should use shared data sources as a best practice. The only reason typically not to use them is when you want a report to be completely self-contained. But otherwise, having one place to manage data source connection information makes a lot of sense when these objects all get shipped off to the report server and are making important things happen out there in Business User Land.

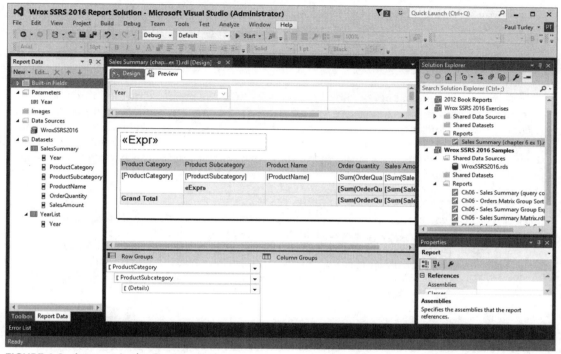

FIGURE 6-3: A report in the Design window.

Shared datasets have advantages under very specific circumstances and are required when designing mobile reports. Therefore, you will use them in chapters 17, 18, 19, and 20. As a default choice, for most paginated reports, I generally recommend using embedded datasets.

The `Wrox SSRS 2016 Exercises` project contains finished copies of all the exercises found at the end of each chapter. The `Wrox SSRS 2016 Samples` project includes many topic-specific examples, each prefixed with the chapter number. For the chapter samples, it is important to realize that explicit instructions are not provided for every single click and menu selection. Because you have already mastered the essentials getting started creating a new report, data source, and dataset, there is no need to repeat those steps. Some unfinished reports are provided with steps completed up to the task or topic that you can finish. You will be instructed as to which report to open. In some of cases, you'll examine a completed report to see how it works.

To follow along, open a copy of the sample report, rather than making changes to the original, so you can go back and start over if necessary. The best way to do that is to copy and paste the report in the Solution Explorer.

> **TIP** *Whenever you use the copy/paste method to back up a report, ensure that you save your changes first, because this technique actually makes a copy of the last saved file, rather than the version of the report sitting in memory that may have unsaved changes.*

This step is pretty simple, but not entirely intuitive at first. My preferred method is to select the report in Solution Explorer (not the report file name as if renaming the file, but just click once to select the report), and then use Ctrl+C (copy) and Ctrl+V (paste). If you right-click to Copy, then you must right-click the project to Paste. I typically remove the Copy of file prefix and then describe the backup state in parentheses at the end of the filename. You can see this pattern in the sample project.

> **TIP** *Making regular backups provides peace of mind by ensuring that you don't lose your work. There are three common backup methods for reports: using a version control system such as TFS, making routine copies of the report files in the project folder to a different storage location, and keeping a secondary report project in the solution. The latter allows you to use the earlier-mentioned copy-and-paste backup method.*

If you are disciplined about using integrated version control, then it can provide a safety net to prevent catastrophic loss. However, it doesn't help with the typical cadence of report design. When working on a challenging report, I often create and keep one or more backup copies of the report I'm working on. This provides a way to experiment with different techniques without messing up a working design. If something goes wrong, rather than trying to untangle it, you can just revert to an earlier copy. After testing to make sure the design is working, you can delete the backup copies.

Graphical Query Designer

The reason there are different query tools is that report developers have varied levels of experience with T-SQL. Therefore, individuals develop strong preferences. When I began my career with databases, at first I relied on graphical query design tools. Now I find it easier to hand-write queries rather than using the graphical Query Designer. These helper tools exist for good reason, and they work well. If you are not a T-SQL aficionado, you should learn how to use the graphical query design tool, but it shouldn't always be your central experience. With a little practice, many find it easier to hand-code simple queries, rather than relying on the Query Designer.

When using SQL Server as a data source, the dataset in Query Designer is more elaborate than in Report Builder. This graphical Query Designer is actually borrowed from the SQL Server client tools, and is also available in SQL Server Management Studio (SSMS).

Open the Sample Report

If you don't already have the Wrox SSRS 2016 Report Solution open in SSDT, open it now.

1. In the Object Explorer, expand the Wrox SSRS 2016 Samples project.

2. Expand the Reports folder.

3. In the Object Explorer, click once to select the Ch06 - Sales Summary (query completed) report.

> **TIP** *There is a subtle difference between selecting an object and selecting the name of the object. For example, when you select a report in Object Explorer, the entire line is highlighted. If you click once and then click again, the name of the report is selected. The same behavior applies to textboxes in the designer where clicking twice will select the text within the object, rather than the object itself. If this happens, click outside the object and then click it once.*

4. Press Ctrl+C and then Ctrl+V to make a copy of the report. The new report should appear in the Object Explorer preceded by the text Copy of in the filename.

5. Double-click the new report copy to open it in the designer.

6. Expand the Datasets node in the Report Data window.

7. Right-click the SalesSummaryMonthProductRegion dataset and select Query… to open the graphical Query Designer.

8. Use this finished query to familiarize yourself with the query design interface as you read the following description about designing a query with this tool. When you're finished, cancel out of the Query Designer and don't save changes.

9. Optionally, create a new dataset in this report and follow these steps to duplicate this query. Save your changes, and then switch back to the original query to check the results.

To design a query in SSDT, create a dataset just like you did previously using Report Builder. Click the Query Designer… button to open the graphical Query Designer. You add tables to the query by using the right-most icon on the toolbar. In the example shown in Figure 6-4 is the end result after completing the following steps. Please note that the following six steps are for reference and are explained in greater detailer in the subsequent steps.

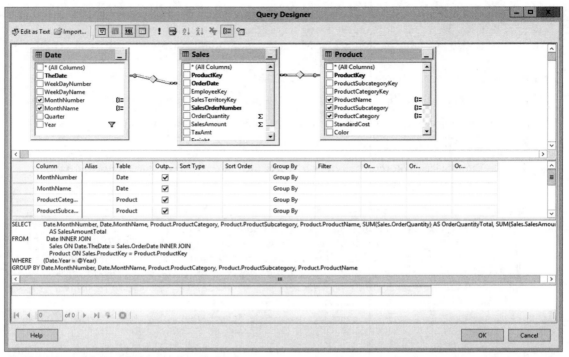

FIGURE 6-4: Tables added to Query Designer.

1. Add the Date, Sales, and Product tables.

2. Verify that the join lines were added by the query designer.

3. Use the check boxes to select the fields you see in the example: MonthNumber, MonthName, ProductCategory, ProductSubcategory, ProductName, OrderQuantity, and SalesAmount.

4. Click the Use Group By button on the toolbar.

5. For the OrderQuantity and SalesAmount fields, use the drop-down list to change the Group By column selection to Sum.

6. For the OrderQuantity and SalesAmount fields, copy and paste the field names (in the "Column" column) to the Alias column.

The designer has four panes separated vertically. The top pane shows the tables that were added to the query, joins, and selected columns. The second pane lets you rename columns, group, aggregate, filter the results, and apply parameters. The query text pane shows the T-SQL script generated by the designer, and the results pane shows the rows returned by the executed query. Test and run the query by clicking the red exclamation mark icon on the toolbar.

Grouping Query Results

Figure 6-4 shows the Group By button on the toolbar (second from the right). This option adds every column to the GROUP BY clause in the query, and displays the text "Group By" in the seventh column of the fields list pane.

Any numeric columns that should be aggregated (rather than grouped in the query) must have the Group By option changed. Figure 6-5 shows the OrderQuantity and SalesAmount columns changed from Group By to Sum. When you do this, a column alias is created for each aggregated column using placeholder names like Expr1. These should be changed to something that makes more sense. You can actually use the original column name for the alias. To differentiate the alias from the original column name, the original names have been appended with the word Total, so the alias names are OrderQuantityTotal and SalesAmountTotal.

Column	Alias	Table	Output	Sort Type	Sort Order	Group By	Filter	Or...	Or...
MonthNumber		Date	☑			Group By			
MonthName		Date	☑			Group By			
ProductCateg...		Product	☑			Group By			
ProductSubca...		Product	☑			Group By			
ProductName		Product	☑			Group By			
OrderQuantity	OrderQuantityTotal	Sales	☑			Sum			
SalesAmount	SalesAmountTotal	Sales	☑			Sum			
Year		Date	☐			Where	= @Year		
			▣						

FIGURE 6-5: Column names modified.

Despite the desire to filter data by the Year, that column doesn't need to be returned in the query results. You can see that the Year column has been included from the Date table and the Output checkbox has been unchecked. To add a parameter, type the parameter name you want to use in the Filter cell preceded by an equal sign (=) and an ampersand (@). In the graphical query designer, a column that is used only for filtering is excluded from the GROUP BY list by changing the selection to "Where." In this case, the designer references the Year column in a HAVING clause to implement filtering.

Query Joins and Join Types

Because these tables have relationships defined in the database, the tables are automatically joined on the key columns. In the example, the Sales table is joined to the Date table using the key column in the Date table named TheDate, and the OrderDate column in the Sales table. Likewise, Sales and Product tables are joined on the respective ProductKey columns.

The designer applies inner joins by default, meaning that there must be matching records on both sides of the join. The Date table contains one record for every day in the years 2005 through 2014, but there are not orders for every date, so the inner join will only return date information for existing orders. An outer join returns all records from a specified table on one side of the join, and then all the matching records from the table on the other side.

Changing the join type is simple. Right-click the diamond on the line between the two tables and select all rows from the table on the outer side. In this case, you right-click the join between Date and Sales tables, and then choose "Select All rows from Date." The join will be designated either LEFT OUTER or RIGHT OUTER, depending on the order they were added in the Query Designer.

Execute the query by clicking the exclamation mark icon in the toolbar. When prompted for the Year parameter, type **2013**, and then click OK. Notice in the results pane, a row for December, 2013, for which there are no existing orders. This is the effect of the outer join.

Report Data Flow

You will find that most objects within the Report Designer have many properties and features, and many of them are only used when necessary. Standard objects you will use in the reports all the time have properties that you probably won't use in most reports, but they provide tremendous flexibility and opportunities to address unique business requirements using creative design techniques.

Some of these properties are depicted in Figure 6-6. You can see (moving left to right) that after query results are processed in a dataset query, an optional filter can be applied after the results are produced. Likewise, conditional filters can be applied as the data enters any data region. After that, the results can be sorted before they are presented to the first group expression. Each data region handles grouping a little differently, but the core concepts are the same. Some data regions support multiple levels of grouping.

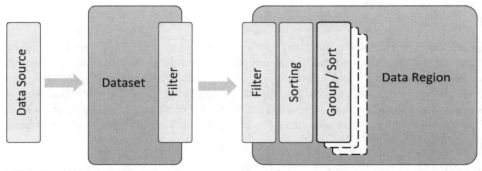

FIGURE 6-6: Using Report Designer properties and features.

REPORT GROUPS

Report groups are one of the most important concepts in fundamental report design. Whether your reports will visualize data in a table, matrix, or any type of chart, you will define group expressions either implicitly by dragging and dropping fields in the designer, or explicitly by writing the expression. Table and list reports do not require a group to be defined, but have limited utility without any groups. Beginning with a table, let's a take a look at how groups work.

1. In SSDT, if you have any unsaved work you want to keep, save that report.

2. From the Object Explorer on the right, open the report named Ch06 - Sales Summary with Groups.

3. You can see that the table is bound to the dataset named SalesSummaryMonthProductRegion.

4. In the Row Groups list below the designer window, use the down arrow button next to the ProductCategory group to choose Group Properties... to open the properties dialog for that group, as shown in Figure 6-7.

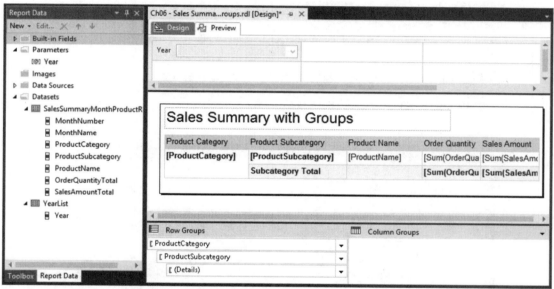

FIGURE 6-7: The Group Properties dialog.

It's probably no surprise that the "Group expression" refers to the ProductCategory field (see Figure 6-8), but there are several optional properties and features associated with groups. For example, page breaks can be managed for each group, so a new page is inserted before or after the grouped field value changes.

5. Use the page list on the left to switch to the Page Breaks page in the Group Properties dialog shown in Figure 6-9.

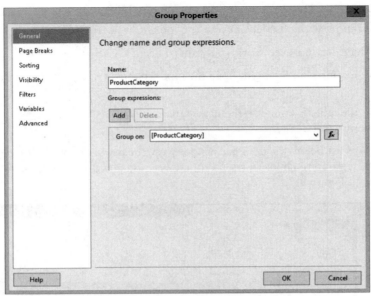

FIGURE 6-8: ProductCategory field as a group expression.

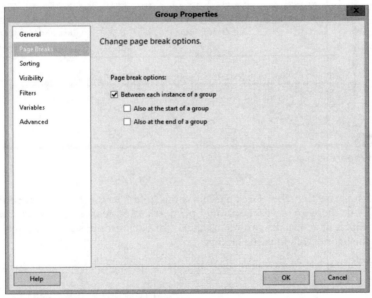

FIGURE 6-9: Managing page breaks.

6. Check the first box to set a page break between each instance of a group.

7. Leave the other checkboxes unchecked.

8. Click the OK button to accept the group changes and close the Group Properties dialog.

 There's no need to inspect the ProductSubcategory group because it's set to group by the ProductSubcategory field. But, what about the (Details) group? This group isn't normally set to group records for a field by default, so let's find out if someone might have changed it.

9. Edit the group properties for the (Details) group and open the Group Properties dialog.

 Hey, look at that! The (Details) group has been changed and set up to group by the ProductName field. Why would this make a difference when that field is already being grouped within the detail rows returned by the query? It seems senseless to explicitly group by the lowest-level value that is being returned in the query results.

10. Now check the behavior in the Table Designer. Hover the mouse pointer over and re-select the two numeric fields for the detail cells in the Order Quantity and Sales Amount columns. You see that the designer applies the SUM function. This is because of the group definition in that (Detail) group.

The first two groups are set up for drill-down navigation by hiding levels that are expanded with toggle items. With any level collapsed, it is important that the value displayed on this line be an aggregated total representing all the hidden details. This will only happen if an aggregate function (such as SUM) has been applied in each expression on the detail row.

Adding Totals to a Table or Matrix Report

The table, matrix, and list data regions are all based on a common object called the Tablix, and many design techniques are similar for each of these data regions. Each of these objects provides different layout options, but the fundamental concept of grouping is the same.

In a table, adding a total to a row group adds a new row that applies an aggregate function (for example, SUM) to all the members of *that* group. The same applies to a total added to a matrix column group. By adding a total row or column, you're actually adding a total that applies to the *parent* of the group. Consider this example. Suppose columns are grouped by quarter and then by year. If you were to add a total to the Quarter column group, the total would be for all the quarters adding into the year. This means that a total applied to the topmost group will always return the grand total for all records in the data region. This is evident in the example shown in Figure 6-10 where the table data region is grouped and totaled by Subcategory.

Product Category	Product Subcategory	Product Name	Order Quantity Total	Sales Amount Total
⊟ Accessories	⊞ Bike Racks	Hitch Rack - 4-Bike	2,617	$182,830.88
	⊞ Bottles and Cages	Water Bottle - 30 oz.	2,336	$6,830.84
	⊞ Cleaners	Bike Wash - Dissolver	2,184	$10,171.38
	⊞ Helmets	Sport-100 Helmet, Black	5,729	$118,103.74
	⊟ Hydration Packs	Hydration Pack - 70 oz.	1,860	$60,151.35
	⊞ Tires and Tubes	Patch Kit/8 Patches	590	$809.79
	Subcategory Total		15,316	$378,897.98

FIGURE 6-10: Grouped table data region with totals.

Defining a total for a group at a lower level would create a subtotal break. Totals can be placed *before* or *after* group values. Adding totals *before* a row group shows the total *above* the group in a heading row, and adding the total *after* shows the total *below* the group in a footer row. Subsequently, for a column group in a matrix data region, inserting a total *before* the group places totals *to the left* of the group. Adding totals *after* the group inserts a total column *to the right* of the group.

Groups, headers, footers, and totals are all related design elements that can take a simple report to the next level and provide significant value. Groups are an essential design concept, and a number of more advanced capabilities have been added as Reporting Services has evolved through newer versions. At the group level, you can now conditionally control things like page breaks and page numbers.

As you continue to review the completed Ch06 - Sales Summary (query completed) report, use the following steps to see how the report was be designed.

1. Switch back to Design view.

2. Take a look at the SalesAmount column. The heading label **Sales Total** was changed from the original field name to make it more readable.

3. The last column was added by right-clicking the header of the column to its left and choosing the option to add a new, blank column. The column label was changed to **Avg Sales**.

4. In the detail row, right-click the Avg Sales textbox and choose Expression....

5. Review the expression that was added: **=AVG(Fields!SalesAmount.Value)**. Before you click OK to complete the expression, select and copy this text to the clipboard.

6. Right-click the textbox in the Total row of the new column and choose Expression....

7. Review this expression that was added by pasting the expression you copied from the detail cell. Click the OK button.

8. Preview and test the report.

Expression Basics

Looking at the last few examples, when you create a field reference in the designer by dragging and dropping or selecting from the field list, you will see a field or expression placeholder in square brackets, such as [ProductCategory] or [SUM(OrderQuantity)]. What you see in the designer is actually a simplified version of the expression that is stored in the report definition. To view the actual expression, right-click the placeholder text and choose Expression.... This opens the Expression Editor, showing the entire expression. Expressions always begin with an equal sign and contain a full object reference. Table 6-1 shows these two examples.

TABLE 6-1: Expression Placeholders

PLACEHOLDER	EXPRESSION
[ProductCategory]	=Fields!ProductCategory.Value
[SUM(OrderQuantity)]	=SUM(Fields!OrderQuantity.Value)

In this chapter's exercise, you will see that expressions can include multiple functions and objects. When used in a data region bound to a dataset, an expression simply references a field or fields in that dataset, but can also reference different datasets, as you will see in more advanced examples in the following chapters. Expressions are the real magic behind both simple and complex report designs. This chapter introduces several features and capabilities that are demonstrated in greater detail in the chapters that follow.

Introducing Aggregate Functions and Totals

When you drop a numeric field into a group or table footer cell, an expression is added applying the SUM() aggregate function. The designer assumes that you will want to sum these values, but this function can be replaced with one of several others. Reporting Services supports several aggregate functions, similar to those supported by the T-SQL query language. For now, let's just consider the concept of basic aggregation using the SUM function.

> **NOTE** *You learn about all the functions in Chapter 7, "Advanced Design Techniques."*

When an aggregate function expression is used in a group detail, header, or footer row, the scope of the current data region or group is assumed. For example, suppose a table contains two nested groups based on the Category and Subcategory fields. If you were to drag the SalesAmount field into the Subcategory group footer, the SUM(SalesAmount) expression would return the sum of all SalesAmount values within the scope of each distinct Subcategory group range.

Sorting

You have a few options to sort data in a report, and the best choice will depend on a few factors. Other features (like grouping) require data to be sorted and may negate the capability to sort data after it is grouped. Be mindful that with a large result set, sorting is a costly operation that will add to the overall report execution time. Options may include the following:

➤ **Sort Records in the Query**—Typically, if records will be presented in a particular order, the most efficient method is to sort the data in the query before it gets to the report. This will aid in grouping as effectively as possible. If other sorting options will be used within the report, presorting in the query may be wasted cycles.

➤ **Table Interactive Sorting**—Normally used in ungrouped table reports, this feature can be applied to any or all columns of the table. Interactive sorting is applied to the textbox in the table heading for each column. Clicking the sort icon displayed in the column header will re-order rows the records displayed in that table. Clicking again toggles between ascending or descending order. In a table or matrix data region with groups, interactive sorting can be applied to the rows within a group.

➤ **Group Sorting**—Every group has an optional Sorting expression. There are times when you may need to group on one set of field values and sort on a different set of corresponding values. This would make sense only when the grouping and sorting fields are distinct within the same set of value ranges.

An example of group sorting can be found in the sample report Ch06 - Orders Matrix Group Sort. The design of this report is quite simple, and Figure 6-11 shows this in the SSDT designer.

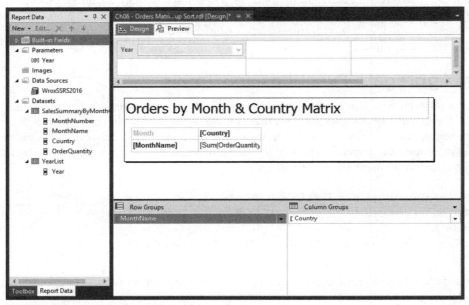

FIGURE 6-11: Design of sample report.

This report began with two datasets. The main query returns the MonthNumber, MonthName, Country, and OrderQuantity columns. Take a look at the Year parameter properties and you'll see that the YearList dataset query is used to populate the parameter list. Edit the SalesSummaryByMonthCountry dataset and you'll see that the Year parameter is used to filter the results in the query's WHERE clause. The matrix is added to the report body. The MonthName field is dragged and dropped onto the Rows header, the Country field is dropped onto the Columns header, and the OrderQuantity field is dropped in the Values cell to create the expression =SUM(Fields!OrderQuantity.Value).

If you were to preview the report at this point in the design process, it would look like Figure 6-12. Out of the box, the rows and column groups are naturally sorted alphabetically.

This is probably fine for the country names, but obviously not for the months, which are in alphabetic order, but not sorted chronologically. This is the reason the MonthNumber column has been included in the query. To fix the group order, you switch to Design view and edit the row group.

Figure 6-13 shows the Sorting page of the Group Properties dialog for the row group.

Orders by Month & Country Matrix

Month	Australia	Canada	France	Germany
April	224	1,704	1,664	836
August	509	1,278	269	279
February	1,235	2,816	714	607
January	415	2,526	2,388	1,184
July	110	960	1,050	503
June	103	699	217	359
March	110	1,213	357	615
May	901	2,108	467	482
November	893	2,018	445	431
October	209	1,660	1,623	785
September	115	1,214	349	543

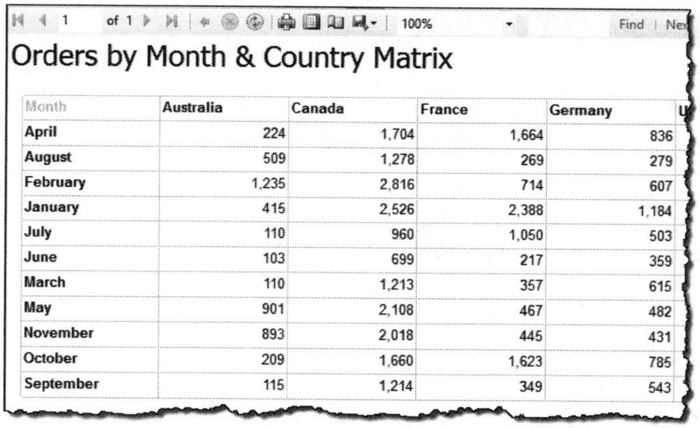

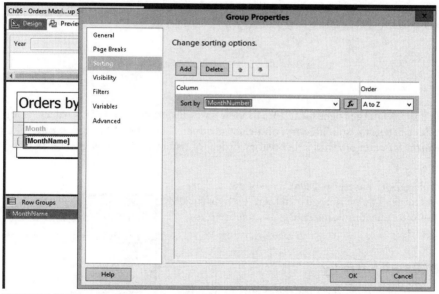

FIGURE 6-12: Previewing the report.

FIGURE 6-13: Sorting page of the Group Properties dialog.

Changing the "Sort by" expression allows you to display one field and sort by another, as you can see with the report previewed in Figure 6-14.

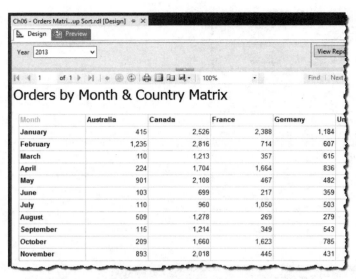

FIGURE 6-14: Displaying by one field and sorting by another.

EXERCISE

In this scenario, the Sales Manager needs a report to view sales orders for the year. Orders should be summarized by product category, subcategory, and each product. The Sales Manager would like to be able to compare product category and subcategory order totals, and then view greater detail only when needed.

You will design a table report based on a Database view and create row groups in the table. The product details will be hidden, so users can drill-down to selected items using a toggle item to expand the group details.

Design the Dataset Query

Begin by designing the query to get data for the report, which is managed in a dataset.

1. Open the `Wrox SSRS 2016 Report Solution` in SQL Server Data Tools.

2. In the Solution Explorer window on the right, expand the `Wrox SSRS 2016 Exercises` project, as shown in Figure 6-15.

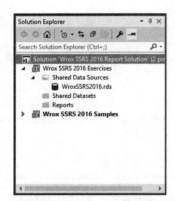

FIGURE 6-15: Expanding the Wrox SSRS 2016 Exercises project.

3. Right-click the Reports folder and choose Add ⇨ New Item.

4. When the Add New Item dialog opens, select Report and enter the filename `Chapter 06 Sales Summary`.

5. Click the Add button.

6. Use the pin icon to ensure that the Report Data window is pinned so it doesn't auto-hide when the mouse is moved away. Auto-hide is a great way to conserve screen real estate, but it is difficult to drag and drop items when the designer window is obscured.

7. In the Report Data window on the left, right-click the `Data Sources` folder and choose Add New Data Source....

8. In the Data Source Properties dialog, choose "Use shared data source reference" and select the existing data source named `WroxSSRS2016`.

9. Copy and paste this data source name into the Name box at the top of the dialog and then click the OK button.

10. Right-click the `Datasets` folder and choose Add New Dataset....

11. Enter `SalesSummary` for the name.

12. Select "Use dataset embedded in my report."

13. Select the `WroxSSRS2016` data source.

14. Click the Query Designer... button.

15. On the toolbar, click the Add Table button on the right.

16. Choose the Views tab and select the `vSalesSummaryYearProduct` view, as shown in Figure 6-16.

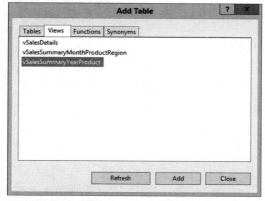

FIGURE 6-16: Selecting the vSalesSummaryYearProduct view.

17. Click the Add button to add the view to the query and close the Add Table dialog.

18. In the field list for the view displayed in the top pane, select every field, but don't select the first item on the list labeled `* (All Columns)`.

19. In the second pane, for the `Year` column, enter the text **`IN(@Year)`** for the Filter.

20. Double-check to ensure that the filter text is correct, as shown in Figure 6-17.

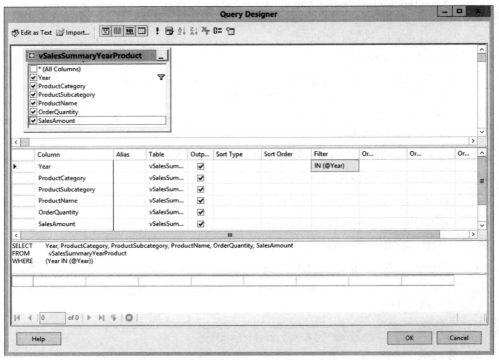

FIGURE 6-17: Filter text added to Query Designer.

21. Click the OK button to accept the query and close the Query Designer window.

22. Click the OK button to close the Dataset Properties window.

Design and Lay Out a Table Report

Next, design and lay out a table report.

1. Add a textbox and a table from the Toolbox window to the same positions on the report as the previous exercise.

2. Enter the title `Sales Summary by Year` into the textbox.

3. Style the textbox so the report looks similar to the previous reports created in Report Builder. After selecting the textbox, use the toolbar to change the font size to 18 points and resize the textbox to fit the text.

4. Expand the dataset to show the fields in the Report Data window. Rather than adding the first two fields to the table directly, drag the `ProductCategory` field into the Row Groups list (located to the left, below the designer) and drop it above the item titled `(Details)`. When you drop the field, you'll see it added to the first column of the table.

5. Drag and drop the `ProductSubcategory` field between the `ProductCategory` and `(Details)` in the Row Groups list and you'll see it added to the second table column.

> **NOTE** *You'll recall from the exercise in Chapter 4, "Report Layout and Formatting," that you can add a field reference to a detail cell using the field list displayed when you hover over the cell. You can also drag-and-drop the field from the dataset field list in the Report Data window.*

6. Drag the `ProductName` field to the detail row in the third column and then, just for variety, use the other technique to add two more fields. Hover over the fourth column detail cell and select the `OrderQuantity` field. Use the same technique to add the `SalesAmount` to the fifth column.

7. Switch between Design and Preview using the tabs above the report design window. In Preview, enter **2013** for the `Year` parameter and click View Report. You can see that the report returns one row per product because that is the detail level of the query, as shown in Figure 6-18.

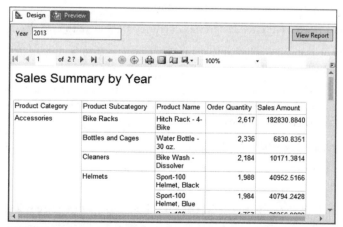

FIGURE 6-18: Report preview showing one row per product.

8. Switch back to Design view.

9. Click any cell in the table to show the gray column and row selection handles.

10. Click the column selection handle above the `Order Quantity` column, as shown in Figure 6-19.

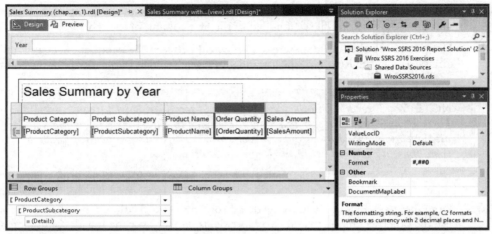

FIGURE 6-19: Selecting the Order Quantity column.

11. In the Properties window on the right, scroll to find the Format property in the Number group.

12. Enter **N0** for the Format property. This designates a number with zero decimals.

13. Select the `Sales Amount` column using the same method.

14. Enter **C2** for the Format property. This designates currency format with two decimals.

15. Select the heading row at the top of the table using the row selection handle. This should select all of the column heading cells.

16. The background color for the selected item is set using the fifth icon (after the two drop-down lists) from the left, as shown in Figure 6-20. Use the Choose Color dialog to select a light colored background such as LightGrey.

FIGURE 6-20: Selecting the background color icon.

17. After each change, switch to Preview to check your work as shown in Figure 6-21, and then switch back to Design.

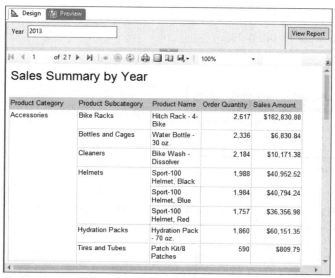

FIGURE 6-21: Previewing the report.

Add Summary Totals and Drill-Down

In this section you apply what you've learned about working with groups, expressions, and totals. A toggle item will be specified in the group to create a drill-down effect by collapsing detail rows into the group header.

You will add totals by using the same steps for the `ProductSubcategory` and `ProductCategory` groups.

1. Back in Design view, click the down-arrow icon next to the `ProductSubcategory` row group.

2. From the menu, choose Add Total ⇨ After.

3. Back in Design view, click the down-arrow icon next to the `ProductCategory` row group, as shown in Figure 6-22.

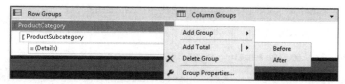

FIGURE 6-22: Clicking the down-arrow icon.

4. From the menu, choose Add Total ⇨ After.

5. Switch back to Preview, as shown in Figure 6-23.

Sales Summary by Year

Product Category	Product Subcategory	Product Name	Order Quantity	Sales Amount
[ProductCategory]	[ProductSubcategory]	[ProductName]	[OrderQuantity]	[SalesAmount]
	Total		[Sum(OrderQu	[Sum(SalesAm
Total			[Sum(OrderQu	[Sum(SalesAm

FIGURE 6-23: Previewing the report.

6. Navigate to the last non-blank page and scroll to the bottom. Note the totals for the last category and the overall total, as shown in Figure 6-24.

		HL Touring Frame - Yellow, 46	73	$43,971.26
		LL Touring Frame - Yellow, 62	310	$62,016.12
	Total		24,381	$5,374,393.77
Total			103,658	$33,574,834.16

FIGURE 6-24: Totals for the last category and the overall total.

In this view, the correspondence of the totals to their respective groups and overall total for the report isn't particularly self-explanatory. A user would need to scroll up and down to match the category heading with the total to match them up, and this would be even more difficult if the groups span multiple pages. To make this easier, you can add the category value to the group footer containing the total value.

7. Switch back to Design view.

8. Right-click the Total cell in the ProductSubcategory column and choose "Expression...". This opens the Expression editor shown in Figure 6-25. This is a tool you will use extensively.

9. To build the expression, place the cursor where you want to insert a function or object reference in the large box at the top of the window. Use the three boxes below to select the category, item, and value below, and then double-click to insert the text.

10. Start by typing an equal sign (=).

11. Select the item labeled `Fields (SalesSummary)`.

12. In the Values list, double-click the `ProductCategory` field to insert the complete field reference.

13. Complete the expression by adding a space followed by an ampersand, space, and then the literal text `" Total"` (including the quotes).

14. Check your expression with Figure 6-25 and make any necessary changes.

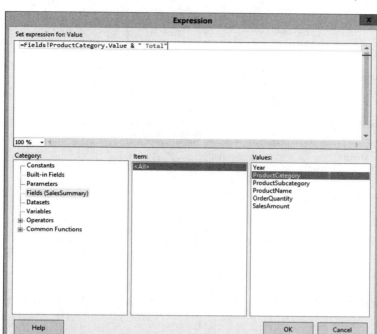

FIGURE 6-25: Expression editor window.

15. Click the OK button to accept the expression and close the Expression editor.

16. On the last row of the table, change the text Total to **Grand Total**, as shown in Figure 6-26.

Sales Summary by Year				
Product Category	Product Subcategory	Product Name	Order Quantity	Sales Amount
[ProductCategory]	[ProductSubcategory]	[ProductName]	[OrderQuantity]	[SalesAmount]
	«Expr»		[Sum(OrderQu	[Sum(SalesAm
Grand Total			[Sum(OrderQu	[Sum(SalesAm

FIGURE 6-26: Changing text to Grand Total.

17. Preview the report and check the group footer rows.

18. At the end of each group of subcategories, the category name is displayed to the left of the category totals for the Order Quantity and Sales Amount columns, as shown in Figure 6-27.

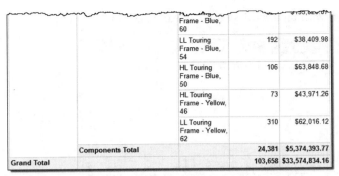

	Frame - Blue, 60		
	LL Touring Frame - Blue, 54	192	$38,409.98
	HL Touring Frame - Blue, 50	106	$63,848.68
	HL Touring Frame - Yellow, 46	73	$43,971.26
	LL Touring Frame - Yellow, 62	310	$62,016.12
	Components Total	24,381	$5,374,393.77
Grand Total		103,658	$33,574,834.16

FIGURE 6-27: Category name and category total.

19. Switch back to Design view.

20. Select the (Details) group in the Row Groups list.

21. Click the down arrow on the right side of the (Details) group row and select Group Properties.

22. In the Group Properties dialog, select the Visibility page.

23. Under Change display options, select the option to Hide under "When the report is initially run."

24. Check the box labeled "Display can be toggled by this report item."

25. Drop down the list and select ProductSubcategory, as shown in Figure 6-28.

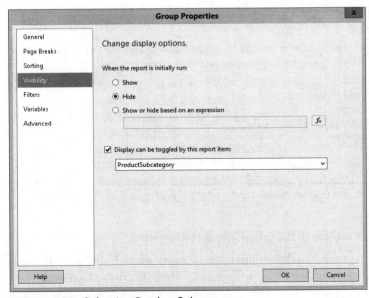

FIGURE 6-28: Selecting ProductSubcategory.

26. Click OK to close the Group Properties dialog.

27. Click the Save All button on the toolbar.

28. Switch to Preview to view the report.

29. You have a problem. With the (Detail) group hidden, the values displayed on each row are for each product subcategory, but the table doesn't have enough information to aggregate the detail rows.

30. Click the plus icon to expand the Helmets subcategory to see that there are three products that had sales during this year, as shown in Figure 6-29.

Sales Summary by Year

Product Category	Product Subcategory	Product Name	Order Quantity	Sales Amount
Accessories	⊞ Bike Racks	Hitch Rack - 4-Bike	2,617	$182,830.88
	⊞ Bottles and Cages	Water Bottle - 30 oz.	2,336	$6,830.84
	⊞ Cleaners	Bike Wash - Dissolver	2,184	$10,171.38
	⊟ Helmets	Sport-100 Helmet, Black	1,988	$40,952.52
		Sport-100 Helmet, Blue	1,984	$40,794.24
		Sport-100 Helmet, Red	1,757	$36,356.98
	⊞ Hydration Packs	Hydration Pack - 70 oz.	1,860	$60,151.35
	⊞ Tires and Tubes	Patch Kit/8 Patches	590	$809.79
	Accessories Total		**15,316**	**$378,897.98**
Bikes	⊞ Mountain Bikes	Mountain-500 Silver, 44	318	$92,341.97
	⊞ Road Bikes	Road-750 Black, 48	1,075	$344,805.48
	⊞ Touring Bikes	Touring-3000 Blue, 58	400	$161,533.51
	Bikes Total		**31,625**	**$26,942,691.15**
Clothing	⊞ Caps	AWC Logo Cap	2,573	$13,483.71
	⊞ Gloves	Half-Finger Gloves, M	1,716	$24,763.77
	⊞ Jerseys	Short-Sleeve Classic Jersey, L	2,247	$71,237.82

FIGURE 6-29: Revealing three products in the Helmets subcategory.

Aggregate Detail Row Summaries

Notice that the values that were displayed in the collapsed row are the same as those in the first row. If no aggregate function is used in the field expression and the group is collapsed like this, the report uses the value for the first row. You can fix this.

1. Switch back to Design view.

2. Right-click and edit the detail cell for the OrderQuantity field adding the SUM function. The modified expressions should match the following:

```
=SUM(Fields!OrderQuantity.Value)
```

3. Make the same change for the SalesAmount field so it matches the following example:

```
=SUM(Fields!SalesAmount.Value)
```

4. Switch back to Preview.

5. Check the subcategory totals and the drill-down details again.

6. Now the `OrderQuantity` and `SalesAmout` values for each subcategory are the sum of each product.

Create Parameter List

The Year parameter requires input from the report user. For this to be convenient, you will create a data-driven list of available Year values for the user to select from.

1. Add another dataset and name it **YearList**.

2. Select the data source.

3. Use Figure 6-30 as a guide and add the simple query script to return a distinct list of `Year` values from the `Date` table.

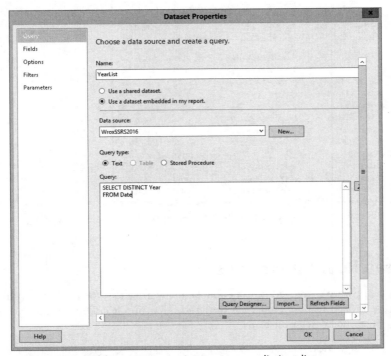

FIGURE 6-30: Adding a query script to return a distinct list.

4. Click OK to accept the new dataset settings.

5. Edit the `Year` parameter from the Report Data window.

6. On the Available Values page, choose "Get values from a query" (see Figure 6-31). Drop-down the Dataset list and choose the new `YearList` dataset.

7. Select the `Year` field for both the "Value field" and "Label field" properties.

8. On the Default Values page, choose "Specific values" and click the OK button.

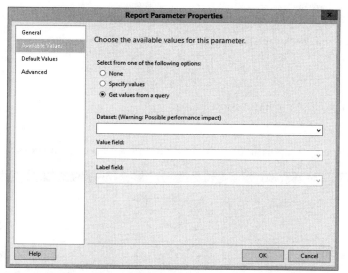

FIGURE 6-31: Choosing "Available Values" and query options.

9. Enter 2013 for the default value.

10. Click OK to close the Report Parameter Properties dialog.

11. Right-click the report title textbox and choose Expression....

12. Modify the expression using Figure 6-32 as a guide.

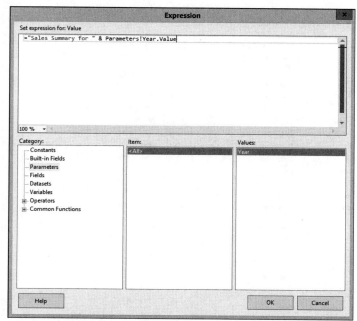

FIGURE 6-32: Modifying the expression.

13. After entering the text, use the Category list to select Parameters.

14. On the Values list, double-click the `Year` parameter to insert the following object reference into the expression.

```
="Sales Summary for " &
```

15. Click the OK button to close the Expression dialog.

16. Preview the report.

17. Figure 6-33 shows the entire report in default view with all product subcategories collapsed.

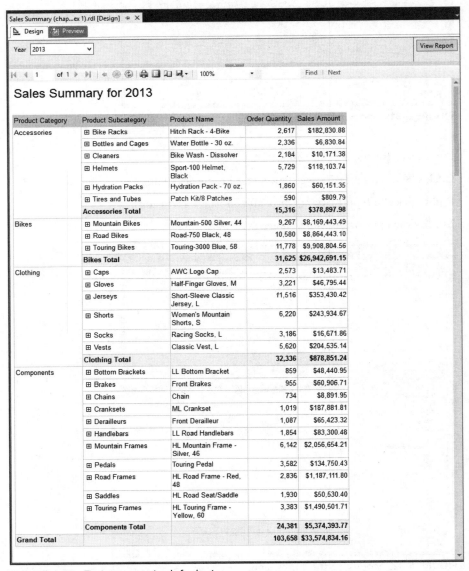

FIGURE 6-33: Entire report in default view.

18. Note that the `Order Quantity` and `Sales Amount` for the `Helmets` subcategory is the sum of all product orders for that year.

19. Expand `Helmets` to see the details.

SUMMARY

Several important concepts introduced in this chapter will be applied at a deeper level in subsequent lessons. Groups are a fundamental and crucial component of nearly all report designs. Here you learned about grouping basics and explored the most essential features, like aggregations, sorting, and visibility. Using a toggle item to control group visibility allows you to create drill-down reports. You learned expression basics using parameters, fields, and aggregate functions

When making the transition from Report Builder to SQL Server Data Tools for Visual Studio, you can think about designing holistic reporting solutions rather than just individual reports. For the remaining report design chapters, use the provided sample reports to follow the examples. You can also use the completed exercises for reference and to check your work.

Chapter 7 builds on these fundamentals by extending report functionality using the techniques you have learned. You will manage report pagination, headers, and footers using expressions to set extended properties in table and matrix data regions, multiple-region reports, master/detail reports, and subreports. You'll learn to use and manage page headers and aggregate function scoping.

PART III
Advanced and Analytic Reporting

This is the "graduate level" set of chapters that will take you from novice to advanced user. In Part II you learned about basic design and the core building blocks that make up reports. Now you are ready to apply these skills to more advanced and functional report designs that provide more business value and capability. The next set of report design skills include grouping and expressions. You will learn to incorporate more advanced queries with parameters, expressions, and programming logic.

Graphical reports are used to visualize data to understand correlation and trends. You will learn to use all of the chart types supported by Reporting Services, which include new chart types introduced in SQL Server 2016. You'll also learn to use KPI indicators, sparklines, and maps to create dashboards and report solutions with navigation and interactive features. You will use SQL Server Analysis Services and the MDX query language with Reporting Services to browse and analyze business data in aggregate and with high-performing queries.

▶ **CHAPTER 7:** Advanced Report Design

▶ **CHAPTER 8:** Graphical Report Design

▶ **CHAPTER 9:** Advanced Queries and Parameters

▶ **CHAPTER 10:** Reporting with Analysis Services

▶ **CHAPTER 11:** SSAS Reporting Advanced Techniques

▶ **CHAPTER 12:** Expressions and Actions

7

Advanced Report Design

WHAT'S IN THIS CHAPTER?

- ➤ Pagination, and page headers and footers
- ➤ Report headers and footers
- ➤ Text formatting and textbox properties
- ➤ Embedded formatting and HTML text styling
- ➤ Master/detail reports
- ➤ Working with subreports
- ➤ Creating a document map

WROX.COM CODE DOWNLOADS FOR THIS CHAPTER

The samples and exercises for this chapter are included in the SSDT solution that was introduced in Chapter 3. If you have not set up the book samples and exercises, return to Chapter 3 and complete those tasks.

The real power behind Reporting Services is its ability to creatively use data groups and combinations of report items and data regions. You can add calculations and conditional formatting by using simple programming code. By programming code, I mean anything from a single line of code to an entire library. Whether you are an application developer or a business report designer, this chapter contains important information to help you design reports to meet your users' requirements and to raise the bar with compelling report features.

PAGINATION AND FLOW CONTROL

With respect to page layout, reports have two sizing modes: interactive and printable. When users run a report in their web browser and use it interactively, they typically don't care that much about the page size. This is particularly true with reports that have wide content like a matrix region that can dynamically grow horizontally with the data. When a report is printed or rendered to a printable format like a PDF or Word file, we need to be mindful about fitting the content on pages.

The report designer does not make page sizing and dimensions particularly obvious so it's an easy thing to miss. Fortunately, the science behind page sizing is pretty simple. Page dimension properties are grouped into two objects that you can select in the designer; these are shown in Figure 7-1. With the Properties window visible, click outside the report body to show properties for the report. Here you will see the `InteractiveSize` and `PageSize` properties. Expand these to see the individual `Width` and `Height` properties for each group.

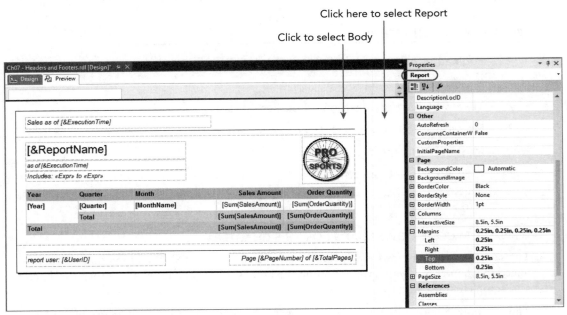

FIGURE 7-1: Report properties in the designer.

If you are not using this default paper size, you can get more options by right-clicking the Report area and choosing the option to show the Report Properties dialog (shown in Figure 7-2). Either way, you will be setting the same properties.

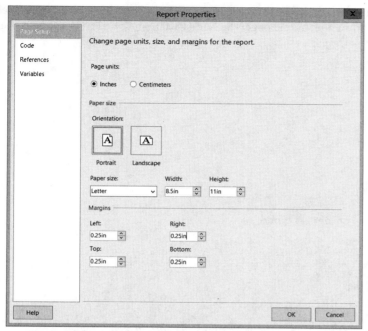

FIGURE 7-2: Report Properties, Page Setup page.

Aside from the default US paper sizes shown here because my machine is set up with an English/US locale, you can also choose from metric sizes or several specialized layouts. The margins are set to 1 inch by default, which means that we lose two inches of printable space in each page. I've changed my margins to a quarter inch, which will maximize the page space and work with most modern printers.

> **TIP** *Quarter-inch margins (about .64 cm) work with most modern printers. Some older laser printers can require up to a half inch of "gripper space" at the top of the page. This is the area of the paper the printer grabs and attaches to the drum during the print cycle. If you are trying maximize the print area, either test the report on each printer model or just be more conservative with the margin settings.*

Click the Body (the area within the designer report boundaries) to check the Size properties, which are shown in Figure 7-3. To fit within a printable page, the body Width must be less than the report width added to the left and right margins.

FIGURE 7-3: Properties window, Size properties group.

> **TIP** *To prevent blank pages:*
>
> *Body Width + Left Margin + Right Margin*
>
> *must be less than Report Width. If not, the page will spill onto a second page. If there is no printable content, just empty space, the printer will feed blank paper between each page of report content. You can test this by saving to a PDF file to see if alternate pages are blank.*

HEADERS AND FOOTERS

The terms "header" and "footer" can refer to three different areas of a report: the report header and footer, the page header and footer, and the header and footer areas of any data region(s) in the report. Table and matrix regions may have headers and footers associated with groups within the region.

> **NOTE** *In this paragraph, I refer to the "effective" report header and footer. My use of this term is important to understand because Reporting Services doesn't actually designate a specific header or footer area. The area of the report body above a table or other repeating data region is "effectively" the page header.*

The report header and the footer each occur only once: on the first page, at the top of the entire report (header), and at the end of the report, on the bottom of the last page (footer). In Reporting Services, there is no designated report header and footer area. The effective report header is simply the blank space containing textboxes and other report items placed above any data regions in the report body. Likewise, the effective report footer is the space below any data regions. If you were to place a table two centimeters below the top of the report body, this would give you a report header two centimeters tall. It's as simple as that and because there is no set limit to the number of data regions or other items you can add to a report (and you can designate page breaks at any location), all the space above, below, and between these items is essentially header and footer space.

Follow along by opening the completed Ch07 - Headers and Footers report, which is in the Wrox SSRS 2016 Sample project.

You have a lot of flexibility when displaying header and footer content. In addition to the standard report and page headers and footers, data region sections can be repeated on each page, creating additional page header and footer content. Figure 7-4 shows a table report with each of the header and footer areas labeled.

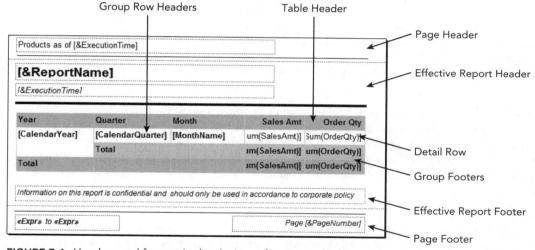

FIGURE 7-4: Headers and footers in the designer for a typical table report.

Figure 7-5 shows the first rendered page of this report. Comparing the design view of the report in Figure 7-4 with the first page rendered in Figure 7-5, note the name of the report in bold text followed by execution date and summary of years and months included in the report, in the (report) header area. The *page* header is omitted from the first page. Below the table, you see the page footer showing the report user's network ID and the page number summary.

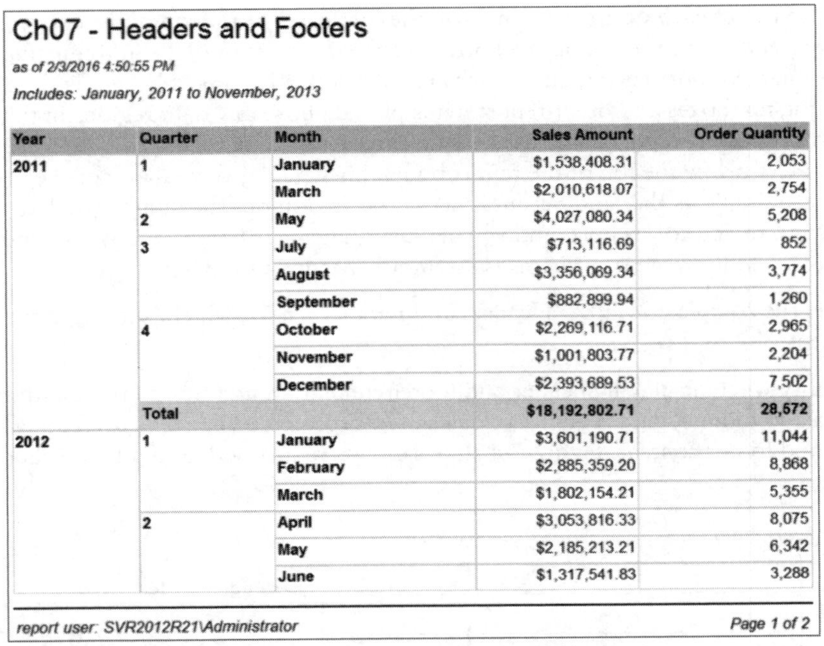

Ch07 - Headers and Footers

as of 2/3/2016 4:50:55 PM

Includes: January, 2011 to November, 2013

Year	Quarter	Month	Sales Amount	Order Quantity
2011	1	January	$1,538,408.31	2,053
		March	$2,010,618.07	2,754
	2	May	$4,027,080.34	5,208
	3	July	$713,116.69	852
		August	$3,356,069.34	3,774
		September	$882,899.94	1,260
	4	October	$2,269,116.71	2,965
		November	$1,001,803.77	2,204
		December	$2,393,689.53	7,502
	Total		$18,192,802.71	28,572
2012	1	January	$3,601,190.71	11,044
		February	$2,885,359.20	8,868
		March	$1,802,154.21	5,355
	2	April	$3,053,816.33	8,075
		May	$2,185,213.21	6,342
		June	$1,317,541.83	3,288

report user: SVR2012R21\Administrator   Page 1 of 2

FIGURE 7-5: Rendered table report with headers and footers.

Figure 7-6 shows the second page, beginning with the page header. Of particular note is the summary of data displayed on this page in "phone book" or "dictionary" style where the year and month of the first and last items on the page are summarized in the header. Also note that even though the group for 2012 is split between pages one and two, the table header is displayed at the top of the page and the year is repeated for quarter 3. In the table, after all four quarters, a group footer shows a total of the year and then a grand total is displayed at the end of the table for all three years.

A common purpose of the page header is to display an abbreviated form of information in the report header. Naturally, you don't want to show redundant information on the first page so it makes sense to hide the page header. Right-click the report body to add a page header and then right-click the page header to show the Page Header Properties dialog, used to set a number of related properties.

Uncheck the "Print on first page" property under "Print options."

> **TIP** *Remember that any property displayed on a property page dialog like this is also available in the Properties window, to the right of the report designer in SSDT. The Properties window can optionally be viewed in Report Builder, enabled from the View ribbon.*

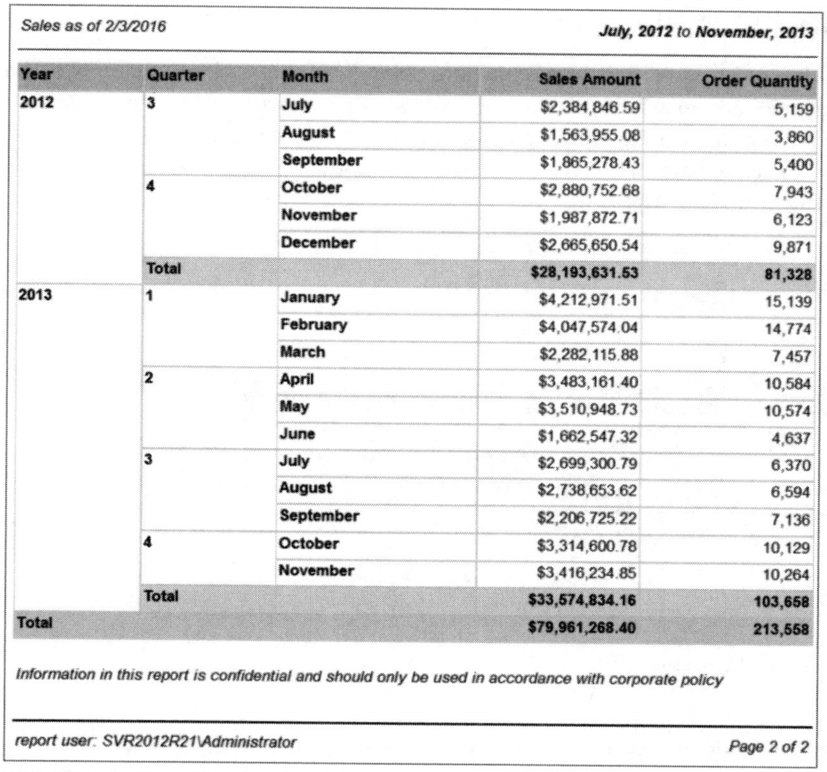

Sales as of 2/3/2016 **July, 2012** to **November, 2013**

Year	Quarter	Month	Sales Amount	Order Quantity
2012	3	July	$2,384,846.59	5,159
		August	$1,563,955.08	3,860
		September	$1,865,278.43	5,400
	4	October	$2,880,752.68	7,943
		November	$1,987,872.71	6,123
		December	$2,665,650.54	9,871
	Total		$28,193,631.53	81,328
2013	1	January	$4,212,971.51	15,139
		February	$4,047,574.04	14,774
		March	$2,282,115.88	7,457
	2	April	$3,483,161.40	10,584
		May	$3,510,948.73	10,574
		June	$1,662,547.32	4,637
	3	July	$2,699,300.79	6,370
		August	$2,738,653.62	6,594
		September	$2,206,725.22	7,136
	4	October	$3,314,600.78	10,129
		November	$3,416,234.85	10,264
	Total		$33,574,834.16	103,658
Total			$79,961,268.40	213,558

Information in this report is confidential and should only be used in accordance with corporate policy

report user: SVR2012R21\Administrator *Page 2 of 2*

FIGURE 7-6: Page header shown on the second page.

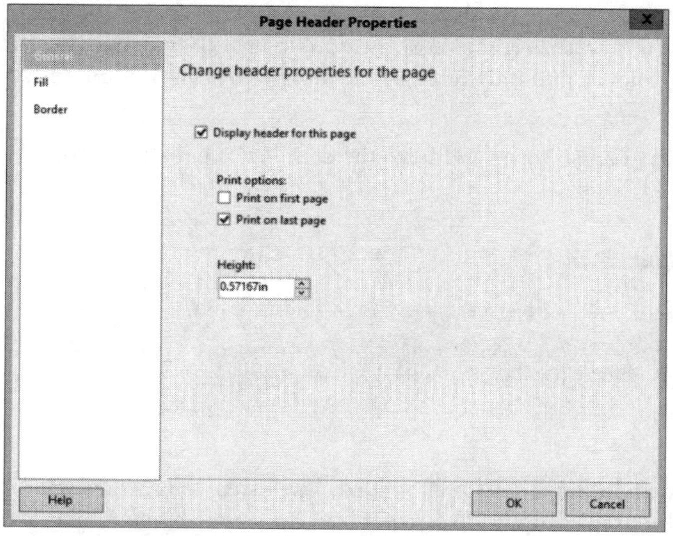

FIGURE 7-7: Page Header Properties dialog.

Tablix Headers and Detail Cells

Listen up: This little golden nugget will help you make more sense of table and matrix reports that you inherit from other developers, or when you resume working on a report you haven't touched for quite a while. When reviewing the sample report created for you, how do you know which cells in the table serve as group headers or are detail cells that aggregate values? Figure 7-8 shows you the secret. This feature is subtle but very useful.

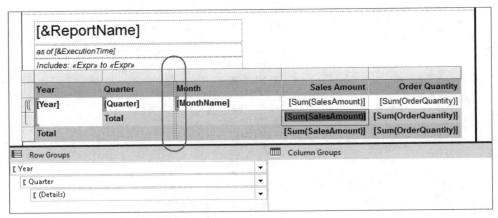

FIGURE 7-8: Row group header boundary.

When designing a table, the fields that you drag into the Row Groups list create groups with row header cells. Fields that you drag into the table columns become ungrouped detail cells. A double broken vertical line (circled in Figure 7-8) is displayed to differentiate between group headers to the left and detail cells to the right of the line. It is apparent in this report that rows are grouped first by Year and then by Quarter. The (Details) group, displayed in the Row Groups list, doesn't have a group header, so the MonthName cell is on the right side of the double-broken line. Because the dataset already groups sales details by month and only returns one month per row, no month-level grouping is necessary in the table.

In a matrix, column group header cells are also separated from the detail cells with a horizontal double-broken line.

Designing the Page Headers

> **NOTE** *As I describe these steps, don't be concerned with following along. You will step through this process in the exercise at the end of the chapter.*

With the Report Data window visible and Built-in Fields expanded, I will step you through the process as I create the header. I can drag-and-drop fields directly into the report body. This is actually a slight misnomer because the "built-in" objects are not really fields per se, but global objects.

The word "field," in this sense, refers to something that returns a value. Regardless, it is useful information you can add to the report header or footer areas. If I were to drag a built-in field, say [ExecutionTime], onto the report body, a textbox will be added at the drop location with a reference to the intended object. If the object or field were dropped into an existing textbox, the inserted value becomes a placeholder for an expression. The expression can coexist with other expression placeholders, and literal text in various formats, within a textbox.

I begin with the Execution Time field, which I will drag to the existing textbox in the top-left corner of the page header region. The textbox already contains the text *Sales as of:* in italicized format.

Next, I drop the Execution Time field/object just to the right of the existing text to create a composite message: *Sales as of: [Execution Time].* Just peachy.

The others are similar. In the lower left-hand corner, I drag the UserID field to the textbox right after the text report user.

In the textbox located in the lower-right corner of the page footer, I add these built-in fields to assemble the following phrase: *Page [&PageNumber] of [&TotalPages]* as shown in Figure 7-9.

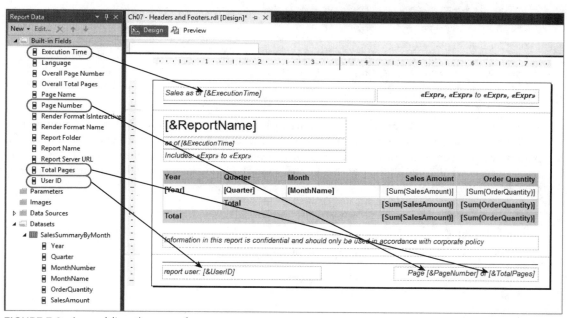

FIGURE 7-9: Assembling the page footer.

You can see that the page header and footer decorations are nearly complete. Our objective is to show the first and last set of month/year values displayed on the page. Well, because the page has already been paginated by the page rendering engine, there is no need to do this work if it's already been done for us.

Instead of using "field" references to get these values, we can use the aggregate functions FIRST() and LAST() with the report items in the table that already return the values. I right-click in the textbox to create a placeholder and then edit the placeholder to add a value expression. I use the callouts in Figure 7-10 to add these expressions in order; first the Month and Year report items are referenced in the range "From" group, with the FIRST functions. In the second, range "To" group, the LAST aggregate function returns the last Year and Month value for that page.

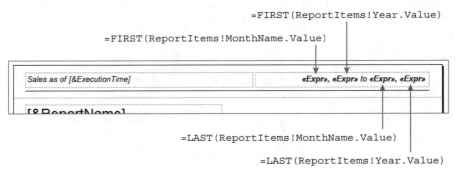

FIGURE 7-10: Assembling the page header.

> **TIP** *Pay close attention to the spaces added to the literal text when assembling static text and expressions in a textbox.*

The textbox below the large report title contains two placeholders with expressions, shown in Figure 7-11. The textbox contains the static text "Includes: " followed by an expression in the first placeholder that concatenates the first month and year in the dataset results. The static text " to " separates the second placeholder with an expression that concatenates the last month and year in the dataset.

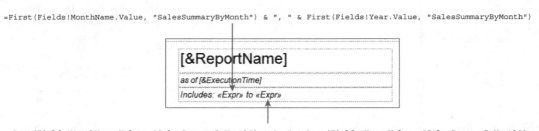

FIGURE 7-11: Assembling the report header.

This example demonstrates how values can be obtained from a dataset outside the boundaries of a data region like a table, list, or matrix. Outside of a data region, an aggregate function must be used to reduce multiple field rows to a single value and the dataset is passed in the second function argument.

Textbox Expressions and Placeholders

When combining values in a textbox, you really have two choices. The previous examples demonstrate the use of multiple placeholders within a textbox. Think of a *placeholder* as if it were a separate textbox embedded in the text for the textbox. The advantage of using multiple text placeholders in a textbox is that each can be styled with separate properties for styling features like the font, weight, and color.

> **NOTE** *Internally, placeholder text is stored as a "textrun" object within the textbox paragraph element. This is important to understand for error reporting and debugging expressions.*

Internally, textboxes contain two levels of objects: paragraphs and textruns, which the visual designer calls a placeholder. When using multiple placeholders in a textbox like the previous example, this is actually a paragraph containing multiple textrun elements. This would be apparent if an incorrect expression were entered, resulting in an error. If you see the text #Error displayed, use the Output window to see the error text, which might look something like this:

```
[rsRuntimeErrorInExpression] The Value expression for the textrun
'Textbox4.Paragraphs[0].TextRuns[3]' contains an error: The expression references
an item 'TotalPages_', which does not exist in the Globals collection. Letters in
the names of Globals collection items must use the correct case.
Preview complete -- 0 errors, 1 warnings
```

> **TIP** *When you see an expression error displayed on the report as #Error, use the Output window in SSDT to view the error or warning information.*

The other approach for combining values in a textbox is to use a single expression to concatenate all the values into a single text value. Rather than the compounded placeholder text used to display the page numbers, the following expression would display the same text without the option for mixed styling features within the text:

```
="Page " & Globals!PageNumber & " of " & Globals!TotalPages
```

The Thing About Repeating Table Headers

You'll notice that the table column headers are repeated on the second page, which is a sensible design pattern. If you look at the Tablix Properties (Figure 7-12), you'll find settings to repeat column and row headers on each page. Seems pretty simple, right?

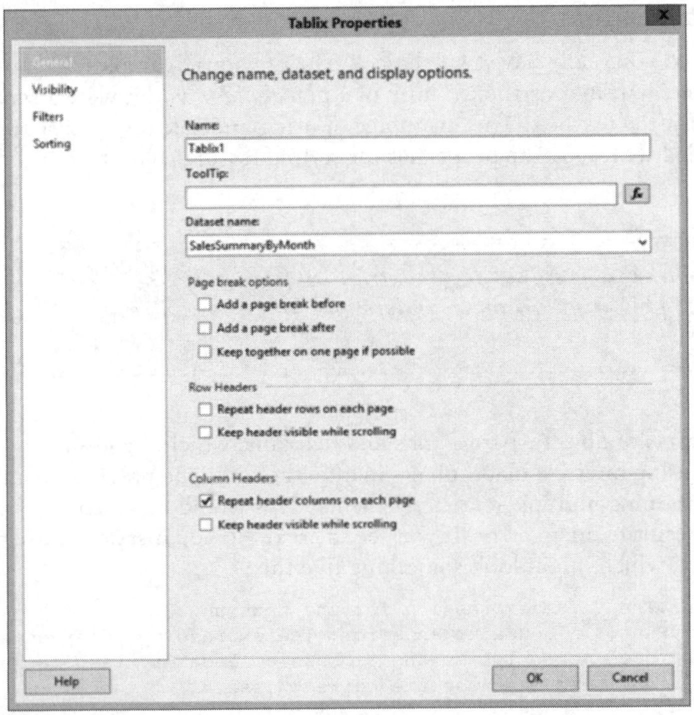

FIGURE 7-12: Tablix Properties dialog.

Somewhere in the product history, as the table and matrix data region evolved into the Tablix (circa 2008), this feature stopped working but it is easy to fix. I do not have a good explanation for why the following step is necessary; and I think we can all agree that this might seem to be overly complicated, but I can at least show you how to get this working.

With the table selected, click the little down arrow icon displayed to the right of the Column Groups in the Grouping Window and switch on Advanced Mode (see Figure 7-13). Advanced Mode shows several hidden objects in the Tablix data region that are used internally to manage header, groups, and cell properties. As you can see, the inner workings of the Tablix are quite complex.

> **WARNING** *I can tell you from experience that the advanced properties of the Tablix can be a Pandora's Box if you don't know exactly what you're doing in there. If you plan to experiment with these properties, I suggest you make a backup copy of the Tablix or your report before you proceed.*

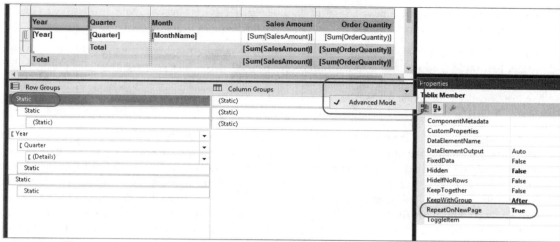

FIGURE 7-13: Setting up repeating page header in Advanced Mode.

Making this change is easy. Just select the first "Static" Tablix Member displayed in the Row Groups list.

In the Properties window, change the `RepeatOnNewPage` property from False to True. That's it!

Use the down arrow icon to switch Advanced Mode off.

Test the report and you'll see that the table header is repeated on each page.

COMPOSITE REPORTS AND EMBEDDED CONTENT

Beyond common, basic report design, more sophisticated reports are created by using more advanced and less common design techniques. In general, these fit into two different categories, which include using advanced properties of different report item components, and by combining multiple data regions to create composite report designs. The composite report design pattern is intriguing because there are virtually limitless options when allowing one grouped data region to repeat instances of another report item or region.

Before opening the door to the mind-blowing possibilities of composite data regions, let's explore the depth of some fundamental report item building blocks. OK, "mind-blowing" might be a stretch but some of the most fundamental report items have considerable capabilities, especially when used as components of a well-constructed solution.

UNLOCKING THE TEXTBOX

The textbox is one of the most fundamental and common report items. Generally, all text and data values are displayed using textboxes. The cells of a table and matrix contain individual textboxes. In addition to the text displayed, several useful properties manage the placement, style, and presentation of data.

The `Font`, `Color`, `BackGroundColor`, and `BackGroundImage` properties make it possible to dress up your report data with tremendous flexibility.

The `BorderStyle` properties of a textbox are similar to those of other report items (such as a rectangle, list, table, and matrix). Once you have mastered the textbox properties, you should be able to use these other items in much the same way. With a table, group separation lines are created by setting the border properties for textboxes in header and footer rows (typically by selecting the entire row and setting the textbox properties as a group).

Three property groups are used for borders. In the Properties window, these groups are expanded using the plus sign (+) icon to reveal individual properties. The group summary text can actually be manipulated without expanding the properties, but it's usually easier to work with specific property values. The `BorderColor`, `BorderStyle`, and `BorderWidth` properties each contain a `Default` value that applies to individual properties (`Left`, `Right`, `Top`, and `Bottom`) that have not otherwise been set. This provides a means to set general properties and then override the exceptions. By default, a textbox has a black `BorderColor` and a 1-point `BorderWidth`, with the `BoderStyle` set to `None`. To add a border to all four sides, simply set the default `BorderStyle` to `Solid`. Beyond this, you can use individual properties to add more creative border effects.

Padding and Indenting

Most report items support padding properties, which are used to offset the placement of text and other related content within the item. Padding is specified in points. A unit of measure from the printing industry, a *PostScript point* is 1/72nd of an inch, or approximately 1/28th of a centimeter.

Figure 7-14 shows the four padding properties, in the Padding group of the Properties pane, applied to all textbox items. The Padding properties provide an offset between textbox borders and the contained text. You can use this to indent text and provide an appropriate balance of white space.

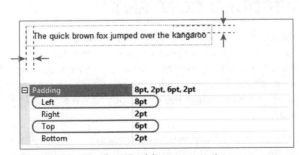

FIGURE 7-14: Textbox Padding properties.

Three similar properties provide more flexibility for text indentation. You can use the `HangingIndent`, `LeftIndent`, and `RightIndent` properties to control paragraph-style text in rich-formatted textboxes. These properties also enable the new Word rendering extension to apply hanging, static text indentations.

Embedded Formatting

This feature allows the text in a textbox to be structured and formatted, much like a document or web page. Textboxes support two modes: a single-value expression or a range of text containing multiple expression placeholders.

To format a range of text, simply highlight the text in the textbox and use the toolbar or Properties window to set properties for the selected text. Figure 7-15 shows a range of highlighted text with the `HangingIndent` and `LeftIndent` properties set to 18 points and 12 points, respectively. Note that certain keywords and phrases within the text are also set using bold and italic. Some title text has also been isolated with bold and larger fonts.

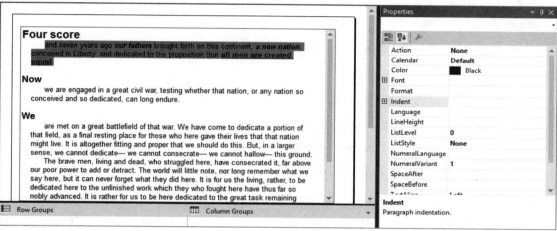

FIGURE 7-15: Text with embedded formatting.

Embedded HTML Formatting

Another option is to embed simple HTML tags within text. This provides a great deal of flexibility for using expressions or custom code to return formatted text. The HTML tags listed in Table 7-1 are supported.

TABLE 7-1: HTML tags supported with embedded formatting

TAG	DESCRIPTION
`<A>`	Anchor. For example: `<A href="http://www.somesite.com">Click Here</A>`
`<FONT>`	Sets font attributes for a group of text. Used with the attributes `color`, `face`, `point size`, `size`, and `weight`. For example: `<FONT color="Blue" face="Arial" size="6">Hello</FONT>`

continues

TABLE 7-1 *(continued)*

TAG	DESCRIPTION
<H1>, <H2>, <H3>, <H4>, ...	Headings.
<SPAN>	Used to set text attributes for a range of text within a paragraph.
<DIV>	Used to set text attributes for a block of text.
<P>	Paragraph break.
 	Line break.
<LI>	List new line.
<B>	Bold.
<I>	Italic.
<U>	Underscore.
<S>	Strikeout.
<OL>	Ordered list.
<UL>	Unordered list.

Embedded tags can be entered directly into a textbox or read from a dataset. When using static text, rather than text fed from a dataset, you must set the MarkupType property for the text placeholder. To do this, highlight the text containing the embedded HTML tags, right-click, and choose Text Properties. In the Text Properties dialog, on the General page, set the Markup type property to the selection shown in Figure 7-16, "HTML - Interpret HTML tags as styles." When working with data-bound text, the difference is subtle; highlight the field placeholder in the textbox, right-click, and choose Placeholder Properties...."

The Text Properties and Placeholder Properties dialogs have identical selections for the Markup type, shown in Figure 7-16.

I have provided an example in the sample report named Ch07 - Sales Order Notes. The SalesOrderNote table contains formatted text with HTML markup tags like this:

```
<h2>Check This Order Before Shipping</h2>
Customer specifically needs 10 <b>RED</b> helmets.<br>She is <i>unhappy</i> that an
earlier order was placed for <b>RED</b> helmets but helmets were <b>MAROON</b>
colored.<br>If product is not bright red color, please:
<ol>
<li>Cancel and <b>do not ship</b> the order</li>
<li>Call the sales person</li>
<li>Do not charge the standard re-stocking fee</li>
</ol>
```

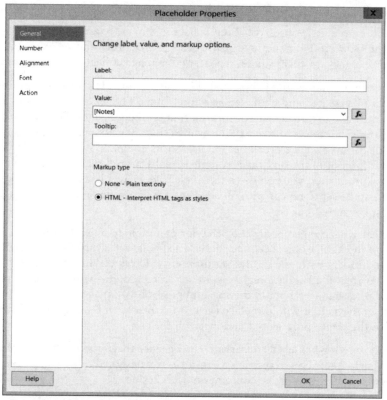

FIGURE 7-16: Placeholder Properties dialog.

When this text is interpreted, the formatting tags are applied and it will appear as it does in Figure 7-17.

FIGURE 7-17: Previewed report with data-bound embedded formatting.

Would You Like Them in a Box? Using a Rectangle as a Container

I love containers. To be honest, I am a little obsessive about collecting boxes, bags, backpacks, and cases. Putting things in the right kind of container provides a sense of order and security. In Reporting Services, containers are used to encapsulate, repeat, and manage collections of content.

The rectangle report item is far more than a simple box to display on a report. It provides containment for multiple items that can be treated and managed as a single unit. The rectangle also has several properties for managing the flow and placement of information on report pages. For example, placing a group of textboxes and other items in a rectangle ensures that they all end up on the same page. You can set the rectangle to force a page break before or after its contents. By default, borders of a rectangle are not displayed, so out of the box the rectangle is really more functional than it is a visual control. By setting a few properties, you can use a rectangle to display a background image, fill color, and borders. It can also be set to repeat with an adjacent Tablix group, and on each page and the table, list, or matrix splits across pages.

The utility of a rectangle is clear when you compare the behavior of a table to a list data region. Both data regions are based on the Tablix object. Functionally, a list acts like a table with a single column and detail row and no headers with one significant difference. Every cell in a table and matrix contains a textbox. The area of a list data region is, in fact, a rectangle—which is the reason that any report items dragged into that area remain the size and position you place them. If you were to drag a rectangle into a table cell, it would replace the cell textbox with the rectangle. Then, constituent items dragged into the same space would no longer fill the cell.

Rectangles can simplify report design when used conservatively. Because the designer shows a rectangle with gray borders, similar to a textbox, returning to a previously designed report may take some poking around to decipher where each of the container objects reside.

Figure 7-18 shows an example of a rectangle used to contain several textboxes to display the report parameters. During design, I may need to adjust the size and placement of the elements, and using the rectangle allows me to move the entire block of items as a group.

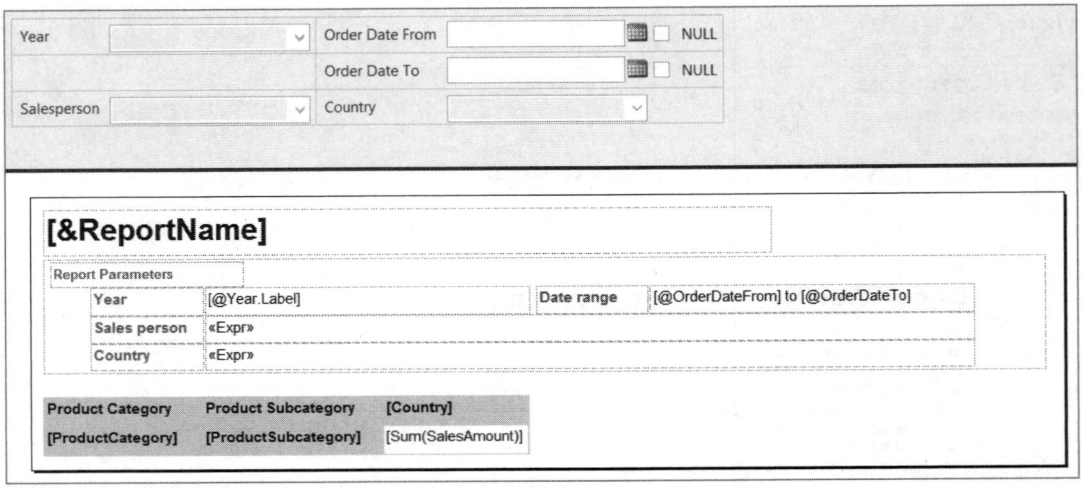

FIGURE 7-18: Report header content contained in a rectangle.

As requirements evolve, I can easily cut and paste the rectangle as a single object and place it in the page header (Figure 7-19) or put it below the matrix.

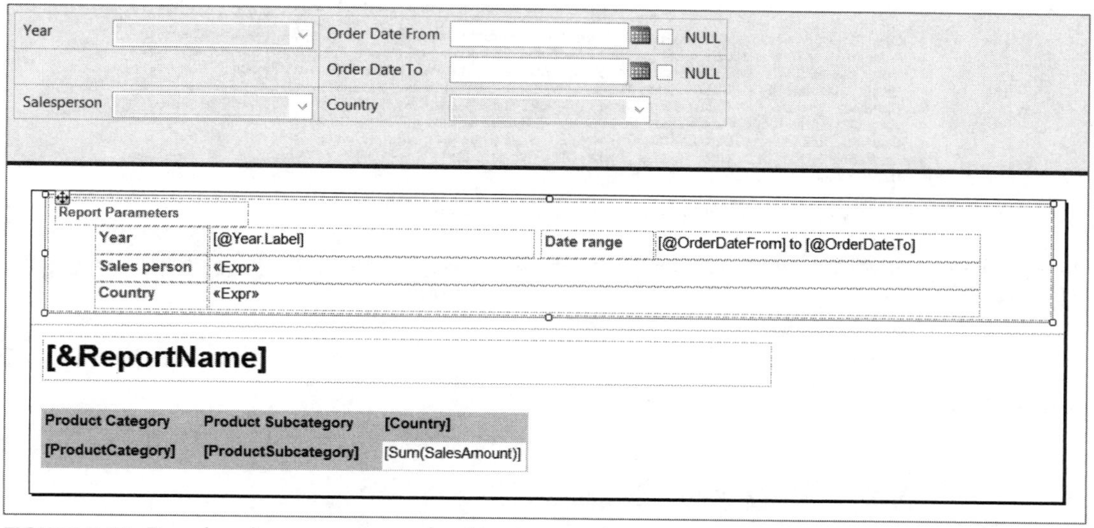

FIGURE 7-19: Page header content contained in a rectangle.

The following example shows how using a rectangle report item container manages page flow. In Figure 7-20, a page break is set with BreakLocation=End. This forces a page break after the rectangle is rendered so the matrix content would be on the next page of the report.

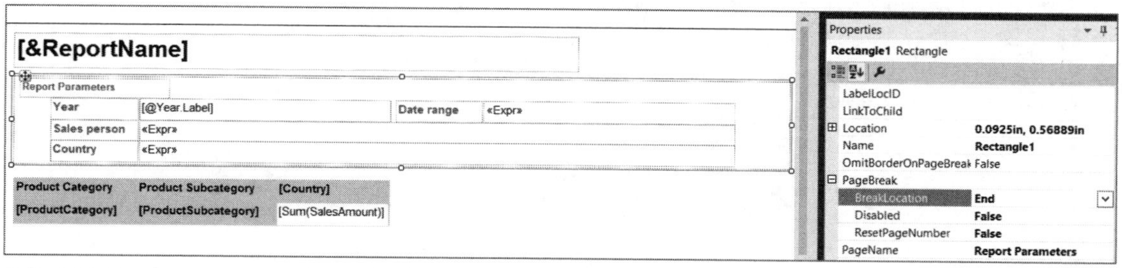

FIGURE 7-20: Setting a page break in the rectangle properties.

The example report uses long parameter lists, which take up a lot of page space. I recently had a consulting client who asked that when a report similar to this one is used in interactive mode, the report header appear as usual, like the one shown in Figure 7-21, but when the report is rendered to Excel, the parameters be displayed only on a separate worksheet.

Using a rectangle to control the page name and conditional page break was quite easy by using an expression on the Disabled property. Figure 7-22 shows the expression that conditionally toggles the Disabled property based on the built-in RenderFormat.Name property. This effectively disabled the page break in all cases where the report is not rendered to Excel.

Ch07 - Sales Order Breakdown

Report Parameters

| Year | 2013 | Date range | (Use selected Year) |

Sales person Syed Abbas, Kim Abercrombie, Hazem Abolrous, Pilar Ackerman, Jay Adams, François Ajenstat, Amy Alberts, Greg Alderson, Sean Alexander, Gary Altman, Nancy Anderson, Pamela Ansman-Wolfe, Zainal Arifin, Dan Bacon, Bryan Baker, Mary Baker, Angela Barbariol, Karen Berg, Karen Berge, Andreas Berglund, Matthias Berndt, Jo Berry, Jimmy Bischoff, Michael Blythe, David Bradley, Alan Brewer, Eric Brown, Jo Brown, Janaina Bueno, David Campbell, John Campbell, Jun Cao, Rob Caron, Jillian Carson, Andrew Cencini, Baris Cetinok, Sean Chai, Sootha Charncherngkha, John Chen, Alice Ciccu, Pat Coleman, Peter Connelly, Stephanie Conroy, Patrick Cook, Ryan Cornelsen, Ovidiu Cracium, Jack Creasey, Barbara Decker, Thierry D'Hers, Brenda Diaz, JoLynn Dobney, Reuben D'sa, Ed Dudenhoefer, Terri Duffy, Maciej Dusza, Shelley Dyck, Terrence Earls, Susan Eaton, Ruth Ellerbrock, Michael Entin, Gail Erickson, Ebru Ersan

Country Australia, Canada, France, Germany, NA, United Kingdom, United States

Product Category	Product Subcategory	Australia	France	Germany	United Kingdom	United States
Accessories	Bike Racks	$2,831	$864	$1,003	$576	$39,450
	Bottles and Cages	$63	$18	$42	$52	$1,591
	Cleaners	$143	$24	$10	$19	$2,343

FIGURE 7-21: Long parameter text in page header.

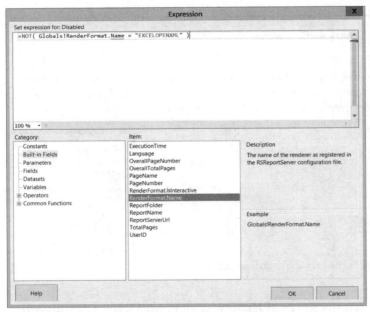

FIGURE 7-22: Setting the PageBreak Disabled property with an expression.

The resulting Excel workbook (shown in Figure 7-23) contains two worksheets, each named as a result of the PageName properties for the rectangle used to manage the parameters and the matrix. The Excel renderer translates any explicit page breaks in the reports as a new worksheet tab.

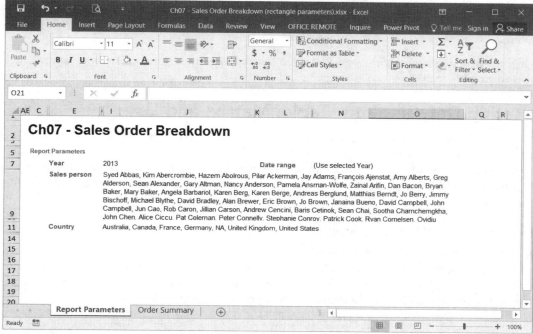

FIGURE 7-23: Report rendered to Excel.

DESIGNING MASTER/DETAIL REPORTS

Most data can be expressed in a hierarchal fashion. Whether stored in related tables in a relational database, as dimensional hierarchies in a cube or tabular structure, or as separate spreadsheets or files, structured data can usually be organized into different levels, which is often a natural way to present information for reporting. Common examples of master/detail data include invoices and line items, customers and orders, regions and sales, categories and products, colors and sizes, and managers and workers. The best way to organize this data in a master/detail report depends largely on how your users want to see it visualized. For each master record, details may be presented in a rigid tabular or spreadsheet-like form or in free-form layout with elements of different sizes and shapes placed at various locations within a repeating section. And, of course, details may also be expressed visually using charts, icons, and gauges.

The last consideration for master/detail report design is whether the data source for the master records and detail records can be combined into a single data stream. If records exist in different tables in the same database, this is a simple matter of joining tables using a query. If the records can't be combined in a query or view, the two result sets should expose the fields necessary to join them, and a subreport can be used. This section about composite reports explores techniques for combining data ranges to filter a single dataset and then uses subreports to combine two separate data sources.

When constructing a hierarchal report, you have a few different techniques at your disposal, including using a table, matrix, list, or subreport.

Repeating Data Regions: Table, Matrix, and List

In Chapter 6, you learned that the purpose of a data region is to repeat rows and columns for each instance of a group or detail record, and you've already seen several examples using a table and matrix. The purpose of a data region is to repeat report items. You can actually add just about anything in place of the default textbox or rectangle container that the designer creates in the detail cells for you.

Table as a Master/Detail Container

By default, all the cells in a table are textboxes unless you drag a different type of item into the cell. Any embedded content will stretch to the dimensions of the cell and will grow vertically if text wrapping in any columns causes that row to grow. To prevent items from stretching, place a rectangle in the cell first and then add the new report item to the rectangle.

> **TIP** *To prevent items embedded in a table detail row from stretching vertically when an adjacent textbox wraps, place a rectangle in the cell first and then add the new report item to the rectangle.*

Regions and items embedded in the detail row are repeated vertically, once for every unique detail group value. Detail rows in a table can be used as a container for all other report items and data regions. There is literally no limit to the number or level of embedded items that can be placed into a table, matrix, or list. All regions and report items contained in the table must be bound to the same dataset.

> **NOTE** *When using embedded data regions and report items within a table, matrix, or list, the contained data regions and items are exclusively bound to the containing dataset via the* DatasetName *property. It is possible to reference a different dataset by using scoped and aggregated field expressions (for example,* FIRST, SUM, *and so on). You can also use* LOOKUP *and* LOOKUPSET *functions or custom code to reference another dataset.*

The sample report named Ch07 - Product Category Sales Profile by Year contains a table data region with drill-down on the first-level group (Year). The detail row contains an embedded column chart with the sales quantity grouped by product category values, as shown in Figure 7-24.

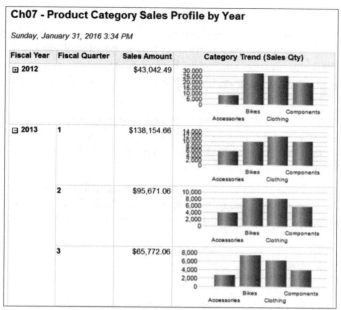

FIGURE 7-24: Multi-level table report with drill-down and repeating chart.

Matrix as a Container

Like using a table as a master/detail container, a matrix can encompass any data region or combination of report items, and repeat an instance of these items both on rows and columns. The detail cells of a matrix are textboxes by default but can be replaced with most any type of report item.

A variation of the theme presented in the previous section, the sample report named Ch07 - Product Category Sales Profile by Year and Country (shown in Figure 7-25) has a matrix based on a dataset containing one additional field, which is used to group columns on the country. The same column chart used in the previous example is repeated both on rows (for each quarter) and on columns for each country.

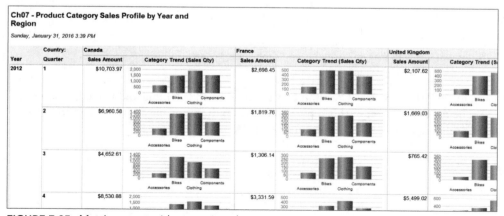

FIGURE 7-25: Matrix report with repeating chart.

List Data Region as a Container

A list is essentially a single-row, single-column table with no headers. Instead of containing a text-box by default, the detail "cell" or area of a list contains a rectangle. Any items placed within the list area will remain the same size and position, rather than stretching to fill the area in the designer. This would roughly be the same thing as if you were to replace a table detail cell textbox with a rectangle and remove the header and footer rows.

A list is a great tool for repeating a region of formatted report items with every group of parent values in a hierarchy. Because a list is based on a Tablix object, like a table and matrix, it has the same essential rules of behavior. The repeated data regions and report items in the list area are bound to the same dataset as the container.

The following examples are sample reports that contain one or more report items contained within the cells or repeated detail area of a data region. The sample report named Ch07 - Product Cost and List Price - Embedded Chart is shown in Figure 7-26. A list data region contains several textboxes and a pie chart.

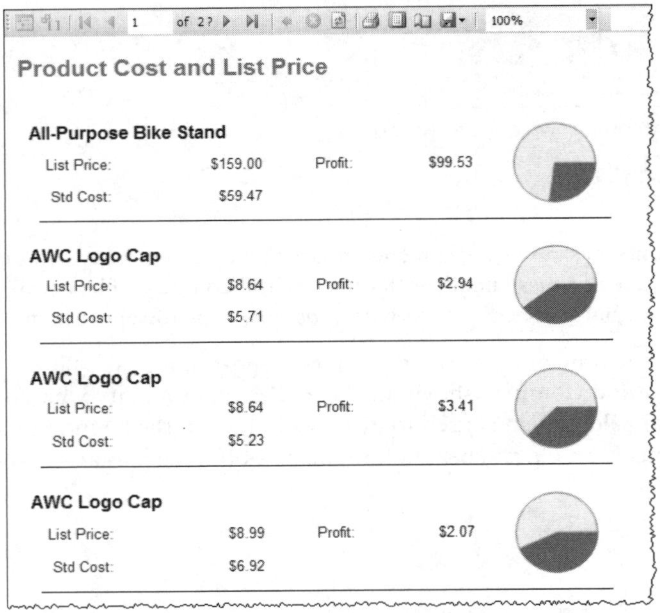

FIGURE 7-26: List report with free-form layout and embedded chart.

The report named Ch07 - Product Cost and List Price - Embedded Table and Chart is shown in Figure 7-27. The list data region in this report contains textboxes, a pie chart, and a table that shows the order detail history for each product.

FIGURE 7-27: Combination report with list, embedded table, and chart.

> **NOTE** *An important design consideration when using multiple, embedded data regions is that all report items are based on only one dataset. The dataset must include fields to group the containing region and the details for the data region it contains.*

Because only one dataset can be used for both data regions (the list and table) in this example, all necessary fields and details are required. The dataset used to drive the list grouped by products must include the order details for the embedded table.

Subreport

A subreport is a container for another report, visually embedded within the main report. As a method of object reuse, subreports can reduce redundant effort and circumnavigate some other barriers but they do impose some compatibility issues with certain rendering formats. Be cautious and test your designs thoroughly. As a rule, I don't use subreports unless they are necessary.

As a master/detail design pattern, subreports allow a data region to encompass detail records from a different dataset, or even an entirely different data source. I will demonstrate how to use them in the "Designing Subreports" section later in this chapter.

Drill-Through Navigation

Actions and report navigation are covered in Chapter 12. I include this topic here because report navigation is often an effective replacement for a complex, multi-level hierarchal report. It can be an effective complement to a summary report that enables report users to get more information and insight by navigating to details rather than including them in a single, comprehensive report. Using navigation actions correctly can help you architect reporting solutions rather than big, cumbersome and monolithic reports.

Consider that a report with four levels of drill-down groups must execute a large query that returns all the records at the detail level, just so the users have the option to drill to a particular branch of detail. Rather than expanding the drill-down branch within the same report, a group item could display a link that allows the user to navigate to another report. In a well-orchestrated solution, the users' perception is that they are simply moving around within their report dashboard solution, instead of moving from report to report.

Groups and Dataset Scope

One of the fundamental reasons that master/detail reports work—and are relatively easy to construct—is the principle of dataset scope. The term *scope* refers to the portion of data from a dataset that is available within a group. When a data region, such as a table, list, or matrix, is rendered, the data is sectioned into the subranges according to a group definition. Any report items or data region items placed in a grouped area, header, or footer are visible only to the data currently in scope. This means that if a table, for example, has a group based on the ProductCategory field and another table is placed in the group header, a table is rendered for each distinct ProductCategory value. Each table instance "sees" a range of detail records filtered by this group value. This can be an incredibly powerful feature, because there is no stated limit on how many items can be embedded within a group; nor is there a limit on group levels and nested embedded data regions. With that said, we have found it impractical to embed several data regions to create overly complex reports.

In this section, we will apply this principle of group embedded data regions for each data region container. This includes the list, table, and matrix.

More Aggregate Functions and Totals

Previously, you saw how the SUM and AVG functions work in a detail group and in group total rows. Reporting Services supports several aggregate functions and each function accepts one or two arguments that are passed in parentheses. The first argument is the field reference or the expression to aggregate. The second, optional argument is the name of a dataset, report item, or group name to indicate the scope of the aggregation. If not provided, the scope of the current data region or group is assumed. For example, suppose a table contains two nested groups based on the Category and Subcategory fields, respectively. If you were to drag the SalesAmount field into the Subcategory group footer, the designer would create an expression like this: =SUM(Fields!SalesAmount .Value). Remember that a field expression appears as a placeholder in the report design. For example, the placeholder text [SUM(SalesAmount)] actually represents the full expression: =SUM(Fields!SalesAmount.Value). Right-click and choose Expression to see the full expression.

The expression would return the sum of all `SalesAmount` field values within the scope of each distinct Subcategory group range. Table 7-2 shows all of the aggregate functions supported by Reporting Services with a brief description of each, for reference.

TABLE 7-2: Aggregate functions supported in report expressions

FUNCTION	DESCRIPTION
AVG()	The average of all non-null values.
COUNT()	The count of values.
COUNTDISTINCT()	The count of distinct values.
COUNTROWS()	The count of all rows.
FIRST()	Returns the first value for a range of values.
LAST()	Returns the last value for a range of values.
MAX()	Returns the greatest value for a range of values.
MIN()	Returns the least value for a range of values.
STDEV()	Returns the standard deviation.
STDEVP()	Returns the population standard deviation.
SUM()	Returns a sum of all values.
VAR()	Returns the variance of all values.
VARP()	Returns the population variance of all values.

In addition to the aggregate functions, some special-purpose functions behave in a similar way as aggregates but have special features for reports, as shown in Table 7-3.

TABLE 7-3: Special-use dataset row functions

FUNCTION	DESCRIPTION
LEVEL()	Returns an integer value for the group level within a recursive hierarchy. The group name is required.
ROWNUMBER()	Returns the row number for a group or range.
RUNNINGVALUE()	Returns an accumulative aggregation up to this row.

To demonstrate scoped aggregates, I start with a copy of the sample report: Ch06 - Sales Summary with Groups. As a refresher, Figure 7-28 shows the first page of the report with callouts containing the aggregate expressions for the last two columns.

Sales Summary with Groups

Product Category	Product Subcategory	Product Name	Order Quantity Total	Sales Total	Sales Avg
Accessories	Bike Racks	Hitch Rack - 4-Bike	2,617	$182,830.88	$16,621
	Bottles and Cages	Water Bottle - 30 oz.	2,336	$6,830.84	$621
	Cleaners	Bike Wash - Dissolver	2,184	$10,171.38	$925
	Helmets	Sport-100 Helmet, Black	1,988	$40,952.52	$3,723
		Sport-100 Helmet, Blue	1,984	$40,794.24	$3,709
		Sport-100 Helmet, Red	1,757	$36,356.98	$3,305
	Hydration Packs	Hydration Pack - 70 oz.	1,860	$60,151.35	$5,468
	Tires and Tubes	Patch Kit/8 Patches	590	$809.79	$74
	Subcategory Total		15,316	$378,897.98	$4,306

=SUM(Fields!SalesAmount.Value) =AVG(Fields!SalesAmount.Value)

FIGURE 7-28: Different aggregate functions used in totals.

The expressions for these two columns are the same for the detail row and the ProductCategory group footer row. With only the field name passed to an aggregate function, SUM and AVG in this case, the current group level is implied. For the details group, the result would be the same as:

```
=Sum(Fields!SalesAmount.Value, "Details")
```

For the ProductCategory group, the implied aggregate value would be the same as:

```
=Sum(Fields!SalesAmount.Value, "ProductCategory")
```

With the group name specified in the second function argument, the expression will always apply to that group level. To demonstrate, I've removed the last column and then added a new column using this expression in the detail row. Figure 7-29 shows the results. As expected, the category total is applied to every calculation.

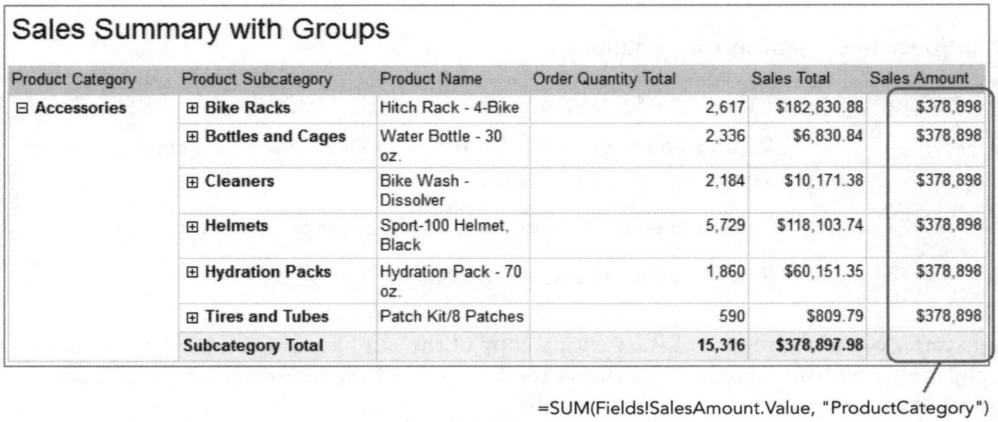

Sales Summary with Groups

Product Category	Product Subcategory	Product Name	Order Quantity Total	Sales Total	Sales Amount
⊟ Accessories	⊞ Bike Racks	Hitch Rack - 4-Bike	2,617	$182,830.88	$378,898
	⊞ Bottles and Cages	Water Bottle - 30 oz.	2,336	$6,830.84	$378,898
	⊞ Cleaners	Bike Wash - Dissolver	2,184	$10,171.38	$378,898
	⊞ Helmets	Sport-100 Helmet, Black	5,729	$118,103.74	$378,898
	⊞ Hydration Packs	Hydration Pack - 70 oz.	1,860	$60,151.35	$378,898
	⊞ Tires and Tubes	Patch Kit/8 Patches	590	$809.79	$378,898
	Subcategory Total		15,316	$378,897.98	

=SUM(Fields!SalesAmount.Value, "ProductCategory")

FIGURE 7-29: Using a scoped aggregation.

Now that we have access to the aggregate value at any level in the group hierarchy, we can calculate the percentage of contribution to the bottom line. Let's see it all the way through now. The final expression is pretty simple:

```
=Sum(Fields!SalesAmount.Value)/Sum(Fields!SalesAmount.Value, "ProductCategory")
```

To assemble the solution in Figure 7-30, The same expression is applied to the detail and group total footer cells in the last column. I've also modified the format property for these cells appropriately to display a percentage value.

Sales Summary with Groups

Product Category	Product Subcategory	Product Name	Order Quantity Total	Sales Total	% Contribution
Accessories	Bike Racks	Hitch Rack - 4-Bike	2,617	$182,830.88	48.25 %
	Bottles and Cages	Water Bottle - 30 oz.	2,336	$6,830.84	1.80 %
	Cleaners	Bike Wash - Dissolver	2,184	$10,171.38	2.68 %
	Helmets	Sport-100 Helmet, Black	1,988	$40,952.52	10.81 %
		Sport-100 Helmet, Blue	1,984	$40,794.24	10.77 %
		Sport-100 Helmet, Red	1,757	$36,356.98	9.60 %
	Hydration Packs	Hydration Pack - 70 oz.	1,860	$60,151.35	15.88 %
	Tires and Tubes	Patch Kit/8 Patches	590	$809.79	0.21 %
	Category Total		15,316	$378,897.98	100.00 %

FIGURE 7-30: Putting the calculations together in a meaningful solution.

DESIGNING SUBREPORTS

When I started using Reporting Services to design reports with nested groups and data regions, my first impulse was to use subreports as much as possible. This seemed like the best approach because I could design simple, modular reports and then put them together. The programming world promotes the notion of reusable objects. However, the downside of this approach is that subreports can create some challenges for the report rendering engine, resulting in formatting issues and poorer performance. In SQL Server 2000 and 2005, subreports didn't render at all in Excel. Improvements have since been made for Excel rendering, but there are inherent challenges for subreports to render consistently for all report rendering formats; particularly with Excel. When using subreports, carefully test the report to be sure that it will render in the target format.

> **NOTE** *Subreports are useful for implementing a variety of design patterns but they are not a cure-all. If you can design a report by embedding data regions into a list, table, or matrix, you are likely to get better results than if you use a subreport to do the same thing.*

A *subreport* is a standalone report that is embedded into another report. It can be independent, with its own dataset, or, using parameters, you can link the contents of a subreport to data in the main report.

> **NOTE** *Subreports fall into a small category of SSRS features that have some limitations that have changed and are likely to continue to change as the product evolves. This is why it is important to test your design in all the rendering formats and scenarios where it will be used.*

There are some limitations to the content and formatting that can be rendered within a subreport. For example, a multicolumn report simply doesn't work in a subreport (depending on the rendering format used). If you plan to use multiple columns in a subreport, test your report with the rendering formats you plan to use.

Subreports generally have two uses. The first is for embedding one instance of a separate report into the body of another report with an unassociated data source. The other scenario involves using the subreport as a custom data region to display repeated master and detail records in the body of the main report. From a design standpoint, this makes perfect sense. Using a subreport allows you to separate two related datasets and perhaps even data sources, linked as you would join tables in a SQL query. It allows you to reuse an existing report so that you don't have to redesign functionality you've already created. However, there may be a significant downside. If the master report will consume more than just a few records, this means that the subreport must execute its query and render the content many times. For large volumes of data, this can prove to be an inefficient solution. Carefully reconsider the use of subreports with large result sets. It may be more efficient to construct one larger report with a more complex query and multiple levels of grouping, rather than assume the cost of executing a query many times.

> **NOTE** *I rarely use subreports in standard scenarios to produce master/detail reports. If I need to use a subreport, the main report is limited to just a few records.*

A subreport can be linked to the main report using a correlated parameter and field reference so that it can be used like a data region, but this is not essential. A subreport could be used to show aggregated values unrelated to groupings or content in the rest of the report.

Creating a subreport is like creating any other report. You simply create a report and then add it to another report as a subreport. If you intend to use the main report and subreport as a Master/Detail view of related data, the subreport should expose a parameter that can be *linked* to a field in the main report. In the following walk-through, you'll build a simple report that lists products and exposes a subcategory parameter. The main report will list categories and subcategories, and the product list report will then be used as a data region, like a table or list in previous examples.

Federating Data with a Subreport

When the data source for a master data region is different from the data source for detail records, using a subreport can be just the ticket for creating a master/detail report. The following example combines report data from two different data sources.

In the sample project, you will find two reports named Ch07 - Product Orders Subreport and Ch07 - Product Details (subreport container). The "container" report contains a list whose data source is the relational sample database: WroxSSRS2016. The other report contains a table with a data source based on the Adventure Works Multidimensional SSAS database.

This literally means that we'll be using two different languages, T-SQL and MDX, and a parameterized expression will provide some translation between the two. Records in the Product table, located in the WroxSSRS2016 database, can be related using the ProductKey column. This column contains values from the Product table in the WroxSSRS2016 database.

The master report, Ch07 - Product Details (subreport container), is shown in Figure 7-31. This report contains a list data region that is bound to the following query and whose data source is the WroxSSRS2016 data warehouse database.

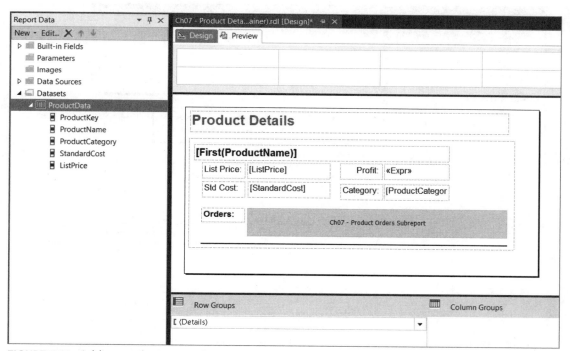

FIGURE 7-31: Adding a subreport to the main report.

The dataset for this report is pretty simple and just returns a set of products that have cost and price information. The `ProductKey` column is present so we can pass it to the subreport as a parameter:

```
SELECT
        ProductKey,
        ProductName,
        ProductCategory,
        StandardCost,
        ListPrice
FROM
        Product
WHERE       (StandardCost IS NOT NULL) AND (ListPrice IS NOT NULL)
ORDER BY ProductName
```

Figure 7-32 shows the child report, Ch07 - Product Orders Subreport, in the Designer. This report is simply a table bound to an MDX query. The data source for this dataset is the Adventure Works Multidimensional SSAS database. I have added a callout to the figure to show the expression used to convert the report parameter to an MDX member reference passed into a query parameter named `ProductUniqueName`.

Within the dataset query expression, the `ProductUniqueName` parameter is used in the WHERE clause using the STRTOMEMBER MDX function. This is a standard filtering convention, commonly used in MDX queries.

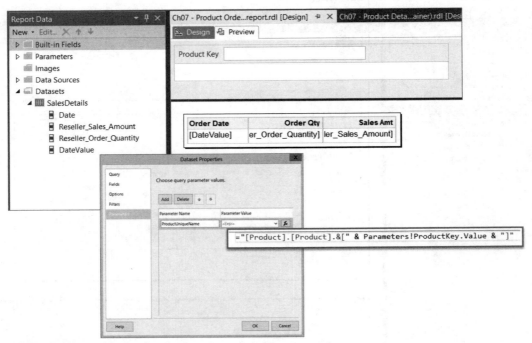

FIGURE 7-32: Modify the dataset parameter using an expression.

> **NOTE** *For more examples of parameter-passing in MDX queries, refer to Chapter 10.*

```
SELECT
     {
     [Measures].[Reseller Sales Amount],
     [Measures].[Reseller Order Quantity]
     } on Columns,
     NON EMPTY
     [Date].[Date].[Date].Members
     DIMENSION PROPERTIES MEMBER_CAPTION, MEMBER_UNIQUE_NAME, MEMBER_VALUE
     on Rows
FROM [Adventure Works]
WHERE
     (
      STRTOMEMBER( @ProductUniqueName ),
      [Date].[Calendar].[Calendar Year].&[2013]
     )
   ;
```

The details group for the master report list data region is set to the `ProductName` field. This satisfies the requirement that, for a data region to contain a nested data region object, it must have a group defined. You create the subreport by dragging and dropping the Ch07 - Product Orders Subreport report from the Solution Explorer into the list area.

Note that regardless of the dimensions of a subreport at design time, when dropped into a containing report, it always appears as a square area that usually takes up more design space than necessary (which also expands the dimensions of its container). After resizing the subreport, I also had to resize the list to appear as it does in Figure 7-33.

Right-click the subreport and choose Subreport Properties to set the parameter/field mapping, as shown in Figure 7-33. The Subreport Properties dialog, shown in Figure 7-33, is used to map a field in the container report to a parameter in the subreport.

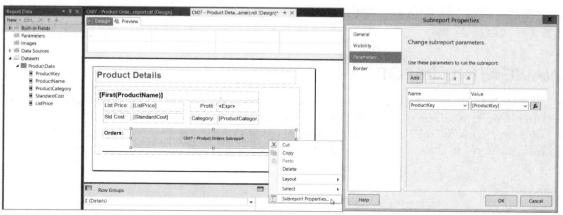

FIGURE 7-33: Product Details report with subreport in designer.

Navigate to the Parameters page, and then click Add to define a parameter mapping. Under the Name column, select the `ProductKey` parameter. Under the Value column, select the `ProductKey` field. Click OK to save these changes and close the Subreport Properties dialog.

This completes the report design. Using lists and subreports typically makes the design process more ad hoc and artful than when you use more rigid tables. Go back and check the size and placement of items so that they fit neatly within the subreport space. You often have to go through a few iterations of preview and layout to make the appropriate adjustments.

At this point, you should be able to preview the report and see the nested table/subreport, as shown in Figure 7-34.

Bike Wash - Dissolver

| List Price: | $7.95 | Profit: | $4.98 |
| Std Cost: | $2.97 | Category: | Accessories |

Orders:

Order Date	Order Qty	Sales Amt
1/28/2013	337	$1,530.67
2/28/2013	276	$1,289.72
3/30/2013	168	$760.28
4/30/2013	228	$1,071.23
5/30/2013	225	$1,064.21
6/30/2013	118	$562.86
7/31/2013	108	$515.16
8/29/2013	105	$498.09
9/29/2013	181	$827.27
10/29/2013	200	$941.94
11/29/2013	238	$1,109.96

Cable Lock

| List Price: | $25.00 | Profit: | $14.69 |
| Std Cost: | $10.31 | Category: | Accessories |

FIGURE 7-34: Product Details report in preview.

NAVIGATING REPORTS

Reports of yesterday were static, designed for print. At best, they could be previewed on a screen. To find important information, users had to browse through each page until they found the information they were looking for. Today, you have several options to provide dynamic navigation to important information—in the same report or to content in another report or an external resource.

Creating a Document Map

The *document map* is a simple navigation feature that allows the user to find a group label or item value in the report by using a tree displayed along the left side of the report. It's sort of like a table of contents for report items that you can use to quickly navigate to a specific area of a large report. You typically will want to include only group-level fields in the document map rather than including the detail rows.

> **NOTE** *The document map is limited to the HTML, Excel, and PDF rendering formats. In the Excel and HTML formats, the document map may not survive when you save report files to an older document format, such as Pocket Excel on an older Windows Mobile device.*

The sample report Ch07 - Products by Category and SubCategory (Doc Map) demonstrates this feature. I've added the ProductCategory and ProductSubcategory groupings to the document map. In the Group Properties dialog for the Category row group, on the Advanced page, I set the Document map property using the drop-down list to the ProductCategory field.

> **WARNING** *Be careful to specify the document map label property only for items you want to include in the document map. For example, if you specify this property for a grouping, don't do the same for a textbox containing the same value. Otherwise, you will see the same value appear twice in the document map.*

Figure 7-35 shows a report with a document map. The report name is the top-level item in the document map, followed by the product category and subcategory names.

You can show or hide the document map using the leftmost icon in the Report Designer's Preview or the Report View toolbar in the Report Manager or SharePoint Report Viewer web part after the report is deployed to the server.

> **NOTE** *My experience has been that the drill-down and document map features usually don't work well together because they duplicate some functionality. Use the document map to navigate to a visible area of the report.*

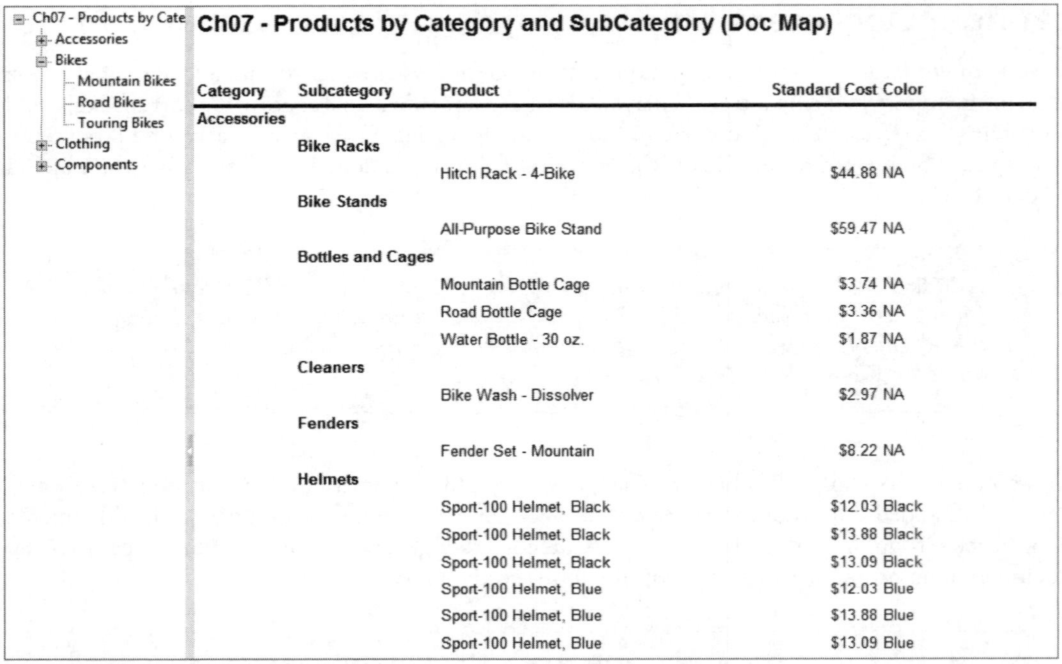

Category	Subcategory	Product	Standard Cost	Color
Accessories				
	Bike Racks			
		Hitch Rack - 4-Bike	$44.88	NA
	Bike Stands			
		All-Purpose Bike Stand	$59.47	NA
	Bottles and Cages			
		Mountain Bottle Cage	$3.74	NA
		Road Bottle Cage	$3.36	NA
		Water Bottle - 30 oz.	$1.87	NA
	Cleaners			
		Bike Wash - Dissolver	$2.97	NA
	Fenders			
		Fender Set - Mountain	$8.22	NA
	Helmets			
		Sport-100 Helmet, Black	$12.03	Black
		Sport-100 Helmet, Black	$13.88	Black
		Sport-100 Helmet, Black	$13.09	Black
		Sport-100 Helmet, Blue	$12.03	Blue
		Sport-100 Helmet, Blue	$13.88	Blue
		Sport-100 Helmet, Blue	$13.09	Blue

FIGURE 7-35: Multi-group table report with document map.

EXERCISES

To apply what you have learned in this chapter, you will work through two exercises. In Exercise 1, you will assemble expressions and titles in the report and page headers and save the resulting report as a template, which you can use to build new reports.

Exercise 1: Create a Report Template

A report template is a standardized report that you can use as the starting point for new reports. It can simply be saved as a report in your project or a folder, to be used as a starting point. The report file can be saved to the project items folder so Visual Studio to manage it as a report template.

Add a New Report and Set Up the Report Body

Well-designed reports are commonly titled and may be decorated with standard branding features, such as a company logo image.

1. Open the Wrox SSRS 2016 Exercises project in SQL Server Data Tools.
2. Add a new report to the project using Add ➪ New Item… from the right-click menu on the Reports folder in the Solution Explorer.
3. Name the report **ProSports Report**.

4. Add a page header and page footer, and resize them to be about .5 inches (1.25 cm) tall.

5. Resize the report body to be 7.5 inches (about 19 cm) wide or less.

6. Right-click the report background outside of the report body to edit the Report properties.

7. Confirm that the Paper size is Portrait and either Letter or A4 like you see in Figure 7-36.

8. Reduce all the margins to .25 inches (about .64 cm) and click the OK button.

> **NOTE** *For this exercise to work with both US and metric standards, I've made a point to use the width of A4 paper, which is slightly less than US letter page size. Screen examples are shown with US sizes but either paper size standard will work.*

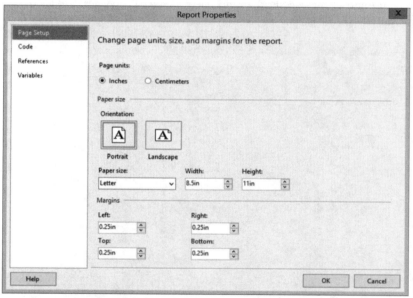

FIGURE 7-36: Report Properties dialog.

Set Up the Report Header

You will add the page number range and set the page header to skip the first page so the header information isn't redundant with information in the report header.

1. In the Report Data window to the left of the designer, expand the Built-in Items node.

2. Drag and drop the ReportName to the left side of the page header.

3. Drag and drop the PageNumber built-in field to the right side of the page header.

4. Resize this new textbox to about 3 inches (7.5 cm) wide.

5. Place the cursor before the [&PageNumber] text and type the word "Page" followed by a space.

6. Place the cursor at the end of the text in this textbox and type a space followed by the word "to" and another space.

7. Drag and drop the TotalPages built-in field to the end of the text in this textbox.

8. Click to select the [&PageNumber] placeholder and use the Report Formatting toolbar to set it to Bold.

9. Click to select the [&TotalPages] placeholder and use the Report Formatting toolbar to set it to Bold.

10. Click outside the new textbox and then once to select the textbox and not the text within it.

11. Use the Report Formatting toolbar to set the text alignment to right justified.

12. Right-click the background of the page header and select Header Properties.... This opens the dialog shown in Figure 7-37.

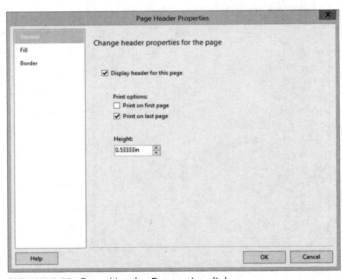

FIGURE 7-37: Page Header Properties dialog.

13. Uncheck the box in the Print options labeled "Print on first page."

14. Click the OK button to accept the changes.

Add Title and Logo to the Report Header

Using a rectangle as a container allows a group of report items to be moved and positioned as a unit.

1. Add a rectangle to the top right-hand corner of the report body. Resize it to fit just within the width of the report body and about .85 inches (2.2 cm) high.

2. Drag and drop the ReportName built-in field to the top-left corner inside the rectangle in the report body, below the ReportName textbox you added to the page header.

3. Select the ReportName textbox in the report body and change the font size to 14pt and change the font weight to Bold.

4. Resize the textbox to fit the height and resize the width to about 5 inches (12 cm) wide. Drag and drop the ExecutionTime built-in field just below the ReportName in the rectangle contained in the report body.

5. Use the Report Formatting toolbar to left align that textbox and italicize the text.

Add the Company Logo in the Report Header Rectangle

You will use an embedded image for the logo, and a textbox in the page footer to display company policy information.

1. Add an image item to the right side of the rectangle. The Image Properties dialog opens.

2. Click the Import... button.

3. Browse to the `Images` folder under the Wrox SSRS 2016 Report Solution folder.

4. In the Open file dialog, in the bottom right-hand corner, drop-down the list of file types and select "All files (*.*)" (see Figure 7-38).

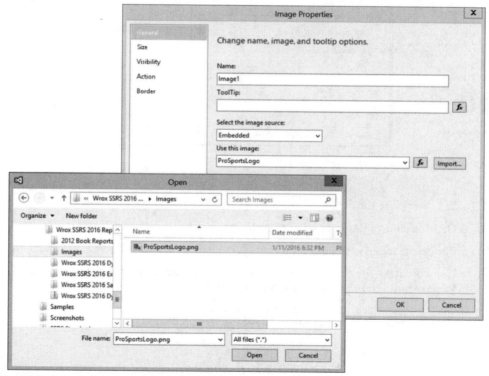

FIGURE 7-38: Adding an embedded image.

5. Select the `ProSportsLogo.png` file and click Open.

6. Click OK to accept the image file selection with the default image properties.

7. Resize the image to be approximately square and fit in the right side of the rectangle.

Add a confidential statement to the report footer and save the report template file.

8. Add a new textbox to the left side of the report footer and stretch it to just within the width of the report.

9. Add a line to the bottom of the page header under the two textboxes.

10. Type the following text into the textbox: **information on this report is confidential according to corporate privacy policy.**

11. Select the textbox and use the Report Formatting toolbar to italicize the text.

12. Add a line to the page footer, just above the new textbox.

13. Use Figure 7-39 to check the report layout and make any necessary changes.

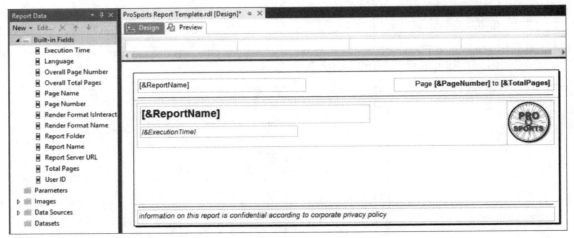

FIGURE 7-39: Completed template report.

14. Save and close the report.

15. Open Windows Explorer or File Explorer.

16. Locate the template report definition file: `ProSports Report.RDL`.

17. Copy the RDL file to the `ReportProject` project items template folder. If you installed Visual Studio to the default installation path, the folder will be located at:

```
C:\Program Files (x86)\Microsoft Visual Studio
14.0\Common7\IDE\PrivateAssemblies\ProjectItems\ReportProject
```

Exercise 2: Create a Report from the Template with Dynamic Expressions

With the template report saved to the Visual Studio report project templates folder, you can use it as a template for new reports.

Create a Matrix Report

Create a new report from the template.

1. In the Wrox SSRS 2016 Exercises project, right-click the `Reports` folder in the Solution Explorer and choose Add ⇨ New Item.

2. In the Add New Item dialog, the new report template is listed. Select the ProSports Report item and change the report name to **Profit by Country and Subcategory** (see Figure 7-40).

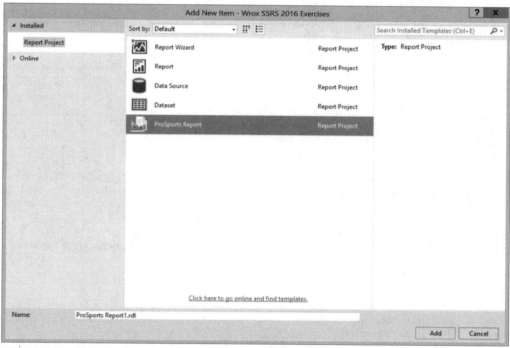

FIGURE 7-40: Select an item from the Add New Item dialog.

3. Click Add to create the new report from the template.

4. When the report opens in the designer, add a new data source referencing the WroxSSRS2016 shared data source in the project.

5. Add a new embedded dataset. Use the query designer to create the query shown in Figure 7-41.

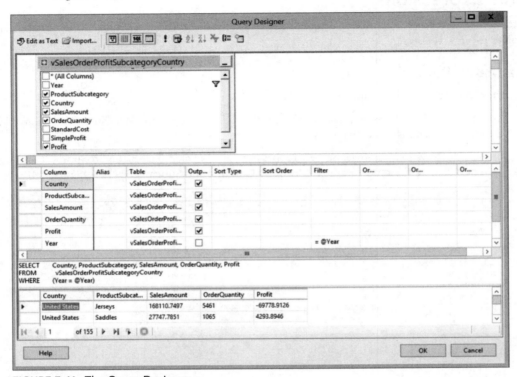

FIGURE 7-41: The Query Designer.

The text for this query should be similar to the following script. The specific text and layout will be a little different depending on how you use the graphical query builder. Carriage returns and tabs are optional and added for readability.

```
SELECT
    Country,
    ProductSubcategory,
    SalesAmount,
    OrderQuantity,
    Profit
FROM vSalesOrderProfitSubcategoryCountry
WHERE (Year = @Year)
```

6. Edit the Year report parameter and set the default value to 2013 as shown in Figure 7-42.

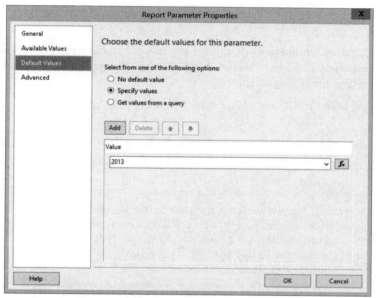

FIGURE 7-42: Report Parameter Properties.

7. Add a matrix data region to the report body just under the header textboxes.

8. In the Report Data window, expand the new dataset.

9. Drag and drop the following fields into the matrix target cells according to the information in Table 7-4.

TABLE 7-4: Matrix cell field mapping

FIELD	TARGET CELL
Country	Columns
ProductSubcategory	Rows
SalesAmount	Values
OrderQuantity	Values
Profit	Values

10. To add the column headers, click in the matrix to show the gray column and row selector handles.

11. Right-click the selection handle to the left of the top row (containing the Product Subcategory and [Country] headings) and select Insert ➪ Inside Group - Below. A row is added with the three columns merged into a single cell.

12. Right-click the cell under the [Country] heading and select Split Cells. The cells are split into three.

13. Make sure that the Properties window is displayed to the right of the report designer.

14. Enter the column header text shown in Figure 7-43 for the Sales Amt, Order Qty, and Profit.

> **TIP** *Depending on the order you perform these steps, the designer will behave a little differently, and with some experience this will become intuitive. For example, if you were to add the row in Step 11 before adding the fields in Step 9, the designer would add the column header for you. I encourage you to experiment with this after you complete the exercise.*

15. Right-align the headings using the Report Formatting toolbar.

16. Select the `Sales Amount` detail cell and set the Format property to C2.

17. Select the `Order Quantity` detail cell and set the Format property to N0.

18. Select the Sales `Profit` detail cell and set the Format property to C2.

19. Compare the report design to Figure 7-43 and make any necessary adjustments to the design.

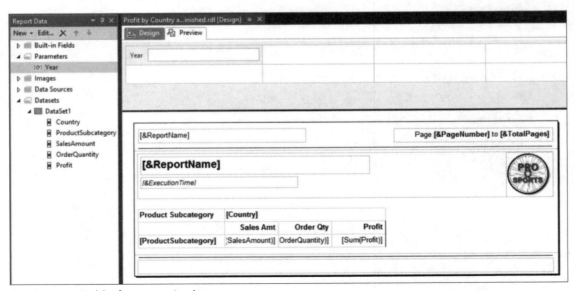

FIGURE 7-43: Add a figure caption here.

Add Alternating Row Shading and Threshold Alert Colors

Long table and matrix style reports are easier to read when rows have alternate background shading for every other row. You will add this effect and change the fore color for negative values to red.

1. Holding the Shift key, click and drag across the `SalesAmount`, `OrderQuantity`, and `Profit` detail cells to select them as a group.

2. In the Properties window, for the `BackgroundColor` property, select Expression....

3. In the Expression editor window, enter the following VB.NET code:

   ```
   =IIF(ROWNUMBER("Country") MOD 2 = 1, "Gainsboro", "White")
   ```

4. Click the OK button to accept the expression.

5. Check Figure 7-44 and make any necessary changes.

FIGURE 7-44: Matrix Design view and BackgroundColor property expresssion.

6. Preview the report. You should see that every other detail row in the matrix is displayed with an alternating gray background.

7. Return to Design view.

8. Select the `Profit` detail cell.

9. In the Properties window, choose the `Color` property and select Expression....

10. In the Expression editor window, enter the following VB.NET code:

    ```
    =IIF(Fields!Profit.Value>=0, "Black", "Red")
    ```

11. Preview the report again. This time, you should see that all negative Profit values are displayed in red.

    The final report is shown in Figure 7-45.

SUMMARY

The report header and footer structure is typically something you can standardize across all of your operational reports. Factoring this mundane work into an organizational report template can save report designers from repeating that effort in future reports. Define report page headers and footers in a report template, where you can reuse the design in all your new reports. You can add built-in fields and summary information to page headers and footers to display and print useful information such as the report name, execution date and time, page numbers, and the report user. These provide important context information if the report is printed or archived.

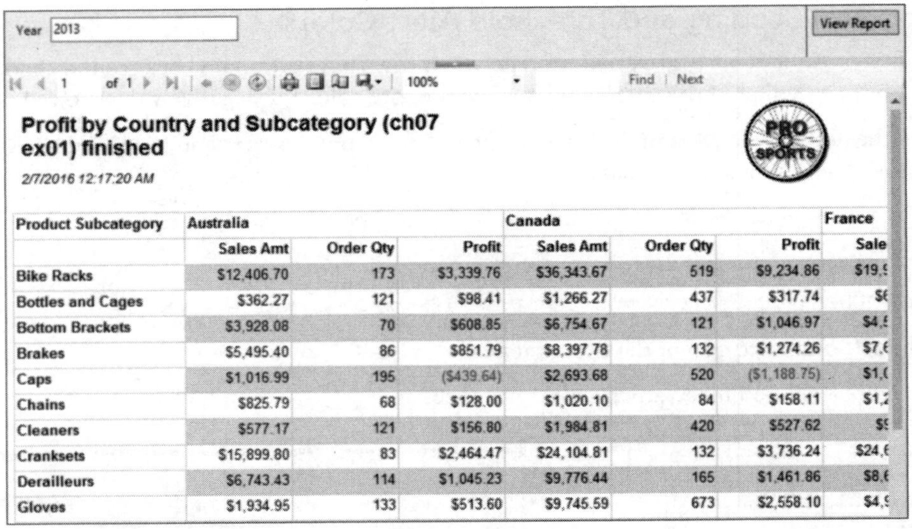

Product Subcategory	Australia			Canada			France
	Sales Amt	Order Qty	Profit	Sales Amt	Order Qty	Profit	Sale
Bike Racks	$12,406.70	173	$3,339.76	$36,343.67	519	$9,234.86	$19,
Bottles and Cages	$362.27	121	$98.41	$1,266.27	437	$317.74	$
Bottom Brackets	$3,928.08	70	$608.85	$6,754.67	121	$1,046.97	$4,
Brakes	$5,495.40	86	$851.79	$8,397.78	132	$1,274.26	$7,
Caps	$1,016.99	195	($439.64)	$2,693.68	520	($1,188.75)	$1,
Chains	$825.79	68	$128.00	$1,020.10	84	$158.11	$1,
Cleaners	$577.17	121	$156.80	$1,984.81	420	$527.62	$
Cranksets	$15,899.80	83	$2,464.47	$24,104.81	132	$3,736.24	$24,
Derailleurs	$6,743.43	114	$1,045.23	$9,776.44	165	$1,461.86	$8,
Gloves	$1,934.95	133	$513.60	$9,745.59	673	$2,558.10	$4,

FIGURE 7-45: Preview of finished report.

The essential design patterns for composite reports include the use of embedded data regions and subreports. Report elements, including complex data regions, can be nested in a list, table, or matrix to create more sophisticated interface paradigms. Subreports can provide this same functionality when a master/detail report must coordinate related information managed in different data sources. Report navigation features take reporting beyond static, passive data browsing. Document maps, as well as drill-down and drill-through techniques, allow users to interact with reports to create a dynamic information analysis and discovery experience.

Chapter 8 will help you apply many of the techniques and design principles you have learned in earlier chapters to graphical reports. You will use different chart types to aggregate and analyze data visually and then create composite charts with different types, with multiple areas and series axes. You'll learn to use the new chart types introduced in SQL Server 2016 and set the stage to build dashboard report solutions in Chapter 14.

8

Graphical Report Design

WHAT'S IN THIS CHAPTER?

➤ Understanding visual design principles and the fashion of visualization

➤ Understanding chart types and design approaches

➤ Getting to know the anatomy of a chart

➤ Creating a multi-series chart

➤ Using multiple chart areas

➤ Learning useful properties and settings

WROX.COM CODE DOWNLOADS FOR THIS CHAPTER

The samples and exercises for this chapter are included in the SSDT solution that was introduced in Chapter 3. If you have not set up the book samples and exercises, return to Chapter 3 and complete those tasks.

By some estimates, 60 to 70 percent of the population are visual thinkers. That means even when consuming numbers and information presented in text, most people perceive a visual representation of the same information in their minds. We have grown accustomed to data displayed in visual form. In fact, we expect important data to be visualized, especially when the presentation communicates comparisons and trends.

When used correctly, a chart more effectively answers questions and empowers consumers to take action on a set of data rather than a grid full of numbers. Conversely, a table filled with details may provide necessary context and balance with the completeness of a detail table. A financial controller or accountant will not balance the books to a chart, but a chart may be a great way for the CEO to see the improved profitability trend based on the same details as the balance sheet.

This chapter begins with the guiding principles of visual report design and discusses how charts are used in analytical reporting. Then we examine the different chart types offered in Reporting Services, and criteria to choose the correct type of chart for different business purposes and data scenarios. The essential components of the most useful and popular charts are explained in simple terms, and then we'll take a look at some of the many detailed properties and features used to create more advanced chart reports. The two exercises for this charter include a time-series chart using a line chart and column chart. You will create a multi-series chart with two separate vertical axis scales and then move to a multi-area chart with synchronized horizontal axis.

VISUAL DESIGN PRINCIPLES

Visual reports are often referred to as *analytic reports* or *dashboard components*. Indeed, the term "dashboard" is used very loosely in different products by different vendors to describe anything from a simple gauge graphic to a huge screen full of visual widgets. So, what, exactly, is the difference between a "visual report" and a "dashboard"? I think the reason that the industry can't offer a precise definition of "dashboard" that can set a boundary between the two terms is because the term "dashboard" is a metaphor for something tangible that we all use, and metaphors are subject to interpretation.

Whatever the specific definition is, the meaning is clear. The purpose of a dashboard or visual report is to summarize and display information for quick and convenient consumption so that users can understand what's going on in their business without taking their eyes off the road.

While working on a product engineering team at Hewlett-Packard, I gained a valuable perspective about successful design that has stayed with me throughout my career. Everything that we design has the following three elements, which exist in balance, and these elements should be considered in everything you design:

➤ **Form**—How does it look and how does it make me feel? Is it attractive, eye-catching, and interesting? People like to use things that are familiar and make them comfortable.

➤ **Fit**—How does it suit the need or solve the issue? Begin with a well-defined problem statement that supports the design, thus creating a useful tool that finds an answer, or completes an important task.

➤ **Function**—Is it easy to use, intuitive, and practical? Does it work in all environments and scenarios where it is needed? In a report or user interface, will the report work on a mobile device with a touch interface away from the office, or is it limited to a desktop? Is it interactive or static; for print or display?

Keep Charts Simple

Basic chart design can be quite simple if the default chart styles suit your needs. After placing the chart in the report body, you can drag fields from the Dataset window directly onto the chart design surface. At the minimum, a chart should have one aggregated field for the value and one grouped field for the category. The category and series groups represent the x-axis and y-axis in bar, column, line, area, and point charts.

Before things get complicated, let's make it simple. Don't go crazy with chart styling at first. Keep charts simple and clean, and use visual properties to emphasize the data, rather than the graphics. Heavy borders, backgrounds, shadows, and three-dimensional (3-D) effects distract from the message and presentation of important information.

> **NOTE** *My rule of thumb for visuals is that the amount of "ink" used in a graphic should correspond to the importance of the information. Generally speaking, dark, heavy borders and large fonts should be used to accentuate important information. Light, thin borders, backgrounds, and fonts should be used for supporting composition. Unnecessary stylings should be eliminated.*

Visual design is art as much as it is science, and thus it is difficult to articulate hard rules for visual design. Sometimes it just needs to look right. Avoid clutter and use white space to provide balance. Work from examples of established design patterns. Experiment and find a presentation style that works for you and your audience, and then work within that theme. You can always fine-tune when the important design work is finished, and then improve the aesthetic design as you go.

You will find several excellent examples in books from Nathan Yao and his website, `FlowingData.com`. Stephen Few provides outstanding guidance about the principles and concepts of effective, simple visual design in his books and website, `PercetualEdge.com`. There you will find many bad examples to avoid, as well as good examples to pursue.

Properties, Oh My!

Reporting Services provides about 60 different chart styles, if you count all the variations. For each, you have fine control of detailed properties used to control border styles, fills, colors, and sizes of just about everything you can imagine. With all this flexibility comes the potential for a good deal of complexity. All told, the chart data region and its constituent objects support nearly 200 individual properties. Some of these properties apply to only certain chart types. But no matter how you look at it, that's a lot of properties to dig through.

Ever since Microsoft acquired the code base for Dundas Software's .NET charting components and added newer versions along the way, they have done a remarkable job of simplifying the design interface. You can take chart design as far as you need to. The necessary effort to design charts may range from simple to tedious. Having been down this road many times, I recommend that after you familiarize yourself with charting basics, you approach the design with specific objectives in mind. Otherwise, you're likely to get lost in the interface.

The Fashion of Visualization

Perfect data visualization is the holy grail of analytic reporting. I've read a lot of books and attended many lectures about "right" and "wrong" data visualization practices. Scores of dashboarding, scorecarding, and visualization products exist, all with the promise of filling a huge gap in the industry left by all the other vendors who, according to competitors, can't seem to get data visualization right.

As I write this, it's only been a few days since the news of pop legend David Bowie's passing. Bowie was synonymous with fashion (and, of course, he performed a song about it). Think of fashion trends over the past few decades—long hair, short hair, big hair; bell-bottoms, straight legs; neon, pastels, plaid, and grunge. Funny thing is that when we look back on the fashions of a previous generation, they seem so incredibly ridiculous that it's hard to believe that people took any of it seriously. But somehow, a few pop stars and celebrities can make extreme fashion look cool and trendy. Charts are like that, too.

When I began using Reporting Services in 2003, 3-D charts were all the rage. Visual reports had big, rounded borders with drop shadows, beveled edges, and gradient-filled backgrounds. Do that now and the reports will immediately be branded as "fluff" and "eye candy." Ten years later, "modern" looking charts were flat with light-shaded bars on a white background. What were we thinking back then? Give us another few years and maybe we'll all be wearing our bell-bottoms and designing 3-D charts.

Visual Storytelling

The purpose of a chart is to highlight important information and let it tell a story. Different report types can effectively convey comparisons or trends, but it's important to use the right chart for your data. Before moving on, I want to make an important point. If you work in a field where specialized visualizations are useful and appropriate, you may find some of the more abstract and special-purpose charts of great value. But for day-to-day business reporting, it's common to use just a handful of traditional chart types to visualize business metrics. So, even though Polar, Stock, and Funnel charts look cool, they may not help you convey an effective message. In business, 99 percent of the industry uses about 5 percent of the available chart types—namely, columns, bars, lines, and a few variations of the same types.

Perspective and Skewing

Hopefully, I've already talked you out of using 3-D charts as a practice, but I suppose there are isolated cases where it might make some sense. Consider a case where you are preparing a PowerPoint presentation. The data is static with the numbers right in front of you. Now, you want to choose the most effective and impactful visual for your presentation, and maybe a bold 3-D chart makes the right statement. You can tweak it, spin it around, and make adjustments so the data points are all visible and in exactly the right place. This is a much different experience than designing a report for changing data. As soon as the values change, the last row of columns in a 3-D perspective chart may no longer be visible.

Here's a rhetorical question. Figure 8-1 shows two renditions of the same chart and the same data in two different styles. Which is easier to read? This is purposely an extreme example, but it makes the point that wasting screen space on visual styling (not to mention ink or toner if printed) is just unnecessary.

The purpose of marketing is to persuade a consumer to perform an action, often by using psychology and emotion, to amplify and de-emphasize certain information. The carefully crafted presentation of information can alter a user's perception, and his or her belief about certain facts. In analysis (which is a tool of science), information is presented in a uniform and standard format so that the consumer can make an honest and unbiased assessment.

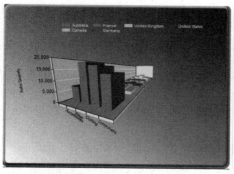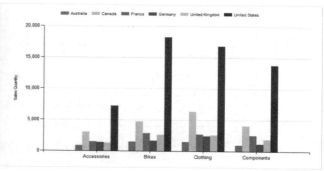

FIGURE 8-1: Two renditions of the same chart.

CHART TYPES

Some of the more common chart types (such as column, bar, line, and area) can be used for different views of the same data. Pie charts present a more simplified view and work well with fewer category values. Other charts are more specialized and may be appropriate for multi-value data points, range values, and variances. All the chart types support dynamic capabilities, such as actions and tooltips. Using these features in report design, a chart user can get more information and details by hovering over or clicking a range, point, or area of the chart. Let's take a brief look all the major chart types.

Chart Type Summary

Twelve general chart types are available, as described in Table 8-1.

TABLE 8-1: Chart Type Categories

CHART TYPE	DESCRIPTION	BEST USE
Column	A classic vertical bar chart with columns representing values along the y-axis. Like-valued items along the x-axis are grouped, and bars representing the same x-axis values in each group have the same colors or patterns. Series values may also be grouped and subgrouped. Columns can have point labels, and the colored bars can be labeled using a legend. Columns can be arranged side by side (along the x-axis) or in front of one another (along the z-axis.) Columns may appear to be extruded from their base using a rectangular or circular (cylindrical) shape.	Discrete group values on the Category (x) axis. Also effective with linear time-series periods broken into discrete buckets (such as days, weeks, or months).

continues

TABLE 8-1 *(continued)*

CHART TYPE	DESCRIPTION	BEST USE
Bar	Functionally the same as a column chart turned 90 degrees. It has the advantage of more accurately depicting value comparisons for layouts in which you have more available horizontal space.	Used only with discrete group values, not for linear series groups.
Line	Like a column chart but with a trend line drawn from one point to the next in the series. This type of chart is appropriate for a series of values that tend to progress over a relatively even plane that describes a "level," "up," or "down" trend. It is inappropriate for series values that tend to jump around. This type of chart is useful for comparing multiple series (along the z-axis) without obscuring trend lines behind a series.	Time-series and linear interval category groups (time, dates, and progressive numeric values).
Area	Like a line chart but the area encompassed by the line is filled. The solid shading of the charted area depicts a volume of data values. Opaque fill colors may be appropriate when the lines don't intersect. Otherwise, transparent fill colors may be useful to discern overlapping fill areas.	Time-series and linear interval category groups.
Pie	The classic pie chart can be an good tool for comparing a small number of relative values but it may not be as accurate as a tree map, bar, or column chart. Unlike these other charts, the aggregate value isn't quantified. For simple comparisons, users understand pie charts because they put comparative values into a proportional context and can drive quick decision support at a glance. Pie chart views can be exploded to visually separate each slice.	Use only for discrete category groups and never for linear series values. However, may be used for discrete bucket values. Typically, use pie charts with no more than 6 to 10 slices.
Doughnut	A doughnut is a pie with a hole in the middle. It's more effective as a bold marketing visual. A 3-D doughnut rendering may expose smaller slices more clearly than a pie chart because each slice has four sides rather than three.	Use with a subtle 3-D effect for conveying a bold statement and not for accurately measuring business metrics. Typically, limit slices to 6 or 10.

CHART TYPE	DESCRIPTION	BEST USE
Scatter	Plots several points in a range (both x and y) to show trends and variations in value. The result is more like a cloudy band of points, rather than a specific aggregated point or line.	Used with dozens to hundreds of data points when analyzing the general trend is of greater value than seeing a specific point.
Bubble	A technique for charting points on three dimensions. Values are plotted using different-sized points (or *bubbles*) on a two-dimensional (2-D) grid. The size of the bubble indicates the related value along the z-axis.	Appropriate when measuring two different series values along two different linear axes where size represents one value and position represents the other.
Range (Gantt)	Range and Gantt charts are often used to visualize project phases and the progress of stages in a process along a linear series.	Used when each data item (project, commodity, unit of work) has a beginning and end value on a linear axis.
Stock	This category of charts (sometimes called *candlestick* or *whisker graphs*) plots values vertically like a column chart having variable start and end points. For each item along the y-axis series, a vertical line indicates a start and end value for the range. A tick mark in the line can indicate a significant value in that range or an aggregation of the range. This type of chart is useful for showing trading stocks with opening, closing, and purchase values; wholesale, retail, and discount prices; and so on.	A specialized kind of visual for discrete data items that have multiple events along a linear axis, typically multiple start and end values.
Shapes	Shape charts like the funnel and pyramid are effectively a single, stacked column chart. These typically are used to model sales and production against goals, and sales opportunity pipelines. The Tree map and sunburst charts are 2016 product additions. The tree map chart is considered by many visualization experts to be a more versatile replacement for pie charts because it provides a more accurate comparison of values and can handle a larger number of data points.	Used in specific business scenarios where data items progress through ranked stages.

continues

TABLE 8-1 *(continued)*

CHART TYPE	DESCRIPTION	BEST USE
Polar (Radar)	Polar and radar charts plot points from a central hub at different angles and distances in a radial fashion. This kind of visual does have some useful applications, but traditional nonlinear charts (such as a column or bar) are often more suitable.	A specialized visual. Can be used with discrete, nonlinear but related categories. Best used to express that no category exists at the beginning or end of the range.

Column and Stacked Charts

With so many variations of this chart type, the right choice will depend on the objective. Is it sufficient to demonstrate that one data point is less than or greater than another, or do these points need to be strictly measurable? An artistic chart might help to make an impact, but a flatter view is usually more appropriate to maintain accuracy.

Stacked charts effectively show the proportion of series values within each category group. The stacked column chart shown in Figure 8-2 demonstrates that each series value increases the column height in proportion, but the trade-off with this visual is that it's more difficult to compare the individual series values across each category.

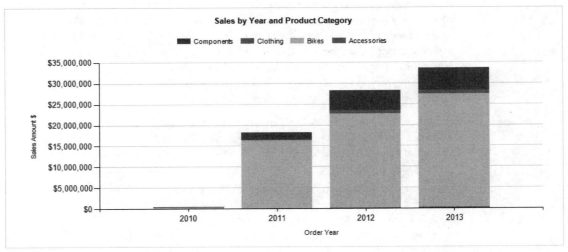

FIGURE 8-2: Stacked column chart.

To emphasize the proportion of like values rather than the comparative accumulation, the 100 percent stacked view makes all the bars in the chart the same length, rather than depicting the sum of all the values in the bar.

Area and Line Charts

As shown in Figure 8-3, an *area chart* plots the values of each point, and then draws a line from point to point to show the progression of values along the series. This is an effective method for analyzing trends, and works well when values tend to climb, decline, or remain level in the series. This type of chart is accurate when data exists for all category values on the x-axis. It typically doesn't work well to express a series of values that are not in a relatively uniform plane.

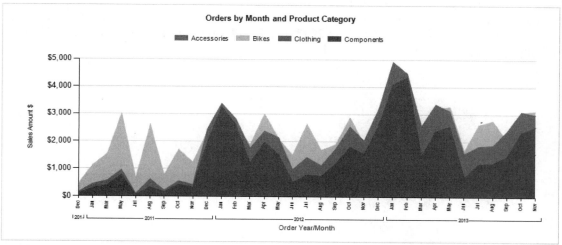

FIGURE 8-3: Area chart.

A *line chart* is a variation of an area chart using a line or ribbon rather than a solid area. The line chart works better than the area chart for comparing multiple categories for a series of values, because one layer may obscure another in the area view. In the preceding example, the area chart works because of how the values are sorted. Larger values are in the background, and other points in the foreground are smaller, and the trend increases back to front.

Pie and Doughnut Charts

A *pie chart* can be a good tool for comparing proportional values when you have a relatively small number of categories, and each group is in an easily comparable range. If your goal is to use screen space effectively, geometry proves that this not the best visual. Simply put, a circle-shaped chart inside a rectangle-shaped page wastes a lot of screen or page space. Pie charts have received very bad press for some good reasons amplified by the strong opinions of a few noted data visualization industry experts. Right or wrong, some people simply don't take this visual very seriously anymore. That said, it's still one of the most effective ways to convey a simple proportion of values in an uncluttered view or public presentation. The bottom line is that you should make sure this is the right visual for your purpose, and consider alternatives if in doubt.

Pie charts have fallen out of vogue in recent years due to their limited ability to visualize relatively similar values. Often, a pie chart is chosen when it works with a sample set of data that has a few categories with drastically different values, but ends up being a poor choice when the actual report data is less suitable for this type of chart. Consider using a tree map, column, or bar chart when more accurate comparisons are needed.

Here's a quick experiment. Open the report named `C08 - Pie and Column Chart` in the `Wrox SSRS 2016 Samples` project. Preview the report and try to quickly determine the sales ranking of the three Bike product categories in 2013. Figure 8-4 shows the data visualized in a pie chart. That's a tough one, huh?

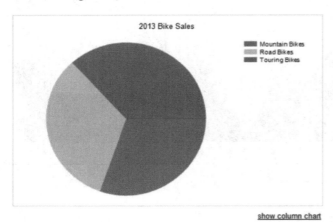

FIGURE 8-4: Pie chart for Bike product categories.

You can see that I've added a report action in a textbox that shows and hides a column chart in the same report. I'm not going to give away the answer so you'll have to use the sample report to find the answer for yourself, but you may be surprised.

Pie charts are also a very poor choice in a number of scenarios where column and bar charts would provide a more accurate presentation.

The purpose of a chart is to tell a complete story about the data, and it's important to label it clearly so that you know what the groups represent. Group values can be titled using point labels, call-out labels, or in a legend.

A *doughnut chart* is a pie chart with a hole. Yes, it's really that simple. Variations of the pie and doughnut charts allow you to separate the slices and, of course, twist and bend them using 3-D effects. Again, under the right conditions, this might be prudent with small, management result sets, but always consider your options before going down this route.

A significant limitation of this chart style is evident when the number of grouped values exceeds single digits. Consider the following example. Open the sample report `Ch08 - Pie and Bar Chart with Many Values`. You will notice I have added a visible parameter that allows you to specify the number of products to display in this sales summary. Figure 8-5 shows that it is difficult to discern between 25 different values. Below the pie chart is a bar chart visualizing the same results. In this case, the bar chart is a much better choice. The text arrangement of the vertical axis is ideal when comparing many values.

Top 25 Product Sales

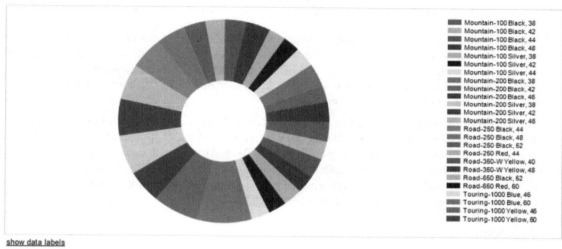

show data labels

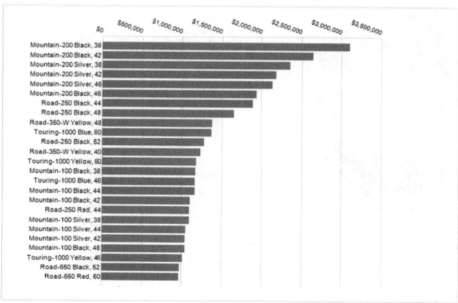

FIGURE 8-5: Doughnut chart versus bar chart.

The advantage of a bar chart over a doughnut chart, in this scenario, is that vertical page space is virtually unlimited in multiple page reports.

But Wait. There's More!

A couple of product versions ago, a nifty trick was introduced that allows column and bar charts to grow dynamically. This feature is not as simple as just switching it on, though. Like most of the cool capabilities in Reporting Services, you have to write a little code. If you take a look at the DynamicHeight property of the bar chart in Design view, you'll see how this works.

```
=(COUNT(Fields!ProductName.Value, "ProductSalesSummary") / 5) & " in"
```

The expression counts the number of rows returned from the dataset used in a calculation and concatenates a string value that resolves to the number of inches for the height of the chart. The result will be one plus the number of rows divided by five. Adding one avoids a division-by-zero error. The chart will allow room for about five rows per inch. I find it necessary to adjust this math in different reports to avoid adding extra white space.

Like the previous sample, I added a textbox with a drill-through action, but this one controls the chart series labels on the pie chart. Having data labels enabled does help you see the value that each slice represents, but, again, this is only useful with a limited number of axis values. Now that you see how this works, preview the report once more. Now, select 200 for the Top Products parameter list and press Enter. Click the "Show data labels" link below the pie chart and, as shown in Figure 8-6, it should be obvious that the bar chart is a better choice.

Top 200 Product Sales

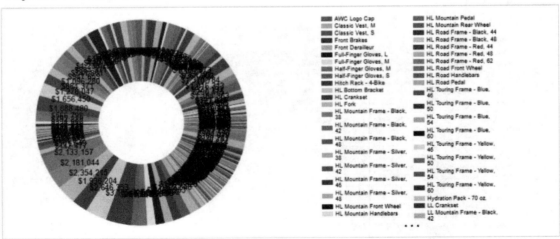

FIGURE 8-6: Top 200 Product Sales report.

Bubble and Stock Charts

Bubble charts are essentially a point plotted in a grid representing three dimensions. The value of the z-axis is expressed by the size of the bubble. Imagine that the bubble exists in a 3-D plane and appears larger if it is closer to you. Actually, the bubble can be a circle, square, triangle, diamond, or cross shape. This also means that a combination of shapes can be used to represent different data elements in the same chart space. The example shown in Figure 8-7 is included in the sample project and is named Ch08 - Bubble Chart Product Subcategory Profit Analysis.

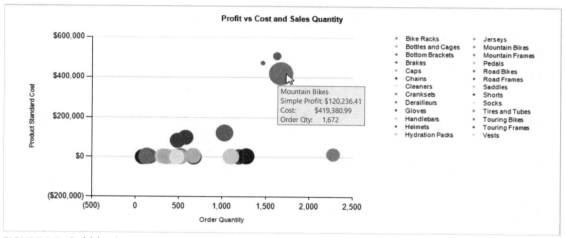

FIGURE 8-7: Bubble chart.

For sales orders grouped by subcategory, for a selected year and country, the product cost is plotted on the vertical axis and order quantity on the horizontal axis. Bubble size represents the simple profit calculated in the query. The example shown in Figure 8-7 helps you discover a valuable insight by revealing that Mountain Bike sales were particularly profitable in Canada.

The bubble chart properties are most easily set in the Series Properties dialog shown in Figure 8-8. With the sample report open in Design view, click the chart to show the Chart Data window and then use the call-out menu for the series in the Values field list. Here, the StandardCost, SimpleProfit, and OrderQuantity fields are assigned to the Bubble, "Bubble size," and Category fields, respectively.

New Chart Types

Two new chart types introduced in SQL Server 2016 Reporting Services are the Tree Map and Sunburst charts. Sample reports are provided for both, which you can see in Figures 8-9 and 8-10.

It is notable the chart designer is generically designed to manage settings for every chart type. Consequently, the Category and Series group assignments, used to visualize fields differently in each chart type, can be quite arbitrary and some experimentation may be necessary to make sense of it.

FIGURE 8-8: Series Properties page for bubble chart.

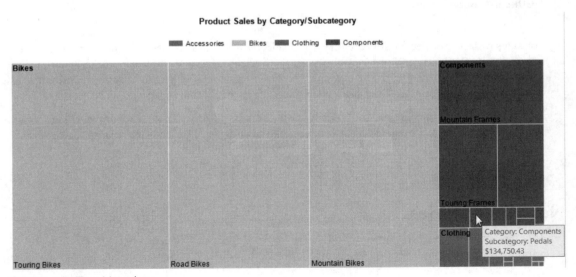

FIGURE 8-9: Tree Map chart.

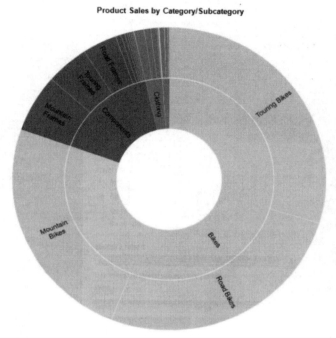

Product Sales by Category/Subcategory

FIGURE 8-10: Sunburst chart.

The Anatomy of a Chart

The best way to learn how to use the charts in Reporting Services is to work through a few examples and exercises. An exhaustive review of all the properties and settings (some of which are shown in Figure 8-11) usually leads to getting lost and confused. Like learning to drive, start with the basic process and rules, and then just do it. You'll figure out the details along the way.

Chart objects are organized into the hierarchy shown in Figure 8-12. Understanding this structure and the relationships between these objects will save you a lot of time and effort.

The Chart object is really is just a container. The Chart Area object does most of the work, and contains most of the useful properties. Take some time to explore the chart objects in the design interface. Because there are so many different objects, selecting the right object can be tricky at first, but with a little experience, you will become comfortable with the interface.

With a chart open in the designer, show the Properties window and then click different areas of the chart to select and view the names of various objects. Use the chart objects hierarchy as a reference as you click different areas to select objects. Additionally, you can right-click an object to reveal menu options that will take you to subordinate objects and collections. For example, if you were to right-click the Chart object, the Properties window and the right-click menu will let you find the Chart Area objects. Taking time to do this now will save you time and effort when you follow the exercise later in this chapter.

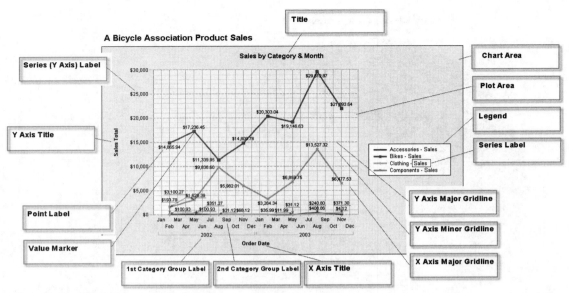

FIGURE 8-11: Chart properties and settings.

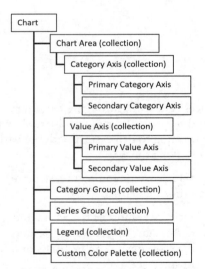

FIGURE 8-12: Hierarchy of chart objects.

Note that many of these objects are organized into collections to make them fit neatly into the standard Properties windows and design interface. As a rule, you can select an object and set its properties in one of two ways.

If you right-click an object in the chart designer, you see a menu item to edit the object's properties. That menu may also include related objects that you can edit. Choosing this menu option opens a custom property page for the object. Choosing an option in a property page to edit another object opens another property page. These are stacked in the order in which they were opened. Some properties are actually object collections. Clicking an ellipsis (...) button for that collection opens a dialog with the object collection and associated properties.

In addition to the custom properties pages for each chart-related object, you can edit properties in the standard Properties window.

Multiple Series, Axes, and Areas

A *series* is any single numeric field, aggregated and plotted along a group of category values. There is no limit to the number of series that can be added to the same chart. Each series can be visualized as a different chart type as long as they are compatible types. Compatible chart types are those that can be visualized along axis scales within the same vertical or horizontal space. For example; column, line, and area charts are compatible, but could not be mixed with a bar or pie chart.

Reporting Services charts support multiple chart areas. This powerful feature enables you to place multiple charts, of different types and characteristics, in the same chart container. Each of these chart areas is based on the same dataset, and can be aligned and correlated with a sibling chart in a variety of ways. The following is a simple example.

In a chart report you can separate two data fields into different chart areas, arranged vertically. When you align the Category Axis, any changes in the data are consistently reflected in both chart areas.

To make room for the second chart area, increase the chart's height by stretching it vertically. Right-click the chart and choose Add New Chart Area, as shown in Figure 8-13.

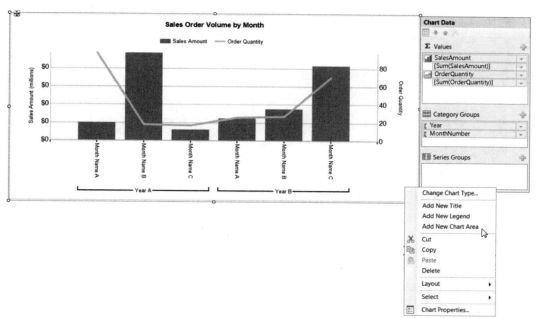

FIGURE 8-13: Adding a new chart area.

The new chart area appears as only white space below the original chart until a series axis is assigned to it. Right-click the `OrderQuantity` field in the Chart Data Values pane, and choose Series Properties, as shown in Figure 8-14.

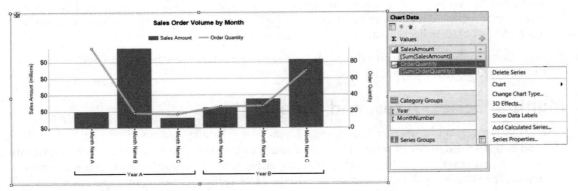

FIGURE 8-14: Series Properties option.

In the corresponding Series Properties dialog, on the Axes and Chart Area page, use the "Change chart area" drop-down list to select the new chart area. Verify your settings with Figure 8-15, and then click OK to close the Series Properties dialog.

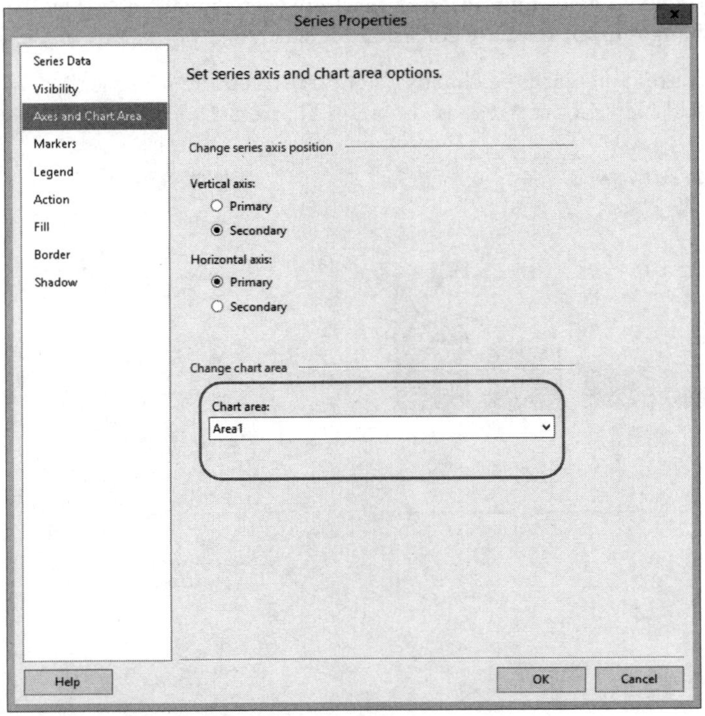

FIGURE 8-15: Selecting a chart area.

As shown in Figure 8-16, the finished report shows a chart visual very similar to the previous example. However, the line chart and its axis have been moved to the second chart area.

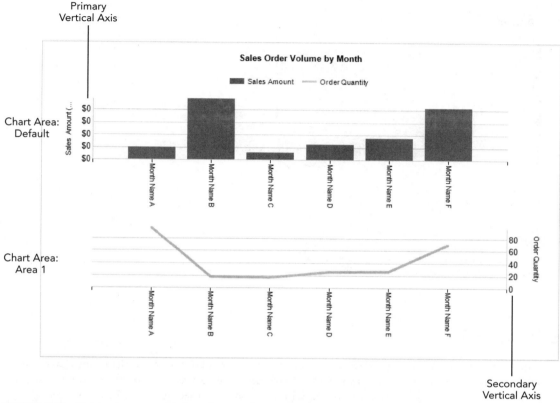

FIGURE 8-16: Finished report with line chart and axis moved.

To set properties for the chart area, right-click the chart in the designer and choose Chart Area Properties. Selecting the chart area can be a little tricky. I have found it easiest to right-click the second chart area without selecting it first. When you right-click, the designer selects the chart area and displays the appropriate menu option. Figure 8-17 shows the Chart Area Properties dialog. On the Alignment page, use the "Align with chart area" drop-down list to choose the Default chart area. Click OK to accept this change, and then preview the report.

This last change ensures that the horizontal axis scales always align. Although the two chart areas appear to be separate charts with distinct chart types, they both use the same scale so that data in the two chart areas can be used for comparison.

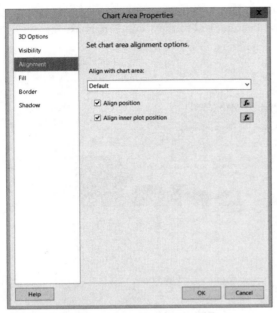

FIGURE 8-17: Chart Area Properties dialog.

EXERCISES

The following two exercises will have you build two reports containing multi-series charts. Both exercises demonstrate techniques to visualize two different series values on two different scales. You will start by using a single chart area with a primary and secondary axis. In the second exercise, you will separate the two series into different chart areas.

Exercise 1: Creating and Styling a Simple Chart

This exercise uses a single chart with a column and line chart in the same chart area. Two different measure values are visualized using a primary and secondary axis, which have different scales.

1. Add a new report to the `Wrox SSRS 2016 Exercises` project by using the Add ⇨ New Item... right-click menu. Name the report **Sales Order Volume by Month**.

2. Add a data source in the Report Data window and use the shared data source `WroxSSRS2016`. Give the new data source the same name.

3. In the report Data window, add an embedded dataset using the data source you just added. Name the dataset **SalesByMonth**.

4. Use the following query script:

```
SELECT
    Year,
    MonthNumber,
```

```
            MonthName,
            OrderQuantity,
            SalesAmount
FROM             vSalesSummaryMonth
WHERE Year IN ( @Year )
```

5. Click OK to close the Dataset Properties dialog.

6. Edit the Year report parameter and change the Data type to Integer.

7. Check "Allow multiple values."

8. Edit the Year property in the Report Data window.

9. Use the Available Values page to add 2011, 2012, and 2013.

10. Use the Default Values page to add 2012 and 2013 as the default values.

11. Use the Toolbox window to add a chart to the report body.

12. In the Select Chart Type dialog, select the first column chart type displayed, and then click OK to close the dialog.

13. Resize the new chart so that you have some comfortable working space.

14. Click the chart to show the Chart Data window.

15. Use the Chart Data window to add the SalesAmount and OrderQuantity fields as values.

16. Add the Year and MonthNumber fields as category groups.

17. Preview the report to make sure the chart is showing sales values for each month in 2012 and 2013.

Axis Titles and Formatting

Attention to detail makes a difference in visual design. With the essential chart design completed, the following steps are used to fine-tune properties used for titles and layout details.

1. Return to Design view.

2. Click to select the vertical axis title and change the text to Sales Amount (millions).

3. Click to select the vertical axis scale values.

4. Right-click the selected vertical axis scale and select Vertical Axis Properties....

5. In the Vertical Axis Properties dialog, select the Number page.

6. Change the Category to Currency, as shown in Figure 8-18.

7. Set the Decimal places to 0.

8. Check "Use 1000 separator."

9. Check "Show values in" and select Millions from the drop-down list.

10. On the Major Tick Marks page, check "Hide major tick marks."

11. On the Line page, change the "Line color" to Light Gray.

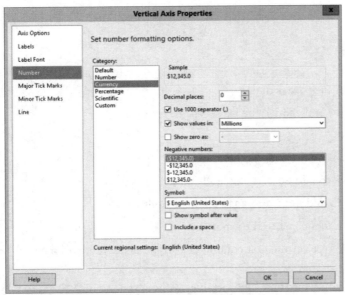

FIGURE 8-18: Changing the Category to Currency.

12. Click OK to close the Vertical Axis Properties dialog.

13. Preview and check the report.

14. In Design view, right-click the Horizontal Axis and select Horizontal Axis Properties....

15. In the Horizontal Axis Properties dialog, on the Axis Options page, change the Interval to 1 (shown in Figure 8-19). This will show a value on every category value regardless of the available room for labels.

16. On the Labels page, choose the "Disable auto-fit radio button."

17. Set the "Label rotation angle" to 90 degrees.

18. On the Major Tick Marks page, check "Hide major tick marks."

19. On the Line page, set the "Line color" to Light Gray.

20. Click OK to close the Horizontal Axis Properties dialog.

21. Preview and check the report.

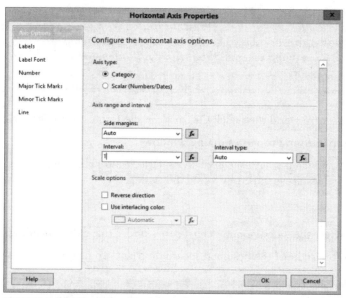

FIGURE 8-19: Changing the Interval to 1.

Change Axis Labels

The horizontal axis is grouped by `Year` and then `MonthNumber`. Even though the chart values are grouped and sorted by the `MonthNumber`, you want to display the name of the month and, to save space, you will abbreviate the month name to three characters.

1. In Design view, click the chart to show the Chart Data window.

2. In the Category Groups list, right-click or use the small down arrow icon for the MonthNumber field and select Category Group Properties....

3. Find the Label property and click the Expression button (fx) to the right.

4. Use the Expression Builder to replace the default field expression with the following:

```
=Fields!MonthName.Value.Substring(0, 3)
```

> **TIP** *If you are familiar with Visual Basic for Applications (VBA), which is used in Office macros, the Visual Basic .NET* `SubString` *method is similar to the* LEFT, RIGHT, *and* MID *functions. Either VBA or .NET style VB code can be used in Reporting Services expressions.*

> **WARNING** *The code completion feature of the Expression Builder can work against you if an object method or property isn't contained in the object reference library, as is the case with the* SubString *method. Always double-check the final code before accepting any changes.*

5. Double-check that the code is correct and then click OK to close the Expression window.

6. Click OK to close the Category Group Properties dialog window.

7. Select the horizontal axis title, which displays the text "Axis Title," and press Delete. It is fairly obvious that the chart values are grouped by Year and Month.

Final Formatting

1. In the Chart Data window, select the SalesAmount chart series under the Values heading.

2. In the Properties window, to the right of the designer, locate the ToolTip property.

> **TIP** *The properties listed in the Properties window can be grouped by category or listed alphabetically. When you know the name of the property, sometimes it's easier to list the properties in alphabetical order using the sorting toolbar button for the docked window.*

3. Use the drop-down list to select <Expression...> to open the Expression Builder window.

4. Assemble the following expression, either by hand or using the Expression Builder tools:

```
=Fields!MonthName.Value & ", " & Fields!Year.Value & " Sales Amount: " &
    FORMAT(SUM(Fields!SalesAmount.Value), "C2")
```

5. Click OK to close the Expression window.

6. Change the Chart Title text to **Sales Order Volume by Month.**

7. Select and drag the legend, containing the Sales Amount field, to the top and center of the chart.

8. Save your work.

9. Preview the report.

10. Hover the mouse pointer over a column to view the tooltip, as shown in Figure 8-20.

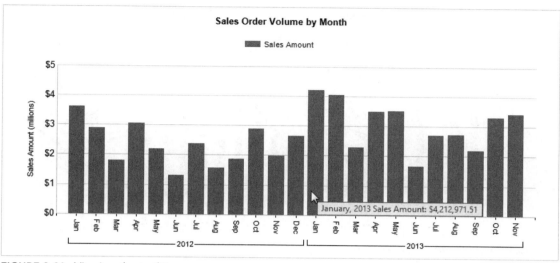

FIGURE 8-20: Viewing the tooltip.

Exercise 2: Creating a Multi-series Chart

Charts can be used to visualize multiple values with different axes and scales. In the following exercise, you will design a chart report with two different series axes that align to a common category axis. One series will show sales currency values on one scale, and the other series will show order quantity values on a different scale within the same chart area. You will also use different chart types to visually separate the two series.

1. Make a copy of the `Sales Order Volume by Month` chart report you completed in the previous exercise and name it `Sales Order Volume and Quantity by Month`.

    > **TIP** *You should remember that the easiest way to make a duplicate copy of a report in the SSDT for Visual Studio designer is to select the report in Solution Explorer and then use Ctrl+C and Ctrl+V. The duplicated report filename will be prefixed with "Copy Of...."*

2. Name the report `Sales and Order Quantity by Month`.
3. Preview the report (see Figure 8-21).

FIGURE 8-21: Previewing the report.

A new chart series is added using a field expression with the Sum function. By default, the new series is added to the primary axis, which means that SalesAmount and OrderQuantity are being measured on the same scale. Because the OrderQuantity values are significantly smaller than the SalesAmount currency values, those columns are barely visible. The left axis values are an irrelevant scale for the OrderQuantity. This should be rectified.

1. In Design view, click any gold OrderQuantity series.

2. Right-click the OrderQuantity series again, choose Change Chart Type..., and change the chart type to a line chart. In the Select Chart Type dialog, select the first chart option under the Line category.

3. Right-click and choose Series Properties....

4. In the Series Properties dialog, Axis and Chart Area page, change the "Vertical axis" to Secondary, as shown in Figure 8-22.

5. On the Border page, change the Line width to 3pt.

6. Click OK to close the dialog and save the properties.

7. Change the Axis Title for the secondary axis, on the right, to **Order Quantity**.

8. Right-click the secondary axis scale and select Secondary Vertical Axis Properties....

9. Style the axis by setting the series border width, series axis number formats, and axis titles so that it is similar to the primary axis. Instead of formatting as Currency, the number format should be a whole, non-currency number without decimals.

10. When completed, click OK to close the Secondary Vertical Axis Properties dialog.

11. Preview the report, as shown in Figure 8-23.

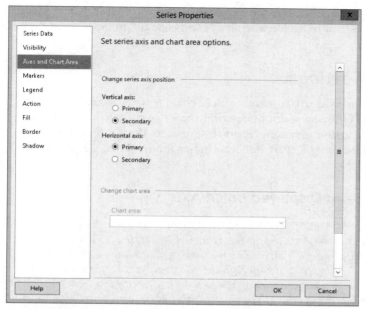

FIGURE 8-22: Changing the "Vertical axis" to Secondary.

FIGURE 8-23: Previewing the revised report.

These two exercises cover the essentials. A number of minor adjustments could improve the presentation. I find that chart and visual design is always a balance of time and priorities. If this chart will be used by a large audience to make important decisions, you may want to do a little more visual tweaking, but in the end, it is important to decide when it's "good enough" to move on to the next design task.

Useful Properties and Settings

Hundreds of chart design variations exist. After many years of chart report design, I have some favorite features and settings. The following sections describe a few I've collected. For a comprehensive guide to chart styles and updated advanced report tips, refer to *Microsoft SQL Server Reporting Services Recipes: for Designing Expert Reports* (Indianapolis: Wrox, 2010) and the authors' respective blog sites.

Controlling the Number of Items Displayed on an Axis

> **TIP** *The easiest way to select the Axis properties is to right-click the axis scale for the chart with the report in design view. The right-click menu will display the option to edit properties for the selected object (like "Vertical Axis Properties..." or "Horizontal Axis Properties..."). The displayed menu will verify that you've selected the correct object. For example, the axis title, axis scale, and chart area are in the same proximity so it is easy to choose one next to the other. If you select the wrong object, just right-click and try again.*

Open Vertical Axis Properties or Horizontal Axis Properties.

Interval property – 1 means to display every value, regardless of whether the text fits when rendering the axis labels.

Managing Axis Text Placement and Rotation

Open Vertical Axis Properties or Horizontal Axis Properties ⇨ Labels group/page.

Disable auto-fit and set the rotation angle. Try 45, or experiment with other values.

Managing the Format of Axis Values

Open Vertical Axis Properties or Horizontal Axis Properties ⇨ Number group/page.

Choose a format option or use a custom format string such as `#,##0` or `$#,##0.00`.

Changing the Color and Width of a Series Line

In a line chart, click a series line or series value in the Chart Data window. Change the `Color` and `BorderWidth` properties.

Setting a Tooltip for a Chart Value

In the chart designer, click a series value or the item in the Chart Data window Values pane.

Set the `ToolTip` property using an expression.

Using the Expression Builder, reference fields and concatenate a string value with formatted text and carriage return characters, as shown in the following example:

```
=Fields!FirstName.Value & " " Fields!LastName.Value & vbCrLf & "Income: "
& Format(Fields!Income.Value, "$#,##0")
```

Controlling the Width and Gap Between Columns or Bars

In the chart designer, click a series value or the item in the Chart Data window Values pane. In the properties for the chart series, select CustomAttributes ➪ PointWidth.

A value of 1 fills the gap between columns or bars. Less leaves a space, and more causes overlap.

Controlling the Exact Position of Each Chart Area (for a Chart with Multiple Chart Areas)

Chart area size and position are managed automatically by default. To override this behavior, edit the chart area properties. Set the CustomPosition ➪ Enabled property to True, and then set the Height, Width, Left, and Top properties. To control the placement of the chart area plotted content, repeat these steps for the CustomInnerPlotPosition properties group.

Dynamically Increasing a Chart's Size

Edit the Chart properties.

Set the DynamicWidth property to expand the size of a column, area, or line chart. Use an expression to increase the width based on the number of records or distinct group values, as shown in the following example:

```
=(1 + COUNT(Fields!Country.Value, "Chart1")) & " in"
```

SUMMARY

With new product versions, the charting capabilities in Reporting Services have improved over the years. New chart types provide different options to visualize business data for information workers. Advanced charts provide the additional capability to deliver actionable information, including compelling new features such as multi-series charts and chart areas.

The chart design skills you've learned in this chapter can be extended to specialized chart types and more advanced styles of chart reports based on the same properties and capabilities. Most of the additional properties you'll find in the designer are used to manage the aesthetic qualities of charts, which you can use to customize the style and fine-tune your chart reports.

In the next chapter we transition from the essentials to advanced design concepts. Chapter 9 introduces techniques used to implement complex query logic, grouping, and filtering using single and multi-value selection parameters.

Advanced Queries and Parameters

WHAT'S IN THIS CHAPTER?

➤ Understanding T-SQL queries and parameters

➤ Understanding MDX queries, parameters, and expressions

➤ Understanding DAX queries, parameters, and expressions

➤ Managing report parameters

➤ Using parameter expressions

Chapter 5, "Database Query Basics," introduced you to query and report parameters. This chapter introduces you to a few simple techniques to parameterize queries. The discussion in this chapter steps through the design of each sample report, and then delves deeper into less-common and more advanced design patterns.

The parameter architecture in Reporting Services has remained the same since the product's inception. But recent enhancements in SQL Server 2016 give you control of the parameter placement in the parameter bar displayed at the top of the browser. In this chapter, you see how to define specialized parameter items you can use to return all (or a range of) dataset records with a single parameter selection. Many of the same techniques can be used with MDX queries for SQL Server Analysis Services (SSAS). However, you will need an understanding of the unique needs and capabilities of the MDX language and query objects.

> **NOTE** *Unlike in previous chapters, this chapter does not walk you through every step of the included exercises, but provides the necessary instructions to apply the skills you have acquired in the previous chapters.*

T-SQL QUERIES AND PARAMETERS

As the native query language of Microsoft SQL Server, Transact-SQL (T-SQL) provides a great deal of flexibility and many creative ways to dynamically filter datasets with parameters. Out of the box, you get several sample reports and instructions to demonstrate different parameter techniques (such as using parameter lists, simple and multi-select parameters, inter-dependent cascading parameters, and so on).

Parameter Lists and Multi-select

The Ch09 - Parameter In List report has two datasets: one to populate a parameter list, and one for the main report query.

The ProductList dataset uses the following query:

```
SELECT
        ProductKey, ProductName
FROM Product
ORDER BY
        ProductName
;
```

Another dataset, named ReportDate, uses the following query:

```
SELECT
        s.OrderDate,
        s.SalesOrderNumber,
        p.ProductCategory,
        p.ProductSubcategory,
        p.ProductName,
        p.ProductKey,
        p.StandardCost,
        p.ListPrice,
        s.OrderQuantity,
        s.SalesAmount
FROM
        vSales2013 s
        inner join dbo.Product p on s.ProductKey = p.ProductKey
WHERE
        p.ProductKey IN ( @ProductKeys )
;
```

When this query is executed in the designer, the ProductKeys parameter is added to the report, and a corresponding dataset parameter is created. These two objects have the same name, so they can be easily confused, but it is important to understand the difference. Starting with the dataset, let's work from the inside out. Figure 9-1 shows the Parameters page of the Dataset Properties dialog where the report parameter, ProductKeys, is mapped to the dataset parameter having the same name.

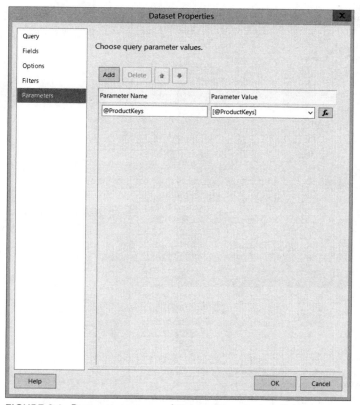

FIGURE 9-1: Parameters page of Dataset Properties dialog.

Inspect the report parameter in the Report Data window and note the following properties (as shown in Figure 9-2):

➤ **The "Data type" should be set to Integer instead of the default Text**—Setting "Data type" to match the filtered field can be more efficient. Certain data types (such as Date and Boolean) change the input control displayed in the parameter bar. Date-type parameters use a calendar picker control, and Boolean-type parameters display a pair of radio buttons to facilitate selecting either True or False values. All other types use a plain input box, unless values are provided in the Available Values page. In that case, a drop-down list is displayed.

➤ **"Allow multiple values" is checked**—The drop-down list (which contains parameter values for selection) shows a check box before each item. This causes a comma-separated list of the selected values to be sent to the query parameter and converted to a single text string. A *multi-select report parameter* is an array of key/value pairs named Value and Label.

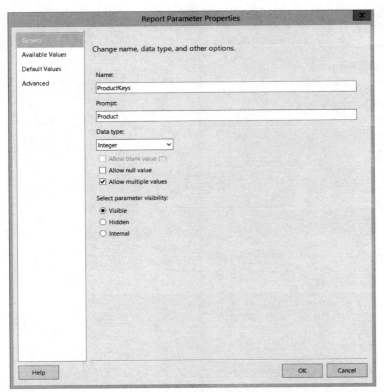

FIGURE 9-2: Report Parameter Properties page of the Report Data window.

On the Available Values page shown in Figure 9-3, you can use the ProductList dataset to provide the product values based on the query. The "Value field" property is set to use the ProductKey and the "Label field" property will use the ProductName. This means that report users will see the names, but key values will be used internally.

You can select any combination of parameter values.

How do you show users what parameter values they selected in the report header? When a report is printed as shown in Figure 9-4, it may be important to capture the parameter selection so that the readers understand the context of the report.

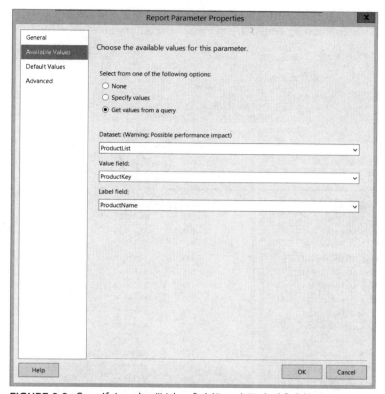

FIGURE 9-3: Specifying the "Value field" and "Label field" properties.

Before looking at the finished expression, here is an experiment for educational purposes. Add a new textbox to the report header area above the table. Right-click and choose Expression... to open the Expression builder dialog. Use the parameter list and double-click the ProductKeys parameter, which creates the following expression:

```
=Parameters!ProductKeys.Value(0)
```

There are two problems with this expression. It will display the numeric product key (rather than the product name) in the textbox, and it will only display the first selected item. To correct this, you use the "Label field" property instead of the "Value field" property. A multi-value parameter is stored as an array, so you can't just display it as a single value. The VB.NET JOIN function will iterate through each array element, and represent the key/value pairs for each selected item. Here's the working expression to display a comma-separated list of every selected parameter value:

```
=JOIN(Parameters!ProductKeys.Label, ", ")
```

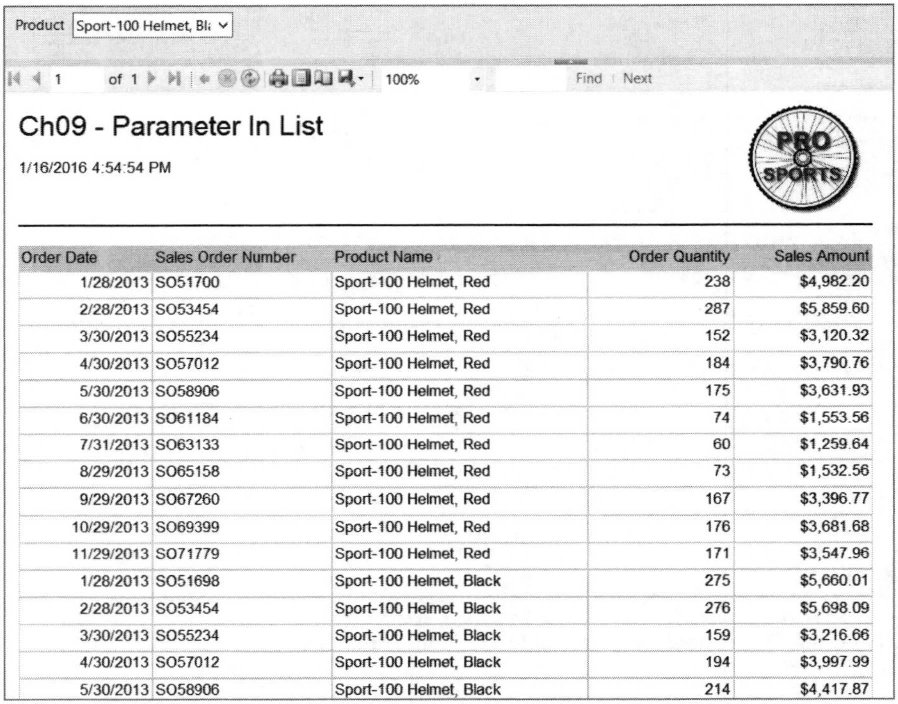

Order Date	Sales Order Number	Product Name	Order Quantity	Sales Amount
1/28/2013	SO51700	Sport-100 Helmet, Red	238	$4,982.20
2/28/2013	SO53454	Sport-100 Helmet, Red	287	$5,859.60
3/30/2013	SO55234	Sport-100 Helmet, Red	152	$3,120.32
4/30/2013	SO57012	Sport-100 Helmet, Red	184	$3,790.76
5/30/2013	SO58906	Sport-100 Helmet, Red	175	$3,631.93
6/30/2013	SO61184	Sport-100 Helmet, Red	74	$1,553.56
7/31/2013	SO63133	Sport-100 Helmet, Red	60	$1,259.64
8/29/2013	SO65158	Sport-100 Helmet, Red	73	$1,532.56
9/29/2013	SO67260	Sport-100 Helmet, Red	167	$3,396.77
10/29/2013	SO69399	Sport-100 Helmet, Red	176	$3,681.68
11/29/2013	SO71779	Sport-100 Helmet, Red	171	$3,547.96
1/28/2013	SO51698	Sport-100 Helmet, Black	275	$5,660.01
2/28/2013	SO53454	Sport-100 Helmet, Black	276	$5,698.09
3/30/2013	SO55234	Sport-100 Helmet, Black	159	$3,216.66
4/30/2013	SO57012	Sport-100 Helmet, Black	194	$3,997.99
5/30/2013	SO58906	Sport-100 Helmet, Black	214	$4,417.87

FIGURE 9-4: Clarifying the context in the printed report.

Figure 9-5 shows the finished report with the parameter list in the heading.

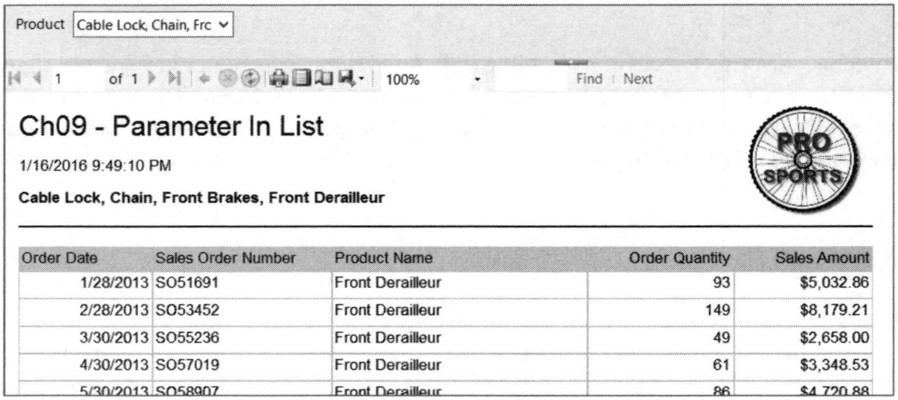

Order Date	Sales Order Number	Product Name	Order Quantity	Sales Amount
1/28/2013	SO51691	Front Derailleur	93	$5,032.86
2/28/2013	SO53452	Front Derailleur	149	$8,179.21
3/30/2013	SO55236	Front Derailleur	49	$2,658.00
4/30/2013	SO57019	Front Derailleur	61	$3,348.53
5/30/2013	SO58907	Front Derailleur	86	$4,720.88

FIGURE 9-5: Finished report with the parameter list in the heading.

Cascading Parameters

In the previous example, the parameter list is a little long and inconvenient. With so many values to choose from, multiple parameters can be used to break a list down into a manageable hierarchy. A parameter can depend on another parameter so that the list of available values is filtered based on another parameter selection. For example, if you offer users a list of product categories and another list of product subcategories, the subcategory list would show only subcategories for a selected category. Figure 9-6 shows an example. A selection from the Categories parameter filters the product subcategories, and that selection filters the products list.

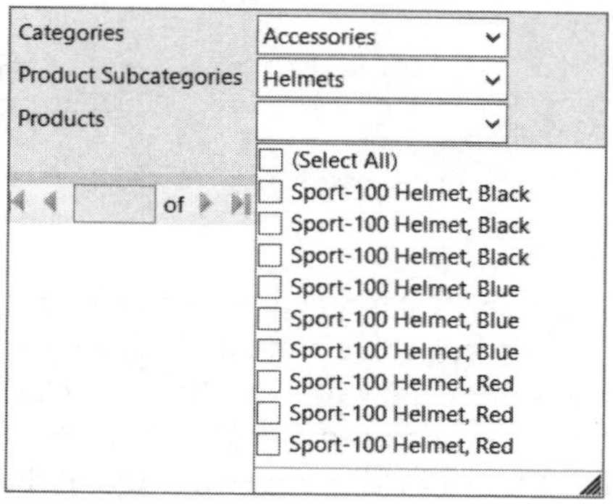

FIGURE 9-6: Filtering product subcategories.

The sample report Ch09 - Cascading Parameters shows how to build this. You start with three separate datasets that are used to populate the parameter lists. Dataset names are listed before query. Note the logical dependencies between each query in order.

➤ CategoryList:

```
SELECT DISTINCT ProductCategory
FROM Product
;
```

➤ SubcategoryList:

```
SELECT DISTINCT ProductSubcategory
FROM Product
WHERE ProductCategory IN ( @Categories )
;
```

➤ ProductList:

```
SELECT ProductKey, ProductName
FROM Product
WHERE ProductSubcategory IN ( @ProductSubcategories )
;
```

The main report dataset (named ReportData in the sample report) uses only the ProductKeys parameter as a predicate to filter sales records.

```
SELECT
    s.OrderDate,
    s.SalesOrderNumber,
    p.ProductCategory,
    p.ProductSubcategory,
    p.ProductName,
    p.ProductKey,
    p.StandardCost,
    p.ListPrice,
```

```
        s.OrderQuantity,
        s.SalesAmount
FROM
        vSales2013 s
        inner join dbo.Product p on s.ProductKey = p.ProductKey
WHERE
        p.ProductKey IN ( @ProductKeys )
    ;
```

Recall from the previous example that the `ProductKeys` parameter used two different fields for the product key value and label. Conversely, for the `Category` and `Product` subcategory parameters, it is unnecessary to have different fields. Figure 9-7 shows the Available Values settings for the `Categories` parameter where the `ProductCategory` field is used for both the "Value field" and "Label field" properties. Using the name rather than a key value to filter from a parameter typically works, as long as the values are unique and it is a relatively short list.

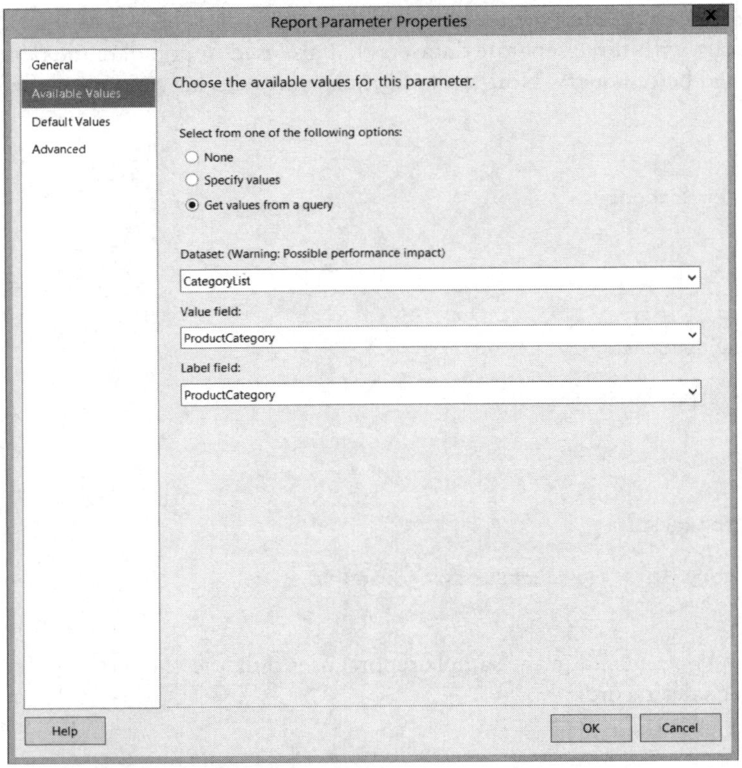

FIGURE 9-7: Available Values settings.

The `ProductSubcategory` parameter settings are similar to the `Category`, with the `ProductCategory` field used for the "Field value" and "Label value" properties. The `ProductKeys` parameter is essentially the same as it was in the previous report example, with the `ProductKey` used for the "Value field" and the `ProductName` for the "Label field." Cascading parameters must be arranged in order of dependency, which, in this case, is `Category`, `Product Subcategory`, and `Product`. Use the up and down arrows in the Report Data toolbar header to change the order if necessary.

Arranging Parameters in the Parameter Bar

SQL Server 2016 introduces a new report design feature that provides control over the placement of report parameters in the parameter bar displayed above a rendered report. Note that the parameter bar is displayed for reports in a report server configured for native mode.

> **NOTE** *In SharePoint integrated mode, parameters continue to be arranged vertically in a panel on the right side of the browser window.*

The parameter bar is customizable. As shown in Figure 9-8, use the right-click menu to add and remove columns and rows to and from the grid, and then drag and drop the parameters into any cell. Right-click and remove unneeded rows and columns.

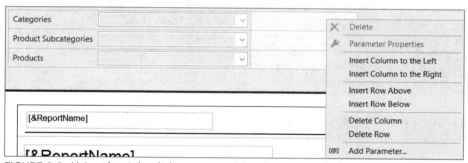

FIGURE 9-8: Using the right-click menu to add and remove columns and rows.

Managing Long Parameter Lists

Multi-select parameters typically work well when the user will select a manageable number of parameter items. There is no stated limit either to the number of items that can be included in a parameter list, or to the number of items that can be selected. The only control that you really have is to limit the items you display in the list. Both the number of values on this list and the number of selected items can affect report performance.

The sample database returns 397 products, which are included in the parameter list shown in Figure 9-9. Any more than this and you would see a noticeably longer report rendering time. Even more impactful is the effect of selecting many values and passing them into the query for filtering.

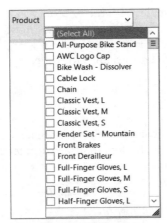

FIGURE 9-9: Products in parameter list.

Multi-select parameters always display a "(Select All)" item at the top of the list. Choosing this item checks the boxes for every item in the list, and unchecking it deselects all of the listed items.

> **WARNING** *Long parameter lists can affect report performance. Multi-select parameters include an item at the top of the list labeled "(Select All)." Choosing this item selects every item on the parameter list and passes all of those values into the report query. You cannot disable this feature, nor limit the number of items selected. You should limit parameter lists to a few hundred items.*

Consider what happens if the "(Select All)" option were used in this sample report. The following query is executed after the parameter values are parsed, which explicitly includes every available ProductKey:

```
SELECT
     s.OrderDate,
     s.SalesOrderNumber,
     p.ProductCategory,
     p.ProductSubcategory,
     p.ProductName,
     p.ProductKey,
     s.OrderQuantity,
     s.SalesAmount
FROM
     vSales2013 s
     inner join dbo.Product p on s.ProductKey = p.ProductKey
WHERE
```

```
p.ProductKey IN ( 486,223,224,225,484,447,559,473,472,471,
485,555,552,470,469,468,466,467,464,465,462,463,451,452,
483,603,558,393,396,304,305,306,296,297,298,299,301,302,
303,300,307,308,309,288,289,290,291,293,294,295,292,412,
401,402,544,421,517,537,439,440,441,442,443,444,210,437,
438,241,242,243,244,245,246,247,248,249,250,251,252,211,
238,239,240,415,407,408,547,424,520,540,497,498,499,500,
494,495,496,492,554,523,487,601,556,391,394,550,531,532,
533,534,551,524,525,526,527,410,397,398,542,419,515,535,
279,280,281,282,283,284,285,286,287,253,254,255,256,257,
258,259,260,261,262,263,264,265,266,267,268,269,270,271,
272,273,413,403,404,545,422,518,538,510,502,503,504,505,
506,507,508,509,493,553,521,232,233,234,229,230,231,226,
227,228,235,236,237,461,460,459,454,453,445,455,448,602,
557,392,395,409,426,427,428,549,511,512,513,411,399,400,
543,420,516,536,274,275,276,277,278,417,418,429,430,431,
432,433,434,435,436,414,405,406,546,423,519,539,522,219,
218,478,449,528,348,349,350,351,344,345,346,347,358,359,
360,361,362,363,352,353,354,355,356,357,364,365,366,367,
587,588,589,590,596,597,598,599,600,591,592,593,594,595,
480,482,481,514,501,479,529,311,312,313,314,310,373,374,
375,376,377,378,379,380,368,369,370,371,372,580,581,582,
583,317,318,319,315,316,381,382,383,384,385,386,387,388,
389,390,338,339,340,341,342,343,332,333,334,335,336,337,
326,327,328,329,330,331,320,321,322,323,324,325,604,605,
606,584,490,489,488,491,215,216,217,220,221,222,212,213,
214,450,416,548,425,541,530,573,574,575,576,561,562,563,
564,577,578,579,560,585,586,565,566,567,568,569,570,571,
572,446,477,476,475,474,458,457,456 )
;
```

This query was tested with and without the FROM clause, which revealed a return of the same set of results. Surprisingly, the difference in performance is negligible, and the verbose query takes only milliseconds longer. Perhaps if you use twice the number of product keys, a larger data volume, or you are running on a production server with other competing operations, you might see a greater impact. The point is that, under certain conditions, queries like this play a role in causing performance issues. So you should take steps to manage them. Using cascading parameters can help, because the user wouldn't be able to select every product at once. The following technique may also be helpful.

All Value Selection

Rather than allowing users to select all of the parameter items if they don't want to exclude any data, adding a custom item to the list can help you manage the query logic with more efficiency. In the next scenario demonstrated in the sample report Ch09 - All Parameter Selection 1, the goal is to provide users with the option either to select a single country or to return results for all countries. Figure 9-10 shows the parameter list showing an item labeled "(All Countries)."

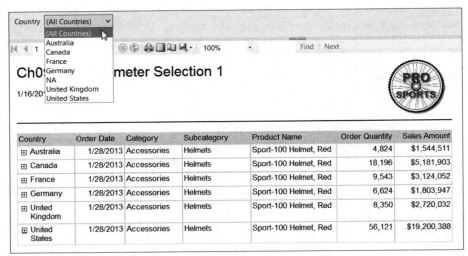

FIGURE 9-10: Using "(All Countries)" to provide users with an option.

The query for my `CountryList` dataset looks like the following. Note that this is actually two `SELECT` statements.

```
SELECT
    '(All Countries)' AS Country
UNION
SELECT DISTINCT
    Country
FROM SalesTerritory
;
```

In T-SQL, two queries that return the same set of columns can be appended using the `UNION` statement. This adds the "(All Countries)" row to the top of the list ahead of the country names from the `SalesTerritory` table.

The magic happens here in the following main report query where a logical decision is performed in the `WHERE` clause:

```
SELECT
    s.OrderDate,
    s.SalesOrderNumber,
    p.ProductCategory,
    p.ProductSubcategory,
    p.ProductName,
    p.ProductKey,
    p.StandardCost,
    p.ListPrice,
    s.OrderQuantity,
    s.SalesAmount
FROM
    vSales2013 s
```

```
        inner join dbo.Product p on s.ProductKey = p.ProductKey
        inner join dbo.SalesTerritory t on s.SalesTerritoryKey = t.TerritoryKey
    WHERE
        t.Country = @Country OR @Country = '(All Countries)'
    ;
```

Using an OR operator, one of two conditions must be met for a given row to be output in this query. Starting on the left side of the OR, the Country column value must match the selected @Country parameter value. If this branch is used, only orders for the selected country would be output. But what about the expression on the right side of the OR operator? That statement says, if the selected @Country parameter value is "(All Countries)," let every row through. The OR operator trumps the other statement and just returns everything.

Here's one more example, which is very similar to the first, but uses a numeric key rather than text. In this scenario, the parameter displays the sales country and region values concatenated together for the "Label field" (Figure 9-11) and returns the TerritoryKey for the "Value field."

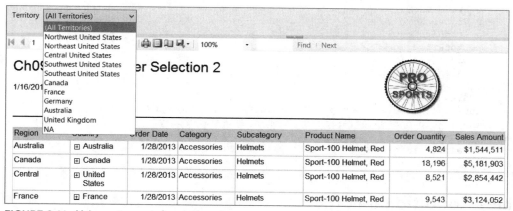

FIGURE 9-11: Using a numeric key rather than text.

The design of the Ch09 - All Parameter Selection 2 sample report uses a slightly different approach.

As shown here, like the previous example, the TerritoryList dataset has an extra row generated using -1 for the TerritoryKey and the text (All Territories). This row is appended to all of the table values in the query using the UNION operator.

```
SELECT
    -1 AS TerritoryKey,
    '(All Territories)' AS TerritoryName
UNION
SELECT
    TerritoryKey,
    CASE WHEN Country = Region THEN Region ELSE Region + ' ' + Country
        END AS TerritoryName
FROM SalesTerritory
;
```

> **TIP** *When adding special-purpose items to a parameter list query, using a negative number for the key can ensure that it doesn't duplicate the key value for an actual record.*

Here is the main report query, which uses an expression on the WHERE clause to test the TerritoryKey query parameter. If the value is -1, this indicates that the user selected the "(All Territories)" item. In this case, the OR operator effectively disregards the first filter clause and returns all rows.

```
SELECT
        s.OrderDate,
        s.SalesOrderNumber,
        p.ProductCategory,
        p.ProductSubcategory,
        p.ProductName,
        p.ProductKey,
        p.StandardCost,
        p.ListPrice,
        s.OrderQuantity,
        s.SalesAmount
FROM
        vSales2013 s
        inner join dbo.Product p on s.ProductKey = p.ProductKey
        inner join dbo.SalesTerritory t on s.SalesTerritoryKey = t.TerritoryKey
WHERE
        s.SalesTerritoryKey = @TerritoryKey OR @TerritoryKey = -1
    ;
```

Handling Conditional Logic

Once you have mastered these essential parameter techniques, you can combine them to address real business reporting challenges. The example report Ch09 - And Or Parameter Logic contains three parameters named MonthNumber, DateFrom, and DateTo. If an actual month value is selected for the MonthNumber, all records for that month should be returned, and the date range for the other two parameters should be ignored. Similar to previous examples, a special item is added to the MonthNumber parameter list, prompting the report user to use the date range parameters DateFrom and DateTo. The query for the MonthList dataset looks like this:

```
SELECT    - 1 AS MonthNumber, '(Select Date Range)' AS MonthName
UNION
SELECT DISTINCT MonthNumber, MonthName
```

```
FROM Date
ORDER BY MonthNumber
;
```

The WHERE clause in the main report query contains two branches of logic with an OR operator.

> **TIP** *When implementing conditional logic in a query with multiple logical operators, keep in mind that the predicate (WHERE clause) is evaluated for each candidate row. That row will be returned if the predicate expression evaluates to* True.

The first condition uses parentheses to control the order of operations. As you can see, if the MonthNumber parameter value is -1 (indicating that the user selected the option to select a date range), rows are returned that meet the date range criteria. If any other MonthNumber is selected, the second branch of the expression (after OR) is implemented, and the first branch is ignored because it logically resolves to False.

```
SELECT
     s.OrderDate,
     s.SalesOrderNumber,
     SUM(s.SalesAmount) AS SalesAmount,
     SUM(s.OrderQuantity) AS OrderQuantity
FROM
     vSales2013 s inner join Date d on s.OrderDate = d.TheDate
WHERE
     (@MonthNumber = -1 AND s.OrderDate BETWEEN @DateFrom AND @DateTo)
     OR
     d.MonthNumber = @MonthNumber
GROUP BY
     s.OrderDate,
     s.SalesOrderNumber
;
```

The MonthNumber parameter data type is set to Integer, to match the type of the MonthNumber column. Using the MonthList dataset for the Available Values property causes the parameter to be presented as a drop-down list. For the DateFrom and DateTo parameters, setting these to a Date data type prompts the report user with date picker controls. Users can either type or select dates.

All three parameters are arranged in the designer parameter bar grid, as you can see in Figure 9-12.

When the report is previewed, you can see in Figure 9-13 that when the month of July is selected, only July records are returned, regardless of the data range.

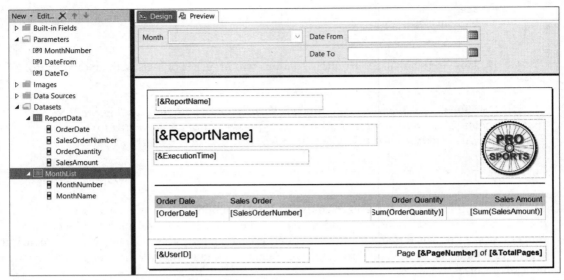

FIGURE 9-12: Designer parameter bar grid arrangement.

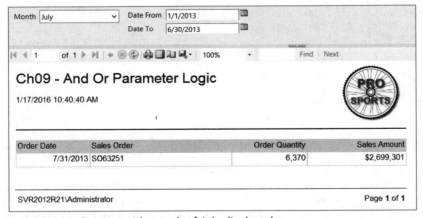

FIGURE 9-13: Preview with month of July displayed.

MDX QUERIES AND PARAMETERS

Chapter 10, "Reporting with Analysis Services," provides an end-to-end examination of report design using SSAS as a data source. If you're new to SSAS, that chapter will help you build a foundation for working with Analysis Services and Reporting Services together, and how parameters are used to pass member key values.

Once you have done a lot of report design work for SSAS cubes and tabular models, you will grow accustomed to the quirks and unique patterns of the query design when working with MDX queries (which are discussed in more detail in Chapter 10). Using the graphical query builder to create SSAS queries will do a lot of the following work for you, but it also has severe limitations and doesn't produce ideal and manageable code in many situations. For the discussion in this chapter, you should review the provided sample reports to view the following solutions. To build them yourself, jump ahead to Chapter 10 to get the lowdown on manually writing MDX queries.

Let's start with a baseline query. You should use SQL Server Management Studio (SSMS) to write and test MDX queries.

```
SELECT
    {
        [Reseller Sales Amount],
        [Measures].[Internet Sales Amount]
    } ON Columns,
    (
        [Product].[Category].Members,
        [Sales Territory].[Sales Territory Country].Members
    ) ON Rows
FROM [Adventure Works]
WHERE
    (
        [Date].[Calendar Year].&[2013]
    )
;
```

The results of this query are visualized in a matrix report, as shown in Figure 9-14. Two variations of the Ch09 SSAS Parameters report are included in the sample reports project.

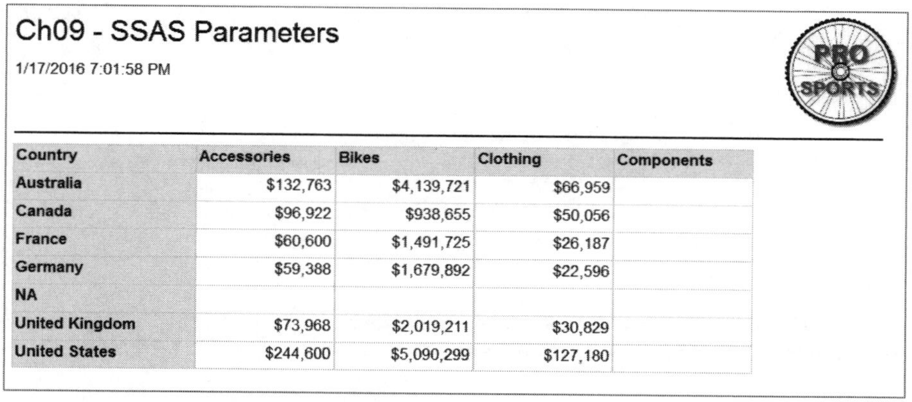

Ch09 - SSAS Parameters

1/17/2016 7:01:58 PM

Country	Accessories	Bikes	Clothing	Components
Australia	$132,763	$4,139,721	$66,959	
Canada	$96,922	$938,655	$50,056	
France	$60,600	$1,491,725	$26,187	
Germany	$59,388	$1,679,892	$22,596	
NA				
United Kingdom	$73,968	$2,019,211	$30,829	
United States	$244,600	$5,090,299	$127,180	

FIGURE 9-14: Matrix report showing results of MDX query.

Beginning with a simple, single-select parameter, the year used in the WHERE clause can be dynamically replaced in one of two different ways. The most conventional method for parameterizing this query is to build a simple parameter list dataset like this one:

```
WITH
MEMBER Measures.YearUniqueName    AS [Date].[Calendar Year].CurrentMember.UniqueName
MEMBER Measures.YearLabel         AS [Date].[Calendar Year].CurrentMember.Name

SELECT
    { Measures.YearUniqueName, Measures.YearLabel } On Columns,
    [Date].[Calendar Year].Members On Rows
FROM [Adventure Works]
;
```

In the properties for the `Year` parameter, the `YearList` dataset provides the available values. `YearUniqueName` is mapped to the "Value field" property and `YearLabel` is mapped to the "Label field," as shown in Figure 9-15.

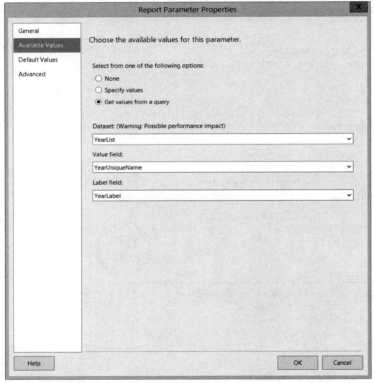

FIGURE 9-15: Mapping to the "Value field" and "Label field".

Rather than using integer values as parameter keys as is done in a typical SQL query, Analysis Services uses a full qualified unique name reference for each key value, similar to those shown in the `YearUniqueName` column in Figure 9-16. Note that this query returns the `All` member (in this case named "All Periods") in addition to a row for each year.

	YearUniqueName	YearLabel
All Periods	[Date].[Calendar Year].[All Periods]	All Periods
CY 2005	[Date].[Calendar Year].&[2005]	CY 2005
CY 2006	[Date].[Calendar Year].&[2006]	CY 2006
CY 2007	[Date].[Calendar Year].&[2007]	CY 2007
CY 2008	[Date].[Calendar Year].&[2008]	CY 2008
CY 2009	[Date].[Calendar Year].&[2009]	CY 2009
CY 2010	[Date].[Calendar Year].&[2010]	CY 2010
CY 2011	[Date].[Calendar Year].&[2011]	CY 2011
CY 2012	[Date].[Calendar Year].&[2012]	CY 2012
CY 2013	[Date].[Calendar Year].&[2013]	CY 2013
CY 2014	[Date].[Calendar Year].&[2014]	CY 2014

FIGURE 9-16: Using a full-qualified unique name reference for each key value.

In the SSMS, values can be copied from a cell or range of cells in the results pane. As shown in Figure 9-17, the unique name value for the All Periods member has been selected and copied to the clipboard to set the parameter default value.

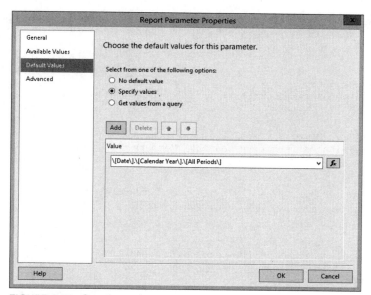

FIGURE 9-17: Copying values.

The Default value is set by pasting the unique name copied from earlier results.

```
[Date].[Calendar Year].[All Periods]
```

When you return to this page, you will see something interesting. In the report definition, this property is stored in a format that requires certain characters to be "escaped" with backslashes that are automatically inserted before each square bracket (as shown in the following example). Don't be concerned about this because it's just a convention that the report designer takes care of for you.

```
\[Date\].\[Calendar Year\].\[All Periods\]
```

Parameter values are always passed into the query as text values. These values must be converted using one of the following MDX functions, depending on the object type, so Analysis Services sees it as the right type of object:

```
STRTOMEMBER
STRTOSET
STRTOTUPLE
STRTOVALUE
```

The first two functions are most commonly used and will handle most parameter needs. The STRTOMEMBER function resolves a text member reference to a single member object, and the STRTOSET function resolves any valid text expression to a set of members.

Single-Valued Parameter

In the query used in the following example, the year is a member, so the parameter is passed to the STRTOMEMBER function like this:

```
SELECT
    {
        [Reseller Sales Amount],
        [Measures].[Internet Sales Amount]
    } ON Columns,
    (
        [Product].[Category].Members,
        [Sales Territory].[Sales Territory Country].Members
    ) ON Rows
FROM [Adventure Works]
WHERE
    (
        STRTOMEMBER( @Year )
    )
;
```

Multi-Valued Parameter

Modifying this solution for multi-valued parameter selection requires only two simple changes. First is to check the "Allow multiple values" option to convert to a multi-valued parameter. The second change is to use the STRTOSET function like this:

```
SELECT
    {
        [Reseller Sales Amount],
        [Measures].[Internet Sales Amount]
    } ON Columns,
    (
        [Product].[Category].Members,
```

```
                [Sales Territory].[Sales Territory Country].Members
        ) ON Rows
FROM [Adventure Works]
WHERE
        (
                STRTOSET( @Year )
        )
;
```

Now, users can select any combination items from the parameter list, causing a comma-separated set of unique name references to be passed into the query. The STRTOSET function parses the list and converts it into a set object, which is used to slice the cube and effectively filter the results.

Date Value Ranges

There are cases where it might make more sense to handle the parameter value using the native data type or otherwise collect a simple value rather than the MDX-style unique member name. A date type parameter is a good example because it is more natural to prompt the user for a date with the date picker calendar control. Because MDX parameters are handled as text and member references, an expression is used to translate the report parameter into the correctly formatted report parameter.

Again, you start with a finished query in SSMS. Note the range notation used to create a set of date members in the WHERE clause.

```
SELECT
        {
                [Reseller Sales Amount],
                [Measures].[Reseller Order Count]
        } ON Columns,
        (
                [Product].[Category].Members,
                [Sales Territory].[Sales Territory Country].Members
        ) ON Rows
FROM [Adventure Works]
WHERE
        (
                { [Date].[Date].&[20130101] : [Date].[Date].&[20130131] }
        )
;
```

There are actually a couple of different techniques that can be used to employ this solution. Two are demonstrated here. Neither is better than the other, but learning how this works will give you a better understanding of the mechanics of the query engine and how parameters work.

Range of Members

Two report parameters are added, named DateFrom and DateTo, exactly the same as were used in previous examples. Both parameters are date types and given a valid default value.

In the properties for the dataset, on the Parameters page, define two query parameters with different names than the two existing report parameters. The names can actually be anything you want, and the choices shown in Figure 9-18 merely demonstrate that the report and query parameter names don't have to be the same.

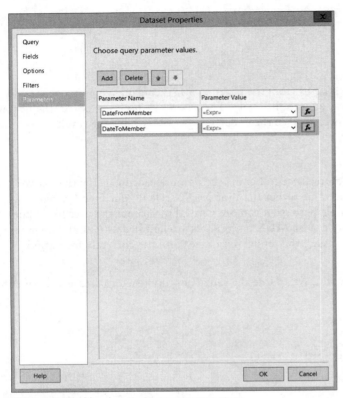

FIGURE 9-18: Naming two query parameters.

The trick here is that the expressions build each of the two member reference values. Because the original expression is copied from the original object reference, the rest is easy to figure out. To create the sample report, follow these steps:

1. Begin the expression with an equal sign as usual.

2. Add a double quote. All MDX parameters are passed as text, so you must concatenate a literal member reference.

3. Paste the entire member reference from the clipboard and add a double quote to the end. This expression would work as it is now so that you know, for troubleshooting purposes, you are at a known state.

4. Delete everything between the last pair of open and closed square brackets. This is where you will add the parameter date. Thus far, the expression should look like this:

```
="[Date].[Date].&[]"
```

5. Close and open the brackets you just orphaned by removing their content (including the double quotes), and then add a couple of ampersands and two spaces to make room for more content. The result should be as follows:

```
="[Date].[Date].&[" &   & "]"
```

6. Place the cursor between the ampersands, with one space on either side, and use the Expression editor to add the parameter contained within the FORMAT function. Because the data must be formatted in a non-standard string, you need to use the FORMAT function to customize the output with a format string to match the Date member key.

7. Use the following two examples to verify that the two query parameter expressions are correct for the DateFrom and DateTo parameters, respectively.

➤ DateToMember parameter:

```
="[Date].[Date].&[" & FORMAT(Parameters!DateFrom.Value, "yyyyMMdd") & "]"
```

➤ DateToMember parameter:

```
="[Date].[Date].&[" & FORMAT(Parameters!DateTo.Value, "yyyyMMdd") & "]"
```

8. Within the query, each of the two parameters is substituted for the member references in the range and wrapped by a STRTOMEMBER function. The resulting query now looks like this:

```
SELECT
    {
        [Reseller Sales Amount],
        [Measures].[Reseller Order Count]
    } ON Columns,
    (
        [Product].[Category].Members,
        [Sales Territory].[Sales Territory Country].Members
    ) ON Rows
FROM [Adventure Works]
WHERE
    (
        { STRTOMEMBER( @DateFromMember ) : STRTOMEMBER( @DateToMember ) }
    )
;
```

Range Expression as a Set

The other technique builds the entire range expression and then passes it to the STRTOSET function as a single query parameter. Because report parameters and query parameters are separate objects, this gives you the freedom to manage this using another approach.

> **TIP** *Before deleting the two existing parameters, copying one of the expressions to the clipboard will save time. While prototyping and working out all the expression code for a report, you should consider using Notepad so that you can keep and reuse expressions until you sort out the ideal solution.*

1. Return to the Parameters page in the Dataset Properties (Figure 9-19) and remove both query parameters.

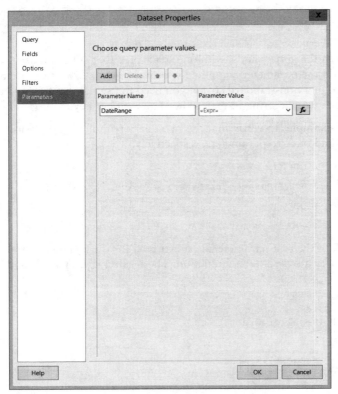

FIGURE 9-19: Dataset Properties page.

2. Copying one of the two expressions to the clipboard first will save some work.

3. Create a new query parameter named `DateRange` and use the following expression for the Parameter Value:

```
="[Date].[Date].&[" & FORMAT(Parameters!DateFrom.Value, "yyyyMMdd")
& "] : [Date].[Date].&[" & FORMAT(Parameters!DateTo.Value, "yyyyMMdd") & "]"
```

4. The revised dataset query uses the `STRTOSET` function with the new parameter.

```
SELECT
    {
        [Reseller Sales Amount],
        [Measures].[Reseller Order Count]
    } ON Columns,
    (
        [Product].[Category].[Category].Members,
        [Sales Territory].[Sales Territory Country].[Sales Territory
            Country].Members
```

```
        ) ON Rows
FROM [Adventure Works]
WHERE
    (
          { STRTOSET( @DateRange ) }
    )
  ;
```

The resulting text of the entire query is exactly the same as the original, non-parameterized query, but the key point is that this MDX expression produces a set object, which is handled by the STRTOSET function:

```
[Date].[Date].&[20130101] : [Date].[Date].&[20130131]
```

SUMMARY

The purpose of this chapter has been to give you a set of survival skills and a collection of useful techniques to add to your bag of standard design techniques. Working with parameters, as well as knowing how to use them in creative ways, will be critical as you prepare to design an entire reporting solution.

This material builds on the design techniques for creating queries acquired in Chapter 5. Looking forward, you will expand on these skills and start thinking about reports as more than a single delivery vehicle for some business information—in particular, as part of a well-orchestrated solution.

In Chapter 10, you will get a well-rounded introduction to all the features used to build an Analysis Services report from the ground up, utilizing some of the parameter-passing techniques used in these past few sections. You will see how parameters are used in expressions to manage visibility, grouping, sorting, and so much more. Parameters are an important element of actions and report navigation.

10

Reporting with Analysis Services

WHAT'S IN THIS CHAPTER?

➤ Using Analysis Services for reporting

➤ Working with Multidimensional Expressions (MDX)

➤ Building queries with the MDX Query Designer

➤ Building queries manually

➤ Adding nonadditional measures

➤ Understanding when to use the Aggregate function

➤ Using MDX and drill-through reports

SQL Server Analysis Services (SSAS) is an industry-leading semantic modeling, calculation, and analytic reporting platform. Today, SSAS comes in two different implementations on the same server platform. The multidimensional version employs optimized storage, data caching, and pre-aggregated calculations to achieve high performance and a rich set of analytical features that have matured over nearly 20 years. To achieve superior performance, SSAS tabular models utilize a modern, streamlined technology that uses in-memory column compression and calculations technology. To a query or data browsing tool, tabular models appear and behave just like multidimensional cubes.

> **NOTE** *Arguably, there are multiple implementations of the tabular in-memory technology employed in SSAS, which also include Power Pivot and Power BI. These expanding choices underscore the versatility of the Microsoft BI platform and this impressive technology.*

Today, both SSAS tabular and multidimensional models can be queried using either of the two languages developed specifically for each of these technologies, namely Data Analysis Expressions (DAX) for tabular, and Multidimensional Expressions (MDX) for multidimensional. Until query design tools are created to better support the DAX query language with parameter passing, MDX will remain the query language of choice for both flavors of SSAS. For the purposes of this discussion, either form of SSAS will be referred to as a semantic data model, or cube. Without getting into the subtleties, from a query and reporting perspective, they are essentially the same. So, from here on, tabular and multidimensional models will be collectively referred to as a cube or online analytical processing (OLAP) database.

Cube data is easy to navigate and it is easy to produce complex, business-relevant results for business leaders and information workers. This chapter introduces some of the basic concepts of OLAP and multidimensional storage systems. You will use the Report Designer to create MDX language queries, both with and without the MDX Graphical Query Builder. You will learn how to build compelling reports using parameters, PivotTables, and KPI indicators in a table or matrix report.

Finally, you will learn to use cube actions and apply best practices and safety checks to your report solutions that use Analysis Services as a data source.

In Chapter 11, "SSAS Reporting Advanced Techniques," you will build on this knowledge to create advanced reports that can change their content (rows, columns, and measures) by simply changing report parameter values.

ANALYSIS SERVICES FOR REPORTING

Relational databases are no longer the only viable choice for managing data for analysis and reporting. True, the vast majority of general-use databases use conventional relational database management system (RDBMS) platforms like SQL Server. Specialized data management systems are faster, easier, and more cost-effective than one product designed to do it all. In this new age of business analytics and data science, self-service analysis tools like Power Pivot and Power BI have proven to be powerful and easier to implement. These tools are based on the same technology as Analysis Services, offering the same advantages of ultra-high-performance and ease-of-use in an enterprise-scale service. After the necessary effort has been expended to build and populate a data warehouse, taking the next step to create a multidimensional or tabular SSAS data model on this data is relatively easy.

Making the leap from the operational data store to a relational data warehouse may be sufficient in a small business with unsophisticated reporting needs. However, for a medium-scale business environment, including Analysis Services in the solution has many advantages. Generally, moving to an SSAS solution enables capabilities in four categories:

> ➤ Data in an SSAS model is "browseable" without your having to write sophisticated queries. Information is organized into dimensional hierarchies so that report designers can simply drag and drop to design report datasets.

➤ Information workers can design their own reports without understanding the underlying data structure. With no query-writing skills, users simply select from predefined measures and hierarchies to create queries and design reports.

➤ Using calculated members, sophisticated calculations are built into the cube. Users and report designers can select from calculated members as easily as they can use standard measures and other cube members.

➤ Queries typically run very fast, even when the data model is derived from large sets of data. The improved performance is primarily because of data being either pre-aggregated or loaded entirely into memory.

The bottom line is that building an SSAS model with Analysis Services is generally easy to do if you have a properly designed relational data warehouse. Navigation is much easier than with a relational database. Cubes enable self-service reporting and effective data exploration. Most importantly, cubes can be faster when compared to other data sources and reporting solutions.

If you work for a small company or in an environment with manageable volumes of data, you will likely find significant advantages. Because Analysis Services is already covered under your SQL Server product license, there is little or no cost to building cubes and realizing these benefits.

If you work for a large company and work with larger volumes of complex business data, you probably do not need much persuasion to recognize the advantages of using cubes to help solve these challenges. Comparatively, making the move to SSAS models will help you take reporting to the next level while solving performance and query design issues.

> **NOTE** *A quick note on dimensional modeling: Keep it simple. The design tools make it easy to add lots of attributes to an Analysis Server cube. As a developer or super-user, you might think you are helping your clients by adding all these attributes. Don't do it. Think carefully about what attributes you want to add, and minimize the number of dimensions. (Ideally, you should use seven to ten.) Keep the overall cube simple and, therefore, easy to use.*

USING REPORTING SERVICES WITH ANALYSIS SERVICES DATA

Reporting Services works natively with several Analysis Services capabilities:

➤ **Native support for nonadditive measures and calculations**—Rather than building sophisticated expressions and calculation logic into reports, Reporting Services lets you take advantage of features already built into the Analysis Services data model.

➤ **Analysis Services and the MDX query language support custom formatting defined for measures in the cube**—Reports may be designed to use this formatting without duplicating this effort in the report design.

➤ **Drill-through reports can work for MDX datasets**—Drill-through reports can be used with some basic knowledge of MDX member reference, formatting, and special field properties present in Reporting Services for MDX reports,

➤ **Data may be protected through user role-based security**—If user credentials are provided to data sources using Windows Authentication, this works without special report provisions.

➤ **Summary reports that would normally aggregate a lot of data run much faster with cubes**— Take advantage of this capability by designing summary reports and dashboards with drill-through actions to lower-level, detailed reports.

Most reports that use Analysis Services as a data source are fairly easy to design for two reasons:

➤ The mission of Analysis Services is to make data easy to use. A properly designed cube simplifies your business data by organizing it into predefined, hierarchical structures with business facts pre-aggregated and ready to use by dragging and dropping into the MDX Query Designer.

➤ The Report Designer is friendly, with an MDX-based dataset. It automatically generates parameter lists, cascading parameters, and filtering logic. In many ways, designing a report for SSAS is easier than for a relational database because of the simplification applied in the cube, and because of these enhancements to the Report Designer.

Most SSAS reports are usually simple in design, just because of the nature of the cube. With predefined drill-down paths, and multiple multilevel hierarchies, it should be natural to visualize this information in a matrix or multi-axis chart. Business leaders now expect to see data presented in standard formats, using key performance indicators (KPIs) to present business metrics in dashboards and business scorecards with gauges and iconic graphical indicators. In the following exercises, you will see how using an SSAS data source with dimensional hierarchies, measures, KPIs, calculated members, and related cube elements make business report design simple and manageable.

WORKING WITH MULTIDIMENSIONAL EXPRESSION LANGUAGE

The MDX query language is part of the OLEDB for OLAP specification from Microsoft. The MDX query language is used in several products from different vendors, such as IBM Cognos, Hyperion EssBase, Business Objects, and, of course, Microsoft SQL Server Analysis Services. Like SQL, the language varies from product to product, but the concepts and core features are the same—or at least very similar in some categories.

MDX: Simple or Complex?

Most IT professionals who want to learn MDX already know a little or a lot of SQL. They have worked through the process of reporting on transactional databases, migrating to a data warehouse, and building queries on a relational/dimensional model. Now, they realize the benefits of a truly dimensional storage engine to solve complex business problems.

This presents an interesting challenge for most of these people. You see, MDX is a simple query language that sits squarely on the multidimensional foundations of OLAP technologies—all of which exists for the sole purpose of simplifying business data. But if Analysis Services and MDX are so *simple*, why does the industry perceive them to be so difficult to learn? There's a simple answer.

MDX is very different from SQL, but on the surface it looks a lot like SQL. This means that anyone making the transition must struggle through a mental paradigm shift—from two-dimensional (2-D), row-set–based thinking to multidimensional, axis-based, cell-set thinking. Making this mental transition is not so difficult with a bit of effort, but it's easy to slip back into a SQL mindset if you don't stay in practice. MDX is not really more difficult than SQL; it is more like the difference between a procedural language and an object-oriented language. Here's the interesting twist. When you're finished working with all these cool, multidimensional concepts, you take the output and pound it back into a 2-D result so that you can display it on a screen or print it on a sheet of paper.

MDX is one of those topics that can't be introduced without sufficient background and an exhaustive set of exercises. So, you will not learn everything you need to know about MDX in this chapter. The purpose here is to give you some exposure to the kinds of things you can do using this powerful query language. For most report work, you shouldn't need to know more than some basic commands and functions. As you shop for books and training, note that the language and query techniques haven't really changed much since SQL Server 2008. There have been some good books written since then, but the language hasn't really changed.

Building Queries with the MDX Query Designer

When you choose the SQL Server Analysis Services data processing provider as you define a report data source, the MDX Query Designer is automatically invoked for any new datasets. Your first objective will be to work with dataset results from a query generated by the MDX Query Designer. After exploring this feature, you will write MDX queries without the aid of the builder.

A common approach is to hand-write the MDX queries for reports in SQL Server Management Studio, and then copy-and-paste them into the text query editor. This is primarily because of individual style and query design patterns for MDX, much like T-SQL experts insist on hand-coding their queries instead of using the query builder. But this doesn't mean you must do the same.

The graphical MDX Query Designer generates relatively well-formed, efficient MDX script. If you design all the necessary calculated members into the model, you shouldn't have to make changes to the report queries. If you do need to write advanced MDX queries, you probably don't need to use the graphical designer anyway. Compared to T-SQL, MDX queries are usually simpler and less verbose, because business rules are resolved in the model rather than in the query. Regardless, the MDX Query Designer works the way it does and has some quirks when things get advanced. You should work with it and take advantage of its capabilities, which when doing so, serves your needs. If the complexity of your SSAS-based reports gets to that point, you will know when you outgrow the Query Designer.

Creating a Data Source

Let's start by creating a shared data source for the `Adventure Works Multidimensional` database.

> **NOTE** *This is one of a few tasks that requires the Visual Studio SSDT designer, rather than Report Builder. If your business users will be using Report Builder to design their own reports, it is necessary for a developer to create and deploy shared data sources using SSDT or the web-based Report Portal. Shared data sources cannot be designed and deployed from Report Builder.*

1. In SSDT, open the `Wrox SSRS 2016 Exercises` project.

2. In the Solution Explorer for a report project, right-click Shared Data Sources, and select Add New Data Source, as shown in Figure 10-1.

FIGURE 10-1: Adding a new data source.

3. The Shared Data Source Properties dialog opens, as shown in Figure 10-2. Select the Microsoft SQL Server Analysis Services data provider from the Type drop-down list.

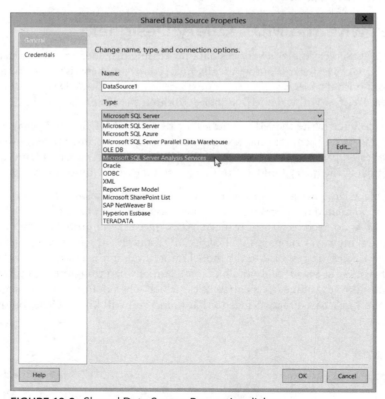

FIGURE 10-2: Shared Data Source Properties dialog.

4. Click the Edit button to the right of the "Connection string" box to open the Connection Properties dialog shown in Figure 10-3.

FIGURE 10-3: Connection Properties dialog.

5. Type `LocalHost` or the name of your Analysis Services server in the "Server name" box. From the drop-down list in the "Connect to a database" section, select the `Adventure Works Multidimensional` Analysis Services database. Test the connection and then click OK to accept these connection settings.

> **TIP** *Chapter 3, "Reporting Services Installation and Architecture," covers the setup and configuration of SSDT, the sample databases (including Adventure Works Multidimensional) and Analysis Services.*

6. Back in the Shared Data Source Properties dialog, change the Name to `AdventureWorksSSAS`, as shown in Figure 10-4. Doing so differentiates between a relational data source and this Analysis Services data source for databases that have the same name or a similar one. You can see that a connection string is generated and placed in the "Connection string" box.

7. Click OK to save the new shared data source. Then, right-click the new shared data source and select Deploy.

You will choose this shared data source for all the examples used in this chapter. Because the data source uses the Analysis Services data provider, the Report Designer generates MDX queries rather than the T-SQL queries you've seen in previous examples using the SQL Server data provider.

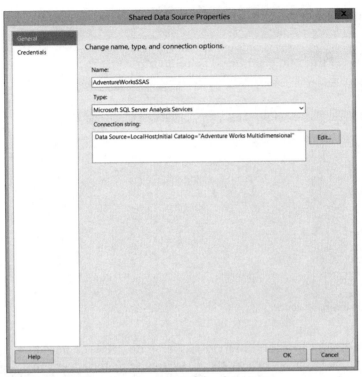

FIGURE 10-4: Changing the name of the data source.

Building the Dataset Query

You've been using the Visual Studio SSDT Report Designer for the previous chapter exercises. One of the objectives of using Analysis Services is to enable capable business users to be self-sufficient. Enabling self-service report design was the original goal behind Report Builder. Frankly, it hasn't been embraced everywhere and by everyone, but there is a pretty good story there. In the previous edition of this book, the author actually had the reader switch gears and use Report Builder at this point. In training classes, we normally decide ahead of time which tool to use, and then provide the appropriate instructions.

Most report design tasks are identical when comparing SSDT and Report Builder. However, the differences are subtle, which makes it difficult to provide side-by-side instructions for both tools. The steps described in the examples for this chapter apply to SQL Server Data Tools for Visual Studio. Where there are differences, they are pointed out in the margin notes.

You will design a report using one of the KPIs defined in the `Adventure Works` cube. A KPI is a standardized set of related members used to report the state of a business metric. In this case, you want to report the current value, goal, and status of Channel Revenue by product category for a selected calendar year. This section does not step you through every click and keystroke, because you already know how to design reports. This section covers the MDX-specific features, and then shows you how to use the report design skills you acquired in previous exercises.

1. Add a new report named `Channel Revenue by Territory`.

2. Add an embedded data source, and give it the same name as the shared data source for the `AdventureWorksSSAS` shared data source.

> **NOTE** *When using Report Builder, you will browse to the server, select the shared data source, and then click Create. Note that if the data source is not available, you must click the "Browse other data sources" option, navigate to* `http://localhost/ReportServer/Data Sources`, *and then open it.*

3. Add a new dataset named `ChannelRevenueByTerritory` and choose the `AdventureWorksSSAS`.

4. Click the Query Designer... button.

    You see that the MDX Query Designer shown in Figure 10-5 is used to construct the query using simple drag and drop. This figure has been labeled to point out the important components of this screen. At first, you will use the Cube metadata pane to select cube members, and then drag them into the cube member drop area (or Data pane). This discussion will refer to other components in this figure as you continue to work with this tool.

> **NOTE** *The author prefers to work from the inside out, dragging in measures and then the dimension members. This seems like the most logical approach.*

5. Using the Cube metadata pane, expand the KPIs node and the Channel Revenue KPI. Drag the Value, Goal, and Status members into the Data pane. Note that a large I-beam bar indicates the drop position of the current member. Use this to position these members in the proper order.

    The metadata pane enables you to explore and select from any member of the cube structure. Figure 10-6 shows various members of the `Adventure Works` sample cube. In short, measures, calculated members, and KPIs represent numeric values for reporting. All other members are used to group, filter, and provide navigational paths to these values. The nodes have been expanded in the metadata pane to demonstrate examples of each of these elements.

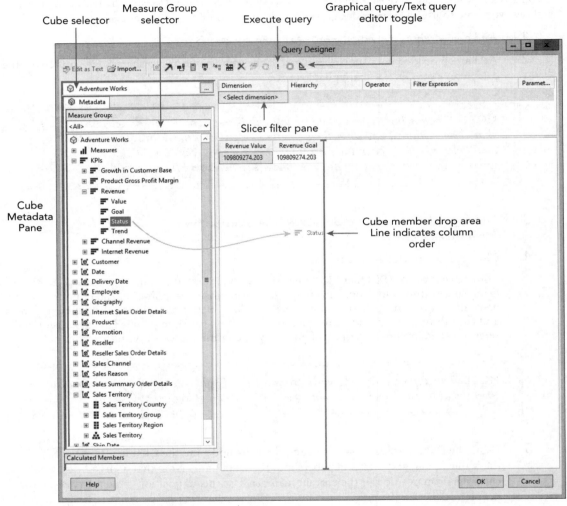

FIGURE 10-5: MDX Query Designer.

Another useful technique is to select a specific option from the Measure Group selector. This restricts information to just the measures and dimensions that relate to that measure group. For example, you can select Reseller Sales to see only measures and members of that group.

All attributes are organized into subject-specific dimensions. Dimensions have two types of hierarchies—attribute and user. An *attribute hierarchy* is simply a flat collection of dimension members derived from a specific data attribute. A *user hierarchy* has multiple levels of attributes organized into a logical drill-down structure. For the most part, you want to use user hierarchies for all drill-down and structured reporting. As a matter of convention, hierarchies consist of levels and members. Members are just the individual attribute values for a level (such as Years, Quarters, or Months). Note that attribute hierarchy levels typically have the same name as the hierarchy (such as `[Date].[CalendarYear].[CalendarYear]`), but user hierarchies do not. The user attribute name typically is more explicit (such as `[Date].[Calendar].[CalendarYear]`). Unless specifically hidden in the design, the members of every user hierarchy level correspond to the members of an attribute hierarchy.

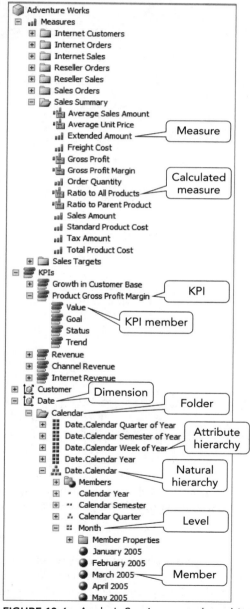

FIGURE 10-6: Analysis Services metadata objects.

6. After dragging the KPI members to the Data pane, expand the Sales Territory dimension.

7. Drag the Sales Territory hierarchy (pyramid shaped icon) to the left-most position in the drop area within the Data pane.

8. Compare the Query Designer to Figure 10-7 and make corrections if necessary.

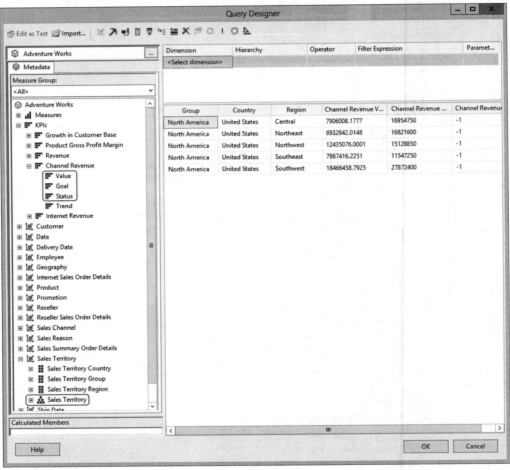

FIGURE 10-7: Query Designer filled in.

The Query Designer parses the hierarchy levels and generates columns for each. The query runs and shows the results grouped by the attribute members, in order of column placement.

Using Parameterized Queries

The query created with the previous steps is complete and usable, but returns results for all the data. To filter data from a cube, you "slice" the cube to limit the query's scope to certain members of a hierarchy. You do so by using the Filtering pane of the MDX Query Designer. Follow these steps to add a parameterized filter to the query you just created:

1. Expand the Date dimension and the `Calendar` folder.

2. Drag the Calendar Year attribute in the Date dimension to the Filter pane.

3. Drop down the Filter Expression list and check the box to select CY 2012, as shown in Figure 10-8. Note that the values in the Data pane change when a different year is selected.

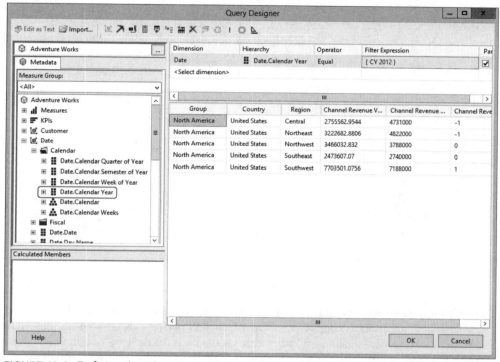

FIGURE 10-8: Defining the Filter Expression.

Use the Filter Expression drop-down window to set the default filter member. Note that every hierarchy has an `All` member, which is used to include all members of the hierarchy.

4. On the Filter Expression drop-down list, uncheck everything and then check `All Periods` to set the filter to include all members. This essentially negates the filter unless you make a different selection.

5. Depending on your screen size, the right-most column may not be in view. If it isn't, scroll and adjust the columns to view the Parameter column. Check this box to generate a related report parameter for this filter.

6. Click OK to close the Query Designer.

Slicing the Cube

The concept of a filter is actually contrary to how MDX works. The term *filter* is commonly used because most people understand this notion based on their experiences with relational database technologies. However, what actually has been defined here is more accurately known as a *slicer*. To limit the results of an SSAS dataset, you won't tell the query engine to scan individual rows, looking for values that match certain criteria. You are actually telling it to "slice off" a portion of the cube, which is already organized into predefined ranges of grouped and sorted attributes.

An important distinction between these two conventions is that slicing doesn't toss out the rest of the cube that doesn't meet the WHERE clause criteria (as a true filter would). It sets the context (or CurrentMember property) for the specified hierarchy. Members of the hierarchy outside this scope are still accessible to functions and operators that may be used in the query. The default slicer (shown in Figure 10-9) is set to use the All member, which returns data for all calendar year members. Of course, users can change this parameter selection when they run the report.

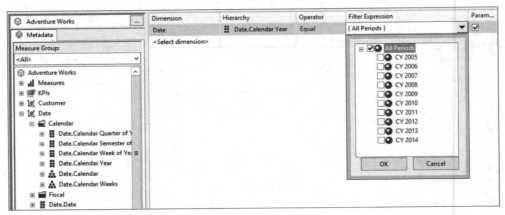

FIGURE 10-9: Default slicer.

The Value and Goal KPIs typically are used to return a measure or calculated value. The Status and Trend members are used to simplify the state of the KPI performance based on some scripted logic, and to drive a graphical dashboard indicator of some kind. In the case of Channel Revenue, the Status KPI member returns an integer with one of three values to indicate the state of channel revenue. The value –1 indicates poor performance, 0 is marginal, and 1 indicates acceptable or exceptional performance.

Reviewing the Finished Sample Report

After you create a dataset, designing a report that uses Analysis Services (for the most part) is not different from designing other reports. Figure 10-10 shows a table report designed for this dataset.

This is the Ch10 - Channel Revenue by Territory report in the sample project. This involved simply defining groups on the sales territory region hierarchy levels and using the fields derived from the Value and Goal KPI members in the table's detail row.

Visualizing a KPI

For the KPI indicator, the Channel_Revenue_Status column was added to the table first. When you drag-and-drop the Indicator item from the Toolbox into the existing Status column detail cell, the designer will set the Value expression using the original textbox. Different indicators have three, four, or five states. The default logic for this three-state indicator is that it will show the red icon if the current value is 0 percent to 33 percent of the maximum possible value, yellow if 33 percent to 66 percent, or green if 66 percent to 100 percent. This might be correct logic in some cases, but the correct states have already been coded in the cube design. To edit the indicator properties, click it in Design view and then use the Gauge Data window to view the Indicator Properties dialog for Indicator1 (shown in Figure 10-11).

Ch10 - Channel Sales by Territory

For   CY 2012

Group	Country	Region	Channel Revenue Value	Goal	Status
North America	United States	Central	$2,755,563	$4,731,000	◆
		Northeast	$3,222,683	$4,822,000	◆
		Northwest	$3,466,033	$3,788,000	△
		Southeast	$2,473,607	$2,740,000	△
		Southwest	$7,703,501	$7,188,000	●
	Total		$19,621,387	$23,269,000	

FIGURE 10-10: Table report.

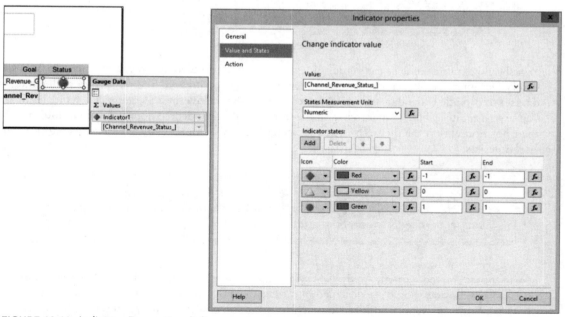

FIGURE 10-11: Indicator Properties dialog.

> **NOTE** *To set properties for an indicator report item, click the indicator to show the Gauge Data window. Click the down arrow next to the name of the indicator, and choose "Indicator properties..." from the menu.*

You learn more about gauges and indicators in greater detail during the discussion about dashboard reports in Chapter 19, "Mobile Report Design Patterns." In this brief overview, you learn how this indicator gets discrete integer values from the KPI definition in the SSAS cube or model—-1 represents Red, 0 is Yellow, and 1 is Green. For this to work, the States Measurement Unit must be set to Numeric rather than Percentage. The icon indicator states must also be mapped to the appropriate state values.

With a KPI indicator in the last column, adding a group total row after the Country group adds the appropriate SUM expressions to the Channel Revenue Value and Goal columns, but not for the Status. The Status value can't be aggregated. It is really up to the business to decide how any measure value should roll-up at a higher level (or whether it should at all). In this case, let's say that the KPI status only applies at the Region level. One option is to take an average of the leaf-level state values and then apply a numeric range to derive a state from the total. This can lead to statistical anomalies, and it is best to calculate the correct value for each hierarchy level within SSAS.

> **NOTE** *Aggregating KPI states can be a tricky business. Don't assume what the business rules are without consulting the business stakeholder. Likewise, some measures are nonadditive and simply can't be totaled.*

You should explore some of the standard features that were added as a result of using the MDX Query Designer. The Parameter drop-down is completely configured and populated with a hidden dataset to provide Calendar Year values. Items on the list below the All member are indented. Had you used a multi-level user hierarchy, all the levels would be indented appropriately to indicate their position within the hierarchy. All parameter lists are automatically generated as multi-value selection lists.

> **TIP** *The graphical MDX Query Designer generates a hidden dataset for each parameter created. To view them, right-click the Datasets node in the Report Data window and select Show Hidden Datasets.*

Most reports created with an Analysis Services data source are this simple. Because the calculation and KPI business logic are designed into the cube, no extra work is necessary when reports are designed. With the Report Builder Designer, information workers can design reports with little or no knowledge of cube design or MDX query scripting. Using practically any MDX-based dataset, reports can be designed with a table, matrix, chart, or combinations of the data ranges and other report items to visualize business information in the most appropriate format.

Modifying an MDX Query

You are now crossing a bridge. On the other side is an environment that is a little more complex and delicate than the one you just left. Reporting Services enables you to do a lot of interesting things with MDX and SSAS data sources, but the Query Designer was not engineered for advanced MDX. The author does a lot of report design using MDX and often steps into client projects where others have tried to implement complex MDX queries and have failed.

Over the years, working on these projects, the author and his colleagues and have discovered what has and has not worked, and have developed techniques for achieving the desired results. One of their most important lessons has been to work within the product's capabilities and not to force it to work otherwise. The author has had numerous conversations with members of the Reporting Services product team on this topic, and the advice often received is, "We didn't intend for you to write an MDX query that way, and we don't support that particular technique. You can achieve the same result by doing it this way." Following are some of these techniques.

The author has not had much luck adding his own parameter logic to handwritten MDX queries. It can be done, but the Query Designer is particular about script changes, and intervenes at the most inconvenient times. You should do one of the following:

➤ Use the MDX Query Designer to design the original query with the built-in parameter logic and supporting datasets, and then modify the query logic, leaving the parameter logic alone.

➤ Hand-write MDX queries in SSMS with hard-coded slicer and filter logic. Paste and execute the query to define the dataset fields, and then add parameters in the Dataset expression window, not the query window.

The second recommendation is the author's standard method. The caveat is, if you make query changes, you cannot execute the modified query including parameters and get the designer to add new fields to the dataset. After you understand the mechanics of the query editor, you can write more complex queries and handle the parameter logic on your own.

> **NOTE** *Advanced MDX is a skill that most casual report designers need not learn. You will find several good examples of advanced, hand-coded MDX queries with embedded parameters in Chapter 11.*

Building a Query Using the MDX Designer

Let's start with a copy of the dataset you just completed. The objective is to define three calculated members based on the same KPI members you used. These calculated members do not exist in the cube. Let's assume you don't have permission to modify the cube structure to add them to the cube design. In addition to the Value, Goal, and Status members for the Channel Revenue KPI, you need to see what these values were for the prior year.

1. Make a copy of `Channel Sales by Territory` report so that you have it for reference.

2. In the new copy of the report in SSDT, open the dataset query `ChannelRevenueByTerritory`.

3. Switch to the query editor to text query view using the Design Mode icon (right-most icon on the Query Designer toolbar). In text view, the query should appear as shown in Figure 10-12.

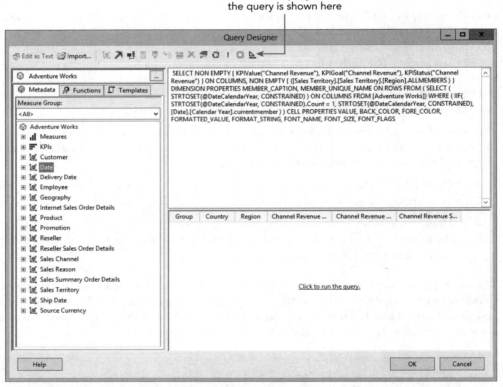

FIGURE 10-12: Switching to the text query view.

4. Select and then copy the MDX script to the clipboard.

5. Open SQL Server Management Studio (SSMS), connect to Analysis Services, and then click the New Query button on the toolbar to open a new MDX query.

6. Paste the query from the Report Designer in the Query window.

7. Use the example in Figure 10-13 to add line returns and tabs to format the query for readability.

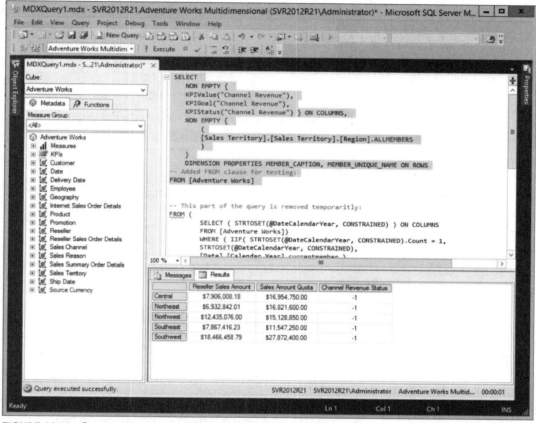

FIGURE 10-13: Query as it appears in Query window.

> **NOTE** *Apparently, the Reporting Services MDX Query Designer was created before carriage returns were invented. A handy tool to reformat MDX query script is MDX Studio, which you can download from* www.sqlbi.com/tools/mdx-studio. *This is a third-party tool and future support isn't guaranteed.*

All the MDX experts have their own styling preferences. Just like T-SQL, MDX is forgiving about carriage returns, tabs, and spaces, so knock yourself out restyling your queries to make them readable and easier to follow. As you read books and search for examples, you are likely to see a lot of variation. The author finds it easier to read a query where each clause (SELECT, FROM, WHERE) is demoted to the left margin, and subsequent operations are indented with container punctuation (like parentheses and set braces) on separate lines and matching tab stops so that it reads to like programming code.

8. The nested parameter references will not work in SSMS, so simplify this query to run without them. The easiest way to do this is to divide the first part of the script, up to the ON ROWS expression, from the rest with a few carriage returns. (This example uses only the first part for testing.) To complete the test query, you just need to add a FROM clause followed by the cube name. Again, your screen should look like Figure 10-13.

9. Highlight only the first query, and click the Execute button on the toolbar.

10. To add the calculated members to the query, type the following into the Query window before the existing script:

```
WITH
  MEMBER Measures.[Last Year Value] AS
    (
       [Date].[Calendar Year].CurrentMember.PrevMember
      ,KPIValue("Channel Revenue")
    )
    ,FORMAT_STRING = "$#,##0.00"
  MEMBER Measures.[Last Year Goal] AS
    (
       [Date].[Calendar Year].CurrentMember.PrevMember
      ,KPIGoal("Channel Revenue")
    )
    ,FORMAT_STRING = "$#,##0.00"
  MEMBER Measures.[Last Year Status] AS
    (
       [Date].[Calendar Year].CurrentMember.PrevMember
      ,KPIStatus("Channel Revenue")
    )
```

> **TIP** *Keep in mind that when copying and pasting query script from a document or online post, quote and double-quote characters often get changed by the software. If you run into errors, try re-typing quotation and punctuation characters.*

To understand the logic for each of these calculated members, let's examine the first one. A new member named Last Year Value is added to the Measures collection, applying this expression:

```
MEMBER Measures.[Last Year Value] AS
  (
    [Date].[Calendar Year].CurrentMember.PrevMember
   ,KPIValue("Channel Revenue")
  )
,FORMAT_STRING = "$#,##0.00"
```

This member returns the Channel Revenue KPI Value for the previous Calendar Year, based on the current member of the Calendar Year hierarchy. If your user selects 2013 for the DateCalendarYear parameter, the WHERE clause uses the parameter to set this as the current member. The PREVMEMBER function causes the expression to return the Channel Revenue

KPI Value for Calendar Year 2012. Because the final report query will be parameterized, this functionality is completely dynamic.

11. You want to add these three new members to the query's COLUMNS axis, which will be interpreted as three new fields in the report. Remove the NON EMPTY directive after the SELECT clause. This ensures that all columns will be returned, even if no data is present. To add the new calculated members to the query, apply the following changes:

```
WITH
  MEMBER Measures.[Last Year Value] AS
    (
      [Date].[Calendar Year].CurrentMember.PrevMember
      ,KPIValue("Channel Revenue")
    )
    ,FORMAT_STRING = "$#,##0.00"
  MEMBER Measures.[Last Year Goal] AS
    (
      [Date].[Calendar Year].CurrentMember.PrevMember
      ,KPIGoal("Channel Revenue")
    )
    ,FORMAT_STRING = "$#,##0.00"
  MEMBER Measures.[Last Year Status] AS
    (
      [Date].[Calendar Year].CurrentMember.PrevMember
      ,KPIStatus("Channel Revenue")
    )
SELECT
  {
    KPIValue("Channel Revenue")
    ,KPIGoal("Channel Revenue")
    ,KPIStatus("Channel Revenue")
    ,[Last Year Value]
    ,[Last Year Goal]
    ,[Last Year Status]
  } ON COLUMNS
  ,
    {
      [Sales Territory].[Sales Territory].[Region].ALLMEMBERS
    }
  DIMENSION PROPERTIES
    MEMBER_CAPTION
    ,MEMBER_UNIQUE_NAME
  ON ROWS
-- Added FROM clause for testing:
FROM [Adventure Works]
```

12. Run the query to verify that it works. You should now see six columns in the results. The reason that the new members don't return a value is that the current member of the Calendar Year has not been set. To do this, add a WHERE clause to slice the cube on Calendar Year 2013:

```
WITH
  MEMBER Measures.[Last Year Value] AS
    (
      [Date].[Calendar Year].CurrentMember.PrevMember
      ,KPIValue("Channel Revenue")
```

```
          )
        ,FORMAT_STRING = "$#,##0.00"
      MEMBER Measures.[Last Year Goal] AS
        (
          [Date].[Calendar Year].CurrentMember.PrevMember
          ,KPIGoal("Channel Revenue")
        )
        ,FORMAT_STRING = "$#,##0.00"
      MEMBER Measures.[Last Year Status] AS
        (
          [Date].[Calendar Year].CurrentMember.PrevMember
          ,KPIStatus("Channel Revenue")
        )
SELECT
  {
    KPIValue("Channel Revenue")
    ,KPIGoal("Channel Revenue")
    ,KPIStatus("Channel Revenue")
    ,[Last Year Value]
    ,[Last Year Goal]
    ,[Last Year Status]
  } ON COLUMNS
  ,
      {
        [Sales Territory].[Sales Territory].[Region].ALLMEMBERS
      }
  DIMENSION PROPERTIES
    MEMBER_CAPTION
    ,MEMBER_UNIQUE_NAME
    ON ROWS
-- Added FROM clause for testing:
FROM [Adventure Works]
-- Added WHERE clause for testing:
WHERE
    [Date].[Calendar Year].&[2013];
```

13. Apply this change, check your query with the following script, and then run the query. You should now see the 2013 values for the new calculated members. You can check this by making note of the values, using 2013 in the WHERE clause rather than 2014, and then running it again.

14. To prepare the query for the report, you must add all the parameter logic from the original query. Comment out the FROM and WHERE lines from the new query, and then merge the two sections of script you previously separated. Your final query should look like this:

```
WITH
  MEMBER Measures.[Last Year Value] AS
    (
      [Date].[Calendar Year].CurrentMember.PrevMember
      ,KPIValue("Channel Revenue")
    )
    ,FORMAT_STRING = "$#,##0.00"
  MEMBER Measures.[Last Year Goal] AS
```

```
        (
          [Date].[Calendar Year].CurrentMember.PrevMember
         ,KPIGoal("Channel Revenue")
        )
       ,FORMAT_STRING = "$#,##0.00"
     MEMBER Measures.[Last Year Status] AS
        (
          [Date].[Calendar Year].CurrentMember.PrevMember
         ,KPIStatus("Channel Revenue")
        )
SELECT
   {
     KPIValue("Channel Revenue")
    ,KPIGoal("Channel Revenue")
    ,KPIStatus("Channel Revenue")
    ,[Last Year Value]
    ,[Last Year Goal]
    ,[Last Year Status]
   } ON COLUMNS
  ,
     {{[Sales Territory].[Sales Territory].[Region].ALLMEMBERS}
   DIMENSION PROPERTIES
     MEMBER_CAPTION
    ,MEMBER_UNIQUE_NAME
     ON ROWS
-- Added FROM clause for testing:
-- FROM [Adventure Works]
-- Added WHERE clause for testing:
-- WHERE
--   [Date].[Calendar Year].&[2013]


FROM
(
  SELECT
    StrToSet
    (@DateCalendarYear
     ,CONSTRAINED
     ) ON COLUMNS
  FROM [Adventure Works]
)
WHERE
  IIF
  (
    StrToSet(@DateCalendarYear,CONSTRAINED).Count = 1
   ,StrToSet
    (@DateCalendarYear
     ,CONSTRAINED
     )
   ,[Date].[Calendar Year].CurrentMember
  )
CELL PROPERTIES
  VALUE
 ,BACK_COLOR
```

```
, FORE_COLOR
, FORMATTED_VALUE
, FORMAT_STRING
, FONT_NAME
, FONT_SIZE
, FONT_FLAGS;
```

15. Now you're ready to update the query in the report. Copy the query from the Management Studio Query window, and paste it over all the script in the Report Designer Query window. If you lose the formatting, paste the query into Microsoft Word or WordPad, and then recopy to the clipboard.

16. Click the Query Parameters toolbar button, and change the parameter value for `DateCalendarYear` to `CY 2013`. Click OK to return.

17. Click the Execute button to test the query and refresh the field collection, as shown in Figure 10-14.

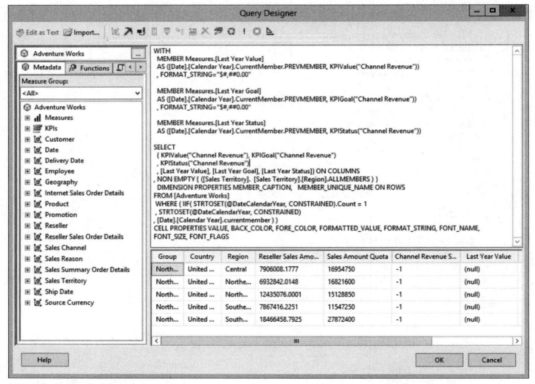

FIGURE 10-14: Testing the query.

18. Click OK to accept changes and save the dataset.

Report design based on this new dataset is pretty straightforward. The three new calculated members are added to the dataset fields collection. They can be used to add columns to the table using the same drag-and-drop technique you have used before.

Figure 10-15 shows the Select Indicator Type dialog, which is displayed when the indicator report item is dragged from the Toolbox to the `Last Year Status` column detail cell. The three-state indicator with different icon shapes has been selected here. When using default red, yellow, and green colors, this is a good choice because the different shapes are distinguishable on monochrome printed reports and by colorblind users. The appropriate use of color is discussed in Chapter 19.

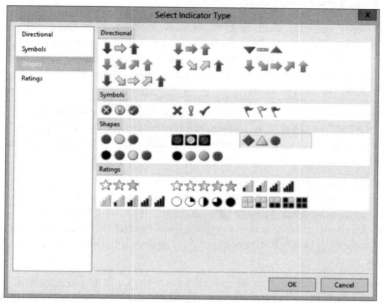

FIGURE 10-15: Three new calculated members in the dataset fields collection.

Figure 10-16 shows the completed report with the additional measure columns and status indicator for the Last Year KPI.

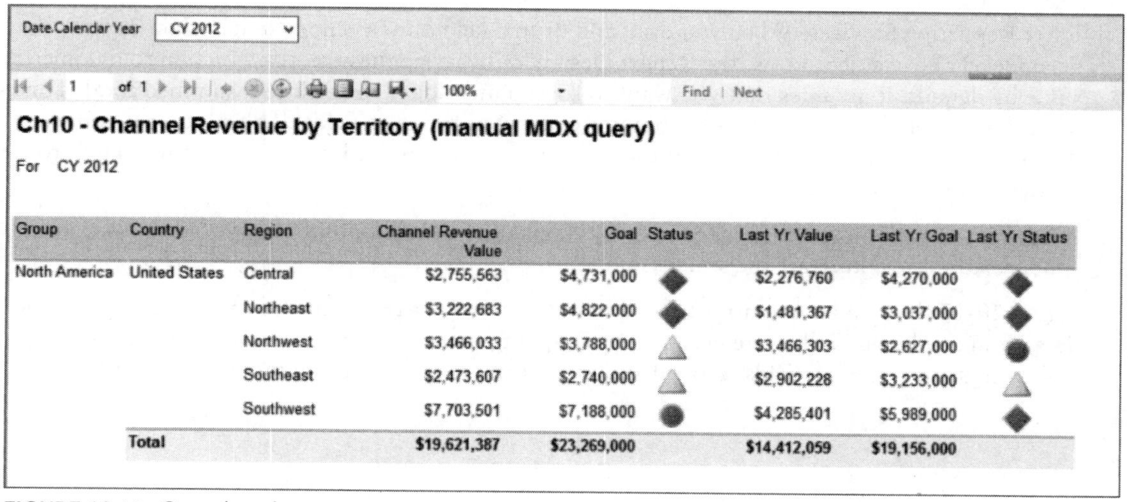

Date.Calendar Year CY 2012

1 of 1   100%   Find | Next

Ch10 - Channel Revenue by Territory (manual MDX query)

For   CY 2012

Group	Country	Region	Channel Revenue Value	Goal	Status	Last Yr Value	Last Yr Goal	Last Yr Status
North America	United States	Central	$2,755,563	$4,731,000	◆	$2,276,760	$4,270,000	◆
		Northeast	$3,222,683	$4,822,000	◆	$1,481,367	$3,037,000	◆
		Northwest	$3,466,033	$3,788,000	△	$3,466,303	$2,627,000	●
		Southeast	$2,473,607	$2,740,000	△	$2,902,228	$3,233,000	△
		Southwest	$7,703,501	$7,188,000	●	$4,285,401	$5,989,000	◆
	Total		$19,621,387	$23,269,000		$14,412,059	$19,156,000	

FIGURE 10-16: Completed report.

The gauges can also be copied and pasted from the original Status column. On the new gauge, click the pointer, and then use the smart tag to update the field binding to use the Last_Year_ Status field.

ADDING NONADDITIVE MEASURES

Some things just don't add up! Often, the values you need to see on reports are calculated using more complex logic than simple sums. Measure values can be based on statistical functions, rolling or weighted averages, or industry-specific standard calculations. Special logic is often required to calculate common metrics such as inventory counts, profit, and ratios. Regardless, these aren't calculations you should have to repeat in every report.

One of the advantages of using SSAS is that all the necessary business logic for reporting and analysis can be designed into the cube. This means that as soon as the business rules are sorted out in the cube design, you simply use the measures, calculated members, and KPIs with full confidence that the results will be accurate and reliable.

Let's use a simple example of an average sales amount calculation. You can use your imagination to extend this scenario to other business cases that would apply to your situation. The Adventure Works cube contains a measure named Reseller Average Sales Amount. The logic behind this calculation relies on the knowledge of individual transaction sales amounts that are actually not present in the cube. In fact, unless you were to go back to the original data source for these sales records, you couldn't calculate this value yourself.

Fortunately, Analysis Services performs some magic when it processes the cube and aggregates this measure value. It figures out which values must be stored in the cube, and which values can be derived at query time. In the case of an average measure, it must store the average at every level of a dimensional hierarchy, because it is not possible to derive an average from a range of average values at a lower level. Although it is interesting to know how Analysis Services performs these aggregations and stores selected values, you can sleep soundly at night knowing that you do not have to worry about it.

Enter Reporting Services. When you drag and drop a field onto a report item or data region at a group level above a detail row, the Report Designer always applies the SUM function to a numeric value by default. It assumes that you want to roll up individual values into a summed total. This is a helpful assumption most of the time, but not when your measure fields don't sum, or if you want to do something else with them. What if the measure were a standard deviation or a weighted, rolling average? How would you roll this up into a group footer?

It doesn't matter. This is Analysis Services' job, and you should not have to worry about it. Here's a simple example to illustrate the simple solution.

Figure 10-17 shows a basic matrix report, named AS Avg Sales in the Chapter 10 samples. The detail and total value cells were designed by dragging the Sales_Amount_Quota and Reseller_ Average_Sales_Amount fields to the detail area of the matrix. The column widths have been expanded so that you can see the expressions. As you can see, the Designer applied the `SUM` function to all four of these cells.

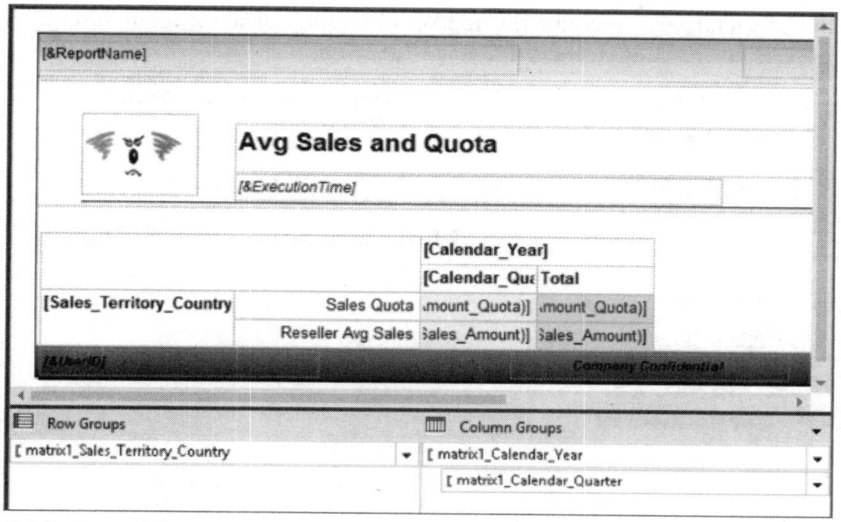

FIGURE 10-17: Basic matrix report.

Figure 10-18 shows the report in preview. See if you can spot the calculation error. Take a close look at the `Total` column for the `Reseller Avg Sales` field.

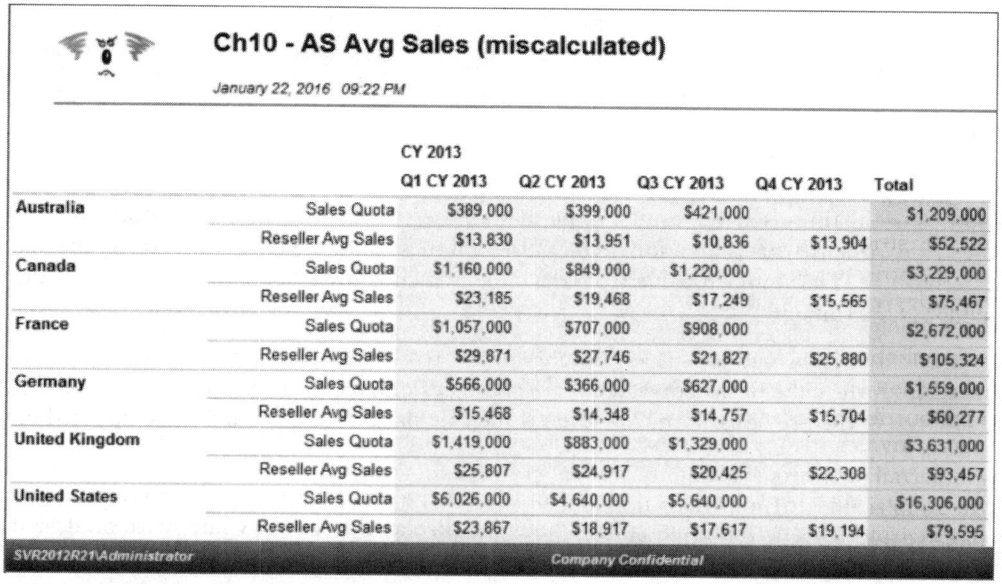

Ch10 - AS Avg Sales (miscalculated)

January 22, 2016 09:22 PM

		CY 2013				
		Q1 CY 2013	Q2 CY 2013	Q3 CY 2013	Q4 CY 2013	Total
Australia	Sales Quota	$389,000	$399,000	$421,000		$1,209,000
	Reseller Avg Sales	$13,830	$13,951	$10,836	$13,904	$52,522
Canada	Sales Quota	$1,160,000	$849,000	$1,220,000		$3,229,000
	Reseller Avg Sales	$23,185	$19,468	$17,249	$15,565	$75,467
France	Sales Quota	$1,057,000	$707,000	$908,000		$2,672,000
	Reseller Avg Sales	$29,871	$27,746	$21,827	$25,880	$105,324
Germany	Sales Quota	$566,000	$366,000	$627,000		$1,559,000
	Reseller Avg Sales	$15,468	$14,348	$14,757	$15,704	$60,277
United Kingdom	Sales Quota	$1,419,000	$883,000	$1,329,000		$3,631,000
	Reseller Avg Sales	$25,807	$24,917	$20,425	$22,308	$93,457
United States	Sales Quota	$6,026,000	$4,640,000	$5,640,000		$16,306,000
	Reseller Avg Sales	$23,867	$18,917	$17,617	$19,194	$79,595

SVR2012R2\Administrator Company Confidential

FIGURE 10-18: Report in preview.

When to Use the Aggregate Function

The solution to this problem is to let Reporting Services know that it should not try to aggregate any values. The measure value at each level represents the appropriate rollup of subordinate levels. This is done by replacing occurrences of SUM with the AGGREGATE function.

Figure 10-19 shows the report with these changes. All the SUM function references have been replaced with AGGREGATE by editing each expression.

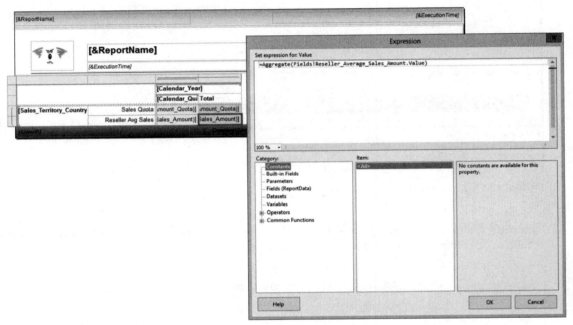

FIGURE 10-19: Report with changes.

Preview the report again to see the results. Note that all the Sales_Amount_Quota total values remain the same, because this is an additive measure and these values were already using the SUM function in the cube. The summed value from the cube (which you see here) and the summed values in the report are the same.

However, the Reseller_Average_Sales_Amount totals are different. This is because the calculation returned from the cube in the corrected report is the calculated average, rather than the sum of averages you saw in the previous example—even if the calculation logic needed to be updated in the SSAS model or cube.

Just for the sake of argument, let's say that the total needed to be the median instead of average. By using the AGGREGATE function, the report would just display the correct values with no design changes necessary. Figure 10-20 shows both the original miscalculated report and the new fixed report juxtaposed so you can see the difference.

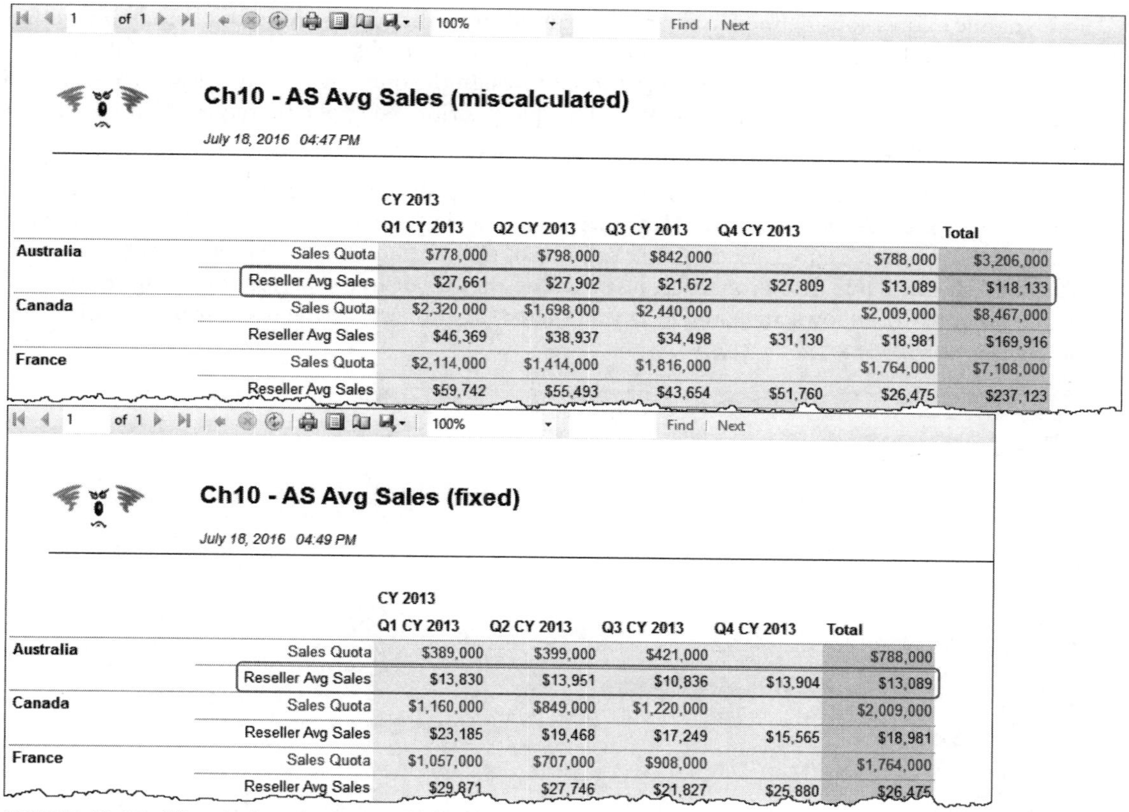

		CY 2013					
		Q1 CY 2013	Q2 CY 2013	Q3 CY 2013	Q4 CY 2013		Total
Australia	Sales Quota	$778,000	$798,000	$842,000		$788,000	$3,206,000
	Reseller Avg Sales	$27,661	$27,902	$21,672	$27,809	$13,089	$118,133
Canada	Sales Quota	$2,320,000	$1,698,000	$2,440,000		$2,009,000	$8,467,000
	Reseller Avg Sales	$46,369	$38,937	$34,498	$31,130	$18,981	$169,916
France	Sales Quota	$2,114,000	$1,414,000	$1,816,000		$1,764,000	$7,108,000
	Reseller Avg Sales	$59,742	$55,493	$43,654	$51,760	$26,475	$237,123

		CY 2013				
		Q1 CY 2013	Q2 CY 2013	Q3 CY 2013	Q4 CY 2013	Total
Australia	Sales Quota	$389,000	$399,000	$421,000		$788,000
	Reseller Avg Sales	$13,830	$13,951	$10,836	$13,904	$13,089
Canada	Sales Quota	$1,160,000	$849,000	$1,220,000		$2,009,000
	Reseller Avg Sales	$23,185	$19,468	$17,249	$15,565	$18,981
France	Sales Quota	$1,057,000	$707,000	$908,000		$1,764,000
	Reseller Avg Sales	$29,871	$27,746	$21,827	$25,880	$26,475

FIGURE 10-20: Miscalculated report and fixed report.

MDX PROPERTIES AND CUBE FORMATTING

As you have looked at the MDX queries generated by the MDX Query Designer, you may have noticed several property references in the MDX script under the headings CELL PROPERTIES, DIMENSION PROPERTIES, and CUBE PROPERTIES. This is evidence of one of the most significant differences between Analysis Services and a relational database product such as SQL Server 2016. When you run a T-SQL query for a SQL Server database, the result set contains very little information aside from the column names and values. The data provider and client components use a bit of metadata, such as data types, numeric scales, and string lengths. The formatting of the query results is entirely in the hands of whichever client application is consuming the data.

MDX-based queries provide a mechanism for returning a variety of useful information about different objects returned from a query. Within the cube design, every measure can be formatted, and every calculated member can have font, color, and other styling characteristics associated with it. Dynamic expressions defined in the cube are used to modify these properties based on threshold values or any other logic. This way, profit-related measures are displayed in green, and losses are in red and bold text. These properties are returned through the query results as metadata tags associated with each cell and dimension member. The query script can explicitly request that certain properties be returned.

Reporting Services uses these query object properties by generating corresponding properties for each field object it derives from an MDX query. These field properties are accessible in the Report Designer Expression dialog. When you select a field, the Value property is referenced by default. To see all the available field properties, just back up the cursor to the period following the field name. Figure 10-21 shows an example setting the Color property of the textbox used to display the Sales_Amount_Quota.

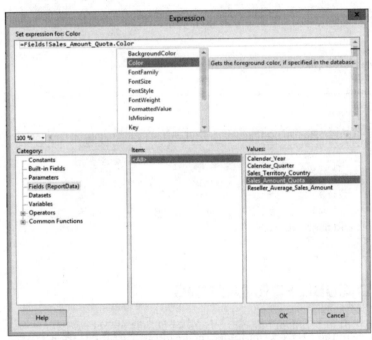

FIGURE 10-21: Modifying field properties.

This is a powerful concept. A consulting client once insisted on having specific colors for specific currencies. By using dynamic logic to conditionally set calculated measure colors in the cube, the Reporting Services report simply consumes this information.

DRILL-THROUGH REPORTS

Drill-through actions are one of the most useful features of Reporting Services. As you know, a *drill-through report* uses a report action to navigate to a second report when the user clicks a report item (often a textbox) that contains a reference value of some kind. The typical scenario for drill-through reports is where a high-level summary report lists dimension members in a data region in a table or matrix. Using the example of a table report showing sales summary information for products, if users were to click a product name, they might expect to see sales details for that product. If a report based on relational tables were used for drill-through, you would expect a key value (such as the `ProductID`) to be passed from the source report to a parameter in the target report, and used to filter records.

MDX-based reports can play this role as well as any other data source. The difference is in how keys and unique identifiers are defined in a cube. Every dimensional attribute does have a key value, but it might not necessarily correspond to a primary key value in a relational data source. Because attributes are organized into hierarchies, the unique value used to describe an attribute preserves the entire hierarchy lineage through a property called `UniqueName`. This is the value passed to any parameters generated by the MDX Query Designer. It is considered a best practice to use the same technique for drill-through reports. The value of a dimension member is derived from the MDX `Name` property for a member by default. For a product, this would just be the product name as it appears on the report. The `UniqueName` property value is derived from the `ProductKey` field in the `DimProduct` table and would look something like this:

```
[Product].[Product].&[470]
```

The example provided in the Chapter 10 samples consists of a source and target report that you can use as an example of this functionality. The `Top 10 Product Internet Sales by Year` report contains a table with an action configured for the Product textbox. The `Product Sales by Year` report has a parameter called `Product` that filters an MDX query bound to a chart. The source report contains an action defined on the Product textbox, which passes a value using the following expression to the target report:

```
=Fields!Product.UniqueName
```

The target report, `Product Sales by Year` (MDX drill-through target), contains a query parameter named `ProductProduct` that was generated by the MDX Query Designer when this report was designed.

Figure 10-22 shows the Action expression settings for the source report product textbox. Note the expression used in the `Values` column of the parameter mapping. Also note that, back on the design surface, the product textbox font color is blue. This is a visual clue to users that they can click on a product because it appears just like a link on a web page.

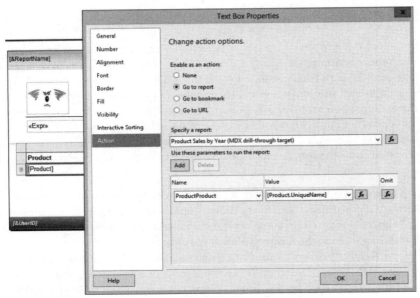

FIGURE 10-22: Action expression settings.

Parameter Safety Precautions

If a drill-through report, URL, or cube report action is exposed to the Internet or an uncontrolled network environment, precautions should be taken to prevent script injection attacks. Two common safety precautions are used when parameters are passed to an MDX query.

The first is implemented by default in the script generated by the MDX Query Designer. Parameters are passed to the function STRTOSET or STRTOMEMBER with the CONSTRAINED optional argument flag. This flag instructs the MDX query processing engine to disallow any dynamic script or function calls in the parameter text.

The other provision that you can implement yourself is the URLEscapeFragment function. Passing any MDX object reference to this function MIME-encodes any characters that could be used to embed script. The query processor decodes any valid characters on the receiving end after validating the unaltered text. This sample code returns a properly escaped form of a dimension member reference:

```
UrlEscapeFragment(SetTostr({[Dim].[MyHierarchy].CurrentMember}))
```

BEST PRACTICES AND PROVISIONS

The following are some important considerations for designing reports for Analysis Services. Keep these factors in mind as you create reports.

➤ **Leverage the cube**—Design business rules and calculations into the cube. Report and query design with a comprehensive cube is a simple matter of dragging and dropping members into the Query Designer.

➤ **Allow empty rows**—By default, the MDX Query Designer eliminates rows that have all empty cells. This may impede certain reports, such as charts and matrices. To include all rows, regardless of empty cells, remove the NON EMPTY directive on the rows axis.

➤ **Let the cube manage aggregation**—Replace the SUM or FIRST aggregate functions added by the Report Designer with the AGGREGATE function. This instructs Reporting Services to let the Analysis Services query engine take care of the aggregate values.

➤ **Sorting months**—When you use the Report Wizard to create a table or matrix report, groups are sorted on the same field as the group. Fields such as Months are sorted in alphabetical order. Because the members are already sorted correctly in the cube dimension, this is resolved by removing the Sort expression for the group.

➤ **Cascading parameters**—Auto-built MDX queries create multiple datasets with interdependent parameters. Removing an unneeded parameter can be challenging. Check each hidden dataset query for references to the parameter, and remove those references or delete the dataset and rebuild it without the parameter.

➤ **Use the Query Designer to create parameters**—Allow the MDX Query Designer to create parameter and filter logic, and then modify the query after making a backup copy.

SUMMARY

SQL Server Analysis Services (SSAS) is a powerful tool for storing and managing critical business information to support business decisions and analytics. If SSAS is used correctly, compelling and useful reports can be created easily using Reporting Services. Business users shouldn't need to understand the MDX language to design day-to-day reports with Report Builder. But with some basic MDX knowledge, business intelligence (BI) solution developers can create advanced visualizations and powerful business dashboards that would be slow and difficult to design with a relational data source.

The advantages afforded by SSAS and the MDX query engine are numerous. Queries are lightning-fast, data is simplified and accessible, and business-specific calculations are managed in a central location. Using Reporting Services to design reports for Analysis Services data can create a fast, secure, and reliable BI solution with uniform results across the business enterprise.

Chapter 11 will take you deep into a real reporting solution utilizing Analysis Services and MDX. You will learn to use advanced techniques like expressions and report navigation to see how multiple reports are used to architect a complete cube browser solution.

11

SSAS Reporting Advanced Techniques

WHAT'S IN THIS CHAPTER?

➤ Dynamically changing report content and navigating hierarchies by changing report parameters

➤ Restricting the number of rows with a parameter

➤ Displaying and allowing users to explore cube metadata

➤ Creating your own cube browser in Reporting Services

In 2005, I presented a session on report design at the PASS Global Summit. After the session, a very distinctive character came up and introduced himself. He was a tall gentleman with an Aussie accent, wearing a leather outback hat and a permanent smile. Grant Paisley and I have been good friends ever since. We found we had much in common, including a passion for taking technologies like Reporting Services to the edge. If there was ever an out-of-the-box thinker, it is Grant. He has done things with SSRS that are simply unimaginable. His cube browser solution, which he has been evolving and improving for years, blew my mind. It is a remarkable example of the flexibility afforded by Reporting Services paired with Analysis Services and some ingenuity.

Grant contributed the content of this chapter in the last edition of our book with a collection of reports sewn together using actions, expressions, and parameters. It all works in SSRS 2016 exactly as it did in 2012 with only minor adaptations to the sample project, which is called Wrox SSRS 2016 Dynamic Cube Browser. Having used these and similar patterns in a number of my projects, I encourage you to review the techniques and glean relevant parts that may be useful in your own solutions.

> **NOTE** *With little or no modification, you should be able to change the data source and use this solution to browse any multidimensional or tabular model. You will need to change the default parameter values for the Cube Browser report and any reports that are initially loaded. Given the complexity and advanced nature of this approach, I can't offer any guarantee or technical support for this solution. After reviewing the solution, review my summary notes at the end of the chapter.*

BUILDING A DYNAMIC CUBE BROWSER WITH SSRS

Years ago, when I attended Tech Ed (Microsoft's annual conference for developers and IT professionals) in Boston, I noticed that the Blue Man Group was in town. I just *had* to see them; they are compelling on stage. This reminds me that when you see blue text in a browser (or report), you are *compelled* to click it. This chapter discusses how you can use this "blue clicking compulsion" to create dynamic and flexible reports that can be navigated simply by clicking blue content.

This chapter describes a series of reports that demonstrate the techniques behind building an OLAP client in SSRS. Along the way you will learn about the following:

➤ Using self-calling drill-through reports to navigate content

➤ Using other reports to collect parameters

➤ Formatting reports to make them easy to navigate

➤ Using cube metadata to drive report content (this will work on any cube)

CUBE DYNAMIC ROWS

I have often observed when I'm creating reports for clients that the reports they want are very similar. The columns stay fairly static, with values such as Amount, Amount Last Year, Growth, Growth Percentage, and Gross Profit. The only difference is the data shown on rows. So two reports could have identical columns, but one has Products on rows and another has Regions.

One of the neat things about Analysis Services is that it lets you move up and down through hierarchies, selecting what you are interested in. In the Product dimension, for instance, you can select Product Category: Bikes or Product Sub-Category: Mountain Bikes. You can even select a single Product Model.

This report uses a parameter that lets you change what hierarchy is displayed on rows and lets you drill up or down within that hierarchy. It also uses a parameter for the measure to display. The final report will behave as shown in Figure 11-1. Simply clicking a hierarchy member allows you to drill down to more and more detail, or similarly drill back up.

Product Categories	Gross Profit
All Products	13 m
Bikes	11 m
Components	1.0 m
Accessories	634 k
Clothing	369 k

Product Categories	Gross Profit
All Products	13 m
Bikes	11 m
Mountain Bikes	5.9 m
Road Bikes	4.4 m
Touring Bikes	217 k

Product Categories	Gross Profit
All Products	13 m
Bikes	11 m
Road Bikes	4.4 m
Road-150 Red, 48	470 k
Road-150 Red, 62	466 k
Road-150 Red, 52	421 k
Road-150 Red, 56	406 k

FIGURE 11-1: Behavior of final report.

The Cube Browser report (an extension of this concept) calls a modified version of the Cube Metadata report. It allows users to dynamically change what measure and hierarchy to display on rows without needing to type a value into the parameter.

Cube Dynamic Rows Anatomy

This report utilizes custom MDX, mainly calculated measures, to present consistent column names to Reporting Services. Therefore, it facilitates dynamically changing rows and the measure by simply changing the parameters.

From SQL Server Data Tools (SSDT), open the report called Cube Dynamic Rows. Figure 11-2 shows the Report Data pane for the Cube Dynamic Rows report.

FIGURE 11-2: Cube Dynamic Rows Report Data.

Parameters

First, let's look at the parameters.

The string report parameter called pMeasure has this default value:

    [Measures].[Gross Profit]

and these available expression values (label / value):

> Gross Profit / = "[Measures].[Gross Profit]"
>
> Sales Amount / = "[Measures].[Sales Amount]"
>
> Amount / = "[Measures].[Amount]"

So this parameter drives the measure value displayed in the report.

The string report parameter called pRowMbr has this default value:

    [Product].[Product Categories].[Subcategory].&[1]

This is the "focus" member of the report. In this case it is Product dimension, Product Categories hierarchy, and Subcategory level Mountain Bikes.

Dataset

Open the Query Designer for DataSet1, as shown in Figure 11-3.

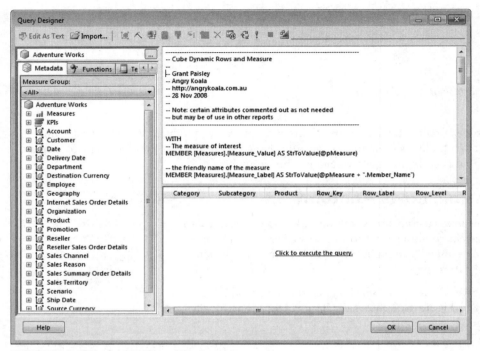

FIGURE 11-3: DataSet1 in Query Designer.

Here is the MDX query:

```
--------------------------------------------------------------------------------
-- Cube Dynamic Rows and Measure
--
-- Grant Paisley
-- Angry Koala
-- http://angrykoala.com.au
-- Nov 2011
--
-- Note: certain attributes commented out as not needed
-- but may be of use in other reports
--------------------------------------------------------------------------------

WITH
-- The measure of interest
```

```
MEMBER [Measures].[Measure_Value] AS StrToValue(@pMeasure)

-- the friendly name of the measure
MEMBER [Measures].[Measure_Label] AS StrToValue(@pMeasure + ".Member_Name")

MEMBER [Measures].[Row_Key]
    AS StrToValue( @pRowMbr + ".Hierarchy.Currentmember.Uniquename" )
MEMBER [Measures].[Row_Label]
    AS StrToValue( @pRowMbr + ".Hierarchy.CurrentMember.Member_Caption" )

MEMBER [Measures].[Row_Level]
    AS StrToValue( @pRowMbr + ".Hierarchy.CurrentMember.Level.Ordinal" )

--MEMBER [Measures].[Row_Level_Name]
--   AS StrToValue( @pRowMbr + ".Hierarchy.Level.Name" )

MEMBER [Measures].[Row_Hierarchy_Name]
    AS StrToValue( @pRowMbr + ".Hierarchy.Name" )

--MEMBER [Measures].[Row_Hierarchy_UniqueName]
--   AS StrToValue( @pRowMbr + ".Hierarchy.UniqueName" )

MEMBER [Measures].[Row_Dimension_Name]
    AS StrToValue( @pRowMbr + ".Dimension.Name" )

--MEMBER [Measures].[Row_Dimension_UniqueName]
--    AS StrToValue(@pRowMbr + ".Dimension_Unique_Name" )

SELECT NON EMPTY {
 -- display the measure and rowmbr attributes on columns

 [Measures].[Row_Key],
 [Measures].[Row_Label],
 [Measures].[Row_Level],
 --[Measures].[Row_Level_Name],
 [Measures].[Row_Hierarchy_Name],
 --[Measures].[Row_Hierarchy_UniqueName],
 --[Measures].[Row_Dimension_Name],
 --[Measures].[Row_Dimension_UniqueName],

 [Measures].[Measure_Label] ,
 [Measures].[Measure_Value]

} ON COLUMNS,

NON EMPTY
        -- if want to display row member parent, self and children
        -- un-comment following code
        --STRTOSET("{" + @pRowMbr + ".parent, "
```

```
        --              + @pRowMbr + ", "
        --              + @pRowMbr + ".children}" )

        -- show the current hierarchy member with its ascendants
        -- together with its children on rows
        STRTOSET(
            "{Ascendants(" + @pRowMbr + " ), "
            + @pRowMbr + ".children}"
        )

    ON ROWS

    FROM [Adventure Works] -- must hard code the cube  :(
    -- the cube name, together with the parameter default values are the only
    -- things required to point this report at a different cube
```

In effect you create a calculated measure for each row member property of interest and display them on columns:

```
[Measures].[Row_Key],
[Measures].[Row_Label],
[Measures].[Row_Level],
--[Measures].[Row_Level_Name],
[Measures].[Row_Hierarchy_Name],
--[Measures].[Row_Hierarchy_UniqueName],
--[Measures].[Row_Dimension_Name],
--[Measures].[Row_Dimension_UniqueName],
```

In addition to the current measure label and value:

```
[Measures].[Measure_Label] ,
[Measures].[Measure_Value]
```

On rows you simply display the "ascendants" of the current member and its children:

```
STRTOSET(
    "{Ascendants(" + @pRowMbr + " ), "
    + @pRowMbr + ".children}"
)
```

If you select the Query Parameters icon from the toolbar you see the following, as shown in Figure 11-4:

➤ pMeasure with a default value of [Measures].[Gross Profit]

➤ pRowMbr with a default value of [Product].[Product Categories].[Subcategory].&[1]

> **NOTE** *You'll need to enter the parameter information shown in Figure 11-4. Make sure this is complete before you continue.*

Execute the query to see the results, as shown in Figure 11-5.

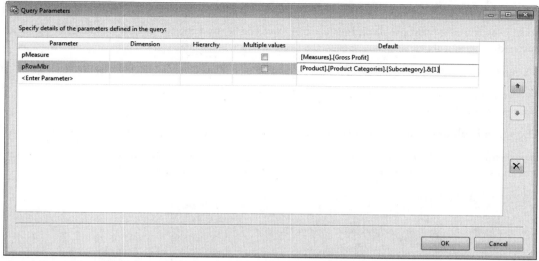

FIGURE 11-4: Query Parameters dialog.

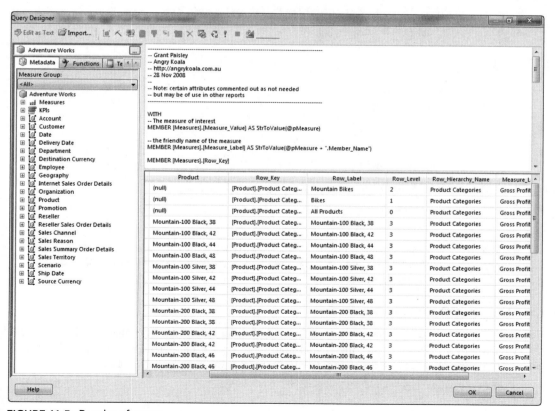

FIGURE 11-5: Results of query.

Matrix Content

So now that you have some data, let's look at how you format the tablix, including a neat trick to better display numbers.

A single table with the detail row shows Row_Label and Measure_Value data fields.

The first column header displays the name of the current hierarchy as it is set to [Row_Hierarchy_Name].

The second column header shows the name of the current measure as it is set to [Measure_Label].

If you right-click the Details group in the Row Groups pane and select Group Properties, you see it has an expression to group on [Row_Key], as shown in Figure 11-6.

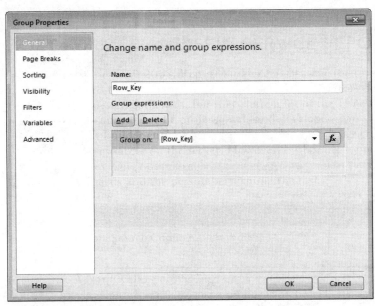

FIGURE 11-6: Expression group on [Row Key].

Go to the Sorting tab. As shown in Figure 11-7, rows are sorted by the Row_Level and then Measure_Value data fields. This ensures that members are displayed in hierarchy level order (ascending) and then by value (descending).

Formatting the Row Label

Right-click the Row_Label textbox, select Text Box Properties, select Alignment options, and click the *fx* button in the Padding Options area, as shown in Figure 11-8. You see an expression for the cell's left alignment. This indents the text four characters for each level in the hierarchy:

```
=str( (Fields!Row_Level.Value * 4) + 2 ) + "pt"
```

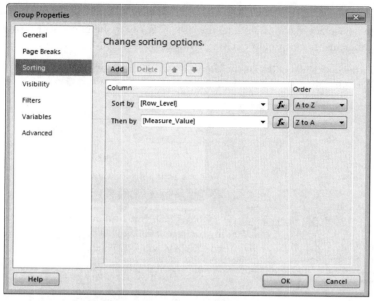

FIGURE 11-7: Seeing how rows are sorted.

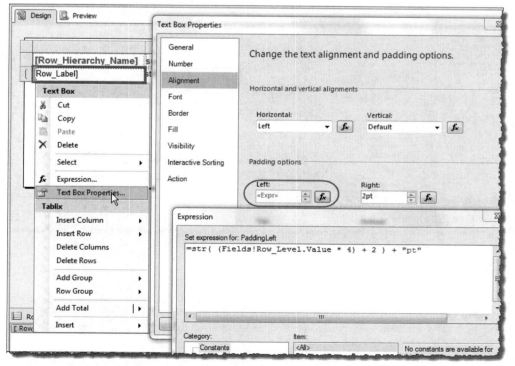

FIGURE 11-8: Changing the text alignment and padding properties.

Highlighting the Current Row

You can highlight the row currently selected to indicate to the user that he or she can select a row by setting its color to blue. (Remember, users can't help clicking something that is blue.)

For both the `Row_Label` and `Measure_Value` cells, in the detail row, set the property `BackgroundColor` to this expression:

```
=iif(Fields!Row_Key.Value=Parameters!pRowMbr.Value,
  "LemonChiffon",
  Nothing
  )
```

This is shown in Figure 11-9.

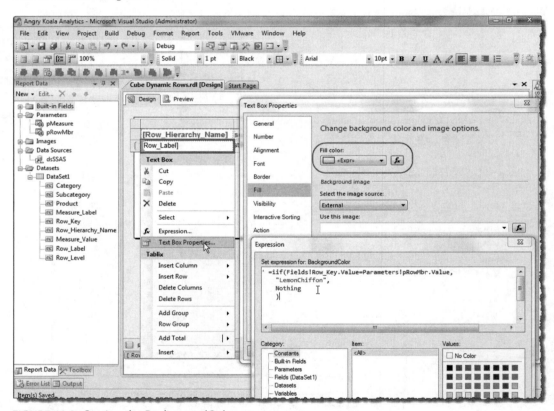

FIGURE 11-9: Setting the BackgroundColor property.

You also need to set the font color to this expression:

```
=iif(Fields!Row_Key.Value=Parameters!pRowMbr.Value,
"DimGray",
"Blue")
```

Notice that the cell property `BorderColor = LightGray` and `BorderStyle` default has been changed from `Solid` to `None` and that `BorderStyle` is set to `Solid`, as shown in Figure 11-10.

This approach to formatting gives the report a clean look. You don't really need vertical lines, because the data/values in the columns already line up.

FIGURE 11-10: Current cell properties.

Dynamic Number Formatting

Our last party trick is creating dynamic formatting for the measure value. Select the properties for the `Measure_Value` textbox. You will see it is formatted by the following expression:

```
=iif(last(abs(Fields!Measure_Value.Value)) > 10000000, "#,, m;(#,, m)",
 iif(last(abs(Fields!Measure_Value.Value)) > 1000000,  "#,,.0 m;(#,,.0 m)",
 iif(last(abs(Fields!Measure_Value.Value)) > 10000,    "#, k;(#, k)",
 iif(last(abs(Fields!Measure_Value.Value)) > 1000,     "#,.0 k;(#,.0 k)",
     "#,#;(#,#)"
))))
```

This is a pretty neat trick. Now you can succinctly display values that range from 1 to into the millions without needing extra-wide cells or having so many digits that it's hard to read.

Let's preview this. You now have rows driven by the `pRowMbr` parameter, and for each row, the value for the measure specified in `pMeasure`.

You can test changing the report content by changing the value of the `pMeasures` parameter combo box from Gross Profit to Sales Amount, as shown in Figure 11-11.

Self-Calling Drill-Through Action

To change the focus to another row, you need to create a self-calling drill-through action. Specifically, you create an action that calls the same report, passing through the member unique name of the row that is clicked.

Modify the properties for the Row_Label textbox. In the Action tab, shown in Figure 11-12, the "Go to report" radio button is enabled, and "Specify a report" is set to the built-in global value `[&ReportName]`. The two parameters (name / value) are as follows:

➤ pRowMbr / [Row_Key]

➤ pMeasure / [@pMeasure]

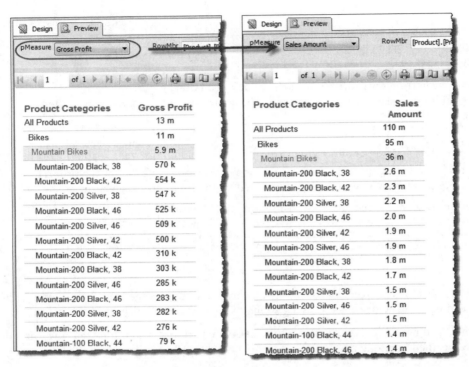

FIGURE 11-11: Testing the changing of the report.

Select the Preview tab, as shown in Figure 11-13, and experiment with drilling up and down the product hierarchy.

Cube Dynamic Rows Summary

This report demonstrates the fundamental content presentation and navigation technique employed by Angry Koala Analytics reports. It allows any dimension hierarchy to be displayed on rows and allows you to navigate up and down through that hierarchy.

In the Cube Browser report you will add columns, a filter, and a date. Then you will hook it up to a modified version of the Cube Metadata report, thus allowing the user to change what is displayed in the report.

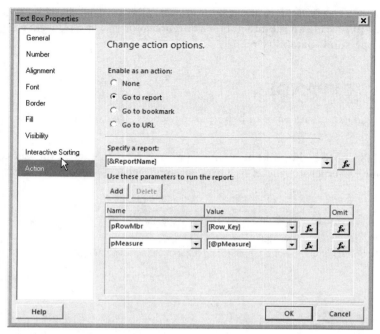

FIGURE 11-12: Changing action.

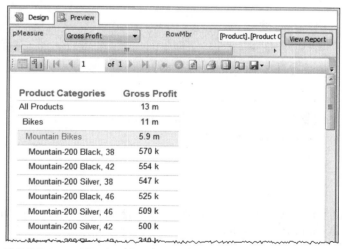

FIGURE 11-13: Viewing the changed report.

So effectively you have the start of a mini OLAP browser built in SSRS. By creating linked reports with different parameters, you can provide an infinite number of reports for your users, from a Profit and Loss report to a Salesperson Profitability report.

CUBE DYNAMIC ROWS EXPANDED

This report demonstrates how you can create an even better, user-friendly way to navigate dimension hierarchy data.

With a quick change to the MDX query and by adding a column group, you can change the Cube Dynamic Rows report to display each hierarchy level in a new column. Figure 11-14 is a preview.

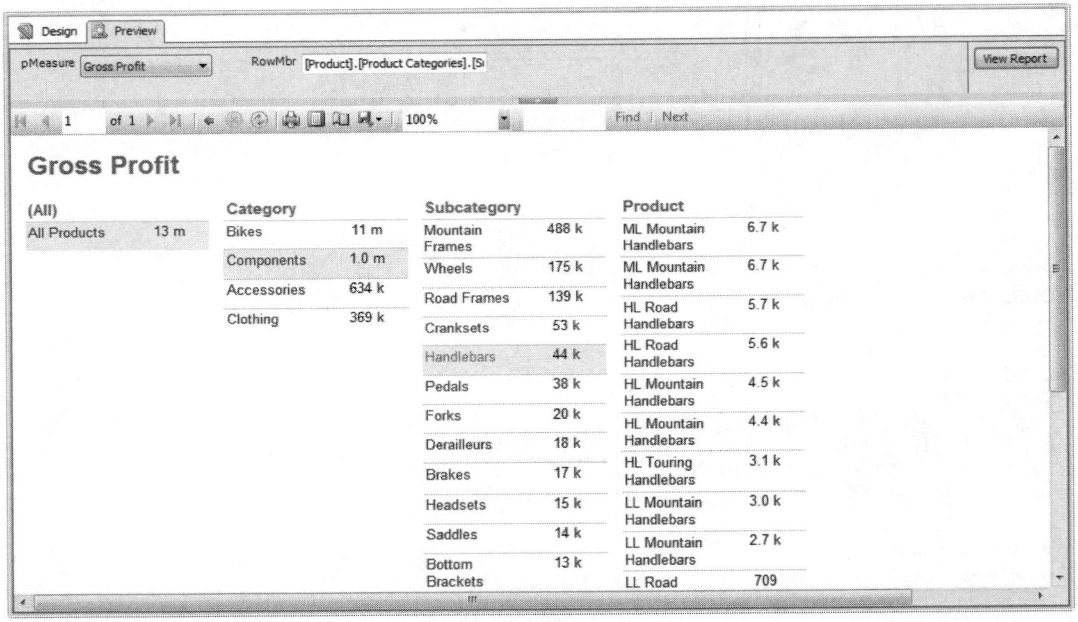

FIGURE 11-14: Viewing each hierarchy level in a new column.

MDX Query Modifications

You add one more measure, MbrIsAncestor, which is referenced to highlight all ancestor members (see the "Visualization Tweaks" section later in this chapter):

```
MEMBER [Measures].[MbrIsAncestor] AS
    StrToValue(
        "IsAncestor( " +@pRowMbr + ".hierarchy.currentmember, "
                    +@pRowMbr + " )"
        + " or ( " + @pRowMbr + ".hierarchy.currentmember is " +@pRowMbr + " )"
    )
```

You change the core part of the query to show the current member (pRowMbr) ancestors. For each ancestor member, you also return its siblings:

```
-- for each ascendant member
-- generate its siblings

STRTOSET(
  "{" +
  GENERATE(
    Ascendants(StrToMember( @pRowMbr) )
    ,StrToValue(@pRowMbr + ".Hierarchy.CurrentMember.Uniquename")
    ,".siblings, "
  )
  + ".siblings,"

-- and add the children

  + @pRowMbr + ".children"
  + "}"
)
```

Design Surface Modifications

You now need to make modifications to the design surface to show multiple columns and indicate the navigation path.

Tablix

In essence, you create a new 1 × 1 table/tablix with a single column group based on Row_Level, as shown in Figure 11-15. This creates one column of data per row level in the hierarchy.

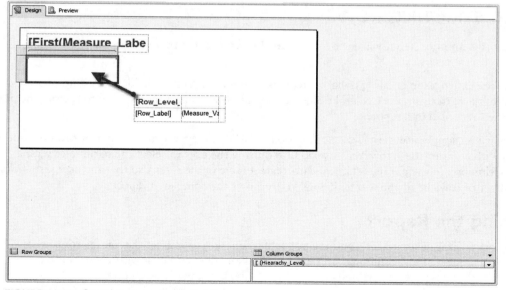

FIGURE 11-15: Creating a new table/tablix.

The existing tablix (with row group on `Row_Key`) is pasted into this cell. In other words, we have a table within a table. This gives the desired behavior of one column per hierarchy level and all the members listed within that level in rows, ordered by the current measure value.

Visualization Tweaks

First you remove the expression for indenting the `RowLabel` textbox (each level is now in a new column, not in the same column):

```
=2pt
```

Insert a title textbox above the two tables to display the current measure name:

```
=First(Fields!Measure_Label.Value)
```

Display the name of the current row hierarchy level in the header:

```
=Fields!Row_Level_Name.Value
```

Highlight not just the current member in the dimension hierarchy, but all ancestors in the hierarchy. This shows the path selected at each level in the hierarchy. Set the `BackgroundColor` property:

```
=iif(Fields!MbrIsAncestor.Value,
  "LemonChiffon",
  Nothing
  )
```

Summary

You can use this style of report to select members of interest within a hierarchy. This has the added benefit that, for the current measure, only members with data are displayed.

CUBE RESTRICTING ROWS

This report is another step toward the SSRS Cube Browser report that you began in the Cube Dynamic Rows report.

One of the challenges in creating dynamic reports is that the user can accidentally request a huge amount of data. In this report you take a quick look at how to add functionality to restrict the number of rows returned in a report.

Effectively you simply use the TOPCOUNT function in MDX to restrict the number of rows the query returns with a parameter. However, instead of requiring the user to select the parameter with a fiddly option box in the parameters, you can create a table in the report so that the user just clicks the number of rows he or she wants. Figure 11-16 shows the completed report.

Designing the Report

This report utilizes custom MDX and the TOPCOUNT function to restrict the number of rows returned in a query. This technique can be utilized on any query against MDX. For this example you start with the report you created earlier in the Cube Dynamic Rows report.

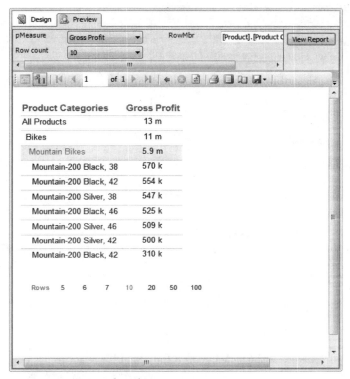

FIGURE 11-16 Completed report.

Essentially you need to make three modifications:

➤ Add a parameter for the number of rows to display.

➤ Modify the MDX query to restrict the number of rows (uses the TOPCOUNT function).

➤ Modify self-calling drill-through actions.

Figure 11-16 shows the final report.

pRowCount Parameter

First you need a new dataset to produce a list of values for the pRowCount parameter.

As shown in Figure 11-17, the following SQL query was used to create a new dataset called CellCount that is based on the shared data source dsAnySQLDB:

```
Select 5 as CellCount union all
select 6 union all
select 7 union all
select 10 union all
select 20 union all
select 50 union all
select 100
```

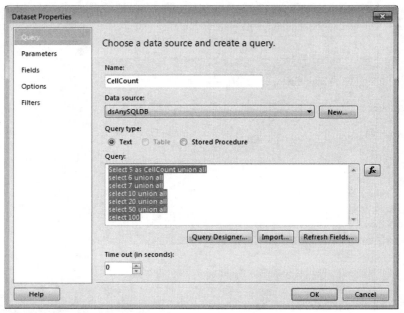

FIGURE 11-17: Creating a new dataset.

On the properties of the pRowCount parameter, both the Value and Label fields are set to CellCount, as shown in Figure 11-18.

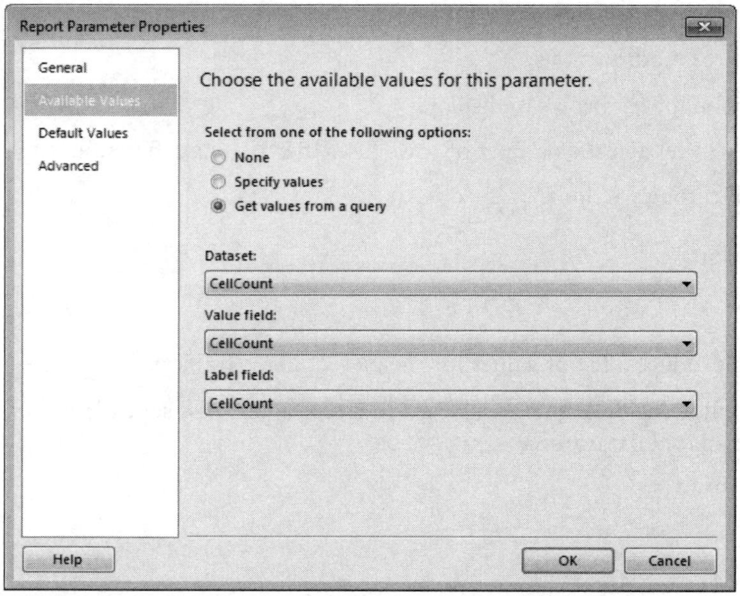

FIGURE 11-18: Setting the "Value field" and "Label field" values.

Restricting the Number of Rows in the MDX Query

Right-click DataSet1 and open the Query Editor. Notice that the MDX query is wrapped with the TOPCOUNT function:

```
-- returns the top n number of rows based on current measure
TOPCOUNT (
    -- show the current hierarchy member with its ascendants
    -- together with its children on rows
    STRTOSET (
        "{Ascendants(" + @pRowMbr + " ), "
        + @pRowMbr + ".children}"
    )
    , StrToValue (@pRowCount)
    , [Measures] . [Measure_Value]
)

ON ROWS
```

Select the Parameter icon from the toolbar, and see that the pRowCount parameter is set to a default of 6, as shown in Figure 11-19.

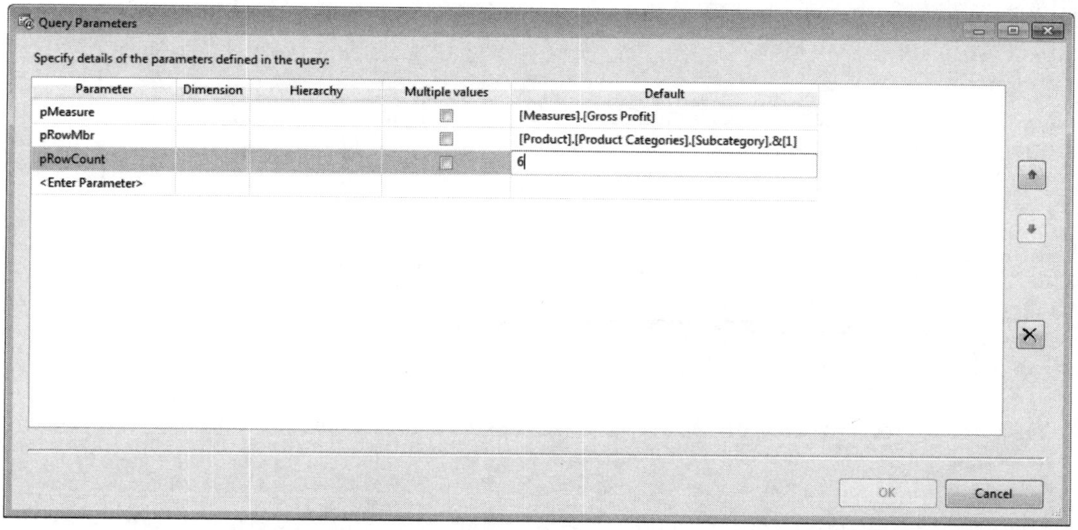

FIGURE 11-19: Default value of pRowCount parameter.

If you execute the query observer, the results should look like Figure 11-20.

If you preview the report, you'll see that you can now change the number of rows displayed, as shown in Figure 11-21.

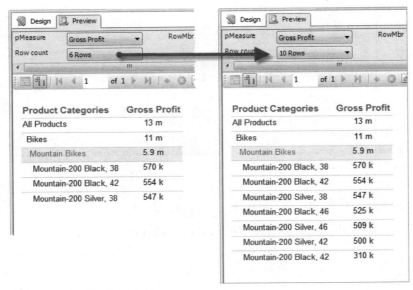

Query Designer window showing:

```
-- returns the top n number of rows based on current measure

TOPCOUNT(

    -- show the current hierarachy member with it's ascendants
    -- together with it's children on rows

    STRTOSET(
        "{Ascendants(" + @pRowMbr + "), "
        + @pRowMbr + ".children}"
    )

    ,StrToValue(@pRowCount)
    ,[Measures].[Measure_Value]
)

ON ROWS
```

Category	Subcategory	Product	Row_Key	Row_Label	Row_
(null)	(null)	(null)	[Product].[Prod...	All Products	0
Bikes	(null)	(null)	[Product].[Prod...	Bikes	1
Bikes	Mountain Bikes	(null)	[Product].[Prod...	Mountain Bikes	2
Bikes	Mountain Bikes	Mountain-200 ...	[Product].[Prod...	Mountain-200 ...	3
Bikes	Mountain Bikes	Mountain-200 ...	[Product].[Prod...	Mountain-200 ...	3
Bikes	Mountain Bikes	Mountain-200 S...	[Product].[Prod...	Mountain-200 S...	3

FIGURE 11-20: Results of execution.

Product Categories	Gross Profit
All Products	13 m
Bikes	11 m
Mountain Bikes	5.9 m
Mountain-200 Black, 38	570 k
Mountain-200 Black, 42	554 k
Mountain-200 Silver, 38	547 k

Product Categories	Gross Profit
All Products	13 m
Bikes	11 m
Mountain Bikes	5.9 m
Mountain-200 Black, 38	570 k
Mountain-200 Black, 42	554 k
Mountain-200 Silver, 38	547 k
Mountain-200 Black, 46	525 k
Mountain-200 Silver, 46	509 k
Mountain-200 Silver, 42	500 k
Mountain-200 Black, 42	310 k

FIGURE 11-21: Previewing the report.

Adding pRowCount to Self-Calling Drill-Through Report Action

Now that you can control how many rows are returned, you need to add the pRowCount parameter to the row hierarchy self-calling drill-through action.

Open the Row_Label textbox properties. Notice that the pRowCount parameter has been added to the existing action, with a value set to [@pRowCount], as shown in Figure 11-22.

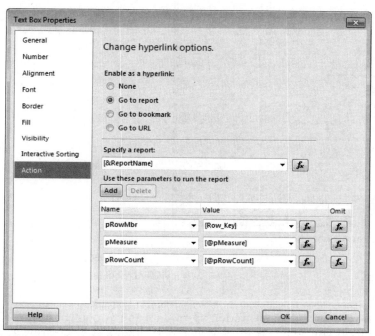

FIGURE 11-22: Adding pRowCount.

A Better Way to Interact with a Report Parameter

This report also has a table displaying the available pRowCount values. The current selected number of rows is highlighted in gray. The self-calling drill-through action on the CellCount textbox, as shown in Figure 11-23, now includes the pRowCount parameter and is set to the column value the user clicked ([CellCount]).

Summary

Another step toward the simple SSRS OLAP browser is complete. Already the user can change rows and measures (at least manually) and drill up and down a cube hierarchy. You have added the ability for the user to control the number of rows returned.

The next step is to build a way to directly interrogate the cube structure. You do so in the Cube Metadata report.

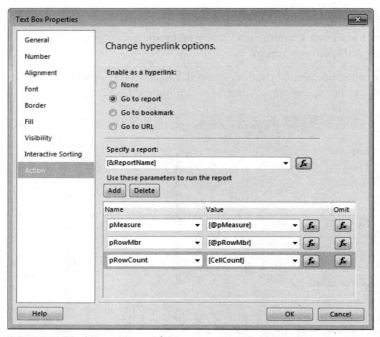

FIGURE 11-23: Interacting with a report parameter.

CUBE METADATA

Wouldn't it be nice to have all your cube documentation up-to-date and available to your users? Wouldn't it be even better if you could create generic reports and, just by creating a linked report in Report Manager and changing a few parameters, generate a completely new report?

So how do you do this? Creating the report in this chapter requires that we combine a few techniques, but first we need to access Analysis Services metadata.

Designing the Report

This solution involves tricking Reporting Services into talking nicely to Analysis Services and taking advantage of the dynamic management views (DMVs) in SQL Server 2012. You use the following DMVs:

➤ MDSCHEMA_CUBES

➤ MDSCHEMA_MEASUREGROUPS

➤ MDSCHEMA_MEASURES

➤ MDSCHEMA_MEASUREGROUP_DIMENSIONS

➤ MDSCHEMA_HIERARCHIES

➤ MDSCHEMA_LEVELS

You might want to explore others (that won't be needed in this report):

➤ DBSCHEMA_CATALOGS

➤ DBSCHEMA_DIMENSIONS

To get the full list of DMVs, run this command:

```
SELECT * FROM $SYSTEM.DBSCHEMA_TABLES
```

Figure 11-24 shows how the finished report will look.

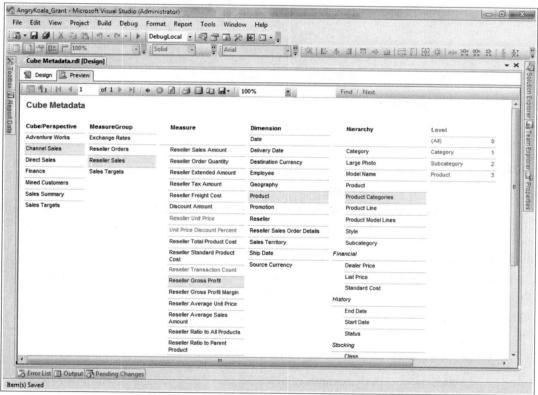

FIGURE 11-24: Finished report.

The following are the steps to list the cubes/perspectives and, after selecting a cube/perspective, displaying the list of related measure groups.

Follow these steps to add the cubes metadata DMV dataset information:

1. Add a dataset, enter the following DMV script as an expression, and click Refresh Fields:

```
SELECT * FROM $System.MDSCHEMA_CUBES WHERE CUBE_SOURCE =1
```

2. Name the dataset **Cubes**. Your dataset properties should look those shown in Figure 11-25.

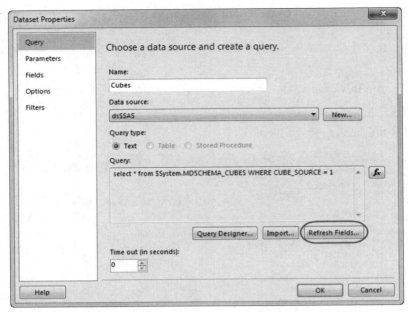

FIGURE 11-25: Dataset properties.

3. Insert a table on the design surface and drag the CUBE_NAME column onto it, to list the cubes/perspectives. When you preview this, you see the cube metadata, as shown in Figure 11-26.

MeasureGroups

Follow these steps to insert another table to display MeasureGroups, filtered by the selected CUBE_NAME (or perspective) in our first table utilizing a self-calling drill-through action:

1. Create a report parameter called pCube, and set the default value as Channel Sales.

2. Create a new dataset called MeasureGroups, and set the query to the following:
   ```
   SELECT * FROM $System.MDSCHEMA_MEASUREGROUPS
   ```

3. Add a parameter with this default value:
   ```
   [CUBE_NAME] = [@pCube]
   ```

4. Add the filter [CUBE_NAME] = [@pCube]. The Dataset Properties dialog shown in Figure 11-27 shows the filter condition.

   Finally, you need to "highlight" the currently selected cube and MeasureGroup and add the self-calling drill-through action.

5. For the CUBE_NAME textbox in the properties window, set the BackgroundColor expression to the following:
   ```
   =iif(Fields!CUBE_NAME.Value=Parameters!pCube.Value,"LemonChiffon","White")
   ```

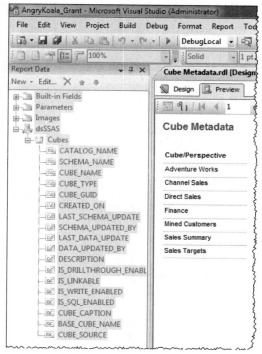

FIGURE 11-26: Cube metadata.

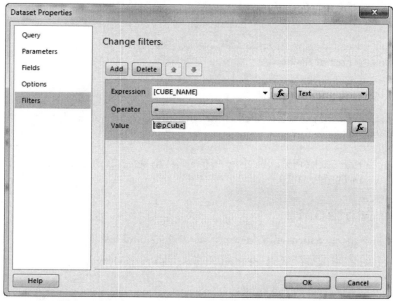

FIGURE 11-27: Dataset Properties dialog showing filter condition.

6. Open the CUBE_NAME Text Box Properties dialog. In the Action tab, set the "Enable action as a hyperlink" radio button to "Go to report." Set "Specify a report" to [&ReportName]. Add the following report parameter name and value, as shown in Figure 11-28:

PARAMETER	VALUE
pCube	[CUBE_NAME]

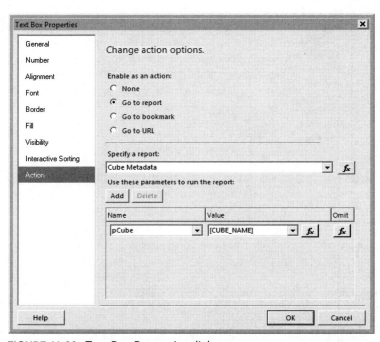

FIGURE 11-28: Text Box Properties dialog.

7. Insert a table on the design surface and drag on the MEASUREGROUP_NAME column, to list the MeasureGroups associated with the selected cube (or Measure Group) and add the filter [CUBE_NAME] = [@pCube], as before.

Preview the report. You can see that clicking a cube (or perspective) to select it displays the associated MeasureGroups, as shown in Figure 11-29.

Adding Other Cube Metadata

Similarly, you can add metadata for measures, dimensions, hierarchies, and levels:

1. Add the following report parameters, and set their default values as shown:

FIGURE 11-29: Clicking a cube to display an associated MeasureGroup.

PARAMETER	VALUE
pMeasure	`[Measures].[Reseller Gross Profit]`
pMeasureGroup	`Reseller Sales`
pDimension	`="[Product]"` This must be an expression because of the special meaning of [ ] in SSRS. `[Product]` is a shortcut for the value of a DataSet column, such as `Product.Value`, where you want the dimension unique name, `[Product]`.
pHierarchy	`[Product].[Product Categories]`

2. Enter the following code to add these datasets.

In each case, enter the sample query and then click Refresh Fields (to populate columns from the query). Then replace the query with the expression. When the dataset is saved, you still receive a message that the field could not be updated, but if you click OK, the fields are in fact there.

Measures

```
="SELECT * FROM $System.MDSCHEMA_MEASURES"
+ " WHERE CUBE_NAME = '" & Parameters!pCube.Value & "'"
+ " AND ( MEASUREGROUP_NAME = '" & Parameters!pMeasureGroup.Value & "'"
+ " OR MEASURE_DISPLAY_FOLDER = '" & Parameters!pMeasureGroup.Value & "' )"
```

Example:

```
SELECT * FROM $System.MDSCHEMA_MEASURES
WHERE CUBE_NAME = 'Channel Sales'
AND ( MEASUREGROUP_NAME = 'Reseller Sales'
OR MEASURE_DISPLAY_FOLDER = 'Reseller Sales' )
```

MeasureGroupDimensions

```
="SELECT * FROM $System.MDSCHEMA_MEASUREGROUP_DIMENSIONS "
+ " WHERE CUBE_NAME = '" & Parameters!pCube.Value & "'"
+ " AND MEASUREGROUP_NAME = '" & Parameters!pMeasureGroup.Value & "'"
```

Example:

```
SELECT * FROM $System.MDSCHEMA_MEASUREGROUP_DIMENSIONS
WHERE CUBE_NAME = 'Channel Sales'
AND MEASUREGROUP_NAME = 'Reseller Sales'
```

Hierarchies

```
="SELECT * FROM $System.MDSCHEMA_HIERARCHIES"
+ " WHERE CUBE_NAME = '" & Parameters!pCube.Value & "'"
+ " AND [DIMENSION_UNIQUE_NAME] = '" & Parameters!pDimension.Value & "'"
```

Example:

```
SELECT * FROM $System.MDSCHEMA_HIERARCHIES
WHERE CUBE_NAME = 'Channel Sales'
AND [DIMENSION_UNIQUE_NAME] = '[Product]'
```

Levels

```
="SELECT * FROM $System.MDSCHEMA_LEVELS "
+ " WHERE CUBE_NAME = '" & Parameters!pCube.Value & "'"
+ " AND [DIMENSION_UNIQUE_NAME] = '" & Parameters!pDimension.Value & "'"
+ " AND [HIERARCHY_UNIQUE_NAME] = '" & Parameters!pHierarchy.Value & "'"
```

Example:

```
SELECT * FROM $System.MDSCHEMA_LEVELS
WHERE CUBE_NAME = 'Channel Sales'
AND [DIMENSION_UNIQUE_NAME] = '[Product]'
AND [HIERARCHY_UNIQUE_NAME] = '[Product].[Product Categories]'
```

You should see the report data shown in Figure 11-30.

3. Insert a table on the design surface based on each dataset, add an expression to highlight the field when it's selected, and create a self-calling drill-through action.

4. For the Text Box Properties of CUBE_NAME, in the Action page, set the "Enable action as a hyperlink" radio button to "Go to report," set "Specify a report" to [&ReportName], and add the following Report Parameter names and values:

PARAMETER	VALUE
pCube	= [@pCube]
pMeasureGroup	= [MEASUREGROUP_NAME]
pMeasure	= [@pMeasure]

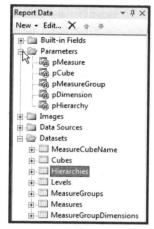

FIGURE 11-30: Complete report data.

5. Now that you have added the extra parameters, go back to the CUBE_NAME Text Box properties and add the following parameters to the Action page:

PARAMETER	VALUE
pMeasureGroup	= [@pMeasureGroup]
pMeasure	= [@pMeasure]

Measures

6. Set the Measure textbox to Gray if the metadata is not visible and you can display additional information with a tooltip. Alternatively, you can add columns to show other metadata.

7. In the Text Box properties of MEASURE_NAME, add a self-calling drill-through action (set "Specify a report" to [&ReportName]) with the following parameter names and values:

PARAMETER	VALUE
pCube	= [@pCube]
pMeasureGroup	= [@pMeasureGroup]
pMeasure	= [MEASURE_UNIQUE_NAME]

The design surface should resemble Figure 11-31 and preview like Figure 11-32.

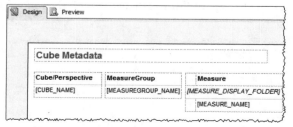

FIGURE 11-31: Design surface.

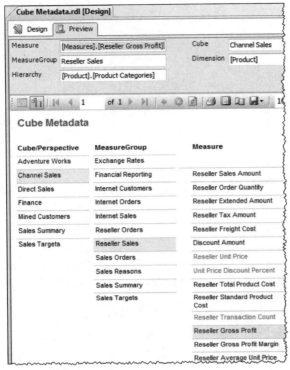

FIGURE 11-32: Preview.

Dimensions

List the dimensions for the selected `MeasureGroup`, and highlight the current dimension.

8. Add a self-calling drill-through action with the following values:

PARAMETER	VALUE
pCube	= [@pCube]
pMeasureGroup	= [@pMeasureGroup]
pMeasure	= [MEASURE_UNIQUE_NAME]

Hierarchies

9. Add a self-calling (report is `[&ReportName]`) drill-through action with the following parameter names and values:

PARAMETER	VALUE
pCube	= [@pCube]
pDimension	= [@pDimension]

Levels

10. To provide complete information, show the level name and number for the selected hierarchy.

Figures 11-33 and 11-34 show the design surface and preview for Dimensions, Hierarchies, and Levels.

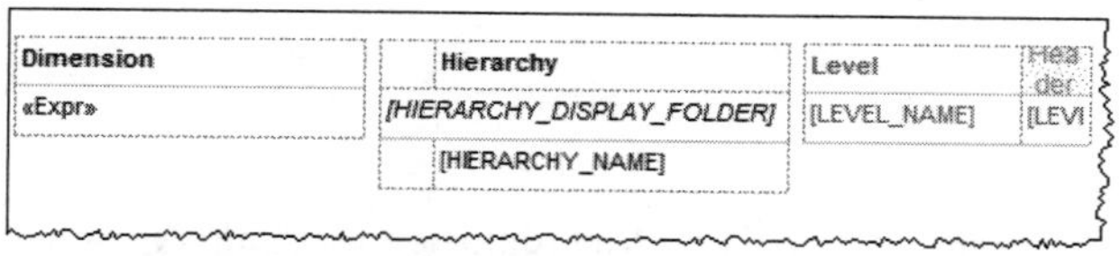

Dimension	Hierarchy	Level	Hea der
«Expr»	*[HIERARCHY_DISPLAY_FOLDER]*	[LEVEL_NAME]	[LEVl
	[HIERARCHY_NAME]		

FIGURE 11-33: Design surface.

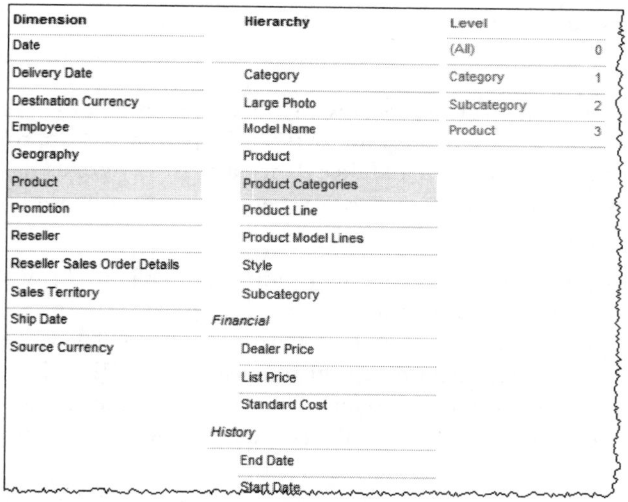

Dimension	Hierarchy	Level	
Date		(All)	0
Delivery Date	Category	Category	1
Destination Currency	Large Photo	Subcategory	2
Employee	Model Name	Product	3
Geography	Product		
Product	Product Categories		
Promotion	Product Line		
Reseller	Product Model Lines		
Reseller Sales Order Details	Style		
Sales Territory	Subcategory		
Ship Date	*Financial*		
Source Currency	Dealer Price		
	List Price		
	Standard Cost		
	History		
	End Date		
	Start Date		

FIGURE 11-34: Preview.

Final Thoughts

You now have a way to discover information about the structure of your cubes so that, if you also populate the description fields within Analysis Server, you can provide users with up-to-date documentation, such as a measure's meaning. You can also enable users to search for a measure by name, or you can add a help button on a standard report to display details of a dimension or measure.

The Cube Browser and the Angry Koala Cube Browser reports in this book use this report. With some modifications, this will enable users to dynamically change the rows, columns, and filters in their Cube Browser reports.

CUBE BROWSER

You can build a simple, functional OLAP browser in Reporting Services by using some of the advanced reporting techniques described earlier in the chapter:

1. Extend the Cube Dynamic Rows report to include dynamic columns.

2. Add a date filter.

3. Add a dynamic filter.

4. Allow users to change the measure.

5. Link the new report with a modified version of the Cube Metadata report to allow users to do the following:

   ➤ Select the measure to display

   ➤ Change the content of rows and columns

   ➤ Change the filter

With these features, developers or power users can create a report with any combination of Rows, Columns, Filter, Date, and Measure by creating a linked report and setting the parameters appropriately. Also, as soon as a report is running, users can slice and dice their data. If they are using the native reporting services manager, they can also create their own version of a report by simply saving the current report as a favorite in Internet Explorer.

This cube browser report is also *fast*. In a traditional report, when you add parameters in the MDX query window, behind the scenes an MDX query is generated for each parameter. This means that when a report is run, 10 to 20 MDX queries can run before the report is rendered. The Cube Browser report has only the MDX query to bring back data for the grid (plus a basic SQL union statement to generate a list of numbers for the row count and column count). You go to other supporting reports to collect parameters. Consequently, when you drill up and drill down, the response time is fantastic.

Figure 11-35 shows a Sales report, and Figure 11-36 shows a Profit and Loss report. Both are examples of the same Cube Browser report, just with different parameters.

Anatomy of the Reports

Rather than going through a step-by-step approach to building the reports in this suite, let's run through the architecture and then the necessary techniques utilized within each report.

The reports are:

➤ Cube Browser

➤ Cube Browser Metadata

➤ Cube Browser Member

First, let's look at the roles of these reports.

Gross Profit for April 2004
Product Categories by Sales Territory
Promotions : All Promotions

Swap rows with

Columns	Filter	All Sales Territories	North America	Europe	Pacific	NA	columns
All Products		667 k	273 k	216 k	178 k		5
Bikes		583 k	219 k	197 k	167 k		6
Mountain Bikes		310 k	151 k	99 k	60 k		7
Mountain-200 Silver, 38		54 k	29 k	15 k	9.5 k		10
Mountain-200 Black, 38		50 k	24 k	16 k	9.4 k		20
Mountain-200 Black, 42		46 k	19 k	13 k	14 k		50
Mountain-200 Silver, 42		41 k	20 k	14 k	6.3 k		100
Mountain-200 Black, 46		40 k	19 k	15 k	6.3 k		
Mountain-200 Silver, 46		37 k	16 k	12 k	8.4 k		
Mountain-400-W Silver, 46		7.7 k	3.1 k	3.1 k	1.4 k		

Rows 5 6 7 10 20 50 100

run by platypus\grantp in < 1 second
11:00:25 PM Monday, December 07, 2009

Cube Browser
Page 1 of 1

FIGURE 11-35: Sales report.

Amount for April 2004
Accounts by Departments
Promotions : All Promotions

Swap rows with

Columns	Filter	Corporate	Research and Development	Quality Assurance	Sales and Marketing	Executive General and Administration	columns
Net Income		226 k	794 k	(21 k)	(18 k)	(9.4 k)	5
Operating Profit		327 k	894 k	(21 k)	(18 k)	(9.5 k)	6
Operating Expenses		960 k	392 k	21 k	18 k	9.5 k	7
Labor Expenses		775 k	281 k	18 k	16 k	8.2 k	10
Commissions		60 k	60 k				20
Telephone and Utilities		32 k	19 k	409	424	212	50
Depreciation		33 k	12 k	724	714	378	100
Travel Expenses		29 k	9.0 k	463	574	263	
Rent		13 k	4.5 k	277	270	139	
Office Supplies		6.4 k	2.1 k	116	132	62	

Rows 5 6 7 10 20 50 100

run by platypus\grantp in < 1 second
11:10:05 PM Monday, December 07, 2009

Cube Browser
Page 1 of 1

FIGURE 11-36: Profit and loss report.

Cube Browser

This Cube Browser is the main report and the only one directly visible to your users. You can have multiple linked reports based on this physical report showing different data on rows, columns, and filters by simply creating a linked report and changing the parameters.

The following list explains what users can do in this report and in any linked reports and how to do it. The key action for each item is listed, as are any supporting parameter settings.

➤ **Change the measure to display**—Click Measure Name in the title to drill through to the Cube Browser Metadata report.

   `driver = Measure`

➤ **Change what hierarchy to display on rows**—Click Hierarchy Name in the title to drill through to Cube Browser Metadata.

   `driver = Rows`

➤ **Change what hierarchy to display on columns**—Click the Column Hierarchy Name to drill through to Cube Browser Metadata.

   `driver = Columns`

➤ **Change what hierarchy to use for a filter**—Click the Filter Hierarchy Name to drill through to Cube Browser Metadata.

   `driver = Filter`

➤ **Change the Filter value (member)**—Click the Filter Member Name to drill through to Cube Browser Member.

   `driver = Filter`

➤ **Change the date period (it can be year, quarter, month, or day)**—Click the Date Member in the title to drill through to Cube Browser Member.

   `driver = Date`

➤ **Drill up and down the hierarchy displayed on rows or columns**—Click a row member to drill-to-self with new selection.

➤ **Change the number of rows or columns to display**—Click the row number to drill-to-self with a new selection.

➤ **Swap rows with filter**—Click the Swap Filter textbox to drill-to-self with the `Row` and `Filter` parameters swapped.

➤ **Swap rows and columns**—Click the Swap Column textbox to drill-to-self with the `Row` and `Column` parameters swapped.

Figure 11-37 shows the key navigation paths from the Cube Browser to the Cube Browser Metadata and the Cube Browser Member.

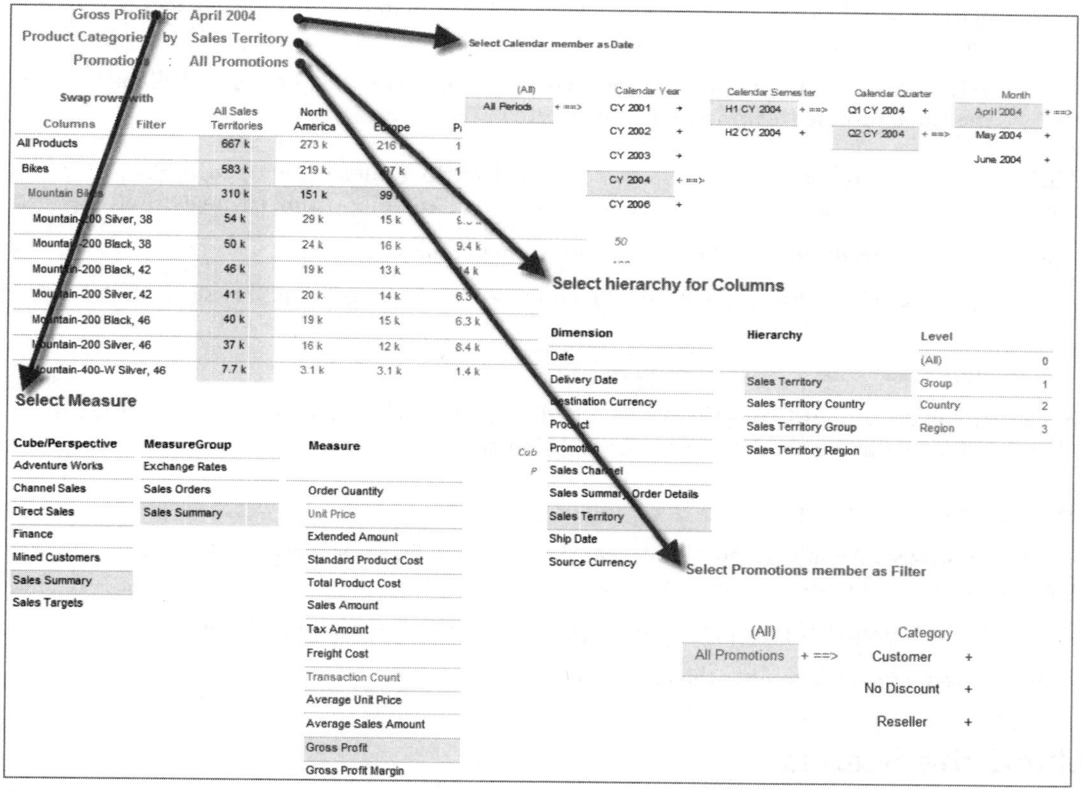

FIGURE 11-37: Key navigation paths.

Cube Browser Metadata

The Cube Browser Metadata report is called from the Cube Browser report and returns a measure or hierarchy. Its design is based on the Cube Metadata report and is called when the user wants to do the following:

➤ Change the measure

➤ Select what hierarchy to display on rows or columns

➤ Select what hierarchy to filter by

It therefore has two distinct behaviors. The following list explains what users can do if the driver parameter value is Measure, and how to do it:

➤ **Select a cube/perspective**—Click the MeasureLabel to initiate drill-to-self action to display measures available in the selected cube.

➤ **Select a measure from the cube/perspective**—Click a measure to fire as a drill-back action to the Cube Browser report passing the selected Measure.

The following list explains what users can do if the driver parameter is Row, Column, or Filter, and how to do it. The key action for each item is listed, as are any supporting parameter settings:

➤ **Select a dimension**—Drill-to-self to display hierarchies.

➤ **Choose a hierarchy for a selected dimension**—Drill back to Cube Browser with the selected hierarchy.

    driver = Rows, Columns, or Filter

Note that you do not hard-code the report you *drill back* to. One of the parameters is the calling report. It allows this report to be called from different linked reports.

Cube Browser Member

The Cube Browser Member report is called from the Cube Browser report and returns a hierarchy member. It is called when the user wants to do the following:

➤ **Select a period of time to filter the report by** (a specific year, quarter, month, or day).

➤ **Select a member to filter the report by.**

Behind the Scenes

Now let's look at the details and the reports utilized.

Cube Browser

The Cube Browser report is based on the Cube Dynamic Rows report. It uses the same basic concept but extends the idea to columns. Date and dynamic filters are added. To add the date and dynamic filters, you need the following parameters (I have included a sample default value):

➤ pCube = Sales Summary (the name of the cube or perspective)

➤ pMeasureGroup = Sales Summary (the name of the MeasureGroup)

➤ pMeasure = [Measures].[Gross Profit] (the UniqueName of the measure)

➤ pDateMbr = [Date].[Calendar].[Month].&[2004]&[4] (the UniqueName of the Date member)

➤ pRowMbr = [Product].[Product Categories].[Subcategory].&[1] (the UniqueName of the member from which ascendants and children are shown on rows)

➤ pRowCount = 10 (the number of rows to show)

➤ pColMbr = [Sales Territory].[Sales Territory].[All Sales Territories]
(the UniqueName of the member from which ascendants and children are shown on columns)

➤ pColCount = 5 (the number of columns to show)

➤ pFilterMbr = [Promotion].[Promotions].[All Promotions] (the UniqueName of the member acting as filter)

If you open the DataSet1 query and select the parameters icon from the Query Designer Toolbar, you'll see the list of parameters together with their default values, as shown in Figure 11-38.

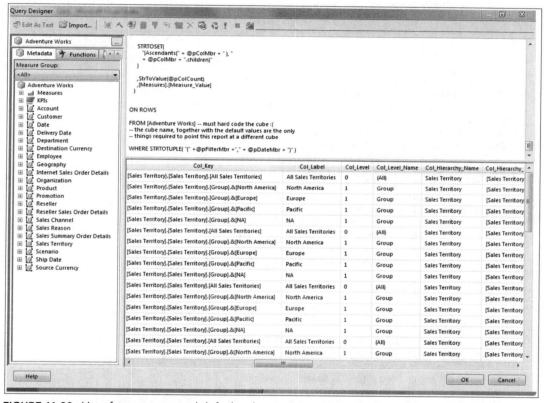

FIGURE 11-38: List of parameters and default values.

Here is the required MDX query, including the necessary additions for extra functionality:

```
----------------------------------------------------------------
-- Cube Browser
--
-- Grant Paisley
-- Angry Koala
-- http://angrykoala.com.au
-- 14 Nov 2011
```

```
    --
    --
    -- Note: certain attributes commented out as not needed
    -- but may be of use in other reports
    -------------------------------------------------------------------

    WITH
    -- The measure of interest
    MEMBER [Measures].[Measure_Value]
      AS StrToValue(@pMeasure)

    -- the friendly name of the measure
    MEMBER [Measures].[Measure_Label]
      AS StrToValue(@pMeasure + ".Member_Name")

    -- Row metadata
    MEMBER [Measures].[Row_Key]
      AS StrToValue( @pRowMbr + ".Hierarchy.Currentmember.Uniquename" )
    MEMBER [Measures].[Row_Label]
      AS StrToValue( @pRowMbr + ".Hierarchy.CurrentMember.Member_Caption" )
    MEMBER [Measures].[Row_Level]
      AS StrToValue( @pRowMbr + ".Hierarchy.CurrentMember.Level.Ordinal" )
    MEMBER [Measures].[Row_Level_Name]
      AS StrToValue( @pRowMbr + ".Hierarchy.Level.Name" )
    MEMBER [Measures].[Row_Hierarchy_Name]
      AS StrToValue( @pRowMbr + ".Hierarchy.Name" )
    MEMBER [Measures].[Row_Hierarchy_UniqueName]
      AS StrToValue( @pRowMbr + ".Hierarchy.UniqueName" )
    MEMBER [Measures].[Row_Dimension_Name]
      AS StrToValue( @pRowMbr + ".Dimension.Name" )
    MEMBER [Measures].[Row_Dimension_UniqueName]
      AS StrToValue(@pRowMbr + ".Dimension_Unique_Name" )

    -- Column metadata
    MEMBER [Measures].[Col_Key]
      AS StrToValue( @pColMbr + ".Hierarchy.Currentmember.Uniquename" )
    MEMBER [Measures].[Col_Label]
      AS StrToValue( @pColMbr + ".Hierarchy.CurrentMember.Member_Caption" )
    MEMBER [Measures].[Col_Level]
      AS StrToValue( @pColMbr + ".Hierarchy.CurrentMember.Level.Ordinal" )
    MEMBER [Measures].[Col_Level_Name]
      AS StrToValue( @pColMbr + ".Hierarchy.Level.Name" )
    MEMBER [Measures].[Col_Hierarchy_Name]
      AS StrToValue( @pColMbr + ".Hierarchy.Name" )
    MEMBER [Measures].[Col_Hierarchy_UniqueName]
      AS StrToValue( @pColMbr + ".Hierarchy.UniqueName" )
    MEMBER [Measures].[Col_Dimension_Name]
      AS StrToValue( @pColMbr + ".Dimension.Name" )
    MEMBER [Measures].[Col_Dimension_UniqueName]
      AS StrToValue(@pColMbr + ".Dimension_Unique_Name" )

    -- Filter metadata
    MEMBER [Measures].[Filter_Key]
      AS StrToValue( @pFilterMbr + ".Hierarchy.Currentmember.Uniquename" )
    MEMBER [Measures].[Filter_Label]
```

```
   AS StrToValue( @pFilterMbr + ".Hierarchy.CurrentMember.Member_Caption" )
MEMBER [Measures].[Filter_Level]
   AS StrToValue( @pFilterMbr + ".Hierarchy.CurrentMember.Level.Ordinal" )
MEMBER [Measures].[Filter_Level_Name]
   AS StrToValue( @pFilterMbr + ".Hierarchy.Level.Name" )
MEMBER [Measures].[Filter_Hierarchy_Name]
   AS StrToValue( @pFilterMbr + ".Hierarchy.Name" )
MEMBER [Measures].[Filter_Hierarchy_UniqueName]
   AS StrToValue( @pFilterMbr + ".Hierarchy.UniqueName" )
MEMBER [Measures].[Filter_Dimension_Name]
   AS StrToValue( @pFilterMbr + ".Dimension.Name" )
MEMBER [Measures].[Filter_Dimension_UniqueName]
   AS StrToValue(@pFilterMbr + ".Dimension_Unique_Name" )

-- Date metadata
MEMBER [Measures].[Date_Key]
   AS StrToValue( @pDateMbr + ".Hierarchy.Currentmember.Uniquename" )
MEMBER [Measures].[Date_Label]
   AS StrToValue( @pDateMbr + ".Hierarchy.CurrentMember.Member_Caption" )
MEMBER [Measures].[Date_Level]
   AS StrToValue( @pDateMbr + ".Hierarchy.CurrentMember.Level.Ordinal" )
MEMBER [Measures].[Date_Level_Name]
   AS StrToValue( @pDateMbr + ".Hierarchy.Level.Name" )
MEMBER [Measures].[Date_Hierarchy_Name]
   AS StrToValue( @pDateMbr + ".Hierarchy.Name" )
MEMBER [Measures].[Date_Hierarchy_UniqueName]
   AS StrToValue( @pDateMbr + ".Hierarchy.UniqueName" )
MEMBER [Measures].[Date_Dimension_Name]
   AS StrToValue( @pDateMbr + ".Dimension.Name" )
MEMBER [Measures].[Date_Dimension_UniqueName]
   AS StrToValue(@pDateMbr + ".Dimension_Unique_Name" )




SELECT NON EMPTY {
-- display the measure and rowmbr attributes on columns

[Measures].[Row_Key],
[Measures].[Row_Label],
[Measures].[Row_Level],
[Measures].[Row_Level_Name],
[Measures].[Row_Hierarchy_Name],
[Measures].[Row_Hierarchy_UniqueName],
[Measures].[Row_Dimension_Name],
[Measures].[Row_Dimension_UniqueName],

[Measures].[Col_Key],
[Measures].[Col_Label],
[Measures].[Col_Level],
[Measures].[Col_Level_Name],
[Measures].[Col_Hierarchy_Name],
[Measures].[Col_Hierarchy_UniqueName],
[Measures].[Col_Dimension_Name],
[Measures].[Col_Dimension_UniqueName],
```

```
    [Measures].[Filter_Key],
    [Measures].[Filter_Label],
    [Measures].[Filter_Level],
    [Measures].[Filter_Level_Name],
    [Measures].[Filter_Hierarchy_Name],
    [Measures].[Filter_Hierarchy_UniqueName],
    [Measures].[Filter_Dimension_Name],
    [Measures].[Filter_Dimension_UniqueName],

    [Measures].[Date_Key],
    [Measures].[Date_Label],
    [Measures].[Date_Level],
    [Measures].[Date_Level_Name],
    [Measures].[Date_Hierarchy_Name],
    [Measures].[Date_Hierarchy_UniqueName],
    [Measures].[Date_Dimension_Name],
    [Measures].[Date_Dimension_UniqueName],

    [Measures].[Measure_Value],
    [Measures].[Measure_Label]


} ON COLUMNS,

-- returns the top n number of rows based on current measure

TOPCOUNT(
-- show the current hierarchy member with its ascendants
-- together with its children on rows

STRTOSET(
"{Ascendants(" + @pRowMbr + " ), "
+ @pRowMbr + ".children}"
)

,StrToValue(@pRowCount)
, [Measures].[Measure_Value]
)

* -- cross product

-- returns the top n number of Columns based on current measure

TOPCOUNT(

-- show the current hierarchy member with its ascendants
-- together with its children on Columns

STRTOSET(
"{Ascendants(" + @pColMbr + " ), "
+ @pColMbr + ".children}"
)
```

```
, StrToValue(@pColCount)
, [Measures].[Measure_Value]
)


ON ROWS

FROM [Adventure Works] -- must hard code the cube :(
-- the cube name, together with the default values are the only
-- things required to point this report at a different cube

WHERE STRTOTUPLE( "(" +@pFilterMbr +"," + @pDateMbr + ")" )
```

Much like how you created calculated measures for the metadata on rows, you now get the same metadata for the Date, Filter, and Column members. For each you collect the following:

➤ Key

➤ Label

➤ Level

➤ Level_Name

➤ Hierarchy_Name

➤ Hierarchy_UniqueName

➤ Dimension_Name

➤ Dimension_UniqueName

Notice that you have done the following:

➤ Added extra measures to display metadata for columns, date, and filter

➤ Created a cross product between rows and columns

➤ Added a tuple in the WHERE clause based on the Date member and the Filter member

As shown in Figure 11-39, when you run the MDX query, you see all the metadata together with the Measure value you want to display: Measure_Value.

Report Body

The main tablix, shown in Figure 11-40, is a matrix with:

➤ Columns grouped by Col_Key and displaying Col_Label

➤ Rows grouped by Row_Key and displaying Row_Label

➤ The Measure_Value in the details cell

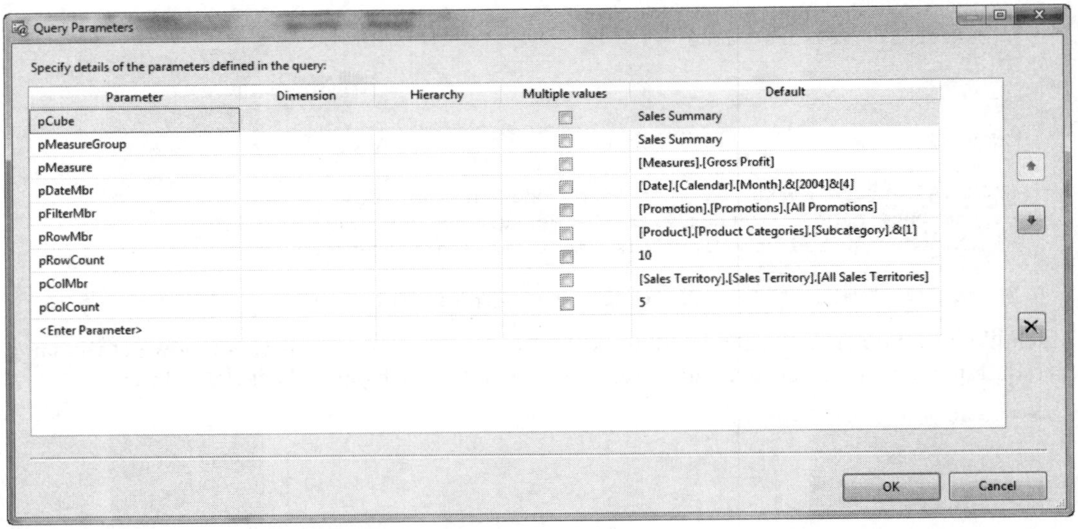

FIGURE 11-39: Metadata and measure value.

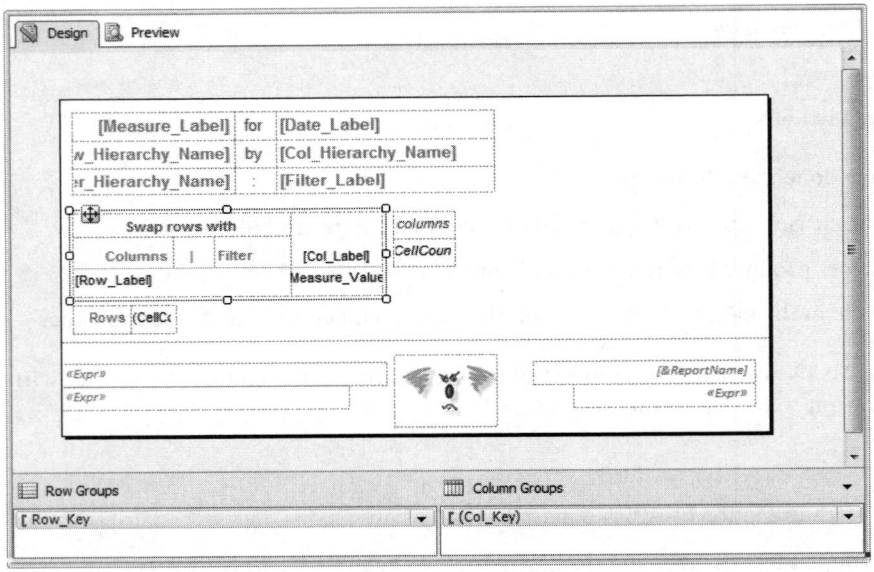

FIGURE 11-40: Main tablix.

In the columns, similar to the rows, the group is by Col_Key and sorted by the Col_Level (the level in the hierarchy) and within the level, descending by Measure_Value. You could enhance the report by adding a parameter to control whether sorting is ascending or descending, as shown in Figure 11-41.

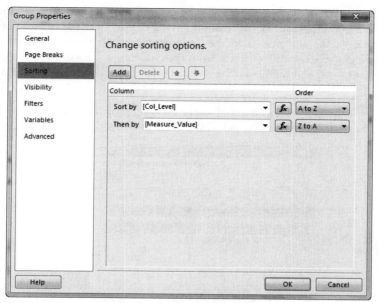

FIGURE 11-41: Adding an ascending or descending control.

The `Measure_Value` textbox is tweaked to highlight the current member (`LemonChiffon`) for rows and columns.

The `BackgroundColor` is set as follows:

```
=iif(Fields!Row_Key.Value=Parameters!pRowMbr.Value, "LemonChiffon",
iif(Fields!Col_Key.Value=Parameters!pColMbr.Value, "LemonChiffon",
 Nothing
 ))
```

Similarly, the font is set to `Black` if this cell corresponds to the current member; otherwise, it is set to `DimGray`:

```
=iif(Fields!Row_Key.Value=Parameters!pRowMbr.Value, "Black",
iif(Fields!Col_Key.Value=Parameters!pColMbr.Value, "Black",
 "DimGray"
 ))
```

On the labels for rows and columns, the same background color is set (`LemonChiffon`), but the text color is `DimGray` if they correspond to the current member. Otherwise, it is `Blue`, indicating that you can click it to drill up and down the hierarchy:

```
=iif(Fields!Row_Key.Value=Parameters!pRowMbr.Value,
"DimGray",
"Blue")
```

Restricting Rows and Columns

The parameter `pColCount` restricts the number of columns displayed in this report.

You use the TOPCOUNT function in MDX to restrict the number of column members returned in the query driven by the parameter pColCount. However, instead of having to select the parameter with a fiddly option box in the parameters, the user just clicks the number of columns he or she wants. The TablixColCount table displays these selectable values from the CellCount dataset. The clickable values are colored Blue except for the numeric matching the current parameter value, and it is DimGray.

Clicking invokes a self-calling drill-through action with all parameters set as their existing values except for pColCount, and that is set [CellCount], which is the value of the cell that is clicked. Figure 11-42 shows the parameter values for this action.

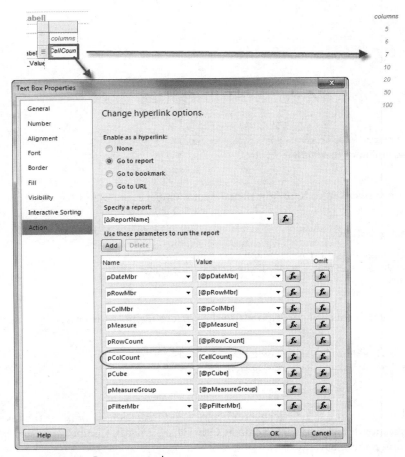

FIGURE 11-42: Parameter values.

Restricting rows works in the same way, but with parameter pRowCount.

Swap Actions

In the top-left cell of the main tablix is the TablixSwap. It contains two blue cells that allow the user to swap the rows with columns or swap the rows with the filter. Again, all that happens is a self-calling drill-through action takes place. For instance, for the rows and columns swap we set up a tooltip:

```
="Swap rows ("
+ Fields!Row_Hierarchy_Name.Value
+ ") with columns ("
+ Fields!Col_Hierarchy_Name.Value
+ ")"
```

We also set up a self-calling drill-through action. Notice the swapping of row and column parameters shown in Figure 11-43.

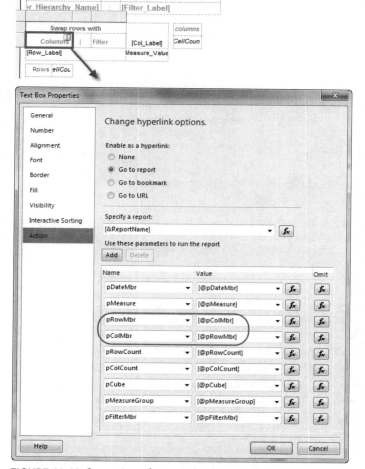

FIGURE 11-43 Swapping of row and column parameters.

Titles

The titles in the report work both as titles and as places where users can change what they see in the report.

Changing the Measure (TextboxMeasureName)

The first textbox in the Titles table includes the Measure to display in the report. When the user clicks it, he or she is taken to the Cube Browser Metadata report to select a different measure from the same cube, or even a measure from a different cube. All parameters are passed to the Cube Browser Metadata report, plus the following:

➤ pCallingReport = is set by the report calling this report. This allows drill-through textbox action to return to the calling report.

➤ pDriver = Measure indicates that the user wants to select a cube and measure. Other possible values are Rows, Columns, Date, and Filter.

Figure 11-44 shows the action, and Figure 11-45 shows how to select a measure.

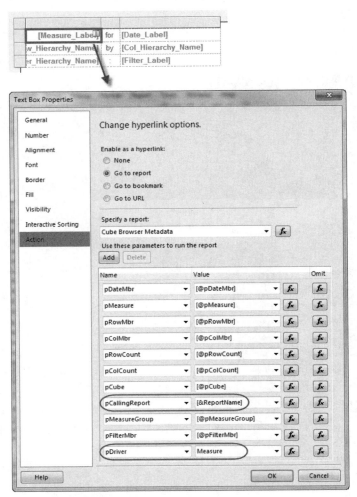

FIGURE 11-44: Action.

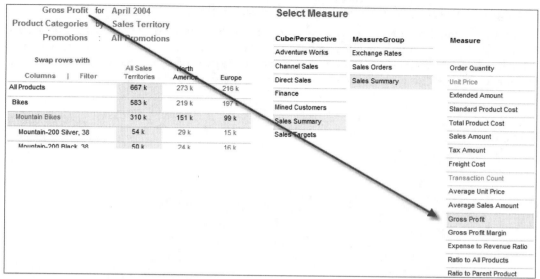

FIGURE 11-45: Selecting a measure.

Changing the Hierarchy on Rows (TextboxRowHierarchyName)

Similarly, if you want to change what is on rows, click the `TextboxRowHierarchyName`. This action calls the same Cube Browser Metadata report, but this time with `pDriver = Rows`. Now the Cube Browser Metadata report displays the Dimensions and Hierarchies for the Measure Group corresponding to the current measure. Figure 11-46 shows `TextboxRowHierarchy` on the design surface and the Action tab of the textbox properties window with the parameter values required to call the Cube Browser Metadata report. Figure 11-47 shows a preview of the result.

Changing the Hierarchy on Columns (TextboxColHierarchyName)

Changing columns works the same way as `TextBoxRowHierarchyName`, except that the `pDriver` parameter is set to `Columns` so that the Cube Browser Metadata report knows to display, and later return, the `pColMbr` parameter.

Changing the Hierarchy for the Filter (TextboxFilterHierarchyName)

Changing the filter also works the same way as `TextBoxRowHierarchyName`, except that the `pDriver` parameter is set to `Filter` so that the Cube Browser Metadata report knows to display, and later return, the `pFilterMbr` parameter.

Changing the Date Member (TextboxDateLabel)

The user can change the period of time the report covers by clicking the `TextboxDateLabel`. This drills through to the Cube Browser Member report, where the user can select another `Date` member in the hierarchy. This can be a year, quarter, month, or even a single day. Figure 11-48 shows the action parameters. This time `pDriver` is set to `Date`. Figure 11-49 shows what the user sees.

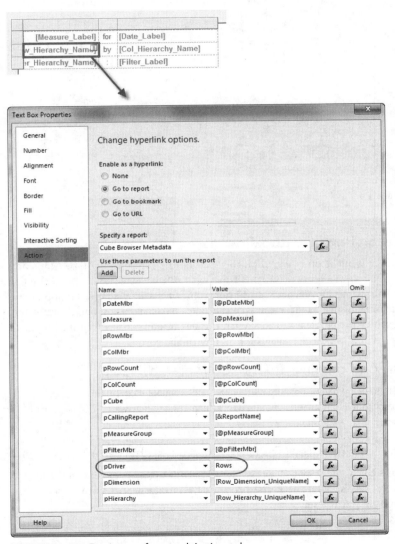

FIGURE 11-46: Design surface and Action tab.

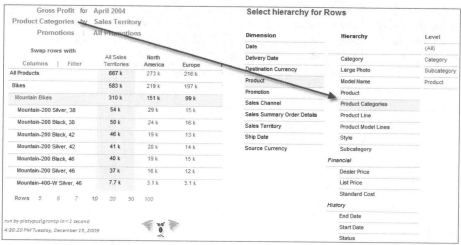

FIGURE 11-47: Preview of result.

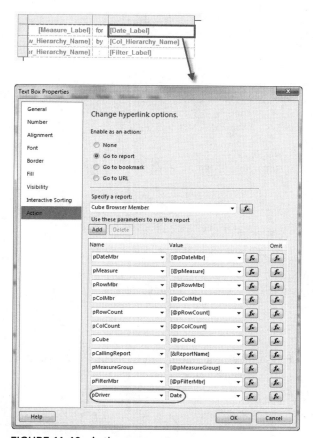

FIGURE 11-48: Action parameters.

> **NOTE** *The date ranges in the newer sample database are newer than those displayed here. Set the* `pDateMbr` *parameter default to a date member in 2013 or 2014 to work with the provided SSAS database.*

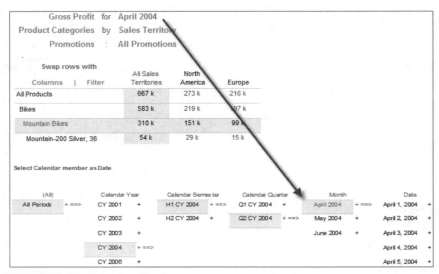

FIGURE 11-49: Selecting the Date parameter.

Footer Information

To round out the report, we have added some interesting information to the footer:

➤ Who ran it

➤ How long it took to execute

➤ Page numbers in 1 of *n* format

➤ The name of the report

In production we always number our reports using the following format:

p*nnn - meaningful name*

For example, p012 - Channel Sales.

So in the footer we would display the report's full number and name, but in the title we would strip the number and just leave the report name.

Figure 11-50 shows a formatted footer.

FIGURE 11-50: Formatted footer.

The following is the code for the first textbox, which displays who ran the report and how long it took to run:

```
="run by " & User!UserID + " in " +

IIf(
 System.DateTime.Now.Subtract(Globals!ExecutionTime).TotalSeconds<1,
    "< 1 second",
 (

IIf(System.DateTime.Now.Subtract(Globals!ExecutionTime).Hours >0,
    System.DateTime.Now.Subtract(Globals!ExecutionTime).Hours
    & " hour(s), ", "") +

IIf(System.DateTime.Now.Subtract(Globals!ExecutionTime).Minutes >0,
    System.DateTime.Now.Subtract(Globals!ExecutionTime).Minutes
    & " minute(s), ", "") +

IIf(System.DateTime.Now.Subtract(Globals!ExecutionTime).Seconds >0,
    System.DateTime.Now.Subtract(Globals!ExecutionTime).Seconds
    & " second(s)", ""))

 )
```

The next textbox shows when the report was run:

```
= FormatDateTime(Globals!ExecutionTime,3)
& " "
& FormatDateTime(Globals!ExecutionTime,1)
```

Then, at the right of the footer comes the report's name:

```
=Globals!ReportName
```

The final textbox holds the page number and total number of pages:

```
= "Page "
& Globals!PageNumber
& " of "
& Globals!TotalPages
```

Now you have a simple OLAP browser. You can create user reports by creating linked reports with different parameters. Interestingly, your users can also configure the report to one they like and then just save it as a favorite in Internet Explorer.

NOTE *Paul here again with my own "final thoughts." Thanks again to Grant Paisley for this contribution to the previous edition of the book. I made some very minor revisions to make sure everything worked with an updated copy of the data source.*

I chose to include this chapter because I think the cube browser solution is pure genius and a great example of a well-crafted complex solution that would simply not be feasible for us to build from the ground-up as an exercise. It is easy to get lost in the details so I offer this advance: Start by running the Cube Browser report and then see how the actions utilize the other reports to collect parameters. After that, run the Angry Koala Cube Browser report and do the same. I hope you find this as educational and valuable as I have.

You can use this solution with different data sources but you should make sure each parameter has a valid default value. Without the book sample SSAS database, make sure the date parameters (such as pDateMbr*) are in the correct ranges with defaults set to 2013 or 2014.*

Final Thoughts

This is a great starting point for creating your own variation on an OLAP Cube Browser. For instance, the Angry Koala Cube Surfer report, shown in Figure 11-51, uses the same basic concept as the Cube Browser. But instead of showing a single measure in each data cell, it shows the following:

> ➤ The measure for the current period (in bold)

> ➤ The measure for the same period in a comparison period (driven by a lag number—for example, 12 means 12 months, and therefore means the same month last year)

> ➤ An Australian sparkline (it has a line down under)

Figure 11-51 shows the Cube Surfer comparing the last three periods to the previous periods—six, five, and four (lag = 3).

Figure 11-52 shows the same report with a lag of 12 for a year-on-year comparison.

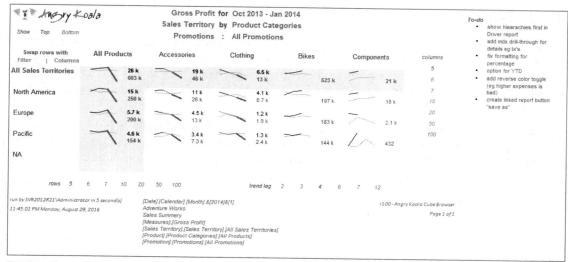

FIGURE 11-51: Angry Koala Cube Surfer report.

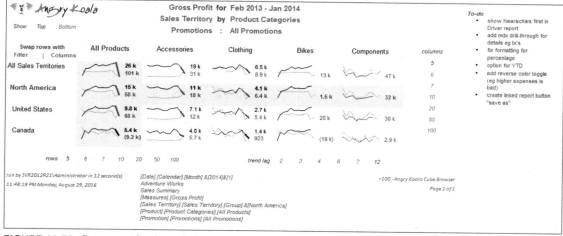

FIGURE 11-52: Report with a lag of 12.

SUMMARY

In this chapter you have harnessed the power of Analysis Services to create compelling reports with dynamic content. You have learned how to use self-calling drill-through reports to navigate cube hierarchies and create helper reports to collect parameters based on Analysis Services metadata utilizing DMVs. As a result, you will now be well placed to meet, and in many cases exceed, the expectations of your business users.

Chapter 12 is about building solutions and not just reports. You will apply techniques such as conditional expressions, parameters, and calculated fields to extend report functionality. We will explore using embedded .NET code within a report to process complex business logic and code programmatic logic to control report output and behavior.

12

Expressions and Actions

WHAT'S IN THIS CHAPTER?

➤ Revisiting expressions

➤ Understanding calculated fields

➤ Using conditional expressions

➤ Getting to know IIF and SWITCH functions

➤ Using custom code

➤ Reporting recursive relationships

➤ Using actions to navigate reports

The real power behind Reporting Services is its ability to creatively use data groups, and combinations of report items. Calculations and conditional formatting can be added by using simple expressions and more advanced programming code. Whether you are an application developer or a report designer, this chapter contains important information to help you design reports to meet your users' requirements and to raise the bar with compelling report features.

Coupled with expressions and parameters, report actions are used to take reporting solutions to the next level and build comprehensive dashboards and report navigation experiences.

BASIC EXPRESSIONS RECAP

In previous chapters, we used expressions for a variety of things but have just scratched the surface. You can do a lot with a little code and some creative design. Recall that we used expressions to create standardized report and page header content. You should remember that any textbox bound to a dataset field or built-in field actually contains an expression.

Also recall that you can build simple composite values in a textbox by dragging items from the Report Data pane into a textbox. For example, if you want to display the page number and total number of report pages in the report footer, insert a textbox into the report footer and drag the `PageNumber` built-in field from the Report Data pane into the textbox. Then, place the cursor at the end of this text, press the spacebar, type the word `of`, press the spacebar, and then drag the `TotalPages` built-in field to the end of the text. This produces an expression that appears like this in the Report Designer:

```
[&PageNumber] of [&TotalPages]
```

If you have worked with versions of Reporting Services prior to 2012, you will notice an improvement in the user experience. After the cursor leaves the textbox, the Report Designer no longer displays the following non-descriptive label in gray:

```
<<Expr>>
```

What value is really stored in this textbox? If the expression is created by using the designer (instead of the Expression Builder), you no longer can right-click and choose Expression to find out. Instead, these types of expressions are built as "text runs" inside a paragraph defined for the textbox. To see what is really going on under the covers, you would need to open the RDL file using a text editor such as Notepad. You will find an XML snippet as follows:

```
<Paragraphs>
    <Paragraph>
        <TextRuns>
            <TextRun>
                <Value>=Globals!TotalPages</Value>
                <Style />
            </TextRun>
            <TextRun>
                <Value> of </Value>
                <Style />
            </TextRun>
            <TextRun>
                <Value>=Globals!PageNumber</Value>
                <Style />
            </TextRun>
        </TextRuns>
        <Style />
    </Paragraph>
</Paragraphs>
```

However, if you prefer to build your expressions in a more "programmatic" way, you can always use the Expression Builder dialog and type in the following:

```
=Globals!PageNumber & " of " & Globals!TotalPages
```

Don't worry; the next section explains the detailed steps to accomplish this task. This type of expression, built by hand-coding in the Expression Builder, is stored slightly differently in the RDL file:

```
<Paragraphs>
    <Paragraph>
        <TextRuns>
```

```
<TextRun>
    <Value>
        =Globals!PageNumber &amp; " of " &amp; Globals!TotalPages
    </Value>
    <Style />
</TextRun>
    </TextRuns>
    <Style />
    </Paragraph>
</Paragraphs>
```

Notice that the RDL generated is slightly less verbose and contains only one `TextRun` element, which holds the expression you typed in the Expression Builder. If you've worked with previous versions of Reporting Services, this will look familiar. It is the same Visual Basic expression code that Reporting Services has used all along.

Reporting Services was originally designed to be an application developer–centric tool, used by programmers in Microsoft Visual Studio. As time went on and the product matured, the powers that be at Microsoft took a good hard look at Reporting Services and realized that the industry was asking for a more information worker–centric reporting tool. Several incremental steps have helped Reporting Services become this dual-identity product that appeals to both programmers and business users. The downside is that, in places, the product can be a bit schizophrenic. In addition to the designer's drag-and-drop expressions and the Expression Editor's expression syntax differences, the built-in fields in the Report Data pane are referred to as members of the Globals collection within true report expressions. The term *built-in fields* is just a friendly term, not a syntax convention.

USING THE EXPRESSION BUILDER

You have already used a few expressions in the basic report design work done so far. Any field reference is an expression. In the Group Properties dialog, you used a field expression. In the previous example, we used an expression to show the page number and total pages so that it reads "X of Y" when the report is rendered. Expressions are used to create a dynamic value based on a variety of built-in fields, dataset fields, and programming functions. Expressions can be used to set most property values based on a variety of conditions, parameters, field values, and calculations. Let's take a quick look at common methods to build simple expressions. We'll explain the previous example, only this time in the Expression Builder.

> **TIP** *You will find finished examples of these expressions in the Product Details report, in the Wrox SSRS 2016 Samples project. To follow along, just create a new textbox alongside the finished one.*

To display the page number and page count, right-click the textbox and select Expression, and then use the Expression window to create the expression. You can use two methods to add expressions to the expression text area. One method is to select items from the category tree and member list and double-click an item to add to the expression. The other method is to simply type text into the expression text area. This uses the IntelliSense Auto List Members feature to provide drop-down lists for known items and properties. Here's the first method:

1. Begin by typing `="Page"` `&` in the Expression box, and then click the Built-in Fields item in object tree view. All related members are listed in the adjacent list box.

2. Double-click the `PageNumber` item in the list.

3. Place the cursor at the end of the text, and type the text `&` `" of "` `&`. Then select and insert the `TotalPages` field.

The finished expression should read as follows:

```
="Page " & Globals!PageNumber & " of " & Globals!TotalPages
```

The Expression window (also called the Expression Builder) should appear, as shown in Figure 12-1.

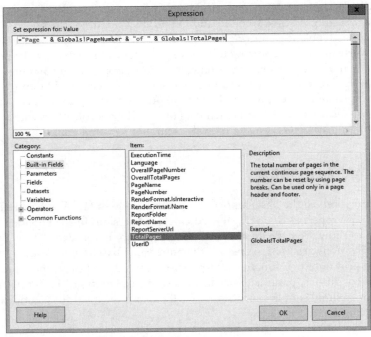

FIGURE 12-1: Expression window.

In previous chapters, you learned how parameter values are passed into a query to limit or alter the result set. Parameters can also be used within the report to modify display characteristics by dynamically changing item properties. For example, we can create grouping expressions for data regions based on values in parameter variables. A report's parameters collection is publicly accessible from the Expression window and can be included as part of expressions.

CALCULATED FIELDS

Custom fields can be added to any report and can include expressions, calculations, and text manipulation. This might be similar in functionality to alias columns in a query or view, but the calculation or expression is performed on the report server after data has been retrieved from the database. Calculated field expressions can also use Reporting Services global variables, custom code, and functions that may be unavailable in a SQL expression.

Let's start with a basic report that displays product details. Again, to see the completed steps, take a look at the Product Details report in the Wrox SSRS 2016 Samples project. You will replace a simple expression previously used in a textbox with a calculated field. Figure 12-2 shows a textbox used to calculate the profit margin for each product by subtracting the StandardCost field from the ListPrice. The Expression dialog is shown for this textbox.

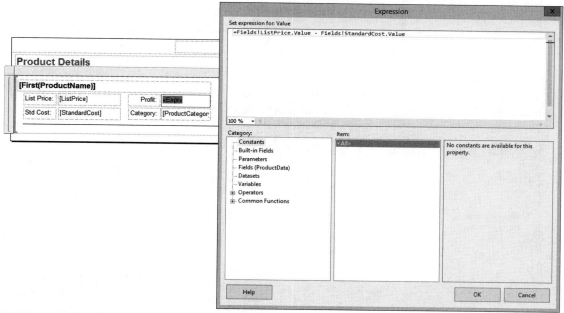

FIGURE 12-2: Textbox used to calculate profit margin.

Rather than performing the calculation on the textbox, let's add a calculated field to the dataset definition so that this calculation can be reused by other objects in the report.

Use the Report Data pane in the Report Designer to select the dataset you want to use. Right-click the dataset and choose Add Calculated Field, as shown in Figure 12-3.

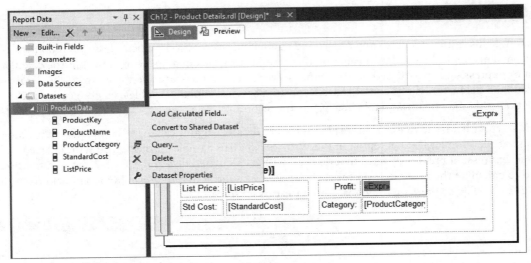

FIGURE 12-3: Selecting the dataset you want to use.

The Dataset Properties dialog opens, as shown in Figure 12-4. On the Fields page, click the Add button to add a new item to the Fields collection. Type the new field name, and then click the expression button (*fx*) next to the Field Source box on this new row.

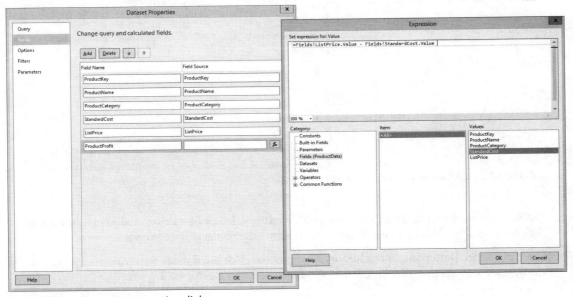

FIGURE 12-4: Dataset properties dialog.

When the Expression dialog opens, simply type or build the same expression as before. Verify the results with Figure 12-4, and then click OK on both of these dialogs to save the newly calculated field to the dataset.

Using the calculated field is no different from using any other field derived from the dataset query. Just drag and drop the new field from the Report Data pane to the textbox on the report. Note the Profit field reference in the textbox, as shown in Figure 12-5.

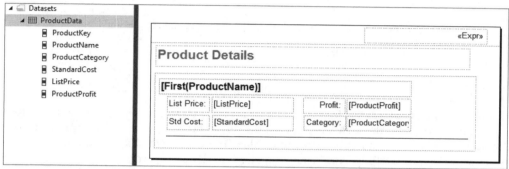

FIGURE 12-5: Field reference in a textbox.

You can use the expression button to invoke the Expression Builder to use any functionality available within the design environment in addition to the database fields exposed by the dataset query. These calculations will be performed on the Report Server rather than on the database server.

CONDITIONAL EXPRESSIONS

You have seen some simple examples of using expressions to set item values and properties. Let's look at one more example of a conditional expression, and then we'll discuss using program code to handle more complex situations. We'll create a simple Product Inventory report that uses conditional formatting. The table in this report returns a list of products with current inventory values. The Product table in the WroxSSRS2016 database contains a ReorderPoint value that informs stock managers when they need to reorder products. If the inventory count falls below this value, you can set the inventory quantity to appear in red next to the name. Using a conditional expression in this manner is similar to using conditional formatting in Excel.

The following example uses a dataset with this SQL query:

```
SELECT
        l.LastInventoryDate,
        l.ProductNumber,
        l.ProductName,
        i.[ReorderPoint],
        i.[Quantity],
        i.[ListPrice]
```

```
FROM
        ProductInventory i
        INNER JOIN
        (
            SELECT
                MAX(i.InventoryDate) AS LastInventoryDate,
                p.ProductNumber,
                p.ProductName
            FROM
                Product p
                INNER JOIN ProductInventory i on p.ProductNumber = i.ProductNumber
            GROUP BY
                p.ProductNumber,
                p.ProductName
        ) l on i.ProductNumber = l. ProductNumber
    ;
```

The table bound to this dataset has four columns: Name, ReorderPoint, Quantity, and ListPrice. On the Quantity textbox in the table's detail row, the Color property is set to an expression containing conditional logic instead of being set to a value. You can use the Expression Builder or just type this expression into the Properties window under the Color property:

```
=IIF(Fields!Quantity.Value < Fields!ReorderPoint.Value, "Red", "Black")
```

I have done the same kind of thing with the Font > FontWeight property for the textbox so that if the inventory quantity for a product is below the reorder point value, the quantity is displayed in both red and bold text:

```
=IIF( Fields!Quantity.Value < Fields!ReorderPoint.Value OR Fields!ListPrice.Value >
    100, "Heavy", "Normal" )
```

THE IIF() FUNCTION

Even if you are not a programmer, learning a few simple Visual Basic commands and functions will prove valuable and will likely meet most of your needs. The most common and useful function you're likely to use in simple expressions is IIF (the name stands for "Immediate IF"). As you saw in the previous example, the IIF() function takes three arguments. The first is a Boolean expression that returns either True or False. If the expression is True, the value passed into the second argument is returned. Otherwise (if the first expression is False), the third argument value is returned. Take another look at the expression used in the previous example:

```
=IIF(Fields!Quantity.Value < Fields!ReorderPoint.Value, "Red", "Black")
```

If the expression Fields!Quantity.Value < Fields!ReorderPoint.Value yields a True result (where Quantity is less than ReorderPoint), the value "Red" is returned. Otherwise, the value returned is "Black".

In cases where an expression may return more than two states, IIF() functions can be nested to form multiple branches of logic. In this example, three different conditions are tested:

```
=IIF( Fields!Quantity.Value < Fields!ReorderPoint.Value, "Red",
    IIF(Fields!ListPrice.Value > 100, "Blue", "Black" )
  )
```

Preview the report to check the results; they should look like Figure 12-6.

> **NOTE** *Because the print edition of this book is printed in black and white, I've added callouts on the right side of this screen image to indicate some of the colored text in the Quantity column. The non-bold text in this column is black.*

Product Inventory / Reorder

Product Name	Reorder Point	Quantity	
All-Purpose Bike Stand	3	**144**	← Blue text
AWC Logo Cap	3	288	
Bike Wash - Dissolver	3	36	
Cable Lock	3	252	
Chain	375	236	
Chain	375	192	} Red text
Chain	375	161	
Classic Vest, L	3	252	
Classic Vest, M	3	216	
Classic Vest, S	3	180	
Fender Set - Mountain	3	108	
Front Brakes	375	347	
Front Brakes	375	**420**	← Blue text
Front Derailleur	375	347	
Front Derailleur	375	236	
Front Derailleur	375	270	
Full-Finger Gloves, L	3	144	
Full-Finger Gloves, M	3	108	

FIGURE 12-6: Report results.

Let's analyze the logic. If `Quantity` is not less than `ReorderPoint`, the third `IIF()` function argument is invoked. This contains a second `IIF()` function, which tests the `ListPrice` field value. If the value is greater than `100`, the value `"Blue"` is returned; otherwise, the return value is `"Black"`. According to the definition of this function, the second argument is the `TruePart` value, and the third argument is the `FalsePart` value. This means that the value in the second position is returned if the expression evaluates to `True`, and the value in the third position is returned if it is `False`.

> **NOTE** *Because* `IIF()` *is a function, it evaluates all its parameters/arguments. In other words, even if the condition expression evaluates to true, the code in the false part also executes. But the function doesn't return it, and vice versa. This is significant, because you might have code that throws* `NullReference` *exceptions on either true or false parts when the condition does not favor that outcome. The best way to circumvent this behavior is to write a custom code function embedded in the report that contains a true Visual Basic (VB)* `If/Then/Else` *statement and returns the expected outcome. Then you can call this embedded code function from the Expression Builder. This topic is covered in the following section.*

Beyond the simplest nested functions, expressions can be difficult to write and maintain. In addition to decision structures, you can use common functions to format the output, parse strings, and convert data types. Count the opening and closing parentheses to make sure that they match. This is yet another example of where writing this code in a Visual Basic class library or forms project is helpful because of the built-in code-completion and integrated debugging tools. Consider using these other functions in place of nested IIF() functions.

The SWITCH() function accepts an unlimited number of expression and value pairs. The last argument accepts a value that is returned if none of the expressions resolves to True. You can use this in place of the previous nested IIF() example:

```
=SWITCH(
    Fields!Quantity.Value < Fields!ReorderPoint.Value, "Red",
    Fields!ListPrice.Value > 100, "Blue",
    TRUE, "Black"
)
```

I have included two versions of this report in the sample project, one using nested IIF functions and one using a SWITCH expression. Unlike the IIF() function, the SWITCH() function has no FalsePart value. Each expression and return value is passed as a pair. The first expression in the list that evaluates to True causes the function to stop processing and return a value. The last expression will always be true because it's, well, true—literally. Because this expression always evaluates to True, it becomes the catchall expression that returns "Black" if no other expressions are True.

Visual Basic supports many of the old-style VBScript and VB 6.0 functions, as well as newer overload method calls. In short, this means that there may be more than one way to perform the same action. Table 12-1 describes a few other Visual Basic functions that may prove useful in basic report expressions.

TABLE 12-1: Visual Basic Functions for Report Expressions

FUNCTION	DESCRIPTION	EXAMPLE
FORMAT()	Returns a string value formatted using a regular expression format code or pattern. Similar to the Format property but can be concatenated with other string values.	=FORMAT(Fields!TheDate .Value, "mm/d/yy")
MID() LEFT() RIGHT()	Returns a specified number of characters from a specified position (if using MID()) and for a specific length. You can also use the .SUBSTRING() method.	=MID(Fields!TheString .Value, 3, 5) =LEFT(Fields!TheString .Value, 5) = Fields!TheString.Value .SUBSTRING(2, 5)

FUNCTION	DESCRIPTION	EXAMPLE
INSTR()	Returns an integer for the first character position of one string within another string. Often used with MID() or SUBSTRING() to parse strings.	=INSTR(Fields!TheString.Value, ",")
CSTR()	Converts any value to a string type. Consider using the newer ToString() method.	=CSTR(Fields!TheNumber.Value) =Fields!TheNumber.Value.ToString()
CDATE() CINT() CDEC() ...	A type-conversion function similar to CSTR(). Converts any compatible value to an explicit data type. Consider using the newer CTYPE() function to convert to an explicit type.	=CDATE(Fields!TheString.Value) =CTYPE(Fields!TheString.Value, Date)
ISNOTHING()	Tests an expression for a null value. May be nested within an IIF() to convert nulls to another value.	=ISNOTHING(Fields!TheDate.Value) =IIF(ISNOTHING(Fields!TheDate.Value), "n/a", Fields!TheDate.Value)
CHOOSE()	Returns one of a list of values based on a provided integer index value (1, 2, 3, and so on).	=CHOOSE(Parameters!FontSize.Value, "8pt", "10pt", "12pt", "14pt")

Hundreds of Visual Basic functions can be used in some form, so this list is just a starting point. For additional assistance, view the Online Help index in Visual Studio, under Functions [Visual Basic]. This information is also available in the public MSDN library at http://msdn.microsoft.com.

USING CUSTOM CODE

When you need to process more-complex expressions, it may be difficult to build all the logic into one expression. In such cases, you can write your own function to handle different conditions and call it from a property expression.

You can take two approaches to managing custom code. One is to write a block of code to define functions that are embedded in the report definition. This technique is simple, but the code will be available to only that report. The second technique is to write a custom class library compiled to an external .NET assembly and reference this from any report on your Report Server. This approach has the advantage of sharing a central repository of code, which makes updates to the code easier to manage. It also gives you the freedom to use any .NET language (C#, VB). The downside of this approach is that the configuration and initial deployment are a bit tedious.

Using Custom Code in a Report

A report can contain embedded Visual Basic .NET code that defines a function you can call from property expressions. The Code Editor window is simple; it doesn't include any IntelliSense, editing, or formatting capabilities. For this reason, you might want to write the code in a separate, temporary Visual Studio project of type "VB class library," to test and debug before you place it into the report. When you are ready to add code, open the Report Properties dialog. You can do this from the Report menu. The other method is to use the Report Designer right-click menu. Right-click the Report Designer outside of the report body and select Properties. On the Properties window, switch to the Code tab, and write or paste your code in the Custom Code box.

The following example starts with a new report. Here is the code, along with the expressions you will need to create a simple example report on your own. The following Visual Basic function accepts a phone number or Social Security number (SSN) in a variety of formats and outputs a standard U.S. phone number and properly formatted SSN. The Value argument accepts the value, and the Format argument accepts the value Phone or SSN. You use it only with phone numbers, so you can omit the SSN branch if you like.

```vb
'*************************************************************
'    Returns properly formatted Phone Number or SSN
'    based on format arg & length of text arg
'    2/20/2016 - Paul Turley
'*************************************************************
Public Function CustomFormat(ByVal text as String, ByVal format as String) as String
     Dim sCleanedInput as String = Replace(text, "-", "")
     '** Remove all spaces and punctuation **
     sCleanedInput = Replace(sCleanedInput, " ", "")
          sCleanedInput = Replace(sCleanedInput, "(", "")
          sCleanedInput = Replace(sCleanedInput, ")", "")


     Select Case format
     Case "Phone"
          '** Remove US international prefix **
          If sCleanedInput.Length = 13
             And sCleanedInput.SubString(0, 3) = "111" Then
                sCleanedInput = sCleanedInput.SubString(3, 10)
          End If
          Select Case sCleanedInput.Length
          Case 7 '** No area code **
               Return sCleanedInput.SubString(0, 3) & "-" _
                    & sCleanedInput.SubString(3, 4)
          Case 10  '** Area code **
               Return "(" & sCleanedInput.SubString(0, 3) & ") " _
                    sCleanedInput.SubString(3, 3) _
                    & "-" & sCleanedInput.SubString(6, 4)
          Case Else  '** Non-std phone number or non-US intl. prefix **
```

```
                    Return text
            End Select
        Case "SSN"
            If sCleanedInput.Length = 9 Then
                Return sCleanedInput.SubString(0, 3) & "-" _
                    & sCleanedInput.SubString(3, 2) & "-" _
                    & sCleanedInput.SubString(5, 4)
            Else
                Return text
            End If
        Case Else
            Return text
        End Select
    End Function
```

The dataset in this report gets its data from the Vendor and related tables in the WroxSSRS2016 database and returns three columns: FirstName, LastName, and Phone. The SQL expression used to retrieve this information is as follows:

```
SELECT
    FirstName + ' ' + LastName AS FullName,
    Phone
FROM SalesPerson
ORDER BY Phone
```

The three columns shown in Figure 12-7 are used in a table bound to the dataset. The Value property of the Phone column uses an expression that calls the custom function preceded by a reference to the Code object:

```
=Code.CustomFormat(Fields!PhoneNumber.Value, "Phone")
```

Custom Formatting with Embedded Code

Sales Person Name	Phone (stored)	Formatted Phone
Ranjit Varkey Chudukatil	1 (11) 500 555-0117	(500) 555-0117
Rachel Valdez	1 (11) 500 555-0140	(500) 555-0140
Jae Pak	1 (11) 500 555-0145	(500) 555-0145
Lynn Tsoflias	1 (11) 500 555-0190	(500) 555-0190
Don Hall	100-555-0174	(100) 555-0174
Gary Altman	102-0112	102-0112
Terrence Earls	102-0115	102-0115
Brian Lloyd	102-0182	102-0182
Anibal Sousa	106-555-0120	(106) 555-0120
Zheng Mu	113-555-0173	(113) 555-0173
Ivo Salmre	115-555-0179	(115) 555-0179
Dragan Tomic	117-555-0185	(117) 555-0185
Andy Ruth	118-555-0110	(118) 555-0110
David Lawrence	118-555-0177	(118) 555-0177
James Kramer	119-555-0117	(119) 555-0117
Barbara Decker	119-555-0192	(119) 555-0192

FIGURE 12-7: Finished report.

Links and Drill-Through Reports

Links and drill-through reports are powerful features that enable a textbox or image to be used as a link to another report by passing parameter values to the target report. The target report can consist of a specific record or multiple records, depending on the parameters passed to the target report. The following example uses the Products by Category and SubCategory (drillthrough source) report in the sample project. The Product Name textbox is used to link to a report that will display the details of a single product record. The Product Details report, shown in Figure 12-8, is simple. It contains only textboxes and an image bound to fields of a dataset based on the Products table. This report accepts a `ProductID` parameter to filter the records and narrow down to the record requested.

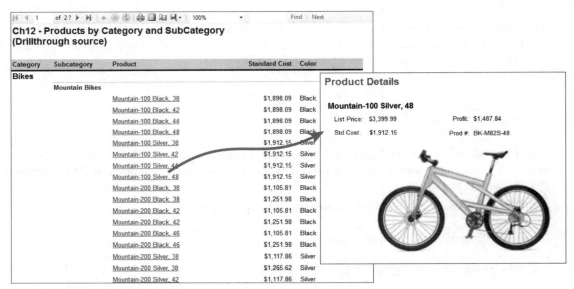

FIGURE 12-8: Product Details report.

Any textbox or image item can be used for intra-report or inter-report navigation, for navigation to external resources such as web pages and documents, and to send e-mail. You enable all these features using navigation properties you can specify in the Text Box Properties or Image Properties dialog. First, open the Text Box Properties dialog by right-clicking the textbox and selecting Properties. In the Text Box Properties dialog, use the Actions page to set the drill-through destination and any parameters you would like to pass.

Figure 12-9 shows the Text Box Properties dialog Action page for the Ch12 - Products by Category and SubCategory (Drillthrough source) report in the sample project.

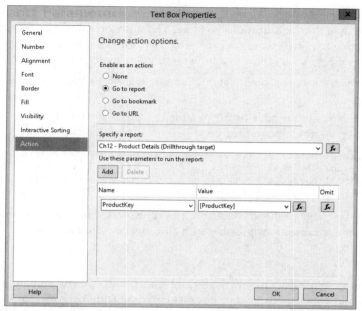

FIGURE 12-9: Action page in the Text Box Properties dialog.

Note the navigation target selections under the "Enable as an action" option list. When you choose "Go to report," the report selection drop-down is enabled, listing all reports in the project. A report selected from this list must be deployed to the same folder on the Report Server as the source report. A drill-through report typically is used to open the report to a filtered record or result set based on the value in this textbox. (Remember that the user clicked this textbox to open the target report.) The typical pattern is to show a user-friendly caption in the textbox (the product name in this case) and then pass a key value to the report parameter to uniquely identify records to filter in the target report. In this case, the ProductID value is passed.

To enable this behavior, add a parameter reference that will be used in the target report to filter the dataset records. All parameters in the target report are listed in the Name column. In the Value column, select a field in the source report to map to the parameter. A new feature is apparent in the rightmost column. An expression can be used to specify a condition in which the parameter is not passed to the target report. Expressions are short pieces of VB.NET code, and can be used to call custom code functions and even code libraries referenced as .NET assemblies.

By default, drill-through reports are displayed in the same browser window as the source report. There are a few techniques for opening the report in a secondary window, but none are out-of-the-box features. My favorite technique is to use the "Go to URL" navigation option and open the target report using a URL request. Although this is a little more involved, it provides a great deal of flexibility.

To navigate to a report in a separate web browser window, call a JavaScript function to create a pop-up window using any browser window modifications you like. The function call script, report folder path, report name, and filtering parameters are concatenated using an expression. Here are two examples. The first is simple and opens the report in a browser window in default view:

```
="JavaScript:void window.open('http://localhost/reportserver?/Sales Reports/
Product Sales Report');"
```

The second, somewhat more elaborate example adds report parameters, hides the report viewer toolbar, and customizes the browser window size and features:

```
="JavaScript:void window.open('http://localhost/reportserver?/Sales Reports/
Product Sales Report&rc:Toolbar=False&ProductID=" & Fields!ProductID.Value &
"', '_blank', 'toolbar=0,scrollbars=0,status=0,location=0,menubar=0,resizable=0,
directories=0,width=600,height=500,left=550,top=550');"
```

The report name can be parameterized and modified using custom expressions. These short examples give you an idea of the kinds of customizations possible with custom code and expressions.

Navigating to a URL

You can use the "Go to URL" option to navigate to practically any report or document content on your Report Server; files, folders, and applications in your intranet environment; or the World Wide Web. With some creativity, this can be used as a powerful, interactive navigation feature. It can also be set to an expression that uses links stored in a database, custom code, or any other value. It's more accurate to say that any URI (Uniform Resource Identifier) can be used, because a web request is not limited to a web page or document. With some creative programming, queries, and expressions, you can design your reports to navigate to a web page, document, e-mail address, web service request, or custom web application, directed by data or custom expressions.

> **WARNING** *Reporting Services does not make any attempt to validate a URL passed in an expression. If a malformed URL is used, the Report Server returns an error. There is no easy way to trap this error or prevent it from occurring. The most effective way to handle this issue is to validate the URL string before passing it to the "Go to URL" property.*

Navigating to a Bookmark

A *bookmark* is a textbox or image in a report that can be used as a navigational link. If you want to allow the user to click an item and navigate to another item, assign a bookmark value to each target item. To enable navigation to a bookmark, set the "Go to bookmark" property to the target bookmark.

Using bookmarks to navigate within a report is easy. Each report item has a BookMark property that can be assigned a unique value. After adding bookmarks to any target items, use the "Go to bookmark" selection list to select the target bookmark in the properties for the source item. This allows the user to navigate to items within the same report.

REPORTING ON RECURSIVE RELATIONSHIPS

Representing recursive hierarchies has always been a pain for reporting and often is a challenge to effectively model in relational database systems. Examples of this type of relationship (usually facilitated through a self-join) can be found in the DimEmployee table of the WroxSSRS2016 sample database. Most reporting tools were designed to work with data organized in traditional multi-table relationships. Fortunately, our friends at Microsoft built recursive support into the reporting engine to deal with this common challenge. A classic example of a recursive relationship (where child records are related to a parent record contained in the same table) is the employee/manager relationship. The Employee table contains a primary key, EmployeeID, that uniquely identifies each employee record. ManagerID is a foreign key that depends on the EmployeeID attribute of the same table. It contains the EmployeeID value for the employee's manager. The only record that wouldn't have a ManagerID would be the president of the company or any such employee who doesn't have a boss.

Representing the hierarchy through a query would be difficult. However, defining the dataset for such a report is simple. You just expose the primary key, foreign key, employee name, and any other values you want to include on the report.

To see how this works, follow these steps:

1. Create a new report, and define a dataset using the WroxSSRS2016 shared data source. The dataset query is simple and includes both the primary key and a recursive foreign key. The ParentEmployeeKey for each employee contains the EmployeeKey value for that employee's supervisor or manager:

```
SELECT
    EmployeeKey,
    ParentEmployeeKey,
    LastName,
    Title
FROM SalesPerson
;
```

2. Add a table data region to the report body, and drag the LastName and Title fields to the detail row. For demonstration purposes, we've also dragged the EmployeeKey and ParentEmployeeKey fields.

3. Insert a column named Org Level in the table. (We'll get to this in a moment.)

4. Edit the (Details) group properties using the drop-down button for this item in the Row Groups pane, as shown in Figure 12-10.

   This action opens the Group Properties dialog, shown in Figure 12-11. To define a recursive group, you must set two properties. First, the group must be based on the unique identifier for the child records. This is typically a key value and must be related to the unique identifier for parent records—usually a parent key column in the table. Second, the Recursive parent property is set to relate the parent key to the table's primary key.

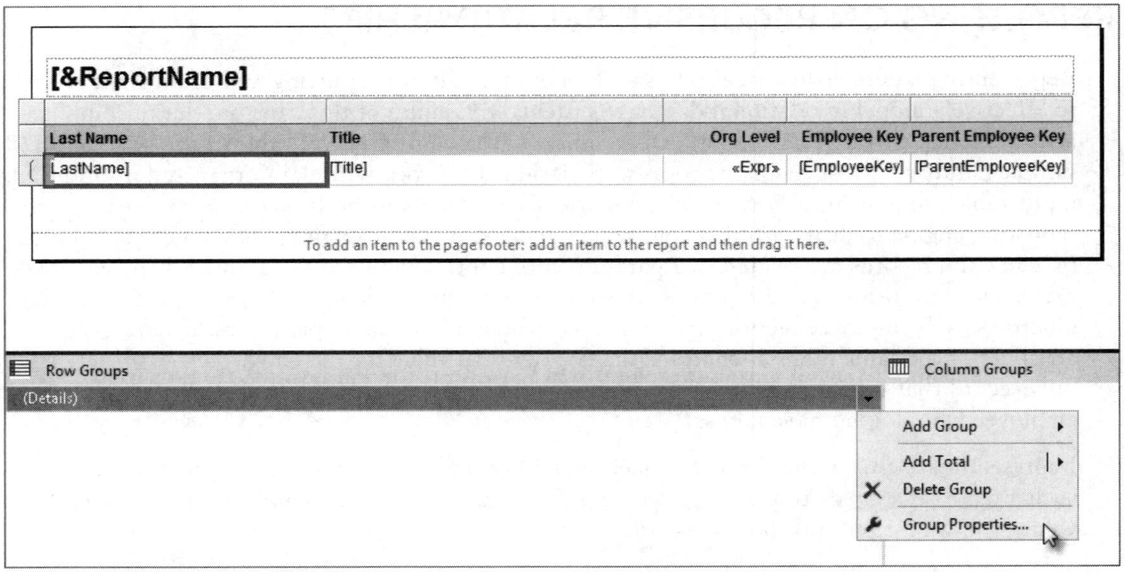

[&ReportName]

Last Name	Title	Org Level	Employee Key	Parent Employee Key
LastName]	[Title]	«Expr»	[EmployeeKey]	[ParentEmployeeKey]

To add an item to the page footer: add an item to the report and then drag it here.

📋 Row Groups		🔲 Column Groups
(Details)	▼	

	Add Group	▶
	Add Total	❘ ▶
✕	Delete Group	
🔧	Group Properties...	

FIGURE 12-10: Row Groups pane.

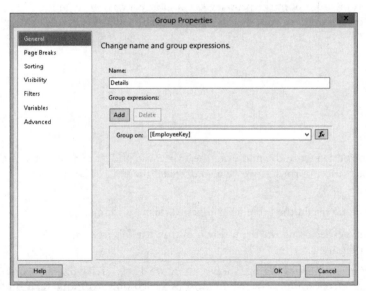

FIGURE 12-11: Group Properties dialog.

5. Use the General page to set the group expression to the EmployeeKey field.

6. Move to the Advanced page on this dialog, and set the Recursive parent property to the ParentEmployeeKey field, as shown in Figure 12-12.

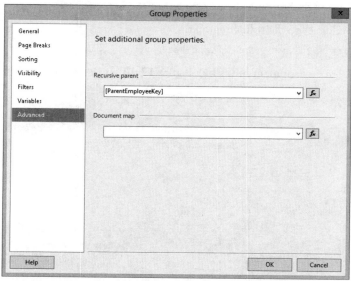

FIGURE 12-12: Setting the "Recursive parent" property.

7. Go ahead and preview the report. Although the records are actually arranged according to each employee's pecking order in the company, it's not very obvious that this recursive hierarchy report is really working. You need to make a change so that the report lets you visualize the employee hierarchy (who reports to whom).

8. Switch back to Design view. Right-click the detail cell in the new Org Level column and select Expression. Type =LEVEL("Details") in the Expression dialog. This expression calls the LEVEL function, passing in the name of the Details group. This function returns an integer value for a row's position within the recursive hierarchy defined for this group.

9. Click OK on the Expression dialog, and then preview the report again. This time, you see numbers in the Org Level column. The CEO (the only employee record without a ParentEmployeeKey value) shows up at level 0. This is Ken Sanchez. The employees who report to Mr. Sanchez are listed directly below and are at level 1 within the hierarchy.

You're not done. The report still isn't very visually appealing, so let's indent each employee's name according to his or her level. The easiest way to do this is to use a little math to set the Left Padding property for the LastName textbox. You'll start with the same expression as before. Padding is set using PostScript points. A point is about 1/72nd of an inch, and there are about 2.83 millimeters to a point. Because this is such a small unit of measure, we'll indent our employee names by 20 points per level.

10. Right-click the `LastName` textbox and choose Textbox Properties.

11. In the Text Box Properties dialog, move to the Alignment page. Under the Padding options section, click the Expression button (labeled *fx*) next to the Left property box.

12. In the Expression dialog, type the following text:

```
=((LEVEL("Details") * 20) + 2).ToString & "pt'
```

13. Verify that your design environment looks like Figure 12-13.

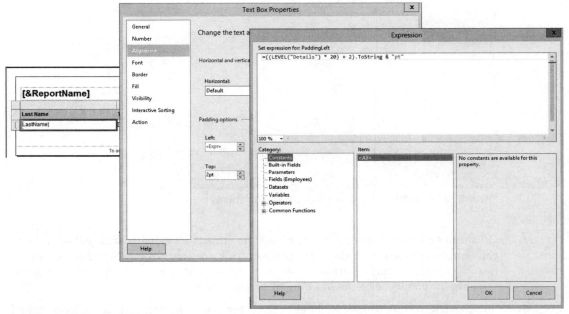

FIGURE 12-13: Correct design environment.

14. Click OK in the Expression Editor window, and then click OK to close the Text Box Properties dialog.

15. Preview the report. In Figure 12-14, you see each employee name indented according to his or her position in the organization. You can verify these results by noting the level value in the `Org Level` column and the correspondence between the `EmployeeKey` and `ParentEmployeeKey` column values. The point of this example is to see the hierarchical relationship between various employee records.

1 of 2? 100% Find | Next

Ch12 - Employee Sales Organization List

Last Name	Title	Org Level	Employee Key	Parent Employee Key
Sánchez	Chief Executive Officer	0	112	
Bradley	Marketing Manager	1	8	112
Duffy	Vice President of Engineering	1	14	112
Tamburello	Engineering Manager	2	3	14
Walters	Senior Tool Designer	3	5	3
Erickson	Design Engineer	3	11	3
Goldberg	Design Engineer	3	13	3
Miller	Research and Development Manager	3	162	3
Margheim	Research and Development Engineer	4	81	162
Matthew	Research and Development Engineer	4	117	162
Raheem	Research and Development Manager	4	221	162
Cracium	Senior Tool Designer	3	267	3
D'Hers	Tool Designer	4	6	267
Galvin	Tool Designer	4	269	267
Sullivan	Senior Design Engineer	3	271	3
Salavaria	Design Engineer	3	274	3
Krebs	Production Control Manager	1	23	112
Dobney	Production Supervisor - WC60	2	9	23
Rapier	Production Technician - WC60	3	39	9
Kramer	Production Technician - WC60	3	78	9

FIGURE 12-14: Finished report.

ACTIONS AND REPORT NAVIGATION

When we interact, navigate, and explore, data comes alive. Reports can either be flat, static lists of data, or they can let users understand the context of the information on a report by exploring details using actions that enable navigation. In Chapter 6 you learned how to create drill-down reports, allowing you to explore details by hiding and showing groups. A drill-through report, by contrast (and in simple terms), is one report that navigates to another report using an action, passing parameter values to the target report. There is tremendous power and flexibility in this pattern, which allows users to view details in the context of a selected item.

In slightly less simple terms, there are really two different applications of report actions that include the ability to drill-through back to the same report and dynamically change the presentation. This is by far my favorite report design pattern. With a little creativity, report actions can be used to gather multiple parameter values and then do some pretty amazing things with visual dashboard-style presentation. You've already seen an extreme example of this pattern in the cube browser Grant presented in Chapter 11.

You've graduated beyond basic report design so the examples I have provided are realistic. The following example demonstrates these techniques in a realistic scenario. This solution, shown in Figure 12-15, is composed of just two reports, which you will find in the examples for Chapter 12. Note that several report parameters are used to filter all the datasets used in these reports.

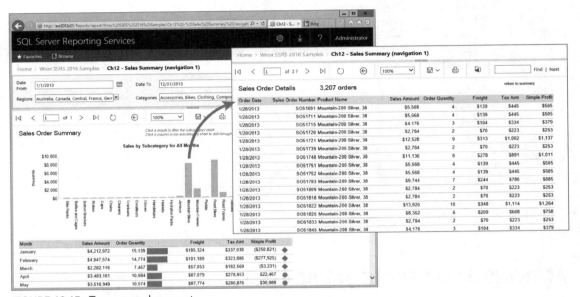

FIGURE 12-15: Two example reports.

The Sales Summary report has two drill-through actions.

> **TIP** *Any text used in an action should appear to the user as a link; however, Reporting Services doesn't automatically change text color as the web browser does for links on a web page. If a textbox contains a navigation action, you should explicitly make the text color blue for users to recognize it as a link.*

The column chart and the table shown in Figure 12-16 are based on two separate datasets. The table has a drill-through action on the month name that passes that month selection back to the same report, passing the selected month as a parameter used to filter the data in the chart. Figure 12-16 shows the table with a drill-through action on the first column.

Month	Sales Amount	Order Quantity		Freight	Tax Amt	Simple Profit	
January	$528,841	998		$13,221	$42,307	($33,458)	◆
February	$641,433	1,403		$16,036	$51,315	($56,292)	◆
March	$390,561	764		$9,764	$31,245	$11,067	●
April	$404,086	652		$10,102	$32,327	($7,130)	◆
May	$685,905	1,116		$17,148	$54,872	$9,418	●
June	$229,271	439		$5,732	$18,342	$6,242	●

FIGURE 12-16: Table with a drill-through action on the first column.

The SalesSummaryMonth dataset is the source for this table, and the query script follows. Aside from the actions, the design of this report is no different from an analytic report you would build for production use, using the skills you've learned so far, with grouped T-SQL queries and multi-select parameters.

I will point out that the MonthNumber column in this query is used for two purposes: to sort the Details row group of the table and to pass into the drill-through action as a parameter. The four query parameters referenced in the WHERE clause are no different than parameters used in most any standard reporting and I've included these to make this scenario realistic:

```
-- Navigation Report (Month):
-- SalesSummaryMonth
SELECT
    d.MonthNumber,
    d.MonthName,
    SUM(SalesAmount)     AS SalesAmount,
    SUM(OrderQuantity)   AS OrderQuantity,
    SUM(p.StandardCost)  AS StandardCost,
    SUM(Freight)         AS Freight,
    SUM(TaxAmt)          AS TaxAmt,
    SUM(SimpleProfit)    AS SimpleProfit
FROM
    [dbo].[vProductOrderSalesProfit] s
    INNER JOIN [dbo].[SalesTerritory] t ON s.SalesTerritoryKey = t.[TerritoryKey]
    INNER JOIN [dbo].[Product] p ON s.[ProductKey] = p.[ProductKey]
    INNER JOIN Date d ON s.OrderDate = d.TheDate
WHERE
    t.TerritoryKey IN( @RegionKeys )
    AND
    p.ProductCategoryKey IN( @CategoryKeys )
    AND
    ( OrderDate BETWEEN @DateFrom AND @DateTo )
GROUP BY
    d.MonthNumber,
    d.MonthName
;
```

The following script is the query for the SalesSummarySubcategory dataset, which provides records for the column chart above the table. Of interest is the @SelectedMonth parameter. This is the parameter used to pass the selected month from the table drill-through action to this query and to filter the dataset for the column chart. By default, the value is –1, which returns data for all months. I designed it this way to easily select one value that would result in effectively clearing the filter and returning all months:

```
-- Navigation Report (category):
-- SalesSummarySubcategory
SELECT
        p.[ProductCategory],
        p.[ProductSubcategoryKey],
        p.[ProductSubcategory],
        SUM(SalesAmount)        AS SalesAmount,
        SUM(OrderQuantity)      AS OrderQuantity
FROM
        [dbo].[vProductOrderSalesProfit] s
        INNER JOIN [dbo].[SalesTerritory] t ON s.SalesTerritoryKey = t.[TerritoryKey]
        INNER JOIN [dbo].[Product] p ON s.[ProductKey] = p.[ProductKey]
WHERE
        t.TerritoryKey IN( @RegionKeys )
        AND
        p.ProductCategoryKey IN( @CategoryKeys )
        AND
        OrderDate BETWEEN @DateFrom AND @DateTo
        AND
        ( MONTH( s.OrderDate ) = @SelectedMonth OR @SelectedMonth = -1 )
GROUP BY
        p.[ProductCategory],
        p.[ProductSubcategoryKey],
        p.[ProductSubcategory]

;
```

Figure 12-17 shows the ReportData window for this report in Design view. All of the report parameters were auto-generated from the queries. Applying the patterns you used in Chapters 6 and 7, parameters were modified with appropriate data types, default values, and simple datasets to provide list selections as you normally would in a parameterized report. Please take a close look at the sample reports to get an understanding of how these parameters are set up to work.

Now for the Month drill-through action. In Design view, select the detail cell in the table containing the MonthName field (yeah, the one with the blue text. That's the one.) Right-click, and then choose Textbox Properties...

The Text Box Properties dialog, shown in Figure 12-18, contains an Action page, and this is where you will find the action with the target report (which happens to be the same report we're working in) and a boatload of report parameters. Each of these parameters except one simply passes the current value or values of that parameter back to itself. This is a simple state-management system that allows the report to keep track of all parameter values between report executions. Frankly, this is a bit of a pain to maintain because every action must pass every parameter but it works quite well. Users can modify parameter values either by using the standard parameter toolbar or one of the custom actions we had created.

FIGURE 12-17: Report Data window.

What happens if we stop at this point and see what we've done? Switch to Preview. With all the parameters in default view, you'll be looking at summary values for a lot of unfiltered data. You can narrow this down some by deselecting some of the Territory Region items and clicking View Report. You can also try selecting only one or two product categories. After you find a parameter selection that tickles your fancy, click one of the blue month names in the table. This will requery the column chart with data for only that month—while applying all the other parameter filters you selected because these selections are preserved in the drill-through action parameter list.

Now that you have a set of filtered data in the context of those things you're most interested in, let's look up all the low-level details that would comprise this data and for a selected product subcategory. You do this by simply clicking a column of interest on the column chart (See Figure 12-19).

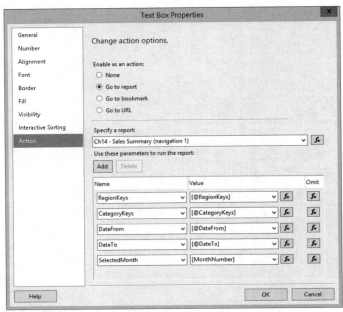

FIGURE 12-18: Text Box Properties dialog.

This action navigates to the detail report, passing the selected subcategory along with all the other selected parameters. The net effect is that the detail report includes the context of the summary report.

Back in Design view, Figure 12-20 shows the report action properties for the `SalesAmount` column chart series.

Take note of the Value column. The placeholder for each parameter expression is preceded with an "@" character. If you view the actual expression for the `@DateFrom` for example, it looks like this:

```
=Parameters!DateFrom.Value
```

When you use the Expression Builder and add a multi-value parameter, the expression will reference only the first item by default. For example, if I were to add the `RegionKeys` parameter, the initial expression will look like this:

```
=Parameters!RegionKeys.Value(0)
```

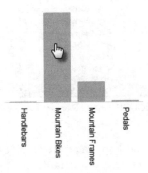

FIGURE 12-19: Clicking a column of interest on the column chart.

Modifying this expression so the parameter passes all selected values is a simple matter of removing the parentheses and ordinal value from the end. The resulting expression should look just like the single-values parameter expression, like this:

```
=Parameters!RegionKeys.Value
```

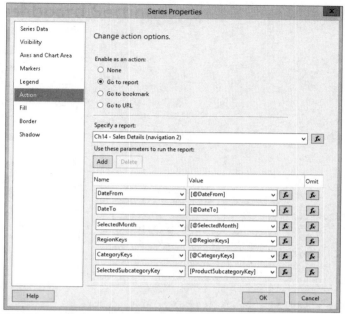

FIGURE 12-20: Report action properties.

On the receiving end of this action is the detail report. Figure 12-21 shows the report in Design view. This report contains the same parameters as the summary report.

> **NOTE** *When I create these dashboard-style report navigation solutions, I often create the first report, making sure all the parameters are in place before using it as a template for the other reports.*

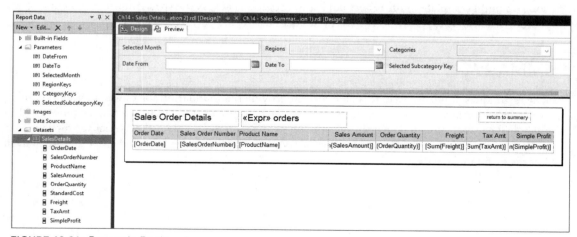

FIGURE 12-21: Report in Design view.

As you can see, the query script for this report simply applies filters based on the parameters and returns a detailed result set:

```
-- Navigation Report detail:
-- SalesDetails
SELECT
        [OrderDate],
        [SalesOrderNumber],
        p.ProductName,
        SalesAmount,
        OrderQuantity,
        p.StandardCost,
        Freight,
        TaxAmt,
        SimpleProfit
FROM
        [dbo].[vProductOrderSalesProfit] s
        INNER JOIN [dbo].[SalesTerritory] t ON s.SalesTerritoryKey = t.[TerritoryKey]
        INNER JOIN [dbo].[Product] p ON s.[ProductKey] = p.[ProductKey]
        INNER JOIN Date d ON s.OrderDate = d.TheDate
WHERE
        t.TerritoryKey IN( @RegionKeys )
        AND
        p.ProductSubcategoryKey = @SelectedSubcategoryKey
        AND
        OrderDate BETWEEN @DateFrom AND @DateTo
        AND
        ( MONTH( s.OrderDate ) = @SelectedMonth OR @SelectedMonth = -1 )
        ;
```

We have one more action. In the top-right corner of the detail report, a textbox labeled "return to summary" uses an action to navigate to the summary report. Figure 12-22 shows how the SelectedMonth parameter is reset back to the default state by passing the literal value −1.

The final solution is a simple but effective orchestration of two reports that work seamlessly together. These reports provide business users with high-level summary information and low-level sales order details. Most users won't even know they are using two reports. With some planning, you can build complete multi-report navigation solutions across the spectrum, from dashboard and scorecard summaries, down to transactional details.

SUMMARY

The techniques you learned in this chapter can provide the foundation for powerful and dynamic reporting solutions. Using report navigation actions, users can start with a summary report and then drill through to details within the context of the parameter values they select for filtering. This pattern can be applied to reports in different styles and business scenarios; whether graphical dashboards or financial ledgers.

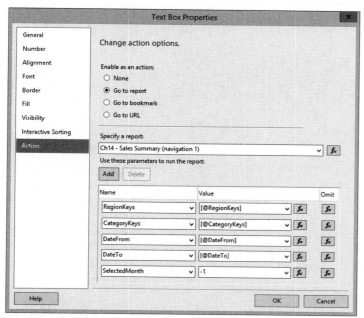

FIGURE 12-22: Parameter reset back to the default state.

Expressions and programming code are the heart of advanced reports. You can use simple expressions to dynamically change content, using styles and color to draw attention to important information. You can write custom functions using .NET code to encapsulate more complex logic. Reporting Services supports several specialized features to address specific business requirements and report layouts, such as document maps and recursive hierarchies.

Chapter 13 is all about managing report projects for teams and advanced report users. You will learn how to manage solutions in SQL Server Data Tools for Visual Studio, and how to deploy and manage shared data sources and datasets. I'll share lessons learned from several reporting projects over the years; defining specifications and requirements, and working with users and business stakeholders to deliver successful reporting solutions. We will also discuss how to effectively use Report Builder for self-service and user-driven reporting.

PART IV
Solution Patterns

The two chapters in this part of the book have us stepping away from the intricacies of individual report features. and provide a solution perspective. You've learned to create nearly every style of report by using different data regions and visual report items. In this part you learn to apply these skills to create solutions and assemble different report building blocks to create super reports, scorecards, and dashboards. By following solution development disciplines and design best practices, you and members of a collaborative development team can build holistic report solutions.

▶ **CHAPTER 13:** Report Projects and Consolidation

▶ **CHAPTER 14:** Report Solutions, Patterns, and Recipes

13

Report Projects and Consolidation

WHAT'S IN THIS CHAPTER?

➤ Understanding SSDT solution patterns

➤ Getting to know report specifications and requirements

➤ Using report templates

➤ Understanding development phases

➤ Using version control

➤ Planning for self-service reporting

➤ Exploring Report Builder solutions

➤ Migrating self-service reports

How to best structure the work in a manner that is both consistent and logical is the first decision facing a report solution developer. In like manner, this becomes particularly important when working as part of a project team; each team member is responsible for delivering a piece of the overall solution.

The chapter looks at ways to organize your report development, and support the full deployment life cycle from requirements to production implementation.

The Reporting Services product has expanded to include different categories of reports, which provides greater opportunity to support different types of reporting scenarios. This also adds to the potential confusion of choices and solution approaches for those architecting and managing solutions and supporting report users. In brief, the Reporting Services umbrella encompasses the following reporting scenarios:

➤ **Paginated Reports**—Conventional SQL Server Reporting Services (SSRS) reports are designed and delivered by the IT organization to the business user community. These reports are typically designed using patterns similar to software development projects, starting with business and functional requirements. A report specification is created, so the report designer/developer has technical requirements. Reports go through quality assurance (QA) testing, and are then delivered to production through a build-and-deployment process. These reports are typically designed and managed within projects and solutions in SQL Server Data Tools (SSDT) for Visual Studio.

➤ **Self-service Reports**—These reports are created by business users with data sources managed by the organization. Users can design these reports using self-service report authoring tools like Report Builder. Reports are saved directly to a designated folder on the report server without a rigid development, QA, and deployment process.

➤ **Mobile Reports**—Mobile reports can be designed, tested, and delivered in a similar manner to paginated reports, as part of a formal solution. The toolset is different simply because Microsoft acquired this technology from a different development company. As the reporting platform continues to evolve, the way these reports are designed may change in the future. As of this writing, mobile reports are designed in a separate tool.

SSDT SOLUTIONS AND PROJECTS

What is a solution? In its most basic form, a *solution* can be thought of as simply a collection of related projects. When you create a new project using the File menu in the Visual Studio environment, a solution is created automatically in the location you specify in the New Project dialog, as shown in Figure 13-1. When creating a project for the first time, you can create a directory on your computer or network hard drive to contain your solutions and projects. Also, you can save your solution to your source control system as it is created. You learn more about that later in this chapter.

With SSDT, you can create SQL Server Integration Services, Analysis Services, Reporting Services, or database projects. Before you start developing a Reporting Services solution, however, you are faced with some important questions:

➤ Should the Reporting Services project be created in its own solution, or be added to an existing solution containing other project types? Adding it to an existing project has the advantage of providing a seamless development environment. Under this scenario, the impact of changes to one area of development can be more readily applied to another. The disadvantage of placing multiple projects into a solution is that it can make the solution unwieldy and slower to open. Also, it can affect version control if several people make changes to the solution (see the "Version Control" section later in this chapter).

➤ How do you intend to separate reports that have been deployed to production from reports you currently are working on, or that have been deployed to your test environment?

Projects and solutions can help manage and organize files for a variety of reasons. The optimal choice for your situation will depend on the size and scope of your work, whether you are working within a team, and the degree of project management formality employed within your organization.

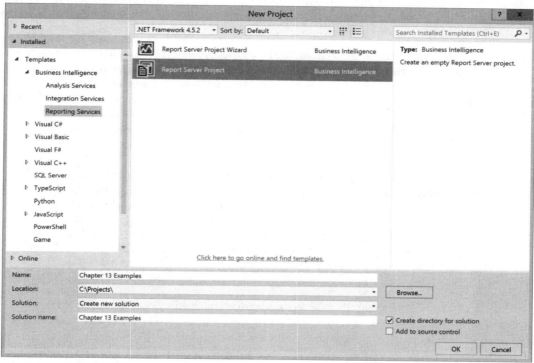

FIGURE 13-1: New Project dialog.

Project Structure and Development Phases

As with any software development project, each component or report should progress through a series of design and development phases. These may include prototyping or proof-of-concept, design, testing, and deployment. You have a couple different ways to keep reports organized—multiple environments, or multiple logical folders and/or projects for each phase.

Multiple Reporting Environments

The multiple-environment approach involves maintaining multiple reporting environments that reflect the phases of design and development. The most common scenario is to have a development report server, a test/QA server, and, finally, the production environment. This is more involved, requiring a well-defined report promotion and deployment path. It also requires that multiple server environments be set up.

The idea is to keep the report development in the development sandbox environment. As report development is complete, the report can be deployed to the next stage—testing. In the testing/quality assurance (QA) environment, analysts can verify the report's integrity and validate report data and layout. After the report has gone through testing and validation, it can be marked ready for production, and go through any formalized promotion processes (such as change control). Visual Studio/ SSDT can be used with an integrated version control solution (such as Team Foundation Server, or a number of third-party versioning applications) to manage the development ownership, archival, and check-in/check-out process of report project files.

Although SSDT is typically the tool of choice for IT developers in these formalized project settings, Report Builder, utilizing the features of SharePoint, can be used in a similar manner. If you have well-established processes in place for managing project asset check-in/check-out and versioning through SharePoint, Report Builder is a viable alternative. With Reporting Services configured in SharePoint integrated mode, designate different document libraries to manage collections of reports. You can then use the versioning and workflow features of SharePoint to manage report definition files.

> **WARNING** *Implementing SharePoint is not only a significant investment in terms of cost and effort, it also requires an investment in adjusting business culture to work within an organization. If you have already adopted SharePoint and are accustomed to using libraries and workflows to manage documents, using SSRS in integrated mode may be a good fit. However, adding SharePoint for the sake of managing report projects or business intelligence (BI) content alone can be a cumbersome task.*

If you are not using SSRS in SharePoint integrated mode and need to manage multiple reports through a proper development, QA, and production life cycle, use SSDT for report design. Using the Visual Studio Configuration Manager, you can define a configuration for each deployment target: one for the development report server and data sources, another for QA, and still another for production. Select the development configuration, and then use the project properties to set your report server deployment.

Multiple Logical Folders and Projects

When following the multiple-folder approach, you might find it helpful to create separate projects and folders, and then graduate reports from one project to another as they are verified and pass testing criteria. For each of the Visual Studio projects within a master solution, create duplicate shared data sources. You can drag and drop reports from one project into another. Note that when you do this, the report definition is not physically deleted from the original report folder, so you may need to clean up the report definition file using Windows Explorer.

For each report project, set the `TargetFolder` property of a deployment folder to a name that corresponds to the project name (such as Prototype Phase, Design Phase, Test Phase, and Completed Reports).

Finally, remember one last thing about what will happen on practically every report project. In the beginning, your sponsor will tell you what reports and features they want, and you'll work with them to capture all the requirements in detail. Things generally will go pretty smoothly until they begin testing and you come up on a deadline. In the eleventh hour, users will start asking for things, and your sponsor will request changes.

You'll learn of some minor misunderstandings you may have had about the early requirements, and this will prompt even more changes. Some last-minute changes are inevitable in any project, but when a change is requested, it must be in writing. Whether changes are requested in handwritten form, in a document, or in an e-mail message, save these requests. You should be able to trace every new request back to an earlier requirement, or understand that it is a new requirement. If users request changes, have the project sponsor approve them. In the end, managing these changes will go a long way toward ensuring the success of your report project.

Report-Naming Conventions

One of the important decisions faced by a reporting solution developer is how to name the reports being produced. Many developers find it useful to include a number in the report name as a short-hand way to refer to a report. For example, this would enable report users to ask questions about "Report four" rather than the "Consolidated income and reconciled expenses" report.

You also need to consider whether you will include the name of the report in the report heading so that any confusion between a report's name and its title can be cleared up. Using `=Replace(Globals!ReportName, ".rdl", "")` as the expression for the report title ensures that the title and report name are the same.

Shared Datasets and Data Sources

Another significant challenge facing a report developer is whether to create and deploy a shared dataset or to use a dataset embedded in each report. Shared datasets are managed in the Solution Explorer shown in Figure 13-2. As with many things in a development project, this question has no right or wrong answer.

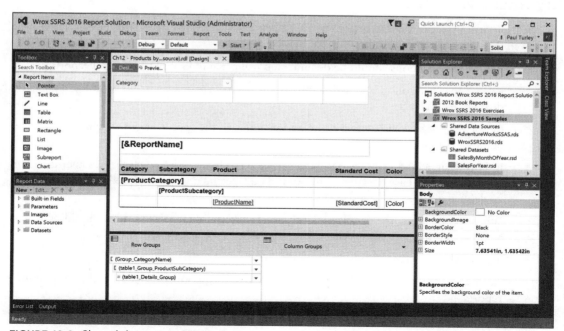

FIGURE 13-2: Shared datasets in SSDT.

Shared datasets have a number of advantages:

➤ They allow the report writer to focus on addressing the report requirements rather than spending time working out the best way to retrieve data from the data store. Data retrieval queries can be written by staff with a closer appreciation of the most efficient ways to access the data.

➤ You can deploy enhancements to the query used to retrieve the required data to multiple reports without needing to change their definition.

Shared datasets have some disadvantages as well:

➤ They can result in more data being retrieved than is strictly necessary to run a given report.

➤ Changes to the query used to retrieve the required data may result in a given report no longer operating, or in returning data that was not part of the report definition.

If you are considering extensive use of shared datasets, you need to follow a couple of best practices:

➤ Make sure that you have a system for rolling back changes to a report and/or shared dataset. It might also be necessary to employ a deployment methodology whereby multiple versions of the same dataset can be deployed to eliminate the unintended consequence of changes on reports that will not be upgraded.

➤ Make sure you have a strong test regime to ensure that all reports are tested when a change to a shared dataset is deployed.

Key Success Factors

Reporting projects have a much better chance of being successful when the business requirements are well defined and clearly communicated. In particular:

➤ Report specifications should be documented using a standard format for all reports.

➤ Report specifications are a "living, breathing" document that will evolve as the report goes through its life cycle.

➤ Report layout should be mocked up and included in the specifications to capture the stakeholder's vision.

➤ Report designers must understand the source data. In cases in which the designer is unfamiliar with the database design and business data, specific queries or stored procedures should be defined and prepared before report design.

➤ Whenever possible, the details of database objects and their relationships should be abstracted into a stored objects or semantic view.

➤ The database schema should be frozen before work begins.

➤ Accurate samples or real data should be available to support the design and testing of all reports.

> ➤ Report designers should update report specifications to reflect any layout, data, and business rule changes that might have occurred during development, and to include further relevant details to assist in future maintenance.

These may seem like lofty goals. The fact is that often you may be unable to control all these factors. Experience will help you figure out where to draw the line between situations in which you should work in less-than-ideal conditions and situations in which you should insist that these conditions be met before you begin work. In any case, be sure to clearly communicate your concerns and the associated risks.

Solution Scope

You should understand the scope of the solution before report work begins. If you lack a clear understanding of all the solution's related components, the project can easily spin out of control, with more work being started than finished.

Here are some common examples of solution scope challenges:

> ➤ Report performance problems that can prompt database schema changes or the construction of denormalized fact tables containing duplicate data.

> ➤ Realizing that changing transactional data doesn't support reporting scenarios, you redesign the database while in production.

> ➤ Database and report features are added as you go, not according to a predefined plan, causing each report to take on different behavior and features.

> ➤ Report designers and users brainstorm new features during the report development and subsequently define new requirements.

When a data warehouse, data mart, or semantic model is unavailable and outside the scope of the report project, you may consider using an *operational data store* (ODS). An ODS reflects transactional data closer to real time, as opposed to the historical volumes in a data warehouse. It has gone through some data cleansing and integrity checking to create more accurate reports.

If these kinds of issues aren't mitigated and managed, even simple projects may be doomed before they start. Ideally, a report designer should be on the receiving side of business requirements and should help clarify the details, rather than making up new requirements as the project moves along. In most cases, the report designer should rely on the business analyst/information worker to be the subject-matter expert on the data in context, allowing for a separation of concerns and better-defined tasks.

Report Specifications

Figure 13-3 shows a requirements document template I use for a lot of report projects. Depending on a few factors, variations can range from simple (like this one) to more detailed and complex. The thing is that there is no perfect report requirements document. Any attempt to create an all-purpose and all-encompassing template to cover every possible reporting scenario will likely be over-engineered and complicated. A template should cover the basics: data sources, data structure, groupings, aggregate measures, and totals. The business and functional requirements describe the behavior, or the report and use cases, but not the implementation; that is covered in the technical requirements.

Dashboard & Reporting Requirements

[client, project]

Prepared by:

[name] [email address]

Date:

[date]

Dashboard & Reporting Requirements

This document will capture the visualization requirements, including reports and dashboards, for the [... project]. It is organized by user role with a brief description of each.

Role 1

(Explanation of Role)

Report Title

If a report has multiple sections based on different queries or data selections, complete a specification for each section.

Report Specification for	(Full Report Name)		
Description			
Report Category or Group	(Reports are often grouped by business function, features or user audience.)		
Priority	(1=High, 2=Medium, 3=Low - relative to other reports in the solution)		
Line Code from Solutions Framework			
Business Problems/Questions Answered			
Data Source	(data mart or data model name)		
Fields (Table columns, dimension attribute members & measures are collectively called fields in Reporting Services. List all fields by name with the related report column title & data format.)	**Schema Field Name** (actual table column or member name)	**Column Title** (report column heading title)	**Format** (currency, percent, date - short/long, decimal places, etc.)
Row Heading(s)	(If report format and data is not all self described, some sections of table row headings may require labels)		
Filtering	(How is data filtered? - I.e. static filters, parameter-based filters, at database server, at report server) List filtered fields and criteria.		
Grouping	(How is data grouped? Static, dynamic based on parameter field selection, subgroups, are groups indented, formatted differently, etc.? If pivot/matrix reports then there may be groups on rows and columns.) List the groups and the field(s) for each group.		
Sorting	(How is data sorted? - static, parameter-based, sub-sorting within groups, clickable column headers, etc.) List the sort field(s)		
Parameters (For each parameter, specify if it should support single-value or multi-value selections. Each parameter prompt may be a textbox, radio buttons or drop-down list [with checkboxes for multi-select values]. Parameters may be used to filter, group, sort, show and hide fields, items, rows or columns)	**Parameter** (Parameter Name)	**Source** (Source of value – i.e. single value, static list, dataset query)	**Default** (Default value)

Calculations (What calculations are performed in the report. Indicate operational order of precedence and conditions - i.e. if one or more values are 0 or null, what to do if divided by 0, negative results, etc.)	(Calculations may be performed in the database, semantic model, dataset query, on custom report fields or in report items.)
Notes	

Visual Mockups & Diagrams

(For visual reports and dashboard components, provide an example; sketch or visual mockup of each visual element)

Report X

Role X

(Explanation of role)

Report Y

Report Z

FIGURE 13-3: Requirements document template.

The perfect, universal report requirements template doesn't exist, because business environments, data sources, and reporting scenarios differ wherever you go. Working for a large consulting firm, at the request of our project methodology development team, I wrote a report specification template. It was simple and flexible, but the content writers turned it into something rigid and unusable. That is how such things often evolve when we try to make them comprehensive and prescriptive.

I am often asked what is the best mock-up diagramming or prototyping tool for Reporting Services. In the end, a report requirements template should serve as a checklist used to define each report. It should include a diagram of the report indicating the layout and function of each section or data region, and it should cover these areas:

➤ Data sources (server, authentication method, principles)

➤ Database objects and fields (tables, joins, views, stored procedures, cubes, dimensions, attributes, measures, KPIs)

➤ Data regions (table, matrix, list)

➤ Groups and group levels

➤ Fields and aggregate functions (SUM, AVERAGE, COUNT, DISTINCT COUNT)

➤ Visualizations (chart, gauge, map, scorecard, sparkline, indicator, bar)

➤ Interactions and actions (drill-down, drill-through, dynamically hidden/displayed, and filtered regions)

➤ Security levels and permissions to access the report and the underlying data sources

Work with your users and project sponsor to design a report specification template that addresses your unique business needs. Some reports may query data from multiple tables, and users may not be familiar enough with the data structures to specify column names and keys for joins. In this case, you may need to involve a database expert to help with these requirements. Other reports may get their data from existing views or stored procedures, making this part of the process much easier.

How Formal and Detailed Is a Specification?

A *specification document* is a contract between you, the report designer, and your stakeholder. It's a document that communicates a business need, as well as the functional (and perhaps the technical) requirements. It also provides a foundation for testing and validating the delivery of the final product. The level of detail and formality of the specification depends on the business culture and the relationship with your stakeholder.

> **TIP** *I have designed reports with little or no requirement documentation when I have the luxury of working shoulder-to-shoulder with the stakeholder. This works when stakeholders are accessible and committed to testing and providing feedback. When that's not the case, and in more formal settings, a report specification document is an absolute necessity.*

Gathering requirements is an iterative process. Keep the first iteration focused on business objectives and user experience. Business users tend to describe systems or products they've worked with. If the report design specifics are locked down too much in the specification, this may not leave you with enough freedom to address business objectives in the most effective way. For example, a user familiar with Excel is going to want reports that behave exactly like Excel. Mobile app users might prefer a user experience similar to their iPad. Reporting Services can mimic some of these behaviors and many of the same features, but it may not be as users imagine.

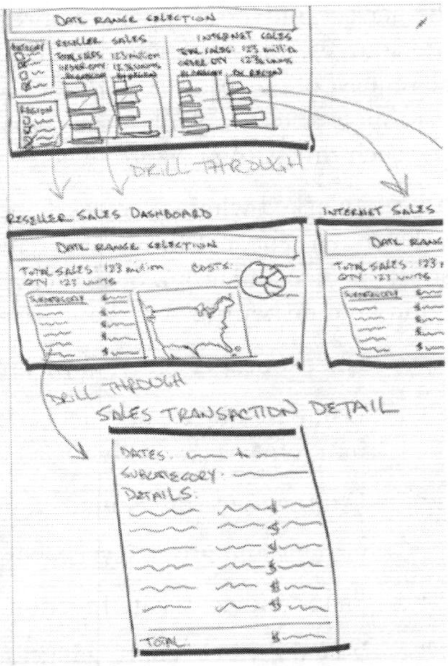

Sometimes the most effective way to envision the right design is to step away from technology and go to the whiteboard or sketchpad. I've even seen some good report mockups on cocktail napkins. This first effort to capture ideas and concepts should lead to a specification with technical details and verifiable test cases.

Figure 13-4 is a sketch of a dashboard report solution created on my tablet using OneNote, which was used to design a report solution. These images are rough by design, but the purpose is to communicate the visual concepts and navigation paths. This effectively demonstrates ideas so that you can quickly get feedback and make changes.

FIGURE 13-4: Sketch of a dashboard report solution.

Report mockups provide a visual reference. Remember that a mockup or prototype should never evolve into a production report. If you have designed a "quick and simple" report with the intention that it not be used in production, ensure that it is a "throw away" design and make a point to start over after the requirements are clear. You can do this by naming the file and adding a textbox as an annotation to the report body. This isn't to say that every report must be mocked-up or prototyped before starting design. Just ensure that you begin the design with the goal either to throw it away or to see it through to production.

> **NOTE** *I get this question on occasion: What's the best tool to mock up report designs quickly so you can get user feedback? Are you ready for the answer? It's Reporting Services. Yep, I can create a simple demo report quicker and more effectively in the report designer than using Visio or any other "mockup" tool.*

Report Template

As soon as you have developed a template that satisfies your business requirements, you can deploy it to the local development environment by copying the .rdl file to the following location:

```
C:\Program Files (x86)\Microsoft Visual Studio 14.0\Common7\IDE
\PrivateAssemblies\ProjectItems\ReportProject
```

> **NOTE** *Consider setting the attributes of your template files to read-only to prevent accidental overwriting.*

> **NOTE** *Note that the directory name quoted here contains a version number that is relevant to the current version of Reporting Services. This is subject to change in future releases, so it's important to find out the folder name for the release you are using.*

You might find that if the project sponsor and users are unfamiliar with the data structures, you are left to make assumptions about how the tables should be joined and queried. In these cases, the report specification becomes more of a checklist and a forum to validate assumptions and to answer questions. This also lengthens the report's development cycle, because you have the onus of learning the details of the data model. Remember that the key to success is effective communication. On larger projects or when reporting on more complex databases, you may need to separate the report's business requirements from the technical specification, perhaps by using two separate documents to gather these requirements. In any case, the key is to involve users and business stakeholders in obtaining buy-off and validating the results.

VERSION CONTROL

One of the key issues that must be addressed when you are working as part of a team is how to ensure that you do not overwrite another developer's changes, and that the changes you make are not overwritten by someone else.

The purpose of this section is to outline the major characteristics of version control in a report development project, and to show how these can be implemented and used in an SSDT environment.

Microsoft Team Foundation Server is a complete solution-management framework for development teams to use to plan and manage the daily build and delivery of software solutions. Team Foundation Server includes the integrated version control and build management. Team Foundation Server must be licensed, installed, and configured on a server. There are also several third-party version control systems that integrate with Visual Studio or simply manage source file version control within the filesystem. Popular free services like GitHub and Subversion are simple to set up. The core concepts of most all version control solutions are the same, but require some practice and ramp-up to use them effectively.

For most development projects, the use of version control is a given because it is the only method of ensuring that multiple developers can work on the same project without overwriting each other's work. It is worth pointing out that a number of administrative and process costs are associated with maintaining a version-control system, so it is worth considering what you are getting for this cost.

Here are some of the benefits of version-control systems:

➤   They ensure that a backup is made of each object as and when it is checked in to the server. This means that any data loss caused by a corruption of the developer's code is limited to the version on which the developer is actively working. If you ensure that the check-in policy states that all code must be checked in no later than the end of the current business day, this significantly reduces the cost of rework after any failures.

➤   They allow a change to be associated with a documented task or bug and therefore encourage developers to ensure that these are documented before work commences.

➤   If used in conjunction with a build process, they ensure that only tested versions of code are deployed to production.

➤   They provide a history of changes to code that helps when trying to distinguish stable reports from volatile ones, and obtain some metrics on the cost of development.

Setting Up Version Control

Version-control systems normally operate by introducing a new menu structure into the Visual Studio/SSDT environment that is used to establish a connection between your project and the version-control server. For example, Team Foundation Server has a "Connect to Team Foundation Server" option on the Tools menu. If you know the URL for your project's server, you can use this menu to establish a connection to your project's code repository on the server.

Whenever you open the project, a connection to the version-control server is established, so it may be necessary to re-enter your username and/or password whenever you open the project. If the server is unavailable when you open the project, normally you have a choice to "Go offline" or "Disable source control for this session." In this case, any changes you make are synchronized with the server the next time you go online.

> **NOTE** *Note that the Visual Studio/SSDT environment normally remembers that the project was opened offline and continues to work disconnected from the server until you select File ▷ Source Control ▷ Go online.*

Getting the Latest Version

One of the first things you should do when working in a version-controlled environment is ensure that you have the latest version of the report in your local workspace before you make any changes. Many version-control systems allow more than one developer to work on the same thing at the same time. You find out that someone has changed your report only when you try to check it back in. When this happens, normally you have at least three alternatives. You can save your local version, use the server version, or merge the two. When this happens, it is good corporate citizenship not to elect to overwrite the server version until you are absolutely certain that the person who changed the report agrees to lose the changes he or she has made.

Viewing a Report's History

You can obtain a history of changes to a report by right-clicking it and selecting "View change history." This displays a window showing the following information for each change:

➤ The date of the change.

➤ Who made the change.

➤ Any comments the developer made when the report was checked in.

➤ A list of work items (bug reports, tasks) associated with the change. You see this by double-clicking the change.

Restoring a Previous Version of a Report

You can restore a previous version of a report by right-clicking it and selecting Get Specific Version. The default version is always the latest version, but you can search for the required version using a date, change number, or label. Note that doing so copies the nominated version to your local workspace only. So, if you want the version you selected to be the latest version, you need to check it back in again.

Setting Check-out and Check-in Policies

Most version-control systems allow the user to specify the policy to employ when checking in and/or checking out reports or code. For example, you might want to set a policy that states that no two developers can work on the same project at the same time, or that a report must be reviewed by another developer before it is checked in.

For example, to prevent two developers from checking out the same report in a Team Foundation Server environment, select Team ➪ Team Project Settings ➪ Source Control and uncheck the "Enable Multiple check out" check box.

Applying Labels

You apply a label to a version of a report when you want to be able to find it again using the label you supply. You add a label to a report by right-clicking the project and selecting Apply Label. You then select the report and version combination to which the label is to applied, supply a label value and an optional comment, and click OK. You can add more than one report to a label by clicking Add.

SYNCHRONIZING CONTENT

When you have completed the development of your report, the next challenge will be to deploy your report to a server environment to allow it to be seen and/or reviewed by your co-workers or business users. This section deals with how to build and deploy either an individual report or a suite of reports to a server environment.

Deploying an Individual Report

Deploying a single report is straightforward; you just right-click the report and select Deploy. Note that the report goes through a build process that checks that the report is valid before it is deployed. If there are no build or deployment errors (see the section "Checking for Build Errors," later in this chapter), a message in the output window tells you that the report has deployed successfully.

Deploying a Suite of Reports

To save time, instead of deploying each report in your project individually, you might choose to deploy all of them at the same time. You can do this in one of two ways:

➤ Right-click the project name and choose Deploy.

➤ Click the first report you want to deploy, hold down the Shift key, click the last report you want to deploy, right-click, and choose Deploy.

Each report you select will go through the same build and deploy process, but this time, a message in the output window tells you how many of the reports were built and deployed successfully.

Checking for Build Errors

Most common errors in reports are displayed in the report preview pane when you preview the report. However, you might also be notified of an error or warning on your report on the Error tab of the SSDT environment. If the Error tab does not appear, you can display it by selecting View ➪ Error List.

Excluding a Report from a Deployment

As noted, you can remove an individual report from an individual deployment by just not clicking it before you select the Deploy option. You can unclick a report by holding down the Ctrl key and clicking the report you want to exclude after the reports you want to include have been highlighted.

But what if you want a report to be excluded on a more permanent basis? You could just delete the report, but this would remove any record of it, which would also remove its history.

Another alternative is to right-click the report and select Exclude From Project. This removes the report from the project without deleting it from either your local workspace or the version-control server. If, in the future, you want to re-include the report, you can add it back to the project by right-clicking it, selecting Add ➪ Existing item, and navigating to the report definition file (.rdl) in your local workspace.

MANAGING SERVER CONTENT

This section deals with how you manage your report content (reports, datasets, and data sources) on a report server that has been installed in either a native mode or SharePoint configuration. In a development environment, you will probably not need to know a great deal about managing reports on the server, because you will be modifying content directly using the Visual Studio/SSDT. However, you might not have the required access to perform a direct deployment in either the test or production environment, so you may need to know how these can be managed on the server. You might also want to check that the way your report has been configured in your Visual Studio/SSDT environment matches the way it has been deployed to the server.

Checking the Deployment Location

The first thing you need to know before you manage content on your Reporting Services server is the server's location. You can discover this by selecting Project ⇨ Properties in the Visual Studio/SSDT environment. You see the window shown in Figure 13-5.

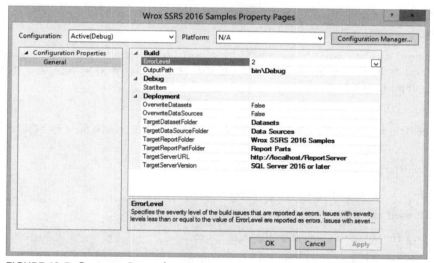

FIGURE 13-5: Property Pages for sample server.

Here are the things you need to review on this screen:

➤ The configuration determines the rest of the settings. In Figure 13-5, the Debug configuration is being used. As a report developer, you can set up a configuration for each of the environments (development, test, and production, for example). You can change these settings automatically by selecting the required configuration from this drop-down menu.

➤ If the `OverwriteDatasets` or `OverwriteDataSources` setting is set to `True`, a dataset/data source is overwritten on the server when a report is displayed that uses the setting. If it is set to `False`, you are warned in the output window that the dataset/data source is not being changed.

➤ You see the `TargetDatasetFolder`, `TargetDataSourceFolder`, `TargetReportFolder`, and `TargetReportPartFolder` object types. Creating a folder for each of these types is a good way to organize them on the server for ease of access and to allow them to be properly secured. Figure 13-5 shows the defaults for these settings. Note that the report folder defaults to the name of your project.

Managing Content in Native Mode

When your report server was set up, it was decided whether your reports would be deployed to a SharePoint environment. Reporting Services ships with a "native" mode deployment option for customers who do not have (or do not want) a SharePoint site. This section deals with the content management options in default (native) mode for Reporting Services.

Managing Shared Data Sources

In native mode, shared data sources are stored in a folder you can view from the Reports URL. This is normally `http://ServerName/Reports`, but it is best to check where it is deployed in your environment by examining the settings by selecting Project ⇨ *Projectname* Properties from SSDT. The folder name is located in the `TargetDataSourceFolder` row of this screen.

You can manage the following from the server:

➤ Whether the report can be viewed by visitors to the report site when in tiled mode. This is the default view used by Reporting Services in native mode. The alternative view is Details view, which displays reports as a list.

➤ Enabling/disabling the data source.

➤ The type of the data source, such as whether the data is stored in an XML file or a SQL Server database.

➤ The folder in which the data source is stored.

➤ The description that appears next to the data source.

➤ The credentials used to run the report.

➤ The connection string used to connect to the data source.

➤ The data-driven subscriptions applied to this data source.

➤ The list of reports, datasets, and data models that depend on the data source. If required, any of these can be deleted from the Dependent Items tab.

➤ The list of users who can view or overwrite this data source on the server.

Note that any changes you make on the server will be overridden by the settings in your project each time a report is deployed if the `OverwriteDataSources` project property is set to `True`.

To manage a data source, select it from the Reports URL and click the down arrow that appears to the right of the data source name when you hover the mouse cursor over the data source. Just ensure that you click the Apply button after you make your changes. If you have trouble applying the changes, you might have to run your browser using local administrator privileges by right-clicking the icon and selecting "Run as administrator."

Another interesting thing you can manage on the server is the creation of a data model from your data source. This will be generated in the folder you nominate. You can download and open it from the SSDT environment by selecting Open ⇨ Existing Project and selecting the downloaded project.

Managing Shared Datasets

In native mode, shared datasets are stored in a folder that can be viewed from the Reports URL. You can check this location in the same way as for data sources, but in the `TargetDataSetFolder` row of the properties screen.

The things you can manage on the server for a dataset include the things you can manage for a data source, except that you can't disable a dataset.

You can additionally set the timeout in seconds for a dataset to respond to a request from a report, and set up and manage dataset caching. This is a way of enhancing a report's performance by using a cached copy of the dataset rather than looking up the data from the data source. This cache can be refreshed after a specified interval or on a schedule. If you elect to have the cache refreshed on a schedule, a SQL Agent job will be created for you when you click Apply on the Caching options.

Note that any changes you make on the server will be overridden by the settings in your project each time a report is deployed if the `OverwriteDataSets` project property is set to `True`.

Managing Reports

In native mode, reports are also stored either in a folder or on the home screen of the Reports URL. The things you can manage on the server include most of the things you can manage on a dataset. You also can manage some additional items:

➤ Create a linked report with a predefined set of parameters.

➤ Create a scheduled and/or data-driven subscription to the report. This can be used to automatically distribute copies of the report to a predefined set of recipients via the filesystem or e-mail.

➤ Create a snapshot of the report either manually or at given intervals.

Managing Content in SharePoint

All the things you can manage in native mode can also be managed from your SharePoint site. You access the SharePoint report management menu, in the same way as you access the native mode menu. Just select the blue down arrow (instead of the yellow one) to see menu options for the familiar report operations.

Here are some additional options:

➤ Edit in Report Builder. Report Builder is a user-friendly tool for developing reports that look more like an Office product than a developer product. You get only a subset of the facilities that are available to you from the Visual Studio/SSDT environment, but, in many cases, this is all you need. If you do not have a copy of Report Builder installed on your local computer, one is automatically downloaded from your server.

➤ Manage Parameters is useful in cases where your report uses default values for parameters and you need to check what those default values are. You should not assume that the values in your development environment match those in SharePoint, even immediately after a report is deployed. It is always best to check.

➤ Send To can be used to download a copy of the report, copy it to a new location, or e-mail it to someone as a link.

> **WARNING** *If you are making changes directly on your reporting server, be sure that these changes are reflected in your local reporting development workspace. Failure to do so may result in any changes being overwritten the next time the project or report is deployed.*

REPORT BUILDER AND SELF-SERVICE REPORTING STRATEGIES

Since Reporting Services 2008, Report Builder has become the primary method for report designers to create standard RDL-based reports. As you know, two report design tools are targeted to serve different report design audiences, but they share a lot of the same functionality and capabilities. In short, SSDT is primarily for IT professionals and developer teams to collaborate and design report solutions. Report Builder enables business-focused report designers to create individual reports using published resources on the server. However, both tools support basic and advanced report design capabilities. One doesn't replace the other, and one isn't necessarily better than the other. It depends on the needs and the person performing the task.

Figure 13-6 shows the major feature differences and similarities between the Report Builder and SSDT design tools.

Report Builder   SSDT / Visual Studio

- Create & edit reports on server
- Use live shared data sources
- Report Part Gallery
- Number format on ribbon

- All report item features
- Data regions & groups
- Multiple & composite report items
- Subreports
- Expressions & expression builder
- Parameters
- Filters
- MDX graphical query designer
- Custom code (VB.NET)
- Deploy to report server
- All other features

- Multiple report projects
- Version control/TFS integration
- Create & managed shared data sources & shared datasets
- Create & publish report parts
- T-SQL graphical query designer
- Edit RDL as XML
- Build & deploy

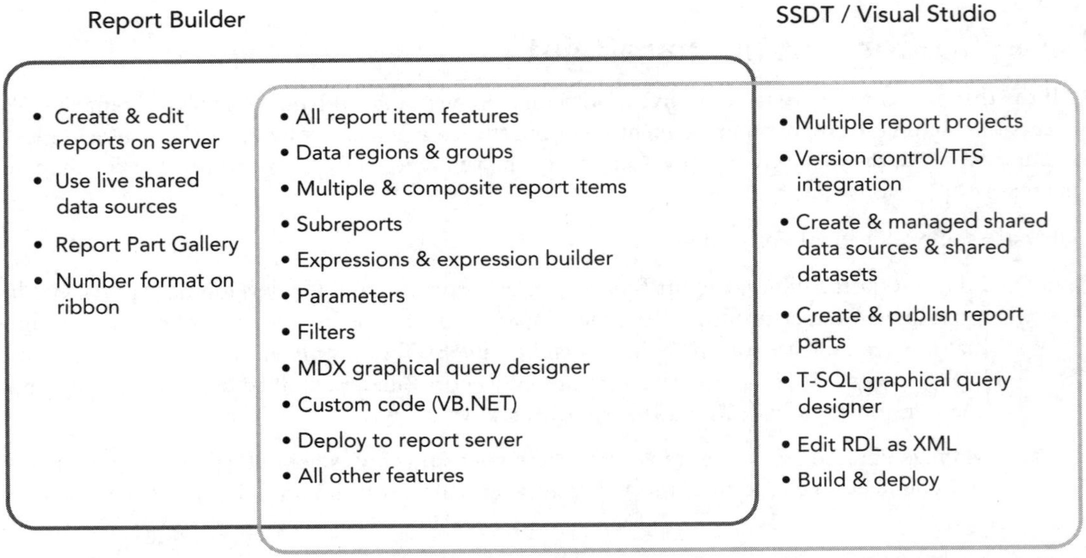

FIGURE 13-6: Feature differences and similarities between the Report Builder and SSDT design tools.

As you can see, these design tools share core capabilities, making them suited to mainstream report design. Many professional designers don't have a strong preference. Some who do simply prefer to use the tool to which they are accustomed. Figure 13-7 shows the tasks and roles that are best suited for each design tool.

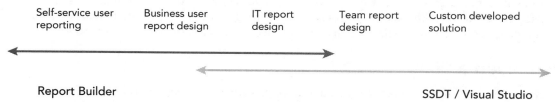

| Self-service user reporting | Business user report design | IT report design | Team report design | Custom developed solution |

Report Builder   SSDT / Visual Studio

FIGURE 13-7: Tasks and roles that are best suited for each design tool.

For purely ad hoc and self-service user report design, Report Builder is more appropriate because of its simplicity and straightforward interface. Experience has proven that nontechnical users get lost in the complexity of the Visual Studio shell as a business user tool. The concepts of managing solutions and projects in SSDT are cumbersome and seem unnecessary for users who just want to create a report. Report Builder is streamlined to eliminate some of the "report development" tasks. For example, to use a shared data source, you don't need to define a separate embedded, named data source to reference the external, named data source. I have had students struggle with this concept for the duration of a week-long class. By contrast, the Report Builder design experience is simple and sleek.

At the opposite end of the spectrum, for team development, the Visual Studio-based SSDT provides integrated version control and report project management capabilities. IT professionals use SSDT to design and deploy shared objects used by business users in self-service reporting scenarios. These include shared data sources, shared datasets, and report parts.

REPORT BUILDER AND SEMANTIC MODEL HISTORY

If you've used earlier versions of Reporting Services, or if you've grown up with the product as I have, you probably know that a little history has brought us to this point in the product's evolution. The 2005 version of Reporting Services included a self-service reporting and data browsing tool called Report Builder. This should not be confused with the report design tool we have today that has the same name—first called Report Builder 2.0, then Report Builder 3.0, and now today the new tool is simply called Report Builder.

> **NOTE** *Report Builder 1.0 consumed data through a semantic object layer known as the Report Model, which is no longer supported. This offered some useful capabilities, but also had some limitations and was not enterprise class by most standards. It was a first step toward a better solution, and many businesses found some value for limited ad hoc reporting. This modern release of the SQL Server product platform is a welcome replacement for Report Models and Report Builder 1.0.*

PLANNING A SELF-SERVICE REPORTING ENVIRONMENT

As the IT and business leader in an organization, you cannot simply turn the user community loose with a set of design tools to use as they please. You may have seen what happens when businesses run without data governance. Heck, I have stepped into organizations with thousands of Access databases, Excel workbooks, and reports strewn throughout the network filesystem, with no understanding of ownership or where reliable data resided. This is clearly not the right answer.

You Need a Plan

A manageable self-service reporting solution begins with a concise plan, well-defined processes, and a clear understanding of who owns what and where reports will reside. Part of that plan should encompass tracking the ownership and ongoing status of each report. At regular intervals (say, once a month or once a quarter), the status of new or evolving reports should be revisited. Some user reports may be considered for migration to IT-supported business reports. Some may be considered for consolidation, to have their features added to an existing report. Other reports may be dismissed as one-off, unsupported, or legacy reports to be deleted or archived.

If you perform these reviews on a regular, scheduled cycle, nothing falls through the cracks. The IT group has a clear understanding of the reports they support, as well as those that are the responsibility of business units, leaders, and individual users.

Design Approaches and Usage Scenarios

Before you over-engineer the solution, you must understand what business users will do with these reports they create. If I have learned anything from years of consulting with many different companies, it is that it is important to have a process in place to manage IT assets, including reports and BI dashboards. Too much process can be a hindrance to getting business done and performing other important tasks. That balance will be different for each organization, but some general principles apply to all. Seek to understand what users need to accomplish with their self-service reporting solution.

From a user reporting perspective, these scenarios may include the following:

➤ **A report created for personal use**—This report may be used by the person who created it at some point in the future, or that person may be done with it after the first use. Because it is a user-owned report, others in the organization will not use it to make critical business decisions based on the information it presents.

➤ **A report or set of reports to be used by a business unit or small group**—These ad hoc reports are used to help a small group of business users perform a task, but they understand that they own these reports and are responsible for the information they provide.

➤ **A report created by a business user to be migrated to production**—After the design is reviewed by an IT professional, this report may be validated and migrated to a production report, or redesigned and then used and supported by the whole organization. These reports are often viewed as prototypes or proofs of concept to be rebuilt from scratch to company IT standards.

➤ **Production reports designed and created by IT for company use**—This is the traditional approach to IT solutions. Users or business unit leaders submit a request, a business analyst gathers and documents requirements, and then IT developers create the solution that is vigorously tested before being deployed to production. Some critical reports may fall into this category, but this doesn't provide the freedom and flexibility required by most organizations.

Allowing business users to own some of the day-to-day report creation can free IT developer resources to build more complex and critical reporting solutions. Because many experienced business users may know their data better than IT pros, who better to do the initial design and prototyping than those who will use the reports? Complex and mission-critical solutions should be developed using IT project standards and development methodology. Using the prototyping approach, certain trained and educated users design proof-of-concept reports that can be reviewed and analyzed to help establish the business and technical requirements. IT developers then redesign the reports from the prototypes and agreed-upon requirements.

Define Ownership

A classic problem in most any business environment is that information tends to move from place to place and person to person. Without a set of governance rules, people gather the information they need to perform their jobs and store it in whatever form works best for them. Over time, people may share their Excel workbooks and other documents with others, and some of these may become de facto standard sources for others. The problem is that the latest version may be in someone's local folder or inbox. In many cases, multiple copies are changed and updated with new information. Local reports work much the same way. If each doesn't have an owner and a home, people will continue to build on their own copies.

The most significant fault in unmanaged business reporting environments is that the administrators don't know who created certain reports, or who is responsible for the reports they have. Over the years, the number of reports grows, with no traceability to the person who requested that a report be created, who designed it, or who last updated it. In part, this problem is aided by Reporting Services' report catalog logging, but having the network ID of the person who originally deployed a report may not be a comprehensive solution. That person may no longer own the report and may not even work for the company anymore.

When called in to consolidate a set of reports, some IT project sponsors commonly say, "We don't know who these reports belong to or how they are used. What do we do?" My response has been, "Make a backup and then delete them from the servers. I'm sure you'll hear from the owners eventually." That's probably not the best solution, but I can assure you it works.

Report ownership really has two components. The first is the person who created, or is responsible for maintaining, a report. The second is the business entity that uses a report—and that may be responsible for the ongoing business and data requirements.

For the first component, ownership may simply fall into the hands of the business entity that created or assumes responsibility for the report. Here are a few possible scenarios:

➤ A single user created a report, and he or she assumes full responsibility for the information it presents.

➤ A business unit or department owns the report. The users within that business entity will use the report for their own needs, and it won't be shared outside that group.

➤ The business enterprise owns the report. The design was conducted in accordance with IT and business standards. The data access method, query, and data have been validated and approved by IT and the business.

Ideally, all reports should be well-designed and reliable, but if you allow business users to create their own reports, they should be suspect until formally validated or redesigned by IT. Until that happens, they should be deployed to an isolated location and branded so that any user understands who the owner is and the conditions of its use. If the CEO is handed a copy of Martha's personal report, she should know to validate any information it contains before making a critical business decision. If she is looking at an IT-sanctioned report, she should know, with confidence, that the information is accurate and reliable.

Every report should have a clear owner and sponsor. If IT owns the report server, they should have a clear and tangible record for each report, including the following:

➤ Who requested that the report be created and defined the business requirements?

➤ Who designed and developed the report?

➤ Who tested and validated the design?

➤ Have the queries and data access methods been validated to be accurate and efficient?

➤ Does the report meet corporate security requirements?

➤ Who should be able to run and get data through the report?

➤ What data should or should not be accessible through this report to specific users or members of Active Directory groups?

Data Governance

Laying down rules often does no good unless people have reasonable alternatives to find what they need and to perform their jobs. Therefore, the first step toward governing the source and storage media for important information should be to provide a convenient and reasonable way to get to it. Enterprise data should be stored in enterprise databases. Department-level documents and reports should be stored in a designated location accessible to that group. Only after a foundation for collaboration exists can you mandate the rules for common use.

When users design their own reports, they should connect to the same data sources using the same methods as others, and then consume the data using a standard approach. Business data entities (such as a product catalog, customer contact list, or employee directory) should be queried from a central location. Or copies should be derived from a central store and then updated at regular intervals. Only when report data is obtained from an authorized source are reports reliable and consistent. This can be achieved by surfacing the appropriate data through an enterprise data warehouse, online analytical processing (OLAP) cubes, and semantic data models.

Data Source Access and Security

All users who will do their own reporting must be able to connect to enterprise data sources. But this doesn't mean that all users must have access to sensitive information. By employing user-level access and managing Active Directory group membership, users are granted access to only the data they should be permitted to read.

Certain reporting capabilities (such as subscriptions and alerting) require report data to be accessed when the user is not online to be authenticated. In these cases, a shared data source should be created with stored credentials and minimal access to data records for a group of users. When reports and queries are executed at scheduled intervals, these results are sent to the user via e-mail, a file share, or are made available in cached result sets.

The use of shared data sources with stored credentials is common in Reporting Services solutions and can be adequately secure. Care should be taken to return only necessary data for the report. Access to the reports should be secured in addition to securing access to the database. In some cases, it may be necessary to manage two sets of shared data sources. One provides fine-grained access to certain data for interactive users, and the other supports these unattended reporting situations.

Create and deploy these shared data sources to a central location on your report server or SharePoint site. By default, a folder named Data Sources is created on the report server. In a SharePoint integrated site, add or use a document library set aside for shared data sources. Because you may use the SharePoint site to host other BI reports and content such as Excel Services reports, PerformancePoint, and Power View reports, you can designate one data source library for all the different data source content types. If the site is created using the Business Intelligence Center site template, a library called Data Connections is created and can be used for this purpose.

User Education

As soon as the report infrastructure is prepared and a plan is in place for your organization's self-service reporting strategy, train your users on the essentials. Start with a pilot user group to help iron out the rough spots, and then show them how to launch Report Builder, search the gallery, and add report parts. Then show them how to use shared datasets and select and use a shared data source (in that order).

With some preparation and planning, many business users can design reports without possessing query language or advanced report design skills. Depending on the sophistication of the need, users might have to acquire only basic skills. Using reports parts, they simply drag and drop pluggable parts onto the report body and then run the report. Using shared datasets, they need not write queries; they just add data regions and bind and group fields.

Optimizing the Report Builder User Experience

If you leave users to figure out how to design reports on their own, they will probably fail. Out of the box, Reporting Services doesn't lend itself to self-exploration, because it contains many features and capabilities that will confuse users if they try it on their own. But with a little guidance, this can be a good experience for the users. Guided, users can learn the basics and then learn more advanced features when they're ready.

Conducting User Training

Start small, keep it simple, and help your users understand the basic, essential tasks to design simple reports. Don't teach these users to write queries and use expressions. For advanced users, you can schedule a second-level training session after they have mastered the basics. In your first training session, teach your users to do the following:

➤   Navigate to the Report Manager or SharePoint site.

➤   Launch Report Builder.

➤   Choose the report type to create.

➤   Choose the data source.

➤   Assemble a dashboard from the report part gallery or design the report using wizards and drag-and-drop tools.

➤   Browse data in the report.

➤   Save the report to a folder or library.

Folder and Library Management

One of the easiest ways to segregate user reports from enterprise reports is to designate a location for each. Users and IT report designers are granted permissions to deploy to appropriate libraries or folders. In a large-scale environment, these may be separate servers. In a smaller solution, they could be separate folders or document libraries on the same server or site.

Report Branding

After a report has been printed or exported to a file, it should also be identifiable. Using a template, brand these reports so that they will be recognizable as user-created or enterprise-standard reports. This could be as simple as a brief textbox in the report header or a designated image or logo.

Formal reports can have a "mark of approval" logo that lets people know at a glance that they are looking at a tested and trusted report. One of my customers took this advice and created three report templates to meet their business needs. Each template had an image in the report header to mark the report with the corporate report conformance level. Here's a summary of their approach:

➤   **Level 1**—Sourced from corporate BI data, but created by anyone without IT controls.

➤   **Level 2**—Sourced from BI data and query/report logic reviewed by a BI team member.

➤ Level 3—Sourced from BI data, query/report logic reviewed by a BI team member, and validated/approved by the business data stewards for the data on the report.

Data Source and Query Options

Reporting Services has the flexibility to connect to a variety of data sources and to use different database objects. Too many choices are confusing, though. Standardize on a data access method and then teach users to work with a set of database objects. Most IT shops have established standards for connecting users to their databases and making data available through various objects. It's important that you establish and enforce these standards before turning your users loose on corporate data. In brief, your options are to encapsulate data using these objects:

➤ Relational database views

➤ Relational database stored procedures

➤ OLAP database cubes and perspectives

➤ Semantic data model

If your users will be reporting directly on a relational database (preferably a data warehouse and not operational transactional schemas), you can provide access through views, stored procedures, or a semantic model.

If you provide access through a view, this simplifies data access by providing a layer of abstraction from multiple table relationships and join operations. Views don't provide parameterization. Users must still write a SELECT statement and a WHERE clause to query this data.

A stored procedure used to select and return data from multiple tables can have parameters built into its design. To use a stored procedure for a report, users need only select it from a list of procedures for the database specified in the report data source. No SELECT clause is necessary, and parameters in the stored procedure are automatically used to derive report parameters by the report designer. There are some minor limitations, such as how multi-value parameters must be handled. But for a relational data source, stored procedures can simplify the user report design experience and provide a simple and efficient way to query data at the source.

Using Shared Data Sources

Report Builder requires shared data sources for deployment. Create a data source for each database or semantic model, and deploy it to the shared data sources folder or library on the server. For all interactive reports that will be run while the user is logged into his or her desktop computer, you can use Windows Integrated security and pass through the user's security credentials. The databases and database servers must be configured to allow access to a role, Windows, or Active Directory group to which all the report users have membership.

A network administrator can create a group for the report users and add each user to the group. For SQL Server, create a login for the group, and then map the SQL Server login to the db_datareader role for the database that a report queries data from. For Analysis Services, create a role for the

OLAP database, and add the group to the role with Read permission granted for the cube, dimensions, and members.

Using Analysis Services to Simplify Data Access

For analytical reporting, pairing Report Builder with SQL Server Analysis Services (SSAS) can simplify user report design even further. When the simplified in-memory tabular technology was added to SSAS in SQL Server 2012, it was referred to as the BI Semantic Model (BISM). Now, in SQL Server 2016, it is just called "SSAS," which encompasses an SSAS OLAP (cube) database (now called a multidimensional database) and SSAS Tabular, an enterprise implementation of the same data storage and aggregation technology used in Power Pivot and Power BI. Both OLAP/multidimensional databases and tabular models are managed using the Analysis Services storage engine, and the security model is the same for both.

To provide user access, a role is defined in the database with a set of permissions, and then one or more Windows users or groups are added to the role. To grant access to an Analysis Services database, define a role with Read permissions, and then add the appropriate Windows or Active Directory group to the role.

Designing and Deploying Report Parts

Report parts are fragments of a report, complete with a data source, dataset, and parameters, that can be reused in another report. A report part may be a single data region, such as a table or chart, or it may be a combination of report items and data regions, such as a complete dashboard. Report parts are published to a folder or library on the report server from any report using SSDT. This is considered to be an IT activity, and should be part of the preparation effort to support user report design.

> **NOTE** *Report Parts is a feature that works as it was designed, but has not had tremendous uptake in the industry since it was introduced in SQL Server 2008 R2. In the right scenarios, this feature enables reusing portions of existing reports. You should carefully evaluate whether report parts are right for your users. This is not a feature that I typically use in my solutions.*

Using Report Parts

In Report Builder, users choose to insert a report part and then search the gallery. If these report parts are used without modification, a user can simply add them to a report and then run the report without having any report design skills beyond the basics.

> **WARNING** *Report Parts can only be used in reports that are authored in Report Builder. This is one of the few capabilities of Report Builder that doesn't exist in the SSDT report designer.*

When a developer updates and republishes existing report parts, users are given the option to update their reports. In this case, a report opened in Report Builder displays a Report Part update notification. If the user chooses to allow an update to take place, the affected report parts are replaced with the new components on the server.

In a SharePoint integrated solution, the server address is set to the SharePoint root-site address. Like all of the target deployment folder properties (data sources, datasets, and reports), the report part folder is set to the full path to the library used for report parts, as you see in Figure 13-8.

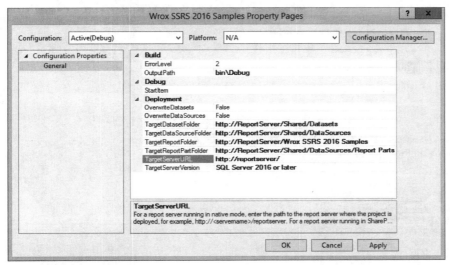

FIGURE 13-8: Report part folder.

Figure 13-9 shows the Options dialog in Report Builder. In a SharePoint integrated solution, the server address is set to the SharePoint root-site address, and the report part folder is set to a relative path to the library used for report parts. Pay close attention to this, because the address formats are different between the two tools.

Report parts can be published from either SSDT or Report Builder. Publish report parts to a designated library, and give each report part an appropriate searchable name.

In SSDT, the report part names are specified in the Publish Report Parts dialog, which is accessible from the report. The selected report parts are then published to the server when the report is deployed. In Report Builder, choose Publish Report Parts from the Report Builder button menu, as shown in Figure 13-10.

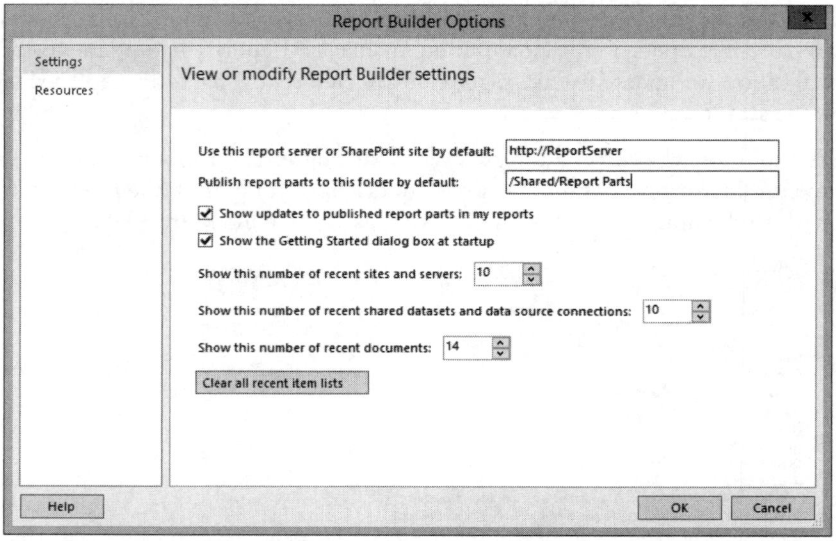

FIGURE 13-9: Options dialog.

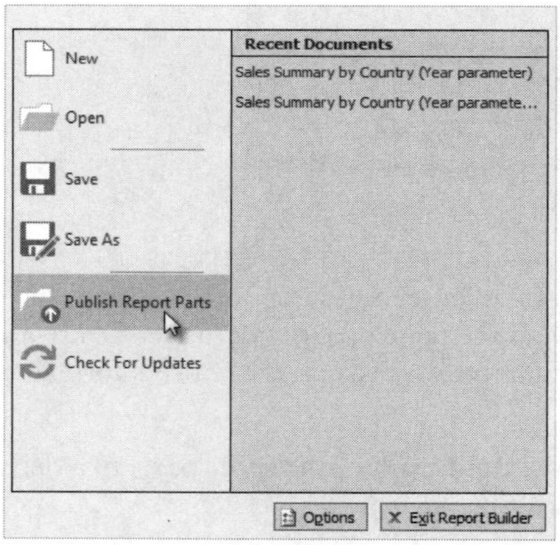

FIGURE 13-10: The Publish Report Parts option.

In either SSDT or Report Builder, the Publish Report Parts dialog is used to select the report-design objects you want to deploy, and to rename these objects as report parts. When a data region is added to a report, you commonly shouldn't worry about giving it a friendly name. But if you choose to publish a table or chart as a report part, you must give it a more recognizable name than `Table3` or `Chart1`. Remember that when naming report parts, eventually several report parts may be deployed. The user will need to know not only what type of report item a part represents, but also exactly what it does. Names should be descriptive, making it easy to discern how they consume or visually present a set of data. A good name might be something like `Sales Amount by Sales Territory Country Chart`.

All the dependent objects that the report part needs to function are included on this list. If you uncheck any of these objects, they are still added to the report, but they are not made available to add individually. You typically don't need to select the datasets, data sources, and parameters when deploying report parts.

Using Shared Datasets

Shared datasets allow for more advanced and granular report design without the need for users to write queries and consume data directly from data sources. A shared dataset is designed by an IT developer and is deployed to the report server in the same way that shared data sources and report parts are deployed and used. When designing a new report, a report user can choose a shared dataset from the server catalog, and then design standard report data regions as they would with a dataset of their own design.

This requires greater aptitude than using report parts, but it also mitigates common mistakes made in query design, and simplifies data access for common users. Users can have more flexibility to use advanced report design techniques without having to deal with the complexities of using SQL and MDX. Shared datasets can have associated parameters, filters, and calculated field definitions that users simply utilize rather than design themselves. Each deployed dataset can be configured with caching options to speed up report execution and minimize redundant database queries.

Shared datasets should be tested thoroughly before they are deployed and generally should not be modified after they have been used.

USER REPORT MIGRATION STRATEGIES

For reports that will serve as prototypes or the starting point for IT-supported business reports, you should consider a formal process. This can be part of the scheduled user report review cycle, or it can be performed for specific reports to let users assist with the design process and proof of concept. The process consists of the following phases:

➤ Review

➤ Consolidate

➤ Design

➤ Test

➤ Maintain

Review

A user-designed report helps IT analysts and developers understand how they want to consume data. If the report is proposed to IT acceptance, it should be reviewed for security, effective query design, and proper use of report design techniques. If the report meets these standards, it may be tested and then promoted to the production IT-supported report server or library for general use by the business. It should be branded so that business users can identify it as a reliable source of business data.

Consolidate

When new reports are introduced, in many cases they may have functionality that duplicates other reports. It's common for new reports to simply be a variation of an existing design that may be sorted, grouped, or filtered a little differently. Using common report design techniques, you can modify existing reports to use parameters and expressions to dynamically sort, group, and filter data. In many organizations, existing user-designed reports can be consolidated to drastically reduce the number of reports that IT must support. For example, I've seen cases where 800 reports were reduced to about 100 by retiring unused reports and consolidating redundant reports with those having more interactive features.

Don't wait until you have hundreds of out-of-control reports. Make this a regular effort in your periodic review.

Design

When reports are created as prototypes, treat them as examples and not as the starting point for a production report. There is great value in throwing away exemplary designs. Only keep a report that was designed from the beginning according to corporate IT project standards. Otherwise, you'll be ahead of the game by learning from it as a proof of concept, tossing it out, and starting over.

Test

Every report should go through the same testing and quality assurance process as custom software. Generally, report development cycles are shorter, and testing need not be a long and expensive ordeal. However, critical business reports should be tested by an objective team, separate from developers and report designers. Each report should be tested by a technical professional for security conformance, query, and presentation.

Maintain

As new requirements are introduced, the entire process can be repeated to decide if features should be added to existing reports, or if new reports should be added to the solution. Database servers may be added or moved, and shared data sources should be updated to reflect these changes. As new features are contemplated or reports are considered for consolidation, you should think about the trade-offs involved with report execution, query efficiency, and reduced functionality. Meeting multiple requirements using a single report must be weighed against the increased cost of maintaining multiple reports. The overall goal is to strike a balance between having reports that are simple to maintain and reducing the overall number of reports by combining features through more advanced design.

SUMMARY

Successful reporting solutions are planned and managed. This chapter considered some of the decisions you face when organizing your report projects, enabling a team of report designers to collaborate, test, and deploy reports to production. Obtaining report requirements is an iterative process that begins with conceptual design and may include creating mock-up sketches. A report design specification is important, especially when the report designer isn't working alongside the stakeholder.

In a team environment, version-control systems help team members work together to share design files and prevent lost work, roll back changes, and manage their work. Separate report servers let report designers and developers make sure their solutions function as designed and deploy correctly. Testers use a QA server environment to test reports and ensure correct results and behavior before the final solution is shipped or deployed to production.

This chapter presented a set of guidelines for planning, designing, and maintaining a solution using Report Builder, thus enabling your business users to design their own reports. It is critical to define and understand the ownership of reports. When users own a report's requirements and design, they must accept responsibility for the data it presents and the business decisions. IT professionals or business leaders must manage user access to important data and tools that provide these capabilities. Data sources should be governed by the business, and users should be trained to use only reliable data sources.

Self-service report design is a partnership between users and IT professionals. Some user-designed reports may be used simply to browse information and for casual observations. Other reports may be used to help IT professionals better understand user reporting requirements and data use patterns. A user report may serve as a proof of concept that can be used to evolve a solution, or to redesign properly developed report solutions using efficient design patterns and industry best practices.

Chapter 14 will show you how to build a composite dashboard report solution with interactive visual components and a drill-through map. It begins with a discussion of working within the strengths and limitations of the Reporting Services architecture. I'll demonstrate best-practice techniques for creating highly visual scorecards with sparklines and KPI indicators. Then, you will assemble a complete dashboard report.

14

Report Solutions, Patterns, and Recipes

WHAT'S IN THIS CHAPTER?

- ➤ Designing super reports
- ➤ Report recipes
- ➤ Dashboard solutions
- ➤ Designing a KPI scorecard
- ➤ Designing an interactive sparkline report
- ➤ Maps with navigation

WROX.COM CODE DOWNLOADS FOR THIS CHAPTER

The wrox.com code downloads for this chapter are found on this book's web page on the Download Code tab. The code is in the Chapter 14 download and individually named according to the names throughout the chapter.

Anyone who does a lot of advanced report design work can appreciate the fact that Reporting Services can be used to build highly customized reports meeting the demands of complex business requirements. Features and properties have been added in each product version improving these capabilities. Some objects have dozens of properties, many of which are used only for very specific needs, namely, to solve specific problems.

The report recipe concept discussed in this chapter was born from a series of conference presentations I have given at the PASS Global Summit over the past few years. The topic of advanced report design led to discussions about practical design patterns and different ways that a single, more capable report could be created to replace many simple reports. Through the use of some well-established design techniques, we have learned to create fewer, more complex and adaptable reports, rather than one report for each user request or individual requirement.

Let's face it—a lot of reporting environments are not meticulously planned. In most organizations, different people create reports to surface information from various data sources. Over time, the reports grow and evolve. To some degree, this situation is inevitable, but that is to not say that we must sit back and watch it turn into chaos.

In Chapter 13, we discussed an approach to conduct regular user report reviews with consideration for consolidation and redesign. This concept isn't exclusively for migrating user reports to those under IT control. We can take a similar approach to dealing with reports developed in more formal settings that may have become redundant or obsolete. The process is much the same: assign ownership and schedule regular reviews, comparing similar reports slated for consolidation or retirement.

SUPER REPORTS

When a set of business requirements is presented for development, they are translated into a set of report capabilities and features. When a set of similar requirements is presented with considerable overlap, this may be an opportunity to combine them into a cohesive set of features. A *super report* combines features to present each set of business users with only the capabilities and information they need.

How can we design one report to present different information for different users? We offer each set of users different report behaviors by enabling elements of the report under unique conditions. This is possible by using the skills and techniques discussed in earlier chapters. These features can be combined to take the user's reporting experience to a whole new level.

Figure 14-1 shows the interdependencies between basic report design elements. The graphic depicts how different design techniques are combined to create advanced report features. Note that expressions are central to this approach and frequently used alongside other techniques.

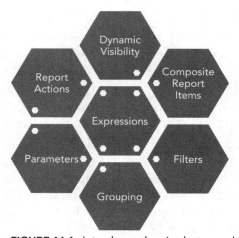

FIGURE 14-1: Interdependencies between basic report design elements.

Through examples, you learn to combine these techniques and features to create more capable, advanced, and useful reports.

Working with the Strengths and Limitations of the Reporting Services Architecture

Before I continue, I want to be clear about something: I love this product. I have found Reporting Services to be extremely powerful, flexible, and capable of solving most business problems I have encountered in about nine years of using it. Given a challenge, I can usually find a way to tackle it with Reporting Services. In learning about the product team's vision and long-term goals for Reporting Services' features and capabilities, we have gained insight into the mechanics of the product's components and why they behave as they do. Without fully understanding the design goals in constructing the architecture of this product, it is easy for a report designer to ask questions such as "Why does it work that way?" and "Why did it do that?" Reporting Services has some limitations that may not make sense to the casual user. I have found that most advanced capabilities that I want to include in reports can be implemented, but not necessarily using my chosen technique. As I have run up against limitations and have discussed these with the product architects and product managers, the answers are often in the vein of "That feature wasn't designed to work that way. You can accomplish the same thing by using this other feature or technique." My goal is to share these techniques and capabilities with you.

One of the chief goals of this product is to render reports in a variety of presentation formats using server-side components. In doing so, a report rendered to a specific format may not take advantage of all the capabilities offered by that format, client tool, or markup language. For example, reports rendered to HTML do not offer all the advanced behavior you might implement in a custom-built web page with cascading style sheets and JavaScript. If you designed a report in Microsoft Excel, you might design the workbook with formulas used to recalculate the spreadsheet rather than using literal values for summaries and totals. The general approach is that Reporting Services renders using methods to address the commonality of all these formats. There's always room for more features and advanced functionality. Some of these may be added to the product in later versions, because this makes sense for mass consumption. Because of the modular architecture of Reporting Services, certain features can be added through custom programming extensions.

> **WARNING** *Developing custom extensions for Reporting Services is a fairly advanced undertaking so adjust your expectations accordingly. I see them used on occasion by large companies with specialized needs and with teams of developers, but rarely on projects with typical time and budget constraints.*

Seeking the Excel Export Holy Grail

A common scenario I find in the business community is when experienced Excel users (usually financial analysts) ask for reports to be rendered to an Excel workbook containing formulas, data sources, pivot tables, and other advanced Excel capabilities. Exactly mimicking Excel's capabilities is not always possible, so don't misunderstand me when I say that extensively formatted reports can be exported to Excel with a great deal of precision. It stands to reason that if Excel users want to use the advanced capabilities of Excel, in many cases they may have a better experience using Excel as their reporting tool rather than Reporting Services. I do not make that statement lightly and appreciate that using Excel instead of Reporting Services introduces a different set of support and maintenance challenges, but I have seen many report designers and developers bend over backward, expending countless hours, trying to get Reporting Services to output exactly what Excel users want.

The issue of exporting reports to Excel with all the desired features is a complicated equation. It seems that nearly every time I encounter someone who wants a particular capability enabled in the workbooks they export from Reporting Services, the question is phrased as "When are they going to *fix* the problem with SSRS not supporting... (some feature)?" The fact is that every Excel user perceives different capabilities as more important than others and in the end, they really just want to use Excel. This is the primary reason that Excel has been enhanced significantly, in recent versions, as a reporting and analytic tool.

> **NOTE** *I could easily go on for several pages with stories about projects involving reports rendered to Excel workbooks. Reporting Services does a good job of formatting a report as a workbook with static data. However, consider starting with Excel if users truly need to leverage Excel's advanced features such as formulas, data connections, filters, slicers, charts, and pivot tables.*

It is not easy to define the limits of most products. For some reason, the specifications and documentation for most products do not contain a list of things they cannot do—at least not in bold type. I have had very little success going to a large software vendor and saying, "Tell me what your product *can't* do." Wouldn't it be nice if, when you shop for a car or house, the salespeople list the comparative shortcomings of their product? It would make the selection process so much easier. For this discussion, that is where I would like to start. Table 14-1 details some of the more recognizable limitations of the Reporting Services architecture. This is by no means a complete list, nor is it a list of bugs and issues. It is simply a guideline of design constraints to be aware of when taking reports to the next level. Given these points, I describe some common alternatives to implement desired functionality.

TABLE 14-1: Common limitations and design alternatives

AREA	LIMITATION	ALTERNATIVES
Data presentation	In the report body or a group section, all fields must be aggregated, even if the dataset returns only one row.	Use an aggregate function even if your query returns one row or if all rows for the field return the same value. Typically, you should use the FIRST() function for character and date data and the SUM() function for numeric data.

AREA	LIMITATION	ALTERNATIVES
Formatting	Conditional formatting expressions can be complicated and difficult to maintain, especially when nesting Boolean logic and when the same expression is repeated for multiple report items and fields.	Write a Visual Basic function in the Report Properties Code window, and call the function as an expression for each report item. For example: `=Code.MyFunction(Fields!MyField.Value)` In certain cases, you might also be able to leverage the newly introduced `Report` and `Group` variables to hold certain values.
	Aggregate functions don't return 0 for summaries on NULL values. Our users want to see 0s.	Use a Visual Basic function to return a 0 in place of a NULL value. For example: `=IIF(IsNothing(SUM(Fields!MyField.Value)), 0, SUM(Fields!MyField.Value))` Or, pass values to a Visual Basic function to convert NULL, empty string, or no value to a 0 or another value. For example: `=Code.NullToZero(Fields!MyField.Value)`
	Some highly formatted reports don't export well to Excel.	Often, only data regions that translate to a grid layout export neatly to Excel. If you need more visual report styles to export to Excel, design two alternate data regions: one optimized for browsing and the other for Excel. Use the built-in Render Format Name field in an expression on the `Hidden` property to conditionally hide each data region, depending on the render format. For example: `=(Global!RenderFormat.Name="Excel")` or `=NOT(Global!RenderFormat.Name="Excel")`
	Grouped column headers can't be hidden using expressions.	Only data columns can be hidden; group header columns cannot. Rather than using group header columns, add the group header fields to the data columns collection (by dragging the field to the right side of the double dash group/data column separator). Then set the cell `HideDuplicates` property to the dataset name. To conditionally hide a column, right-click the column header, choose Column Visibility, and set an expression for the `Hidden` property. For example, if you want to hide the column for the Tax Amount field if the dataset doesn't return that column, use this expression: `=(Fields!TaxAmt.IsMissing)`

continues

TABLE 14-1 *(continued)*

AREA	LIMITATION	ALTERNATIVES
Rendering	HTML rendering doesn't support some table design formatting. For example, narrow columns used for spacing and borders are padded with extra space.	This is a characteristic of HTML rendering and is generally not considered a bug. HTML rendering is constantly being adjusted and improved in product updates. Provide specific feedback to the SSRS product development team through the Microsoft Connect site (`connect.microsoft.com`) If reports require more exact tolerances for printing or layout, users should be instructed to use printer-friendly rendering formats such as PDF and TIFF.
	Using images in place of borders causes extra vertical and horizontal padding and column misalignment.	Most rendering formats were not designed to use images in place of borders. Images placed in table cells typically are padded. Report design is a little different from web design, and some of the techniques may not work. Reports should be tested in all common rendering formats when using image borders.
	Reports don't support events like Access does. I want to count pages, rows, groups, and report item values.	Reporting Services supports the concept of on-demand processing and `Report` and `Group` variables. These variables are set once and can be retrieved from within their scope. With the combination of these new variable types and some custom code, you can re-create those counts.
Actions	Code variables aren't tracked across multiple "postings" of an interactive report. I need to keep track of values that are modified by code as my user interacts with a report.	You can use report parameters and set the action of the interactive item to "post" to the same report, passing the changed value in the parameter collection. Although cumbersome, the best way to preserve the "state" of non-default parameter values between report actions is to set the target value of each parameter to an expression referencing that same parameter.
Excel rendering	Exported reports do not output formulas but static values for each cell, including group totals.	Several options are available depending on your requirements and the sophistication of your Excel audience. Read the recommendations that follow for alternative approaches. The simple fact is that exported reports output the resulting values of expressions and not the acual expression formula.

AREA	LIMITATION	ALTERNATIVES
	Excel columns and cells don't align perfectly and some cells are merged in the final worksheet.	To output an entire report to a worksheet, the Excel rendering extension must create columns to contain every report item and data region. Items placed near but not exactly in the same horizontal space will produce multiple small columns. In the report design, make sure that each report item and Tablix column is aligned so they fall into the same column space. Use a table as a container, and avoid using subreports and uncontained textboxes. Rather than placing header items in the report's page header, use cells in the table header and set the table header rows to repeat on a new page. The settings are a little tricky and covered in this post: `http://www.sqlchick.com/entries/2011/8/20/repeating-column-headers-on-every-page-in-ssrs-doesnt-work-o.html`
	We'd like to use all the features of Excel PivotTables and advanced formatting without the limitations imposed by Excel rendering through SSRS.	Use the Atom Feed feature on the report toolbar. This generates a live feed from published SSRS reports that can be used in an Excel workbook through Power Pivot. This allows you to treat a published report as a data source for Excel, using the datasets and parameters you've defined in the report. I demonstrate this ability in this post: `https://sqlserverbiblog.wordpress.com/2015/05/04/how-to-get-reports-in-excel-without-exporting-from-reporting-services/`
	We'd like to divide report content into separate worksheets.	Create page breaks at the start or end of tables and other data regions. Use the `Page Name` property of a group or data region to name the resulting worksheet.

REPORT RECIPES: BUILDING ON BASIC SKILLS

In 2010, Robert Bruckner from Microsoft and I collaborated on a book titled *SQL Server Reporting Services Recipes* (Wrox). We invited several professional associates to contribute and we showcased report design patterns and techniques for solving many common business problems. We demonstrated how SSRS may be used in creative ways to design unique report solutions. The book highlights various design methods through the application of games and puzzles developed using Reporting Services. Most of those techniques are still valid in the current product version.

A *recipe* is a design pattern based on the design components and basic skills acquired by creating simple reports. Many of the following examples are based on solutions created for clients and demonstrate some of the learning and best practices acquired from many years of field experience. To implement these solutions, you need to apply the skills you learned in the previous chapters.

To illustrate a complete, working solution, I will step through the process to create a series of reports. Each self-contained report will be published as a report part that you will use to assemble a dashboard. Each example shows you how to use a different technique and design pattern. This exercise applies techniques and skills that have been demonstrated in earlier chapters.

> **NOTE** *In an effort to keep things simple, I don't show you every little step and, as a result, certain styling details may not match exactly what you see unless you modify all of the same properties as the completed exercise sample provided in this book's download files for comparison.*

Before you get started, I just want to set expectations. Dashboard report design is a very detailed and iterative process. If you can get these features working the first time you try, you should get a prize (because I can't). In fact, this is a process that requires even the most experienced report designers to spend considerable time in trial-and-error design and debugging iterations. Good report designers are patient and persistent.

To describe every property used in the completed report for this exercise would make these instructions very long and tedious, so I've included only the essential steps. At the end of each section, compare your work with the completed copy of the Internet Sales KPI Dashboard report and then make adjustments. Of course, you always have the option to simply review the completed sample as you step through the instructions.

Dashboard Solution Data Sources and Datasets

The completed dashboard report for this exercise is shown in Figure 14-2. This report contains the following sections:

➤ Three gauges display the value of two KPI values compared to target values. The Orders gauge measures the total orders against a parameterized goal.

➤ The KPI scorecard is grouped by Fiscal Year and Month. It displays the Gross Profit Margin percent value followed by two indicators that show the KPI status and monthly trend using calculations performed in the Analysis Services multidimensional cube.

➤ To the right of the scorecard is a grouped table showing the calendar year and product category. For each category, a sparkline displays the monthly sales trend. Each Category label is a drill-through action that will display the sparkline details in a line chart located to the right of the table. When a user clicks a category, the chart is refreshed with corresponding details.

➤ A map of the United States is located in the top-right corner of the dashboard. This shows the location of the top customers ranked by sales orders.

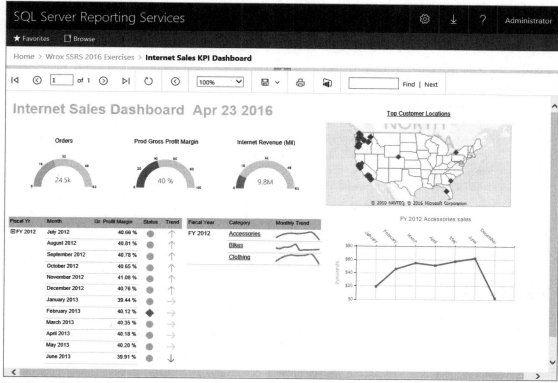

FIGURE 14-2: Final dashboard.

When I prepared an earlier version of this solution in the previous edition of the book, I made extensive use of the newly introduced report parts feature. After using report parts on several projects and introducing them to some of my clients, I've decided not to promote this feature. The concept of report parts was proposed as a self-service reporting feature that would enable Report Builder users to assemble reports from parts, or fragments, of a completed report published to the report server. It's not that report parts don't work as designed; in fact, they do. I have just discovered that most Reporting Services users who have mastered Report Builder are perfectly capable of designing their own reports and in many cases, the effort that it saves doesn't offset the flexibility of simply building the report from scratch.

KPI Scorecard

A *scorecard* is a standard in the business community for displaying the status of metrics and key performance indicators. A typical scorecard is a table report with optional row groups and drill-down capability to allow users to progressively discover more details.

Our scorecard report will show product gross margin summaries by fiscal years and the months within each year for selected product categories. Figure 14-3 shows the finished report with the first fiscal group expanded to reveal the details for each month. The calculations and business logic for the Gross Profit Margin KPI are encapsulated in the cube. The purpose of the report is to simply surface these values.

Fiscal Yr	Month	Gr. Profit Margin	Status	Trend
FY 2012	July 2012	19.31 %	●	⬆
	August 2012	20.58 %	●	⬆
	September 2012	19.32 %	●	⬆
	October 2012	19.04 %	●	⬆
	November 2012	20.08 %	●	⬆
	December 2012	8.24 %	◆	⬇
	January 2013	13.58 %	▲	⬊
	February 2013	15.18 %	▲	⬊
	March 2013	21.87 %	●	➡
	April 2013	20.40 %	▲	➡
	May 2013	21.35 %	●	➡
	June 2013	26.01 %	●	➡

FIGURE 14-3: Final scorecard report.

We will start with a shared data source for the Adventure Works Multidimensional database in Analysis Services:

1. Open the Wrox SSRS 2016 Exercises project in SSDT.

2. Create a new report named Internet Sales KPI Dashboard.

3. Add a data source to the report that uses the AdventureWorksSSAS shared data source.

4. Create a new dataset named FiscalInternetSales based on this data source and use the graphical query builder to design the query shown in Figure 14-4.

5. Expand the `Date` dimension, expand the `Fiscal` folder, and then drag the `Fiscal` hierarchy to the data grid.

6. Expand KPIs and drag the `Product Gross Profit Margin` KPI to the rightmost column in the grid. This action will add the `Value`, `Goal`, `Status`, and `Trend` columns.

7. Drag the `Internet Revenue` KPI to the data grid.

8. Expand `Measures`, expand the `Internet Sales` measure group, and then drag the `Internet Order Quantity` measure to the right side of data grid.

9. Add the `Date.Fiscal Year` hierarchy to the filter pane, above the data grid.

10. Drop down the Filter Expression list box, check `FY 2012`, and click OK.

11. In the Filter pane, scroll to the right and check the box in the `Parameters` column.

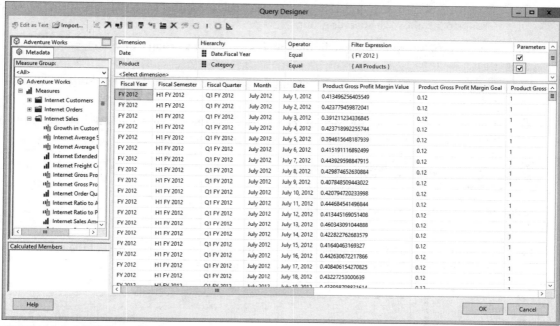

FIGURE 14-4: MDX Query Designer.

12. From the `Product` dimension, drag the `Category` attribute hierarchy to the Filter pane, set the Filter Expression to include all four leaf level members (Accessories, Bikes, Clothing, and Components), and check the Parameters box.

13. Close the Query Designer and Dataset Properties dialog.

14. Add a new table data region to the report body in preparation to complete the following steps. Figure 14-5 shows the table's groups in the finished report so you can see where I'm heading with this.

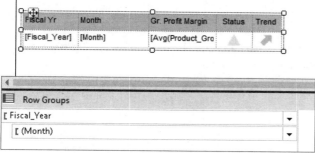

FIGURE 14-5: Completed scorecard table in report designer.

15. With the table selected, drag the `Fiscal Year` field from the Report Data pane to the Row Groups pane above the details group.

16. Use the drop-down arrow to edit the details group, add a group expression, and select the `Month` field.

17. Drag the `Gross Profit Margin Value`, `Status`, and `Trend` fields to separate detail columns.

18. Change the expressions for each of these cells to use the `AVG` function instead of the `SUM` function. Figure 14-6 shows the report in design view at this stage.

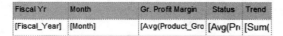

Fiscal Yr	Month	Gr. Profit Margin	Status	Trend
[Fiscal_Year]	[Month]	[Avg(Product_Gro	[Avg(Pr	[Sum(

FIGURE 14-6: Score table with AVG expressions.

19. From the toolbox, drag an Indicator to the Status cell in the details row of the table. The Select Indicator Type dialog opens, shown in Figure 14-7.

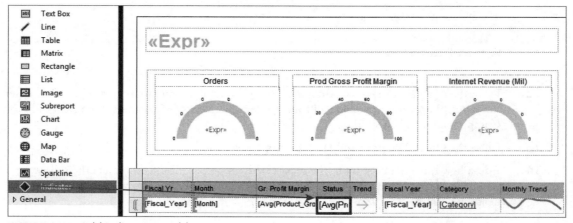

FIGURE 14-7: Add indicator to table.

20. Select an appropriate three-state KPI indicator. I prefer the red, yellow, and green state indicators that use the diamond, triangle, and circle shapes.

21. Click OK to close this dialog. These icons, shown in Figure 14-8, correspond to the state field values –1, 0, and 1, respectively.

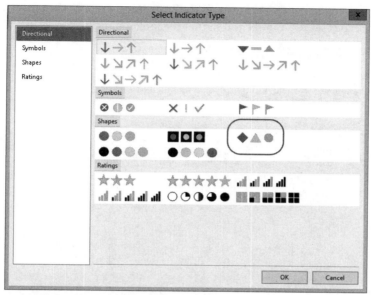

FIGURE 14-8: Select Indicator Type dialog.

22. Drag another indicator to the Trend detail cell, and select a five-state trend directional arrow set. The arrow icons will correspond to the trend state values –2, –1, 0, 1, and 2, respectively.

23. Configure the details group to hide and toggle visibility, using the Fiscal Year textbox as a toggle item.

For a refresher on creating a drill-down table, refer to the section "Add Summary Totals and Drill-Down" in Chapter 6.

Gauges

The three gauges are bound to the same dataset as the scorecard table. Because the gauge properties are fairly self-explanatory and we'll focus the exercise on more complex elements, I'm going to have you copy and paste them from the completed sample. Before you do that, let's take a quick look at the updated gauge selection in SQL Server 2016:

1. Drag and drop a gauge from the toolbox to a blank area of the report body.

This opens a window titled Select Gauge Type, shown in Figure 14-9. If you have worked with earlier versions of SSRS, you will recognize a selection of newer, modern-looking gauges. These are actually the same gauges we have had since SQL Server 2008 R2, but with default properties set to simplify and flatten the look and feel.

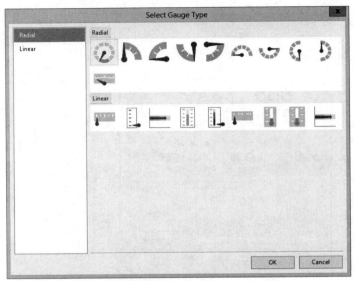

FIGURE 14-9: Select Gauge Type dialog.

2. Select the last linear gauge on the list. This places a bullet graph gauge on the report without the outdated styling of the previous gauges.

3. Delete the new gauge.

4. Open the completed sample report named Internet Sales KPI Dashboard (ch14) in design view.

5. Select and copy the title textbox and the rectangle containing the three gauges to the clipboard using Ctrl+C.

6. Make room on your new report for these items in the same location on the report body.

7. Use Ctrl+V to paste the copied report items and then reposition them to fit on your report.

8. Preview the report to make sure it executes correctly. Make corrections if necessary, using the completed report for comparison.

9. Return to the design view.

10. Click the first gauge to show the Gauge Data window.

Gauges contain two essential elements to work correctly: Scale and Pointer. The Scale contains a `MaximumValue` property, which defines the range of values for one or more pointers and for optional markers.

11. Click the numeric scale, just outside the gray ring area. The Properties window should display `RadialScale1`.

12. Scroll to the top and note the (MaximumValue) property expression. For this gauge, a parameter named InternetOrdersGoal is used to set the maximum scale value.

> **NOTE** *Note that the* InterntOrdersGoal *parameter is added only as a report parameter. Unlike the query parameters defined in the query designer, this report parameter is created from the Parameters node of the Report Data pane.*

13. Click the RadialPointer1 item in the Gauge Data window. Note the Value expression:

```
=Sum(Fields!Internet_Order_Quantity.Value)
```

14. Find and view the FillColor expression. This uses a SWITCH function to change the pointer fill color to indicate the state of the order quantity relative to the orders goal target value:

```
=SWITCH(Sum(Fields!Internet_Order_Quantity.Value, "FiscalInternetSales")
        /Parameters!InternetOrdersGoal.Value < .4, "Red",
        Sum(Fields!Internet_Order_Quantity.Value, "FiscalInternetSales")
        /Parameters!InternetOrdersGoal.Value >= .75, "Teal",
        True, "Orange")
```

Explore the same properties of the other two gauges. In a similar fashion, they apply KPI value and target elements to set the pointer value and scale maximum properties.

Interactive Sparkline and Chart

This addition to the report will include a grouped table that contains an embedded sparkline. You will also add a separate line chart to the report. On any row representing the summary of product category sales for a year, the user can click the sparkline or row label to see a detailed view of the same data in the chart. Figure 14-10 shows the finished report in design view.

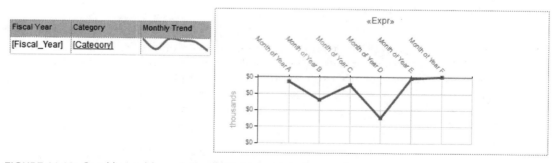

FIGURE 14-10: Sparkline table and chart in the report designer.

1. Add another dataset to the report that uses the AdventureWorksSSAS shared data source. Name the dataset FiscalYearSales.

2. Use the query designer to create the query shown in Figure 14-11.

As a challenge, now that you have had some practice building MDX queries, use the graphical query builder and drag the measure and dimension members to assemble this query. Switch the query designer to text mode to view the generated MDX script.

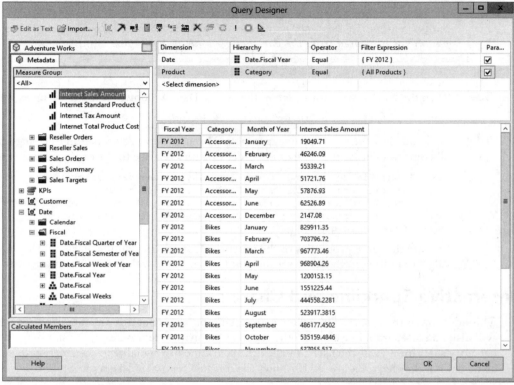

FIGURE 14-11: MDX query designer.

For reference, the MDX query for the generated query should be similar to the following script. (Line breaks and indents have been added to aid readability.) If you prefer, you can switch the query designer to text mode and type this script:

```
SELECT
NON EMPTY { [Measures].[Internet Sales Amount] } ON COLUMNS,
NON EMPTY
{
  (
    [Date].[Fiscal Year].[Fiscal Year].ALLMEMBERS
  * [Product].[Category].[Category].ALLMEMBERS
  * [Date].[Month of Year].[Month of Year].ALLMEMBERS )
} DIMENSION PROPERTIES MEMBER_CAPTION, MEMBER_UNIQUE_NAME ON ROWS
FROM
  ( SELECT
  ( STRTOSET(@ProductCategory, CONSTRAINED) ) ON COLUMNS
    FROM ( SELECT ( STRTOSET(@DateFiscalYear, CONSTRAINED) )
```

```
  ON COLUMNS
  FROM [Adventure Works]
  )
)
CELL
  PROPERTIES VALUE, BACK_COLOR, FORE_COLOR, FORMATTED_VALUE,
  FORMAT_STRING, FONT_NAME, FONT_SIZE, FONT_FLAGS
```

3. Close the Dataset Properties dialog when completed.

4. Add two report parameters named `ChartFiscalYear` and `ChartCategory`. You can leave all the default properties and settings for the parameters. However, check the "Allow null value" box on the General page for each parameter, as shown in Figure 14-12.

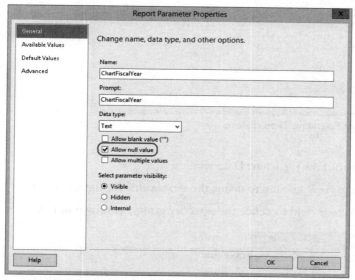

FIGURE 14-12: Parameter properties.

5. Add a table to the report to the right of the scorecard table.

6. Click the table to show the grouping pane in the bottom of the report designer.

7. Drag and drop the `Fiscal Year` field from the dataset to create a row group.

8. Drag and drop the `Category` field from the dataset in the Report Data pane to create a row group after the previous group

9. In the Row Groups list, right-click the (Details) group and delete it.

10. When prompted, choose the option to only delete the group and not the associated rows and columns.

11. Drag and drop the sparkline to the blank table detail cell.

12. When prompted, select a smooth line type sparkline (see Figure 14-13) and click OK.

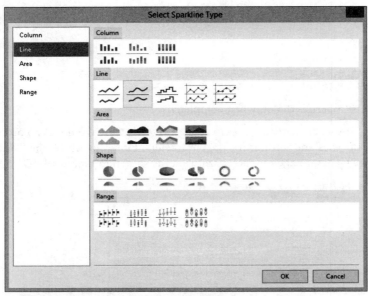

FIGURE 14-13: Select Sparkline Type dialog.

13. Click the sparkline to show the Chart Data window.

14. Add the `Internet_Sales_Amount` to define the series value for the sparkline.

15. Add the `Month_of_Year` field to define the category group, as shown in Figure 14-14.

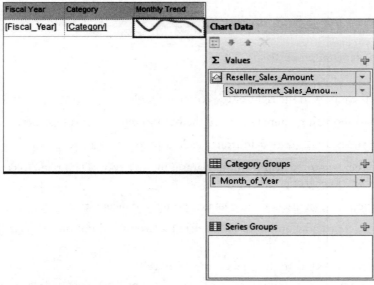

FIGURE 14-14: Chart Data window.

16. Edit the category group expression so that it uses the Key property rather than the Value of the Month_of_Year field. You need to use the Expression Editor to make this change. In the expression, backspace over the Value, and type or choose Key from the property list. Close the Expression Editor and save the change.

The Category Group Properties dialog should look similar to Figure 14-15.

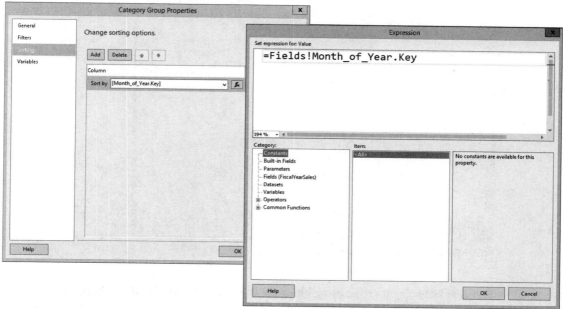

FIGURE 14-15: Category group expression.

Next, you will use a chart to show the same values as one of the selected sparklines in detail.

17. Add a line chart next to the table.

18. Use the same category group and series value as the sparkline.

19. Format the chart to your liking.

20. Edit the chart properties and add the two filter expressions shown in Figure 14-16. The chart is filtered to restrict records matching the ChartFiscalYear and ChartCategory parameters.

21. For each filter expression, use the Expression drop-down list to select the field. Then use the expression builder button to the right of the Value box to open the expression editor and build an expression using the appropriate parameter. For each Value expression, close the editor and save the expression.

Do the following to create the report action used to pass these parameters and filter the chart:

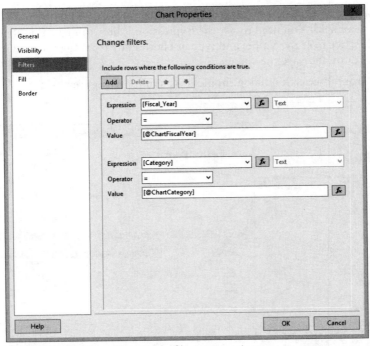

FIGURE 14-16: Chart Properties filter expressions.

22. Style the Category textbox using blue text and underline to resemble a hyperlink. This just lets the user know that it's a clickable link.

23. Right-click the Category textbox to the left of the sparkline.

24. Choose Text Box Properties... from the menu to show the Text Box Properties dialog shown in Figure 14-17.

25. Use the Actions page to set a report action. Select the "Go to report" radio button.

26. Select (or type) the name of the report you are designing. This causes the same report to be executed when the user clicks this report item.

27. Add two items to the list of parameters for the report action.

28. Select or type the name of each parameter. Parameter names are case-sensitive. For each parameter, select the corresponding field, as shown in Figure 14-18.

29. Test and make sure that the drill-through action works as expected. Hover the mouse pointer over the category name until the pointer changes to a hyperlink pointer. When you click the series line, the report should re-render, showing a chart with data that matches the sparkline.

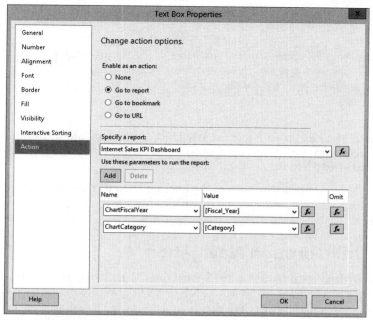

FIGURE 14-17: Text Box Properties Action page.

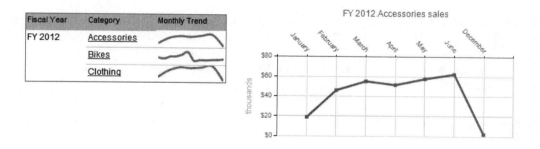

FIGURE 14-18: Sparkline table and chart in preview.

> **TIP** *When using a drill-through action for the same report, if you can replace the report name with an expression for the ReportName built-in field,* =Globals!ReportName, *the action will continue to work if the report is renamed.*

30.   Click the link for the sparkline or text for the year and category you want to see.

> **TIP** *When you hover the mouse pointer over the sparkline or the Category text, the hyperlink "finger" pointer is displayed. I always tell my students that the web browser will give you the finger if it's working.*

The report should re-render and display a filtered chart. The chart line should show the same trend as the sparkline, with the added axis details. If you click a different row, you should see a different chart trend line for each.

31.   Compare your report with the completed version of the Internet Sales KPI Dashboard report. Compare the properties and behavior of the elements you've added up to this point and make any necessary adjustments.

Thumbnail Map with Drill-Through Navigation

The map report item can help you visualize geographic and spatial data. A map may get its data from an external file (in a standard format such as TIGER/LINE or ESRI), from spatial shapes or point objects stored in a SQL Server database, from SQL Server functions used to calculate or derive geospatial objects, or from an external source such as the Bing Maps web service. A single map may be assembled from data and metadata obtained from any combination of these sources.

> **WARNING** *The Map is by far the most complicated report item in the Reporting Services repertoire. When I design maps, I usually find it necessary to cycle through the Properties windows multiple times in order to get everything working. I recommend that you keep a working map report on hand as a reference guide for future map reports.*

In the following example, you will add a map report item to the dashboard consisting of the following elements:

➤   Geographic boundaries in a polygon layer

➤   Geographic polygon objects colored using grouped aggregate values

➤   Locations stored as SQL Server geographic points

➤   A tile layer showing imagery from Bing Maps

> **NOTE** *You need to have an Internet connection in order to use the Bing Maps layer in this report. If you do not, it's OK but the map will display an error in the background until you are connected.*

1. Add a data source to the report that uses the WroxSSRS2016 shared data source.

2. Create a dataset to the report named CustomerAddresses using the following query:

> **TIP** *To save time, you can copy this query script from the completed sample report in the exercises project.*

```
WITH CustOrderTotal
AS
(
        SELECT CustomerID,
        SUM(SubTotal) AS OrderTotal
        FROM OrderDetails
        GROUP BY CustomerID
)
SELECT  TOP( @TopCustomers )
        AccountNumber,
        CustomerName,
        Title,
        PersonType,
        AddressLine1,
        City,
        StateProvinceCode,
        PostalCode,
        CountryRegionCode,
        AddressType,
        SpatialLocation,
        o.OrderTotal
FROM
        CustomerLocations c
        INNER JOIN CustOrderTotal o ON c.CustomerID = o.CustomerID
WHERE       (@CountryRegionCode IS NULL) OR
                        (CountryRegionCode IN (@
CountryRegionCode))
ORDER BY o.OrderTotal DESC
;
```

3. Execute the query. You'll be prompted for the `TopCustomers` and `CountryRegionCode` parameters.

4. Enter `1000` for the `TopCustomers` and `US` for `CountryRegionCode`.

5. Modify the two new report parameters. Set defaults using the values in the previous step.

6. Add a Map report item in the upper-right area of the report body. The New Map Layer dialog opens, which prompts for the initial properties. You will build most of this report using the designer and Properties window.

7. In the first page of the New Map Layer dialog, leave the default option to use map shape data from the map gallery.

The map gallery is a set of report files installed with the product that include maps of the United States and other geographic regions. You can obtain additional map shape files for different geographies from many online resources and fee-based services.

8. Use the USA by State Inset map gallery selection, shown in Figure 14-19, and click Next.

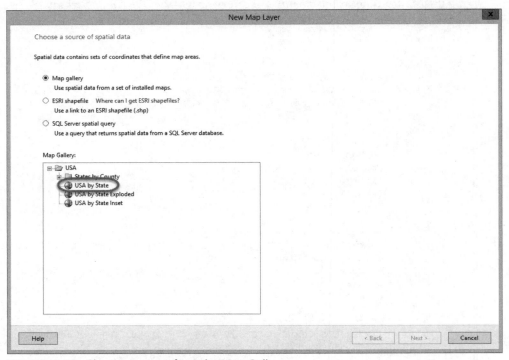

FIGURE 14-19: Choosing a map from the Map Gallery.

9. On the second page, check "Crop map as shown above," and reposition and zoom the map to show the continental United States.

10. Check the box to add a Bing Maps layer.

11. Click Next.

12. This adds a tile layer to the map to stream live map imagery from the Bing Map service when the user or report server has the necessary Internet connectivity. (This depends on whether the report is viewed in the designer or deployed to the report server.)

13. Accept the default, Basic Map, and click Next.

14. Check Single color map for the theme, and then click Finish to complete the wizard.

15. In the report designer, click to select and then delete each of the three default scales and legends on the map.

16. Click the map outside of the state shapes. This should select the Map Viewport object in the Properties window.

17. Click again to show the Map Layers window to the right of the view port designer, as shown in Figure 14-20.

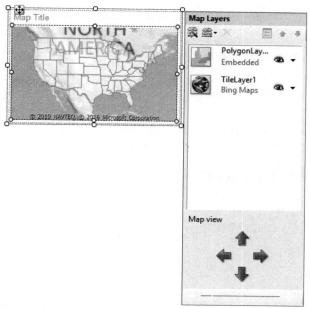

FIGURE 14-20: Map Layers window.

18. Use the second toolbar drop-down button to add a point layer.

The map port now has three layers:

➤ The polygon layer is used to display geographic shapes that the map wizard imported from the U.S. map gallery file. This content is now embedded in the report file.

➤ The tile layer visualizes bitmap content from the Bing Map web service when the report is executed.

➤ The point layer is used to plot shapes on the map using geospatial coordinates stored in the database.

In the Map Layers window, each of these layers can be shown or hidden to make the design effort easier. To focus on each layer, I hide the other layers so that I can easily see the results of my work. After all the layers are designed, I make them all visible before deploying the report.

Geographic Shape Colors

Polygon shapes typically are used to visualize geographic boundaries, such as the U.S. states in our example. Each polygon is bound to data using key/value pairs. Several properties may be used to visualize data-bound values in the form of center point markers that may be sized, colored, or labeled to express relative or proportional values. You will use the background color of each state to show the relative number of customers in that state:

1. Choose the polygon layer in the Map Layers window. Make sure you have the polygon layer selected by checking the title in the Properties window.

2. In the Properties window, choose the CustomerAddresses dataset you created earlier in the drop-down list for the DatasetName property.

3. Select the Group property, and then click the ellipsis button (...) to open the Group Properties dialog.

4. Add a group expression, and then select the StateProvinceCode field. Close the Group Properties window to accept the changes.

5. Select the BindingFieldPairs property, and click the ellipsis to open the MapBindingFieldPair Collection Editor, shown in Figure 14-21.

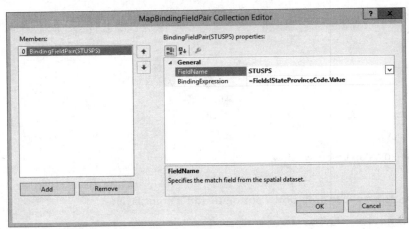

FIGURE 14-21: MapBindingFieldPair Editor dialog.

6. Add a binding field collection member.

7. For the FieldName property, select the STATEUSPS polygon identifier.

8. For the BindingExpression property, select the StateProvinceCode dataset field.

9. Compare your selections to Figure 14-21, and then close the dialog window to accept the changes.

Adding Spatial Point Markers

You can use a lot of very creative features with point markers using the many properties organized into various groups. However, the appropriate choice of properties may not seem very intuitive until you've had a chance to work with these features for a while. It's easy to get lost and spend hours on trial-and-error design, trying to find the right property settings.

> **NOTE** *The CustomerLocation table in the sample database stores the customer location as a SQL Server spatial point data type. The map will use this value to plot a marker in the point layer for each customer location.*

If you want the marker shape, size, or color to be consistent for all points, use the properties in the `PointTemplate` group. If you want to vary the shape, size, or color based on different values, use the corresponding properties in each subgroup under the `PointRules` group. Use `ColorRule` to apply color ranges and stock or custom color palettes, `MarkerRule` to change the shapes of markers (which can include using custom graphics and icons), and `SizeRule` to vary the marker sizes based on data values. These properties are disabled by default; you will leave them that way for this exercise:

1. Return to design view, and select the map to view the Map Data window as you did before.
2. Select the point layer, and view the Properties window.
3. Set the `DataSetName` property, using the drop-down list, to the name of the dataset you created earlier.
4. Expand the `SpatialData` group, change the (Type) to `Dataset`, and select the `CustomerAddresses` dataset you created earlier from the `DataSetName` property drop-down list.
5. For the `SpatialField` property, choose the `SpatialLocation` field. This field in the database contains a geospatial point value that the map view port can use to plot a point on the map.
6. Select the `BindingFieldPairs` property and click the ellipsis to open the MapBindingFieldPair Collection Editor.
7. If a binding pair member exists in the Members list, edit it. Otherwise, click Add.
8. Set the `FieldName` property to `AccountNumber`.
9. For the `BindingExpression` property, use the drop-down list to select = `Fields!AccuntNumber.Value`.
10. Close the editor dialog.
11. Expand the `PointRules` property group.
12. Expand the `ColorRule` group.
13. Set (Enabled) to `True`.
14. Set (Type) to `Custom`.
15. Use the (`CustomColors`) collection to add a single color. Click the ellipsis to add Lime to the `MapColor` collection.
16. Expand the `MarkerRule` group, and select the `Markers` collection property.

17. Enable the `MarkerRule`.

18. Click the ellipsis to open the Marker Collection dialog.

19. Remove all the default marker shapes, but leave a single diamond marker in the collection. Then close and accept the changes.

20. Use the `PointTemplate` properties group to set the marker's Size to 8pt.

21. Select the `ToolTip` property, and then use the Expression Builder to concatenate a list of fields to be displayed in the tooltip for each marker, which represents a customer's location. For example, I've added the following expression:

```
=Fields!CustomerName.Value & vbCrLf
& vbCrLf & Fields!AddressLine1.Value
& vbCrLf & Fields!City.Value & ", " & Fields!StateProvinceCode.Value
```

Again, you can use several properties to make visual adjustments; this can be time-consuming. When you have a working baseline map report, you can return to the designer and experiment with these properties.

22. Preview the report. You should see a working map report with colored and labeled states, and lime green diamond markers showing the location of the top 1,000 customers by default.

> **NOTE** *Mapping many data points can be time-consuming so be as conservative as possible. On my system, it takes about seven seconds to plot the top 1,000 customer locations and over a minute for all 18,000 customers.*

Entering a larger value for the `TopCustomers` parameter will show more customer locations on the map but will take longer to render.

> **NOTE** *As I mentioned, because of the intricacies of the map report item, it is not uncommon to miss a step or property setting on the first pass through your design. Use the finished sample report for comparison if you run into any issues.*
>
> *I've provided a larger version of this map in a standalone report named Customer US Map. In the completed Internet Sales KPI Dashboard report, clicking the title of the thumbnail report invokes a report action that navigates to the larger map report.*

SUMMARY

Congratulations; you finished the extended tour of advanced report design solution patterns. You may not use every one of these designs in your professional reports to meet the immediate needs of your business. However, I bet you will find similar applications allowing you to apply the same or similar techniques.

We started with a high-level discussion of report solution requirement gathering; you learned that report design solutions are successful when you can clearly define the scope and purpose of a request. Reports are best designed from a detailed, written specification from the business owner. We designed a reporting solution in phases including planning, design, implementation, testing, and validation. Advanced reports should be deployed to a test server for inspection and testing before they are migrated to production servers for the entire business to use.

This chapter has given you some valuable tools that you can take with you to help you create the right report solutions for your business and users. Download and use the samples to practice these techniques and then go out and solve some tough data problems with high-value report designs.

PART V
Reporting Services Custom Programming

The chapters in this part of the book are for the application and solution developer. These two chapters demonstrate how to integrate Reporting Services into custom applications using programming code, web services, and APIs. Chapter 16 shows you how Reporting Services can be enhanced using custom data access, security, delivery, and rendering extensions.

▶ **CHAPTER 15:** Integrating Reports into Custom Applications

▶ **CHAPTER 16:** Extending Reporting Services

15

Integrating Reports into Custom Applications

WHAT'S IN THIS CHAPTER?

➤ Leveraging URL access and web services to render reports

➤ Building a custom Windows Forms application to enter parameters and render reports

➤ Integrating report viewer controls in Windows and Web Forms applications

➤ Rendering reports from within your web applications as HTML or as other downloadable formats such as PDF

➤ Creating custom parameter input interfaces for Reporting Services

This chapter is relatively unchanged from the previous edition of the book. The application integration capabilities of Reporting Services have not changed significantly in SQL Server 2016.

Reporting Services was designed to be a flexible reporting technology that can be easily integrated into a variety of scenarios. Many reporting needs will never expand beyond the out-of-the-box functionality provided by Reporting Services. However, if the requirement arises, Reporting Services includes endless opportunities for integration with custom-built applications, as well as SharePoint.

Within a SharePoint portal, Reporting Services leverages the framework to deliver reports via Report Libraries. However, many organizations maintain a custom corporate reporting portal instead of SharePoint. In these situations, developers might need a way to display numerous reports in a web environment. Reporting Services can also be embedded into line-of-business applications. Developers might want to use Reporting Services to create invoices or purchase orders directly from their applications. Some organizations may decide that the default Web Portal is not robust enough for their needs. In this situation, a custom reporting management application can be built that replaces and expands on the functionality of the out-of-the-box Web Portal.

All these issues can be solved with the features available in Reporting Services. This chapter looks at the following three methods of rendering reports from Reporting Services:

➤ Using URLs to access reports via HTTP

➤ Using the Reporting Services web service to programmatically render reports

➤ Using the `ReportViewer` controls to embed reports

URL access allows you to quickly incorporate Reporting Services reports in custom applications such as websites and portals, and even Windows applications. Programmatic rendering lets you create custom interfaces. Developers can do anything from implementing their own security architecture around Reporting Services to creating their own input parameter interface. The code samples and exercises in this chapter are designed for an intermediate or skilled developer and will not go into the details of how to create and set up projects within Visual Studio.

> **NOTE** *The programming examples included in this chapter are sufficient for a developer with moderate .NET programming skills to follow along and re-create a working solution with the provided sample reports and databases. Unlike exercises in earlier chapters, I have not included detailed step-by-step instructions for every required task. If you get stuck or need help, please review the completed sample projects.*

In this chapter, you learn about the following:

➤ The syntax and structure for accessing Reporting Services through the URL

➤ The reporting items that can be accessed through the URL

➤ The parameter options that can be passed to the URL to control report output

➤ Creating a Windows application that renders reports to the filesystem

➤ Creating a web application that returns rendered reports to the browser

➤ Easily embedding reports in a Windows application using controls

URL ACCESS

Reporting Services' primary means of accessing reports is through HTTP requests. These requests can be made through URLs in a web browser or a custom application. By passing parameters in the URL, you can specify the report item, set the output format, and perform various other tasks. In the next few sections, you look at the features available through URL requests, URL syntax, passing parameters, and setting the output format.

URL Syntax

The basic URL syntax is as follows:

```
protocol://server/virtualroot?[/pathinfo]&prefix:param=value
[&prefix:param=value]...n]
```

The parameters in the syntax are as follows:

➤ `Protocol` specifies the URL's protocol, such as HTTP or HTTPS (if an SSL certificate is applied to the report server).

➤ `Server` specifies the name of the Report Server you want to access. This can also include a fully qualified domain name. To access your local machine, you can either type the machine name or use the `localhost` alias.

➤ `Virtualroot` specifies the IIS virtual directory you specified during setup. When installing Reporting Services, you must enter two virtual directories: one for the Web Portal and one for the Report Server (for URL and web services). By default, the virtual directory you would access is `reportserver`.

➤ `Pathinfo` specifies the full path to the item you want to access within the Report Server database. To access the root of the Report Server, you can simply place a single forward slash (/).

After you have listed the path, you can pass various parameters. These parameters depend on the type of object you are referencing. Reports have a number of parameters to specify properties such as the rendering format. Each parameter is separated by an ampersand (&) and contains a `name=value` pair for the parameter.

You can retrieve the list of items under the Professional SQL Reporting Services folder using this URL:

```
http://localhost/reportserver?/Wrox SSRS 2016 Samples&rs:Command=ListChildren
```

> **NOTE** *Note that some of the examples in this chapter take up two lines simply because they are too long to fit on one line.*

Now that you're familiar with the basic URL syntax, let's see how it is implemented in each of the Reporting Services objects.

Accessing Reporting Services Objects

URL requests are not limited to reports. You can access various Reporting Services items, including:

➤ Folders

➤ Data sources

➤ Resources (such as images)

➤ Reports

The following sections describe accessing each of these items. You go through sample URLs and look at items provided in the sample databases and reports that accompany this book.

Folders

Accessing folders will be your starting point for looking at URL requests. Here is the simplest URL request you can make:

```
http://localhost/reports
```

That URL is redirected to the Favorites page in Web Portal. With this request, you can see a listing of all reports, data sources, resources, and folders in the root directory of the Report Server, as shown in Figure 15-1. To access another server, simply replace `localhost` with the server's name.

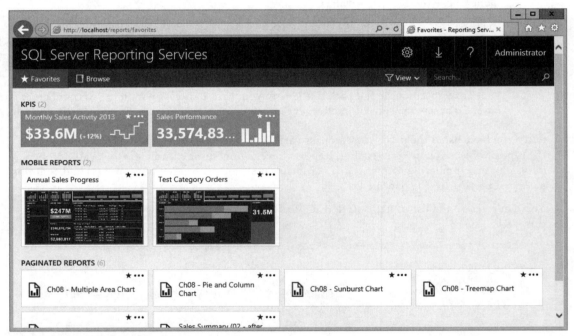

FIGURE 15-1: Web Portal Favorites page.

To see how folder URL requests work, simply enter the Report Server's URL:

```
http://localhost/reportserver
```

A list of directories hosted by the Report server is displayed. Clicking the `Wrox SSRS 2016 Samples` folder link gives you the following URL, as shown in Figure 15-2:

```
http://localhost/reportserver?/Wrox SSRS 2016 Samples&rs:Command=ListChildren
```

This URL contains the following items:

➤ **Path to the report**—/Wrox SSRS 2016 Samples (the browser escapes the URL accordingly)

➤ **Command to list the directory's contents**—rs:Command=ListChildren

You take a closer look at the URL parameters in the section "Reporting Services URL Parameters."

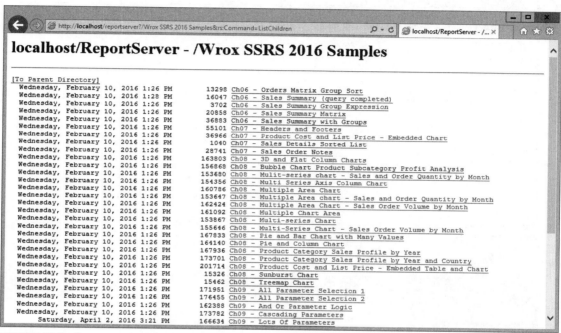

FIGURE 15-2: Report server page.

Data Sources

Through URL requests, you can also view the contents of data sources. Let us examine the Data Sources folder inside the Sample Reports folder. You can access the Data Sources folder by either clicking it from the parent folder or entering the following URL:

```
http://localhost/reportserver?/Data Sources&rs:Command=ListChildren
```

You see the listing of items, as shown in Figure 15-3.

If you have deployed the sample reports, you will notice one of the items listed is WroxSSRS2016. You can tell that this item is a data source by the <ds> tag next to the item name. If you follow the WroxSSRS2016 link, you can view the contents of that data source. Figure 15-4 shows the data source contents.

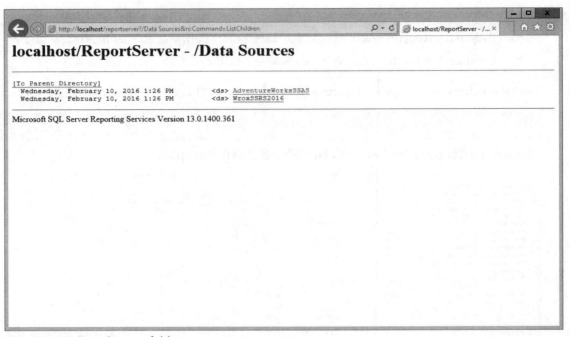

FIGURE 15-3: Data Sources folder.

FIGURE 15-4: Data source contents.

Here's the URL used to view the WroxSSRS2016 data source:

```
http://localhost/reportserver?/Data Sources/
WroxSSRS2016&rs:Command=GetDataSourceContents
```

This URL contains the following items:

➤ **Path to the data source**—/Data Sources/ WroxSSRS2016

➤ **Command to view the data source content**—rs:Command=GetDataSourceContents

Viewing the data source enables you to quickly see how your data source is configured. Notice that this information is returned in XML format, making it easy to work with. If you have your own reporting application that shares a single connection, you could use this URL to dynamically load this data source information. This information could then be used to make other database connections in your application.

Resources

Resources are items used within your reports, such as images or additional resources that have been added to a Report server folder, such as Word and Excel documents. You can use URLs to access resources stored on the Report server. Depending on the type of resources you reference, either you will be prompted to open or save a file, such as a Word or Excel document, or the resource will be rendered directly in the browser. The GetResourceContents command can be used in the URL to reference the resource. For example, if an image is stored in a directory called Images, the URL to the directory and the command GetResourceContents can be used to reference that resource:

```
http://localhost/Reportserver?/Images/
MyImage.jpg&rs:Command=GetResourceContents
```

The URL contains the following contents:

➤ **Path to the resource**—/Images/MyImage.jpg

➤ **Command to retrieve the resource content**—rs:Command=GetResourceContents

You can use this information in other applications. If you want to reference the image from a web page, you could simply set the src attribute of an image tag (<img>) to reference the earlier URL.

Resources can also be incredibly handy for storing documents. In your reporting solution, you might want to store readme files to accompany your reports. You can store these documents as resources on the Report server and then apply different properties to them, such as security. Your application could then point to the resource URL to allow downloading of the document. Keep in mind, however, that these resources are stored in the Report server database along with the report definitions. As such, you should carefully plan for storage if you intend to store several large files, or use an external server to serve up such resources.

Reports

The most important objects you can access through the URL are your reports. This section covers the syntax for accessing reports. The next section discusses the various parameters you can pass to change things such as report parameters, output formats, and other items.

The basic syntax for accessing a report is very similar to accessing all your other resources. You should first specify a path to the report and then provide the commands for its output. Here's the basic URL for accessing the Internet Sales KPI Dashboard report:

```
http://localhost/ReportServer?/Wrox SSRS 2016 Samples/
Internet Sales KPI Dashboard&rs:Command=Render
```

View the Internet Sales Dashboard report, as shown in Figure 15-5.

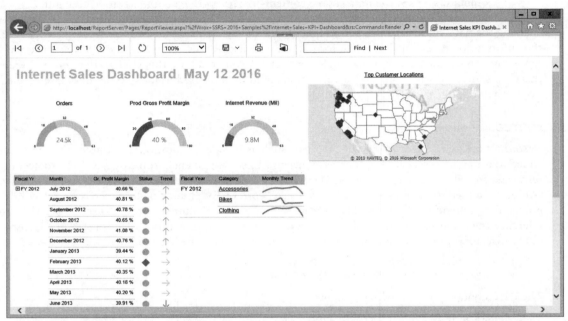

FIGURE 15-5: Sales Dashboard report.

The URL contains the following contents:

➤ **Path to the resource**—`/Wrox SSRS 2016 Samples/ Internet Sales KPI Dashboard`

➤ **Command to retrieve the resource content**—`rs:Command=Render`

You will also notice that the link URL changes to a `ReportViewer.aspx` page via redirection (notice the browser address bar in Figure 15-5) when requesting a report. The report server takes the user to a page that has a report viewer configured for the requested report.

Using URLs is the easiest and most convenient way to embed Reporting Services reports into custom applications. A custom application can point to the desired report either by creating a simple hyperlink or by using an HTML rendering object such as the `WebBrowser` component to render the report within a Windows client application. A special Windows Forms control designed for viewing reports is covered in the section "Programmatic Rendering."

The following section looks at the parameters that can be passed through the URL, including setting report parameters and output format.

Reporting Services URL Parameters

Now that you have seen the basics of obtaining items from your Report server using URLs, let's take a look at passing some parameters. The next few sections move through how parameters are passed to Reporting Services and what values are available for these parameters. The majority of the parameter functionality focuses on report rendering, but some items also apply to your data source, resources, and folder.

Parameter Prefixes

The first thing you need to consider is the different parameter prefixes in Reporting Services. Reporting Services has five main parameter prefixes: rs, rc, rv, dsp, and dsu. The following sections describe these prefixes in detail.

rs Prefix

In the earlier examples, you saw the parameter rs:Command, which contains the prefix rs. The rs prefix is used to send commands to the Report server. The following URL shows an example of the rs prefix being used to call the Command parameter and pass the ListChildren argument to it:

```
http://localhost/reportserver?/Wrox SSRS 2016 Samples&rs:Command=ListChildren
```

rc Prefix

The second main parameter prefix in Reporting Services is rc. It provides device-information settings based on the report's output format. For example, if you are outputting your report as HTML, you can control the HTML Viewer. You can use this prefix to pass parameters that do things such as hide toolbars or control the initial state of toggle items. The following URL calls the Employee Sales Summary report and turns off the parameter inputs:

```
http://localhost/ReportServer?/Wrox SSRS 2016 Samples/
Internet Sales KPI Dashboard&rs:Command=Render&rc:Parameters=False
```

rv Prefix

The rv prefix was introduced with SQL Server 2008. It is used to pass parameters to reports that are stored in a SharePoint document library. In such a library, a SharePoint Report Viewer Web Part is used to display a report, so the rv prefix should be used for these reports.

dsu and dsp Prefixes

Parameter prefixes can also be used to send database credentials. Use the dsu prefix to pass the data source username, and use the dsp prefix to pass the data source password. In any Reporting Services report, you can incorporate multiple data sources. So, you need a way to specify which data source the credentials should be passed to. That's where the prefixes come in. The full syntax to use these prefixes is as follows:

```
[dsu | dsp]:datasourcename=value
```

For example, to pass the username `guest` with a password `guestPass` to your WroxSSRS2016 data source, you would use the following URL parameters:

```
&dsu:WroxSSRS2016=guest&dsp:WroxSSRS2016=guestPass
```

Be aware that these credentials are submitted as clear text over HTTP. You can encrypt the HTTP Request (which contains the URL parameters) using a Secure Sockets Layer (SSL) certificate on your web server and making the URL request over HTTPS. This prevents the information from being sent unencrypted, but it does not prevent the end user from viewing the credentials you pass. Make sure that you consider these factors in your reporting solution architecture.

Now that you have seen the different parameter prefixes in Reporting Services, we'll move on to the available parameters that can be used with the `rv`, `rs`, and `rc` prefixes.

Parameters

First, let's examine the new SharePoint endpoint parameter that can be used with reports that are hosted in a SharePoint Integrated mode Report server configuration. This chapter does not go into detail about SharePoint integration, but let's look at the parameters that can be used with the `rv` prefix. Table 15-1 describes the four available values.

TABLE 15-1: SharePoint "rv" URL Parameters

PARAMETER	DESCRIPTION
Toolbar	Modifies the toolbar display of the SharePoint Report Viewer Web Part. The default value, `Full`, displays the entire toolbar. The `Navigation` value displays only the page navigation in the toolbar. The `None` value removes the toolbar.
HeaderArea	Modifies the header area of the SharePoint Report Viewer Web Part. The default value, `Full`, displays the complete header. The `BreadCrumbsOnly` value displays only bread crumbs in the header. A value of `None` removes the header from view.
DocMapAreaWidth	Displays the width of the parameter area of the SharePoint Report Viewer Web Part. The value should be a nonnegative number and defined in pixels.
AsyncRender	Tells the SharePoint Report Viewer Web Part whether to render the report asynchronously. The value must be a Boolean flag of `True` or `False`, with `True` meaning that the report will render asynchronously. If this parameter is not specified, the default value of `True` is used.

Now that you have seen the different `rv` parameters, let's examine the `rs` parameters. Table 15-2 describes the four available values.

TABLE 15-2: Web service "rs" URL Parameters

PARAMETER	DESCRIBES
Command	Sends instructions to the Report server about the item being retrieved. Available values return the report item and set session time-out values.
Format	Specifies the target output format when rendering reports. Any rendering format available on the Report server can be passed using this parameter.
ParameterLanguage	Passes a language in the URL that is different from the language specified in the browser. If this parameter is not specified, the default is to use the browser culture value.
Snapshot	Retrieves historical report snapshots. Once a report has been stored in snapshot history, it is assigned a time/date stamp to uniquely identify it. Passing this time/date stamp returns the appropriate report snapshot.

Now that you have seen the different rs parameters, let's take a look at some of their available values.

Command Parameter

The Command parameter is the main parameter with which you set the output of a given report item. It can also be used to reset a user's session information, which guarantees that a report is not rendered from the session cache. Table 15-3 describes the possible values that can be passed to the Command parameter.

TABLE 15-3: Command Parameter Values

VALUE	DESCRIPTION
GetComponent Definition	Returns a published report item's XML definition. You must have Read Contents permission on the report item to use this command value.
GetDataSource Contents	Returns data source information in an XML format. You use this parameter on shared data sources.
GetResourceContents	Returns the binary of your Reporting Services resources, such as images, via the URL.
GetSharedDataset Definition	Returns shared dataset information in an XML format. You must have Read Report Definition permission on the shared dataset to use this command value.

continues

TABLE 15-3 *(continued)*

VALUE	DESCRIPTION
ListChildren	Used in combination with a Reporting Services folder. This lets you view all the items in a given folder.
Render	Allows you to render the report using the URL. Probably the most frequently used command.
ResetSessionTimeout	Can be used to refresh a user's session cache. Because Reporting Services typically works via HTTP, it is crucial for the server to maintain state information about the user. However, if you want to ensure that a report is executed each time the user views a report, this state information needs to be refreshed. Use this parameter to reset the user's session and remove any session cache information.

Format Parameter

The Format parameter is the main parameter for controlling the report output. The available values for this parameter are determined by the different rendering extensions installed on your Report server. Table 15-4 shows the output formats available with the default installation of Reporting Services.

TABLE 15-4: Rendering Format Parameters

VALUE	OUTPUT
Web Formats	
HTML4.0	HTML version 4.0. This format is supported by older browsers, such as Internet Explorer 4.0 and above.
HTML5	HTML version 5. This format is supported by newer "modern" browsers, such as Internet Explorer 10 and newer, Windows Edge, Google Chrome, and Apple Safari.
MHTML	MHTML standard output. This output format is used to send HTML documents in e-mail. Using this format embeds all resources, such as images, into the MHTML document instead of referencing external URLs.
Print Formats	
IMAGE	Allows you to render your reports to several different graphical device interfaces (GDIs), such as BMP, PNG, GIF, and TIFF.
PDF	Portable Document Format (PDF) can be used to view and print documents.
Data Formats	
WORD	Word output. Users can use this format to output a report into a standard Microsoft Word document format.

VALUE	OUTPUT
EXCEL	Excel output. Users can use this format to output a report into a standard Microsoft Excel document format, version 2003 and prior.
EXCELOPENXML	New Open XML Excel output. Users can use this format to output a report into a standard Microsoft Excel document format, version 2007 and after.
PPTX	PowerPoint output. Users can use this format to output a report into a standard Microsoft PowerPoint document format.
CSV	Comma-separated value (CSV) format. CSV is a standard data format that can be read by a wide variety of applications.
XML	eXtensible Markup Language (XML) format. XML has become a standard data format, used by many different applications.
Control Format	
NULL	The NULL provider allows you to execute reports without rendering. This can be useful when you work with reports that have cached instances. You can use the NULL format to execute the report for the first time and then store the cached instance.

When you set the rendering formats via the URL, either the report is rendered directly in the browser, or you are prompted to save the output file. Let's take a look at rendering the Internet Sales KPI Dashboard report in PDF format. Enter the following URL using the rs:Format=PDF parameter:

```
http://localhost/ReportServer?/Wrox SSRS 2016 Samples/
Internet Sales KPI Dashboard&rs:Command=Render&rs:Format=PDF
```

Figure 15-6 shows the output.

Note that the browser prompts you to save/open the rendered report PDF. You can easily incorporate this into your own custom applications or portals. You can simply give your users a link containing the rs:Format parameter and automatically output the correct format.

Setting Device Information

Now that you have seen the various output formats available in Reporting Services, you need to see the different device information settings for the various formats. The Format parameter enables you to specify the type of format you want, but each format has specific settings that can be useful to you. For example, if you specify the IMAGE format, you get an output in TIFF. What if you wanted a bitmap or JPEG image? To output in a different image format, you just specify device information when passing the URL. You can output the Internet Sales KPI Dashboard report in JPEG format using the following URL:

```
http://localhost/ReportServer?/ Wrox SSRS 2016 Samples/
Internet Sales KPI Dashboard&rs:Command=Render&
rs:Format=IMAGE&rc:OutputFormat=JPEG
```

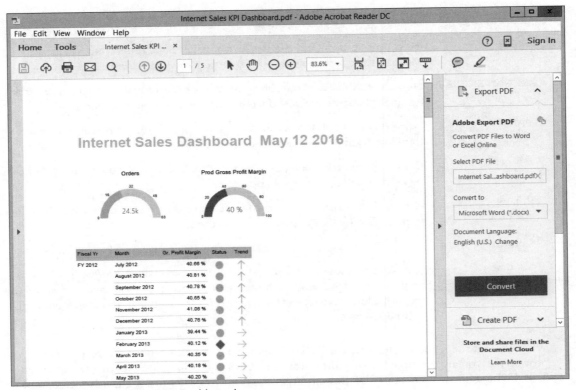

FIGURE 15-6: Internet Sales KPI Dashboard.

Notice that the file type sent back to you is a JPEG image. You can use numerous device information settings for each of the rendering extensions. Each device information setting is prefixed using `rc`. The following syntax can be used to pass device information:

```
http://server/virtualroot?/pathinfo&rs:Format=format&rc:param=value
[&rc:param=value...n]
```

Now that you have seen the different output formats and commands you can pass to Reporting Services, let's discuss passing information to your individual reports.

Passing Report Information Through the URL

The previous sections illustrated how a URL can be used to control report rendering. This section describes how a URL can be used to control report execution. It first explains how to pass report parameters. These are the parameters that you define while authoring your report. Then you see how historical snapshots of reports can be rendered using the URL.

Report Parameters

Many of your reports have parameters to control all kinds of behavior. You can use parameters to alter your query, filter and group datasets and tables, and even change the appearance of your reports. In some cases (although it isn't recommended), parameters can be used to insert data into SQL tables via the executing query. Reporting Services allows you to pass this information directly via a URL request. In the previous section, you read about the parameter prefixes and the available values that can be sent to Reporting Services. With report parameters, you simply need to remove the prefix and call the parameter name directly.

> **TIP** *The Internet Sales KPI Dashboard report has eight parameters so any parameters that are not explicitly passed to the report will have default values.*

In this example, we pass two parameters to the Internet Sales KPI Dashboard report. In a custom solution, you could allow your users to update these parameters through a custom interface that you define. When you call the report, you need to provide the parameter values in the URL, as shown here:

```
http://localhost/ReportServer?/Wrox SSRS 2016 Samples/
Internet Sales KPI Dashboard
  &rs:Command=Render
  &InternetOrdersGoal=60000
  &RevenueGoal=59000000
```

> **TIP** *Make sure that you remove spaces from the example I have provided on multiple lines for readability. The URL should contain no returns or spaces.*

Notice that when the parameters in your URL are passed, the HTML Viewer updates to reflect the values, which you can see in Figure 15-7. The parameter name you use in the URL is defined in the report definition as the parameter Value rather than the Label.

Although you can use URL access to submit multi-value parameters to your report, there is a hard limit on the size of a permitted URL within browsers, IIS, and even ASP.NET during an HTTP GET request. As a rule of thumb, it is best to restrict URLs to around 2,000 characters if using GET. This restriction does not apply when using HTTP POST and a form with key-value pairs for each of the parameters.

It is also worth mentioning that if a parameter is configured to allow null values, you can provide the following syntax to pass null from the URL:

```
parameterName:isnull=true
```

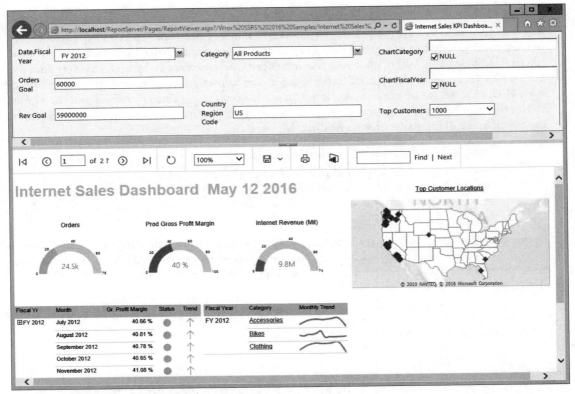

FIGURE 15-7: Dashboard report with parameters.

Now that you have seen how to pass report parameters to the URL Access of Reporting Services, let's look at passing snapshot IDs to render historical execution snapshots.

Rendering Snapshot History

One of the major features of Reporting Services is the ability to create execution snapshots of reports. Say you have a report in which the data updates on a monthly basis. After the data is updated, it does not change for another month. A perfect example of this is monthly financial statements. If your data changes only once a month, there is no reason to query your database every time you need a report. Therefore, you can use execution snapshots to store this information after the query has been executed. Similar to a monthly report, what should happen when your data updates from, say, January to February? You don't want to lose the January snapshot as soon as the February information is available. That is where historical snapshots come into play. When you create the February snapshot, you add January to the snapshot history, and so on for each subsequent month.

Now that you have execution snapshots stored in history, you need some way to access them. Reporting Services gives you an easy way to do so. As you have seen, each report has a report path that can be used to render the report. To render a historical snapshot, you simply need to add a parameter for the historical snapshot ID along with the rs prefix.

The syntax to pass your snapshot ID is as follows:

```
http://server/virtualroot?[/pathinfo]&rs:Snapshot=snapshotid
```

The snapshot ID of your historical snapshot is the date and time stamp of when the report was added to the history, formatted according to the ISO 8601 standard YYYY-MM-DDTHH:MM:SS. For example:

```
http://localhost/ReportServer?/Wrox SSRS 2016 Samples/Internet Sales KPI
Dashboard&rs:Snapshot=2016-05-31T23:59:21
```

> **TIP** *To find the snapshot history information for a report, use the Web Portal to manage the report. The Snapshot History page is accessible from the menu bar on the left side of the window that opens when managing a report.*

URL Rendering Summary

Through URL rendering, you have seen the various commands that can be passed to Reporting Services and that can be used to control the report item display, the format to use, and snapshot information using the rs prefix. After you have created your commands for the Report server, you can pass parameters specific to the output format. Using the rc prefix and the device information parameters, you can specify things such as encoding and which items to display in the HTML Viewer. After you have specified the report item, you need to know how to output it. You can pass parameters to your report by simply passing the parameter name and value combination.

The next section covers the second part of rendering Reporting Service reports. You can use URLs for simple web applications and web portals, but sometimes you need finer control over report access and rendering. To achieve this, you use the Reporting Service web service to programmatically render your reports.

PROGRAMMATIC RENDERING

Reports can be integrated into custom Windows Forms and web applications in several ways:

- ➤ Link to a report in a web browser window using a URL rendering request.
- ➤ An HTTP form via GET or POST to the Report server URL.
- ➤ Replace web page content with a report by using SOAP Web Service rendering to write binary content to the web HttpResponse object.
- ➤ Use SOAP Web Service rendering to write report content to a file.
- ➤ Embed a report in an area of a web page by setting the source of an HTML frame or an IFrame tag.

➤ Use the Microsoft `ReportViewer` control in a Windows Forms or Web Forms .NET application.

➤ Use the Microsoft `ReportViewer` control in a WPF application by wrapping it inside a `WindowsFormsHost`.

> **WARNING** *A general word of caution when considering programmatic rendering solutions: Reporting Services includes very specific optimizations that occur when reports are rendered on the report server within the* `ReportViewer` *web control. Circumnavigating the native report server rendering facility can negatively impact performance, especially for large, multi-page reports. Certain interactive report features are not supported in different rendering formats. Consider these trade-offs when taking control of report rendering.*

Rendering using a URL is handy and easy to implement in many situations, but it does have its limitations. When rendering from the URL, you have to make sure that you use the security infrastructure provided with Reporting Services. For some applications, such as public websites, you might want to implement your own security layer. In that case, rendering from the URL does not provide the functionality you need. This section describes rendering reports using the Reporting Services web service.

You connect to the Reporting Services web service, return a list of available reports, retrieve their parameters, and render the report. Let's look at three implementations of programmatic rendering. The first uses a Windows Forms application to render reports to a file. This will help you understand the basic principles without a lot of interface work. The second implementation demonstrates rendering through an ASP.NET page. You will see some of the items you need to consider when working through a web application. Last, you will read about how the `ReportViewer` control can embed reports in Windows and Web Forms applications for viewing.

Common Scenarios

Before looking at the actual programming code for rendering reports, it is important to understand a couple of scenarios in which it is reasonable to write your own rendering code. These scenarios commonly are experienced while working with clients and consuming low-to-moderate query results. They do not represent the only scenarios in which you would write your own rendering code, but they do illustrate how and when custom code can be used. Let's consider each of these scenarios.

Custom Security

One of the biggest questions around Reporting Services involves how to use Reporting Services without its standard security infrastructure. Reporting Services requires you to connect to reports using a Windows identity, also known as Windows Integrated Authentication. In many organizations, this is just not possible (as is the case with a public Internet reporting solution). They have mixed environments or untrusted domains that do not allow for identification to the Report server. Some clients also have large-scale authentication and authorization infrastructures already implemented.

You can still use Reporting Services in these situations. Using your own security infrastructure involves creating both authentication and authorization code in your environment. After you have determined that a user can access a report, a Windows identity that you define can be used to connect to reports. To hide this security implementation, the Reporting Services web service can be used, and the Report server can be abstracted and behind a firewall. You can render reports directly to a browser or file without passing the original user identity to the Report server.

When you execute reports by passing a default set of credentials via the web service proxy, you are running what is known as a "trusted subsystem." Your application's configuration maintains the credentials for the Windows Identity that can access reports on the Report server.

Server-Side Parameters

Although URL rendering is by far the easiest way to incorporate Reporting Services in your applications, it does have some limitations. When you send information via a URL, it is easy for a user to change that URL or see what you pass. If you are shrewd enough, you might try to obscure the URL parameters by using an HTTP POST instead of GET. However, this is easily circumvented with the use of browser developer tools (Firebug, Internet Explorer Developer Tools) or an HTTP proxy such as Fiddler.

By using the Reporting Services web service, you can easily hide the details of how you retrieve report information within your code. Parameters are passed through code instead of the URL. This gives you complete control over how that information is retrieved without exposing it to the users. The next section describes your first rendering application.

Rendering Through Windows

This section covers the mechanics of rendering using the Reporting Services web service. You build a simple Windows application that returns a list of reports from the Report server. As soon as you have the list of reports, you use the web service to return a list of report parameters. After entering any report parameters, you render the report to a file. These steps illustrate the main components of rendering through program code.

Building the Application Interface

First you need to build your application interface. Let's start by building a simple Windows form. For this example, I've added labels, textboxes, and buttons for basic functionality. Figure 15-8 shows the form's design view.

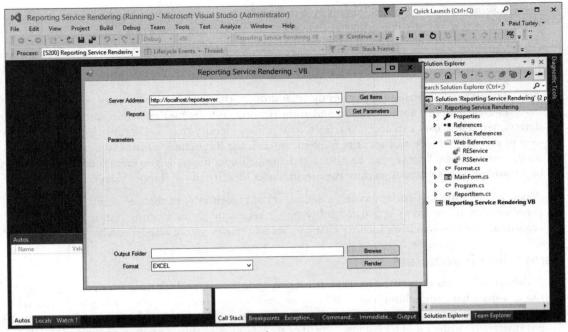

FIGURE 15-8: Custom rendering application interface.

This form allows you to query a given Report server to return a list of reports. After it returns the reports, you can use it to access a list of parameters for the reports. Finally, you need to render the report to a given folder location.

Setting Up the Web Services

Before you can begin rendering reports, you need to set up a reference to the Reporting Services and Report Execution web services. After you create your web references, you can start to develop the application. The next few figures show you how to create references to the web services. Start by adding the web references to your project.

Open the Solution Explorer. Right-click the References folder and select Add Service Reference, as shown in Figure 15-9. In the bottom-left corner, click the Advanced button to open the Service Reference Settings dialog box, which is shown in Figure 15-10. Make sure the check box "Generate asynchronous operations" is checked. We will leverage the asynchronous web service capabilities to provide a more responsive UI. Click the Add Web Reference button at the bottom left to open the Add Web Reference dialog.

In the Add Web Reference dialog, shown in Figure 15-11, enter the location of the web service in the URL box. This URL depends on the Report server name and the installed location of the Report server virtual directory. By default, the Report server virtual directory is located under the root at /ReportServer. For the default virtual directory on a local machine, enter the following URL:

```
http://localhost/ReportServer/ReportService2010.asmx
```

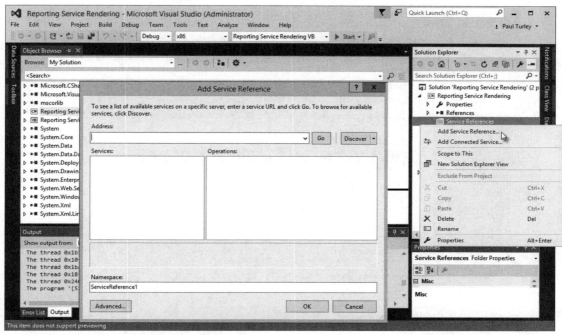

FIGURE 15-9: Add Service Reference dialog.

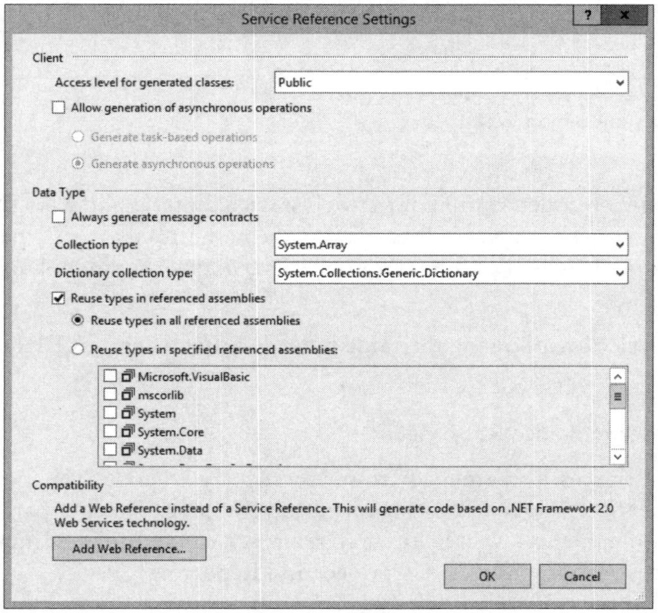

FIGURE 15-10: Service Reference Settings dialog.

> **NOTE** *The old endpoints,* `ReportService2005.asmx` *(Native mode) and* `ReportService 2006.asmx` *(SharePoint Integrated mode), were deprecated in version 2008 R2 but are installed with the product for backward-compatibility purposes. The newer (and still the most current) endpoint, ReportService2010, was introduced to include functionalities from both endpoints, as well as to offer additional management features.*

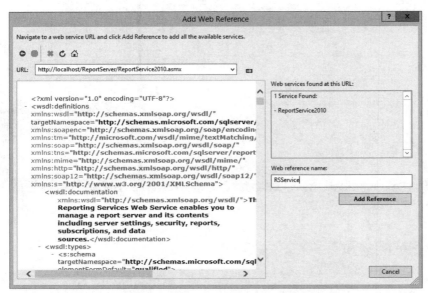

FIGURE 15-11: Add Web Reference dialog containing WSDL.

After you enter the URL, press Enter to view a description of the web service. Enter a name for the new web reference and click Add Reference. This name will be used as the namespace for all types defined by the proxy assembly. This example uses the name RSService. The dialog should look like Figure 15-11 when filled in.

Now add the Report Execution web service by following the same procedure but using this URL:

```
http://localhost/ReportServer/ReportExecution2005.asmx
```

In the example, we name this web service reference RSService.

Now that you have referenced the web services, you are ready to start writing your code. The first thing you can do is add a `using` (C#) or `Imports` (VB) statement to your code. The first part of the `using` statement is the application name followed by the web reference name. In the example, the project is called Reporting_Service_Rendering for the C# project and Reporting_Service_Rendering_VB for the Visual Basic project.

C#

```
using System;
using System.Collections.Generic;
using System.IO;
using System.Linq;
using System.Windows.Forms;
using Reporting_Service_Rendering.RSService;
using Reporting_Service_Rendering.REService;
```

VB

```
Imports Reporting_Service_Rendering_VB.RSService
Imports Reporting_Service_Rendering_VB.REService
```

After you have added the `using` or `Imports` statement, you need to create an instance of the `ReportingService2010` and `ReportExecutionService` objects. These are the main objects that will be used to retrieve a list of reports and their associated parameters and then render the report. At the top of the Windows Forms class code for the MainForm, create the declarations shown in the following sections. The class declaration is included for clarity.

C#

```
public partial class MainForm : Form
{
        ReportingService2010 _rs = new ReportingService2010();
        ReportExecutionService _rsExec = new ReportExecutionService();
        bool _reportHasParameters = false;
        const string _REPORT_SERVICE_ENDPOINT = "ReportService2010.asmx";
        const string _REPORT_EXECUTION_ENDPOINT = "ReportExecution2005.asmx";
```

VB

```
Public Class MainForm
    Private _rs As New ReportingService2010
    Private _rsExec As New ReportExecutionService
    Private _reportHasParameters As Boolean = False
    Private Const _REPORT_SERVICE_ENDPOINT As String = "ReportService2010.asmx"
    Private Const _REPORT_EXECUTION_ENDPOINT As String = "ReportExecution2005.asmx"
```

Next, you need to set the security credentials that these objects will use. In your code, pass the credentials of the currently logged-on user. If you already have your own custom authentication and authorization method in place, you could pass a system identification that you define instead of the current user.

Open the `Form Load` event in the Windows Form. This is a suitable place for setting the credentials. Inside this event, set the `ReportingService2010` and `ReportExecutionService` objects' `Credentials` property to `System.Net.CredentialCache.DefaultCredentials`. This gives the web services the credentials of the currently logged-on user (Windows Integrated Authentication).

C#

```
_rs.Credentials = System.Net.CredentialCache.DefaultCredentials;
_rsExec.Credentials = System.Net.CredentialCache.DefaultCredentials;
```

VB

```
_rs.Credentials = System.Net.CredentialCache.DefaultCredentials
_rsExec.Credentials = System.Net.CredentialCache.DefaultCredentials
```

The final piece you need to add to the `Form Load` event is the code to populate your drop-down list. This code adds all the format names to the list, along with an appropriate extension for each. Begin by adding a new class file to your project to create a small class that helps you populate the drop-down. To add a new class, click Project ➪ Add class (or use the shortcut Shift+Alt+C):

C#

```
internal class Format
{
    public Format(string name, string extension)
    {
        Name = name;
        Extension = extension;
    }

    public string Name { get; private set; }
    public string Extension { get; private set; }

    public static IList<Format> GetFormatsList()
    {
        List<Format> formats = new List<Format>{
        new Format("EXCEL", ".xlsx"),
        new Format("WORD", ".docx"),
        new Format("PPTX", ".pptx"),
        new Format("HTML4.0", ".html"),
        new Format("HTML5", ".html"),
        new Format("XML", ".xml"),
        new Format("CSV", ".csv"),
        new Format("PDF", ".pdf"),
        new Format("IMAGE", ".tif")
        };

        return formats;
    }
}
```

VB

```
Friend Class Format

    Public Sub New(ByVal name As String, ByVal extension As String)
        Me.Name = name
        Me.Extension = extension
    End Sub

    Public Property Name As String
    Public Property Extension As String

    Public Shared Function GetFormatsList() As IList(Of Format)
```

```
        Dim formats As New List(Of Format) From {
            New Format("EXCEL", ".xlsx"),
            New Format("WORD", ".docx"),
            New Format("PPTX", ".pptx"),
            New Format("HTML4.0", ".html"),
            New Format("HTML5", ".html"),
            New Format("XML", ".xml"),
            New Format("CSV", ".csv"),
            New Format("PDF", ".pdf"),
            New Format("IMAGE", ".tif")
        }

        Return formats

    End Function

End Class
```

With this class, you can finish your `Form Load` event code. Add the few last lines of code to populate your format combo box:

C#

```csharp
private void MainForm_Load(object sender, EventArgs e)
{
    _rs.Credentials = System.Net.CredentialCache.DefaultCredentials;
    _rsExec.Credentials = System.Net.CredentialCache.DefaultCredentials;

    reportFormatComboBox.DataSource = Format.GetFormatsList();
    reportFormatComboBox.DisplayMember = "Name";
    reportFormatComboBox.ValueMember = "Name";
}
```

VB

```vb
Private Sub MainForm_Load(sender As System.Object, _
e As System.EventArgs) Handles MyBase.Load
    _rs.Credentials = System.Net.CredentialCache.DefaultCredentials
    _rsExec.Credentials = System.Net.CredentialCache.DefaultCredentials

    reportFormatComboBox.DataSource = Format.GetFormatsList()
    reportFormatComboBox.DisplayMember = "Name"
    reportFormatComboBox.ValueMember = "Name"
End Sub
```

You have now created an instance of the `ReportingService2010` object, passed the logged-on user's credentials to it, and populated the format drop-down list. The next section discusses connecting to the Report server and retrieving a list of available reports.

Retrieving Report Information

Now that you have set up the Reporting Services web service, you need to retrieve your list of reports. To do this, specify the Report server that you want to query, and then call the `ListChildren` method of the `ReportingService2010` object. `ListChildren` returns a list of all items, including data sources, resources, and reports. After you have retrieved the list, you need to pull out only report items. Finally, you add the report items to the drop-down.

As pointed out earlier, you ensure that your web-reference proxy was generated with asynchronous operations. When you create a web reference using the Visual Studio IDE, it generates both the synchronous and asynchronous operations. Due to the nature of this application—a Windows form UI—it is best practice to ensure that calls to the Report Services are performed on a different thread than the UI thread. This prevents the UI thread from being blocked while the web service operation completes, providing a much better user experience.

The asynchronous pattern may seem a bit complex or overwhelming at first, but in essence all it does is register an event handler that invokes a delegate function (the "callback") when the asynchronous operation is completed. In other words, you fire a call to the operation and return from the method. The execution happens on a background thread that waits for the event notification when the operation completes and invokes the callback function.

In addition to the asynchronous operations, you can always call the synchronous methods directly without having to worry about delegates and events. This is fine in scenarios such as server-side code, where there's no user interface to be concerned with.

Let's start by setting the URL to your Report server. Open the click event of the Get Items button to start your code. You'll keep your UI event handlers pretty lean and perform the bulk of operations in separate methods. Remember that _rs is your private object reference to the web service, as defined at the top of the class definition. Also, this event handler will need to call a function that loads the reports list box, which will be implemented later on. So for now, just use a "TODO:" comment as a placeholder and reminder.

C#

```csharp
private void btnGetItems_Click(object sender, EventArgs e)
{
    GetItems();
}
private void GetItems()
{
    if (!String.IsNullOrEmpty(txtServer.Text))
    {
        _rs.Url = String.Format("{0}/{1}", txtServer.Text.TrimEnd('/'),
        _REPORT_SERVICE_ENDPOINT);

        _rs.ListChildrenCompleted += new
        ListChildrenCompletedEventHandler((sender, e) =>
        {
            if (e.Error == null && e.Result != null)
                // TODO: Load the list box with e.Result
            else
                MessageBox.Show(e.Error.ToString());
        });

        _rs.ListChildrenAsync("/", true, Guid.NewGuid ());
    }
    else
```

```
        {
            MessageBox.Show("Enter a server string first.. " +
    "Example: http://localhost/reportserver");
        }
    }
```

VB

```vb
    Private Sub btnGetItems_Click(sender As System.Object, e As System.EventArgs)_
      Handles btnGetItems.Click
        GetItems()
    End Sub

    Private Sub GetItems()
        If (Not String.IsNullOrEmpty(Me.txtServer.Text)) Then

            _rs.Url = String.Format("{0}/{1}", txtServer.Text.TrimEnd("/"),
            _REPORT_SERVICE_ENDPOINT)

            AddHandler _rs.ListChildrenCompleted, Sub(sender As Object, args As
            RSService.ListChildrenCompletedEventArgs)
              If (IsNothing(args.Error) AndAlso Not IsNothing(args.Result)) Then
                'TODO: Load the list box with args.Result
              Else
                MessageBox.Show(args.Error.ToString())
              End If
            End Sub

            _rs.ListChildrenAsync("/", True, Guid.NewGuid())

        Else
            MessageBox.Show("Enter a server string first... Example:
            http://localhost/reportserver")
        End If

    End Sub
```

The preceding code uses the server location specified in the Server Address textbox (txtServer) concatenated with the reference to the Reporting Services web service URL endpoint.

As soon as the URL for the web service is set, you can get the list of reports. Create an array of CatalogItem objects, and then call the ListChildren or ListChildrenAsync method. These methods take two parameters in their synchronous form: the folder path on the Report server and a Boolean value indicating whether to recurse through the directory. The asynchronous flavor adds a third parameter that allows you to provide the unique state object. This is required to prevent errors when multiple asynchronous operations are outstanding. To ensure uniqueness, you create an instance of type System.Guid. In the preceding code, you already implemented the asynchronous version. For completeness, here is how both the synchronous and asynchronous code look when calling the ListChildren web service method:

SYNCHRONOUS C#

```csharp
    CatalogItem[] items;
    items = _rs.ListChildren("/", true);
```

SYNCHRONOUS VB

```
Dim items() As CatalogItem
items = _rs.ListChildren("/", True)
```

ASYNCHRONOUS C#

```
_rs.ListChildrenCompleted +=
    new ListChildrenCompletedEventHandler((sender, e) =>
    {
        if (e.Error == null && e.Result != null)
            // TODO: Load the list box using e.Result
        else
            MessageBox.Show(e.Error.ToString());
    });

_rs.ListChildrenAsync("/", true, Guid.NewGuid());
```

ASYNCHRONOUS VB

```
AddHandler _rs.ListChildrenCompleted, Sub(sender As Object, args As _
RSService.ListChildrenCompletedEventArgs)
    If (IsNothing(args.Error) AndAlso Not IsNothing(args.Result)) Then
        ' TODO: Load the list box using args.Result
    Else
        MessageBox.Show(args.Error.ToString())
    End If
End Sub

_rs.ListChildrenAsync("/", True, Guid.NewGuid ())
```

As soon as the operation returns with an array of Report Items, the last step is to loop through the resulting array and add each item to a drop-down list (ComboBox). Similar to how the formats were loaded, create a class to help data-bind the report items. Let's take a look at the code for this class:

C#

```
internal class ReportItem
{
        public ReportItem(string name, string path)
        {
                Name = name;
                Path = path;
        }

        public string Name { get; private set; }
        public string Path { get; private set; }
}
```

VB

```
Friend Class ReportItem
    Private _name As String
    Private _path As String

    Public Sub New(ByVal name As String, ByVal path As String)
```

```
                _name = name
                _path = path
        End Sub

        Public ReadOnly Property Name() As String
            Get
                Return _name
            End Get
        End Property

        Public ReadOnly Property Path() As String
            Get
                Return _path
            End Get
        End Property
    End Class
```

Using the `ReportItem` class just created, you can add the report catalog items to the combo box. In the `MainForm` class, you'll implement a new method that does just that. The following code is for the `LoadReportsBox` method, which is invoked by the asynchronous delegate-callback method to the `ListItemsAsync` operation (where you had originally put a TODO: comment line to load the list box):

C#

```csharp
private void LoadReportsBox(CatalogItem[] items)
{
    reportsComboBox.Items.Clear();

    foreach (var item in items)
    {
        if (item.TypeName == "Report")
        {
            reportsComboBox.Items.Add(new ReportItem(item.Name, item.Path));
        }
    }

    reportsComboBox.DisplayMember = "Name";
    reportsComboBox.ValueMember = "Path";
    reportsComboBox.DroppedDown = true;
}
```

VB

```vb
Private Sub LoadReportsBox(ByVal items As RSService.CatalogItem())
    'populate report combo box
    reportsComboBox.Items.Clear()
    For Each item As RSService.CatalogItem In items
        If (item.TypeName = "Report") Then
            reportsComboBox.Items.Add(New ReportItem(item.Name, item.Path))
        End If
    Next

    reportsComboBox.DisplayMember = "Name"
```

```
                reportsComboBox.ValueMember = "Path"
                reportsComboBox.DroppedDown = True
        End Sub
```

Don't forget to replace the TODO comment line inside GetItems with the invocation of LoadReportsBox. The Result property of the callback argument object should contain the CatalogItem array expected by LoadReportsBox:

C#

```
    rs.ListChildrenCompleted +=
        new ListChildrenCompletedEventHandler((sender, e) =>
        {
            if (e.Error == null && e.Result != null)
                LoadReportsBox(e.Result);
            else
                MessageBox.Show(e.Error.ToString());
        });
```

VB

```
    AddHandler _rs.ListChildrenCompleted, Sub(sender As Object, args As
    RSService.ListChildrenCompletedEventArgs)
        If (IsNothing(args.Error) AndAlso Not IsNothing(args.Result)) Then
            LoadReportsBox(args.Result)
        Else
            MessageBox.Show(args.Error.ToString())
        End If
    End Sub
```

You now can open your form and return a list of report items. The next section describes retrieving the parameters for a report.

Retrieving Report Parameters

The next area of programmatic rendering consists of retrieving a list of parameters for your report. This bit of code can be used in various scenarios. The parameter interface that is provided by Reporting Services works well for simple parameters. However, it does not handle many things, such as advanced validation based on business rules, or even fancier input interfaces such as dials and sliders. Being able to return a list of parameters allows you to create your own dynamic user interface.

In the following example, you create a simple list of parameters. For each parameter, you dynamically add a label control and either a textbox, check box, or date/time picker to your form, based on the parameter type. The following line of code is the first thing you should do within the GetParameters method, which is called from the respective button-click event handler. This line of code identifies the report that is selected in your report drop-down list:

C#

```
    ReportItem reportItem = (ReportItem)reportsComboBox.SelectedItem;
```

VB

```
Dim reportItem As ReportItem = DirectCast(reportsComboBox.SelectedItem, ReportItem)
```

This creates a new `ReportItem` variable using the selected item of your combo box. The `ReportItem` class created in the preceding section contains a `Name` and a `Path` property. You can use this `Path` property to retrieve your list of parameters.

To return your list of parameters, call the `GetItemParameters` method of the `ReportingService2010` object. This method has two purposes. It returns a list of parameters and can validate parameters against the available values defined when creating the report. Here are the arguments for the `GetItemParameters` method:

➤ `ItemPath` is the path to the report for which you want to retrieve parameters.

➤ `HistoryID` is the ID used to identify any historical snapshots of your report.

➤ `ForRendering` is a Boolean argument that can be used to retrieve the parameters that were set when the report was executed. For example, you might create a snapshot of your report or receive it in an e-mail subscription. In both cases, the report is executed before the user views it. By setting the `ForRendering` property to `true`, you can retrieve these values and use them in your own custom interface.

➤ `Values` is an array of `ParameterValue` objects that can be used to validate the values assigned to a parameter. This can be useful to guarantee that the parameter values you pass to your report match the parameter values the report definition accepts.

➤ `Credentials` are the database credentials to use when validating your query-based parameters in case you have to execute a query to populate available values.

➤ `userState` (async only) is an optional parameter that is available only in the asynchronous version of the operation. It provides a unique state object to prevent errors when multiple asynchronous operations are outstanding. Typically, a new GUID is used for this parameter.

Because you are not working with historical reports or validating values in this exercise, a number of the properties will not be set. The following code can be used to call the `GetItemParameters` method synchronously:

C#

```
ItemParameter[] parameters;
parameters = _rs.GetItemParameters(reportItem.Path, null, false, null, null);
```

VB

```
Dim parameters() As ItemParameter
parameters = _rs.GetItemParameters(reportItem.Path, Nothing, False, _
                      Nothing, Nothing)
```

Because you are using the asynchronous pattern in this sample exercise, here is how to use the asynchronous version, calling the `GetItemParameterAsync` method. The following code should be implemented inside of a private method named `GetParameters`. This method, in turn, is invoked by the "Get Parameters" button click event handler:

ASYNCHRONOUS C#

```csharp
_rs.GetItemParametersCompleted +=
new GetItemParametersCompletedEventHandler((sender, args) =>
{
    if (args.Error == null && args.Result != null)
        LoadParametersGroupBox(args.Result);
    else
        MessageBox.Show(args.Error.ToString());
});
_rs.GetItemParametersAsync(reportItem.Path,
null, false, null, null, Guid.NewGuid());
```

ASYNCHRONOUS VB

```vb
AddHandler _rs.GetItemParametersCompleted, _
    Sub(sender As Object, args As RSService.GetItemParametersCompletedEventArgs)
        If (args.Error Is Nothing AndAlso Not args.Result Is Nothing) Then
                LoadParametersGroupBox(args.Result)
        Else
                MessageBox.Show(args.Error.ToString())
        End If
    End Sub

    _rs.GetItemParametersAsync(reportItem.Path, Nothing, False, Nothing, _
Nothing, Guid.NewGuid())
```

The last task is to create a user interface for your parameters. The `ReportParameter` objects returned by Reporting Services contain information useful for creating a custom interface. Some of the key properties include the parameter data type, prompt, and valid values. All of these can be used to define your own interface. Finish your code by simply adding a label and either a textbox, check box, or date/time picker to your form for each `ReportParameter`.

Following is the code for the `LoadParametersGroupBox` method, which is invoked inside the callback delegate upon successful execution of the web operation. Also, the logic to build the appropriate control type based on parameter type was refactored into a separate method, as shown in the method named `GetParameterControl`:

C#

```csharp
private void LoadParametersGroupBox(ItemParameter[] parameters)
{
    // Let everyone know this report has parameters.
    _reportHasParameters = (parameters.Length > 0);

    //add the parameters to the parameter list UI
    int left = 10;
    int top = 20;
    paramInfoGroupBox.Controls.Clear();

    foreach (var parameter in parameters)
    {
        Label label = new Label
```

```csharp
                {
                    Text = parameter.Prompt,
                    Left = left,
                    Top = top
                };

                paramInfoGroupBox.Controls.Add(label);
                paramInfoGroupBox.Controls.Add(
                    GetParameterControl(parameter, left, top));
                top += 25;
            }
        }

    private Control GetParameterControl(ItemParameter parameter, int left, int top)
    {
        Control parameterControl;
        switch (parameter.ParameterTypeName)
        {
            case "Boolean":
                parameterControl = new CheckBox
                {
                    Checked = parameter.DefaultValues != null ?
                    Boolean.Parse(parameter.DefaultValues[0]) : false
                };
                break;
            case "DateTime":
                parameterControl = new DateTimePicker
                {
                    Text = parameter.DefaultValues != null ?
                    parameter.DefaultValues[0] : String.Empty
                };
                break;
            default:
                //there are other types, such as float and int,
                //and you can also retrieve default values and
                //populate as dropdown, but
                //it's beyond scope of this exercise
                parameterControl = new TextBox
                {
                    Text = parameter.DefaultValues != null ?
                    parameter.DefaultValues[0] : string.Empty
                };
                break;
        }
        parameterControl.Name = parameter.Name;
        parameterControl.Left = left + 150;
        parameterControl.Top = top;

        return parameterControl;
    }
```

VB

```vb
    Private Sub LoadParametersGroupBox(ByVal parameters As ItemParameter())
        'let everyone know this report has parameters
        _reportHasParameters = (parameters.Length > 0)
```

```
    'add the parameters to the parameter list UI
    Dim left As Integer = 10
    Dim top As Integer = 20

    paramInfoGroupBox.Controls.Clear()

    For Each parameter As ItemParameter In parameters
        Dim label As New Label With
        {
            .Text = parameter.Prompt,
            .Left = left,
            .Top = top
        }
        paramInfoGroupBox.Controls.Add(label)
        paramInfoGroupBox.Controls.Add( _
            GetParameterControl(parameter, left, top))
        top += 25
    Next
End Sub

Private Function GetParameterControl(ByVal parameter As ItemParameter, _
                                     ByVal left As Integer, _
                                     ByVal top As Integer) As Control
    Dim parameterControl As Control

    Select Case parameter.ParameterTypeName
        Case "Boolean"
            parameterControl = New CheckBox With {
                .Checked = If(parameter.DefaultValues IsNot Nothing, _
                            Boolean.Parse(parameter.DefaultValues(0)), False)
            }
        Case "DateTime"
            parameterControl = New DateTimePicker With {
                .Text = If(parameter.DefaultValues IsNot Nothing, _
                            parameter.DefaultValues(0), String.Empty)
            }
        Case Else
            'there are other types, like float and int,
            'and you can also retrieve default values and populate as a drop-down
            'but it's beyond the scope of this exercise
            parameterControl = New TextBox With {
                .Text = If(parameter.DefaultValues IsNot Nothing, _
                            parameter.DefaultValues(0), String.Empty)
            }
    End Select

    parameterControl.Name = parameter.Name
    parameterControl.Left = left + 150
    parameterControl.Top = top

    Return parameterControl
End Function
```

Now that you have retrieved your list of reports and built a parameter list, we'll discuss rendering and outputting the report to a file.

Rendering a Report to a File on the Filesystem

This section describes rendering a report to a file on the filesystem. Using the `ReportExecution2005` web service, you can retrieve a byte array that contains the final report. This byte array can be used in a variety of ways. This example writes the byte array to a file by using the filesystem object. Another example in a later section writes the byte array to the HTTP `Response` object.

You set up the `ReportExecution2005` web service in the previous sections, so now you can use it to render a report to a file on the filesystem. In `btnRender_Click` you call a new method, `RenderReport`, which sets the URL by concatenating the server text the user entered with the `ReportExecution2005.asmx` string:

C#

```
_rsExec.Url = String.Format("{0}/{1}",
    txtServer.Text.TrimEnd('/'), "ReportExecution2005.asmx");
```

VB

```
_rsExec.Url = String.Format("{0}/{1}", _
    txtServer.Text.TrimEnd("/"), "ReportExecution2005.asmx")
```

Next, you need to set a string argument that will be used for the report's path.

Before you get into the rendering code, let's look at the `Render` method that is contained within the `ReportExecutionService` object of the `ReportExecution2005` web service. Table 15-5 shows the different parameters.

TABLE 15-5: Report Execution Web Service Parameters

PARAMETER	DATA TYPE	DESCRIPTION
Format	String	The report's output format.
DeviceInfo	String	Information used by a specified rendering format, such as specifying the image type (GIF, JPEG) with the `IMAGE` format.
Extension (out)	String	The file extension of the rendered report.
MimeType (out)	String	Output returned from Reporting Services containing the MIME type of the underlying report. Useful when rendering a report to the web. The MIME type can be passed to the `Response` object to ensure that the browser correctly handles the document returned.
Encoding (out)	String	The encoding used to render the report.
Warnings (out)	Warning Array	The output of any warning returned from Reporting Services during report processing.
StreamIDs (out)	String Array	The output of the stream IDs that can be used with the `RenderStream` method.

The `Render` method returns an array of bytes that represents the rendered report. The array can then be used just like any other byte array, such as writing it to a file on the filesystem or sending it over a TCP connection.

The parameters of the `Render` method are similar to the values that can be passed using URL rendering.

Now that you have seen the basics of the `Render` method, let's examine the code you need to write for your `Render` button-click event. The first thing you must do in your code is retrieve the selected report and output format. Use the `Format` and `ReportItem` classes created earlier to retrieve the selected items in your drop-downs:

C#

```csharp
Format selectedFormat = (Format)reportFormatComboBox.SelectedItem;
ReportItem reportItem = (ReportItem)reportsComboBox.SelectedItem;
```

VB

```vb
Dim selectedFormat As Format = _
    DirectCast(reportFormatComboBox.SelectedItem, Format)
Dim reportItem As ReportItem = _
    DirectCast(reportsComboBox.SelectedItem, ReportItem)
```

You need to retrieve the input parameters the user specified. Then you must create a new function that loops through the controls you created earlier to retrieve their values and return an array of `ParameterValue` objects:

C#

```csharp
private REService.ParameterValue[] GetReportExecutionParameters()
{
    var controlList = new List<Control>();

    //get the values from the parameter controls that are not labels
    controlList.AddRange(paramInfoGroupBox.Controls
        .OfType<Control>()
        .Where(c => c.GetType() != typeof(Label)));

    //add the control information to parameter info objects
    var parameterValues = new List<REService.ParameterValue>();
    foreach (var control in controlList)
    {
        parameterValues.Add(new REService.ParameterValue
        {
            Name = control.Name,
            Value = (control is CheckBox) ?
            ((CheckBox)control).Checked.ToString() : control.Text
        });
    }

    return parameterValues.ToArray();
}
```

VB

```
Private Function GetReportExecutionParameters() As REService.ParameterValue()
    Dim controlList = New List(Of Control)()

    'get the values from the parameter controls that are not labels
    controlList.AddRange(paramInfoGroupBox.Controls.OfType(Of Control)() _
                        .Where(Function(c) c.[GetType]() <> GetType(Label)))

    'add the control information to parameter info objects
    Dim parameterValues = New List(Of REService.ParameterValue)()
    For Each ctrl As Control In controlList
        parameterValues.Add(New REService.ParameterValue() With {
          .Name = ctrl.Name,
          .Value = If((TypeOf ctrl Is CheckBox), _
                    DirectCast(ctrl, CheckBox).Checked.ToString(), ctrl.Text)
        })
    Next

    Return parameterValues.ToArray()
End Function
```

You can now use the GetReportExecutionParameters function to build an array of input parameters. You can add the following code to your RenderReport method to retrieve the input parameters:

C#

```
REService.ParameterValue[] parameters = GetReportExecutionParameters();
```

VB

```
Dim parameters As REService.ParameterValue() = GetReportExecutionParameters()
```

Now that you have your list of input parameters, you are almost ready to call the Render method. For this, you need to declare variables that will be used for the output parameters HistoryID, DeviceInfo, Encoding, MimeType, Extension, Warnings, and StreamIDs. Not all of these variables are needed, because they are set to null and are not used. However, they have been declared here to show the syntax of the Render method. The final variable you need for the Render method is an array of bytes. This byte array can then be written to the filesystem:

C#

```
byte[] result = null;
string historyID = null;
string devInfo = null;
string encoding;
string mimeType;
string extension;
REService.Warning[] warnings = null;
string[] streamIDs = null;

// Load the report, set the parameters and then render.
_rsExec.LoadReport(reportItem.Path, historyID);
_rsExec.SetExecutionParameters(parameters, "en-us");
result = _rsExec.Render(selectedFormat.Name, devInfo,
```

```
        out extension,
        out encoding,
        out mimeType,
        out warnings,
        out streamIDs);
```

VB

```
Dim result As Byte() = Nothing
Dim historyID As String = Nothing
Dim devInfo As String = Nothing
Dim encoding As String
Dim mimeType As String
Dim extension As String
Dim warnings As REService.Warning() = Nothing
Dim streamIDs As String() = Nothing

' Load the report, set the parameters and then render.
_rsExec.LoadReport(reportItem.Path, historyID)
_rsExec.SetExecutionParameters(parameters, "en-us")
result = _rsExec.Render(selectedFormat.Name, devInfo, extension, _
                        encoding, mimeType, warnings, streamIDs)
```

Finally, you need to take the byte array returned from the Render method and write it to the filesystem. Use the output path specified in the output textbox, along with the report name and format file extension, to open a file stream. Following is the entire RenderReport method, along with the final piece of code for writing the file to the filesystem:

C#

```
private void RenderReport()
{
    _rsExec.Url = String.Format("{0}/{1}",
        txtServer.Text.TrimEnd('/'),
        "ReportExecution2005.asmx");

    Format selectedFormat = (Format)reportFormatComboBox.SelectedItem;
    ReportItem reportItem = (ReportItem)reportsComboBox.SelectedItem;

    REService.ParameterValue[] parameters = GetReportExecutionParameters();

    byte[] result = null;
    string historyID = null;
    string devInfo = null;
    string encoding;
    string mimeType;
    string extension;
    REService.Warning[] warnings = null;
    string[] streamIDs = null;

    // Make sure the report either has parameters
    // that are set or has no parameters.
    if ((_reportHasParameters && parameters.Length != 0) || !_reportHasParameters)
    {
        _rsExec.LoadReport(reportItem.Path, historyID);
        _rsExec.SetExecutionParameters(parameters, "en-us");
```

```
        result = _rsExec.Render(selectedFormat.Name,
            devInfo,
            out extension,
            out encoding,
            out mimeType,
            out warnings,
            out streamIDs);

        // Make sure there is an output path then
        // output the file to the file system.
        if (txtOutputFolder.Text != "")
        {
            string fullOutputPath = txtOutputFolder.Text + "\\" +
            reportItem.Name + selectedFormat.Extension;
            FileStream stream = File.Create(fullOutputPath, result.Length);
            stream.Write(result, 0, result.Length);
            stream.Close();
            MessageBox.Show("Report Rendered to: " + fullOutputPath);
        }
        else
        {
            MessageBox.Show("Choose a folder first");
        }
    }
    else
    {
        MessageBox.Show("Click Get Parameters button and then set values.");
    }
}
```

VB

```
Private Sub RenderReport()
    _rsExec.Url = String.Format("{0}/{1}", txtServer.Text.TrimEnd("/"),
    "ReportExecution2005.asmx")

    Dim selectedFormat As Format =
    DirectCast(Me.reportFormatComboBox.SelectedItem, Format)
    Dim reportItem As ReportItem =
    DirectCast(Me.reportsComboBox.SelectedItem, ReportItem)

    Dim parameters As REService.ParameterValue() = GetReportExecutionParameters()

    Dim result As Byte() = Nothing
    Dim historyID As String = Nothing
    Dim devInfo As String = Nothing
    Dim encoding As String
    Dim mimeType As String
    Dim extension As String
    Dim warnings As REService.Warning() = Nothing
    Dim streamIDs As String() = Nothing

    ' Make sure the report either has parameters that are set or has no parameters.
    If ((_reportHasParameters AndAlso Not parameters.Length = 0) OrElse Not
    _reportHasParameters) Then
```

```
_rsExec.LoadReport(reportItem.Path, historyID)
_rsExec.SetExecutionParameters(parameters, "en-us")
result = _rsExec.Render(selectedFormat.Name, devInfo, extension, _
                        encoding, mimeType, warnings, streamIDs)

' Make sure there is an output path then output the file to the file
system.
If (Not txtOutputFolder.Text = "") Then
    Dim fullOutputPath As String = txtOutputFolder.Text & "\" & _
                                  reportItem.Name & _
                                  selectedFormat.Extension
    Dim stream As System.IO.FileStream = _
      System.IO.File.Create(fullOutputPath, result.Length)
    stream.Write(result, 0, result.Length)
    stream.Close()
    MessageBox.Show("Report Rendered to: " & fullOutputPath)
Else
    MessageBox.Show("Choose a folder first")
End If
Else
    MessageBox.Show("Click Get Parameters button and then set values.")
End If
End Sub
```

Now that you have completed the code for rendering the application, let's try it. You need to build and run the project. When the form opens, enter your server information in the Server Address textbox, and click the Get Items button, as shown in Figure 15-12.

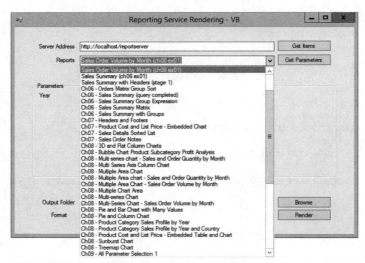

FIGURE 15-12: Reporting Service Rendering application report list.

Select a report that takes parameters (the example uses the Sales Order Volume by Month report from Chapter 8 exercise 1), click the Get Parameters button, and then fill in the parameters, as shown in Figure 15-13.

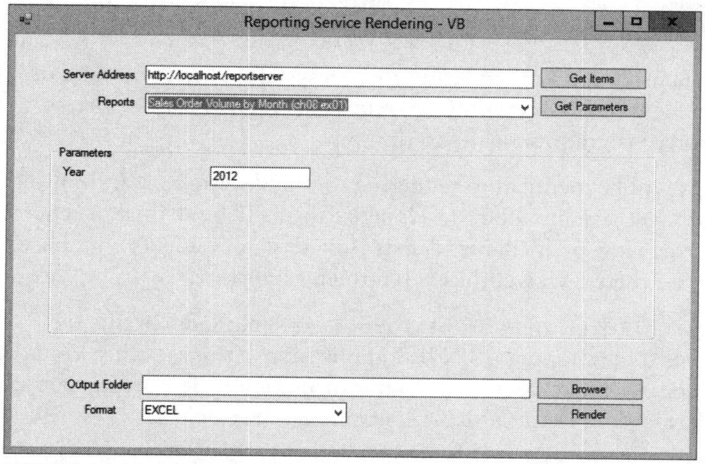

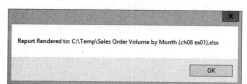

FIGURE 15-13: Reporting Service Rendering application.

Finally, select an output folder and the rendering format EXCEL. After specifying these items, you can click the Render button to render your report. When the rendering is complete, you see a message box saying that the file has been written to the specified location, as shown in Figure 15-14. You can now open your saved file using Microsoft Excel.

FIGURE 15-14: Confirmation message box.

Rendering a Report to the Filesystem Summary

In this section, you have learned the basic steps of rendering a report to the filesystem:

➤ Using the `ReportingService2010` object's `ListChildren` method to return a list of reports

➤ Using the `ReportingService2010` object's `GetItemParameters` method to return a list of report parameters

➤ Using the `Render` method of the `ReportExecutionService` object to output your report in a given format

These basic steps can be used in numerous applications to render a report. Using these methods, users can create their own custom list of reports and customer-report parameter pages and output the report using the returned byte array. In the next section, you use some of these steps to render a report to the web via the `Response` object.

Rendering to the Web

In the preceding section, you saw the mechanics of rendering to a filesystem. However, most of today's applications are written for the web. Along with URL requests, you can use Reporting Services web services to render reports programmatically to the web.

While doing this, most of your steps will be identical to rendering to the filesystem; you simply change the interface. Using the ListChildren method, developers can easily bind a list of reports to an ASP.NET GridView or create a tree view of available reports. Likewise, developers could use the GetItemParameters method to create their own web-based parameter interface.

Because you have seen both the ListChildren and GetItemParameters methods, in this section you work more with the specifics of developing ASP.NET applications. You see what kinds of changes you can make to the web.config file to pass credential information to Reporting Services. Then you look at the mechanics of rendering to the ASP.NET HttpResponse object.

Using Integrated Windows Authentication

Every security model has two main components: authentication and authorization. In Reporting Services, you can use Windows Integrated Authentication within an ASP.NET application to authenticate users. Before you start this example, you need to ensure that your application is configured to use Integrated Windows Authentication.

When deploying an ASP.NET web application to leverage Windows Authentication, you need to open IIS and change some settings of the virtual directory for your website. Make sure that Anonymous Access has been turned off and that Integrated Windows Authentication has been turned on in IIS. Also, if you are not impersonating users in your web application, you will want to configure the application pool identity for your website with a service account and password that has access to the Reporting Services catalog.

Using Integrated Windows Authentication in an ASP.NET web application is the easiest way to take advantage of the security features in Reporting Services. Using this method allows developers to concentrate on other areas of an application without having to build their own authentication mechanism. It also lets you take full advantage of the Reporting Services role-based security model.

In addition to updating the target IIS web server settings for your website to use Integrated Windows Authentication, you have to make some modifications to your ASP.NET web application.

While developing for ASP.NET, you can leverage the Visual Studio Development Server to quickly debug your application. The only caveat is that the web application will run under the identity of the user account that started the Visual Studio devenv.exe process. In most cases, this will be your own user account, so you must be sure to grant yourself permissions in the Reporting Services catalog accordingly.

For this demonstration, you need to create a new ASP.NET Web Application using your .NET language of choice (for example, C# or VB).

Modifying the web.config File

In the web application created for this demonstration, you want to pass the user's security credentials to the Reporting Services web service. To accomplish this, you have to allow your ASP.NET application to impersonate the currently logged-on user. Setting up impersonation requires adding the following line of code to the `web.config` file. Place this line after the authentication element in the file:

```
<identity impersonate="true" />
```

If your `web.config` file does not contain an authentication element, you must first add this element with the appropriate mode attribute for Windows authentication, and place the identity element inside of it:

```
<authentication mode="Windows" />
<identity impersonate="true" />
```

> **NOTE** *On newer systems using VB.NET code, we have found it necessary to add the following element to the Web.Config file within the system.webServer element:*
>
> ```
> <validation validateIntegratedModeConfiguration= "false" />
> ```
>
> *Adding this element should prevent the system from generating a migration error message.*

Setting Up the Report Execution Web Service

The example needs only Rendering functionality, so you will use only the Report Execution web service. However, you generally need to also interact with the `ReportingService2010.asmx` web service, as discussed in the previous section.

For this example, I've added a web reference to `http://localhost/reportserver/reportexecution2005.asmx` and named it `REService`.

Rendering to the Response Object

Now that you have set up Windows Integrated Authentication, modified the `web.config` file, you're ready to write some code. In this simple application, you will have one page that takes in a report path and format from the URL. You'll use this information to call the `Render` method of the Report Execution web service object and write that information back to the response stream.

This example uses one ASP.NET page called `Render.aspx`. Place your code sample in the page's `Page_Load` event. This would be a logical approach when developing an application around Reporting Services. It allows you to have one point of entry to the Report server. The page could then be referenced from other areas of an application. For the entry page, you will use a simple `Default.aspx` page that has the path and format as a textbox and drop-down box. The `Default.aspx` page passes the `Format` and `Path` parameters to the `Render.aspx` page on a button event. Although the input for this example is simple, a more robust example could be built using the same technique that was shown in the previous section.

Let's add some code to the page's Page_Load event to retrieve the report path and format from the HTTP Request object:

C#

```
string path = Request.Params["Path"];
string format = Request.Params["Format"];
```

VB

```
Dim path As String = Request.Params("Path")
Dim format As String = Request.Params("Format")
```

Now that you have the report path and format, you can start setting up the ReportExecutionService object. This is an instance of the Web Service reference, similar to what you did in the Windows Forms application. You will create an instance of the ReportExecutionService object and then set the credentials to the credentials of the currently logged-on user:

C#

```
//create the ReportExecutionService object
ReportExecutionService _rsExec = new ReportExecutionService();

//set the credentials to be passed to reporting services
_rsExec.Credentials = System.Net.CredentialCache.DefaultCredentials;
```

VB

```
'create the ReportingService object
Dim _rsExec As New ReportExecutionService

'set the credentials to be passed to Reporting Services
_rsExec.Credentials = System.Net.CredentialCache.DefaultCredentials
```

As soon as the ReportingService object has been created and your credentials are set, you can render the report. You will create variables to pass any report parameters (none in this example) and capture the report's encoding, MIME type, parameters used, warnings, and stream IDs. The key output parameter, through which you'll render your report, is the MIME type. This parameter tells the HTTP Response object which type of document is being passed back. The following code renders your report to the web application. Notice that it is identical to the code used in the Windows Forms application:

C#

```
ParameterValue[] parameters = new ParameterValue[0];

byte[] result = null;
string historyID = null;
string devInfo = null;
string encoding;
string mimeType;
string extension;
REService.Warning[] warnings = null;
string[] streamIDs = null;
```

```
_rsExec.LoadReport(path, historyID);
_rsExec.SetExecutionParameters(parameters, "en-us");
result = _rsExec.Render(format, devInfo, out extension,
                out encoding, out mimeType, out warnings, out streamIDs);
```

VB

```
Dim parameters As ParameterValue()
Dim result() As Byte
Dim historyID As String
Dim devInfo As String
Dim encoding As String
Dim mimeType As String
Dim extension As String
Dim warnings() As Warning
Dim streamIDs() As String

_rsExec.LoadReport(path, historyID)
_rsExec.SetExecutionParameters(parameters, "en-us")
result = _rsExec.Render(format, devInfo, extension, encoding, _
        mimeType, warnings, streamIDs)
```

The Render method of the ReportExecutionService object returns a byte array that can be used in several ways. For the web, you write this information directly back to the HTTP Response object. Before you write back the data, however, you need to set some information about the report—namely, a filename. To do this, you use the name of the report followed by an extension that you determine using the value returned in the extension variable.

Now construct the filename using the following code. The code uses the information returned from the Render method:

C#

```
string reportName = path.Substring(path.LastIndexOf("/") + 1);
string fileName = reportName + "." + extension;
```

VB

```
Dim reportName As String = path.Substring(path.LastIndexOf("/") + 1)
Dim fileName As String = reportName & "." & extension
```

Finally, you need to put it all together by writing the data and file information back to the HttpResponse object. Do the following:

1. Clear any information that is already in the response buffer.

2. Set the content type of the response equal to the MIME type of your rendered report.

3. Attach your filename information to the response if your report is in a format other than HTML.

4. Use the BinaryWrite method to write the rendered report byte array directly to the Response object.

The following is the completed code for the `Page_Load` event:

C#

```csharp
protected void Page_Load(object sender, EventArgs e)
{
    if (!Request.Params.HasKeys())
        Response.Redirect("</Default.aspx");

    //get the path and output format from the query string
    string path = Request.Params["Path"];
    string format = Request.Params["Format"];

    var _rsExec = new ReportExecutionService();
    _rsExec.Credentials = System.Net.CredentialCache.DefaultCredentials;

    // Prepare report parameter.
    // The GetParameters method could be implemented as was shown in
    // the previous section on rendering to the file system.
    ParameterValue[] parameters = new ParameterValue[0];

    // Variables used to render the report.
    byte[] result = null;
    string historyID = null;
    string devInfo = null;
    string encoding;
    string mimeType;
    string extension;
    REService.Warning[] warnings = null;
    string[] streamIDs = null;

    // Load the report, set the parameters and then render.
    _rsExec.LoadReport(path, historyID);
    _rsExec.SetExecutionParameters(parameters, "en-us");
    result = _rsExec.Render(format, devInfo, out extension, out encoding,
            out mimeType, out warnings, out streamIDs);

    string reportName = path.Substring(path.LastIndexOf("/") + 1);
    string fileName = reportName + "." + extension;

    //Write the report back to the Response object.
    Response.Clear();
    Response.ContentType = mimeType;

    //Add the file name to the response if it is not a web browser format.
    if (mimeType != "text/html")
        Response.AddHeader("Content-Disposition", "attachment; filename=" +
                        fileName);

    Response.BinaryWrite(result);
}
```

VB

```vb
Protected Sub Page_Load(ByVal sender As Object, ByVal e As System.EventArgs)
    Handles Me.Load
```

```vb
Dim path As String = Request.Params("Path")
Dim format As String = Request.Params("Format")

'create the ReportingService object
Dim _rsExec As New ReportExecutionService

'set the credentials to be passed to Reporting Services
_rsExec.Credentials = System.Net.CredentialCache.DefaultCredentials

'prepare report parameters
Dim parameters(0) As ParameterValue

'variables used to render the report
Dim result() As Byte
Dim historyID As String
Dim devInfo As String
Dim encoding As String
Dim mimeType As String
Dim extension As String
Dim warnings() As Warning
Dim streamIDs() As String

_rsExec.LoadReport(path, historyID)
_rsExec.SetExecutionParameters(parameters, "en-us")
result = _rsExec.Render(format, devInfo, extension, encoding, _
         mimeType, warnings, streamIDs)

Dim reportName As String = path.Substring(path.LastIndexOf("/") + 1)
Dim fileName As String = reportName & "." & extension

'write the report back to the Response object
Response.Clear()
Response.ContentType = mimeType
'add the file name to the response if it is not a web browser format
If mimeType <> "text/html" Then
    Response.AddHeader("Content-Disposition", "attachment; " _
                       & "filename=" & fileName)
End If
Response.BinaryWrite(result)

End Sub
```

This example demonstrates some of the key pieces of code you can use to render reports to the web. You first need to set the application's security context by configuring Windows Integrated Authentication and allowing impersonation from your application (or provide credentials for the application pool that can access the Report server). Next, you retrieve a report from Reporting Services by specifying the report path and format. Finally, you use the rendered report data along with its associated MIME type to render the report using the HTTP Response object.

Now that the code for your web application is complete, let's take a look at using your Render.aspx page. You can use a simple query string to render a report. Here's a sample query string that renders the Internet Sales KPI Dashboard report from the sample reports in HTML5 format:

```
http://localhost/Render.aspx?Path=/Wrox SSRS 2016 Samples/Internet Sales KPI
Dashboard&Format=HTML5
```

This URL does the following:

➤ It calls the `Render.aspx` page from your C# project.

➤ It passes in the required parameters: the path (`/Wrox SSRS 2016 Samples/Internet Sales KPI Dashboard`) and the Format (HTML5).

Notice that when you enter HTML 4.0 as the output format, the report data is rendered directly in the browser. In your code, the MIME type of your HTTP `Response` is `text/html` in this scenario. When the browser receives the response, it recognizes the MIME type and renders it directly to the browser.

> **NOTE** *Depending on your security settings, the web browser asks if you want to save the HTML page or open it. You can click Open to view the report in the browser.*

Let's take a quick look at rendering in a format that does not go directly to the browser. Use the following URL to render the same Employee List report, but in `EXCELOPENXML` format:

```
http://localhost/Render.aspx?Path=/Wrox SSRS 2016 Samples/Internet Sales KPI
Dashboard&Format=EXCELOPENXML
```

> **NOTE** *When rendering to Excel, it's a good idea to use the EXCELOPENXML format, which is the standard format for Excel 2007 and newer. Files are saved with an `.xlsx` file extension. The EXCEL format renders to the older binary format with an `.xls` file extension.*

When you set the format to a document format, you are prompted to save to the filesystem. In this case, the MIME type needs to be set to `application/vnd.ms-excel`. You also need to add header information to the `HttpResponse` object that contains the filename `Internet Sales KPI Dashboard.xlsx`. The MIME type notifies Internet Explorer or Edge browsers that you are sending a file, and the added header gives it the appropriate filename.

In this section, you have seen some of the base mechanics of rendering a report using an ASP.NET application. To start, you need to pass the currently logged-on user's credentials (or the credential of the application pool). You do this by setting the application's virtual directory to use Windows Integrated Authentication and then modifying the `web.config` file for the application to use impersonation. In the code, you need to call the Report Execution web service to retrieve the report along with content information such as MIME type. As soon as you have the binary report data, you can write that information directly back to the `HttpResponse` object.

USING THE REPORTVIEWER CONTROL

The `ReportViewer` control enables you to integrate reports into custom applications with little program code. It also affords detailed management of many properties and report behavior using program code.

A quick history of the `ReportViewer` control is in order. Since it was released, many improvements were made in the version for Visual Studio 2010 for SSRS 2008 but only a few changes were made up to Visual Studio 2015 and the initial release of SQL Server 2016. Future versions will be available for download separately from Visual Studio, and it is likely that a new version will be released after this book is published. Because of the necessity for the Microsoft teams to coordinate product versions, the `ReportViewer` has historically supported features of Reporting Services that are one version behind the current release. (This is particularly true of local mode RDLC reports.)

The examples in this section use version 11 (called the Report Viewer 2012 Runtime), which was updated in 2014 and can be downloaded from `https://www.microsoft.com/en-us/download/details.aspx?id=35747`.

> **NOTE** *RDLC reports generated with this version of the* `ReportViewer` *control support RDL version 2008, which is currently two versions behind 2016.*

For starters, an out-of-the-box Reports Application project is listed in the New Project list, as shown in Figure 15-15.

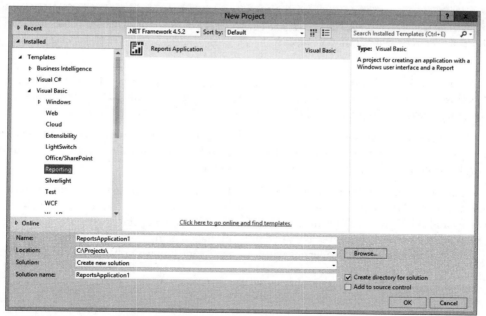

FIGURE 15-15: New Project dialog.

When the Reports Application project template is selected, it creates a new Windows Forms application project with a form containing the `ReportViewer` control and a Report RDLC file. It also automatically starts the Report Wizard, as shown in Figure 15-16.

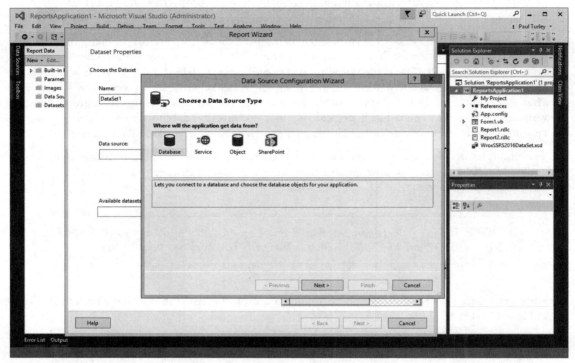

FIGURE 15-16: Data Source Configuration Wizard.

The Report Wizard walks you through creating a data source, selecting an existing data source, saving the connection information to the configuration file, choosing the database objects you want to report on, and then creating a report based on those objects.

The Reports Application project is a great starting point, but the `ReportViewer` control can also be added to any custom application. In Visual Studio, the control is automatically made available under a grouping in the toolbox called Reporting, as shown in Figure 15-17.

The `ReportViewer` control is by far the most flexible and, in most cases, the easiest technique for adding a report to your .NET application. Two separate but similar controls are available—.NET Windows Forms and ASP.NET Web Forms applications. All the user-interface attributes you have seen in the Web Portal and Designer Preview tab can be managed using properties of the control and can be set at design time in the Properties window, or at run time using program code. You can even dynamically create an instance of the control, set its properties programmatically, and render a report without adding it to a form in the designer.

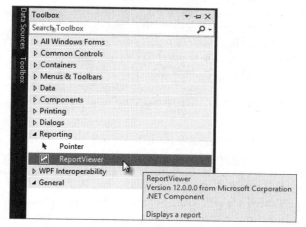

FIGURE 15-17: ReportViewer control properties.

The `ReportViewer` controls are client-side controls that do not need a SQL Server instance to be used. Their only dependency is the .NET Framework 3.51 or newer.

The source data used by the controls can come from any data source, not just SQL Server. The `ReportViewer` controls themselves don't know where the data comes from. Your application brings in the data from whichever source you choose and makes it available to the `ReportViewer` controls in the form of an `IEnumerable` collection, such as ADO.NET `DataTables`, `IQueryable` objects, or custom collections. The `ReportViewer` controls don't even know how to connect to databases or execute queries. By requiring the host application to supply the data, you can use the `ReportViewer` controls with any data source, including relational, nonrelational, and nondatabase data sources.

Two different report execution scenarios are supported in both types of the `ReportViewer` control:

➤ Remote Mode

➤ Local Mode

In Remote mode, standard RDL reports are deployed and executed on the Report server and then are viewed in the control as you would expect. This is similar to the approach used by the Web Portal's `ReportViewer.aspx` page when accessing reports as HTML via URL access.

In Local mode, the `ReportViewer` control acts as a mini report-hosting engine that allows reports to execute in your application without needing a connection to the Report server. In fact, the control hosts a complete version of the SSRS processing and rendering engine, which makes this possible. However, this requires a different version of the report definition file that has been retrofitted for client-side execution. The file is an RDLC file, where the C stands for client-side processing.

> **NOTE** *The* `ReportViewer` *control version 11 supports the RDL 2008 schema while in local processing mode. However, when executing server reports in Remote mode, it does not support the SSRS 2005 version of the Report server. Also, for reports created with the RDL 2010 or 2016 schema, the report processing and rendering are done on the server. Therefore, you can leverage newer features, such as maps, sparklines, KPI indicators, and report parts (introduced in 2008 R2) and parameter layout (introduced in 2016), from within the report viewer.*

Both RDL and RDLC formats have the same base XML schema, but the latter allows some of its XML elements to contain empty values. RDLC also ignores the `<Query>` element of the RDL schema. Actually, the `<Query>` element is included in the XML file only if the file began its life as an RDL format and was later manually converted to an RDLC. When client-side processing files are created using the Visual Studio wizards, the generated file will already have omitted unnecessary elements. RDLC files may also contain design-time information that the `ReportViewer` control uses to generate data-binding code.

You can create an RDLC report by manually converting an RDL report into RDLC by using the Report Creation Wizard, by using the Add New Item dialog in Visual Studio, or by generating the RDLC programmatically.

The last option opens a world of opportunities for custom applications. You can create a custom user interface to allow users to generate new reports on the fly by interacting with your own business/domain data model and then serialize your in-memory report to XML based on the RDL schema. As soon as you have the XML, you can simply provide it to the `ReportViewer` control, along with the data, during execution. In fact, this is similar to how the Report Designer works inside Visual Studio, except that it adds the missing XML elements related to data querying and saves the serialized XML to a file on disk.

Embedding a Server-Side Report in a Windows Application

In the following exercise you view a server-side report in a Windows Forms application using the `ReportViewer` control in Remote mode. The properties and methods of the Web Forms version of the control are nearly identical, making your code transportable between Windows and web application projects. You start by just viewing a report in your custom application and then move on to working with the report's parameters in your code.

As you know, the report rendering interface can generate several toolbar options and parameter prompts when rendering a server report. You can either use these default UI elements or replace them with your own. When you start working with the report parameters, you hide the default prompts and force the user to enter the parameters through your custom application. This gives you much control over how the user interacts with the report and allows you to introduce robust parameter validation according to your business requirements.

To get started, open up Visual Studio, and select File ⇨ New ⇨ Project. Select the Windows Forms Application project template for either C# or VB. This will create a new project with a blank Windows Form and the required references.

The example uses the Sales_by_Region report used throughout this section. First, you will add a form to your Visual Studio Windows Application project. Drag and drop the ReportViewer control onto the form. Resize and anchor it to meet your needs.

The first thing to notice about the ReportViewer control is the drop-down Context menu used to configure the control's most important aspects. The drop-down allows you to choose a specific report or choose a report from a Report server. You can also set the Report server URL and the report path, as well as kick off the Report Wizard to design a new report and dock the report in the current container.

Set the Report Server property to the local report server, and then set the report path to the Sales_by_Region report. You can do this quickly by clicking the smart tag button to the right of the ReportViewer control (the little arrow) to open the common tasks dialog, as shown in Figure 15-18.

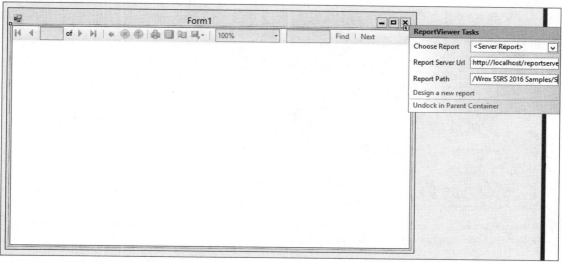

FIGURE 15-18: ReportViewerTasks smart tag panel.

The ReportPath property is the report location in the Report server catalog. In this case, we've selected a report on the local server to display in the ReportViewer control. The location of the Report server is set using the ReportServerUrl property. The ReportPath and ReportServerUrl properties can also be accessed under the ServerReport grouping in the Properties pane of the Visual Studio IDE when the control has focus in the designer.

Because you will use the Report server for processing, set the ProcessingMode property to Remote. This will cause the Report server to query and retrieve source data that will be used in the report. In Remote mode, the ReportViewer controls display reports that are hosted on a SQL Server Reporting Services server. The source data for those reports can come from any appropriate data source, not just SQL Server. This behavior is normal report processing behavior—specific not to the viewer controls, but rather to the Reporting Services platform.

You are now ready to run the custom application and view the report in a Windows Form, as shown in Figure 15-19.

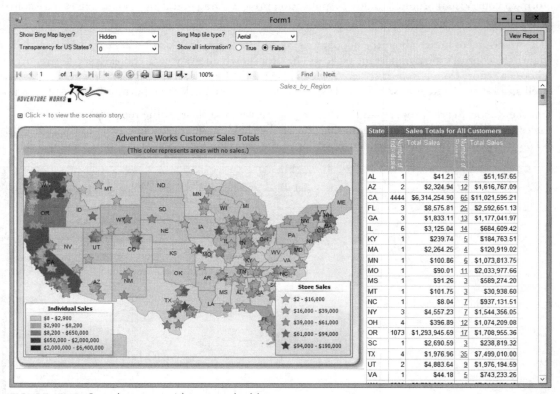

FIGURE 15-19: Sample report with map and table.

You have seen a simple example of running a report in a custom application; however, you might also want to add functionality to control the parameters that the users see and select. For example, let's introduce a slider (TrackBar) that controls the opacity parameter for the Bing Maps layer of this report to replace the standard drop-down values.

Because the available list of values for the opacity parameter is a nonlinear set of six values (0, 10, 25, 35, 50, 75), you must create an array that maps these values to an indexer to correspond to the slider's ticks. Let's add this array as a private member to our form. Then we can load it with values in the form constructor. The following code is from the code-behind for the Form1 class (partial class):

C#

```
private int[] _trackBarValues = new int[6];
public Form1()
{
```

```
        InitializeComponent();
        _trackBarValues[0] = 0;
        _trackBarValues[1] = 10;
        _trackBarValues[2] = 25;
        _trackBarValues[3] = 35;
        _trackBarValues[4] = 50;
        _trackBarValues[5] = 75;
    }
```

VB

```
    Private _trackBarValues As Integer() = New Integer(5) {}
    Public Sub New()
        ' This call is required by the designer.
        InitializeComponent()

        _trackBarValues(0) = 0
        _trackBarValues(1) = 10
        _trackBarValues(2) = 25
        _trackBarValues(3) = 35
        _trackBarValues(4) = 50
        _trackBarValues(5) = 75
    End Sub
```

Next, we will add our new controls to the form, above the ReportViewer control, to collect parameter input from the user. We will need to add a label and combo box (name it ShowMapLayerComboBox) for the parameter ShowBingMaps and specify the values Hidden and Visible as the items for the combo box by entering these values in the Items property of the combo box.

Now, add another label and a TrackBar control, located in the All Windows Forms toolbox group, to the form to correspond to the USStatesTransparency parameter, which controls the opacity level of the Bing Map layer when it is visible. For the TrackBar, be sure to set the properties TickFrequency to 1, Minimum to 0, and Maximum to 5. This ensures that we have a total of only six ticks on the slider to map to the number of available values for this report parameter. In addition, we'll set the Enabled property to false so that the slider is enabled only when the user chooses to set the Bing Maps layer parameter to visible.

Finally, we'll add a new button to the form, give it the text "View Report," and create an empty click-event handler method by double-clicking it. We'll add code in there later.

Your form design surface should look like Figure 15-20.

Now we need to edit the Form Load event and remove the line of code that automatically refreshes the ReportViewer control. Because we first will give the users a chance to select parameters, we don't want the report to run when the form opens. Also, we'll add the following line of code to preselect the first item in the combo box:

C#

```
    private void Form1_Load(object sender, EventArgs e)
    {
        this.ShowMapLayerComboBox.SelectedIndex = 0;
    }
```

VB

```
Private Sub Form1_Load(sender As Object, e As EventArgs) Handles MyBase.Load
    Me.ShowMapLayerComboBox.SelectedIndex = 0
End Sub
```

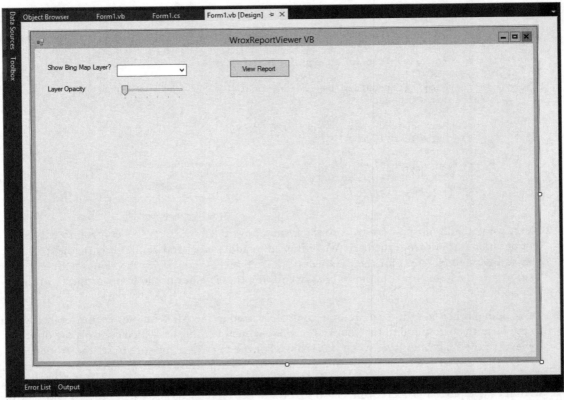

FIGURE 15-20: WroxReportViewer form running.

With every property of the ReportViewer control (except the parameters that we are providing via our user interface) set using the Properties window, the only necessary code is to set our two parameters and execute the report.

Parameters are managed as an array of ReportParameter objects. Because we are overriding two of the required parameters, we will create an array of two elements. Each element is populated by passing the parameter name and value to each ReportParameter constructor.

To use the ReportParameter object, you need to either add the following using/Imports statement to your code, or instantiate the object using the full Microsoft.Reporting.WinForms namespace. Adding the using/Imports statement provides for much cleaner and easier-to-read code, so add the following statements to your form's code-behind file:

C#

```
using Microsoft.Reporting.WinForms;
```

VB

```vb
Imports Microsoft.Reporting.WinForms
```

The report parameters are populated by passing the array to the SetParameters method of the ServerReport object.

Finally, the ReportViewer's RefreshReport method causes report execution to begin.

The last two event handlers are for the combo box, to enable or disable the slider based on the selection, and the button click event. Here is the form's complete code section:

C#

```csharp
using System;
using System.Windows.Forms;
using Microsoft.Reporting.WinForms;

namespace WroxReportViewer
{
    public partial class Form1 : Form
    {
        private int[] _trackBarValues = new int[6];
        public Form1()
        {
            InitializeComponent();
            _trackBarValues[0] = 0;
            _trackBarValues[1] = 10;
            _trackBarValues[2] = 25;
            _trackBarValues[3] = 35;
            _trackBarValues[4] = 50;
            _trackBarValues[5] = 75;
        }

        private void Form1_Load(object sender, EventArgs e)
        {
            this.ShowMapLayerComboBox.SelectedIndex = 0;
        }

        private void ShowMapLayerComboBox_SelectedIndexChanged(object sender,
        EventArgs e)
        {
            this.trackBar1.Enabled =
                (sender as ComboBox).SelectedItem.ToString()
                    .Equals("visible", StringComparison.OrdinalIgnoreCase);
        }

        private void button1_Click(object sender, EventArgs e)
        {
            ReportParameter[] parameters = new ReportParameter[2];

            parameters[0] = new  ReportParameter("ShowBingMaps",
            this.ShowMapLayerComboBox.SelectedItem.ToString());

            parameters[1] = new ReportParameter("USStatesTransparency",
            _trackBarValues[this.trackBar1.Value].ToString());
```

```
                    reportViewer1.ServerReport.SetParameters(parameters);
                    reportViewer1.ShowParameterPrompts = false;
                    reportViewer1.ShowPromptAreaButton = false;
                    reportViewer1.RefreshReport();
                }
            }
        }
```

VB

```
    Imports System
    Imports Microsoft.Reporting.WinForms

    Public Class Form1
        Private _trackBarValues As Integer() = New Integer(5) {}
        Public Sub New()
            ' This call is required by the designer.
            InitializeComponent()

            _trackBarValues(0) = 0
            _trackBarValues(1) = 10
            _trackBarValues(2) = 25
            _trackBarValues(3) = 35
            _trackBarValues(4) = 50
            _trackBarValues(5) = 75
        End Sub
        Private Sub Form1_Load(sender As Object, e As EventArgs) Handles MyBase.Load
            Me.ShowMapLayerComboBox.SelectedIndex = 0
        End Sub

        Private Sub ShowMapLayerComboBox_SelectedIndexChanged(sender As Object, e _
        As EventArgs) Handles ShowMapLayerComboBox.SelectedIndexChanged
            Me.trackBar1.Enabled = DirectCast(sender,
            ComboBox).SelectedItem.ToString().Equals("visible",
            StringComparison.OrdinalIgnoreCase)
        End Sub

        Private Sub button1_Click(sender As Object, e As EventArgs) _
          Handles button1.Click
            Dim parameters As ReportParameter() = New ReportParameter(1) {}
            parameters(0) = New ReportParameter("ShowBingMaps",
            Me.ShowMapLayerComboBox.SelectedItem.ToString())
            parameters(1) = New ReportParameter("USStatesTransparency",
            _trackBarValues(Me.trackBar1.Value).ToString())

            ReportViewer1.ServerReport.SetParameters(parameters)
            ReportViewer1.ShowParameterPrompts = False
            ReportViewer1.ShowPromptAreaButton = False
            ReportViewer1.RefreshReport()
        End Sub
    End Class
```

Figure 15-21 shows the result. The report is displayed in the `ReportViewer` control embedded on the form. The standard report parameter bar and prompts are not displayed in the top of the viewer because they were suppressed using the related `ReportViewer` properties.

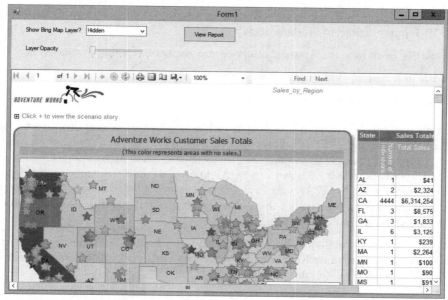

FIGURE 15-21: Report in viewer application.

The `ReportViewer` controls provide an easy-to-implement way to embed reports in your custom web and Windows applications. They also give you complete control over the code for the rest of the application to provide users with an all-around solution.

SUMMARY

This chapter showed you three ways to render reports from Reporting Services. The first part of the chapter focused on rendering reports via URL requests. The second part looked at rendering reports programmatically through the Reporting Services web services. In the last part, you used the `ReportViewer` control to easily embed reports in a Windows Forms application.

URL rendering gives you a quick way to add Reporting Services reports to your own applications. You can add Reporting Services reports to custom portals or create your own custom report links in other applications.

Rendering reports directly through an ASP.NET application can be helpful. It allows developers to create their own interface for items such as parameters using well-known UI constructs in HTML. A key point to remember is that Web Portal uses the same Reporting Services web services used in the examples in this chapter. Therefore, anything you can do from the Web Portal can also be done through your own code. This adds an incredible amount of flexibility for developers of custom applications.

This chapter has shown you how to do the following:

➤ Use simple URL query strings to access reports.

➤ Programmatically work with the Reporting Service and Report Execution Service APIs.

➤ Embed reports into custom Windows and web applications.

➤ Work with the `ReportViewer` control in Visual Studio.

Because the Reporting Services APIs are implemented as web services, you can call them from various types of applications, including .NET Windows applications, ASP.NET web applications, and .NET console applications. You can even use these web services from older applications created with Visual Basic 6.0, VBA applications using Microsoft's SOAP library, or essentially any application that can send a properly formatted SOAP request to the Report server. This flexibility lets you create a number of applications, including those that use custom security or pass parameter information stored in other application databases.

You learn to extend the core functionality of Reporting Services in Chapter 16. You explore extensibility options and reasons for extending Reporting Services with custom extensions for accessing data, authenticating users, rendering, and delivering content.

16

Extending Reporting Services

WHAT'S IN THIS CHAPTER?

➤ Leveraging extensibility options

➤ Reasons for extending SQL Server Reporting Services

➤ Creating custom extensions

➤ Installing custom extensions

When I teach Reporting Services and work with teams to build reporting solutions, I find that certain analogies help put topics into perspective. When the average person buys a car, only a small fraction of that group would consider swapping out the engine or putting in a different exhaust system. Such endeavors require a lot of time and patience. I am not a serious grease monkey but I have disassembled and installed my fair share of car components, and learned quite a lot in the process. Likewise, learning how reporting extensions work internally will give you a better understanding of the core SSRS product. With respect to Reporting Services, if you are a serious mechanic and need to retrofit your reporting solution; this chapter is for you.

> **NOTE** *Before you get into this topic, I will give you some context. In even the most serious, large-scale reporting solutions, developing custom extensions for Reporting Services is quite rare in practice. I will caution you to approach this option only if absolutely necessary, after you have achieved a firm understanding of the native capabilities in the SSRS platform.*

As you learned in previous chapters, Reporting Services is a robust and scalable product for enterprise report processing. In addition, Microsoft has created Reporting Services using a modular extensible architecture that allows users to customize, extend, and expand the product to support their enterprise business intelligence (BI) reporting needs. This chapter introduces you to most of the areas within Reporting Services that allow customization and explains some of the reasons that you might want to extend the product. The Reporting Services extension libraries and application programming interfaces have not really changed since version 2008 R2. Therefore, this chapter is relatively unchanged from the previous edition of the book. I have updated and tested the examples to work with SSRS 2016 and Visual Studio 2015.

The basic requirements for implementing each type of extension are discussed, followed by a detailed example of creating and deploying a data processing extension.

Reporting Services currently supports extending its behavior in the following areas:

➤ **Data processing extensions (DPEs)**—Custom DPEs enable you to access any type of data using a consistent programming model. This option is for you if you cannot access your data using one of the currently supported providers (Analysis Services, Hyperion Essbase, ODBC, OLE DB, Oracle, Report Model, SAP BI NetWeaver Business Intelligence, SQL Server, Teradata, SQL Azure, Parallel Data Warehouse, SharePoint List, and XML). Microsoft has also released a Feature Pack for SQL Server that provides customized extensions, such as SAP Relational DB and DB2, in addition to the ones built into the product.

➤ **Delivery extensions**—Do you want the report sent to your cell phone in PDF format, or perhaps delivered to a file share for your perusal at a later date? The ability to extend SSRS with delivery extensions allows you to manage the delivery mode and vehicle for sending report content for consumption.

Delivery extensions allow you to deliver reports to users or groups of users according to a schedule. E-mail, network file shares, and SharePoint content are the delivery mechanisms currently built into the product. There is also a delivery extension that preloads the cache with pre-rendered parameterized reports. This extension, known as the "null delivery" extension, is not exposed to users, but rather it is leveraged by administrators of data-driven subscriptions. Creating a delivery extension is really a two-part process. You must create the extension itself, as well as a UI tool to manage the extension if you want it to be usable from the SSRS Report Manager. The difficulty in creating a delivery extension is primarily a function of the delivery mechanism.

➤ **Rendering extensions**—These control the type of document/media that gets created when a report is processed. Theoretically, you could have Reporting Services create any type of media given the ability to extend the product in this area. Microsoft provides the following rendering extensions out of the box:

➤ **HTML**—The HTML extension generates HTML5. Support for HTML 4.0 continues but HTML 3.2 has been discontinued in this version of Reporting Services.

➤ **Excel**—The newer Excel extension creates Excel 2007–2016 compatible files using the Open XML Office format (XLSX). The older Excel rendering extension, which generates XLS files compatible with Excel 97 and later, using the Binary Interchange File Format (BIFF), is still available but is hidden by default via the `RSReportServer.config` file. Page breaks defined in the report cause separate worksheets to be rendered in the resulting workbook file.

➤ **Word**—The new Word rendering extension creates Word 2007–2016 compatible files using the Open XML Office format (DOCX). The older Word rendering extension, which generates DOC files compatible with Word 97 and later, is still available but has been hidden by default via the `RSReportServer.config` file.

➤ **PowerPoint**—The new PPTX rendering extension creates PowerPoint 2007–2016 compatible files using the Open XML Office format (PPTX). Page breaks are applied is if the report were printed and renders one slide per page.

➤ **Image**—The Image extension allows you to export reports as images in the BMP, EMF, GIF, JPEG, PNG, TIFF (default), and WMF formats.

➤ **PDF**—This extension allows the generation of reports in the Adobe PDF format.

➤ **CSV**—Comma-separated values emit the data fields separated by commas as plain text files. The first row of the CSV results contains the field names for the data.

➤ **XML**—This extension renders the report in XML format and allows for optional transformations to manipulate the output of the rendered markup.

➤ **Security extensions**—These allow you to authenticate and authorize users and groups into a report server. In its first release, Reporting Services supported only Integrated Windows Security for report access. This was a pretty big problem for some enterprise players. Most companies have heterogeneous networks with multiple operating systems and products. In a perfect world, all our networks, applications, and resources would support some form of "single sign-on," or at least would allow us to build this ourselves. If Microsoft wanted SQL Server to be a key part of an Enterprise Business Intelligence platform, it had to play nicely with others. Microsoft fixed this problem in Service Pack 1 for SQL Server 2000 and made it a part of SQL Server 2005. The release contained fully documented security extension interfaces and an example using ASP.NET forms-based authentication. You can implement your custom security model using SSRS, but only one security extension can be used per Reporting Services instance.

➤ **Report processing extensions (Custom Report Items)**—This extension type came with the 2005 release of Reporting Services. It enabled the creation of custom report items that were processed by the report processing engine. This enables us to extend the RDL standard to include functionality not natively supported by the RDL, such as custom maps and horizontal lists. Developers can also extend current report items to provide alternative versions that better fit their needs.

➤ **Report definition customization extensions**—This extension type, which was introduced with the 2008 release, provides a hook into the preprocessing of the report definition. You can plug in custom code that can modify the report definition stream before it gets processed. This is handy, for example, if you need to modify the report's layout based on a culture, locale, or user identity that is specified with the report request. Note that you are not guaranteed where or when in the request pipeline the customization will occur, but you *are* guaranteed that it will always happen before the processing of the report definition takes place. For this extension, a new interface was included and is required to be implemented:

```
IReportDefinitionCustomizationExtension
```

EXTENSION THROUGH INTERFACES

Reporting Services uses common interfaces or "extension points" to allow expanding the product in a standard way. Enforcing the requirement that RS extension objects must implement certain interfaces allows Reporting Services to interact with different object types without knowledge of their specific implementation. This is a common object-oriented programming technique used to abstract the design from the implementation.

> **NOTE** *For an in-depth study of this topic, look at Chapter 3, "Creational Patterns," of* Design Patterns: Elements of Reusable Object-Oriented Software, *by Erich Gamma, Richard Helm, Ralph Johnson, John M. Vlissides, and Grady Booch (Addison-Wesley, 1994).*

What Is an Interface?

Most C/C++ developers are intimately familiar with *interfaces*. Seasoned .NET developers know about interfaces because we use them to interact with Framework Class Libraries (FCLs) and to program to contracts for loosely coupled code. In fact, Reporting Services itself is exposed to developers through a web service interface. To provide complete coverage of extending Reporting Services, a definition and an explanation of interfaces are required.

So what is an interface? An *interface* is a predefined code construct that forms a contract between software components and defines how they communicate. The interface provides an abstraction layer of its entity to the outside.

That sounds great, but what does it mean? It simply means that to adhere to the contract defined by an interface, all extension components must contain certain methods, properties, and so on.

In Reporting Services specifically, it means that every extension component must contain certain methods defined by the IExtension interface. Other interface implementations may be required as well, depending on the type of extension you are trying to create.

Interface Language Differences

There are differences in how VB.NET and C# require interface methods to be declared. C# supports "implicit" interface definitions. If the method names and signatures match those of an interface that the class implements, the class methods are automatically mapped to their associated interface definitions. We chose System.IDisposable for this example because many of the classes you will create are required to implement it:

C#

```
public class TestClass : System.IDisposable
{
  //this method is automatically mapped to IDisposable.Dispose
  public void Dispose()
  {
      //write some code to dispose of non-memory resources
  }
}
```

VB.NET requires explicit interface implementation. To be mapped correctly, VB.NET requires that you specify that the method is implementing a certain interface. You do this with the `Implements` keyword:

VB.NET

```vbnet
Public Class TestClass
    Implements IDisposable

    Public Sub Dispose() Implements IDisposable.Dispose
        'write some code to dispose of non-memory resources
    End Sub
End Class
```

Visual Studio provides code refactoring features that assist with interface implementation—specifically, a feature called Interface AutoComplete. When you indicate that a class should implement a certain interface, Visual Studio can generate wrapper methods for all the properties, methods, and so on that are required for that interface. This is evident when viewing a class in the Visual Studio Object Explorer, shown in Figure 16-1. This saves a lot of typing and is a great productivity enhancement when you're creating objects designed to "plug in to" an existing framework.

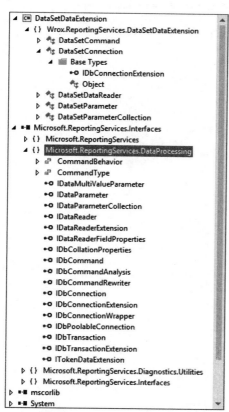

FIGURE 16-1: Reporting Services interfaces in Visual Studio.

Microsoft is also attempting to build "best practices" into Visual Studio. Although the two examples just shown are technically correct in that they implement IDisposable, they do not implement the IDisposable design pattern shown in the .NET Framework SDK. Allowing Visual Studio to do the heavy lifting creates a more feature-complete implementation that includes consideration for cascading object chains and explicit release of memory and non-memory resources. Visual Studio would create code similar to the following for IDisposable. We did take liberties with the comments to make it easier to read:

C#

```csharp
public class TestDispose : System.IDisposable
{
    private bool disposed = false;

    //IDisposable
    private void Dispose(bool disposing)
    {
        if (! this.disposed)
        {
            if (disposing)
            {
                // TODO: put code to dispose of managed resources here
            }
            // TODO: put code to free unmanaged resources here
        }
        this.disposed = true;
    }

    //IDisposable Support
    //Don't change
    public void IDisposable.Dispose()
    {
        // Don't change. Put cleanup code
        // in Dispose(bool) above.
        Dispose(true);
        GC.SuppressFinalize(this);
    }

    // Don't change
    protected void Finalize()
    {
        Dispose(false);
        base.Finalize();
    }

}
```

VB.NET

```vbnet
Public Class TestDispose
    Implements System.IDisposable

    Private disposed As Boolean = False
```

```
'IDisposable
Private Overloads Sub Dispose(ByVal disposing As Boolean)
    If Not Me.disposed Then
        If disposing Then
            ' TODO: put code to dispose of managed resources here
        End If
        ' TODO: put code to free unmanaged resources here
    End If
    Me.disposed = True
End Sub

'IDisposable Support
'Don't change
Public Overloads Sub Dispose() Implements IDisposable.Dispose
    ' Don't change. Put cleanup code
    ' in Dispose(ByVal disposing As Boolean) above.
    Dispose(True)
    GC.SuppressFinalize(Me)
End Sub

' Don't change
Protected Overrides Sub Finalize()
    Dispose(False)
    MyBase.Finalize()
End Sub

End Class
```

You will be using this Interface AutoComplete feature for the remainder of this chapter. Extensions for Reporting Services must be compiled using the .NET Framework 3.5 or newer. The generated code for `IDisposable` is suitable for demonstration purposes, so we won't repeat this code for each object; we'll simply indicate that it is required.

A Detailed Look at Data Processing Extensions

Reporting Services allows you to access data from traditional data sources such as relational databases using the existing .NET data providers. The following providers are supported as part of the .NET Framework supplied by Microsoft:

➤ ODBC

➤ OLE DB

➤ SqlClient

DPEs are components that allow you to access data for use within Reporting Services. If that implies a ".NET data provider" to you, congratulations are in order. These two types of data access objects are very similar and are based on a common set of interface definitions. If you have already built a custom .NET data provider, you can use that provider with Reporting Services with no modification. However, you also can extend your existing provider to offer additional functionality.

To begin, we need to discuss the similarities and differences between a standard .NET data provider and a Reporting Services DPE. Let's start with some architectural information about data providers in general and then dive into the details of creating a custom DPE. The .NET Framework has a data access object model named ADO.NET, as shown in Figure 16-2.

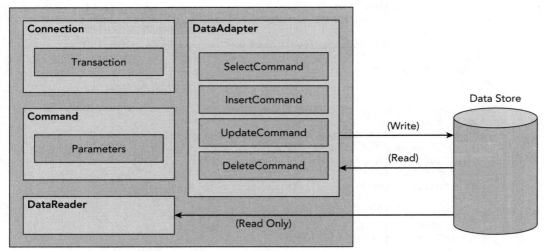

FIGURE 16-2: ADO.NET object model.

Ever since Service Pack 1 of SSRS on SQL Server 2000, it has been possible to customize and extend the security model of Reporting Services. This required adding a few things to the object model.

Here are the basic steps for working with a data source:

1. Connect to a data source.

2. Issue a command to manipulate data.

3. Retrieve the results of your query.

These actions map directly to the objects just described, although a `DataAdapter` implementation is not needed because Reporting Services only reads the data.

Table 16-1 lists the objects that are normally created in a DPE and describes their responsibilities.

TABLE 16-1: Data Processing Extension Objects

OBJECT	DESCRIPTION
`Connection`	Establishes a connection to a specific data source.
`Command`	Executes a command against a data source. Exposes a `Parameterscollection` and can execute within the scope of a transaction.
`DataReader`	Provides access to data using a forward-only, Read Only stream.
`DataAdapter`	Retrieves data and resolves updates with the data source. This object is not required for a DPE because SSRS only needs to read the data to create reports.

Each of these objects contains implementation-specific code needed to create a connection, issue commands, or read and update data. Microsoft has enforced a consistent data access mechanism by basing these objects on a set of standard interfaces. You can use the Object Explorer to explore the interfaces that may be implemented when creating a DPE, although not all of them are required. You can build a minimalist `DataExtension` by implementing the required interfaces listed in Table 16-2 and add additional behavior by implementing the optional interfaces listed in Table 16-3.

TABLE 16-2: Data Processing Extensions Required Interfaces

REQUIRED INTERFACE	DESCRIPTION
IDataParameter	Methods to support passing parameters to a Command object
IDataParameterCollection	Collection of parameters
IDataReader	Methods used to read a forward-only, Read Only data stream
IDbCommand	Represents query command methods to be executed against a data source
IDbConnection	Unique session with a data source
IExtension	Reporting Services–specific interface that supports localization and is implemented by all SSRS extensions

TABLE 16-3: Data Processing Extensions Optional Interfaces

OPTIONAL INTERFACE	DESCRIPTION
IDataReaderExtension	Provides Resultset-specific aggregation information
IDbCommandAnalysis	Analysis Services–specific extension
IDbConnectionExtension	Unique session with a data source
IDbTransaction	Local transaction (nondistributed)
IDbTransactionExtension	Reporting Services–specific interface that supports localization and is implemented by all SSRS extensions

CREATING A CUSTOM DATA PROCESSING EXTENSION

Creating a full-blown data provider is no trivial task. The goal of this walkthrough is to familiarize you with the .NET data access mechanism, as well as help you create and install a custom Reporting Services DPE. Our implementation is simplified in that it does not support transactions or the use of parameters, and many of the methods are empty unless code is explicitly required. The code snippets are given in both C# and VB unless there is a reason to do otherwise.

The Scenario

The first release of Reporting Services (with SQL Server 2000) lacked support for consuming existing ADO.NET DataSet objects. After the release of Service Pack 1, the Books Online documentation contained a sample extension that used some of the dataset's intrinsic properties to allow you to query a DataSet object and limit the resulting rows based on certain criteria. The only problem was that you couldn't do complex filtering or limit the columns that a query returned.

In SQL Server 2005, Reporting Services gained a new data processing extension—the XML data extension. This enabled reports to retrieve data from XML content, which could be located in a file, hosted on a web or file server, or even better, from web services. This new extension provided an XPATH-like syntax for the command text, giving it greater flexibility for searching through data within the XML as well as supporting schemata and namespaces. This DPE has remained largely unchanged through to the current SQL Server 2016 release.

Interestingly, many companies have data stores that never really talk to each other directly, and remain isolated. These companies usually have requirements to query those data sources and create reports that join all that data. SSRS does not provide an explicit mechanism to federate data across multiple servers, besides SQL Server's Linked Server features. If linked servers are just not an option for you, you are left to come up with a creative solution for the situation.

The XML data extension may be useful in this scenario. You can set up a web service that does the dirty work of joining data from multiple tables in memory using ADO.NET. Then all that SSRS needs to provide to the web method is a collection of command texts to be executed, such as SQL statements or stored procedure names, and the relationship details, such as key columns and types of joins. Once the web service has executed the commands and joined the data tables in memory, it returns the XML dataset ready for SSRS to consume.

In our example, we'll provide a similar but more simplistic extension that shows the fundamental pieces required to implement the Reporting Services Interfaces and consume data from an XML dataset file. The ADO.NET DataSet type contains a method that allows it to read in the data from XML and build the internal data table that Reporting Services will consume.

Creating and Setting Up the Project

Let's start by creating our project. Launch Visual Studio, and create the project by choosing File ⇨ New Project. Change the name of the project to DataSetDataExtension. Use the Class Library template with the language of your choice.

> **NOTE** *By default, your project will target a recent version of the .NET Framework. As of the current build of the Reporting Services components, .NET Framework 3.5 is required and my Visual Studio 2015 project works by default with version 4.5.2. You can change the target .NET Framework on the Application page of the project properties.*

After you create your project, you need to set up your environment to help you work. The Visual Basic IDE tends to hide some things from you, so you will make some changes to help our C# brethren follow along. The first thing you want to do is show all your references. The default behavior of

VB.NET is to hide them. Choose Project ➪ Show All Files. The Explorer tab should now show all your project references.

Next, you need to add the references to the required Reporting Services DLL file. The `Microsoft.ReportingServices.DataProcessing` namespace is needed to implement the DPE interfaces, and the `Microsoft.ReportingServices.Interfaces` namespace is needed to implement the `IExtension` interface. Both of these namespaces are defined in the same assembly file, `Microsoft.ReportingServices.Interfaces.dll`.

The extensions and their dependencies are located in a subdirectory below the installation directory of SQL Server itself. We will call the SQL Server installation path `<InstallPath>`. You need the following directory for the SSRS extensions DLL:

```
<InstallPath>\MSRS13.MSSQLSERVER\Reporting Services\ReportServer\bin
```

> **NOTE** *On my machine, this directory is* `C:\Program Files\Microsoft SQL Server\MSRS13.MSSQLSERVER1400\Reporting Services\ReportServer\bin`.

Choose Project ➪ Add Reference. Select the Browse tab, find the appropriate directory, and add the reference. Your Solution Explorer window should now look something like that shown in Figure 16-3.

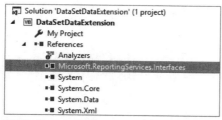

FIGURE 16-3: Reference added to ReportingServices.Interfaces.

Change the name of the project assembly to reflect your custom namespace for the project. Choose Project ➪ Properties. At this point, you can either fill in the root namespace for your components or put it in your code. The sample code contains the namespaces directly. This was another way to avoid IDE problems, as shown in Figure 16-4.

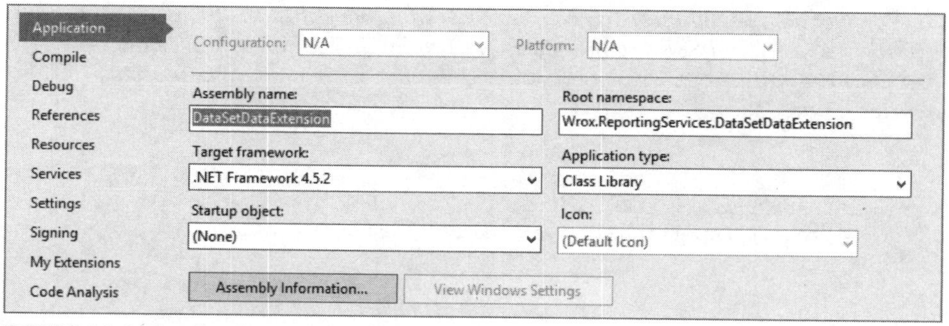

FIGURE 16-4: Application page and assembly information.

Most of the classes created for this project have common requirements. Several of them have empty, default constructors, and all of them require the use of some common namespaces. The code shown next is a skeleton of how each class should look after you create it. Replace the *ClassName* with the name of the class you are working on. This will allow you to concentrate on only the differences between the objects that will be created in your data extension project.

In this example, you will work with `DataSet` objects that are defined in the `System.Data` namespace. To support the SSRS interface requirements, you should include the `Microsoft.ReportingServices.DataProcessing` namespace at the top of your classes. This is the namespace where the interface `IExtension` is defined. Because the common data interfaces are defined in both ADO.NET and SSRS namespaces, you should fully qualify one of them to avoid name collisions and ambiguous reference errors. For the sake of saving keystrokes, we will fully qualify `System.Data` object types instead of the SSRS one when we use it. This namespace, however, is not needed in the `DataSetParameter` and `DataSetParameterCollection` classes.

C#

```csharp
using System;
using Microsoft.ReportingServices.DataProcessing;
using System.Data;

namespace Wrox.ReportingServices.DataSetDataExtension
{
    public class DataSetClassName
    {
    }
}
```

VB.NET

```vbnet
Imports System
Imports Microsoft.ReportingServices.DataProcessing
Imports System.Data

Namespace Wrox.ReportingServices.DataSetDataExtension
    Public Class DataSetClassName

    End Class
End Namespace
```

> **NOTE** *You can also use namespace aliases to avoid name collisions between types in the* ADO.NET *and SSRS namespaces. The following snippet shows how you can alias the* Microsoft.ReportingServices.DataProcessing *namespace to a shorter name:*
>
> **C#**
>
> ```csharp
> using RSDataProc =
>     Microsoft.ReportingServices.DataProcessing;
> ```

```
VB.NET
        Imports RSDataProc =
            Microsoft.ReportingServices.DataProcessing;
```

Creating the DataSetConnection Object

The DataSetConnection object is responsible for connecting to the data source and providing a mechanism for accessing both the DPE-specific Transaction and Command objects. These responsibilities are enforced through the IDbConnection interface. The DataSetConnection object is the extension entry point and will be the first object in the extension that will deal with Reporting Services. As such, it also is required to implement the IExtension interface, as discussed earlier.

Because the DataSetConnection object is usually responsible for connecting to an unmanaged resource, it is required to implement IDisposable. The aggregate interface for all these others is IDbConnectionExtension, which is what you will implement. Figure 16-5 shows a diagram created with the Visual Studio class designer. Having the class designer within Visual Studio makes it easier to implement and understand the relationships between objects in a complex system.

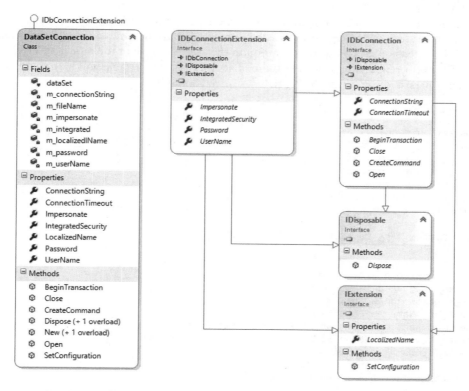

FIGURE 16-5: Interfaces in Visual Studio Class Designer.

To add the `DataSetConnection` class to the project, choose Project ➪ Add Class. Change the name of the class to `DataSetConnection`. Open the file and indicate that the class should implement the `IDbConnectionExtension` interface, as just discussed. Visual Studio creates all the wrapper methods for you. Because you will be doing file I/O and using regular expressions to parse your `ConnectionString` property, you need to add those namespaces to this class:

C#

```
using System;
using System.IO;
using System.Text.RegularExpressions;
using Microsoft.ReportingServices.DataProcessing;
```

VB.NET

```
Imports System
Imports System.IO
Imports System.Text.RegularExpressions
Imports Microsoft.ReportingServices.DataProcessing
```

Variable Declarations

To maintain state for your connection object, you need to declare some member variables. The `m_connectionString` variable will hold the connection string that will be used to connect to the data source. The `m_localizedName` variable should hold a localized name of the current extension used to list the extension as a data source option in the user interface of tools such as Visual Studio Report Designer or SQL Management Studio. The `m_fileName` variable will hold the path to the `DataSet` object persisted (serialized) as XML.

C#

```
private string m_userName;
private string m_password;
private bool m_integrated;
private string m_impersonate;
private string m_connectionString = String.Empty;
private string m_localizedName = "DataSet Data Source";
private string m_fileName;

internal System.Data.DataSet dataSet;
```

VB.NET

```
Private m_impersonate As String
Private m_integrated As Boolean
Private m_password As String
Private m_userName As String
Private m_connectionString As String = String.Empty
Private m_localizedName As String = "DataSet Data Source"
Private m_fileName As String

Friend dataSet As System.Data.DataSet = Nothing
```

Constructors

The `DataSetConnection` object has an empty default constructor. It also has an overloaded constructor that allows the developer to create the object and initialize the connection string in one line of code.

C#

```csharp
public DataSetConnection(string connectionString)
{
        this.m_connectionString = connectionString;
}
```

VB.NET

```vbnet
Public Sub New(ByVal connectionString As String)
        Me.m_connectionString = connectionString
End Sub
```

Implementing IDbConnectionExtension

IDbConnectionExtension adds support for extending the SSRS security model, which is used to authenticate and authorize the connection to the data source. The interface definition is shown next. Notice the unusual use of WriteOnly properties:

C#

```csharp
public interface IDbConnectionExtension : IDbConnection, IDisposable, IExtension
{
        // Properties
        string Impersonate { set; }
        bool IntegratedSecurity {get; set; }

        string Password { set; }
        string UserName { set; }
}
```

VB.NET

```vbnet
Public Interface IDbConnectionExtension
        Implements IDbConnection, IDisposable, IExtension

        ' Properties
        WriteOnly Property Impersonate As String
        Property IntegratedSecurity As Boolean
        WriteOnly Property Password As String
        WriteOnly Property UserName As String
End Interface
```

Impersonate Property

Windows supports the concept of impersonation, in which a process of execution can "assume" the identity of a set of assigned security credentials. The Impersonate property lets you assign a string representing the user account whose security context the process should run under.

C#

```csharp
public string Impersonate
{
        set { m_impersonate = value; }
}
```

```
Public WriteOnly Property Impersonate() As String
   Implements IDbConnectionExtension.Impersonate
      Set(ByVal value As String)
          m_impersonate = value
      End Set
End Property
```

IntegratedSecurity Property

The IntegratedSecurity property indicates whether you want the extension to run using Windows security for both authentication (identifying the user) and authorization (denying/granting a user permission to perform certain actions).

C#

```
public bool IntegratedSecurity
{
    get{ return m_integrated;}
    set {m_integrated = value;}
}
```

VB.NET

```
Public Property IntegratedSecurity() As Boolean
    Implements IDbConnectionExtension.IntegratedSecurity
      Get
          Return m_integrated
      End Get
      Set(ByVal value As Boolean)
          m_integrated = value
      End Set
End Property
```

UserName and Password Properties

The UserName and Password properties are used during the Reporting Services authentication process. The UserName/Password pair is authenticated against either the Windows credential store or some custom store you provide. Next, a principal object that implements IPrincipal is created and assigned to the current thread of execution. That object contains the user's identity and role membership information and is used to authorize user access to system resources (the data source). Good security practice dictates that this information be available for the shortest time possible—thus the use of Write Only properties.

C#

```
public string Password
{
    set { m_password = value; }
}

public string UserName
{
    set { m_userName = value; }
}
```

VB.NET

```vbnet
Public WriteOnly Property Password() As String
  Implements IDbConnectionExtension.Password
        Set(ByVal value As String)
            m_password = value
        End Set
End Property

Public WriteOnly Property UserName() As String
  Implements IDbConnectionExtension.UserName
        Set(ByVal value As String)
            m_userName = value
        End Set
End Property
```

Implementing IDbConnection

The IDbConnection interface is the standard mechanism that data providers use to control the use of the DataSetConnection object. These properties and methods help you change the connection settings, open and close the connection, and associate the connection with a valid transaction. Your connection object does not support transactions because of its Read Only nature and because, in this DPE example, you are working against a filesystem, which is not a resource manager. Here is the definition of the IDbConnection interface:

C#

```csharp
public interface IDbConnection : IDisposable, IExtension
{
        IDbTransaction BeginTransaction();
        IDbCommand CreateCommand();
        void Open();
        void Close();
        string ConnectionString { get; set; }
        int ConnectionTimeout { get; }
}
```

VB.NET

```vbnet
Public Interface IDbConnection
    Inherits IDisposable, IExtension
        Function BeginTransaction() As IDbTransaction
        Function CreateCommand() As IDbCommand
        Sub Open()
        Sub Close()
        Property ConnectionString() As String
        Property ConnectionTimeout() As Integer
End Interface
```

After adding the DataSetConnection class to your project, you will need to implement the IExtension interface as shown here:

C#

```csharp
public string LocalizedName
{
```

```
        get
        {
            return m_localizedName;
        }
    }
    public void SetConfiguration(string configuration) {}
```

VB.NET

```
    Public ReadOnly Property LocalizedName() As String Implements
    IDbConnection.LocalizedName
        Get
            Return m_localizedlName
        End Get
    End Property

    Public Sub SetConfiguration(ByVal configuration As String) Implements
    IDbConnection.SetConfiguration
    End Sub
```

Because the IDbConnection interface implements IDisposable, you must provide an implementation for its Dispose() method:

C#

```
    public void Dispose()
    {
        Dispose(true);
        GC.SuppressFinalize(this);
    }

    protected virtual void Dispose(bool disposing)
    {
        if (disposing)
        {
            this.Close();
        }
    }
```

VB.NET

```
    Public Sub Dispose() Implements IDisposable.Dispose
        Dispose(True)
        GC.SuppressFinalize(Me)
    End Sub

    Protected Overridable Sub Dispose(ByVal disposing As Boolean)
        If disposing Then
            Me.Close()
        End If
    End Sub
```

BeginTransaction Method

The BeginTransaction method is primarily responsible for initiating a new transaction and returning a reference to a valid, implementation-specific Transaction object. The filesystem, which is our data store, does not support transactions, but the interface requires this method. You need to ensure that the developer who will use your object in code knows this. You do so by throwing a NotSupportedException.

C#

```csharp
public IDbTransaction BeginTransaction()
{
    // this example does not support transactions
    throw new NotSupportedException("Transactions not supported");
}
```

VB.NET

```vbnet
Public Function BeginTransaction() As IDbTransaction _
    Implements IDbConnection.BeginTransaction
        ' example does not support transactions
        Throw New NotSupportedException("Transactions not supported")
End Function
```

CreateCommand Method

The CreateCommand method is responsible for creating and returning a reference to a valid implementation-specific Command object. The method uses an overloaded constructor of your custom Command object to pass that object a reference to the current connection. Also, notice that it will create and return a new instance of the DataSetCommand type, which you will be creating later on.

C#

```csharp
public IDbCommand CreateCommand()
{
    // Return a new instance of the implementation-specific command object
    return new DataSetCommand(this);
}
```

VB.NET

```vbnet
Public Function CreateCommand() As IDbCommand _
    Implements IDbConnection.CreateCommand
        ' Return a new instance of the implementation-specific command object
        Return New DataSetCommand(Me)
End Function
```

Open Method

In a full data provider implementation, the Open method is used to make a data source–specific connection. This sample implementation uses the Open method to create an instance of a generic dataset object from ADO.NET and fills it from the XML file provided in your ConnectionString property.

C#

```csharp
public void Open()
{
    this.dataSet = new System.Data.DataSet();
    this.dataSet.ReadXml(this.m_fileName);
}
```

VB.NET

```
Public Sub Open() Implements IDbConnection.Open
     Me.dataSet = New System.Data.DataSet
     Me.dataSet.ReadXml(Me.m_fileName)
End Sub
```

Close Method

The Close method is used to close your data source–specific connection. You will use the Close method to release the DataSet object you have in memory.

C#

```
public void Close()
{
     this.dataSet = null;
}
```

VB.NET

```
Public Sub Close() Implements IDbConnection.Close
     Me.dataSet = Nothing
End Sub
```

ConnectionString Property

The ConnectionString property allows you to set the connection string through code. This property uses a private variable to store the current connection string, which provides the information needed to connect to the data source. Most developers are familiar with this property because of its frequent use in both traditional ADO and ADO.NET. In this DPE example, the ConnectionString property is used to indicate the XML dataset file that you will parse for data. The user of your DPE should input the path to the file he or she wants to parse into the connection string textbox of the Report Designer's Dataset dialog or the shared data source's Properties page. You will store the connection string value in the private member variable m_connectionString.

C#

```
public string ConnectionString
{
     get {return m_connectionString;}
     set {m_connectionString = value;}
}
```

VB.NET

```
Public Property ConnectionString() As String _
   Implements IDbConnection.ConnectionString
     Get
          Return m_connectionString
     End Get
     Set(ByVal Value As String)
          m_connectionString = Value
     End Set
End Property
```

You want to enforce that the value passed into the `ConnectionString` property meets your criteria for supplying the information needed to connect to the data source. You want to enforce that the string is in this format:

```
FileName=c:\FileName.xml
```

The easiest way to validate the string format is to use regular expressions. You need to modify the default `Set` accessor of the `ConnectionString` property to reflect this change. First, you will execute the static/shared `Match` method of the `Regex` class.

> **NOTE** *You are passing in an expression that basically says "Parse the connection string and make matches on character arrays that are preceded by* `FileName=` *and are not composed of beginning-of-line characters or semicolons."*

All that is left is to test to see if the filename is valid and, if so, assign it to your private filename variable. Your code should resemble the following:

C#

```csharp
set
{
    this.m_connectionString = value;

    Match m = Regex.Match(value, "FileName=([э;]+)",RegexOptions.IgnoreCase);
    if (!m.Success)
    {
        string msg = "\"FileName=<filename>\" must be present in the connection"+
                "string and point to a valid DataSet xml file";
        throw (new ArgumentException(msg, "ConnectionString"));
    }

    string filename = m.Groups[1].Captures[0].ToString();
    if (!File.Exists(filename))
    {
        string msg = "Incorrect file name, or file does not exist";
        throw (new ArgumentException(msg, "ConnectionString"));
    }

    this.m_fileName = filename;
}
```

VB.NET

```vbnet
Set(ByVal Value As String)
    Me.m_connectionString = Value

    Dim m As Match = Regex.Match(Value, "FileName=([э;]+)",
                RegexOptions.IgnoreCase)
    If Not m.Success Then
        Dim msg As String = "'FileName=<filename>' must be present string " &
                        "and point to a valid DataSet xml file"
```

```
                    Throw (New ArgumentException(msg, "ConnectionString"))
            End If
            If Not File.Exists(m.Groups(1).Captures(0).ToString) Then
                    Throw (New ArgumentException("Incorrect FileName", "ConnectionString"))
            End If
            Me.m_fileName = m.Groups(1).Captures(0).ToString
        End Set
```

ConnectionTimeout Property

The ConnectionTimeout property allows you to set the connection's time-out property. This is used to control how long the interval for connecting to the source should be before an error is thrown. Your sample class does not actually use this value, but it is implemented for consistency and because of interface requirements. Returning a value of 0 indicates that there is an infinite time-out period.

C#

```csharp
public int ConnectionTimeout
{
        get
        {
                // Returns the connection time-out value.
                // Zero indicates an indefinite time-out period.
                return 0;
        }
}
```

VB.NET

```vbnet
Public ReadOnly Property ConnectionTimeout() As Integer _
        Implements IDbConnection.ConnectionTimeout
        Get
                ' Returns the connection time-out value.
                ' Zero indicates an indefinite time-out period.
                Return 0
        End Get
End Property
```

Creating the DataSetParameter Class

The DataSetParameter class is not needed until the command class is created, but because of that dependency, you do need to create it. The parameter object is used to send parameters to the command object that can be used to execute commands against the data source. Despite the fact that this class is not used to perform any work, the interface requirements of the command class force you to create it. This class also has interface requirements; it is required to support the IDataParameter interface defined in the Reporting Services DPE assembly.

To add the DataSetParameter class to the project, choose Project ➪ Add Class, and change the name to DataSetParameter.

Declarations

The following declarations are used internally to hold the parameter's value and name. The name is stored in a string variable called m_parameterName. Because the value variable might contain any type of value, m_parameterValue is declared as an Object type.

C#

```
String m_parameterName = string.Empty;
Object m_parameterValue;
```

VB.NET

```
Dim m_parameterName As String
Dim m_parameterValue As Object
```

Implementing IDataParameter

The IDataParameter interface enforces that your custom parameter class allows a programmer to get and set the name and value of the current parameter.

C#

```
public interface IDataParameter
    {
        string ParameterName { get; set; }
        object Value { get; set; }
    }
```

VB.NET

```
Public Interface IDataParameter
    Property ParameterName() As String
    Property Value() As Object
End Interface
```

Begin by adding a using (C#) or Imports (VB) statement to include the Microsoft .ReportingServices.DataProcessing namespace in the DataSetParameter class file. Modify the class code to force the DataSetParameter class to implement IDataParameter using the Interface AutoComplete technique discussed at the beginning of the chapter. Your code should resemble the following. The wrappers for all your interface methods should have been created automatically and surrounded by region tags. Here is what your parameter class definition should look like:

C#

```
namespace Wrox.ReportingServices.DataSetDataExtension
{
    public class DataSetParameter : IDataParameter
    {
        string m_parameterName = string.Empty;
        object m_parameterValue;
```

```
Namespace Wrox.ReportingServices.DataSetDataExtension
    Public Class DataSetParameter
        Implements IDataParameter

        Private m_parameterName As String = String.Empty
        Private m_parameterValue As Object = Nothing
```

ParameterName Property

The `ParameterName` property is used to store the parameter's name in a string variable called `m_parameterName`. This field is typically used to map to parameters in stored procedures but is unused in this implementation.

C#

```csharp
public string ParameterName
{
    get { return m_parameterName; }
    set { m_parameterName = value; }
}
```

VB.NET

```vbnet
Public Property ParameterName() As String Implements IDataParameter.ParameterName
    Get
        Return m_parameterName
    End Get
    Set(ByVal Value As String)
        m_parameterName = value
    End Set
End Property
```

Value Property

The `Value` property is similar to the name just created in that it is not actually used in this example. The value is stored in an object variable called `m_value`. You will need to include the `System.Diagnostics` namespace at the top of the class file, via the `using` (C#) or `Imports` (VB) keyword, in order to use the `Debug.WriteLine()` method.

C#

```csharp
public object Value
{

    get
    {
        Debug.WriteLine(string.Format("Getting parameter [{0}] value: [{1}]",
        this.m_parameterName, this.m_parameterValue.ToString()));
        return (this.m_parameterValue);
    }
    set
    {
```

```
          Debug.WriteLine(string.Format("Setting parameter [{0}] value: [{1}]",
          this.m_parameterName, this.m_parameterValue.ToString()));
          this.m_parameterValue = value;
      )}
```

VB.NET

```
    Public Property Value() As Object _
        Implements IDataParameter.Value

    Get
        Debug.WriteLine(String.Format("Getting parameter [{0}] value: [{1}]", _
        Me.m_parameterName, _
        Me.m_parameterValue.ToString))
        Return (Me.m_parameterValue)
    End Get
    Set(ByVal Value As Object)
        Debug.WriteLine(String.Format("Setting parameter [{0}] value: [{1}]", _
        Me.m_parameterName, _
        Me.m_parameterValue.ToString))
        Me.m_parameterValue = Value
    End SetEnd Property
```

Creating the DataSetParameterCollection Class

The DataSetParameterCollection class is simply a collection of parameter objects. Although you could have created a custom collection class that implements all the required methods, an easier route exists. The IDataParameterCollection interface is basically a subset of the IList<T> interface that is used to define other generic collections in the .NET Framework. By using an available object, you significantly reduce the required coding effort. In our example, T is the type IDataParameter, which is implemented by our custom DataSetParameter class.

To add the DataSetParameterCollection class to the project, choose Project ➪ Add Class. Change the name of the class to DataSetParameterCollection.

There is no need to create custom constructors or member variables for use in your collection class. This is because you can use the internal variables and constructors that exist inside the List<T> base class that this class inherits from. The properties that you create will be mapped directly to properties and methods that exist in the List<T> class.

Namespaces

The DataSetParameterCollection class uses the standard namespaces just discussed. An additional namespace is needed because of the use of List<T>. You must add the System.Collections .Generic namespace and a private variable for your internal collection.

C#

```
    using System;
    using Microsoft.ReportingServices.DataProcessing;
    using System.Collections.Generic;
```

VB.NET

```
Imports System
Imports Microsoft.ReportingServices.DataProcessing

Imports System.Collections.Generic
```

Implementing IDataParameterCollection

We have created the DataSetParameterCollection class by using an object wrapper around an IList<T> generic collection. Generics are a feature available starting with .NET 2.0 and later versions, so our example will not compile or run within earlier versions of the .NET Framework run time. The IDataParameterCollection interface defines a custom Add method and provides methods to access the members of this collection through the IEnumerable interface. The List<T> base class implements this interface. Your class will use the internal List<IDataParameter> class properties and methods to service its needs. You will need to include the System.Collections namespace at the top of the class file, via the using (C#) or Imports (VB) keyword, in order to use the IEnumerable interface.

C#

```
public interface IDataParameterCollection : IEnumerable
{
    int Add(IDataParameter parameter);
}
```

VB.NET

```
Public Interface IDataParameterCollection
    Inherits IEnumerable
    Function Add(ByVal parameter As IDataParameter) As Integer
End Interface
```

Here's the modified code in C#:

```
namespace Wrox.ReportingServices.DataSetDataExtension
{

    public class DataSetParameterCollection : IDataParameterCollection
    {
        List<IDataParameter> paramList;
        public DataSetParameterCollection()
        {
            paramList = new List<IDataParameter>();
        }

        public IEnumerator GetEnumerator()
        {
            return paramList.GetEnumerator();
        }
```

Here's the modified code in VB.NET:

```
Namespace Wrox.ReportingServices.DataSetDataExtension

    Public Class DataSetParameterCollection
```

```
Implements IDataParameterCollection
Private paramList As List(Of IDataParameter)

Public Sub New()
    paramList = New List(Of IDataParameter)
End Sub

Public Function GetEnumerator() As IEnumerator _
    Implements IEnumerable.GetEnumerator
    Return (paramList.GetEnumerator)
End Function
```

Because most of the functionality of the DataSetParameterCollection class exists through the paramList reference, all you need to do is to create the wrapper Add method required by the IDataParameter interface. The internal collection uses this method to add parameters to an instance of the collection object.

C#

```csharp
public int Add(IDataParameter parameter)
{
    paramList.Add(parameter);
    return paramList.IndexOf(parameter);
}
```

VB.NET

```vbnet
Public Overloads Function Add(ByVal parameter As IDataParameter) As Integer _
    Implements IDataParameterCollection.Add

    paramList.Add(parameter)
    Return paramList.IndexOf(parameter)

End Function
```

Creating the DataSetCommand Class

The command object is responsible for sending commands to the data source. This is enforced by making the object implement the IDbCommand interface, which supplies a standard mechanism for passing in commands to be executed against the data source. It also supplies parameters that might be needed in the process of executing these commands. Finally, it defines a property that allows the developer to associate the command with a Transaction object. Your implementation is simplified in that it does not support transactions or parameters.

In your implementation, this class is where the majority of the work is done. You need to process the command text to know what data the user wants. You must validate that this text conforms to your requirements, and then you need to create the internal data reference that will supply the data for the data reader object to process. You will use some of the built-in behaviors of the System.Data .DataSet class to satisfy your needs.

To add the DataSetCommand class to the project, choose Project ⇨ Add Class. Change the name of the class to DataSetCommand. Use the Interface AutoComplete feature to have Visual Studio create the wrappers for the methods you will implement. Most of the functionality that exists in this extension will live in this class. You will need to include the `Microsoft.ReportingServices` `.DataProcessing` namespace at the top of the class file, via the `using` (C#) or `Imports` (VB) keyword, in order to use the `Debug.WriteLine()` method.

Variable Declarations

Because most of our work is done in this class, it makes sense that most of our code is also in it. First, you need to create variables to hold your property data. This class actually will be a wrapper around some of the built-in `DataSet` functionality, so you will need reference variables for the dataset objects as well as other variables used for text parsing and the like. To avoid being repetitive, we'll discuss the variables in more depth where they are used. You will need to include the `System` `.Text.RegularExpressions` namespace at the top of the class file, via the `using` (C#) or `Imports` (VB) keyword, in order to use the regular expression–specific types.

C#

```
//member variables
int m_commandTimeOut = 0;
string m_commandText = string.Empty;
DataSetConnection m_connection;
DataSetParameterCollection m_parameters;

//dataset variables
string tableName = string.Empty;
System.Data.DataSet dataSet = null;
internal System.Data.DataView dataView = null;

//regex variables
MatchCollection keywordMatches = null;
Match fieldMatch = null;

//regex used for getting keywords
Regex keywordSplit = new Regex(@"(Select|From|Where| Order[ \s] +By)",
    RegexOptions.IgnoreCase | RegexOptions.Multiline
    | RegexOptions.IgnorePatternWhitespace | RegexOptions.Compiled);

// regex used for splitting out fields
Regex fieldSplit = new Regex(@"([∧,\s]+)",
    RegexOptions.IgnoreCase | RegexOptions.Multiline
    | RegexOptions.Compiled | RegexOptions.IgnorePatternWhitespace);

//internal constants
const int SELECT_POSITION = 0;
const int FROM_POSITION = 1;
const string TEMPTable_NAME = "TempTable";

//these variables can change
int keyWordCount = 0;
int wherePosition = 2;
int orderPosition = 3;

bool filtering = false;
bool sorting = false;
bool useDefaultTable = false;
```

VB.NET

```vbnet
'property variables
Private m_cmdTimeOut As Integer = 0
Private m_commandText As String = String.Empty
Private m_connection As DataSetConnection
Private m_parameters As DataSetParameterCollection = Nothing

'dataset variables
Private tableName As String = String.Empty
Private dataSet As FCLData.DataSet
Friend dataView As FCLData.DataView

'regex variables
Private keywordMatches As MatchCollection
Private fieldMatch As Match
Private tableMatch As Match
Private keywordSplit As Regex = New Regex("(Select|From|Where| Order[ \s] +By)",_
        RegexOptions.IgnoreCase Or RegexOptions.Multiline Or _
        RegexOptions.IgnorePatternWhitespace Or RegexOptions.Compiled)
Private fieldSplit As Regex = New Regex("([∧ ,\s]+)", RegexOptions.IgnoreCase Or _
        RegexOptions.Multiline Or RegexOptions.Compiled Or _
        RegexOptions.IgnorePatternWhitespace)

'constants
Private tempTableName As String = "TempTable"
Private selectPosition As Integer = 0
Private fromPosition As Integer = 1
Private wherePosition As Integer = 2
Private orderPosition As Integer = 3

'internal variables

Private keyWordCount As Integer = 0
Private filtering As Boolean = False
Private sorting As Boolean = False
Private useDefaultTable As Boolean = False
```

Constructors

You want the users of your processing extension to be forced to create the Command object either through the CreateCommand method of the IDbConnection interface, or by passing in a valid DataSetConnection object as a parameter. The purpose is to ensure that you have access to the underlying DataSet object created and parsed in the connection process. You can do this by deleting or not providing an empty default constructor. This prevents the developer from creating the DataSetCommand object without the correct initialization. In the constructor, you want to get a reference to the DataSet that you opened from the filesystem in your connection object.

C#

```csharp
internal DataSetCommand(DataSetConnection conn)
{
    this.m_connection = conn;
    this.dataSet = this.m_connection.dataSet;
    this.m_parameters = new DataSetParameterCollection();
}
```

VB.NET

```
Friend Sub New(ByVal conn As DataSetConnection)

        Me.m_connection = conn
        Me.dataSet = Me.m_connection.dataSet
        Me.m_parameters = New DataSetParameterCollection
End Sub
```

Implementing IDbCommand

The required interface for all Command objects is called IDbCommand. It consists of methods that allow the developer to pass commands and parameters to the Command object. The most interesting method in our implementation is the CommandText method, where you will parse the command string provided by the user and return the appropriate data.

C#

```csharp
public interface IDbCommand : IDisposable
{
        void Cancel();
        IDataReader ExecuteReader(CommandBehavior behavior);
        string CommandText { get; set; }
        int CommandTimeout { get; set; }
        CommandType CommandType { get; set; }
        IDataParameter CreateParameter();
        IDataParameterCollection Parameters { get; }
        IDbTransaction Transaction { get; set; }
}
```

VB.NET

```vbnet
Public Interface IDbCommand
    Inherits IDisposable
        Sub Cancel()
        Function ExecuteReader(ByVal behavior As CommandBehavior) As IDataReader
        Property CommandText() As String
        Property CommandTimeout() As Integer
        Property CommandType() As CommandType
        Function CreateParameter() As IDataParameter
        Property Parameters() As IDataParameterCollection
        Property Transaction() As IDbTransaction
End Interface
```

Now that you have created the method wrappers and all the variables you need to work, you can begin implementing your IDbCommand methods.

Cancel Method

The Cancel method is typically used to cancel a method that has been queued. Most implementations of data providers are multithreaded and support the issue of multiple commands against the data store. You created this method only to support the IDbCommand interface requirements. You should inform the developer of your lack of support by throwing a NotSupportedException. You will need to include the System.Diagnostics namespace at the top of the class file, via the using (C#) or Imports (VB) keyword, in order to use the Debug.WriteLine() method.

C#

```
public void Cancel()
{
    Debug.WriteLine("IDBCommand.Cancel");
    throw (new NotSupportedException("IDBCommand.Cancel currently not supported"));}
```

VB.NET

```
Public Sub Cancel() _
        Implements IDbCommand.Cancel

    Debug.WriteLine("IDBCommand.Cancel")
    Throw New NotSupportedException("IDBCommand.Cancel currently not supported")
End Sub
```

ExecuteReader Method

The ExecuteReader method returns an extension-specific reader object to the caller so that it can loop through and read the data. The DataSetCommand object creates an instance of your custom reader object by executing this method. A reference to your custom data reader is then returned. Your implementation actually builds a temporary table with a schema built based on the query issued by the user. You don't want to fill this temporary table unless the user actually requests the data, so you are checking to see if it is a schema-only command.

You are also checking to see if the users indicated that they want all the fields available from the data source. If that is the case, you use a view of the default DataTable, which already contains all the data. Notice that you will return a new DataSetDataReader, which you will create later in the chapter.

C#

```
public IDataReader ExecuteReader (CommandBehavior behavior)
{
    if(!(behavior == CommandBehavior.SchemaOnly) && !useDefaultTable)
    {
        FillView();
    }
    return (IDataReader) new DataSetDataReader(this);
}

private void FillView()
{
    System.Data.DataRow tempRow = null;
    string[] tempArray = null;
    int count;

    count = this.dataSet.Tables[TEMPTable_NAME].Columns.Count;
    tempArray = new string[count];
```

```
        foreach (System.Data.DataRow row in this.dataSet.Tables[this.tableName].Rows)
        {
            tempRow = this.dataSet.Tables[TEMPTable_NAME].NewRow();

            foreach (System.Data.DataColumn col in this.dataSet.Tables[TEMPTable_NAME]
              .Columns)
            {
                tempArray[col.Ordinal] = row[col.ColumnName].ToString();
            }

            tempRow.ItemArray = tempArray;
            this.dataSet.Tables[TEMPTable_NAME].Rows.Add(tempRow);
        }

        // go ahead and clean up the array instead of waiting for the GC
        tempArray = null;
    }
```

VB.NET

```
    Public Function ExecuteReader(ByVal behavior As CommandBehavior) As IDataReader _
      Implements IDbCommand.ExecuteReader
        If Not (behavior = CommandBehavior.SchemaOnly) AndAlso Not useDefaultTable Then
            FillView()
        End If
        Return CType(New DataSetDataReader(Me), IDataReader)
    End Function

    Private Sub FillView()
        Dim tempRow As System.Data.DataRow = Nothing
        Dim tempArray As String() = Nothing
        Dim count As Integer
        count = Me.dataSet.Tables(tempTableName).Columns.Count
        tempArray = New String(count - 1) {}
        For Each row As System.Data.DataRow In Me.dataSet.Tables(Me.tableName).Rows
            tempRow = Me.dataSet.Tables(tempTableName).NewRow
            For Each col As System.Data.DataColumn In _
Me.dataSet.Tables(tempTableName).Columns
                tempArray(col.Ordinal) = row(col.ColumnName).ToString
            Next
            tempRow.ItemArray = tempArray
            Me.dataSet.Tables(tempTableName).Rows.Add(tempRow)
        Next
    End Sub
```

CommandText Property

Reporting Services does not manually create a separate Command object. It uses the CreateCommand method of the IDbConnection interface to return an implementation-specific Command object. We will use the CommandText property to help us build the data schema that we will return, as well as fill our data source for use of Reporting Services. This method has been broken into methods reflecting the actual work being done and to facilitate this discussion. Notice the ValidateCommandText method. It is the entry point for your text-parsing and table-building process and you will create it later in the chapter. You will need to include the `System.Diagnostics` namespace at the top of the class file, via the `using` (C#) or `Imports` (VB) keyword, in order to use the `Debug.WriteLine()` method.

C#

```
public string CommandText
{
    get
    {
        Debug.WriteLine("IDBCommand.CommandText: Get Value =" +
        this.m_commandText);
        return this.m_commandText;
    }
    set
    {
        Debug.WriteLine("IDBCommand.CommandText: Set Value =" + value);
        ValidateCommandText(value);
        this.m_commandText = value;
    }
}
```

VB.NET

```
Public Property CommandText() As String Implements IDbCommand.CommandText
    Get
        Debug.WriteLine("IDBCommand.CommandText: Get Value =" &
        Me.m_commandText)
Return (Me.m_commandText)
    End Get
    Set(ByVal value As String)
        Debug.WriteLine("IDBCommand.CommandText: Get Value =" &
        Me.m_commandText)
        ValidateCommandText(value)
        Me.m_commandText = value
    End Set
End Property
```

The `ValidateCommandText` method is used to parse the command text to ensure that it meets the requirements for the extension. The first step is to apply the `keywordSplit` regular expression that was defined in the member variable section. The regular expression is `(Select|From|Where|Order [ \s] +By)`, which could be translated into English as follows: "Match the keywords `Select`, `From`, `Where`, and `Order`, where each is followed by the word `By`, but allow spaces and nonvisible characters between them." After you have parsed the statement, you can make some basic assumptions based on the number of matches. At a minimum, you require that the user tell you the Field names and the table name that he or she wants to pull the information from. This means that you must have a `Select` keyword, followed by a Field List, and a `From` keyword, followed by a table name. Thus, the minimum keyword count is 2. If you have a keyword count greater than 2, you know that the user has given you either a filtering criterion such as `Where userID = 3` or a sort criterion such as `Order by lastname ASC`. You can find out which by checking the value in the third position. If that value is a `Where` clause, you can assume that the user wants filtering. If it is not, assume that sorting is the order of the day. If the count is 4, you know that both filtering and sorting are needed. The `ValidateCommandText` method will also call other `Validate` methods, which are discussed and implemented in the following paragraphs.

C#

```csharp
private void ValidateCommandText(string cmdText)
{
    keywordMatches = keywordSplit.Matches(cmdText);
    keyWordCount = keywordMatches.Count;
    switch (keyWordCount)
    {
        case 4:
            sorting = true;
            filtering = true;
            break;
        case 3:
            if (keywordMatches [keyWordCount - 1]
                .ToString()
                .ToUpper() == "WHERE")
                filtering = true;
            else
            {
                sorting = true;
                orderPosition = 2;
            }
            break;
        case 2:
            break;
        default:
            string msg = "Command Text should start with 'select <fields> " +
                         "from <tablename>'";
            throw new ArgumentException(msg);
    }

    ValidateTableName(cmdText);
    ValidateFieldNames(cmdText);

    if (filtering)
    {
        ValidateFiltering(cmdText);
    }

    if (sorting)
    {
        ValidateSorting(cmdText);
    }
}
```

VB.NET

```vbnet
Private Sub ValidateCommandText(ByVal cmdText As String)
    keywordMatches = keywordSplit.Matches(cmdText)
    keyWordCount = keywordMatches.Count
    Select Case keyWordCount
        Case 4
            sorting = True
            filtering = True
            ' break
```

```
            Case 3
                If keywordMatches (keyWordCount - 1).ToString.ToUpper = _
                    "WHERE" Then
                    filtering = True
                Else
                    sorting = True
                End If
            Case Else
                Dim msg As String = "Command Text should start with 'select " & _
                                    "<fields> from <tablename>'"
                Throw (New ArgumentException(msg))
        End Select
        ValidateTableName(cmdText)
        ValidateFieldNames(cmdText)

        If filtering Then
            ValidateFiltering(cmdText)
        End If

        If sorting Then
            ValidateSorting(cmdText)
        End If
    End Sub
```

The next step in the process is validating that the table name and Field names provided by
the user are valid. You have created methods specifically for this purpose. Shown next is the
ValidateTableName method. In the member declaration section, constant values were created, indicating the assumed positions of the keywords within the command text. The table name must immediately follow the From keyword. You then use that keyword's position to locate the table name.
Next, you check to see if your internal DataSet contains this table. If so, the table name is valid;
otherwise, it is invalid.

C#

```csharp
private void ValidateTableName(string cmdText)
{
    //Get tablename
    //get 1st match starting at end of from
    fieldMatch = fieldSplit.Match(cmdText,
                    (keywordMatches [FROM_POSITION].Index)
            + keywordMatches [FROM_POSITION].Length + 1);
    if(fieldMatch.Success)
    {
        if(this.dataSet.Tables.Contains(fieldMatch.Value))
        {
            this.tableName = fieldMatch.Value;
        }
        else
        {
            throw new ArgumentException("Invalid Table Name");
        }
    }
}
```

VB.NET

```
Private Sub ValidateTableName(ByVal cmdText As String)
    fieldMatch = fieldSplit.Match(cmdText, _
    (keywordMatches (FROM_POSITION).Index) + _
        keywordMatches (FROM_POSITION).Length + 1)
    If fieldMatch.Success Then
        If Me.dataSet.Tables.Contains(fieldMatch.Value) Then
            Me.tableName = fieldMatch.Value
        Else
            Throw New ArgumentException("Invalid Table Name")
        End If
    End If
End Sub
```

The next step is to validate the Field names. You also want users to be able to use the * character to indicate that they want all the fields without having to list them individually. This is standard SQL syntax. You need to parse all the text between the Select statement and the From statement. You do this using the constant values created earlier to signify character position and a regular expression to pull out exactly what you are interested in.

The fieldSplit regular expression looks like ([^ ,\s]+). In English, this reads as follows: "Match all character groups that do not contain spaces, commas, and nonvisible white space and that have spaces at the end." If the first field is an asterisk, you know that the user wants all fields. This means that you do not have to build a temporary table to reflect the schema and that you can use the table she requested in the From portion of the text. If the first field is not an asterisk, you must build a temporary table reflecting the schema of the data you will return. To avoid problems with a user changing the fields, and the temp table previously existing, you will simply test for its existence each time and remove it if you must.

Next, you check to see whether the Field names exist in your main table by testing to see whether the column names exist. If they do, the column is valid, and you add a column with this name to your new temp table. You continue to do this as long as the Field names are valid. If an invalid field is submitted, you throw an exception to make the user aware of her mistake.

C#

```
public void ValidateFieldNames(string cmdText)
{
    //get fieldnames
    //get first match starting at the last character of the Select
    // with a length from that position to the from
    fieldMatch = fieldSplit.Match(cmdText,
    (keywordMatches [SELECT_POSITION].Index +
        keywordMatches [SELECT_POSITION].Length + 1),
    (keywordMatches [FROM_POSITION].Index -
        (keywordMatches [SELECT_POSITION].Index +
            keywordMatches [SELECT_POSITION].Length + 1)));

    if (fieldMatch.Value == "*")  // all fields, use default view
    {
        this.dataView = this.dataSet.Tables[this.tableName].DefaultView;
        this.useDefaultTable = true;
```

```
    }
    else   //custom fields : must build table/view
    {
        //don't use default table
        this.useDefaultTable = false;

        //remove table if exists - add new
        if (this.dataSet.Tables.Contains(TEMPTable_NAME))
        {
            this.dataSet.Tables.Remove(TEMPTable_NAME);
        }

        System.Data.DataTable table = new System.Data.DataTable(TEMPTable_NAME);

        //loop through column matches
        while (fieldMatch.Success)
        {
            if (this.dataSet.Tables[this.tableName]
                        .Columns.Contains(fieldMatch.Value))
            {
                System.Data.DataColumn col = this.dataSet.Tables[this.tableName]
                        .Columns[fieldMatch.Value];
                table.Columns.Add(
                        new System.Data.DataColumn(col.ColumnName, col.DataType));
                fieldMatch = fieldMatch.NextMatch();
            }
            else
            {
                throw new ArgumentException("Invalid column name");
            }
        }

        //add temptable to internal dataset and set view to tempView;
        this.dataSet.Tables.Add(table);
        this.dataView = new System.Data.DataView(table);
    }
}
```

VB.NET

```
Private Sub ValidateFieldNames(ByVal cmdText As String)
    fieldMatch = fieldSplit.Match(cmdText, _
(keywordMatches (selectPosition).Index + _
keywordMatches (selectPosition).Length + 1), _
(keywordMatches (fromPosition).Index -  keywordMatches (selectPosition).Index _
 + keywordMatches (selectPosition)
.Length + 1)))

    If fieldMatch.Value = "*" Then
        Me.dataView = Me.dataSet.Tables(Me.tableName).DefaultView
        Me.useDefaultTable = True
    Else
        Me.useDefaultTable = False
        If Me.dataSet.Tables.Contains(Me.tempTableName) Then
            Me.dataSet.Tables.Remove(Me.tempTableName)
```

```
            End If
            Dim table As DataTable = New DataTable(Me.tempTableName)
            While fieldMatch.Success
                If Me.dataSet.Tables(Me.tableName).Columns _
                                        .Contains(fieldMatch.Value) Then
                    Dim col As DataColumn = dataSet.Tables(tableName) _
                                        .Columns(fieldMatch.Value)
                    table.Columns.Add(New DataColumn(col.ColumnName, col.DataType))
                    fieldMatch = fieldMatch.NextMatch
                Else
                    Throw New ArgumentException("Invalid column name")
                End If
            End While
            Me.dataSet.Tables.Add(table)
            Me.dataView = New System.Data.DataView(table)
        End If
    End Sub
```

Assuming that the table name is valid and that all the requested fields are valid, you will use the temp table you have built to satisfy data access requirements. The only thing left to do is add the new table to the existing dataset.

You have now validated all the parts of your query except the filtering and sorting criteria. In the CommandText method, you test whether filtering and sorting are enabled based on your keyword count. If they are enabled, you execute a method that uses the internal behavior of the DataSet class to do the work. In the ValidateFiltering() method, you need to parse the text based on the keyword count. You need to either grab all the text after the Where clause or, if an order clause exists, stop there.

C#

```csharp
public void ValidateFiltering(string cmdText)
{
    if(filtering)
    {
        int startPos =0;
        int length =0;

        startPos = keywordMatches [wherePosition].Index +
            keywordMatches [wherePosition].Length + 1;
        if(keyWordCount == 3)  //no "order by" - Search from Where till  end
        {
            length = cmdText.Length-startPos;
        }
        else // "order by" exists -  search from where  position to "order by"
        {
            length = keywordMatches [orderPosition].Index - startPos;
        }

        this.dataView.RowFilter = cmdText.Substring(startPos,length);
    }
}
```

VB.NET

```vbnet
Private Sub ValidateFiltering(ByVal cmdText As String)
    If filtering Then
        Dim startPos As Integer = 0
        Dim length As Integer = 0
        startPos = (keywordMatches (wherePosition).Index + _
            keywordMatches (wherePosition).Length + 1)
        If keyWordCount = 3 Then
            length = cmdText.Length - startPos
        Else
            length = keywordMatches (orderPosition).Index - startPos
        End If

        Me.dataView.RowFilter = cmdText.Substring(startPos, length)
    End If
End Sub
```

After you parse the text, you will use the `DataView.RowFilter` property to filter the results. Simply apply the string you extracted to the `RowFilter`, and the `DataView` class takes care of the rest. The same technique is applied to get ordering.

C#

```csharp
public void ValidateSorting(string cmdText)
{
    if(sorting)
    {
        int startPos =0;
        int length =0;

        //start from end of 'Order by' clause
        startPos = keywordMatches [orderPosition].Index +
            keywordMatches [orderPosition].Length + 1;
        length =  cmdText.Length - startPos;

        this.dataView.Sort = cmdText.Substring(startPos,length);
    }
}
```

VB.NET

```vbnet
Private Sub ValidateSorting(ByVal cmdText As String)
    If sorting Then
        Dim startPos As Integer = 0
        Dim length As Integer = 0
        startPos = (keywordMatches (orderPosition).Index + _
            keywordMatches (orderPosition).Length + 1)
        length = cmdText.Length - startPos

        Me.dataView.Sort = cmdText.Substring(startPos, length)
    End If
End Sub
```

CommandTimeout Property

The CommandTimeout property specifies how long the Command object should wait for the results of an executed command before throwing an exception. You do not actually use this value, but it must be implemented because of interface requirements. Just return a 0 value to indicate that time-outs are not supported.

C#

```csharp
public int CommandTimeout
        {
            get
            {
                Debug.WriteLine("IDBCommand.CommandTimeout: Get");
                return this.m_commandTimeOut;
            }
            set
            {
                Debug.WriteLine("IDBCommand.CommandTimeout: Set");
                //throw new NotImplementedException("Timeouts not supported");
            }
        }
```

VB.NET

```vb
Public Property CommandTimeout() As Integer Implements IDbCommand.CommandTimeout
            Get
                Debug.WriteLine("IDBCommand.CommandTimeout: Get")
                Return Me.m_cmdTimeOut
            End Get
            Set(ByVal value As Integer)
                Debug.WriteLine("IDBCommand.CommandTimeout: Set")
            End Set
        End Property
```

CommandType Property

Most DPEs allow the developer to pass in a command as text, or they can pass in a fully initialized Command object for the Execute reader method to examine and use. The DataSetCommand class accepts only text; any other type will cause your component to throw a NotSupported exception.

C#

```csharp
public CommandType CommandType
{
    // supports only a text commandType
    get { return CommandType.Text; }
    set { if (value != CommandType.Text) throw new NotSupportedException(); }
}
```

VB.NET

```vb
Public Property CommandType() As CommandType _
        Implements IDbCommand.CommandType
            Get
```

```
                    Return CommandType.Text
                End Get
                Set(ByVal Value As CommandType)
                    If Value <> CommandType.Text Then
                        Throw New NotSupportedException
                    End If
                End Set
            End Property
```

CreateParameter Method

The CreateParameter method returns an extension-specific parameter to the Command object. The method must be supported because of the interface requirements, although it is not actually used. The DataSetParameter object is a simple class that implements another interface called IDataParameter, which allows it to be returned as an object of the interface type.

C#

```csharp
public IDataParameter CreateParameter()
{
    //return DataSetParameter
    return new DataSetParameter();
}
```

VB.NET

```vbnet
Public Function CreateParameter() As IDataParameter _
        Implements IDbCommand.CreateParameter
            Return New DataSetParameter
End Function
```

Parameters Property

The Parameters property returns a collection that implements the IDataParameterCollection interface. Your custom collection class is DataSetParameterCollection and satisfies these requirements. The Parameters property allows the developer to index into the Parameters collection to set or get the parameter values.

C#

```csharp
public IDataParameterCollection Parameters
{
    get
    {
        return this.m_parameters;
    }
}
```

VB.NET

```vbnet
Public ReadOnly Property Parameters() As IDataParameterCollection _
    Implements IDbCommand.Parameters
            Get
                Return Me.m_parameters
            End Get
End Property
```

Creating the DataSetDataReader Object

The data reader in our implementation does nothing more than read properties of our internal `DataView`. The data reader's behavior is enforced by the `IDataReader` interface, which supplies methods to indicate the number, names, and types of the fields that will be read. It also allows the object to actually access the data.

To add the `DataSetDataReader` class to the project, choose Project ➪ Add Class. Change the name of the class to `DataSetDataReader`. After adding the class, add the custom namespace, and edit the class definition.

Declarations

The members of the `DataSetDataReader` class hold all the information that you will use to build the properties it supports. The `currentRow` variable is used to store the value of the current row as the data is being read from your data file. The `dataView` variable holds a reference to the current view of data from the `DataSetCommand` that is passed in via the constructor. Finally, the `dataSet-Command` variable holds a reference to the command that is passed in via the constructor.

C#

```
System.Data.DataView dataView;
DataSetCommand dataSetCommand = null;
int currentRow = -1;
```

VB.NET

```
Private dataView As System.Data.DataView = Nothing
Private dataSetCommand As dataSetCommand = Nothing
Private currentRow As Integer = -1
```

Implementing IDataReader

The `IDataReader` interface exposed by Reporting Services enforces consistency in working with data. It provides properties and methods that allow you to examine the data and its types as well as the `Read` method that actually does the dirty work. Following is the definition of this interface, which shows all methods and properties that will need implementation:

C#

```
public interface IDataReader : IDisposable
{
    Type GetFieldType(int fieldIndex);
    string GetName(int fieldIndex);
    int GetOrdinal(string fieldName);
    object GetValue(int fieldIndex);
    bool Read();
    int FieldCount { get; }
}
```

VB.NET

```
Public Interface IDataReader
    Inherits IDisposable
```

```
        Function GetFieldType(ByVal fieldIndex As Integer) As Type
        Function GetName(ByVal fieldIndex As Integer) As String
        Function GetOrdinal(ByVal fieldName As String) As Integer
        Function GetValue(ByVal fieldIndex As Integer) As Object
        Function Read() As Boolean
        Property FieldCount() As Integer
    End Interface
```

You need to modify your class definition to force the custom `DataSetDataReader` class to support (implement) the interface requirements.

C#

```csharp
namespace Wrox.ReportingServices.DataSetDataExtension
{

    public class DataSetDataReader : IDataReader
    {
        internal DataSetDataReader(DataSetCommand command)
        {
            //set member variables based upon command object
            this.dataSetCommand = command;
            this.dataView = command.dataView;
        }

        public void Dispose() {}
```

VB.NET

```vbnet
Namespace Wrox.ReportingServices.DataSetDataExtension
    Public Class DataSetDataReader
        Implements IDataReader

        Friend Sub New(ByVal command As dataSetCommand)
            Me.dataSetCommand = command
            Me.dataView = command.dataView
        End Sub

        Public Sub Dispose() Implements IDisposable.Dispose
        End Sub
```

GetFieldType Method

The `GetFieldType` method returns the type of data at a particular position within the stream that is being read. This data is used to allow the developer to store the data being read in the correct data type upon retrieval from the data reader.

C#

```csharp
public Type GetFieldType (int fieldIndex)
{
        return this.dataView.Table.Columns[fieldIndex].DataType;
}
```

VB.NET

```
Public Function GetFieldType(ByVal fieldIndex As Integer) As Type _
    Implements IDataReader.GetFieldType
        Return Me.dataView.Table.Columns(fieldIndex).DataType
End Function
```

GetName Method

The GetName method allows the developer to retrieve a data field from the DataReader object by passing in the name of the field to be read.

C#

```
public string GetName(int fieldIndex)
{
        return this.dataView.Table.Columns[fieldIndex].ColumnName;
}
```

VB.NET

```
Public Function GetName(ByVal fieldIndex As Integer) As String _
    Implements IDataReader.GetName
        Return Me.dataView.Table.Columns(fieldIndex).ColumnName
End Function
```

GetOrdinal Method

The GetOrdinal method allows the developer to index the data based on its position within the DataReader stream.

C#

```
public int GetOrdinal(string fieldName)
{
        return this.dataView.Table.Columns[fieldName].Ordinal;
}
```

VB.NET

```
Public Function GetOrdinal(ByVal fieldName As String) As Integer _
    Implements IDataReader.GetOrdinal
        Return Me.dataView.Table.Columns(fieldName).Ordinal
End Function
```

GetValue Method

The GetValue method retrieves the actual value from the data stream. All of these methods are typically used together. The developer pulls the type information from the stream, creates variables of the correct type to hold this data, and gets the data's values using the GetValue function.

C#

```csharp
public object GetValue(int fieldIndex)
{
    return this.dataView[this.currentRow][fieldIndex];
}
```

VB.NET

```vbnet
Public Function GetValue(ByVal fieldIndex As Integer) As Object _
    Implements IDataReader.GetValue
        Return Me.dataView(Me.currentRow)(fieldIndex)
End Function
```

Read Method

The Read method is the workhorse of the DataSetDataReader class. The function loops through the current DataView. If a line is read successfully, this is indicated to the user of your extension by incrementing the row count variable currentRow and by returning a Boolean value. As long as true is returned, data is read successfully. false is returned when the internal view hits the end of the result set. Notice that we use a thread-safe increment function available in the .NET Framework to ensure that the current row variable is safely locked during the increment operation and won't yield a race condition.

C#

```csharp
public bool Read()
{
    System.Threading.Interlocked.Increment(ref this.currentRow);
    if (this.currentRow >= this.dataView.Count)
    {
        return false;
    }
    return true;
}
```

VB.NET

```vbnet
Public Function Read() As Boolean Implements IDataReader.Read
        System.Threading.Interlocked.Increment(Me.currentRow)
        If Me.currentRow >= Me.dataView.Count Then
            Return False
        End If
        Return True
End Function
```

FieldCount Property

The FieldCount property returns the number of fields or columns available in each row of data that the Read method returns.

C#

```csharp
public int FieldCount
{
        // Return the count of the number of columns,
        get { return this.dataView.Table.Columns.Count; }
}
```

VB.NET

```vbnet
Public ReadOnly Property FieldCount() As Integer Implements IDataReader.FieldCount
    Get
        Return Me.dataView.Table.Columns.Count
    End Get
End Property
```

Installing the DataSetDataProcessing Extension

After creating your custom DPE, you must install it to enable access. The installation process has two steps:

1. Install and configure the extension.

2. Configure extension security.

This particular extension is used by both the Report Server and the Report Designer itself, which requires us to install it in two locations. It must be installed on the report server and the workstation used to design the reports (using SSDT/Visual Studio).

Server Installation

Reporting Services has a standard location where extensions should be installed. This location is a subfolder below the installation directory of SQL Server itself. We refer to the SQL Server installation path as `InstallPath`. On my machine, this directory is `C:\Program Files\Microsoft SQL Server\`.

Depending on the different SQL Server products you have installed on the machine, the subdirectories under `InstallPath` may vary. The naming convention for the `Reporting Services` subdirectory is `MSRS11.MSSQLSERVER`, where `MSRS13` represents the product and version name (Microsoft Reporting Services version 13).

The directory into which you will install the extension is the bin directory of the report server: `InstallPath\MSRS13.MSSQLSERVER\Reporting Services\ReportServer\bin`. Copy your custom DPE assembly into this directory. The extension is now in the correct location, but you need to inform the report server of its presence. You do so by editing the configuration file that Reporting Services uses for its settings. This file is called `RSReportServer.config` and is located in the parent directory. Open this file and look for the `<Data>` section. Within this section, you should see entries similar to the following:

```
<Data>
    <Permissions>
        <PermissionSet class="System.Security.NamedPermissionSet" version="1"
                Unrestricted="true" Name="FullTrust"
                Description="Allows full access to all resources"/>
```

```
    </Permissions>
    <Extension Name="SQL"
        Type="Microsoft.ReportingServices.DataExtensions.SqlConnectionWrapper,
            Microsoft.ReportingServices.DataExtensions"/>
    <Extension Name="OLEDB"
        Type="Microsoft.ReportingServices.DataExtensions.OleDbConnectionWrapper,
            Microsoft.ReportingServices.DataExtensions"/>
    <Extension Name="ORACLE"
        Type="Microsoft.ReportingServices.DataExtensions.OracleClient
            ConnectionWrapper,Microsoft.ReportingServices.DataExtensions"/>
    <Extension Name="ODBC"
        Type="Microsoft.ReportingServices.DataExtensions.OdbcConnection
            Wrapper,Microsoft.ReportingServices.DataExtensions"/>
    <Extension Name="DATASET"
        Type="Wrox.ReportingServices.DataSetDataExtension.DataSetConnection,
            Wrox.ReportingServices.DataSetDataExtension"/>
</Data>
```

Add the `DataSet` entry shown in the highlighted code snippet. The `Name` tag is the unique name you want users to see when they select your extension. The `Type` element contains the entry point class for your extension (the first object created and the one that is required to implement the `IExtension` interface), followed by the fully qualified name of your extension.

Save the file. Reporting Services will now recognize your extension, but you must change the Code Access Security (CAS) policy to give the extension the permissions it needs to do its job. CAS is a constraint security model used by the .NET Framework to restrict which system resources and operations that code can access and perform, regardless of the caller.

Server Security Configuration

The security policy file is located in the same directory as the server configuration file. Simply locate the file called `rssrvpolicy.config`, which contains the security policy information for SSRS. Make an entry that looks similar to the following, replacing `<INSTALLPATH>` with the appropriate installation path of the SQL Server Reporting Services instance on the server:

```
    </CodeGroup>
    <CodeGroup  class="UnionCodeGroup"
        version="1"
        PermissionSetName="FullTrust"
        Name="WroxSRS"
        Description="Code group for Wrox DataSet data processing extension">
        <IMembershipCondition class="UrlMembershipCondition"
            version="1"

Url="<INSTALLPATH>\Reporting Services\ReportServer\bin\
DataSetDataExtension.dll" />
    </CodeGroup>
```

> **NOTE** *On my machine, the Url attribute is:* C:\Program Files\Microsoft
> SQL Server\MSRS13.MSSQLSERVER1601\Reporting Services\ReportServer\
> bin\DataSetDataExtension.dll.

> **WARNING** *Be mindful of the build number of SQL Server Reporting Services installed as this will affect the folder name. My example was created using build 1601 which will change with future updates.*

This `CodeGroup` policy specifies that we grant `FullTrust` to our assembly to execute its code. As a best practice, though, you should grant only the permission set required by your code to execute appropriately, thus reducing the possible attack surface.

WorkStation Installation

The next task is installing the extension on your development machine so that you can use it in the Report Designer within SSDT/Visual Studio. The process for installing the extension into the Report Designer is much the same as that for the server, with the exception of the filenames and locations. You can also do this by copying the file to a specific directory of your development machine and making an entry in the configuration file so that the designer is aware of the extension.

Copy your extension to the `C:\Program Files(x86)\Microsoft Visual Studio 14.0\Common7\ IDE\PrivateAssemblies` folder. All the files needed for workstation configuration are located here. The designer's configuration file is called `RSReportDesigner.config`. Insert the same information that you inserted at the server-side extension at the end of the `<Data>` section in this file:

```
<Data>
    <Extension Name="ODBC"
        Type="Microsoft.ReportingServices.DataExtensions.OdbcConnection
        Wrapper, Microsoft.ReportingServices.DataExtensions"/>
    <Extension Name="DATASET"
        Type="Wrox.ReportingServices.DataSetDataExtension.DataSetConnection,
        Wrox.ReportingServices.DataSetDataExtension"/>
</Data>
```

This file has an additional requirement. You must also tell Visual Studio what designer to use with your extension. We chose not to implement a custom designer class but to use the Generic Query Designer provided by Microsoft instead. Your query is based on SQL, so this works well. Make an entry in the `<Designer>` section that immediately follows the `<Data>` section:

```
<Extension Name="DATASET"
    Type="Microsoft.ReportingServices.QueryDesigners.GenericQueryDesigner,
          Microsoft.ReportingServices.QueryDesigners"/>
```

WorkStation Security Configuration

The next step is to set up the security policy so that the extension will run in the designer correctly. The required file is called `rspreviewpolicy.config`. After the last existing `</CodeGroup>` tag, add an entry resembling the following to this file, replacing `<InstallPath>` with your actual Visual Studio installation path:

```
<CodeGroup class="UnionCodeGroup" version="1"
    PermissionSetName="FullTrust"
    Name="WroxSRS"
    Description="Code group for my DataSet data processing extension">
```

```
<IMembershipCondition class="UrlMembershipCondition"
        version="1"
    Url="<InstallPath>\Common7\IDE\PrivateAssemblies\DataSetDataExtension.dll" />
</CodeGroup>
```

> **NOTE** *On my machine, the* Url *attribute is:* C:\Program Files (x86)\
> Microsoft Visual Studio 14.0\Common7\IDE\PrivateAssemblies\
> DataSetDataExtension.dll.

Testing DataSetDataExtension

To test the DataSetDataExtension extension, you must create a report that uses the custom extension. You must also create a DataSet file to contain your data or use the one provided in the sample code. The code is generic enough that you can use it against any serialized dataset. The file included in the example was extracted from a sample database but could, in fact, contain any set of data.

Add a new project to your existing solution. Create the project by choosing File ➪ Add Project ➪ New Project. Choose the Report Server Project template. Change the project's name to TestReport, and click OK. This launches the Report Designer with a blank report. Click the link on the Designer canvas to add a new data source and dataset for the report. The Data Source Properties page appears, as shown in Figure 16-6. Leave the default data source name, and click the Type drop-down box. Your new DataSetDataExtension should now be available as DATASET. Using a FileName attribute, enter the physical path to your serialized dataset into the Connection String textbox. When you are done, the result should resemble Figure 16-9.

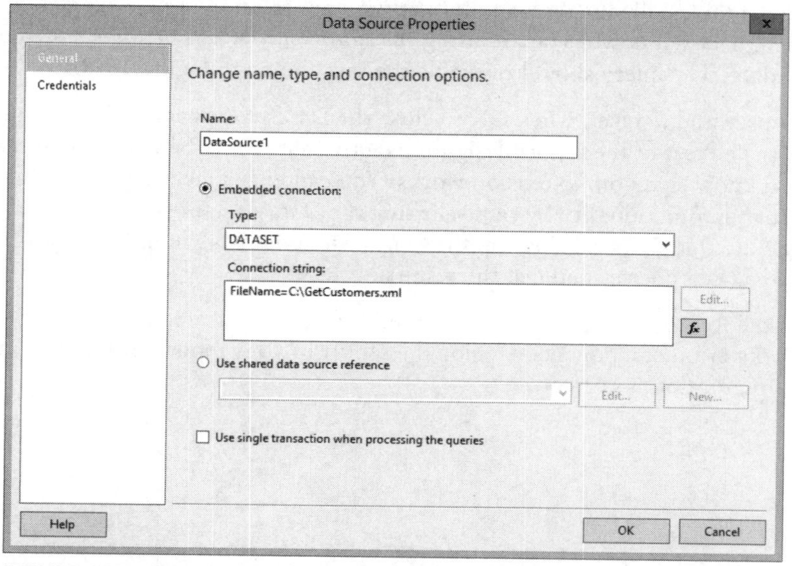

FIGURE 16-6: Data Source Properties with DATASET type selected.

Next, you need to indicate the credentials you want to use. Click the Credentials menu on the left side of the Data Source Properties page; the Credentials window appears, as shown in Figure 16-7. Instruct the data source to "Use Windows Authentication (integrated security)" by selecting the radio button.

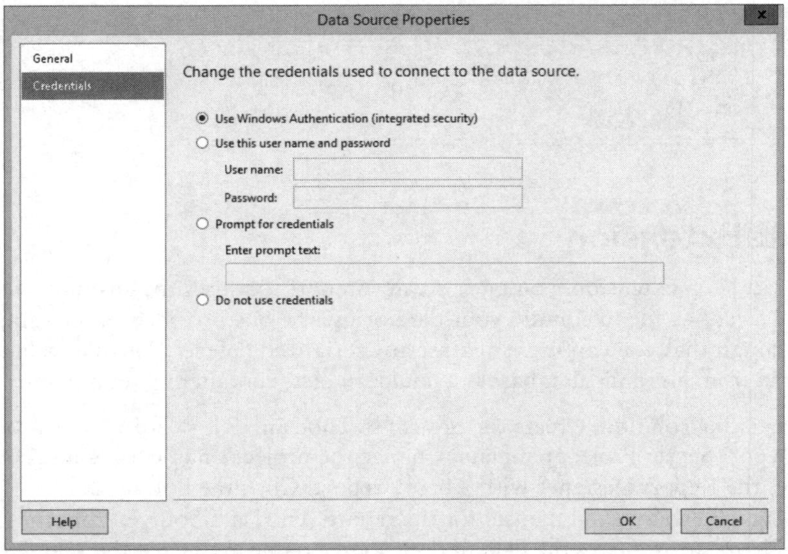

FIGURE 16-7: Credentials page.

After you have set both the type and connection strings, you are ready to set up the basic data query. The dataset we used included a table called DimCustomer that we want to query. Enter SELECT * FROM DimCustomer into the Query window if you are using the sample provided, or some statement that works on your specific data. The query should resemble the text shown in Figure 16-8.

Finish setting up the data source and dataset. Click OK to close the Dataset Properties dialog and add fields to the new dataset. The rest of the report design is exactly as it would be with any of the stock data sources. Now you know that your extension works. You can experiment with the field-limiting/filtering and field-sorting functionality by right-clicking the Dataset name in the Report Data window and selecting Edit Query. This brings up the Query Designer, shown in Figure 16-9, where you can enter more advanced queries and test the results.

By previewing the report in the Report Designer, you have effectively demonstrated the installation and configuration of the workstation components. Deploy the report to your report server and run it to make sure your server configuration is correct.

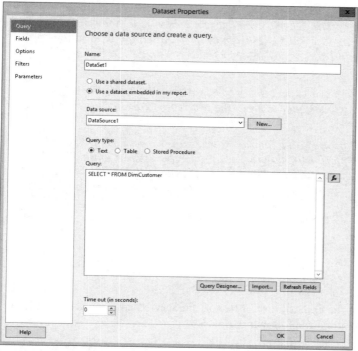

FIGURE 16-8: Query command in Dataset Properties.

CustomerKey	GeographyKey	CustomerAlter...	Title	FirstName	MiddleName	LastName	NameStyle	BirthDate
11000	26	AW00011000		Jon	V	Yang	false	1966-04-08T0
11001	37	AW00011001		Eugene	L	Huang	false	1965-05-14T0
11002	31	AW00011002		Ruben		Torres	false	1965-08-12T0
11003	11	AW00011003		Christy		Zhu	false	1968-02-15T0
11004	19	AW00011004		Elizabeth		Johnson	false	1968-08-08T0
11005	22	AW00011005		Julio		Ruiz	false	1965-08-05T0
11006	8	AW00011006		Janet	G	Alvarez	false	1965-12-06T0
11007	40	AW00011007		Marco		Mehta	false	1964-05-09T0
11008	32	AW00011008		Rob		Verhoff	false	1964-07-07T0
11009	25	AW00011009		Shannon	C	Carlson	false	1964-04-01T0
11010	22	AW00011010		Jacquelyn	C	Suarez	false	1964-02-06T0
11011	22	AW00011011		Curtis		Lu	false	1963-11-04T0
11012	611	AW00011012		Lauren	M	Walker	false	1968-01-18T0
11013	543	AW00011013		Ian	M	Jenkins	false	1968-08-06T0
11014	634	AW00011014		Sydney		Bennett	false	1968-05-09T0
11015	301	AW00011015		Chloe		Young	false	1979-02-27T0
11016	329	AW00011016		Wyatt	L	Hill	false	1979-04-28T0
11017	39	AW00011017		Shannon		Wang	false	1944-06-26T0
11018	32	AW00011018		Clarence	D	Rai	false	1944-10-09T0

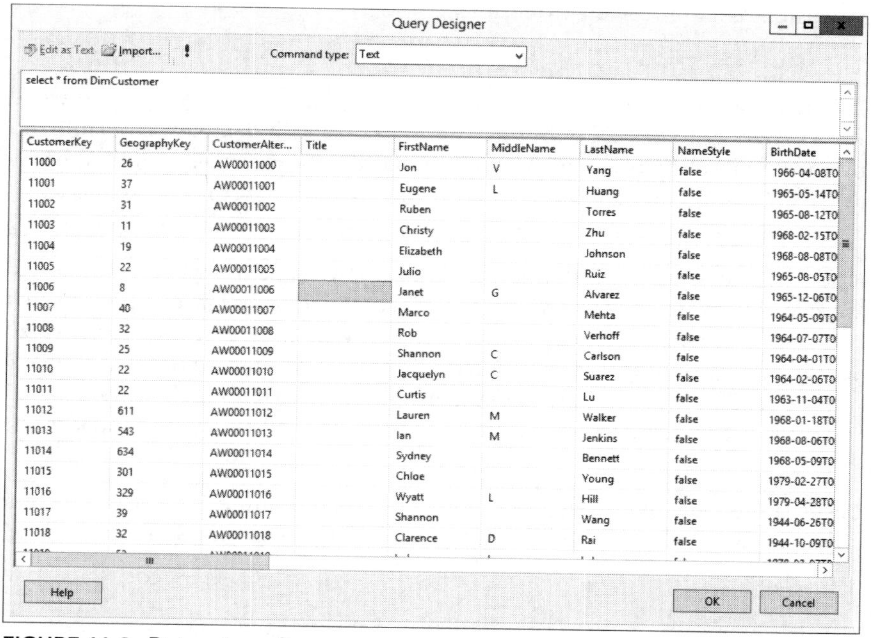

FIGURE 16-9: Dataset results.

> **NOTE** *Another option for testing the custom data extension is to open a new instance of Visual Studio and load the extension project. Add a breakpoint on a line of code that you want to step into, and then select Debug ⇨ Attach to process.*
>
> *In the Attach to Process window, select the process for the Visual Studio instance that has the Report Designer open to the test report consuming the data extension.*
>
> *Finally, click the Attach button. Visual Studio attaches the project code to the Report Designer. To step into the breakpoint, just preview the report in the Report Designer. As soon as Reporting Services hits the line of code with the breakpoint, you are taken to the code view, where you can use all the debugging features of the Visual Studio IDE.*

SUMMARY

In this chapter, you learned about the extensibility of Reporting Services and the areas that currently support customization, including the following topics:

- ➤ Which extensibility options are available
- ➤ Reasons for extending SQL Server Reporting Services
- ➤ How to create custom data processing extensions
- ➤ How to install custom extensions

Along with the extensibility options available in SQL Server Reporting Services, you also learned about some of the business opportunities created. Microsoft has created a flexible, powerful reporting solution that allows you to modify its behavior by implementing the interfaces required by the particular extension type. This functionality has created a third-party market for tools and has allowed enterprise developers to create custom solutions for their businesses' unique needs.

Also discussed were the data access methods that the .NET Framework uses—specifically, how to create a custom data processing extension to work with non-relational data. The example given was simple and cannot stand alone as an application; conversely, it can easily be extended to provide additional functionality including support for parameters. The primary purpose of the example was to familiarize you with the requirements for creating and installing an extension. This type of extension was chosen because it is used on the server for report processing, and on the developer machine for report creation.

This chapter concludes Part 5 about Reporting Services custom programming. The next part of the book introduces and then explores the new Mobile Report capabilities added in SQL Server 2016.

PART VI
Mobile Report Solutions

In the next four chapters, you become acquainted with the new mobile reporting and dashboard capabilities introduced in SQL Server 2016. We begin with an introduction to the features and capabilities, as well as a discussion about the best use cases for Mobile Reports. You learn more advanced applications as you progress through a series of exercises.

Additionally, you learn about the use for each visual control, which enables you to apply the knowledge and design simple reports to address specific business needs. Starting with the unique pattern of "design-first development," you prototype report designs and capabilities, and furthermore, add datasets to support the behavior of those reports. We continue with a tour of sophisticated capabilities used to integrate reports into a complete business intelligence and enterprise reporting solution. You learn how parameters and expressions are used to pass selections and context to another mobile report, paginated report, or website.

In this part, you learn:

- ➤ Basic mobile report design approaches and applications
- ➤ Appropriate use of navigators, selectors, gauges, charts, maps, and data grids
- ➤ Advanced report design techniques with complex visual controls
- ➤ Filtering and interactions
- ➤ Report navigation
- ➤ How to use parameters for dashboard filtering
- ➤ User parameters for drill-through navigation
- ➤ How to drill-through to other reporting tools with URL paths and parameters

▶ **CHAPTER 17:** Introducing Reporting Services Mobile Reports

▶ **CHAPTER 18:** Implementing a Mobile Report with Design-First Development

▶ **CHAPTER 19:** Mobile Report Design Patterns

▶ **CHAPTER 20:** Advanced Mobile Report Solutions

17

Introducing Reporting Services Mobile Reports

WHAT'S IN THIS CHAPTER?

- ➤ Using Mobile Report Publisher
- ➤ Designing datasets for mobile reporting
- ➤ Learn when to use mobile reports
- ➤ Understanding visual control categories

The purpose of this chapter is to introduce Mobile Reports and the best use for different types of visual controls. We begin by comparing the capabilities of mobile and paginated reports, and then explore the essential building blocks of mobile report design. This chapter introduces each of the visual control categories and explains the best use of each control in a mobile report solution.

Having choices and options provides freedom to use different tools to create reporting and data presentation experiences for different purposes. Freedom and flexibility bring the need to make more decisions, and sometimes choosing the right tool is a trade-off between the strengths of one tool and the limits of another that is used to achieve different results. As I have used SQL Server Reporting Services and watched the platform mature over the past fourteen years or so, one thing became very clear: Reporting Services was primarily intended for and is optimized to be used in a web browser on a desktop computer. I have used previous versions of SSRS to create reports for smaller screens and mobile devices. It met the basic need to display information in a simple layout with bold graphics and text and with sufficient rendering fidelity and navigation, but it was not a truly modern mobile experience.

Responding to the proliferation of mobile devices used by business professionals who consume data and make decisions, Microsoft created multiple tools for the mobile professional.

A partner company in the Microsoft development community had created a mobile business intelligence report and dashboard delivery product called Datazen. Microsoft acquired Datazen from ComponentArt in 2015. Much like Reporting Services, Datazen was built on Windows services, ASP.NET web services, and had a server architecture very similar to SSRS, with the notable exception that reports were delivered client-side using installed mobile applications freely distributed in all the mobile device app stores. Going forward, the Datazen product will be the Mobile Reports feature of Reporting Services, managed entirely with the report server and Web Portal installed with SQL Server 2016.

THE MOBILE REPORT EXPERIENCE AND BUSINESS CASE

An important thing to understand about Mobile Reports is that it is not the same thing as conventional SSRS paginated reports, and one is not a replacement for the other. Mobile reports are simple and bold, optimized for touch on mobile devices. Secondarily, a mobile report can be used in a web browser and viewed on a desktop computer.

> **NOTE** *Shortly after Datazen was acquired by Microsoft in 2015, I had numerous conversations with consulting clients who were convinced that they could use it as a replacement for their reporting platform. Before the integration with Reporting Services in SQL Server 2016, Microsoft made it available free for SQL Server Enterprise customers. Those who thought they would replace SSRS and other operational reporting tools soon learned that Datazen, and now SSRS Mobile Reports, serves a specific purpose alongside paginated reports.*

Using the Power BI Mobile app on my iPad, I can open a mobile report that resides on an SSRS report server. Figure 17-1 shows a simple mobile report running in my iPad using full screen layout.

The touch experience is very responsive. I can touch and hold on a data point to see large callouts with more information. The Time navigator allows me swipe and drag across a range of date values or tap to drill down to the next level. Tapping a country in the selector on the left immediately filters the chart and summary values. On my iPad or other tablet device, I see a simplified view of the report when I hold the device in vertical orientation, but if I want to see more details, I can rotate the device horizontally as shown in Figure 17-1 to see the full desktop layout. We explore this capability in the following chapters.

The same report can be opened in the web browser on a mobile device or desktop computer. Figure 17-2 shows a simple mobile report in the browser that I opened from the Web Portal on my server.

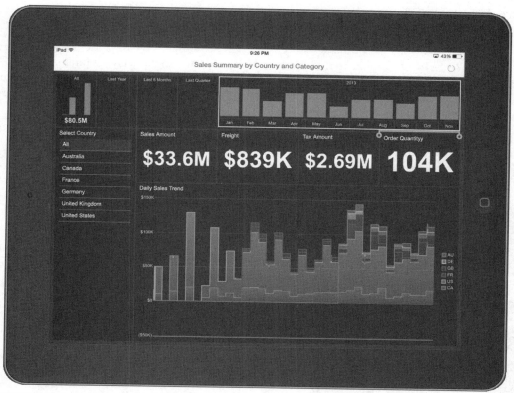

FIGURE 17-1: A running mobile report in full-screen mode on an iPad.

FIGURE 17-2: A simple mobile report displayed in a web browser.

As you will see in the following chapters, you can use several visual controls to assemble more intricate and complex mobile report designs. However, the essence of effective mobile reporting is simplicity and ease of use.

The user experience is very similar to that on the tablet but with a slight delay, as filter selections and data are delivered through HTML from the web server. The report behavior is nearly the same, but some differences are noticeable between the immediate and tactile response in the mobile app and a bit of latency when rendered for the web.

On my mobile phone, the differences are not as subtle, where I have a smaller screen and less available space. On this report, shown in Figure 17-3, the most important information is displayed in fewer visual controls that I navigate by tapping and swiping with my finger or thumb.

FIGURE 17-3: Report viewed in the phone app.

You can see that the controls are arranged differently and are simplified for the smaller screen. The experience of tapping, swiping, and holding a point on the screen is slightly different, adapted for smaller screen resolution and hand-held navigation. Some controls behave a little bit differently on each device because users are accustomed to using the native controls that are inherently part of the device operating system. For example, here on my iPhone, tapping the drop-down list displays the "slot-machine" vertical scrolling selector familiar to mobile iOS users.

Report Drill-Through Navigation

As you have already seen in my previous paginated report designs, I am a big proponent of report navigation. For report users to access more content, you can either put more on a report or allow the user to navigate to other reports to progressively reveal more detail or more specific context. Drill-through navigation is a strong theme in mobile report design.

We have less screen real estate on mobile devices and we have fewer intricate features in mobile report controls, so we can chain reports together to provide a rich navigation experience. One mobile report can navigate to another mobile report within the context of the filters and selected items on a report. Similar to paginated reports, each visual control can have a separate drill-through navigation target. For example, tapping a bar on a chart can send the user to a report filtered on the item represented by the bar in the chart. Additionally, a mobile report can navigate to a paginated report, which might be a better choice for displaying details and transactional source records, enabling users to see the numbers behind charts and aggregated totals.

When to Use Mobile Reports

Before we explore the capabilities of Mobile Reports and talk about what they are, let's talk about what they are not. I find that having this discussion with consulting clients and students helps to define boundaries and simplify trade-off decisions between different tools.

I am not going to sugar-coat this message. The fact is, the Mobile Reports toolset is not as mature or feature-rich as conventional paginated reports in some respects, but it fills an important need in the reporting portfolio. When Datazen was a completely separate product, crafted by a different company, it was easy for me to accept that it employed a different design philosophy than anything from Microsoft. Now that it is part of SQL Server Reporting Services, the differences are more apparent; at the same time the fact remains this tool brings unique value and capability to the Microsoft BI and reporting platform. Do not get hung up on the differences; learn to use the two products together. To some degree, you will need to unlearn some techniques you have acquired for paginated reports in order to embrace different design patterns in mobile reports. That is just the way it is.

Having worked with the Datazen for a couple of years prior to the Microsoft acquisition, I have some specific thoughts about using this tool successfully. Specifically, it is important to use Mobile Reports in a scenario appropriately suited for the product. In that context, you can add capabilities and business value not previously possible. It should be no surprise that the Mobile Reports feature is designed to primarily deliver mobile reporting capabilities to business users in layouts and screen resolutions optimized for modern mobile devices. Simply put, do not cram a lot of detailed information on mobile reports. Keep them simple.

To appreciate the value of mobile reports, you need to use them on a mobile device. Because you design mobile reports on a desktop computer, when you preview and test reports, they may seem to be big and overly simplified. Mobile reports are optimized for small screens and for touch interaction.

As a long-time SSRS practitioner, I am accustomed to a reporting tool that handles a lot of the data grouping and aggregation work for me. Additionally, I am accustomed to using expressions extensively, and these are simply not features of this tool. Rather than wrestling with the design tool, use queries to shape the data.

Mobile Reports Are Not Self-Service BI

Although the fundamental report design experience is not that difficult, data preparation is necessary. Most reports require queries to be written so data is shaped correctly for different visual controls. Query design and preparation requires technical expertise. Although the actual report design effort is relatively simple, this task is typically performed by a report design professional. Users navigate and interact with reports but not in an ad hoc fashion, as they would with Power BI or Excel.

In particular, some visual controls do not group and aggregate the rows in a dataset so you must create a dataset specifically suited for that control. You still have the flexibility to present data in the right shape and format but you may need to create multiple datasets rather than relying on groups and expressions like you would in paginated report data regions, pivot tables, or Power BI visuals.

Mobile Reports Are Not Paginated Reports

Mobile report visuals are prepackaged with properties and layout options that adapt to their size and placement on the page. Consequently, they do not have properties that can be fine-tuned and modified when the report is designed in the same manner as paginated reports. As a long-time SSRS report designer, I am accustomed to tweaking and adjusting properties to make a report look the way I want. This has always been a time-consuming and tedious process, but it is the way the tool works. By contrast, mobile report visuals have very few styling properties, so they take far less time to design but you do not have fine control over the styling and layout of each control.

Mobile reports are not intended for printing or exporting to a file for consumption. Operational reports like transaction lists, balance sheets, and contracts are best designed as paginated reports.

Cached and On-demand Results

The primary design philosophy behind Mobile Reports is that a dataset produces a static result set that is cached and then filtered on the client. Cached dataset results may be scheduled to refresh at regular intervals or can be manually refreshed on-demand. This results in faster report execution and supports an interactive experience within the limits of the cached dataset. As with virtually any scheduled query execution, queries do not run in the user's security context so cached datasets are not always ideal for user-specific filtering and security.

Furthermore, datasets can be parameterized to run live queries, but some interactive features, such as navigators and selectors, are not supported. Oftentimes, the best way to combine interactive mobile reports with on-demand capabilities is to build at least two different reports with navigation actions from one to the other. The first report uses a cached dataset with interactive selectors and navigators to query aggregated data and the second report uses query parameters to return live results.

CONNECTION AND DATASET DESIGN BASICS

The Mobile Report Publisher, which is the design tool for mobile reports, does not include a query design tool. Queries are designed using either an SSDT report project or Report Builder to publish shared datasets to your report server. This requires some planning and iterative design. I will demonstrate an effective design pattern you can use to build datasets to support mobile report features.

Shared datasets have parameters used for filtering data, and can be used to run live queries against data sources or to cache data for more responsive report performance. Because mobile reports on a mobile device run client-side using installed mobile report viewer applications, data can also be securely cached on the device to improve performance and support offline reporting. When a user is online, cached datasets can be refreshed with newer query results.

INTRODUCING MOBILE REPORT PUBLISHER

One of the first impressions you are likely to have when you use the Mobile Report Publisher for the first time is that it has a different look and feel from SSDT or Report Builder. This is primarily because this product was designed with a "mobile-first" mindset. The original Datazen Dashboard Publisher was developed when Microsoft released Windows 8 and fully embraced the "Metro" or "Modern" user experience. In the same way that Windows 10 brought users back to a more familiar desktop Windows behavior, Mobile Report Publisher has a more conventional desktop feel with modern Windows styling.

> **NOTE** *We hear the term "modern" used freely to describe new tools and user experiences. Modern is a very relative term and what is considered "modern" by our standards today will probably have a very different perception in a short time, and might soon be considered "legacy." The mobile report product will undoubtedly change quickly to adapt to a changing user community, newer devices, and the fashion of the industry. It will also likely maintain the title of a modern reporting tool through these adaptations. In short: be prepared for changes.*

Mobile Report Publisher consists of four pages that are accessed using the large tabs on the top-left side of the report design window shown in Figure 17-4.

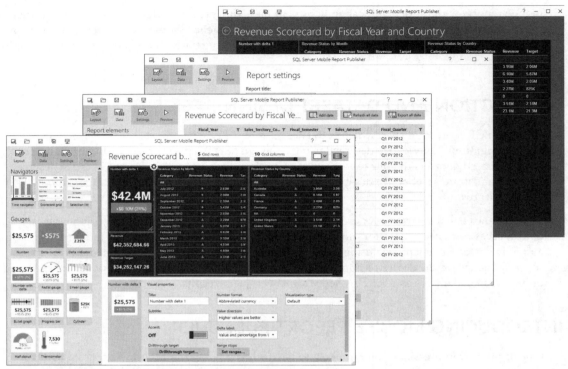

FIGURE 17-4: Pages on Mobile Report Publisher.

Layout View

Layout view is where you arrange controls and set visual properties for those controls. Drag-and-drop controls from the toolbox on the left to the design grid in the body of the report. The grid dimensions are defined using two sliders at the top of the designer and to the right of the report title.

When you initially add a control, a table of simulated data is automatically generated so you can preview the control with data values. This "design-first" approach is a radical shift in report design, and can be a marvelous rapid-design tool for testing prototypes and getting quick user feedback. You build an entire mobile report using this approach in Chapter 18.

Data View

Data view is where you wire up the controls to datasets and set properties related to data consumption and field-mapping. Each control has a unique set of data properties that enable it to group, aggregate, and filter data. First, datasets are imported so they become available to the controls. After controls are added to the grid in the Layout page, you can select each of those controls on this page so you can set the data properties.

Dashboard Settings

Use the Dashboard Settings page to set properties related to the report name, deployment destination, dates, and regional formatting. The metadata you set on this page is saved into the deployed report or file on the filesystem that affects the behavior of certain controls. The Currency property applies regional formatting to the report. The Fiscal year start, First day of the week, and Effective date properties all modify the behavior of Time navigators and time charts. In the US and without needing to deal with fiscal date reporting, I can leave these properties with default settings, but you should set them according to your needs.

Preview

The Preview page is intended for testing your report in the design environment. It approximates how the report will appear after it has been saved and run from the server.

Using the icons on the toolbar in the top-left hand side of the window, you can save locally or publish to server. Figure 17-5 shows the Layout page with the design controls and features used to design a report.

> **TIP** *Saving copies of a report is fairly easy but be careful as you save different version if the report locally and to the server. I advise saving a master copy locally as a backup. Continue to save changes as you go and then save the same version to the server. By keeping these copies in sync, you will always have a backup and there will be no confusion about having old and new versions of the report in different places.*

Use the small icons in the top-left toolbar to create a new report, open, save, and connect to a report server. You can save reports to a folder in the filesystem or to a report server much as you would any document file.

Using the layout selection drop-down, you can create an alternate layout for tablet and phone devices after designing the report in the master layout, which is optimized for a desktop or tablet display in landscape orientation. If no device-specific layout exists, the mobile app will make a best-effort to fit the master layout controls to the device in the order they are arranged.

You can resize the grid in any layout. The default grid size for each of the layouts is as follows:

➤ Master is optimized for horizontal layout, 6 x 12 max grid

➤ Tablet is designed for rotation, 8 x 8 max grid

➤ Phone is designed for vertical layout, 6 x 4 grid

The tablet layout is for a tablet device rotated to portrait orientation. Generally, it's a good idea to keep the grid dimensions relatively close to the defaults and then make adjustments to fit the selected visual controls.

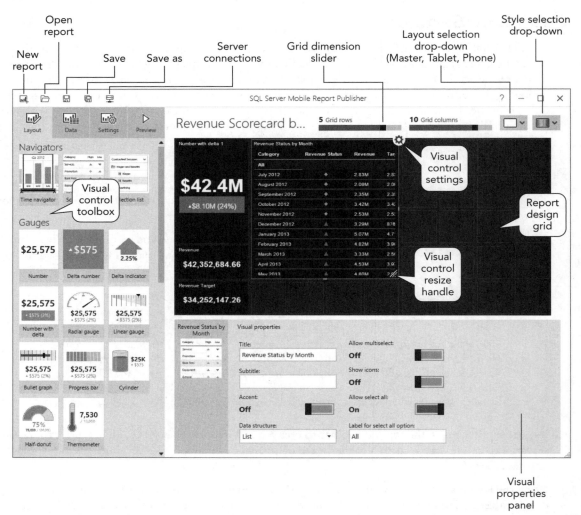

FIGURE 17-5: Mobile Report Publisher Layout page.

The style selection drop-down includes thumbnail images of each of style defined in the site branding theme. Style colors and other properties are dynamically applied to reports if the site branding theme is updated.

VISUAL CONTROL CATEGORIES

On the left side of the page, controls are organized into the following categories, which are explained in the following sections:

➤ Navigators

➤ Gauges

➤ Charts

➤ Maps

➤ DataGrids

Navigators

The Time navigator is essentially a dynamic column, area, or line chart grouped by a selected date or time hierarchy. It also specifies a set of time members that filter another dataset. You can specify the valid date parts for inclusion in the drill-down tree. For example, I chose a year that presents all the month periods for that year; the chart will then visualize days at the next level. In addition to selecting a single value to move down the hierarchical tree to the next level, you can swipe across or hold the Shift key to specify a range and select multiple days (or any other date part). Figure 17-6 shows controls in the Navigator category.

FIGURE 17-6: Navigator controls.

These controls are used to filter the data displayed in other controls:

➤ **Time navigator**—Displays a range of time/date values. It supports years, quarters, months, days, hours. This control requires a column of date and/or time type values. Using the first date/time column in the dataset, it auto-generates each date/time level value in the range and doesn't require a date lookup or "dimension" reference table to fill in any missing values. The Time navigator supports multiple metric fields that are visualized as a time-series chart using a column chart, stepped area, or line chart. You see examples of the Time navigator beginning in the next chapter.

➤ **Scorecard grid**—Combines a selection list with a multi-field value KPI scorecard. This is a versatile control that groups and aggregates column values for a dataset. Optionally, a second table can be joined with a pair of key values and used for aggregation and comparison purposes. The selector functionality works exactly like the Selection list control.

➤ **Selection list**—Groups like-valued rows in the dataset based on a single column and presents them in a list for selection. The selector supports single-select, multi-select, and an additional item at the top of the list titled All. When the All item is selected, the selection list is effectively not used to filter data.

Depending on the mobile device and the available screen real estate, the selector is displayed either as a scrollable list box or as a compact drop-down list control.

For the following examples, I have used the dataset shown in Figure 17-7 as the source table for a number of controls.

	OrderYear	Category ▼	CountryRegionCode ▼	SalesTarget	SalesAmount
1	2013	Accessories	AU	5598000	23,947.53
2	2013	Bikes	AU	6551000	1,283,918.23
3	2013	Clothing	AU	1445000	42,592.78
4	2013	Accessories	CA	1350000	75,888.88
5	2013	Bikes	CA	936000	4,046,454.65
6	2013	Clothing	CA	359000	174,780.30
7	2013	Accessories	DE	1835000	32,504.00
8	2013	Bikes	DE	1300000	1,418,700.92
9	2013	Clothing	DE	898000	64,829.43
10	2013	Accessories	FR	2415000	37,875.79
11	2013	Bikes	FR	1691000	2,426,590.64

⊞ TestSalesAndTargets2013 ⚙

FIGURE 17-7: The dataset shown in the Data page.

Figure 17-8 shows an example of a Scorecard grid and a Selection list using the same set of data. Note that both of these controls present consolidated Category values rather than the repeated rows you see in the source data.

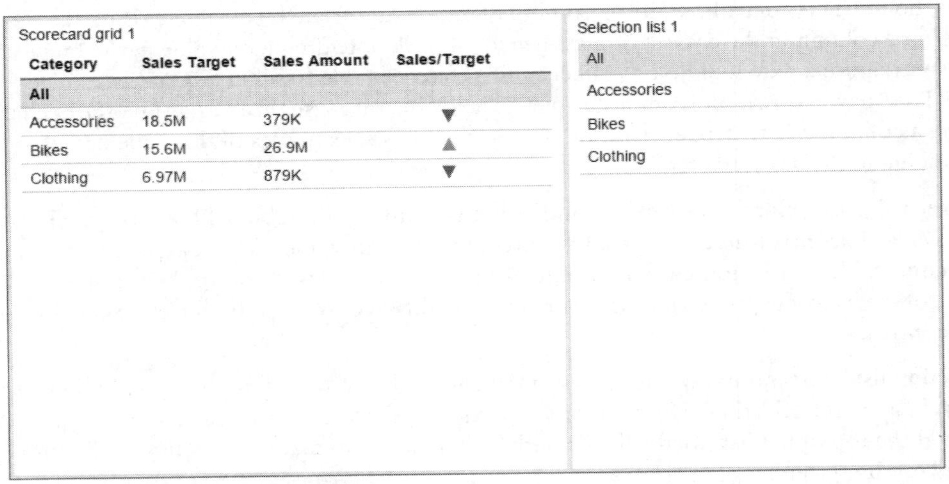

Scorecard grid 1

Category	Sales Target	Sales Amount	Sales/Target
All			
Accessories	18.5M	379K	▼
Bikes	15.6M	26.9M	▲
Clothing	6.97M	879K	▼

Selection list 1

All
Accessories
Bikes
Clothing

FIGURE 17-8: Grid and Selection list controls.

Gauges

This group of controls displays a single numeric field value rather than multiple values. The gauges shown in Figure 17-9 aggregate a numeric column into a single value and can consume a single row or multiple rows.

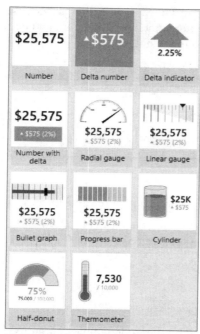

FIGURE 17-9: Gauge type controls.

➤ **Number control**—Displays a single value with no target. This is the only gauge control that takes only one field. Like other controls, several named formats can be used to display numeric values.

All of the other gauge controls display a main value compared to a target value, and these two field values can come from one or two different datasets. These controls essentially do the same thing, presenting the main, target, and comparison values using different visual metaphors. For each control, the comparison of main value and target can be expressed in one of three different ways, using the Delta label property:

➤ Percentage from target

➤ Percentage of target

➤ Value and percentage of target

Charts

The items shown in Figure 17-10 include ten chart controls which are used to analyze data in different ways.

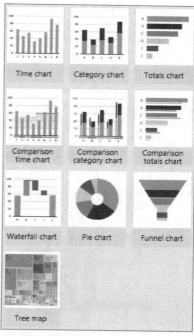

FIGURE 17-10: Chart controls.

The Time chart and Comparison time chart are similar to Time navigator but are not used for selection and filtering. Additionally, they support more time units including auto and decade levels, which are derived from a date or date/time type column in the dataset.

These chart types are used to segment a numeric field by a category field:

➤ The Category chart

➤ Comparison category chart

➤ Waterfall chart

➤ Funnel chart

➤ Tree map

These charts are flexible and can be used to segment or group a measure value by a category or to compare multiple field values:

➤ Totals chart

➤ Comparison totals chart

➤ Pie chart

➤ Funnel chart

Figure 17-11 shows four sample charts that are all based on the same sample dataset used for the other charts in this section. From left to right, the Category and Totals charts both group the Category field values and display the aggregated Sales Amount totals. The main difference between the two controls is that the Totals chart could also be used to show different measure field values side-by-side rather than grouping on the Category field. On the bottom row, the Comparison category and Comparison totals charts are essentially variations of the first two charts that show and compare the main and target values.

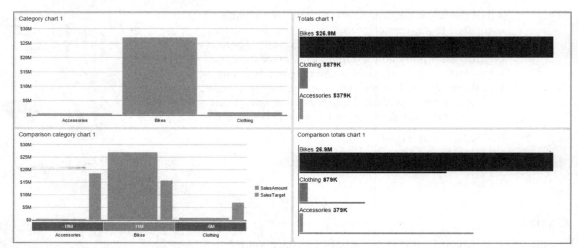

FIGURE 17-11: Same data using different chart types.

The difference between a Category chart and a Totals chart is the way they segregate values into columns or bars. In Mobile Reports, we don't have the same differentiation between column and bar charts as we do in paginated reports. The two Category charts, which are both shown as vertical/column charts here, can be presented either vertically, as a "column chart," or horizontally, as a "bar chart." The Total charts can serve one of two different purposes: either displaying one bar per numeric field selected from the dataset, or as a category-type chart by grouping on a non-numeric value and then aggregating values from a numeric field, similar to conventional charts in paginated reports. This behavior is controlled by the Data structure property. Choose "By columns" to display multiple fields (or dataset columns) or choose "By rows" to categorize values using the field selected in the Series name field property.

The Tree map control does not group detail data. If you have detail data to roll up in a Tree map chart, you will need to handle the grouping in the dataset. The Group by property might seem to be a bit misleading because it simply collects all the details into a container. To demonstrate, using our sample dataset, I have created a Tree map and set the Group by property to use the Category field. The report preview, shown in Figure 17-12, shows that the rectangles within the Bikes category include combinations of Category and CountryRegionCode values.

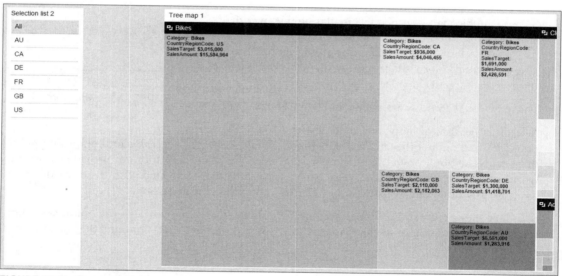

FIGURE 17-12: Report with Tree map.

By combining the Tree map with a Selection list, if a single country code is selected, this would filter the dataset and reduce the rectangles to one distinct value per category group.

Maps

The map visualizations in Mobile Reports are quite simple. A map consists of multiple named shape definitions. Internally, each shape is really a series of points used to "connect-the-dots" and form boundaries. Multiple shapes fit together like a jigsaw puzzle to create the map. Maps are based on the de facto industry standard developed by the Environmental Systems Research Institute (ESRI), a well-known producer of Geographical Informational Systems and mapping software.

Unlike the mapping capabilities for paginated reports, mobile report maps do not support multiple layers, positional data (like latitude and longitude), and cannot consume SQL Server spatial types. Map reports do not require an Internet connection like Power BI maps that use the live Bing Map service.

Three map controls are available:

➤ **Gradient heat map**—Fills map shapes with graduated shades of a color based on the relative value of an aggregated measure field. This type of map visual is useful when you need to visualize values related to different regions for comparison and works well when there are several neighboring regions, like states or counties.

➤ **Range stop map**—Employs KPI-like numeric thresholds to a range of aggregated values for each shape. The resulting values are visualized as solid red, yellow, and green shape fills to indicate whether the value for a geographic region or shape meets the predefined threshold criteria.

➤ **Bubble map**—Displays a circular bubble over the center of each shape. The size of the bubble represents the relative value for the shape and, optionally, the backfill color visualizes the main field value compared to a target field value.

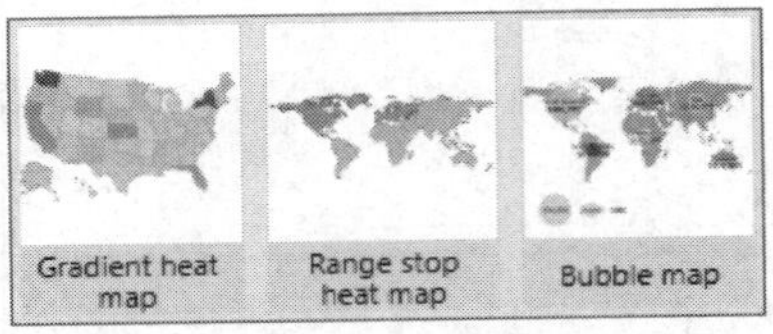

FIGURE 17-13: Map controls.

The map visual controls are shown in Figure 17-13.

A small collection of maps is provided with Mobile Report Publisher and many other maps are available. I have collected several useful maps and provided them with the book download files. For legal reasons, Microsoft does not provide maps of many world countries. Because boundaries can change, any maps provided with the book downloads (or from any other source) should be verified and updated if necessary.

Standard maps consist of two paired files. The shape file (.shp) contains the boundary definition for all of the shapes in the map, and the dBase data file (.dbf) contains the shape names and keys.

> **NOTE** *Yes, you read that correctly… the universal map shape standard uses the old dBase data file format to store map name key/value information. Does this give you an idea about how long this standard has been around?*

To add a new map, add a map control to the report and use the Map property drop-down list. At the bottom of the list (shown in Figure 17-14), click the Custom map... button and then locate one of the two map definition files. Map shape files are currently limited to 500 KB.

The geographic region values in the report dataset must match the shape key identifiers stored in the map. This can be a challenge if you are not familiar with all the shape key values obtained from the map shape file. For this reason, I have included a reference table in the database provided with the book downloads. You can use this reference table to perform the mapping between your data and the shape information stored in both maps that install with the product and the additional maps provided with the book download files.

FIGURE 17-14: Map selection list.

> **TIP** *A reference table of map shape names is included in the database provided with the book download files. This will help you map shape names to the geography regions in your data. I've included shape names for the installed maps and those provided with the book download files.*

Data Grids

Three data controls are used to display detailed information in a grid layout, along with several enhancements:

➤ **Simple Data grid**—Useful when you have multiple rows and columns to display in columnar form—straight and simple. Data is based on one table and displays selected fields. This is the closest we get to transactional reporting in Mobile Reports.

➤ **Indicator Data grid**—Based on one table but it displays selected fields as either columns or indicators/gauges.

Indicators require two fields for metric and target/comparison.

➤ **Chart Data grid**—Supports features of Indicator DataGrid and is based on two tables with matching key fields. The second table is used for the category chart.

In Figure 17-15, you can see that the indicator column contains red and green filled cells in the Value column. This is driven from two columns—a main value and a Target value in order to calculate the relative status.

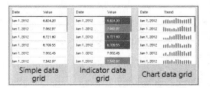

FIGURE 17-15: Data grid controls.

The last control, the Chart data grid, requires two tables that are related using matching key values. The first table drives the columnar table layout and the second produces aggregated chart columns grouped along a specified category. You see a specific example and learn how to use this control in Chapter 20.

SUMMARY

The next three chapters demonstrate how to use the majority of these controls to establish the design techniques required to build working Mobile Report solutions.

You learned how the mobile and paginated report toolsets and features have some common elements, but the design experience is significantly different due to their history and their intended purpose.

Controls on a mobile report are used to navigate, select, and filter data and to interact with other controls. Drill-though actions allow a user to navigate to another report and pass the filtering context and selections made in the original report.

We briefly described and explored differences between every visual control available to report design. We examined the capabilities, data and design needs, and significant features for each control used to create an entire reporting solution.

18

Implementing a Mobile Report with Design-First Development

WHAT'S IN THIS CHAPTER?

➤ Using design-first report development

➤ Creating and using shared datasets

➤ Using Time navigators

➤ Using Selectors

➤ Using Number gauges and charts

➤ Applying mobile layouts and color styling

➤ Deploying and testing a completed mobile report

The purpose of the exercise in this chapter is to introduce mobile report design from start to finish. Using a very simple mobile report scenario and sample sales data, we step through a simplified example exercising the design-first report development pattern.

DESIGN-FIRST MOBILE REPORT DEVELOPMENT EXERCISE

To compete all of the steps for this exercise, you need the following:

➤ SQL Server 2016

➤ Native mode report server

➤ Samples and exercise projects used in earlier chapters

➤ Mobile Report Publisher

➤ Optionally, a mobile device (tablet or phone) with the Power BI mobile app installed

Create a new mobile report from the Web Portal by following these steps:

1. Navigate to your Reporting Services Web Portal.

    If your report server was installed with default settings, the address is `http://myreportserver/Reports` (where `myreportserver` is the name of your report server).

2. Click the Browse icon in the toolbar to show the contents of the `Home` folder rather than your Favorites.

3. Use the "+New" (or "+") menu to add a folder named `Sales Reports`.

4. Navigate to the `Sales Reports` folder.

5. Use the "+New" menu to select Mobile Report (Figure 18-1).

> **NOTE** *When the browser window for the Web Portal is wide enough to show the entire toolbar, the menu items are displayed with the icons along with a short description (for example "+New") but when the window is smaller, the menu items are compacted and only show the icons like you see in Figure 18-1. In the figure, the "+New" menu is displayed as simply "+".*

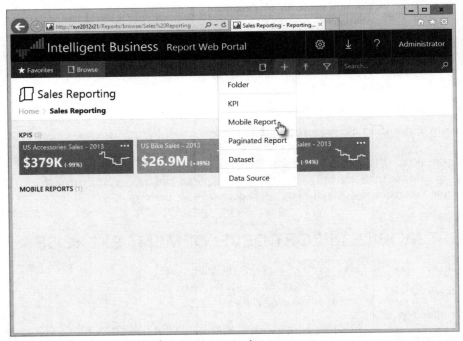

FIGURE 18-1: Web Portal with compact menu items.

The Mobile Report Publisher opens or you are prompted to download and install it. If the Report Publisher has not been previously installed, use the link shown in Figure 18-2 to install the application. If Mobile Report Publisher does not open a few seconds after installing, choose the Mobile Report menu option again.

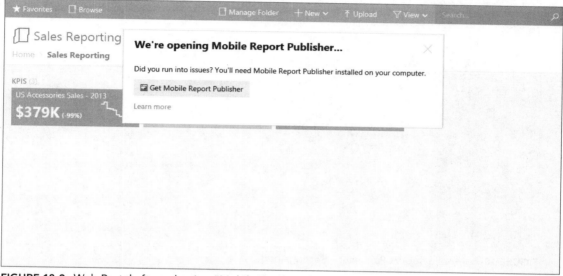

FIGURE 18-2: Web Portal after selecting "Mobile Report."

The Mobile Report Publisher, shown in Figure 18-3, includes toolbar icons and tabs with larger icons, used to navigate between pages.

Common file management options listed on the toolbar include:

➤ Create new mobile report

➤ Open an existing mobile report

➤ Save mobile report

➤ Save mobile report as ...

➤ Connect and manage server connections

Larger icons on the tabs displayed on the left side of the Mobile Report Publisher design window include:

➤ Layout

➤ Data

➤ Settings

➤ Preview

6. Click the Settings icon to open the Settings page for the new mobile report.

7. For the Report title, enter the text **Sales Summary by Country and Category,** as shown in Figure 18-3.

FIGURE 18-3: Mobile Report Publisher—Settings page.

8. Click the "Save mobile report as …" icon on the toolbar to display the options shown in Figure 18-4.

> **TIP** *Before the report is saved the first time, both "Save mobile report" and "Save mobile report as …" icons will perform the same operation, prompting for the location to save the report. After that only the "Save as …" option will prompt for a new location.*

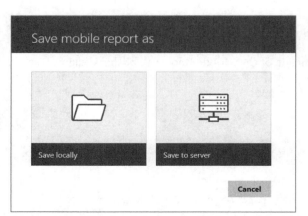

FIGURE 18-4: "Save mobile report as" destination options.

9. Click "Save to server" (Figure 18-5), navigate to the `Sales Reporting` folder on your report server, and then save the report.

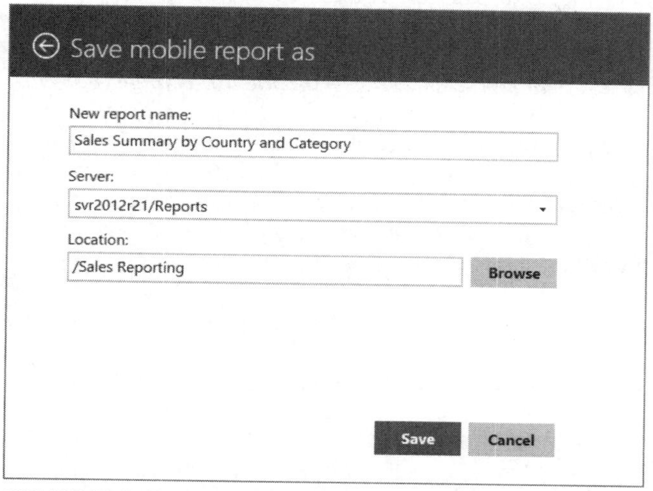

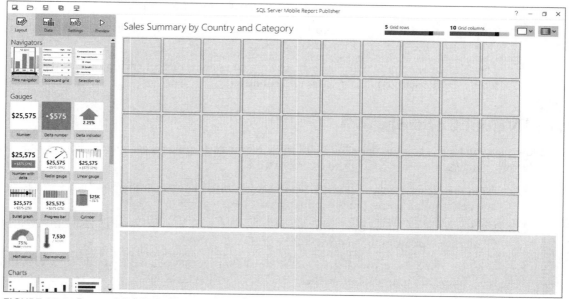

FIGURE 18-5: Report server and location properties.

10. Switch to the Layout page using the left-most tab in the upper left-hand side of the designer.

As you can see in Figure 18-6, a grid is displayed on the report design surface. You can drag and drop visual controls from the panel on the left to any cell in the grid. After you drop a control, use the handle displayed in the bottom-right corner of the control to resize it, stretching it to the right or down, to fill as many cells as you wish.

FIGURE 18-6: Report Mobile Publisher—Layout page.

You can change the number of grid rows and columns using the sliders in the top right-hand side of the designer. Next to the row and column sliders are drop-down lists used to select different mobile device layouts and color palettes. You'll use these a little later on in this exercise.

> **WARNING** *Experienced SSRS report designers are inclined to change the grid rows and columns, adding as many controls as possible. Before you give in to this urge, consider this: the purpose is to design mobile reports optimized for small screens and touch interaction. When viewing a mobile report on a desktop computer, the report might appear overly simple if it has unusually large controls. For this reason, be sure to test mobile reports on a phone or tablet device to ensure that you are providing the best mobile user experience and screen layout.*

Before you start adding controls to the mobile report, let's review the high-level report requirements:

> **NOTE** *Normally, the high-level business and functional report requirements are gathered by interviewing business user stakeholders. The tenets of design-first report development allow you to start designing with only functional requirements and perhaps a modest understanding of the available data.*

➤ Mobile users should be able to select a date period (years, months, or days) or any range of date periods to see aggregated sales metrics.

➤ Users should be able to select the country, or any combination of countries, to see the aggregated sales for those countries within the selected date period range.

➤ The total sales amount, freight cost, taxes, and unit order quantity should be displayed as abbreviated and correctly formatted values.

➤ The sales amount should also be visualized to compare totals for each product category, filtered by the selected date periods and countries.

Add Visual Controls

Now that you have a basic understanding of these requirement guidelines, you can add navigators, selectors, gauges, and other controls to the report:

1. From the Navigators group at the top of the controls panel, drag the Time navigator to the first cell (top-left corner) in the mobile report design grid.

2. Use the resize handle in the bottom-right corner of the Time navigator to resize the control to fill all the columns in the first row of the grid.

3. With the Time navigator selected, use the Visual properties panel displayed below the mobile report designer to update properties with the following tasks, using Figure 18-7 as a guide:

    a. Use the Time levels drop-down list to select Years, Months, and Days.

b. Use the Time range presets drop-down list to deselect all items except All and Last Year.

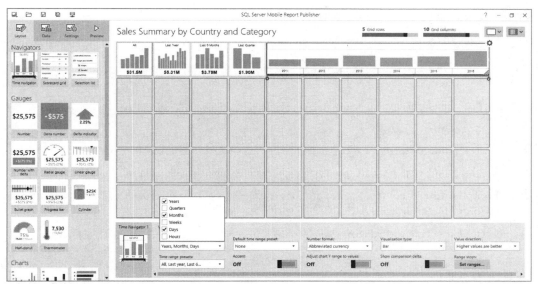

FIGURE 18-7: Time navigator Time level presets.

4. Leave all other properties set to default selections.

5. Drag the Selection list to the left-most cell below the Time navigator and then resize it like Figure 18-8.

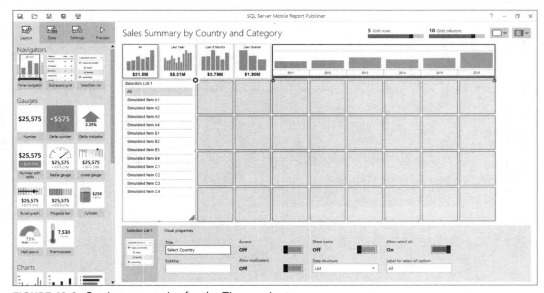

FIGURE 18-8: Setting properties for the Time navigator.

6. In the Visual properties panel, change the title to **Select Country**.

7. From the Gauges control group, add four Number gauges as shown in Figure 18-9.

8. Resize each gauge to be two cells wide.

9. Change the Title for each of the gauges to:

   ➤ Sales Amount

   ➤ Freight

   ➤ Tax Amount

   ➤ Order Quantity

10. Set the Number format for the first three gauges to Abbreviated currency.

11. Set the Number format for the Order Quantity gauge to Abbreviated.

12. From the Charts control group, drag the Category chart and resize it to fill the remaining space on the grid. Use Figure 18-9 to verify the chart properties.

13. Change the Title to Category Sales.

FIGURE 18-9: Category Sales chart added.

Preview the Mobile Report

View the report as it will appear when deployed to the server, and then test the control interactions.

1. Click the Preview icon on the right-most tab to run the report with simulated data.

As you see, simulated data is generated with values appropriate for each visual control. A range of date periods is generated with several years of usable date periods up to the current date.

Remember that this is a simulation of a mobile touch screen interface. On a tablet device, the large controls on this mobile report are better suited for touch navigation and may be presented a little differently so they are familiar to users accustomed to using different devices. If you are using a touch screen computer, you can use the screen to navigate. Otherwise, use the mouse.

2. Touch or click a year on the Time navigator to drill down to the months for the selected year. Note that the number gauges and chart filter values apply the data filtered for the selection.

3. Click and hold or swipe and drag across a range of months to select sales for a given range.

4. Click or touch an item in the Select Country list to filter the values even further. See Figure 18-10.

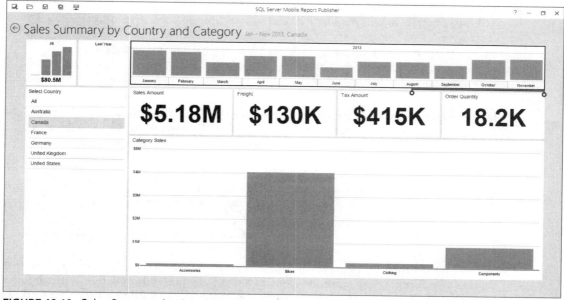

FIGURE 18-10: Sales Summary by Country and Category report with selected Country.

What you have experienced is that by simply adding visual controls to the report, simulated data is generated that can be used to interact with all the controls.

> **NOTE** *Don't underestimate the impact of this simple but powerful feature. Using design-first mobile report development, you can easily demonstrate functionality, report controls, and layout ideas with simulated data. Use this approach to demonstrate design concepts and to get user feedback.*

This report is a very simple example that demonstrates the power of design-first mobile report development.

Add Data to the Report

With a working report using automatically generated simulated data, you can now replace the simulated datasets with real data:

1. Switch to the Data page and note the two datasets named SimulatedTable and Simulated FilterTable. The presence of the two datasets suggests that the best dataset design approach for this report might be to create two different datasets.

> **TIP** *The criteria for using a single dataset or multiple datasets are primarily based on the requirements of each control, and the interactions between controls. Use different datasets when one selector or navigator should filter a dataset.*

In this example, a single dataset can be used for the Time navigator and all the visual controls on the report, except for the Country selector. We don't want the Country selector to be filtered by the Time navigator so it should be driven by an independent dataset.

> **NOTE** *Some controls require a dataset with records grouped at the appropriate level of detail to support the visual. Other controls, which we explore later, also require two datasets correlated using matching key columns.*

We will review the data requirements for all of the visual controls a bit later. The controls on this mobile report can consume datasets having various levels of detail. With an understanding of how these controls work and the data structure required for them to work, you can create the necessary dataset queries.

2. Review the two simulated datasets shown in Figure 18-11. The SimulatedTable has a column of date, time, or date/time type values.

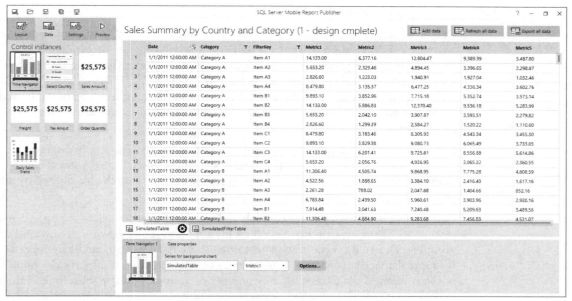

FIGURE 18-11: Data page with simulated datasets.

3. Review the controls in the mobile report, shown in Figure 18-12.

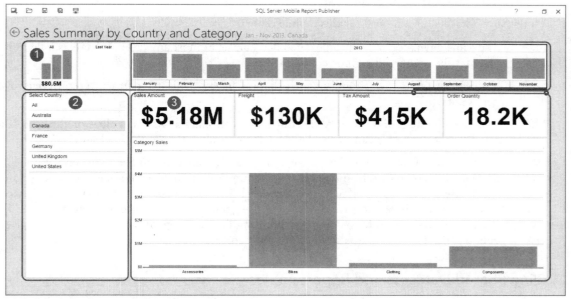

FIGURE 18-12: Visual controls on the report.

Referring to the callout areas in Figure 18-12:

➤ **Callout area 1: Time navigator**—A Time navigator is the combination of both a date or time period selector and a categorized chart. It will generate (depending on the Time levels property selection) a contiguous range of date or time periods between the earliest and latest date/time values existing in a dataset. Unlike a date dimension table, a contiguous range of dates is not required in the query result. The Time navigator will actually fill in gaps left in the data and create all of the date or time periods for the range.

➤ **Callout area 2: Country Selection list**—A Selection list control simply displays one item per row and does not group or aggregate values. A separate dataset is commonly used to drive this control and to avoid having items on the list filtered by other selector or navigator controls in the report.

➤ **Callout area 3: Number gauge controls and Category chart control**—A gauge control simply aggregates all the row values for a numeric column without any kind of grouping. Due to its versatility, gauges often share datasets that can be optimized for more demanding controls. If the dataset returns one row, it displays the value of the column. If the dataset has any number of multiple rows, it rolls up the values in the column using a specified aggregate function.

Not all mobile report chart controls play by the same rules and behave the same way. The Category chart you used in this report is similar to charts in paginated reports. It consumes a dataset with multiple rows, groups all the records on a specified field value, and then aggregates numeric columns of the detail rows within the groupings.

How many datasets do you need for this mobile report?

➤ The Time navigator can consume a detailed dataset at most any level of detail as long as it includes the range of date/time column values.

➤ The Select Country Selection list control should have a dedicated dataset to return one row per country.

➤ The number gauge and category chart in area 3 can share a dataset. Values of all controls in this area should be filtered by the Time navigator and by the Country selector.

➤ If it were important for the Time navigator to remain independent from the controls in area 3, and perhaps not be filtered by the Country selection, it would make sense to isolate the datasets for areas 1 and 3. For simplicity's sake, you will use one dataset for these two controls. The only possible consequence of using a filtered table for both controls would be that, if no data existed for a country or if only a limited range of records existed for a given country, the Time navigator would only show corresponding dates.

Adding Shared Datasets and Report Tables

Adding a shared dataset to a mobile report is quite simple. Figure 18-13 shows the Sales Summary by Country and Category mobile report after completing the steps in the next section, with tables from two new datasets added and the simulated tables removed. Removing the simulated data is not important from the perspective that they add very little processing and storage overhead to the report. However, I typically remove simulated data to ensure that all of the controls have been bound to the actual tables I added after importing replacement datasets. If you attempt to remove a table that has controls bound to it, the designer displays a warning and does not allow the table to be removed.

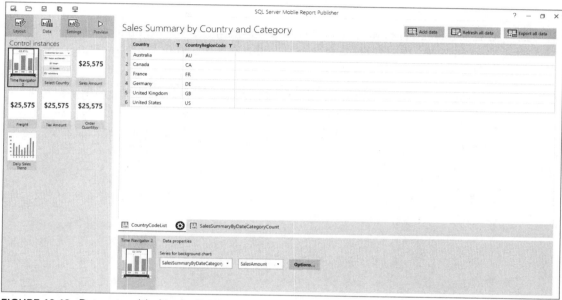

FIGURE 18-13: Datasets added in the Data page.

> **NOTE** *You can create shared datasets using either SSDT for Visual Studio or Report Builder. The only reason I have instructed you to use both is to provide experience with both tools.*

Create a Shared Dataset with Report Builder

You can design shared datasets using two different tools. If you are a report project developer using Visual Studio and SSDT, you can use a shared data source in the SSDT project, add datasets, and deploy them from SSDT. You can also design and deploy shared datasets directly from Report Builder. Either way, the process is relatively similar. In the next steps and those in the following section, I give you a little experience using both tools. Let's start with Report Builder:

1. In Web Portal, navigate to the Home folder and then to the Datasets subfolder.

> **NOTE** *By default, SSDT creates a Datasets folder so if you have previously deployed a report project, the Datasets folder will exist. If not, use the Web Portal to create a folder named Datasets in the Home folder. It really doesn't matter in what folder your shared datasets reside as long as you know where to find them.*

2. On the toolbar, click the "+New" menu item and then select the option to create a shared dataset. Report Builder opens with the New Report or Dataset dialog, shown in Figure 18-14.

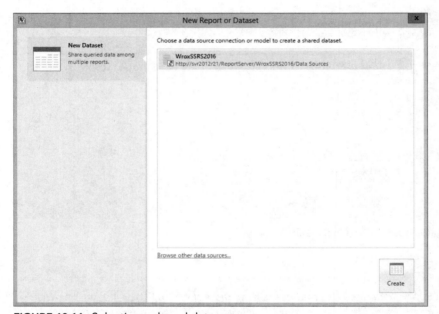

FIGURE 18-14: Selecting a shared data source.

3. Click the WroxSSRS2016 shared data source and then click the Create button.

4. Enter this query directly into the Query box (or use the "Edit as Text" toolbar option in the query designer) and test it, and then save it to the Datasets folder on the report server. Name the dataset **Country Code List**.

```
SELECT DISTINCT
    Country,
```

```
                CountryRegionCode
    FROM    SalesTerritory
    WHERE   Country <> 'NA'
```

Create a Shared Dataset with SSDT

Beginning in the SSDT project, Wrox SSRS 2016 Exercises, add a new shared dataset to the project that references the shared data source named WroxSSRS2016:

1. Name the dataset **SalesSummaryByDateCategoryCountry**.

2. Enter and test the following query in the query designer. I prefer to use the Edit as Text option:

```
SELECT
        [OrderDate],
        [ProductCategory],
        CountryRegionCode,
        [Country],
        SUM([OrderQuantity]) AS [OrderQuantity],
        SUM([SalesAmount]) AS [SalesAmount],
        SUM([TaxAmt]) AS [TaxAmt],
        SUM([Freight]) AS [Freight]
FROM [vSalesDetails]
GROUP BY
        [OrderDate],
        [ProductCategory],
        CountryRegionCode,
        [Country]
ORDER BY
        [OrderDate],
        [ProductCategory],
        CountryRegionCode,
        [Country]
    ;
```

3. After the query has been written, tested, and named correctly in the Shared Dataset Properties dialog shown in Figure 18-15, close and save the query.

4. Right-click the dataset and deploy it to the Datasets folder on the report server.

   The destination should be set as the default deployment path in the project.

5. Use the Web Portal to inspect the Datasets folder. Refresh the browser windows if necessary and make sure that the two new shared datasets are there, similar to Figure 18-16.

Add Data Tables to the Mobile Report

The reason mobile reports use only shared datasets is that, unlike SSRS paginated reports, query definitions are not stored in the report definition files. The Mobile Report Publisher refers to the data structure object based on query results as a "table." Subsequently, there is no query designer in the design tool.

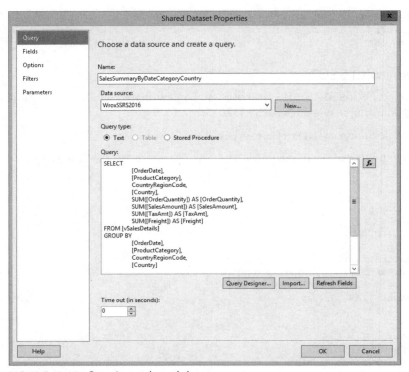

FIGURE 18-15: Creating a shared dataset.

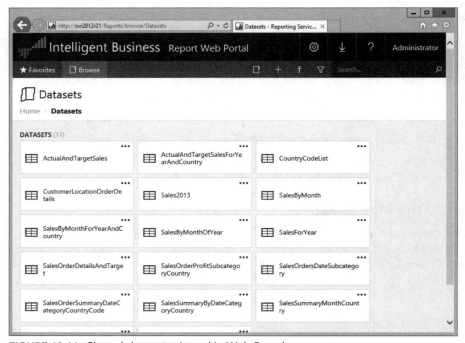

FIGURE 18-16: Shared datasets viewed in Web Portal.

Add tables from the shared datasets using these steps:

1. Return to the Mobile Report Publisher.
2. On the Data page, click the Add Data button on the top-right side of the window. The Add Data options are displayed, as you see in Figure 18-17.

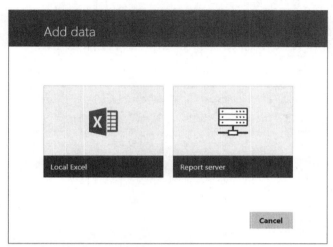

FIGURE 18-17: Add data options.

3. Choose the Report Server option on the right side to select a server. You can see my development server in Figure 18-18.

FIGURE 18-18: Select the report server.

A connection to your report server is added the first time you open Mobile Report Publisher from the Web Portal. You should see your report server and any other report servers you may have added in previous sessions.

4. Select your report server from the list and then browse to the CountryCodeList dataset in the `Datasets` folder. Selecting the dataset adds it to the mobile report.
5. Click the Add Data button again and add the SalesSummaryByDateCategoryCountry dataset to the report.

On the Data page of the Mobile Report Publisher, shown in Figure 18-19, you should see the two new tables imported from the selected datasets.

	OrderDate	CountryRegionCode	ProductCategory	Country	TaxAmt	Freight	
1	12/29/2010 12:00:00...	CA	Accessories	Canada	24.22	7.57	1
2	12/29/2010 12:00:00...	US	Accessories	United States	111.43	34.82	6
3	12/29/2010 12:00:00...	CA	Bikes	Canada	7,939.28	2,481.03	1
4	12/29/2010 12:00:00...	US	Bikes	United States	28,319.26	8,849.77	3
5	12/29/2010 12:00:00...	CA	Clothing	Canada	58.89	18.40	4
6	12/29/2010 12:00:00...	US	Clothing	United States	171.12	53.48	1
7	12/29/2010 12:00:00...	CA	Components	Canada	1,206.48	377.03	4
8	12/29/2010 12:00:00...	US	Components	United States	1,315.60	411.12	6
9	1/29/2011 12:00:00...	CA	Accessories	Canada	67.83	21.20	4
10	1/29/2011 12:00:00...	US	Accessories	United States	219.63	68.63	1
11	1/29/2011 12:00:00...	CA	Bikes	Canada	23,486.52	7,339.54	2
12	1/29/2011 12:00:00...	US	Bikes	United States	89,573.75	27,991.80	8
13	1/29/2011 12:00:00...	CA	Clothing	Canada	104.39	32.62	8
14	1/29/2011 12:00:00...	US	Clothing	United States	458.70	143.34	3
15	1/29/2011 12:00:00...	CA	Components	Canada	1,699.75	531.17	8
16	1/29/2011 12:00:00...	US	Components	United States	7,462.10	2,331.91	2
17	3/1/2011 12:00:00 AM	CA	Accessories	Canada	72.67	22.71	4
18	3/1/2011 12:00:00 AM	US	Accessories	United States	187.33	58.54	1

SimulatedTable   SimulatedFilterTable   CountryCodeList   SalesSummaryByDateCategoryCount ⚙

Time Navigator 1   Data properties

Series for background chart:

| SimulatedTable ▾ | Metric1 ▾ | **Options...** |

FIGURE 18-19: New tables added to report datasets.

6. Verify that you are setting the data properties for the Time navigator.

You should see the control instance named Time Navigator 1 displayed to the left of the properties panel below the data grid. To switch controls, use the Layout page, select the visual control, and then switch to the Data page.

Set Data Properties for the Time Navigator

In the steps in this section, carefully check the figures to make sure you have the correct control selected. To select a different control, return to the Layout page using the tabs on the left side of the mobile report designer grid. In the Data page, the control is displayed on the left-hand side of the Data properties panel.

The Time navigator control automatically detects date and time values and generates time periods for dates between the earliest and latest date/time values in the corresponding data table.

1. Ensure that you have selected the Time Navigator 1 control. If a different control is selected, return to the Layout page and select the Time navigator.

2. In the Data properties panel, shown in Figure 18-20, drop down the "Series for background chart" list and select the SalesSummaryByDateCategoryCountry dataset.

3. Use the drop-down list to the right and check the SalesAmount field, as you see in Figure 18-20.

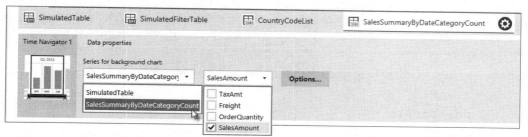

FIGURE 18-20: Time navigator background chart properties.

Set Data Properties for the Selection List

Selection list controls are used to filter other datasets on a mobile report. One dataset is needed to populate the selection list and another dataset is filtered using the items selected from the list. A set of matching key columns is used to perform matching and filtering between the two datasets.

1. Return to the Layout page and click the Select Country selection list on the report design grid.

2. Select the Data page and refer to Figure 18-21 to set the Data properties.

FIGURE 18-21: Filter options in the properties for the Select Country control.

3. From the Keys drop-down list, select the CountryCodeList table.

4. In the field drop-down list to the right, select the CountryRegionCode field.

You can ignore the two Options buttons. The data for this control will not be filtered by any other selection nor are there any numeric fields to be aggregated.

A panel is located to the right, titled The Tables Filtered by Select Country.

5. In the table filtering panel, check only the SalesSummaryByDateCategoryCountry dataset and drop down the adjacent list.

6. Choose the CountryRegionCode field. This is the key column in the target table that will be filtered using key values in the selection list table.

Set Data Properties for the Number Gauges

The most basic of all the visual controls, the number gauge simply aggregates all values in a specified column. All the other gauge controls require another column that is used for comparison, as a KPI or progress indicator. Values should be formatted appropriately, whether currency, percentages, decimal, or whole values.

1. Return to the Layout page and select the Sales Amount number gauge on the report design grid.

2. Select the Data page.

3. From the Main Value drop-down list, select the SalesSummaryByDateCategoryCountry table.

4. From the adjacent field drop-down list, select the SalesAmount field.

5. Click the Options button to display the Filter and Aggregation options, shown in Figure 18-22.

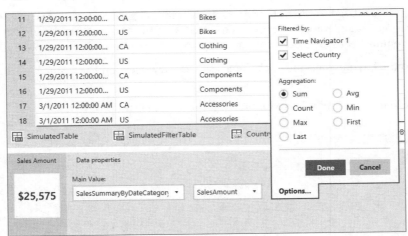

FIGURE 18-22: Number gauge data filter properties and aggregating function selection.

6. Check both the Time Navigator 1 and Select Country controls. These navigator and selection controls are used to filter data for the number gauge.

7. Verify that the Sum aggregation is selected.

8. Repeat the same steps for the three remaining number gauge controls. Choose the corresponding fields for the Freight, Tax Amount, and Order Quantity number gauge controls.

Set Data Properties for the Category Chart

The category chart is similar to charts and other data regions used in paginated reports. The Category Coordinate properties define a group for aggregation, similar to the group expression in paginated reports.

1. Return to the Layout page and select the Category Sales category chart.

2. Select the Data page and follow Figure 18-23 to complete the property assignments.

FIGURE 18-23: Category Sales chart Data properties.

3. Drop down the Category Coordinate list and select the SalesSummaryByDateCategoryCountry table.

4. Drop down the corresponding field list and select the ProductCategory field.

5. Use the field list to the right of the Main Series and select the SalesAmount field.

6. Use each of the Options buttons to check both the Time Navigator 1 and Select Country controls for filtering, and verify that the Sum aggregation is used.

Apply Mobile Layouts and Color Styling

The color palette options are defined in the brand package applied to the report server. To style the report, you select a color palette and a layout for mobile devices.

1. Return to the Layout page.

2. Use the color palette drop-down in the upper-right corner to select a themed style for the mobile report. See Figure 18-24 for some examples.

Color palettes correspond to the custom branding theme applied to the Web Portal.

3. Use the Preview tab to view the mobile report with data.

This time you see the real sales data from the SQL Server database.

4. Test the report by interacting with the Time navigator and "Select Country" Selection list. Click or tap and hold on a column in the chart to see more information about the data point.

5. Switch to Layout view and then use the drop-down control to the left of the color palette selector (see Figure 18-25) to show the Master, Tablet, and Phone layouts.

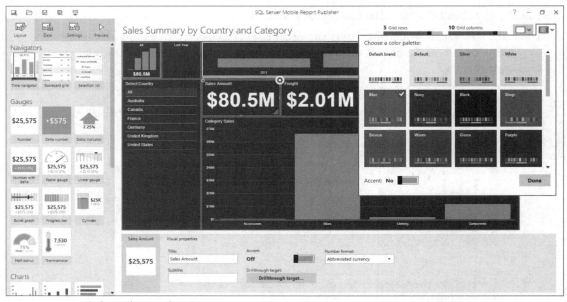

FIGURE 18-24: Color palette selection.

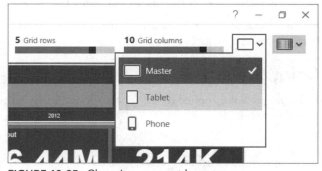

FIGURE 18-25: Choosing a report layout.

Creating alternate mobile device layouts is very easy to do. The control instances that you had added to the original Master layout are displayed in the panel to the left of the mobile report design grid. The default Tablet layout for portrait orientation is five cells wide by ten cells tall.

6. Click the layout drop-down list and choose the Tablet layout.

7. Drag and drop controls into the grid, and resize and arrange them to resemble the example in Figure 18-26.

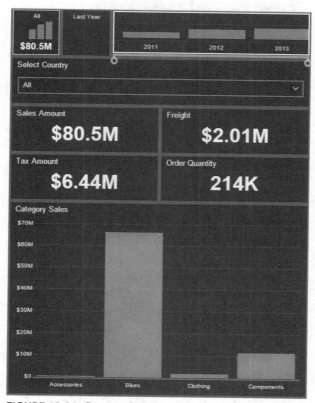

FIGURE 18-26: Report shown in phone layout.

8. Preview the mobile report in this layout to see how it will look and behave on a tablet in portrait orientation.

9. Switch back to Layout view.

10. Select the Phone layout and arrange the control instances to resemble Figure 18-27.

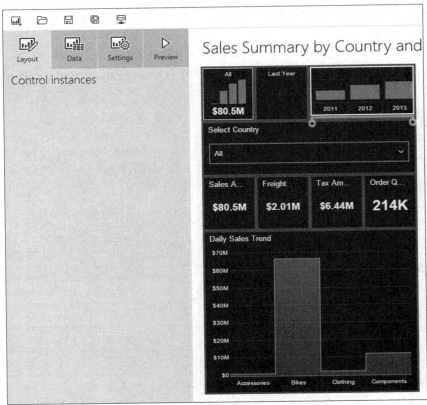

FIGURE 18-27: Report optimized for the phone layout.

11. Preview the mobile report in this layout to see how it will look when used on a smart phone. Figure 18-28 shows the preview.

Test the Completed Mobile Report from the Server

Although previewing a mobile report in the Mobile Report Publisher should approximate a user's experience with published reports, it is always a good idea to test the actual report in a production-like environment:

1. Save the mobile report to the report server before closing the Mobile Report Publisher.

   If you had previously saved the report to the server, clicking the floppy disk icon in the toolbar is sufficient.

2. Navigate to the published mobile report in the Web Portal and click to open the report in the browser.

3. Use the Time navigator and Selection list controls to explore and interact with the report data.

4. If you have a touch screen, use the touch interface to navigate the report, which is shown in Figure 18-29.

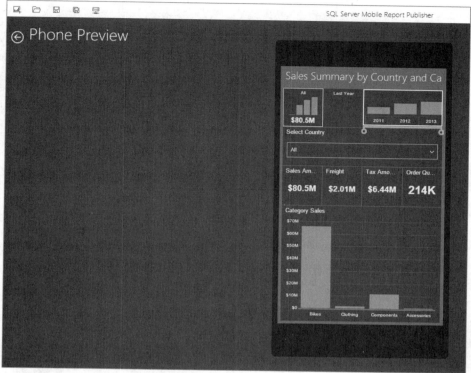

FIGURE 18-28: Phone layout preview.

FIGURE 18-29: Sales Summary by Country and Category report in Web Portal.

If you have Wifi network access to the report server from a mobile device, such as a tablet or smart phone, follow these steps to connect to the mobile report.

If your report server is behind a firewall or if Windows Firewall is running on the report server, you may need to follow the steps in the following article to open port 80 and allow report connectivity to the Internet or wireless network: https://msdn.microsoft.com/en-us/library/bb934283.aspx.

> **TIP** *If you are using a development report server that has inbound traffic exposed to the Internet, you can quickly test report connectivity by temporarily turning off the firewall. Just remember to turn it back on when you are finished.*

5. On your tablet or phone device, use the mobile vendor's app store to find and install the Power BI Mobile app. The mobile application can be installed, free of charge, from the Apple, Google, or Microsoft app store.

6. Run the app and choose the option to connect to a server. Figure 18-30 shows the Power BI Mobile running on my iPad. To add the server connection, I expand the menu bar and tap Connect Server.

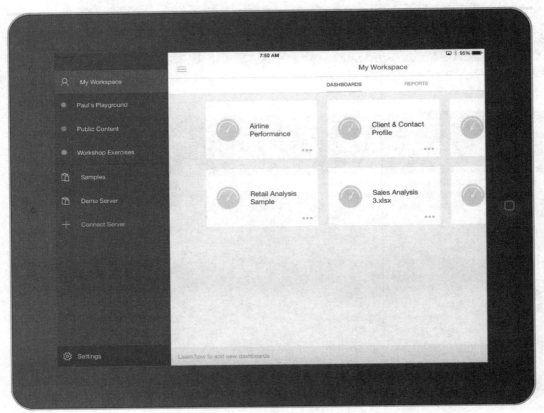

FIGURE 18-30: Power BI Mobile app on tablet.

7. Add the web address of your report server.

8. This will be the same address you use to access the report Web Portal on your web browser but without the `http://` prefix. The default address is `servername/Reports`. You can also use the server's IP address in place of the server name.

9. Enter a username and password to connect to the server. Depending on your network environment, you may need to prefix the username with the domain name and a backslash (like `domain\username`). Figure 18-31 shows the server connection configuration on my iPad.

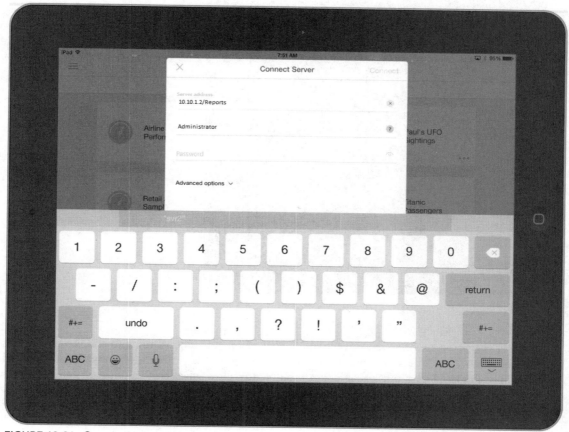

FIGURE 18-31: Connecting to server.

10. On your mobile device, use the new server connection to navigate to the report server, locate the mobile report, and open it.

11. If you are using a tablet device, rotate the screen to transition from Master to Tablet layout.

12. Figure 18-32 shows the live mobile report in portrait orientation. Interact with the report by using the Time navigator to drill down and select different time periods and select combinations or ranges of countries. Tap and hold the chart columns to view more details about the selected data point.

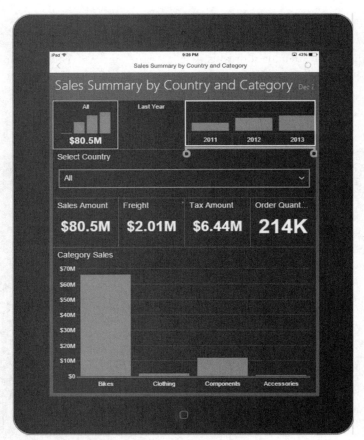

FIGURE 18-32: Report viewed in the mobile app.

This is a very simple mobile report that you have developed from beginning to end, using a design-first approach. By adding combinations of visual controls to the report, the Mobile Report Publisher generated simulated data that provided an example to follow when creating queries and shared datasets to support the actual user reporting experience. You will see in examples in the following chapters that this pattern is useful when designing more sophisticated reporting solutions with significant business value.

SUMMARY

Design-driven development helps solve one of the most vexing problems in report solution design by helping report designers quickly move past the common roadblock of getting the data structure right before adding controls to the report. We have covered the basics of design-driven mobile report development with realistic data and some of the most rudimentary controls to get the feel of the design and usability experience. Use this pattern to quickly build simple prototypes and get user feedback. In your prototyping plan, you should plan to use iterative cycles, toss out designs that do not meet requirements, and try again until you find a design that works for your users. When presenting and demonstrating mobile report solutions, use actual mobile devices, using either screen sharing software or hands-on demonstrators, so users can realize the value of mobile reporting first-hand.

Building on the basics we just covered, Chapter 19 will explore the design patterns applied to mobile reports. You will create dataset queries to support KPIs and trends and then use more sophisticated visual controls to design a report with multiple trends and a map to analyze sales by region.

19

Mobile Report Design Patterns

WHAT'S IN THIS CHAPTER?

- ➤ Introducing KPIs
- ➤ Setting KPI target, status, and trends
- ➤ Creating a time-series mobile report
- ➤ Using a Time navigator, Number gauge, and Time chart
- ➤ Implementing design-first report development
- ➤ Configuring server access
- ➤ Using reports on mobile devices

Now that you have seen how to design a simple mobile report using the design-first development pattern, we turn our attention to a realistic business report design. You start with a KPI, and then create a mobile report with a Time navigator, Selection list, Number gauges, Time charts, and a gradient heat map using a custom map shape file. Like the example in Chapter 18, you will apply mobile device layouts and then test the report on a phone device. In Chapter 20, you create a series of drill-through reports that provide a navigation path from the KPI, to the new sales trend report, and then all the way down to transactional details.

KEY PERFORMANCE INDICATORS

A *key performance indicator*, or KPI, is a measurement of an organization's success in a certain area. KPIs typically indicate the status of performance across specific business metrics that may be organized into a visual scorecard or dashboard.

Each KPI is displayed as a tile in a Web Portal folder. Like paginated reports and mobile reports, KPIs are displayed on each user's Favorites page. Figure 19-1 contains call-outs to describe the elements of the "US Bike Sales - 2013" KPI.

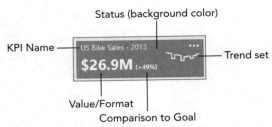

Status (background color)

KPI Name

Trend set

Value/Format

Comparison to Goal

FIGURE 19-1: Elements of a KPI.

Think of a KPI as a separate report with very simple element values that can be obtained from either a query or entered manually when the KPI is created or modified. A KPI consists of the following elements:

➤ Value

➤ Goal

➤ Status

➤ Trend set

The Value, Goal, and Status elements are scalar values, expressed as a single data point. A query written specifically to populate these elements will typically only return one row; however, the Value and Goal elements can be aggregated from a multiple row result set using common aggregate functions like SUM or Average. The Status element expects one of three integer values, which are interpreted as:

1 = good

0 = neutral

−1 = bad

The Status values are used to set the background color of the KPI tile according to presets in the branding package applied to the report server. In the default branding package, 1 (good) is green, 0 (neutral) is amber, and −1 (bad) is red. It is typically not a good idea to try to aggregate the status values from a multiple row query because the resulting value must be an integer with exactly one of these three states.

Let's try it out:

1. Make sure the shared dataset named "Actual And Target Sales" and "Sales By Month For Year And Country" in the Wrox SSRS 2016 Samples projects are deployed to the Datasets folder.

> **NOTE** *The T-SQL script for this dataset is provided here just for reference. The shared datasets are included in the sample project so you don't need to type long queries like this one.*

In addition to the `SalesAmount` and `SalesTarget` columns, the query contains business logic that reduces a comparison between those two column values to a three-state integer for the Status value:

```
-- Actual And Target Sales
With ActualSales as
(
        select
                p.ProductCategory,
                YEAR(s.OrderDate) as OrderYear,
                SUM(s.SalesAmount) SalesAmount
        from
                [dbo].[Sales] s
                inner join Product p on s.ProductKey = p.ProductKey
                inner join SalesTerritory st on s.SalesTerritoryKey =
st.TerritoryKey
        group by
                p.ProductCategory,
                st.CountryRegionCode,
                YEAR(s.OrderDate)
)
select
        t.Category,
        SUM(a.SalesAmount) as SalesAmount,
        SUM(t.SalesTarget) as SalesTarget,
         (SUM(a.SalesAmount)-SUM(t.SalesTarget))/SUM(t.SalesTarget) as
ActualOverTarget,
        CASE
                WHEN (SUM(a.SalesAmount)-SUM(t.SalesTarget))/SUM(t.SalesTarget) <
-.25 THEN -1
                WHEN (SUM(a.SalesAmount)-SUM(t.SalesTarget))/SUM(t.SalesTarget) > 0
THEN 1
                ELSE 0
        END as Status
from [dbo].[SalesTarget] t
        inner join ActualSales a on t.Category = a.ProductCategory
        and t.OrderYear = a.OrderYear
where
        t.OrderYear = @Year
        and t.Category IN(@Category)
        and t.CountryRegionCode IN(@CountryCode)
group by
        t.Category
;
```

2. To create a KPI, navigate to the `Sales Reporting` folder in the Web Portal, click "+ New" to drop down the menu, and select KPI.

Figure 19-2 (shown after step 7) shows the KPI page with the following steps completed. Use it to validate the KPI design.

3. Enter the KPI name **US Bike Sales - 2013**.

4. Add a description to be displayed when a user chooses the KPI in the Web Portal or their mobile device.

5. For the Value format, choose Abbreviated currency... .

6. Verify that USD is selected for the Currency.

7. For the Value, choose Dataset field and then click the ellipsis (three dots) next to the dataset field box.

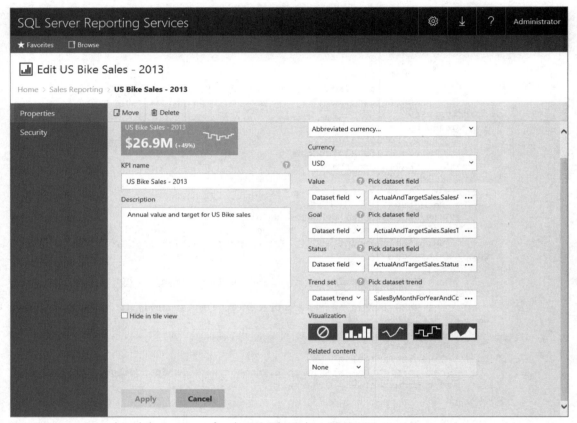

FIGURE 19-2: Completed design page for the US Bike Sales - 2013 KPI.

8. Navigate to the `Datasets` folder and select the Actual And Target Sales dataset.

9. The Parameters window is shown in Figure 19-3. Enter the parameter values shown here and then click the Next button.

    In Figure 19-4, you can see the results of the query with the parameter values you entered in the previous window. Because there is only one row returned by the query, the Aggregation selection actually doesn't matter and any aggregate function will return the right value. If the query returned multiple rows, this selection would be important.

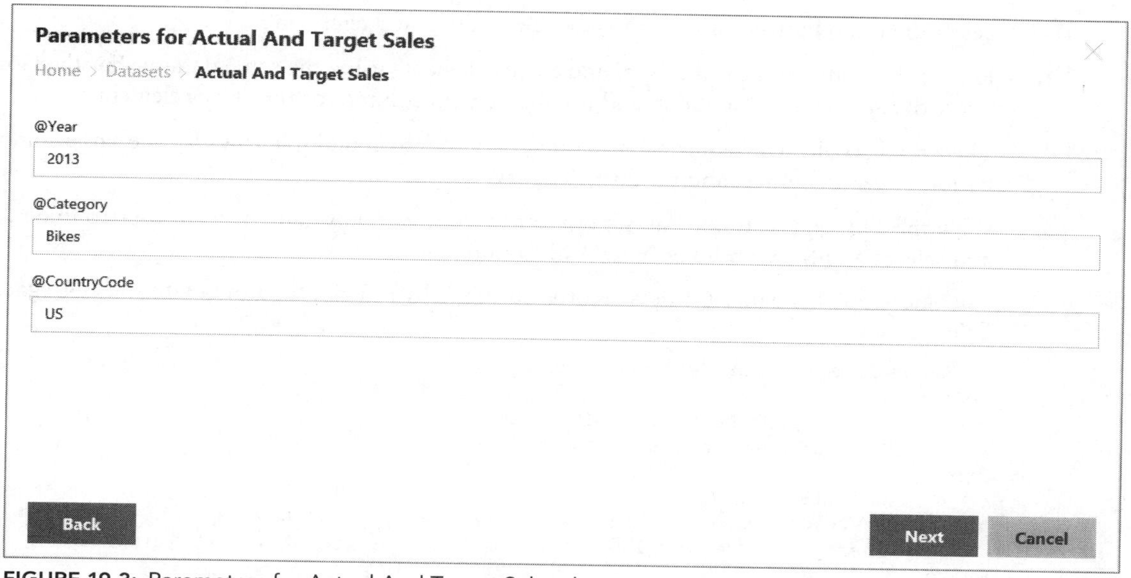
Parameters for Actual And Target Sales
Home > Datasets > Actual And Target Sales
@Year
2013
@Category
Bikes
@CountryCode
US
Back
Next
Cancel

FIGURE 19-3: Parameters for Actual And Target Sales dataset.

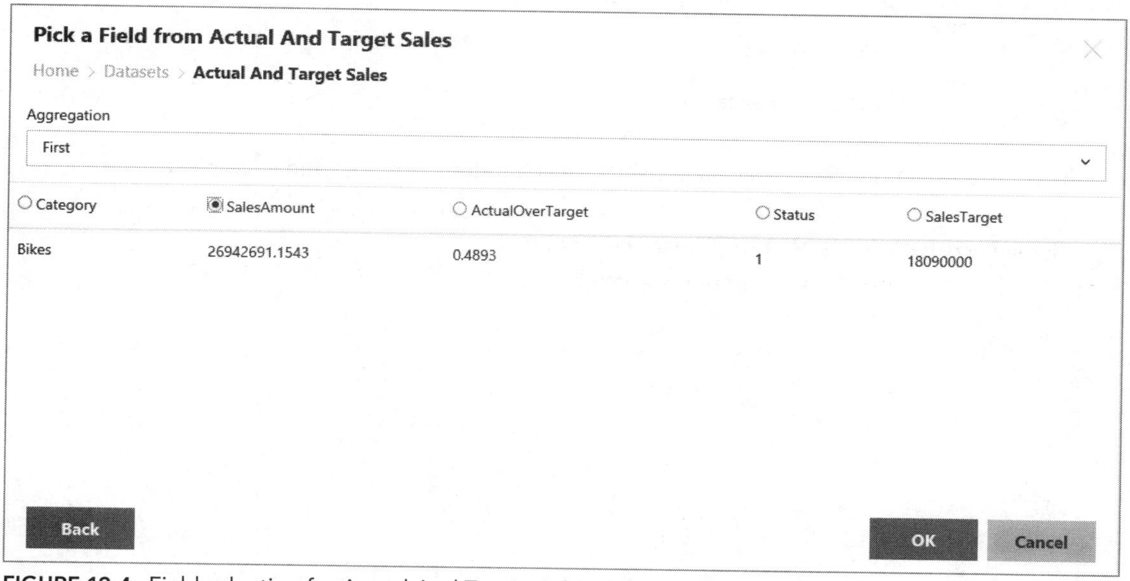
Pick a Field from Actual And Target Sales
Home > Datasets > Actual And Target Sales
Aggregation
First
○ Category
◉ SalesAmount
○ ActualOverTarget
○ Status
○ SalesTarget
Bikes
26942691.1543
0.4893
1
18090000
Back
OK
Cancel

FIGURE 19-4: Field selection for Actual And Target Sales dataset.

10. Select the radio button for the `SalesAmount` column and click OK.

11. Repeat the same steps for the Goal and Status elements using the same dataset. For the Goal, select the `SalesTarget` column and use the `Status` column for the Status element.

12. The Trend set element requires a separate query to return multiple rows for the same combination of year, country, and product category.

13. Click the ellipsis next to the dataset box for this element, navigate to the `Datasets` folder, and select Sales By Month For Year And Country.

The query for this dataset orders records correctly by the month, along with the aggregated SalesAmount:

```
-- Sales By Month For Year And Country
select
        MONTH(s.OrderDate) as OrderMonth,
        SUM(s.SalesAmount) SalesAmount
from
        [dbo].[Sales] s
        inner join Product p on s.ProductKey = p.ProductKey
        inner join SalesTerritory st on s.SalesTerritoryKey = st.TerritoryKey
where
        YEAR(s.OrderDate) = @Year
        and st.CountryRegionCode IN(@CountryCode)
        and p.ProductCategory IN(@Category)
group by
        MONTH(s.OrderDate)
order by
        MONTH(s.OrderDate)
;
```

14. As in Figure 19-5, enter the same parameter values as before and click Next.

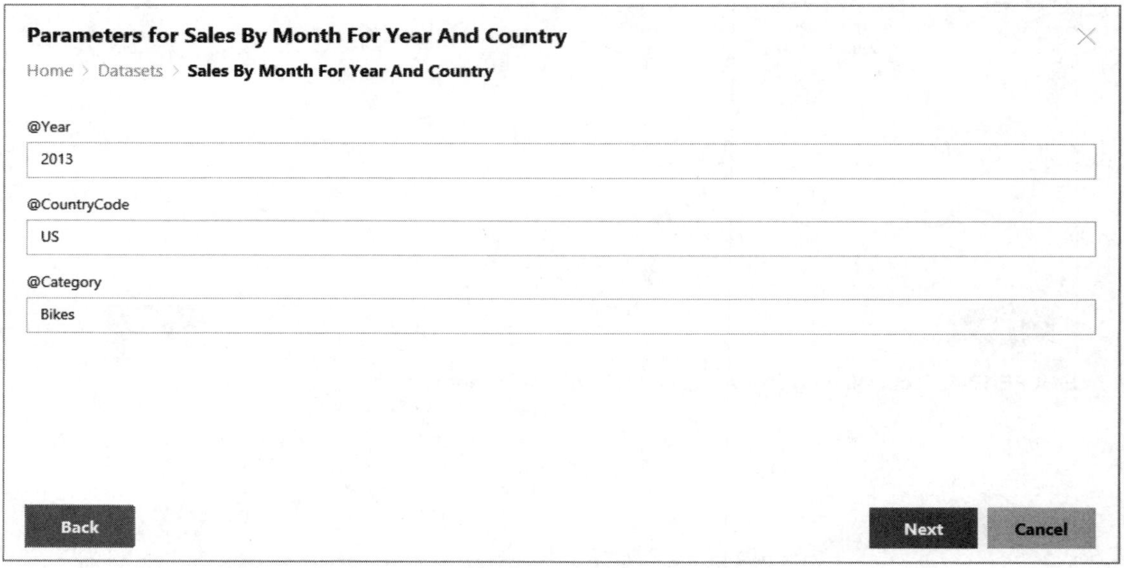

Parameters for Sales By Month For Year And Country   ✕

Home › Datasets › **Sales By Month For Year And Country**

@Year

| 2013 |

@CountryCode

| US |

@Category

| Bikes |

Back   Next   Cancel

FIGURE 19-5: Parameter values for Sales By Month For Year And Country dataset.

15. Select the SalesAmount radio button shown in Figure 19-6 and click OK.

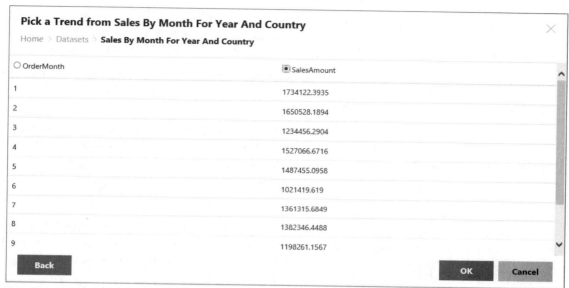

FIGURE 19-6: Field selection for Sales By Month For Year And Country dataset.

16. Select the Stepped Visualization.

> **NOTE** *The Related content property is used to create a drill-through action for the KPI. This allows navigation to a mobile report, web page, or any URL-addressable resource. You will set this property after creating the next reports.*

17. Double-check the properties you set in the US Bike Sales - 2013 KPI design page in Figure 19-2.

18. Click the Create button when completed.

Figure 19-7 shows three sample KPIs that use the same two datasets, passing different parameter values. In addition to the Category, you could also pass different years and countries.

FIGURE 19-7: KPIs in the Web Portal.

THE THING ABOUT KPIs

Key performance indicators are really at the heart of a true Business Intelligence solution, and are used to manage a metric-driven business. Often simple in concept, but challenging to truly implement in practice, KPIs provide business leaders actionable key metrics to drive business decisions.

Software-based decisions are often not as simple as they seem and can be prone to errors and misguided calculations. Business process and culture may not naturally support the KPI paradigm. Following are two examples where this was the case.

The Washington State Department of Corrections implemented a data-driven system for all prisons and jails in the state to calculate the release dates for inmates in 2002. Some prisons are full and there is a need to expedite the release of eligible inmates.

The system tracks an inmate's original sentence, factors based on the severity of crimes, and credits for good behavior, education, and community service. The system calculated a key metric that told Department of Corrections officials when a prisoner was up for early release. Twelve years after the system had been in regular use, one victim's family questioned an inmate's release date. The ensuing investigation found a gross logic error in the calculation for good behavior credit that varied wildly by different correctional facilities; as much as 600 days. Before the error was corrected, 3,200 inmates had been released too early.

Please do not misunderstand my purpose in sharing this example. Used effectively, business scorecards, dashboards, and KPIs are powerful and important. You are likely to find some, perhaps most, KPIs to be uncomplicated. Understand the potential impact of boiling a lot of data and potentially, complex business rules, down to a simple indicator used to make important decisions. I can't emphasize how important it is to make sure those values are accurate and reliable.

You Need Goals

Here is another example. One of my consulting clients, a Fortune 500 manufacturing company, contracted us to architect a large BI solution. Executives wanted "dashboards with KPIs" so we went to work digging up business requirements and wrangling data sources to map out the solution architecture. I led the discussion in one of the investigation meetings with an executive stakeholder to define the first round of KPIs. We had a list of key metrics used in the order fulfillment and manufacturing process. I said, "What are your targets for these metrics?" The executive said, "We would like to see them improve." "That's great," I said. "What goals do you have for improvement?" He said, "This one should be better than it was last year." It became apparent that their process for measuring success was not target-driven. Leaders had been running the business the same way for decades. They knew when the business was or wasn't profitable but they were not really measuring success as much as they were measuring profitability against their balance sheet. For this business unit, the KPI paradigm was a tough fit.

Meeting with the sales director, I expected the answers to be different. Any sales leader worth their salt sets goals and measures sales performance against well-defined targets and quotas. I asked the same questions and was relieved when he told me that every account manager has a set of quarterly sales goals for their regions and product lines. When I asked where these goals were stored, I learned that each sales manager had them in personal spreadsheet files and not in a central database. We also learned that the individual spreadsheets had different variables for calculating and maintaining the sales targets. It took a considerable effort and data cleansing process to get these into a unified database to build organizational KPIs.

From these examples and plenty of others, we learn that KPIs are simple in concept but some can be challenging to put into production. Having simple KPI design tools in SQL Server Reporting Services gives you the flexibility to architect the right solution to fit your organization's business needs. Features as simple as having the ability to manually set KPI goals can be used to get you started and work in iterations to build the ideal solution.

Time-Series Calculations and Time Grain

A KPI, by technical definition, is one metric value compared with another metric, which is used to determine the status or success of some kind of business objective. Simple concept, right? One of the most common challenges with time-based measurements is that metrics often relate to different levels of time or frequencies. For example, if we track widget sales daily but restock them only twice during the month, inventory will fluctuate and the sales-vs-inventory calculations will vary wildly throughout the month.

If the sales director sets quarterly sales volume goals for each region and account manager, who are assessed for daily or weekly progress, how do we measure their daily activity against the quarterly targets? These KPI calculations will yield very different results when calculated daily, weekly, monthly, and finally, at a quarterly level. Some metrics are only relevant at a certain level within the date/time hierarchy, while some others may just have different rules. In this example, the simple answer might be that sales transactions can be summed up at any level (daily, weekly, monthly) but can only be compared to the quarterly target value after all the sales transactions are aggregated to the quarter. One could argue that after one month, the accumulated sales transactions should be comparable to one-third of the quarterly sales target. There are plenty of reasons that this kind of reasoning may or may not be a valid means to measure business success.

In a simple world, we record and report on data metrics at the same level in the Date hierarchy. Targets and Actuals are included and there are few if any exceptions to the simple mathematical rules used to sum up each business metric across the same time periods and then compare them straight across. The rules of success would also be clear in this utopia, where, when the aggregate actual metric value is the same as or any higher than the aggregate target value, the KPI reports indisputable success by displaying a green flag, thumbs-up, or happy face. In the same scenario, if the actual aggregate value is, say, 25% lower than the aggregated target value, there is no dispute that this condition is determined to be bad news or a failing grade. It is a red flag, thumbs-down, and a stern-looking frowny face. And what about the margin between "just good enough" and "25% less than what we wanted"? Is that a middle-of-the-road B− grade where someone gets credit for trying but not failing miserably? These are all important questions that must be decided by business stakeholders and then carefully written and put into practice by trusted technical solution architects and testers to make sure that nothing important in all the business logic falls between the cracks.

> **TIP** *SQL Server Analysis Services, Power Pivot, and Power BI are specifically engineered to address the challenge of matching KPI actual-to-target values across different date and time grains. You will find that DAX and MDX functions, and semantic modeling features that manage unique KPI business rules, are more efficient and easier than relational queries. You see how this works in Chapter 20.*

Create actual value measures and target value measures that are comparable and relevant at the correct, compatible levels of date and time hierarchies. Once defined, storing these predefined calculations as measures hides the complexity and makes report design easier. Matching actual-to-target values across different time grains is what SQL Server Analysis Services is engineered to do. Whether using SSAS multidimensional or Tabular, Power Pivot or Power BI, these semantic modeling and formula language tools are specifically suited to address this challenge where relational databases and SQL are not. Get well-defined rules from the business about the status derived from comparing those metric values and you will be good to go with a rockin' business KPI solution.

CREATING A TIME-SERIES MOBILE REPORT

First, you will create a new report using Mobile Report Publisher.

1. In Web Portal, navigate to the `Mobile Reports` folder you created in the previous exercise.

2. In the `Sales Reporting` folder, click the item on the menu bar titled "+ New" and then from the drop-down menu, click Mobile Report as shown in Figure 19-8.

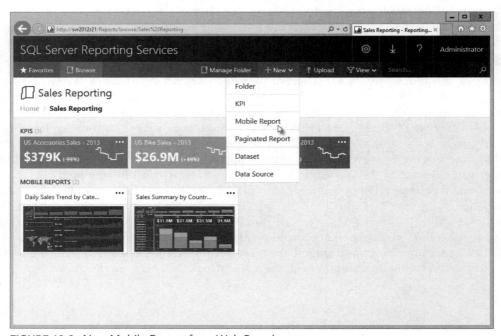

FIGURE 19-8: New Mobile Report from Web Portal.

Mobile Report Publisher opens. You may recall from Chapter 18 that when you see the box containing the message "We're opening Mobile Report Publisher …" (Figure 19-9) just wait for the application to load. It is only necessary to use the Get Mobile Report Publisher button the first time this box opens and then only if it has not been previously installed.

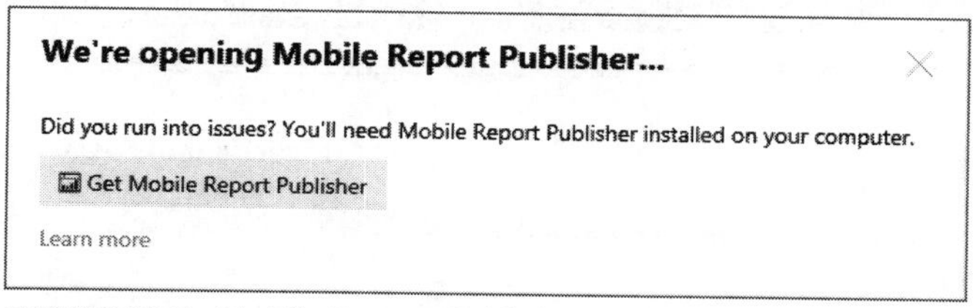

We're opening Mobile Report Publisher...

Did you run into issues? You'll need Mobile Report Publisher installed on your computer.

Get Mobile Report Publisher

Learn more

FIGURE 19-9: Mobile Report Publisher message.

Lay Out the Report Using Design-First Report Development

Next, you will create the essential report using a design with the necessary visual controls.

1. After the new report opens, on the Layout page, drag and drop the following visual controls onto the grid:

   ➤ A Time navigator from the Navigators group

   ➤ A Selection list from the Navigators group

   ➤ Three Number gauges from the Gauges group

   ➤ Three Time charts from the Charts group

   ➤ A gradient heat map from the Maps group

2. Position and resize them so the layout appears similar to Figure 19-10.

Time Navigator Properties

Select the Time navigator and set the following non-default properties, similar to Figure 19-11:

➤ Time levels: Year, Months, Days

➤ Time range presets: All (only)

➤ Number format: Abbreviated currency

➤ Visualization type: Bar

Selection List Properties

Set the Selection list title property by following these steps:

1. Choose the Selection list.

2. In the Visual properties panel, change the Title to **Select Country**.

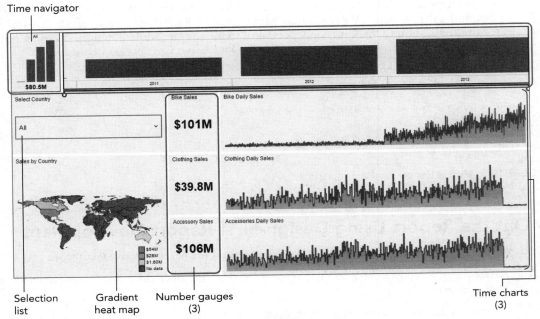

FIGURE 19-10: Report layout example for control positioning.

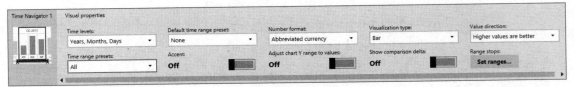

FIGURE 19-11: Time navigator Visual properties in the Layout page.

Number Gauge Properties

Set the properties for the Number gauge controls:

1. For each of the Number gauge controls, change the Title property to:

    ➤ Bike Sales

    ➤ Clothing Sales

    ➤ Accessory Sales

2. For each of the Number gauge controls, set the Number format property to Abbreviated currency.

Time Chart Properties

Set the chart control properties:

1. For each of the Time chart controls, change the Title property to:

- ➤ Bike Daily Sales
- ➤ Clothing Daily Sales
- ➤ Accessory Daily Sales

2. For each of the Time charts, set the Time unit to Day and the Number format to Abbreviated currency.

> **NOTE** *You will set the Layout properties for the map after the Data properties for the other controls.*

Add Data and Set Control Data Properties

1. Switch to the Data page and then click the Add Data button. The Add Data page is displayed, prompting for the location of your dataset. Options include a local Excel document and a report server (Figure 19-12).

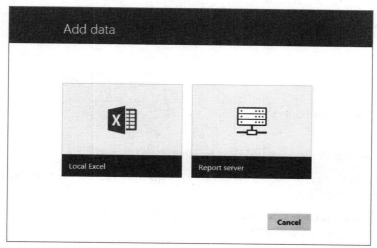

FIGURE 19-12: Add data page.

2. Click the Report server tile.

Add the following four datasets to the report:

➤ Sales By Date Category Country

➤ Sales And Target By Country For Bikes

➤ Sales And Target By Country For Clothing

➤ Sales And Target By Country For Accessories

3. For each dataset, navigate to the `Datasets` folder (see Figure 19-13) and select the item from the folder.

When a dataset is selected, this adds a table to the report definition. Resulting table names have the spaces removed, may be truncated and a numeral added, if necessary, to make the name unique.

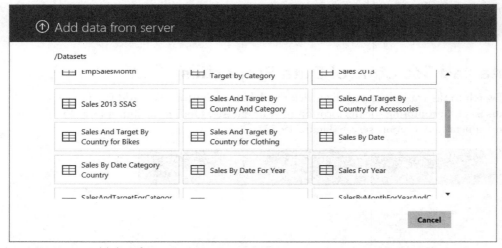

FIGURE 19-13: Add data from server page.

4. Repeat steps 1 through 3 for the remaining datasets.

5. Switch to the Settings page, shown in Figure 19-14, and enter the Report title **Daily Sales Trend by Category and Country**.

6. Click the Save icon on the left side of the toolbar (it's the single floppy disk icon) to display the location options page. Choose "Save to Server."

7. The next page displays the information shown in Figure 19-15, titled "Save mobile report as."

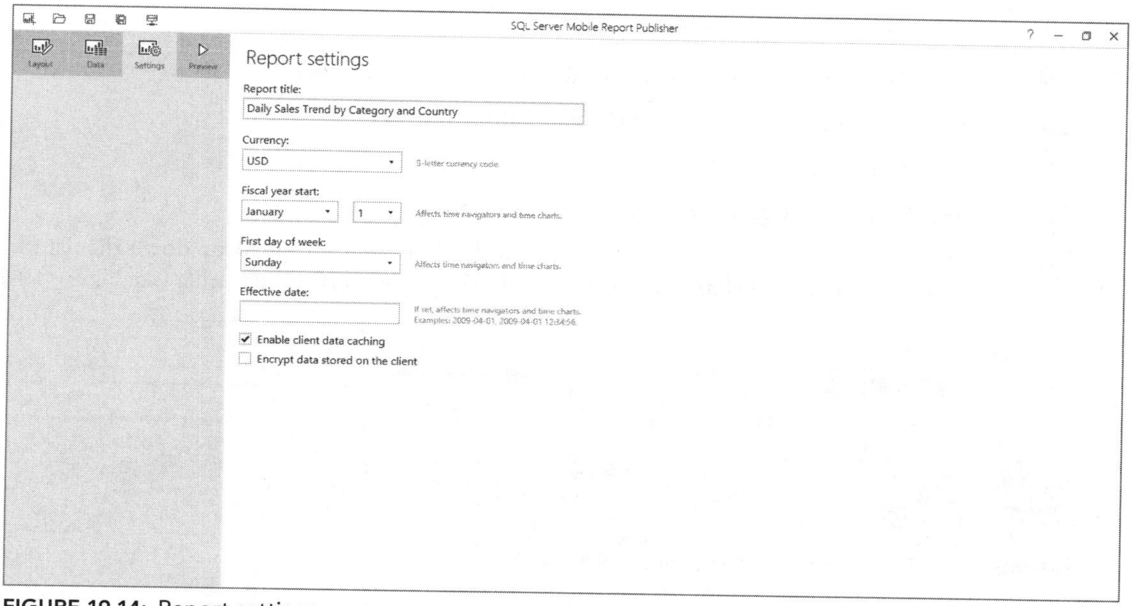

FIGURE 19-14: Report settings page.

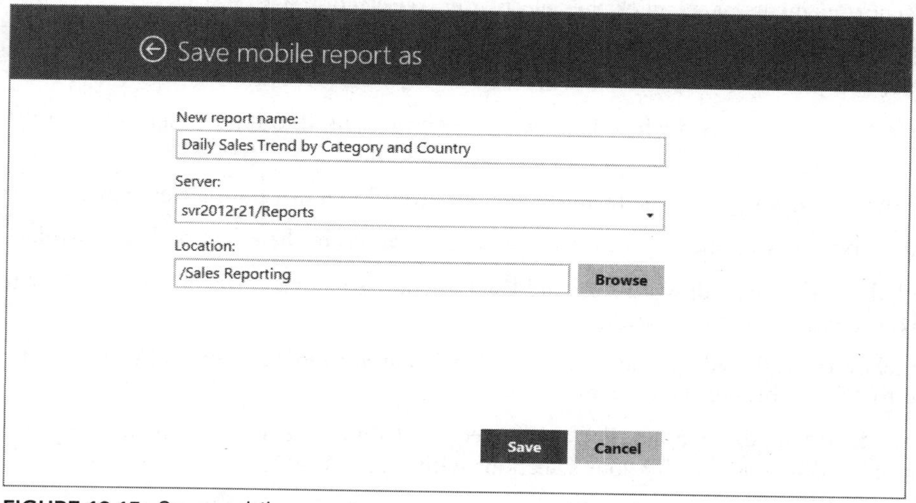

FIGURE 19-15: Save mobile report as page.

8. Verify that the New report name is correct.

9. Use the Browse button to navigate to the `Sales Reporting` folder.

10. Click the Save button to save the mobile report to the server.

11. Return to Data page.

12. Select the Time navigator from the Control instances panel.

13. In the Data properties panel at the bottom of the designer window, drop down the list for the Series for background chart. Select the SalesByDateCategoryCountry table (see Figure 19-16).

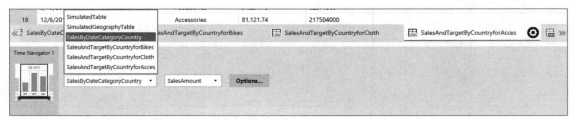

FIGURE 19-16: Time navigator Data properties panel.

14. Drop down the second list box and check only the SalesAmount field.

15. In the Report elements panel, click the Select Country selection list.

16. For the Data properties, choose the SalesByDateCategoryCountry table from the Keys drop-down list.

The Keys property defines the field used for the key value used to filter other tables in the report.

17. Choose the CountryRegionCode from the second drop-down list, on the Keys row.

The Labels property defines the field used to display values in the selection list control.

18. On the Labels row, drop down the second list and choose Country. Check Figure 19-17 to verify your control property selections.

The panel on the right side of the properties panel is used to match key field values for the selector to other tables in the report.

19. Check the following three tables. For each, select the CountryRegionCode field from the adjacent drop-down list. Verify your selections with Figure 19-17.

➤ SalesAndTargetByCountryforBikes

➤ SalesAndTargetByCountryforClothing

➤ SalesAndTargetByCountryforAccessories

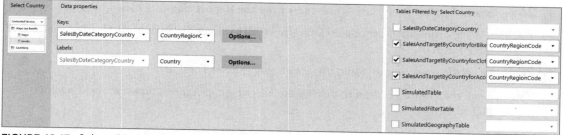

FIGURE 19-17: Select Country Selection list Data properties.

19. Select the Bike Sales control from the Report elements panel.

20. Under Data properties, use the drop-down list to select the SalesAndTargetByCountryforBikes table for the Main Value.

21. From the second drop-down list, select the SubTotal field.

22. Click the Options button to display the Filter by and Aggregation options shown in Figure 19-18.

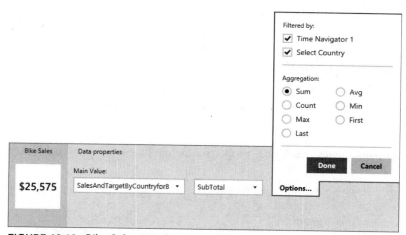

FIGURE 19-18: Bike Sales Number gauge Data properties.

23. Check the boxes for the Time Navigator 1 navigator and the Select Country selection list.

24. Click Done to close the Options window.

25. Repeat the steps 19 through 24 for the Clothing Sales and Accessory Sales Number gauge controls, choosing the appropriate tables.

26.   Select the Bike Daily Sales Time chart from the Report elements panel.

27.   Use the drop-down list under Data properties to select the SalesAndTargetByCountryforBikes table for the Main Series.

28.   From the second drop-down list, select only the SubTotal field.

29.   Click the Options button to display the Filter by and Aggregation options shown in Figure 19-19.

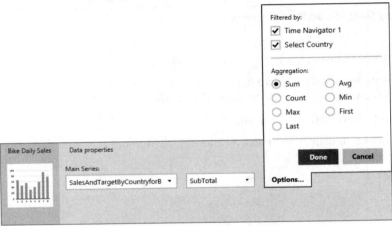

FIGURE 19-19: Bike Daily Sales chart Data properties.

30.   Check the boxes for the Time Navigator 1 navigator and the Select Country Selection list.

31.   Click Done to close the Options window.

32.   Switch to the Layout page to view the Visual properties for the Bike Daily Sales control, shown in Figure 19-20.

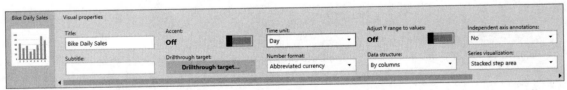

FIGURE 19-20: Bike Daily Sales chart Visual properties.

33.   Check each of the properties and make adjustments to match the Title, Time unit, Number format, Data structure, and Series visualization properties shown in the figure.

Map Properties

Our dataset includes the name of countries where customers have purchased products. You will display sales by country using a gradient heat map of the world where the color of each country represents the relative sales totals for the selected date range.

> **NOTE** *Microsoft doesn't distribute maps for all regions of the world for legal reasons. This is because political and geographic boundaries can change over time and some boundaries may be disputed. I have provided additional maps in the book sample files with the understanding that the map information may change and is not guaranteed to be accurate.*

The world countries map is not included with Reporting Services but I have provided this and several other useful maps in the book sample files.

1. Select the gradient heat map.

2. In the Visual properties panel, drop down the Map list shown in Figure 19-21.

3. Click the Custom Map button.

4. An Open dialog, similar to Figure 19-22, is displayed.

5. Navigate to the Mobile Report Maps folder in the book sample files.

6. Locate the two worldcountries files.

7. Hold down the Ctrl key and then click the .dbf and .shp file.

FIGURE 19-21: Map Selection list.

8. Click the Open button.

9. Select the Sales by Country control in the Layout page and then switch to the Data page in the designer, shown in Figure 19-23.

10. In the Data properties panel, set the SalesByDateCategoryCountry dataset from the Keys drop-down list.

11. Choose the Country field from the adjacent drop-down list.

12. Click the Options button to show the Filtered by property and make sure Time Navigator 1 is checked.

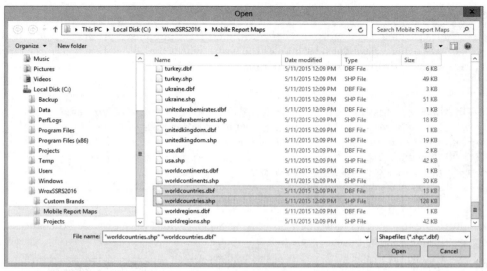

FIGURE 19-22: Selecting shape and data files for custom maps.

13. For the field drop-down list to the right of the Values: label, select the SalesAmount field.

FIGURE 19-23: Sales by Country map Data properties.

Set Color Palette and Mobile Device Layouts

In the following steps you will style the report using a color palette and create custom layouts for different mobile devices.

1. Switch to Preview and check the control interaction. The functionally complete report is shown in Figure 19-24.

You should be able to select different date ranges from the Time navigator and the Selection list to see controls filtered by the selections.

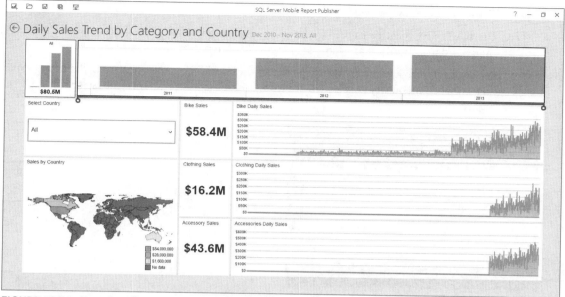

FIGURE 19-24: Functionally complete mobile report.

2. In Layout view, drop down the Color palette selection window and select a suitable color palette. Figure 19-25 shows the black color palette before confirming the Navy selection.

FIGURE 19-25: Report after color palette selection.

3. Return to the Preview page.

4. Use the Time navigator to drill into a year, select months, and drill into a month to select a range of dates. Verify that each visual control is filtered by the date selection.

5. Select different countries by using the Selection list. All controls except for the map should be filtered when a country is selected. An example of the Select Country list selection is shown in Figure 19-26.

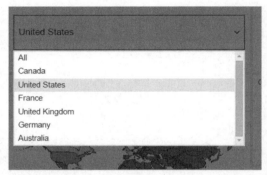

FIGURE 19-26: Using the Select Country Selection list.

Figures 19-27 and 19-28 show the interactive behavior of the map and chart controls when you click-and-hold, scroll, or tap-and-hold or move over various data points.

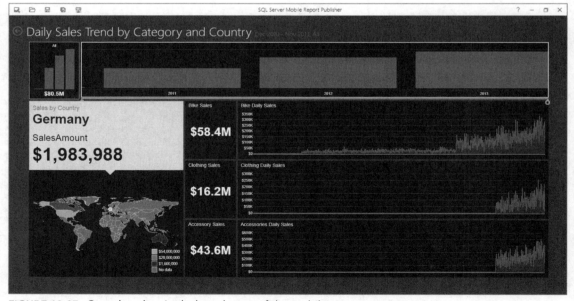

FIGURE 19-27: Completed main desktop layout of the mobile report, testing map interactions.

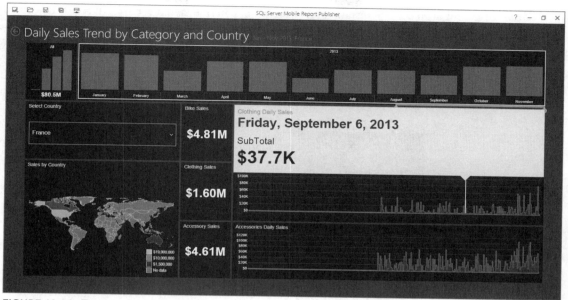

FIGURE 19-28: Testing chart interactions.

6. When you're happy with the default mobile report layout, click the Save icon on the toolbar.

7. Using the layout icon, drop down the Layout window and select the Phone layout.

The Portrait phone layout is 6 tiles tall by 4 tiles wide, by default, as shown in Figure 19-29.

Controls that you used in the master layout design are available in the Report elements pane on the left. These control instances already have their properties set and are ready to be added to the mobile layout with no modification. Every control will adapt to any size or dimensions.

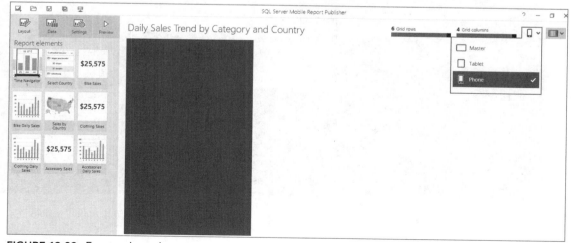

FIGURE 19-29: Empty phone layout.

8. Drag and drop control instances onto the mobile phone layout report. All controls will work but you may need to prioritize the controls that are most important to include in the smaller screen size. You can arrange controls similar to the layout I used in the Figure 19-30. In any case, the navigator and selector controls will continue to function as filter data for the other visual controls as you can see in Figure 19-31.

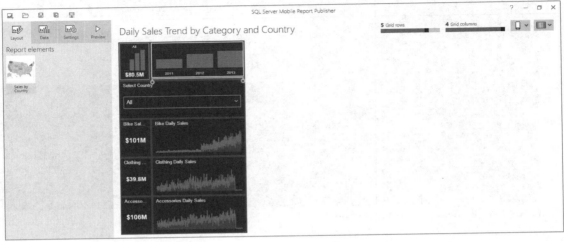

FIGURE 19-30: Completed phone layout.

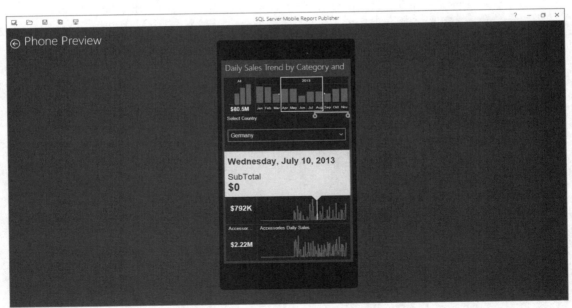

FIGURE 19-31: Testing the phone layout in preview.

Server Access and Live Mobile Connectivity

Similar to the way we connected my iPad to the demo server over the local WiFi network in Chapter 18, we can do the same with an iPhone. If there are no network or firewall restrictions, you should be able to connect from your phone. Make sure both the computer running Reporting Services and your phone device are on the same wireless network. Having the IP address for the report server might be necessary for testing purposes.

Give it a try first and if you can't connect, follow the steps in this article to check and configure your server firewall with the necessary rules and port exceptions for devices to communicate with the report server: https://msdn.microsoft.com/en-us/library/bb934283.aspx.

> **TIP** *If you are using a development report server that has inbound traffic exposed to the Internet, you can quickly test report connectivity by temporarily turning off the firewall. Just remember to turn it back on when you are finished.*

1. If you haven't yet, go to your vendor's app store and download the Power BI Mobile App for your device.

   I've installed this on both of my Windows tablets, my iPad, my Windows phone, and my iPhone. Figure 19-32 shows my iPhone with the Power BI Mobile app. A version of the app is also available on the Google store for Android devices.

   If you have a simple standalone server as I do that is not joined to a corporate domain, just use the server's IP address to connect. Figure 19-32 shows a Command window running on the report server.

2. Open a Command window on the report server by typing **CMD** in the search box near the Windows Start button.

3. Type **IPCONFIG** and press Enter.

4. Locate the section for the wireless network adaptor and the IpV4 Address, shown in Figure 19-32.

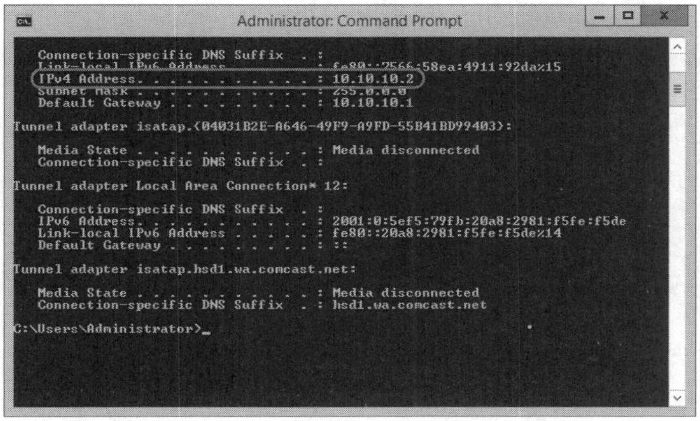

FIGURE 19-32: Command prompt with IPCONFIG results.

5. Write down this number.

Because I'm using a private network to connect to my server, the IP address for the server is only accessible on the same network. I am connected the same WiFi network as the server, which will allow me to connect within my test environment. You may not have this restriction if you are on a wide-area network and your server is assigned a public IP address.

Figure 19-33 shows the Power BI mobile app installed on my iPhone, which is used to access both content hosted in the Power BI service and mobile report content on one or more on-premises report servers.

FIGURE 19-33: Power BI mobile app on an iPhone.

Let's use the Power BI mobile app to open this report and explore the data. We need to create a connection to the report server, connect and navigate folders on the server, open and run the report.

6. Open the Power BI Mobile app by tapping the app tile.

A series of four screens are shown in Figure 19-34 to demonstrate the screen navigation on my iPhone.

When the app opens, tap the menu icon in the top-left corner to display the menu panel.

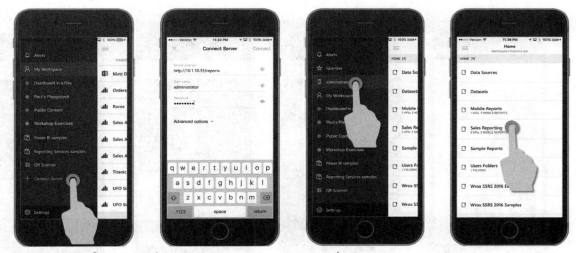

FIGURE 19-34: Steps to navigate to report server content on phone app.

7. Tap the item labeled Connect Server to provide the server address and user account information.

8. On the Connect Server page, enter the Web Portal address for your report server using the IP address (you wrote this down in step 5) or server name in the form of `http://serveraddress/Reports`.

9. Enter the username and password, and then tap Connect in the top-right corner of the screen.

A user can add any number of server connections. By default, a connection is identified by the username but the name and description can be updated on the Advanced options page.

10. Tap the new server connection (named "administrator" in my example).

11. The Power BI Mobile app connects to the report server and displays a list of folders.

12. Tap the `Sales Reporting` folder to see the content. These steps are shown in Figure 19-35.

Now that you have navigated to the report on the phone, let's actually use the report the way it was intended to be used in the mobile app.

13. Tap the thumbnail for the Daily Sales Trend by Category and Country report. An animated progress indicator is displayed while the report opens.

14. Use the Time navigator to filter sales by year. Tap the 2013 column to apply the filter and display the months for the selected year.

15. Tap the Select Country Selection list. On an iOS device, a familiar scrolling list is displayed.

16. Use your thumb to scroll through the list and select a country. Tap Done to apply the filter. Notice that the Number gauges and charts are updated.

17. Tap and hold your finger over one of the Time charts to display details in a pop-up window. While holding, slide to the left or right to view details for dates at different points along the chart.

FIGURE 19-35: Steps to navigate mobile report in phone app.

Each version of the Power BI mobile app renders visuals using platform-specific controls. This means that the user experience will be slightly different across operating systems and platforms and will be familiar to users of that device, whether iOS, Android, Windows apps, or a web browser. For example, the Country Selector on a Windows Phone is rendered as drop-down combo box, whereas the slot-machine style vertical scroll list is rendered on an iPhone or iPad.

SUMMARY

You have learned that mobile report design is fundamentally different than designing paginated reports. Most importantly, although the Mobile Report Publisher is used on a full-screen PC, reports are optimized for small mobile device screens. A single report has three different layouts including the master layout for larger screen landscape orientation, tablet in portrait orientation, and phone.

Mobile reports are simple by design and governed by a unique set of design rules. Reports and visual controls are designed to be responsive, adapting to the size and dimensions of their environment. This behavior and design approach is in contrast with paginated report components that accept and require many property settings. Filters and interactive selectors are designed to work with cached data, which means that you generally cannot pass dataset parameters and use selectors and navigators in the same report.

Chapter 20 continues to explore the capabilities of mobile reports by introducing more advanced features. You will learn to pass parameters between reports using report and URL drillthrough actions. We will use custom maps and shape files and then create a multi-report solution using navigation paths to explore details.

20

Advanced Mobile Report Solutions

WHAT'S IN THIS CHAPTER?

➤ Introducing the Chart data grid visual control

➤ Correlating two datasets in a control

➤ Using parameters in a shared dataset

➤ Drill through to a mobile report with dataset parameters

➤ Drill through to a paginated report with dataset parameters

➤ Adding custom maps and managing shapes

This chapter develops two themes. First, you learn to use some of the most advanced mobile report features, which include the Chart data grid, drillthrough navigation, and maps. Second, since you now have the skills to create mobile reports without detailed instructions, you'll do some of the easy work on your own.

DESIGNING A CHART DATA GRID MOBILE REPORT

In Chapter 17 I mentioned that there are cases for which you will need to design datasets specifically suited for certain controls and this is one of those cases. The Chart data grid control requires two datasets; one to populate the rows of the grid and another for the chart. This is a classic master/detail relationship where a pair of key values is used to correlate the two datasets.

Exercise: Chart Data Grid

The exercises in Chapters 18 and 19 have provided you with all the basic skills to create mobile reports. To move a little faster through this exercise, I am not providing all the detail steps for skills you have already learned. You can use the completed datasets and report in the Samples project.

Create Datasets

You will create four shared datasets. These include two queries used for election lists and two more queries that are used for the Chart data grid: one for the grid and the other for the chart. You can create shared datasets in either SSDT or Report Builder. You'll use SSDT in this exercise.

1. Open the Wrox SSRS 2016 Exercises project in SSDT.

2. Create these four shared datasets for each of the queries in the following script. Each query is concluded with a semicolon. Name queries using the commented name preceding each block of query script:

➤ YearList

➤ CategoryList

➤ SalesBySubcategory

➤ SalesBySubcategoryAndMonth

3. Deploy all four datasets to the `Datasets` folder on the report server:

```
-- YearList
select distinct cast(Year as smallint)
From Date
;

-- CategoryList
select distinct
        [ProductCategory],
        [ProductCategoryKey]
from [dbo].[Product]
order by [ProductCategory]
;

-- SalesBySubcategory
select
        [Year],
        [ProductCategory],
        [ProductCategoryKey],
        [ProductSubcategory],
        [ProductSubcategoryKey],
        sum([SalesAmount]) as SalesAmount,
        sum([OrderQuantity]) as OrderQuantity
from [dbo].[vSalesDetails]
```

```
group by
        [Year],
        [ProductCategory],
        [ProductCategoryKey],
        [ProductSubcategory],
        [ProductSubcategoryKey]
order by
        [Year],
        [ProductCategory],
        [ProductSubcategory]
;


-- SalesBySubcategoryAndMonth
select
        [Year],
        [ProductCategory],
        [ProductCategoryKey],
        [ProductSubcategory],
        [ProductSubcategoryKey],
        [MonthNumber],
        [MonthName],
        sum([SalesAmount]) as SalesAmount
from [dbo].[vSalesDetails]
group by
        [Year],
        [ProductCategory],
        [ProductCategoryKey],
        [ProductSubcategory],
        [ProductSubcategoryKey],
        [MonthNumber],
        [MonthName]
order by
        [Year],
        [ProductCategory],
        [ProductSubcategory],
        [MonthNumber]
;
```

Create a Report and Import Datasets

Create the basic report structure with two selectors and a Chart data grid.

1. Create a new report in Mobile Report Publisher.

2. Add two Selection list controls to the left side of the report design grid: "Years" and "Categories."

3. Add a Chart data grid named "Subcategory Sales Monthly Trend" to fill the remaining space in the report design grid.

   The control placement should be similar to the example shown in Figure 20-1.

FIGURE 20-1: Report shell showing control placement.

4. Add all four datasets to the report using the Add data button to import each from the shared datasets you deployed earlier. You can see these in Figure 20-2

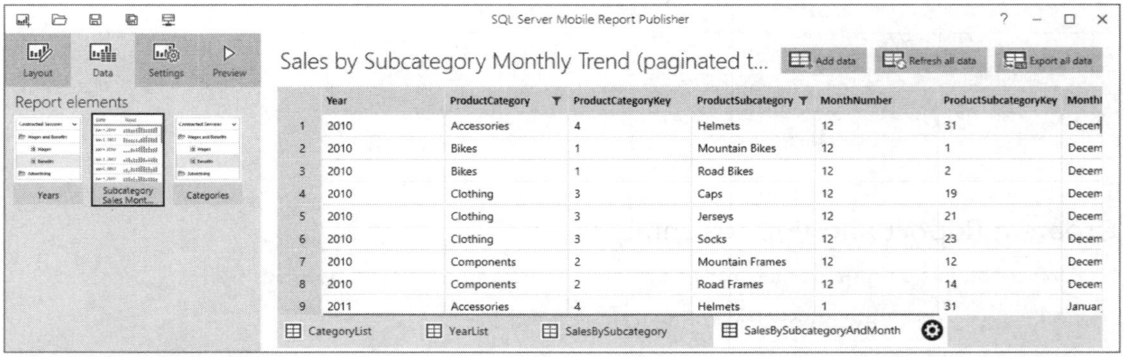

FIGURE 20-2: Report datasets.

Set Properties for the Selection List Controls

Use the drop-down lists to select datasets and fields for the Keys and Labels properties, and then set the filter options for the other datasets in the reports by following these steps.

1. Choose the Years selector in the Data page.

2. Choose the YearsList dataset and verify that the Keys and Labels field properties are set to use the Year field.

3. On the right side of the page, in the section titled "Filter these datasets when a selection is made," check the boxes for the SalesBySubcategory and SalesBySubcategoryAndMonth datasets.

4. For each of the selected datasets, choose the Year field.

5. Ensure that the settings are similar to Figure 20-3.

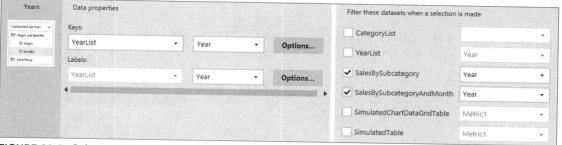

FIGURE 20-3: Selection list "Years" Data properties.

> **NOTE** *For the Data properties, both the "Keys" and "Labels" properties each have two selection lists. The drop-down list on the left is used to select a dataset and the drop-down list on the right is used to select a field from the specified dataset containing the key or label value.*

6. Choose the CategoryList selector.

7. Select the CategoryList datasets from the Keys drop-down list on the left.

8. Select the ProductCategoryKey field for the Keys (list on the right).

9. Select the ProductCategory field for the Labels properties (list on the right).

> **TIP** *The field selection drop-down lists shown in Figure 20-4 are not wide enough to differentiate between the ProductCategoryKey and ProductCategory fields. Drop down each field list to verify the selection.*

10. On the right side of the page, in the section titled "Filter these datasets when a selection is made," check the box for the SalesBySubcategory dataset.

11. Select the ProductCategoryKey field.

12. Ensure that the settings are similar to Figure 20-4.

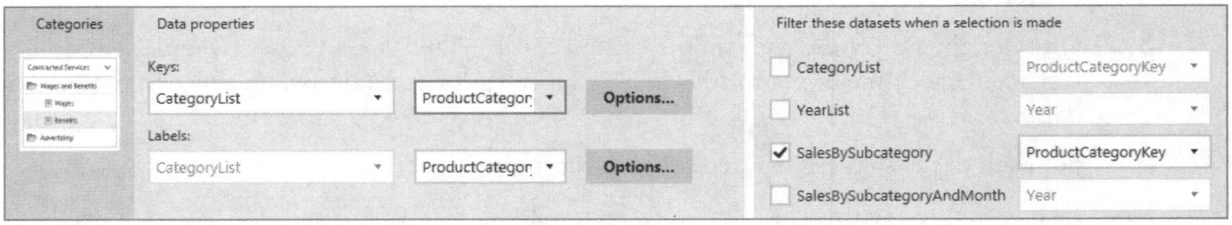

FIGURE 20-4: Selection list "Categories" Data properties.

13. Switch to the Layout page and for each of the "Years" and "Categories" selection list controls, ensure that Allow multiselect is set to "On."

Set Field Properties for the Chart Data Grid Control

Set the field properties using these steps:

1. Choose the Subcategory Sales Monthly Trend control in the Data page.

2. Select the SalesBySubcategory dataset from the drop-down list titled "Data for the grid view."

3. Select the SalesBySubcategoryAndMonth dataset from the drop-down list titled "Reference data for the chart visualizations."

4. On the right side of the page, in the section titled "Data grid columns," check the boxes for the following fields:

➤ ProductSubcategory

➤ SalesAmount

➤ OrderQuantity

5. Optionally, add spaces or abbreviate the field names in each textbox corresponding to a selected field.

Set Chart Properties for the Chart Data Grid Control

Set the chart properties using these steps:

1. At the bottom of the "Data grid columns" section click the "Add chart column" button.

2. Use the textbox to rename the new column to **Monthly Sales.**

3. Click the Options button next to the new column.

4. Set properties in the pop-up dialog as you see in Figure 20-5. The individual property values are provided in Table 20-1.

TABLE 20-1: Data Grid Chart Properties

PROPERTY	VALUE
Chart type	Area
Chart data	SalesAmount
Source lookup	ProductSubcategoryKey
Destination lookup	ProductSubcategoryKey

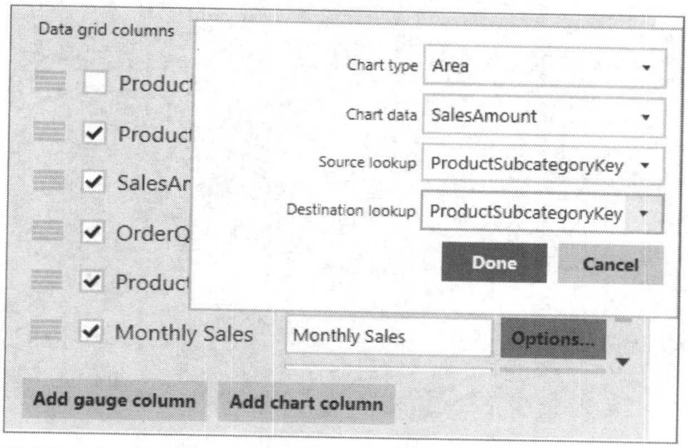

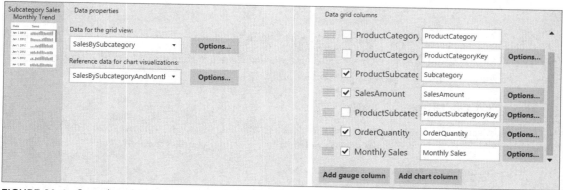

FIGURE 20-5: Data grid columns and Chart properties.

5. Use Figure 20-6 to check the properties and settings on this page and make any necessary adjustments.

FIGURE 20-6: Completed Data properties for "Subcategory Sales Monthly Trend" Chart data grid control.

6. Use the Option... button next to the "Data for the grid view" title.

7. Check both the Years and Categories boxes and then click Done.

8. Use the Option... button next to the "Reference data for chart visualizations" title.

9. Check the Years box and then click Done.

10. Switch to Layout view (shown in Figure 20-7) and choose a color palette for the report.

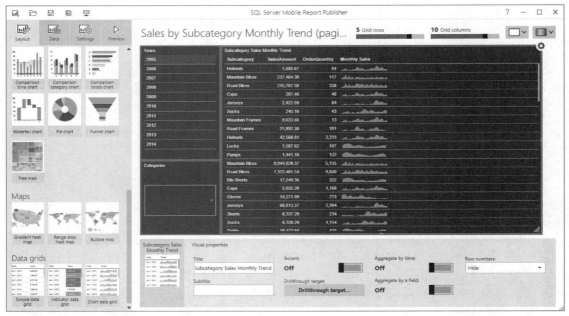

FIGURE 20-7: Chart data grid control Layout properties.

11. Use the Preview page to test the report (Figure 20-8).

12. Select combinations of Years and Categories to ensure that the data grid is filtered correctly. Data should change with each selection.

Fit the Grid for Phone Layout

The main report layout is optimized for a desktop browser window so it must be simplified for a smaller phone screen. You've done this before but this time, there is a catch.

1. Switch to Layout view.

2. Use the Layout drop-down list to choose the Phone layout and arrange controls so they fit in the Phone layout.

3. Preview the report again.

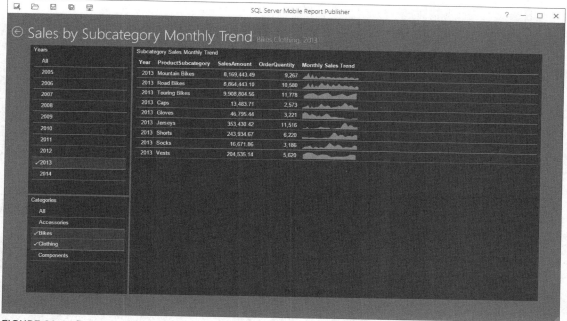

FIGURE 20-8: Report preview.

Although the screen size and control placement adapts to the phone layout, the Chart data grid is too wide and doesn't fit in the phone screen without scrolling the grid horizontally. This is a trade-off when designing a single report to work on multiple devices. An easy remedy is to arrange the grid columns left to right in order of priority so the most important information is visible before scrolling the grid to view items to the right.

4. Switch to the Data page and select the Chart data grid.

5. Using the items listed in the Data grid columns on the right side of the Data properties, rearrange the columns according to the example shown in Figure 20-9.

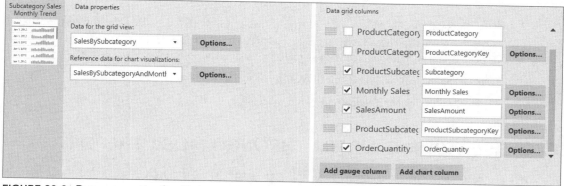

FIGURE 20-9: Data properties for "Subcategory Sales Monthly trend" Chart data grid.

6.   Preview the report in the Phone layout again and compare it to Figure 20-10.

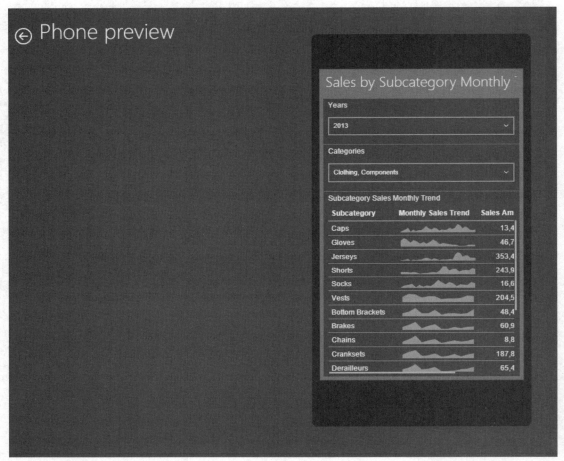

FIGURE 20-10: Phone preview.

7.   Use the Save mobile report as… button (double floppy disk icon) on the top-left toolbar to save the report to the `Sales Reporting` folder on the report server. Save two copies of the report that you will use in the next exercises using the following names:

➤   Sales Subcat Trend (mobile target)

➤   Sales Subcat Trend (paginated target)

EXERCISE: ADDING A DRILL-THROUGH MOBILE REPORT

We're going to create another report that will serve as the drill-through target from the report we just created. Rather than grouping and charting the sales order data at a high level, this report will show details roll-up to the order date.

1. Use SSDT to create another shared dataset named **SalesOrderDetailsForYearAndSubcategory** using the following query script:

```
-- SalesOrderDetailsForYearAndSubcategory
select
        [OrderDate],
        [ProductSubcategory],

        sum([SalesAmount]) as SalesAmount,
        sum([TaxAmt]) as TaxAmt,
        sum([Freight]) as Freight,
        sum([OrderQuantity]) as OrderQuantity
from [dbo].[vSalesDetails]
where
        YEAR([OrderDate]) = @Year
        and
        [ProductSubcategory] = @Subcategory
group by
        [OrderDate],
        [ProductSubcategory],
order by
        [OrderDate],
        [ProductSubcategory]
;
```

   Before saving the new dataset, you need to assign default values to the parameters.

2. On the Parameters page of the Shared Dataset Properties dialog, assign a default value to both parameters as you see in Figure 20-11.

3. Set the data type for both parameters to Integer and then click OK to save the dataset.

> **NOTE** *You may notice that we are using the ProductSubcategory rather than the ProductSubcategoryKey field value for a parameter. The reason for this is that we can only pass the visible field values from a mobile report as parameters. Since the Subcategory is a column in the Chart data grid, I chose to use that column value as a parameter.*

4. Deploy the dataset. The project properties are already set to save it to the `Datasets` folder on the report server.

5. Use Mobile Report Publisher to create a new report named **Sales Order Details by Subcategory and Year**. Alternatively, you can use the completed report provided in the book samples.

6. Add the new dataset to the report.

7. Use Figure 20-12 as a guide to add controls to visualize the dataset. The specific design elements for this report are not critical to this exercise. It simply needs to accept the two parameters and visualize the results.

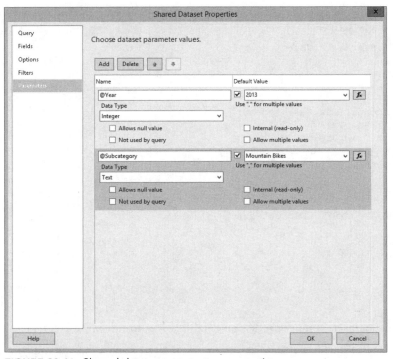

FIGURE 20-11: Shared dataset parameter properties.

FIGURE 20-12: Completed report ready for deployment.

8. Deploy the Sales Order Details by Subcategory and Year report to the `Sales Reports` folder (or any other folder you prefer).

9. Open the previous report you named Sales Subcat Trend (mobile target).

10. Choose the Chart data grid (named Subcategory Sales Monthly Trend) on the Layout page and click Drillthrough target... (see Figure 20-13).

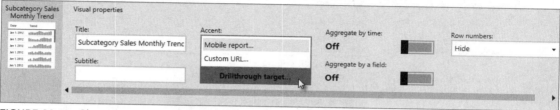

FIGURE 20-13: Chart data grid Visual properties.

11. Choose Mobile report....

12. Navigate to the `Sales Reporting` folder and select the Sales Order Details by Subcategory and Year report. The "Configure target report" page is displayed, as you see in Figure 20-14.

13. Scroll to the bottom of the list of Report parameters to view the parameters for the SalesOrderDetailsForYearAndSubcategory dataset.

14. For the @Year parameter, use the drop-down list to choose the SelectedItem property of the Years Selection list control.

15. For the @Subcategory parameter, use the drop-down list to choose the ProductSubcategory field for the Subcategory Sales Monthly Trend control. You can see the two selections in Figure 20-14 (although the entire control and field name is not visible for the second selection).

16. Use the Save as... icon in the top-left toolbar to save a copy of the report with a name that indicates that it uses a mobile report as the drill-through target. I have named my report Sales Subcat Trend (mobile target).

> **TIP** *The Web Portal only shows the first 20–30 characters of a mobile report name in the standard tiles view, which can be challenging for reports with similar log names. Consider abbreviating report names for readability.*

17. Save the report to the same report server folder and close the Mobile Report Publisher.

18. You can test the drill-through action in the web browser. In Web Portal, locate and open the Sales by Subcategory Monthly Trend report. Select a year, such as 2013, and one or more categories (I have selected Bikes and Components in Figure 20-15). You can also open this on a mobile device.

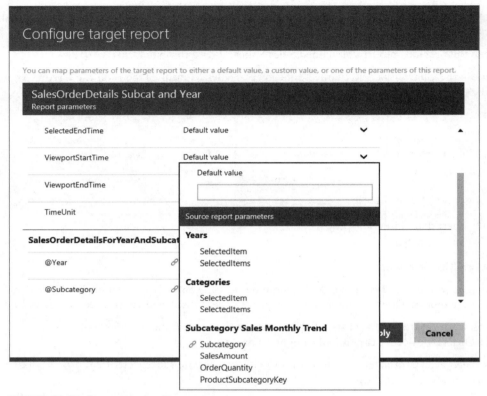

FIGURE 20-14: Report parameters page.

19. Click or tap one of the subcategories. I have clicked the row for Derailleurs. This should navigate to the target report showing only sales order details for the selected year and subcategory, which you can see in Figure 20-15.

20. Test the report navigation in the web browser and on a mobile device to make sure it is working as expected.

EXERCISE: ADDING A DRILL-THROUGH PAGINATED REPORT

Now you will do the same thing as before by designing a drillthrough navigation, but this report will drillthrough to a paginated report using a custom URL.

1. In the Wrox SSRS 2016 Exercises project in SSDT, create a new blank paginated report named **Sales Order Detail**.

2. Create a dataset in the report based on the SalesOrderDetails shared dataset in the project.

Like the mobile report in the previous section, the details of this report design are less important. What is important is that it accepts the Year and Subcategory parameters and displays the filtered results of the SalesOrderDetails.

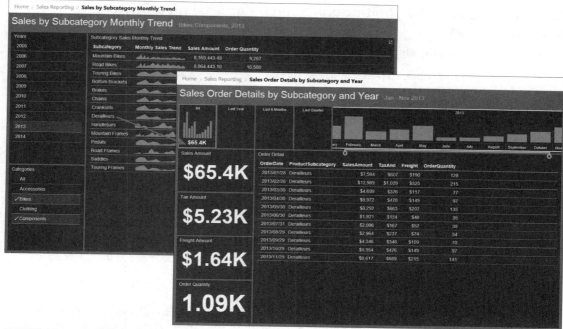

FIGURE 20-15: Drillthrough reports.

3. Design a simple table report like the example shown in Figure 20-16 or add the completed Sales Order Details report from the Wrox SSRS 2016 Ch 20 project.

FIGURE 20-16: Simple Order Details report.

4. Deploy the Sales Order Details to the `Sale Reporting` folder on the report server.

Open and Update the Drillthrough Source Report with a Custom Drillthrough Action

You will start with the mobile report you saved earlier and add drillthrough navigation.

1. Return to Mobile Report Publisher.

2. Open the report named Sales Subcat Trend (paginated target).

3. Choose the Chart data grid and click Drillthrough target....

4. Choose Custom URL... (see Figure 20-17).

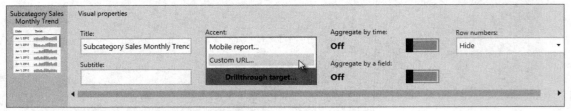

FIGURE 20-17: Chart data grid drillthrough property.

The Set drillthrough URL dialog opens, which is where you will enter the path to the target report. The following web address is the path to the target report on my server. You will need to substitute the name of your server, the folder, and report name if there are any differences. If you are running a local, default SSRS instance, you can use `localhost` as the server name.

```
http://svr2012r21/Reports/report/Sales Reporting/Sales Order
Details?rs:Embed=true&Year=2013&Subcategory=Mountain Bikes
```

> **TIP** *Using a text editor to manage the web address avoids the need to deal with character encoding that the web browser will add to the address text. I prefer to use NotePad++, which you can download free from* `https://notepad-plus-plus.org`.

3. Open NotePad or your preferred text editor and enter the path to your deployed report on your server using this address as an example. Make any necessary changes for your server, folder, or target report name.

4. Copy and paste the address into the address bar of your web browser. Press Enter and verify that the report is displayed. Make corrections if necessary and capture the correct address in the text editor.

5. Copy and paste the valid address into the box titled "Enter a URL to go to when this visualization is clicked."

Now for the tricky part. You can see the list of selector and navigator controls in the Available parameters list on the right side of the Set drillthrough URL dialog in Figure 20-18. The internal control names are used rather than the friendly names you used for the titles. The names are generated and numbered in the order the controls are added. Aside from that evidence, it may take some trial-and-error to verify that you're using the right control references.

> **WARNING** *Since the Mobile Report Publisher uses the internal control names rather than the friendly names, the control names in your report may be different from mine in this example.*

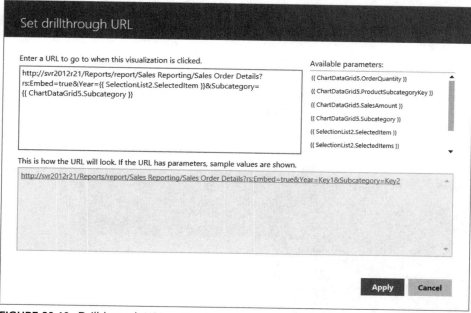

FIGURE 20-18: Drillthrough URL options.

6. Highlight the Year parameter value (2013) and click the item for the SelectedItem property of the Year selector. In my report it's named SelectionList2.

7. Highlight the Subcategory parameter value (Mountain Bikes) and click the item for the Chart data grid Subcategory field. In my report it's named DataGrid5.Subcategory.

> **TIP** *After you have deployed this report, you should test it in the web browser to verify that the correct parameter values were passed.*

8. Apply the changes.

9. Save the report.

10. Open the updated mobile report in the web browser.

11. Use the selectors to choose a year and category to see the filtered set of summary rows and the monthly sales trend for each subcategory.

12. Click one of the subcategory rows in the grid to navigate to the detail paginated report.

13. Check the parameters that are passed to the target report to make sure they were mapped correctly in the URL.

> **TIP** *In addition to observing the data as evidence of parameter values passed to the report, you can also check the parameter values in the browser address bar.*

14. If corrections are needed, change the SelectionList and ChartDataGrid references in the drillthrough URL, apply the changes, and resave the report.

Figure 20-19 shows the target mobile report and the paginated detail report depicting the drill-through action. Once deployed, the drill through should work on any device that has access to the report server. When a user taps a subcategory row in the installed mobile device app, the action should open a web browser with the filtered paginated report.

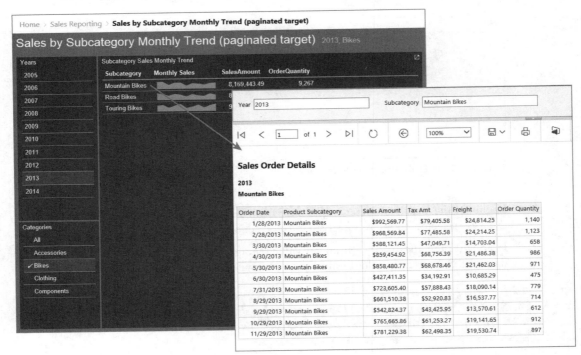

FIGURE 20-19: Mobile and paginated report drillthrough.

Getting Serious with Maps

Providing comprehensive mapping capabilities in a reporting tool seems like a fairly simple thing but, in fact, it is not. In my experience, basic map reporting can be fairly simple but many of the mapping requirements I have encountered over the years were difficult to satisfy with out-of-the-box features and took quite a lot of extra effort.

I have provided 72 map files in the book downloads, which include 51 maps that are not supplied by Microsoft. Because boundaries can change over time (so there is no guarantee that map definitions are perfectly accurate), please verify the region names and boundaries, and use them at your own risk.

Purely by strange coincidence, the maximum number of controls on a mobile report is 72, the same as the number of map files. Not to question fate, I've created a sample report shown in Figure 20-20 containing every single map in the collection as a reference.

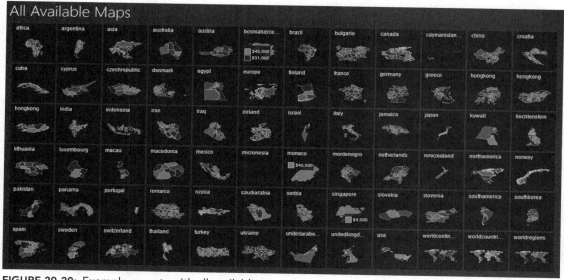

FIGURE 20-20: Example reports with all available maps.

One of the challenges with mapping solutions is that the place names in your data must exactly match the shape name keys in the map shape files. This is particularly challenging when they are not documented. I have gone to great effort to extract the shape names from all the map files included in the book downloads and provide them for reference. You will find the map name and shape information for 72 maps containing 1626 shapes, in the MapShapes table in the WroxSSRS2016 database. Table 20-2 shows a summary of the map names and the number of shape records included in this table. You can reference this table in your queries and build your own reference tables to match up region and place names from your source data to the shape names in the maps. To get the correct shape names, just the return the ShapeNames column from a query on the MapShapes table filtered on the MapName.

TABLE 20-2: MapShapes Table Summary

MAPNAME	SHAPES
Africa	55
argentina	24
Asia	50
australia	8
Austria	9
bosniaherzegovina	2
Brazil	28
bulgaria	28
canada	13
caymanislands	7
China	31
Croatia	21
Cuba	15
Cyprus	6
czechrepublic	7
denmark	15
Egypt	26
europe	46
Finland	5
France	22
germany	16
greece	14
hongkong	18
hungary	20
iceland	8
India	31
indonesia	27

MAPNAME	SHAPES
Iran	30
Iraq	18
Ireland	26
Israel	7
Italy	20
jamaica	14
Japan	47
Kuwait	5
liechtenstein	11
lithuania	10
luxembourg	3
Macau	5
macedonia	8
mexico	32
micronesia	4
monaco	1
montenegro	21
netherlands	12
newzealand	14
northamerica	23
norway	19
pakistan	7
panama	10
portugal	19
romania	41
Russia	88
saudiarabia	13
Serbia	26

continues

TABLE 20-2 *(continued)*

MAPNAME	SHAPES
singapore	1
slovakia	4
slovenia	12
southamerica	14
southkorea	14
Spain	16
sweden	24
switzerland	27
thailand	72
Turkey	73
ukraine	27
unitedarabemirates	8
unitedkingdom	4
Usa	51
worldcontinents	6
worldcountries	178
worldregions	9

Here is a very simple example using the worldcountries map. If you were to query the SalesTerritory table joined to Sales, you would see that we have sales for six countries. If you query the MapShapes table where MapName is worldcountries, you will see that not all the country names match the shape names in the map. In this example, I have created a bridge table named SalesTerritoryCountyMapShapes that matches CountryRegionCode values from the SalesTerritory table to ShapeName values from the MapShapes table. The script to add a bridge table is quite simple, like this example:

```
insert into SalesTerritoryCountyMapShapes ( CountryRegionCode, ShapeName )
values
    ( 'US', 'United States' ),
    ( 'CA', 'Canada' ),
    ( 'FR', 'France' ),
    ( 'DE', 'Germany' ),
```

```
    ( 'AU', 'Austria' ),
    ( 'GB', 'United Kingdom' )
;
```

Now I can write a dataset query for the report that joins the Sales and SalesTerritory tables with the new SalesTerritoryCountyMapShapes bridge table, like this:

```
-- CountryMapShapeSalesOrders
select
        m.ShapeName,
        sum(s.SalesAmount) as SalesAmount
from
        Sales s
        inner join SalesTerritory t on s.SalesTerritoryKey = t.TerritoryKey
        inner join SalesTerritoryCountyMapShapes m on t.CountryRegionCode =
            m.CountryRegionCode
group by
        m.ShapeName
;
```

Creating a simple report, you can add the worldcountries custom map from the downloaded files and then match the map keys to the ShapeName field, as you can see in Figure 20-21.

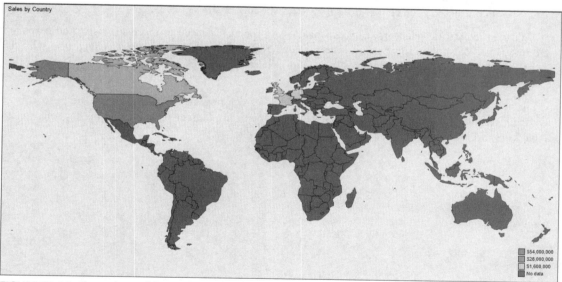

FIGURE 20-21: Example world countries map

Now you have everything you need to create mobile map reports for several different stock maps, world continents, countries, regions, and states. I hope the additional map files and the MapShapes reference table are useful resources for you.

SUMMARY

This chapter took basic summary and details to the next level by introducing you to the Chart data grid control, which you used to create an area chart to show monthly sales summaries grouped and repeated for selected product subcategories.

You worked through three exercises. Starting with the Chart data grid, you created a report with Selection lists to filter the summary grid and show trend information. Next, you added mobile report navigation so that tapping the grid navigated the users to a detail report, showing them sales details by date for the yearly sales information they selected by product subcategory. Finally, you added drill-through navigation to a paginated detail report and used a URL to drill through and pass parameter values from the selectors, navigators, and selected data grid in the mobile report.

I showed you how to use provided map shape and data files to implement custom maps. You used a reference table of geographical shape names to match up location information in your database and visualize it as a map.

The four chapters in Part 6 introduced you to the mobile report visual by category and then in detail. You learned to design reports using the "design-first development" pattern and built proof-of-concept reports to demonstrate functionality with simulated data. You created shared datasets and then completed each report design to meet specific business needs.

We used navigators, selectors, gauges, charts, and then graduated to more sophisticated maps and data grids. We applied filtering and interactions and then implemented report navigation with drill-through navigation and parameters from a mobile report to a paginated report that works in the web browser and on a mobile device.

The two chapters that follow, in Part VII, will show you how to manage content and perform administration tasks on the report server. You learn to implement security and management utilities, backup and recovery, monitoring, and troubleshooting.

PART VII
Administering Reporting Services

In the twenty preceding chapters, our focus has been design and deployment. That means that a lot of time and effort has so far gone into creating and delivering reports for the business to use. Now what do you need to do to make sure they always run, perform well, and work when they are expected? How do you restrict or enable access to users or members of an Active Directory group? Who can create subscriptions or snapshots and who can't? If someone writes a horrendously slow query and then schedules the report to run every night, how do you find it and prevent it from stalling your server?

The two chapters in this part of the book will show you how to manage report content on your server and perform administration tasks to keep your report server healthy and running. You'll learn to identify and troubleshoot problems, isolate issues, and manage them to a resolution. You'll learn the core administration skills to configure and manage security, user access, and manage report content. You'll also learn to set up and monitor report and execution logs, monitor server resources, and tune your report server for optimal report performance.

▶ **CHAPTER 21:** Content Management

▶ **CHAPTER 22:** Server Administration

21

Content Management

WHAT'S IN THIS CHAPTER?

➤ Using web portal

➤ Content management activities

➤ Item-level security

➤ Content management automation

In this chapter, we explore the management of Reporting Services content. Reporting Services content includes:

➤ Reports

➤ Mobile reports

➤ KPIs

➤ Shared data sources

➤ Shared datasets

➤ Report resources

➤ Shared schedules

In Native mode, Reporting Services content management is performed primarily through the Web Portal application. Additionally, some administrative tasks may be managed in SQL Server Management Studio (SSMS). Scripts executed through the RS utility provide an alternative means of performing these tasks.

> **NOTE** *A set of PowerShell commandlets, which essentially duplicate some of the RS utility features, were introduced for Reporting Services; as of this writing, they are still in preview. Check for an update by searching for SSRS PowerShell Provider on CodePlex.com. With efforts to expand PowerShell support for Reporting Services by the community and the product team, I suspect that a comprehensive set of commandlets will be available in the near future, if not by the time you read this book.*

In SharePoint Integrated mode, content management activities are performed in a similar manner but through the SharePoint site or through the ReportServer web services endpoint. In this mode, Web Portal and the RS utility are unavailable.

USING WEB PORTAL

Web Portal is the primary content management tool for Reporting Services installations running in Native mode. As you know, the application provides an easy-to-use and responsive graphical interface to navigate the Reporting Services objects ad folder structure. Through web portal, various items can be accessed or even altered, assuming you have the appropriate permissions.

For default installations, web portal is accessed through the following URL:

```
http://<servername>/reports
```

If you've installed Reporting Services as a named instance, the URL you will use has this form:

```
http://<servername>/reports_<instancename>
```

If you are unable to connect to web portal, check with your administrator that its URL reservation is not configured for an alternative address. Make sure that the Reporting Services Windows service has started. A convenient way to restart the service is to open the Reporting Services Configuration Manager, connect to the server, and then from the Report Server Status page, stop and restart the service. After this, refresh the web browser to view Web Portal.

> **NOTE** *In the preview and release candidates for SQL Server 2016, the report server service did not properly start on some machines on boot-up. This is easy to remedy by using Reporting Services Configuration Manager to stop and restart the service.*

When you first open Web Portal, you see one of two views depending on whether you have previously added objects to your personal Favorites. The Favorites view is shown in Figure 21-1.

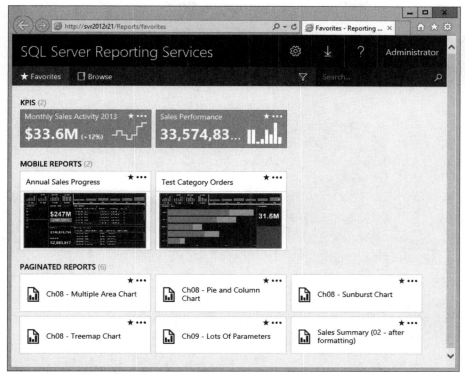

FIGURE 21-1: Web portal Favorites view.

> **TIP** *The familiar concept of Favorites is introduced in web portal, simplifying report navigation. To avoid navigating through long lists of reports and folders, encourage your users to "favorite" reports and other items they routinely use.*

Note that the server redirected the browser to the Favorites page and displays the word "favorites" in the web address. You can explicitly set a link to the Favorites page using this URL. If you had not previously added any objects to your Favorites or if you click the Browse link in the page heading, you are presented with the Browse page, shown in Figure 21-2.

Icons and menu options in the header area of the page provide navigational assistance and access to site-level functionality. On the Home page you see a list of reports, folders, and data sources contained in the current web portal environment.

By clicking an item on the page, you can navigate to that item. For example, if you click a report, the report loads for you to view. If you click a folder, you enter that folder. Clicking the Home link always takes you back to the Home page so you can start over.

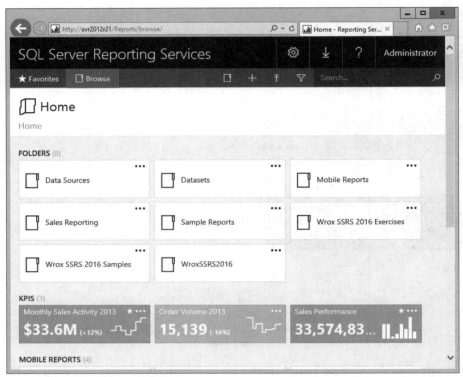

FIGURE 21-2: Web portal Browse view.

Use the gear icon to display a drop-down menu with links to setting options. Available options may depend on your rights on the system. Table 21-1 lists default options available to a user with administrative access to the report server.

TABLE 21-1: Home Folder Setting Options

LINK	DESCRIPTION
My settings	Takes you to the Settings page of the Home folder. Power BI subscription integration is managed from this page.
My subscriptions	Takes you to the My Subscriptions site-level page. This page displays all the subscriptions on the site that you own.
Site settings	Provides access to the Site Settings pages. From these pages you can modify general site-level settings, site-level security, and shared schedules.

To the right of the gear icon is a download icon, which you can use to download and install applications. Table 21-2 shows these options.

TABLE 21-2: Application Downloads

LINK	DESCRIPTION
Report Builder	Installs the most current version of the Report Builder application, which is used to design and publish paginated reports, shared datasets, and other shared objects.
Mobile Report Publisher	Installs the most current version of Mobile Report publisher, used to design and publish visual reports optimized for mobile devices.
Power BI Desktop	Installs the current version of Power BI Desktop. The Power BI analytic data toolset is used to import and transform data, create data models, define calculations, and to create drag-and-drop visual reports.
Power BI Mobile	Provides links to download mobile applications for iOS, Android, and Windows mobile devices. Mobile apps may be used to explore mobile reports and Power BI content.

The Help icon opens a separate browser window displaying the Web Portal Help and Support pages. Just below these links is a Search box. When you enter text in the box and click the button to its right, Web Portal performs a case-insensitive search for items with names and descriptions matching the text you entered.

Every item displayed in web portal has an ellipsis (three dots) in the upper right-hand corner. Clicking the ellipsis displays a pop-up window with options to manage the object, view context-specific information, and other menu options. The ellipsis enables reports and KPIs to be added or removed from your Favorites.

Click the folder, report, or other item to open or navigate to that item. The behavior of clicking the object or clicking the "MANAGE" option varies depending on the object type. These options are intuitive and easy to discover with just a little exploration. For example, clicking a folder navigates to the folder and displays the contents. Clicking a report runs the report. Clicking the ellipsis and then "MANAGE" for a folder enables properties and security, whereas clicking "MANAGE" for a KPI displays the KPI design page.

CONTENT MANAGEMENT ACTIVITIES

Now that you are familiar with web portal basics, it is time to look at the management of various Reporting Services items through the application. The following sections explore the management of these items:

➤ Folders

➤ Shared data sources

➤ Shared datasets

➤ Reports

➤ Report resources

➤ Shared schedules

Several features of the web portal menu bar enable content discovery and management. Click the filter icon on the menu bar to control the visibility of items in the folder that are set to be hidden. The web portal menu bar is shown in Figure 21-3.

FIGURE 21-3: View and Visibility menu.

All of the content types displayed on this list are recognized by Reporting Services and have specific management features. This means that items are displayed with a unique icon and have context-specific features when you choose "MANAGE" after clicking the ellipsis. The Resources content type is a catch-all for miscellaneous file types. You can store practically any type of file and access it through web portal but these items do not have content-specific management features.

> **NOTE** *You can manage Power BI Desktop Reports and Excel Workbook files through web portal. Microsoft has stated that these items will be supported with server-side rendering and management capabilities in a later product version. However, in the initial product release (RTM version), both of these file types will simply open the file on the user's desktop with Power BI Desktop or Microsoft Excel. If you are running a later update of Reporting Services, this behavior may be different for you.*

Folders

All Reporting Services items are stored within a folder hierarchy. This provides a simple, familiar structure for organizing content. The folder hierarchy is a virtual structure; in other words, you will not find these folders in the server's filesystem. Instead, the structure exists as a set of self-referencing records in the ReportServer database.

On the Home page, items within the folder, including any child folders, are presented in a list of folders. The items on the Home page are identified by name, an optional description, and an icon denoting the item's type, such as Folder, Report, Mobile Report, KPI, Linked Report, Shared Data Source, Dataset, Resource, Standard Subscriptions, or Data-Driven Subscriptions.

The menu bar at the top of the folder page list presents buttons for creating new folders and shared objects and for uploading items to the folder. You explore creating new shared data sources and uploading items later in this chapter. New objects are added to a folder using the "+New" icon. Clicking the "+New" button and then selecting Folder takes you to the New Folder page. On this page, you enter a name for your new folder.

> **NOTE** *Depending on the available screen resolution or web browser window size, some menu items change. For example, the "+New" menu will change to "+" if there is limited screen space.*

Under the "MANAGE" option, you have additional properties. You can delete, move, and set role-based security permissions on a folder. The Delete option confirms and then drops the items you have selected. The Move option takes you to Move Items page, which requires you to select where in the site's folder structure the items are to be moved. If you are deleting or moving a folder, the operation succeeds only if you have the required permissions on each item it contains.

Now that you know how to create, alter, and remove folders, what kind of folder structure should you build for your site? Different schools of thought include organizing content by organizational unit, functional area, and user role.

> **NOTE** *Where report duplication between folders might make sense, use linked reports to reference the same report in multiple folders without actually duplicating the report.*

Opinions vary about object and folder naming conventions, standard folder locations, and the complexity of folder hierarchies. I can't tell you exactly how to name folders and other objects. Dad always said "keep it simple" so that's what I do.

You ultimately must decide how to organize your report server but I recommend that it be driven by a set of guidelines adopted before you jump in. Consulting my peers (with whom I have designed countless report solutions in developing guidelines), we recommend that you keep the user experience at the forefront of your thought process and consider the maintenance and security implications of your scheme. You should review the guidelines with administrators, report developers, and user stakeholders to obtain support and educate those who will be working with the guidelines.

Shared Data Sources

Shared data sources hold connection information in a secure manner, allowing this information to be centrally administered while being shared among reports and report models throughout the site.

Report authors often create shared data sources as part of the report development process. In SQL Server Data Tools (SSDT), you can add these to the Report Server project by right-clicking the

`Shared Data Sources` folder in the Solution Explorer, selecting Add New Data Source, and providing the required information in the Shared Data Source dialog. The shared data source item is deployed to the site folder identified by the project's `TargetDataSourceFolder` property. You can access this property by right-clicking the project in Solution Explorer and selecting Properties.

To create a shared data source item without the help of a report-authoring tool, open web portal and navigate to the folder within which the item will be housed. Use the +New menu and click the Data Source button. In the resulting New Data Source page, shown in Figure 21-4, enter a name and description for the new item. Set the options that control whether the item is displayed in its parent folder's Contents page list view and/or enabled for use on the site. Then select the registered data extension to be used, and enter an appropriate connection string. Which data extension you select determines the syntax of the connection string.

> **NOTE** *It is important to note that web portal does not automatically verify the connection. To test the connection, click the Test Connection button on the creation screen.*

Below the connection string, set the security context to be used when establishing the connection. You have four basic options, a couple of which support one or more variations.

The "By prompting the user viewing the report for credentials" option allows you to configure a prompt to be presented to the user. This option instructs Reporting Services whether to treat these as Windows user credentials.

The "Using the following credentials" option allows you to enter a username/password combination that will be encrypted and stored in the primary Reporting Services application database. Again, you have the option to have Reporting Services treat these as Windows or source-specific credentials. The associated "Impersonate the authenticated user after a connection has been made to the data source" option allows database-user impersonation to be employed after the connection has been established. This option provides support for the use of SETUSER functionality within SQL Server.

The "As the user viewing the report" option allows the user to be impersonated when making the connection to the external data source. For this feature to work, the external data source must be local to the Reporting Services server, or Kerberos must be enabled on the domain.

> **NOTE** *In addition, Reporting Services must have support for integrated security enabled for this option to be employed.*

The final option, "Without any credentials," instructs Reporting Services to use the Unattended Execution Account when establishing the connection. This account is not enabled by default and is not recommended for use against most data sources. Whether or not the Unattended Execution Account is enabled, the "Credentials are not required" option is provided. If you attempt to leverage a data source with this option set and the Unattended Execution Account not enabled, you receive an error indicating an invalid data source credential setting. The Unattended Execution Account is configured using the Reporting Services Configuration Manager.

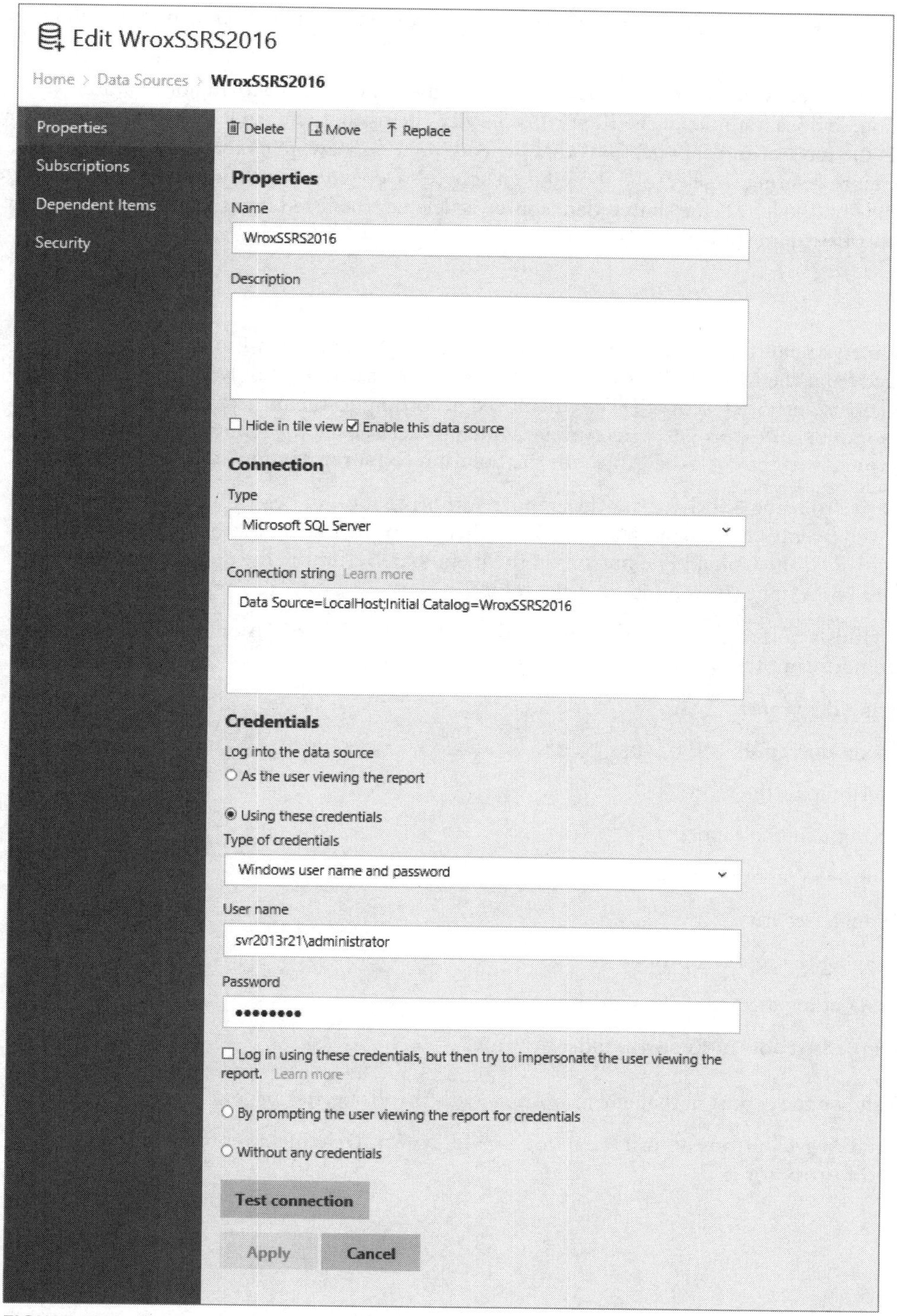

FIGURE 21-4: Data source properties page.

Clicking OK creates the data source item. Clicking the new shared data source item takes you to its Properties page.

On the Properties page, you can move, rename, or delete the data source. Moving or renaming a shared data source does not impact the Reporting Services items that refer to it. Deleting a shared data source breaks the reports and subscriptions that depend on it. To view items that refer to the shared data source before deleting it, select the shared data source's Dependent Items and Subscriptions page navigation links on the left. If the shared data source is deleted, the listed items are broken until they are pointed to a new data source.

Reports

Paginated reports are authored and deployed using either SSDT or Report Builder. You can edit a report in-place from the MANAGE page of a report and then select Edit in Report Builder from the menu bar. Reports authored with SSDT are deployed according to the project properties in SSDT. The `TargetReportFolder` property determines which folder is used for report deployment. To access this property, right-click the project in the Solution Explorer window and select Properties.

As an alternative to using SSDT (or another report authoring tool) to deploy a report to the site, you can use web portal's file upload feature. To do this, open the folder where you want to place the report, and click the Upload File button on the menu bar. Select the file and then click OK to upload. The file now appears as an item in the folder.

Clicking the ellipsis button on a report icon and then "MANAGE" displays a context menu that allows you to perform other actions on the report that include:

➤ Moving the report

➤ Deleting the report

➤ Subscribing to the report

➤ Creating a linked report

➤ Viewing the report's history

➤ Managing security

➤ Managing the report's properties

➤ Downloading a copy of the report

➤ Editing the report in Report Builder

Figure 21-5 shows the report management options with the Properties page selected.

The Delete and Move buttons do just what you would expect. Deleting a report removes any subscriptions and history for it.

> **TIP** *Before deleting a report, remove any linked reports that rely on the deployed report.*

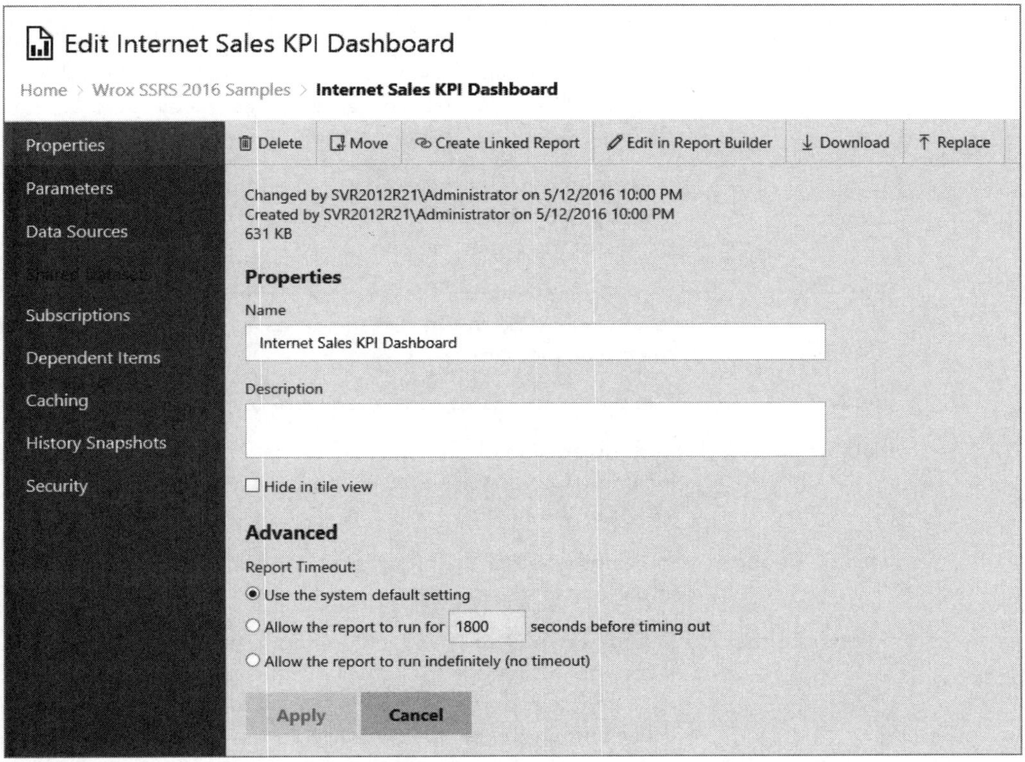

FIGURE 21-5: Report properties pages in web portal.

After the report server is configured for email delivery in Reporting Services Configuration Manager, you can subscribe to the report, which provides you with updates via e-mail or to a shared file location. Using this functionality, you can choose to run the report at a specific time or select a shared schedule that is already set up.

Clicking the Subscriptions page opens the report's Subscriptions page. On this page, existing subscriptions associated with the report are presented in a sortable table.

Clicking the New Subscription button allows you to set up a new standard subscription. On the New Subscription page, you specify the subscription delivery mechanism for the report, which then determines which additional information is needed. Table 21-3 lists the settings for e-mail and file share subscription delivery.

TABLE 21-3: Email Subscription Delivery Options

DELIVERY METHOD	SETTING	DESCRIPTION
E-mail	To	A semicolon-delimited list of e-mail addresses to which the report will be delivered. These addresses will be listed on the To line of the e-mail message.
	Cc	A semicolon-delimited list of e-mail addresses to which the report will be delivered. These addresses will be listed on the Cc line of the e-mail message.
	Bcc	A semicolon-delimited list of e-mail addresses to which the report will be delivered. These addresses will not be listed in the e-mail message.
	Reply-To	The e-mail address to which replies should be directed.
	Subject	The subject line of the e-mail message. The default subject line includes two variables that will be replaced with appropriate values at the time of execution.
	Include Report	Indicates whether the report should be rendered and included in the e-mail message.
	Render Format	Specifies the format to which the report should be rendered if it is to be included in the e-mail message. If you specify Web Archive, the report is embedded in the message body. For any other format, the report is included as an attachment.
	Include Link	Indicates whether a link to the report on the Reporting Services site should be included in the e-mail message.
	Priority	Indicates the flag to be used for the message's importance.
	Comment	A message to be included in the body of the e-mail message.
Windows file share	File Name	The name of the file to deliver. You can supply an extension or select the "Add a file extension when a file is created" option to add an extension based on the rendering format you select.
	Path	The UNC path of the folder to which the file will be delivered.
	Render Format	A rendering format selected from a drop-down list of those available on the site.

DELIVERY METHOD	SETTING	DESCRIPTION
	Credentials Used to Access the File Share	The username/password combination used as credentials when accessing the file share specified in the Path setting.
	Overwrite Options	One of three options indicating how to respond to the existence of a file with the name identified in the File Name setting. Options allow the file to be overwritten; the subscription to fail if the file exists; or the file to be written to the share but under a name with a sequential, numeric value appended.

The subscription processing options determine whether the subscription is delivered based on a subscription-specific or shared schedule. If the report includes parameters, values for these are entered in the Report Parameter Values section at the bottom of the New Subscription page. Clicking OK creates the new subscription.

Choosing the Data-driven subscription option from the report Subscriptions page prompts you for a number of additional options which enable reports to be delivered to a broad audience. The key to a data-driven subscription is a query used to provide user and destination-specific property values. You will typically create your own table in any database of your choice to populate with any of the property subscription values you elect to provide. Any properties that are not set from fields in the table may be set with static values.

Give the subscription a name and identify its delivery type. All subscribers to this data-driven subscription will use this delivery method.

Specify the data source through which subscription data will be retrieved. Use a shared data source or elect to create a subscription-specific data source. These data sources, as with those supporting any other unattended features, must use stored credentials.

Enter a query that retrieves the information required by the subscription. The columns you return from the query depend on how you intend to map fields to various options, properties, and parameters.

Map delivery method settings to fields returned by your query. Alternatively, you can map these settings to constants or, in some cases, elect to provide no value.

If the report contains parameters, map the parameters in the report to fields in the query. Again, you can also map a parameter to a constant or elect to provide no value if appropriate.

Specify whether a subscription-specific or shared schedule will be used to control the timing of subscription delivery. You can also elect to have the subscription delivered whenever data for the snapshot associated with the report is updated. If you choose to use a subscription-specific schedule, you define the schedule.

The Create Linked Report context menu item takes you to the New Linked Report page, as shown in Figure 21-6. You can think of a linked report as a kind of shortcut to a standard report, except that you can configure the linked report's properties differently from those of the report it references. This includes setting alternative processing options, cache refresh options, snapshot options, and security options. In addition, if the report has parameters or uses a shared data source, you also see pages to configure those.

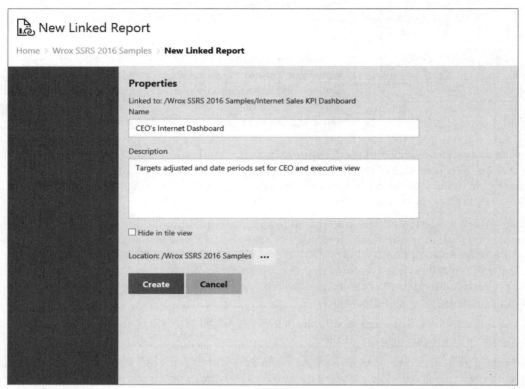

FIGURE 21-6: New Linked Report page.

The View Report History context menu item takes you to a page that shows you the report's history, such as the most recent snapshots and subscriptions. In addition, you can use this page to create a new snapshot of the report.

> **NOTE** *For a report to support history, its data sources must use stored credentials, and all parameters must have been assigned default values.*

The Security functionality allows you to manage the report's security, including assigning roles to users or groups. By default, the report's security is inherited from the parent container. You can break this inheritance to create item-level security, or you can restore this inheritance for an item with unique security settings.

If a report, linked or otherwise, has parameters, a Parameters Properties page is available on the left for that report's management page. On this page, you can set the default value, nullability, visibility, and prompt settings for each report parameter. These settings can be different from those specified during the report authoring phase.

If a report uses a data source, the Data Sources Properties page is available on the left. On this page, you can configure the report-specific and shared data sources that a report uses. You can also swap out report-specific and shared data sources in use by the report.

The Caching page is used to configure a report's use of the Reporting Services caching features. By default, the "Always run this report with the most recent data" option is selected, which means that neither report execution caching nor snapshots are employed. (Session caching, discussed in Chapter 3 and configured at the site level, is still in effect.)

Selecting either "Cache copies of this report and use them when available" or "Always run this report against pregenerated snapshots" enables report execution caching. Using either of these options, a copy of the report is cached when the report is run unless a valid cached copy already exists. That cached copy is held in the `ReportServerTempDB` database to fulfill subsequent requests until the cache expires. The second option, "Cache copies of this report and use them when available" instructs Reporting Services to expire the cached copy after a fixed number of minutes. The third option, "Always run this report against pregenerated snapshots" instructs Reporting Services to expire the cached copy at a fixed point in time. This allows you to set a report-specific schedule or use a shared schedule.

The set of suboptions instruct Reporting Services to create and render the report from a snapshot. The snapshot is a historical copy of a scheduled execution of the report. Snapshots eliminate the potentially long run times experienced by the first user of a report when a cached copy has expired. You can specify a report-specific or shared schedule for the timing of the snapshot and can elect to run the snapshot immediately following its configuration. The snapshot remains valid until the next snapshot is executed.

> **NOTE** *To leverage either report execution caching or snapshots, the report must use data sources with stored credentials in order to authenticate as an unattended user (also discussed in Chapter 3.)*

Settings under each of the two caching options allow you to manage the cache expiration, refresh plans, snapshot schedule, and manual caching options.

The report timeout option under Site Settings provides a safety net for run-away scheduled caching and report executions. If you override the default limit of 1800 seconds, it is advisable to carefully monitor the report server for time-outs and long-running reports.

The Cache Refresh Options page allows you to create a caching plan if one does not exist. When creating a new plan, you are required to set default parameters, if any exist, and specify a time or schedule for refreshing the cached report. Because report parameters require a default value with caching, this can limit your ability to use snapshots as an execution option. However, in many scenarios, using dataset filters can allow you to make wider use of a report snapshot.

The History snapshots page allows you to manage the snapshots for the specific report. Each snapshot stores the intermediate rendering (data and layout) of the report in the database. Storing report history can use considerable space within the ReportServer database. You can limit the number of historical snapshots maintained for a report. The "Use the system default setting" option instructs Reporting Services to retain history for this report according to the site-level history setting. This setting has a default value of 10 days. The other two options override the site-level setting with a report-specific value, allowing you to keep history indefinitely or for simply an alternative number of days.

To actually see historical snapshots for a report, navigate to the History page by clicking the report's History snapshots page. Report snapshots recorded to history are presented here in a detailed, tabular view.

Clicking an entry's Created value opens a new window showing the report rendered using data from this snapshot. You can remove a snapshot from the history using this page. The New history snapshot button is available when snapshots are enabled and when the report has a data source with stored credentials. This button generates an on-demand report snapshot for inclusion in the report history.

Report Resources

Resources are files referenced by a report. Image files are the most commonly used reporting resources, but HTML, XML, XSLT, text, PDF, and Microsoft Office files are often employed as well. Reporting Services does not restrict what kind of resource a report can leverage, so the possibilities are endless. That said, there are practical limitations to what may be used as a reporting resource.

Reporting Services is simply a way to store and return the binary image of a resource file. The consuming application, whether the Reporting Services report processor or a custom report processing extension, must understand how to consume the resource item for it to be incorporated into the report. Otherwise, your only option is to provide a link to the resource and depend on the report-viewing tool, typically a web browser, to handle the binary image for you.

In addition, the binary image of the resource file is stored in an Image data type field in the ReportServer database. This imposes a 2 GB limitation on the file size. If you exceed this limit, an error is returned as you attempt to upload it to the site.

To upload a resource to Reporting Services, open the parent folder's Contents page and click the Upload File button. Locate the file to upload, and click the OK button. After it is uploaded, you should see the item displayed within the folder.

Clicking the item takes you to the resource's View page. If your web browser can render a resource, such as a JPEG or GIF file, the item is displayed within the body of the web portal page. If your web browser cannot render a resource, such as a TIFF file, the browser prompts you to save the file to your local system. The resource item's General Properties page allows you to perform basic maintenance on the item.

Shared Schedules

Shared schedules allow you to define and administer schedules in a centralized manner for use throughout the site.

Shared schedules are managed at the site level, outside the folder structure. To access these, click the Site Settings link in the upper-right corner of the web portal header. Move to the Schedules page to see a tabular representation of Shared Schedules on the system.

The table on the Schedules page shows Name, Schedule (description), Creator, Last Run, Next Run, and Status fields, all of which can be used to sort the table's contents. Selecting one or more items in the table enables the Delete, Pause, and Resume buttons within the menu bar.

Clicking the New Schedule button in the menu bar on this page takes you to the New/Edit Schedule page. This page allows you to enter a name for the schedule and set its frequency of execution. You can also set a date range during which this schedule is executed, as shown in Figure 21-7.

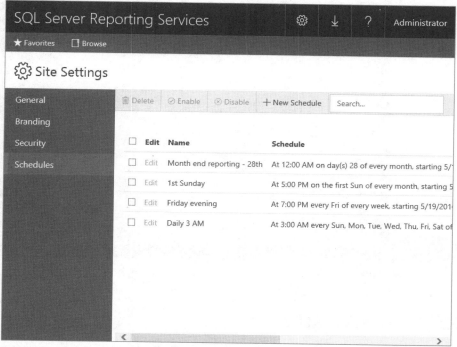

FIGURE 21-7: Schedules page in Site Settings.

Clicking the OK button submits the request to create the schedule. Behind the scenes, Reporting Services attempts to create a scheduled job through SQL Agent. If the SQL Agent Windows service is not started, you receive an error message.

Back on the Schedules page, clicking a schedule item's name or schedule value takes you back to the New/Edit Schedule page, where you can edit the item's configuration. Before making changes, it is a good idea to review the schedule's Reports page to identify reports dependent on it.

Shared schedules can also be created and managed through SQL Server Management Studio. Open SQL Server Management Studio, connect to the Reporting Services instance, and locate the Shared Schedules folder under the instance icon. You can right-click the Shared Schedules folder to create or delete a shared schedule. You can also right-click an individual schedule to delete it or access its properties page. The properties page, shown in Figure 21-8, provides access to the same properties presented through web portal.

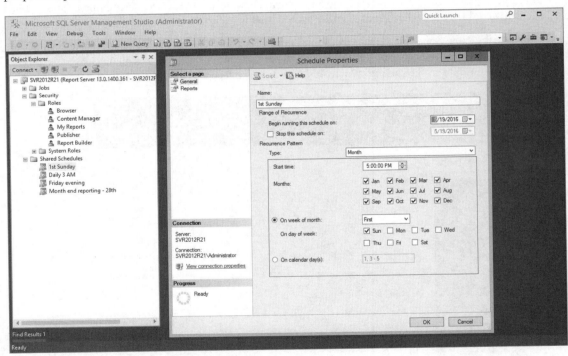

FIGURE 21-8: Schedule Properties in SSMS.

SITE AND CONTENT SECURITY

All content security in Reporting Services is role-based, which is actually quite simple in concept. Users or Windows groups (to which users belong) are assigned to security roles for different objects, and roles have permission sets to perform different actions. Default role assignments are defined at the site level for administrators and at the Home folder level for users. Pretty simple, right? Usually it is.

Site Security

By default, members of the built-in Windows administrators group have permission to manage the report server content and settings through web portal, which you see in Figure 21-9. You can give additional Windows groups or users administrative permission to the server by adding a new role assignment in the Site Settings area, on the Security page.

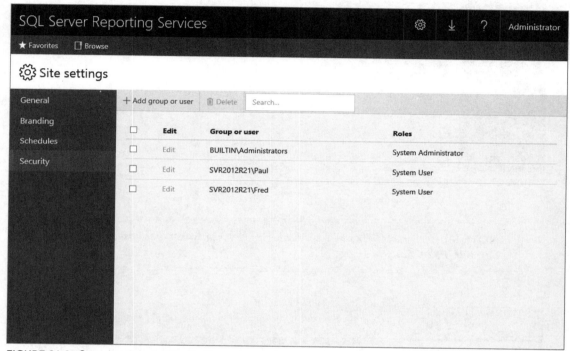

FIGURE 21-9: Security page in Site Settings.

Click +Add group or user to show the page displayed in Figure 21-10. Add the Windows group or username preceded with the domain name and a backslash. If the report server is not joined to a domain, you can use the machine name instead of the domain. Check the System Administrator box to assign this principal administrative rights to the report server and then click OK.

Item-Level Security

To perform any action on a Reporting Services item, a user must be granted permissions. Connecting to the report server with SSMS allows you to view the predefined content roles for the server, shown in Figure 21-11. It is not necessary to modify these roles or to assign new roles but you have the freedom to do so. Creating a new role would allow you to assign user permission sets at a more granular level than the predefined roles that install with Reporting Services.

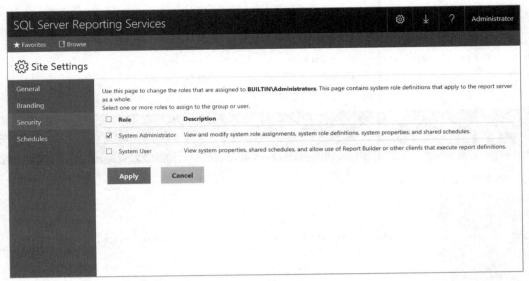

FIGURE 21-10: Assigning roles to a user or group.

NOTE *I have rarely defined custom roles and typically use these predefined roles without making any changes.*

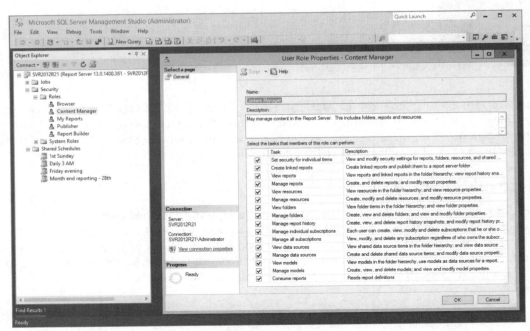

FIGURE 21-11: Role permission mapping in SSMS.

Reporting Services supports a fixed set of permissions associated with each type of item, as shown in Table 21-4.

TABLE 21-4: Fixed Role Permissions

ITEM	PERMISSIONS
Report	Create Any Subscription
	Create Link
	Create Report History
	Create Subscription
	Delete Any Subscription
	Delete Report History
	Delete Subscription
	Delete Update Properties
	Execute Read Policy
	List Report History
	Read Any Subscription
	Read Content
	Read Data Sources
	Read Properties
	Read Report Definition
	Read Report Definitions
	Read Security Policies
	Read Subscription
	Update Any Subscription
	Update Data Sources
	Update Parameters
	Update Policy
	Update Report Definition
	Update Security Policies
	Update Subscription
Shared Data Source	Delete Update Content
	Read Properties
	Read Security Policies
	Update Properties
	Update Security Policies

continues

TABLE 21-4 *(continued)*

ITEM	PERMISSIONS
Reporting Resource	Delete Update Content
	Read Content
	Read Properties
	Read Security Policies
	Update Properties
	Update Security Policies
Folder	Create Data Source
	Create Folder
	Create Model
	Create Report
	Create Resource
	Delete Update Properties
	Execute and View
	List Report History
	Read Properties
	Read Security Policies
	Update Security Policies

Explicitly assigning the right combinations of permissions required to perform an action on the site would be challenging. To simplify things, Reporting Services organizes these permissions into a more condensed set of item-level tasks. These tasks more naturally align with the kinds of activities users need to perform. Table 21-5 lists the task-to-permission mappings. Although it's important to understand these permissions as the underlying mechanism behind item-level security, Reporting Services does not expose these permissions and does not allow tasks to be created or altered.

TABLE 21-5: Task-Level Permissions

ITEM	TASK	PERMISSIONS
Folder	Manage data sources	Create Data Source
	Manage folders	Create Folder
		Delete Update Properties
		Read Properties
	Manage reports	Create Report
	Manage resources	Create Resource

ITEM	TASK	PERMISSIONS
	Set security for individual items	Read Security Policies
		Update Security Policies
	View folders	Read Properties
		Execute and View
		List Report History
Reports	Consume reports	Read Content
		Read Report Definitions
		Read Properties
	Create linked reports	Create Link
		Read Properties
	Manage all subscriptions	Read Properties
		Read Any Subscription
		Create Any Subscription
		Delete Any Subscription
		Update Any Subscription
	Manage individual subscriptions	Read Properties
		Create Subscription
		Delete Subscription
		Read Subscription
		Update Subscription
	Manage individual subscriptions	Read Properties
		Create Subscription
		Delete Subscription
		Read Subscription
		Update Subscription
	Manage report history	Read Properties
		Create Report History
		Delete Report History
		Execute Read Policy
		Update Policy
		List Report History

continues

TABLE 21-5 *(continued)*

ITEM	TASK	PERMISSIONS
	Manage reports	Read Properties Delete Update Properties Update Parameters Read Data Sources Update Data Sources Read Report Definition Update Report Definition Execute Read Policy Update Policy
	View reports	Read Content Read Properties
	Set security for individual items	Read Security Policies Update Security Policies
Data Sources	Manage data sources	Update Properties Delete Update Content Read Properties
	View data sources	Read Content Read Properties
	Set security for individual items	Read Security Policies Update Security Policies
Resources	Set security for individual items	Read Security Policies Update Security Policies
	Manage resources	Update Properties Delete Update Content Read Properties
	View resources	Read Content Read Properties

Take a moment to consider the users of a particular section of your Reporting Services site, such as a folder. Some users will simply need to browse the folder's contents. Others may need to both browse and publish items to the folder. A few may even need the rights to manage the folder's security. These users can be described as having one or more roles within this portion of the site. Each of those roles requires a set of rights for its members to perform their expected tasks. This is the basic model for applying item-level security in Reporting Services.

In Reporting Services, roles are defined at the site level and are assigned tasks, as described earlier. Reporting Services comes with five preconfigured item-level roles, as described in Table 21-6.

TABLE 21-6: User Item-Level Roles

ROLE	DESCRIPTION	TASKS
Browser	Run reports and navigate through the folder structure.	View reports View resources View folders View models Manage individual subscriptions
Content Manager	Define a folder structure for storing reports and other items, set security at the item level, and view and manage the items stored by the server.	Consume reports Create linked reports Manage all subscriptions Manage data sources Manage folders Manage models Manage individual subscriptions Manage report history Manage reports Manage resources Set security policies for items View data sources View reports View models View resources View folders
My Reports	If the "My Reports" feature is enabled on the server, enables consuming and managing items in the user's virtual My Reports folder.	(same as Content Manager)

continues

TABLE 21-5 *(continued)*

ROLE	DESCRIPTION	TASKS
Publisher	Publish content to a report server.	Create linked reports Manage data sources Manage folders Manage reports Manage models Manage resources
Report Builder	Build and edit reports in Report Builder.	Consume reports View reports View resources View folders View models Manage individual subscriptions

To modify the tasks assigned to these roles, open SQL Server Management Studio and connect to the Reporting Services instance. In the Object Explorer pane, expand the Security folder and its Roles subfolder.

Right-click a role and select Properties to open its User Role Properties dialog. Here you can change the role's description and tasks assigned to it. Clicking OK saves your changes.

To create a new role, right-click the Roles subfolder in the SQL Server Management Studio Object Explorer pane and select New Role. In the resulting New User Role dialog, provide the name, description, and task assignments for this role. Click OK to create the role.

To drop a role, right-click it, and select Delete. You are asked to confirm this action before the role is dropped. You can drop both custom and predefined Reporting Services roles.

Because roles are simply named sets of tasks (which themselves are nothing more than named sets of permissions), item-level security is implemented by linking users with one or more roles for a given Reporting Services item.

Assigning Users to a Role

In web portal, you assign a user or Windows group to an object (typically a folder) by creating a new role assignment for that object. The easiest way to give a user permission to all content on the report server is to add the role assignment to the Home folder. If the user should only have access to a specific folder or report, add the role assignment to that object and not to the parent folder.

In the Home folder, role assignments are managed using the Manage Folder item on the menu bar. You can manage other folder assignments the same way or by using the MANAGE option from the item icon.

Managing user access to individual folders or content items at a more granular level is performed beneath the Home folder but requires just a little more work. When you add a role assignment for items within the Home folder, you see the message box in Figure 21-12. By clicking OK, the role assignments for the parent folder will no longer apply and you must assign new role-based security for the item or folder.

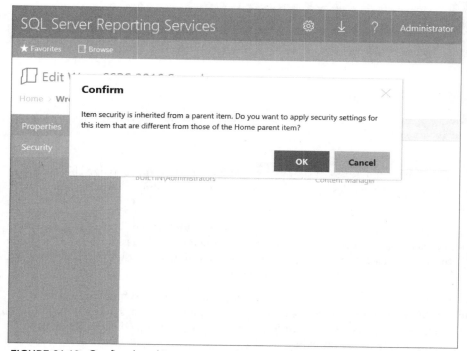

FIGURE 21-12: Confirm breaking security inheritance.

Clicking the New Role Assignment button takes you to the New Role Assignment page, as shown in Figure 21-13. The "Group or user" box accepts any valid Windows principal. Assuming the report server is joined to a domain, enter a group or user as domain\name. On a server not joined to a domain, you can simply enter the group or username or enter the machine name in place of the domain. You can assign any group or user the permissions of any combination of roles by checking one or more boxes on this page.

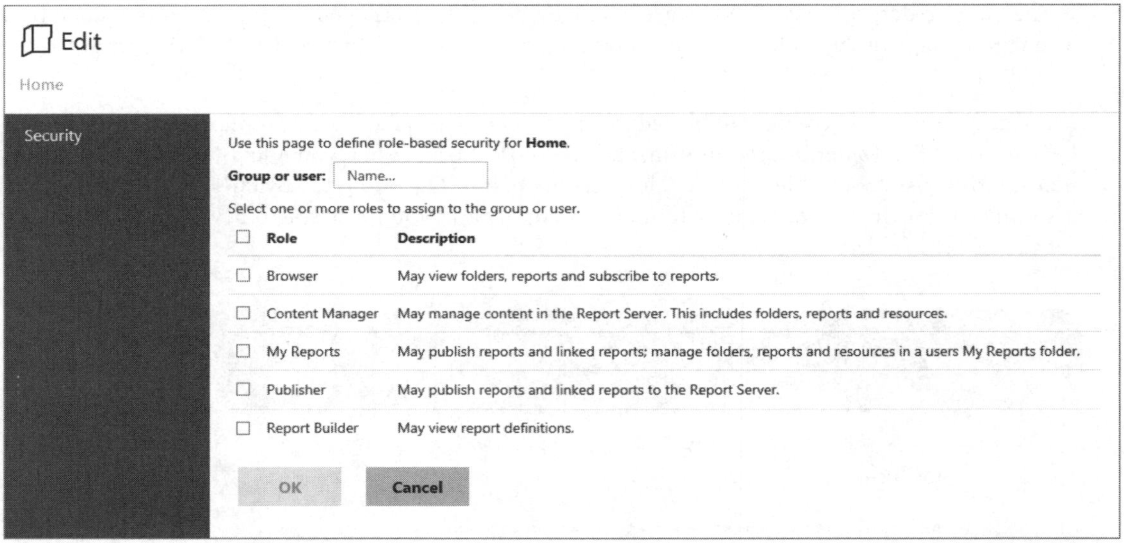

FIGURE 21-13: Edit Security page.

Here, you enter the account name for the user or group to which you want to assign this access and then select one or more of the roles as appropriate. Clicking OK submits the assignment to Reporting Services.

Creating item-user-role assignments for every item on the site would get old quickly. So, instead, Reporting Services uses inheritance for item-level security. When a user is assigned to one or more roles on a folder, this assignment is inherited by that folder's child items. If these child items include folders, the inheritance cascades down the folder hierarchy.

Inheritance makes administering security much easier, but you may need to break inheritance to assign permissions on an item appropriately. To do this, navigate to the item's Security page in web portal. When inheritance is in place, you see an Edit Item Security button. Clicking this button causes a warning to appear about breaking inheritance.

After inheritance is broken, you will notice that the New Role Assignment button is available, allowing you to create user-role assignments for this item.

Also notice that the user-role assignments that would have been inherited from this folder's parent are preassigned to this item. Selecting the check box for any unnecessary assignments and clicking the Delete button on the menu bar removes these.

Finally, if you want to reset this item's security to use inheritance, again click the "Use same security as parent folder" button in the menu bar. The item reverts to inherited security, and any non-inherited assignments are dropped.

SITE BRANDING

The new site branding feature uses a very simple approach to allow the Web Portal, mobile reports, and KPIs to be customized with a branded color theme. You can customize the colors and add a logo graphic to style your report server to match your company brand. A brand package consists of a zipped archive file containing three files, shown in Figure 21-14.

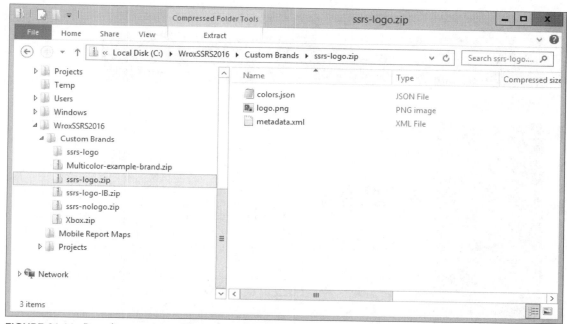

FIGURE 21-14: Branding package file contents.

I have provided example brand package files with the book downloads and you will find these in the Custom Brands folder. You can get started with one of these or download the current theme to a brand package file using the Download option on the Site Settings Branding page. To customize a brand package, make a copy of the file you want to use as the starting point for your brand package. Unzip the files to a folder, modify the colors.json file with your own theme colors, replace the logo.png file with your company logo, and then zip the updated files into a new archive file. All of the modified files must have the original filenames.

Applying a new brand package is quite simple. Figure 21-15 shows the Branding page under Site Settings. Click the "Upload brand package" button, browse to the brand package .zip file, and upload the file. You will immediately see the new brand applied to your web portal, mobile reports, and KPIs.

> **NOTE** *Site branding is a feature Reporting Services inherited from Microsoft's acquisition of the Datazen product from ComponentArt. This is the reason it applies to KPIs and mobile reports, which were also part of the Datazen retrofit. Branding does not apply to paginated reports in the current release of SSRS 2016.*

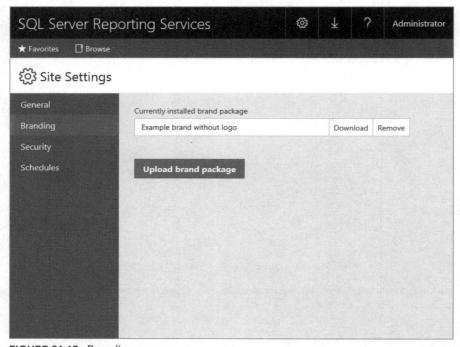

FIGURE 21-15: Branding page.

To help you identify colors you may want to update in your custom brand package, I have created a report with all the elements and colors of the default package, which is shown in Figure 21-16. This report is in the Wrox SSRS 2016 Samples project called Default Branding Colors.

Use this report as a guide to modify the hex color values in the `color.json` file. Although you can download a backup copy of the brand package, you can use the Remove button to revert the site branding back to the default brand package. If your objective is to brand the surface of the web portal, you may need to update only a few of the major color elements. However, updating every one of the 73 color properties and matching them to all the background fills, object borders, hover-over colors, and other properties can be time-consuming work. For reference, Figure 21-17 shows some of the element names that are mapped to objects on the Site Settings page of the web portal. In this simple modification of the default brand package, I have replaced the PrimaryContrast element with yellow (#ffff00) and the logo.png file with the Microsoft logo.

Default Brand Package Colors

Interface Colors

Element Name	Hex Color	Sample Color
danger	#bb2124	
dangerContrast	#fff	
info	#5bc0de	
infoContrast	#fff	
kpiBad	#de061a	
kpiBadContrast	#fff	
kpiGood	#4fb443	
kpiGoodContrast	#fff	
kpiNeutral	#d9b42c	
kpiNeutralContrast	#fff	
kpiNone	#333	
kpiNoneContrast	#fff	
neutralPrimary	#fff	
neutralPrimaryAlt	#f4f4f4	
neutralPrimaryAlt2	#e3e3e3	
neutralPrimaryAlt3	#c8c8c8	
neutralPrimaryContrast	#000	
neutralSecondary	#fff	
neutralSecondaryAlt	#eaeaea	
neutralSecondaryAlt2	#b7b7b7	
neutralSecondaryAlt3	#acacac	
neutralSecondaryContrast	#000	
neutralTertiary	#b7b7b7	
neutralTertiaryAlt	#c8c8c8	
neutralTertiaryAlt2	#eaeaea	
neutralTertiaryAlt3	#fff	
neutralTertiaryContrast	#222	
primary	#bb2124	
primaryAlt	#d31115	
primaryAlt2	#671215	
primaryAlt3	#bb2124	
primaryAlt4	#00abee	
primaryContrast	#fff	
secondary	#000	
secondaryAlt	#444	
secondaryAlt2	#555	
secondaryAlt3	#777	
secondaryContrast	#fff	
success	#2b3	
successContrast	#fff	
warning	#f0ad4e	
warningContrast	#fff	

Theme Colors

Element Name	Hex Color	Sample Color
altBackground	#f6f6f6	
altForeground	#000	
altMapBase	#f68c1f	
altPanelAccent	#fdc336	
altPanelBackground	#235378	
altPanelForeground	#fff	
altTableAccent	#fdc336	
background	#fff	
bad	#e90000	
foreground	#222	
good	#85ba00	
mapBase	#00aeef	
neutral	#edb327	
none	#333	
panelAccent	#00aeef	
panelBackground	#f6f6f6	
panelForeground	#222	
tableAccent	#00aeef	

Data Point Colors

Element Name	Hex Color	Sample Color
Datapoint 01	#0072c6	
Datapoint 02	#f68c1f	
Datapoint 03	#269657	
Datapoint 04	#dd5900	
Datapoint 05	#5b3573	
Datapoint 06	#22bdef	
Datapoint 07	#b4009e	
Datapoint 08	#008274	
Datapoint 09	#fdc336	
Datapoint 10	#ea3c00	
Datapoint 11	#00188f	
Datapoint 12	#9f9f9f	

FIGURE 21-16: Brand package color example report.

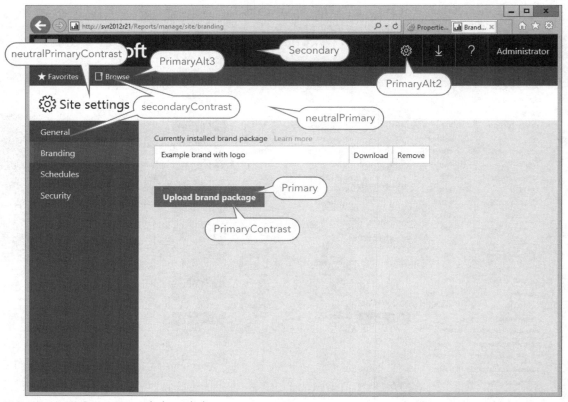

FIGURE 21-17: Some example brand elements.

CONTENT MANAGEMENT AUTOMATION

Content management consists of many repetitive actions. Performing these manually can be time-consuming and can risk introducing errors. Scripts allow these frequently performed actions to be automated. If implemented correctly, scripts can produce significant time savings and minimize the risks associated with changes to your environment. To support automation through scripts, Reporting Services comes with the rs.exe command-line application, also known as the RS utility.

The RS Utility

The RS utility, rs.exe, allows scripts to be run against local and remote instances of Reporting Services. The application is typically located in the *drive*:\Program Files (x86)\Microsoft SQL Server\130\Tools\Binn folder. It is responsible for creating an environment within which a Reporting Services script can be executed.

As part of this responsibility, the RS utility handles communications with an instance of the Reporting Services web service. It also handles the declaration and instantiation of variables supplied through the command-line call. These features allow flexible scripts to be developed with relative ease.

The following is a simple call to the RS utility. Note the use of the `-i` parameter to identify the Reporting Services script. The script file is a simple text file with an RSS file extension. The content of the text file is Visual Basic .NET code.

> **NOTE** *The RSS script file that contains Visual Basic .NET code is written against a proxy based on Web Service Description Language (WSDL). The WSDL defines the Reporting Services SOAP API. RSS Scripts are covered in the next section. However, if you want to learn more about writing scripts for* `rs.exe`, *check out the MSDN guidance at* `http://msdn.microsoft.com/en-us/library/ms154561(v=SQL.130).aspx` *or search for "Reporting Services Script File" using your favorite search engine. Make sure you select SQL Server 2016 when you find the MSDN article because previous versions provide examples to endpoints that are deprecated.*

Also note the identification of the web service URL with the `-s` parameter. In this example, the script is pointed to the web service presented by the local, default instance of Reporting Services:

```
rs.exe -i "c:\my scripts\my script.rss" -s http://localhost/reportserver
```

The connection to the web service is established using the current user's identity. To specify an alternative identity, you can specify a username/password combination with the `-u` and `-p` parameters. In the next example, the connection is made through the fictional `MyDomain\SomeUser` account, which has a password of `pass@word`:

```
rs.exe -i "c:\my scripts\my script.rss" -s http://localhost/reportserver
-u MyDomain\SomeUser -p pass@word
```

In Native mode, the Reporting Services web service presents an endpoint with the name ReportService2010.

> **NOTE** *In past versions of SQL Server, the web service endpoints were broken down into different endpoints depending on the type of install. These were called ReportService2005, which was designed for Reporting Services in Native mode, and ReportService2006, which was designed for Reporting Services in SharePoint Integrated mode. These endpoints were deprecated in SQL Server 2012 and have been combined into a new endpoint called ReportService2010. As of SQL Server 2016, the previous endpoints are deprecated but still available for backward compatibility. It is important to note, however, that when using the* `rs.exe` *utility without the* `-e` *flag you are actually using the ReportService2005 endpoint. This seems contradictory, but I imagine it was designed this way for backward compatibility.*

> **NOTE** *Access to the ReportService endpoints in previous releases of Reporting Services is available using the -e flag. Note that the Reporting Services 2000 endpoint is deprecated and no longer available.*

As mentioned at the start of this section, the RS utility declares and instantiates variables on behalf of the script. Variables are specified with the -v parameter followed by one or more variable/value combinations. Variable/value combinations are separated by an equals sign. Values containing spaces should be enclosed in double quotes. These quotation marks are not part of the variable's value. Here is a sample call to the utility with three variables that illustrates these concepts:

```
rs.exe -i "c:\my scripts\my script.rss" -s http://localhost/reportserver
-v VarA=1 VarB=apple VarC="keeps the doctor away"
```

Table 21-7 is a complete list of parameters that the rs.exe command-line utility supports.

TABLE 21-7: RS Utility Parameter Switches

PARAMETER	DESCRIPTION
-i	Identifies the script file to execute.
-s	Identifies the URL of the Reporting Services web service.
-u	Supplies the username used to log in to the Reporting Services site.
-p	Supplies the password associated with the username used to log in to the Reporting Services site.
-e	Identifies which Reporting Services web service endpoint to employ: Mgmt2010: Used in SQL Server 2012 to customize report processing and rendering. This endpoint can be used in either mode of Reporting Services. Mgmt2006: Used in previous versions of SQL Server to manage objects when Reporting Services is installed in Native mode. Mgmt2005: Used in previous versions of SQL Server to manage objects when Reporting Services is installed in Integrated mode. Exec2005: Used in previous versions of SQL Server to customize report processing and rendering. This endpoint can be used in either mode of Reporting Services.
-l	Specifies the number of seconds before the connection with Reporting Services times out. The default is 60 seconds. A value of 0 indicates an infinite connection time-out.
-b	Indicates that the script should be executed as a batch.
-v	Provides variables and values to pass to the script.
-t	Instructs the utility to include trace information in error messages.

Reporting Services Scripts

Reporting Services scripts are implemented in VB.NET. Only a few namespaces are supported, making the scripts fairly limited but still powerful enough to handle most content-management tasks. Supported namespaces include System, System.Diagnostics, System.IO, System.Web.Services, and System.Xml.

Every script must contain a Sub Main code block. This serves as the script's entry point. The Sub Main block does not have to be the first or only code block in the script. This allows you to move code to additional subroutines and functions you declare in the script.

Within the script, the Reporting Services web service is engaged through the rs object. You do not need to declare this object. The RS utility handles the details of setting up a web reference to a particular endpoint presented by a specific instance of the Reporting Services web service. More details are provided in the preceding section.

The requirement for the script developer is to call the appropriate classes and methods exposed by this endpoint through the rs object. To understand the classes and methods available for each endpoint, refer to the documentation available through Books Online.

Variables specified at the command line are automatically declared and initialized for use within the script. Variables in the script are aligned with those at the command line using a case-insensitive name match. If a variable is not declared in the script or does not match a variable supplied from the command line, you receive an undeclared variable error. All variables passed from the command line are passed in as strings.

The following code sample is a simple demonstration of these concepts. The script consists of a single code block, Sub Main. The ReportService2010 endpoint is accessed through the rs object to recursively read the site's contents starting from a folder identified by the MyFolder variable. The MyFolder variable is passed in from the command line.

```
Sub Main

    'Write the starting folder to the screen
    Console.WriteLine("The starting folder is " + MyFolder)

    'Open the Output File
    Dim OutputFile As New IO.StreamWriter( _
                        "c:\my scripts\contents.txt", False)

    'Obtain an array of Catalog Items
    Dim Contents As CatalogItem() = rs.ListChildren(MyFolder, True)

    'Loop through Array of CatalogItems
    For i As Int32 = 0 To Contents.GetUpperBound(0)

        'Write CatalogItem Type & Path to Output File w/ Pipe Delimiter
        OutputFile.Write(Contents(i).Type.ToString)
        OutputFile.Write("|")
        OutputFile.WriteLine(Contents(i).Path)
```

```
     Next

     'Close Output File
     OutputFile.Close()

  End Sub
```

This script is saved to a file named `List Contents.RSS` located in the `C:\my scripts` folder and is executed against the local Reporting Services instance through the following command-line call:

```
rs.exe -i "c:\my scripts\list contents.rss" -s http://localhost/reportserver
-v MyFolder="/"
```

The `"/"` value represents the `Home` folder in the Reporting Services folder hierarchy.

This is a simple script. It is presented in this form simply to demonstrate the basics of Reporting Services script development. You can find more information about building applications for Reporting Services using the web services at the following URL or by searching for the text "Building Applications Using the Web Service and the .NET Framework":

```
https://msdn.microsoft.com/en-us/library/ms152787(v=sql.130).aspx
```

> **NOTE** *A detailed explanation of the Report Server Web Service Endpoints architecture including how the scripting components fit in is available on MSDN at the following location:*
>
> ```
> https://msdn.microsoft.com/en-us/library/ms152787(v=sql.130).aspx
> ```

SUMMARY

In this chapter, you explored various aspects of web portal. You saw how web portal works and how it is used to manage Reporting Services content. You learned that web portal is available only when Reporting Services is installed in Native mode. You looked at how security works in web portal, including item-level security. You also looked at some of the endpoints that are available when scripting and automating tasks.

This chapter covered the following topics:

➤ Managing reports using web portal

➤ Viewing reports, models, and other content in web portal

➤ Configuring the web portal environment

➤ Automating reporting services with the RS utility

➤ Configuring web portal, including caching, schedules, and subscriptions

The final chapter is all about server administration, where we cover the essentials and details related to managing your report servers. Chapter 22 covers security and account management, backups and disaster recovery, managing the application databases, configuration information, monitoring and logging. We explore server resource management, troubleshooting and performance tuning, extension management and email delivery.

22
Server Administration

WHAT'S IN THIS CHAPTER?

➤ Enforcing security

➤ Account management and system-level roles

➤ Implementing surface area management

➤ Planning for backup and recovery

➤ Managing application databases

➤ Managing encryption keys

➤ Using configuration files

➤ Monitoring and logging

➤ Using performance counters and server management reports

➤ Understanding memory management

➤ Configuring URL reservations

➤ Administering e-mail delivery

➤ Managing rendering extensions

With any mission-critical service, it is important to properly configure and administer your report server. If you have Reporting Services configured in Native mode and not integrated into SharePoint, you will use tools that are specific to Reporting Services.

> **NOTE** *In previous editions of this book, we provided some guidance and high-level configuration information for SharePoint integration. Now that SSRS integration with SharePoint is managed entirely within SharePoint, this is a topic that falls squarely within the discipline of SharePoint site planning and administration. For the Reporting Services administrator, this means that after Reporting Services is installed in SharePoint Integrated mode, service management, content management, and security is all managed within SharePoint.*

This chapter addresses the administration tasks for a report server configured in Native mode. It does not apply to SharePoint Integrated mode. The integrated report server is managed completely within the SharePoint Central Administrator and other SharePoint user interfaces. The Reporting Services Configuration Manager and configuration files are no longer used in that case. Reporting Services no longer runs as a Windows Service in Integrated mode. That version of the core report server is now managed as a SharePoint service application and is managed entirely in SharePoint.
By contrast, although SSRS has been enhanced with newer features, little has changed for the Native mode configuration since SSRS 2008.

An administration plan should address the following general concerns:

➤   Security

➤   Backup and recovery

➤   Monitoring

➤   Configuration

This chapter explores these topics as they relate to Reporting Services in Native mode. This gives you the basic knowledge you need to engage users, developers, and IT administrators in developing a plan tailored to your organization's specific needs.

SECURITY

Properly securing your Reporting Services environment requires you to find the right balance between risk, availability, and supportability. Following good network, system, and facilities management practices goes a long way toward securing your installation. Specific to Reporting Services, you should consider how to best approach the following:

➤   Account management

➤   System-level roles

➤   Surface area management

Account Management

Reporting Services must interact with various resources. To access these resources, Reporting Services must present its requests as originating from a specific, valid user. Reporting Services stores credentials, typically username and password combinations, for the following three accounts, each of which is used to handle specific interactions with resources:

➤ The service account

➤ The application database account

➤ The unattended execution account

Whenever possible, it is recommended that you use Windows domain user accounts as the source of the credentials for these three application accounts. This allows you to leverage the Windows security infrastructure for credential management.

In addition, it is recommended that you employ accounts dedicated for use in these roles. Reuse of credentials can make long-term management of these accounts more difficult and can lead to unintended resource access. This can also lead to the accumulation of permissions associated with an account. An account used for one of these roles should have no more permissions than those required for it to successfully complete its operations.

Finally, you should limit the number of trusted individuals who have knowledge of these credentials. As individuals move out of roles requiring them to have this knowledge (or leave the organization), these accounts should be updated to maintain a secure environment. If you use Windows accounts (as recommended), you can prevent their inappropriate use by prohibiting interactive logins to Windows systems.

The Service Account

During installation you are asked to specify the account under which the Reporting Services Windows service operates. This is called the *service account*. Through this account, the Reporting Services Windows service accesses various system resources. If your installation runs in SharePoint Integrated mode, this is the account that Reporting Services also uses to access the SharePoint databases.

The Reporting Services service account can be one of three built-in accounts or a Windows user account that you define, as described in Table 22-1.

TABLE 22-1: Service and Account Types

ACCOUNT	DETAILS
Local System	A built-in account that behaves as a member of the local Administrators group. When accessing resources on the network, it uses the computer's credentials. It is not recommended that you use this for the service account.
Local Service	A built-in account that behaves as a member of the local Users group. It accesses resources on the network with no credentials.

continues

TABLE 22-1 *(continued)*

ACCOUNT	DETAILS
Network Service	A built-in account that behaves as a member of the local Users group. When accessing resources on the network, it uses the computer's credentials. It is no longer recommended that you use this for the service account.
User Account	Allows you to enter the credentials of a local or domain Windows user account. If a local account is used, access to network resources is with no credentials. If a domain account is used, access to network resources is through the domain account. This is the recommended account type for the service account.

The service account requires permissions to specific resources on the system on which the Reporting Services Windows service runs. Instead of granting these rights to the service account itself, the service account obtains them through membership in a local group created by the SQL Server setup application during installation.

There is no need to directly alter membership to this group when making changes to the service account. Instead, you are strongly encouraged to make any changes to the service account using the Service Account page of the Reporting Services Configuration Manager, shown in Figure 22-1. The tool handles the details of managing membership to this group, updating the Windows service, adjusting encryption keys, altering URL reservations, and granting access to the Reporting Services application databases (if the service account is used as the application database account). All these tasks must be performed when a service account is changed.

Finally, if you are running in SharePoint Integrated mode and you switch the service account, make sure that the account has appropriate access to the SharePoint databases. To do this, open SharePoint Central Administration. In the Reporting Services section, click "Grant database access," and enter the Reporting Services service account information in the resulting dialog. After this change is saved, it is recommended that you restart the SharePoint Services service to ensure that the appropriate credentials are being used.

The Application Database Account

Reporting Services depends on content stored in its application databases. These databases are hosted by a local or remote instance of SQL Server. To connect to its databases, Reporting Services must maintain connection string data along with valid credentials for establishing a connection. The credentials are called the *application database account.*

You have three options for the application database account. You can specify a SQL Server authenticated username and password, provide the credentials for a valid Windows user account, or elect to have Reporting Services simply use its service account when establishing the connection.

The SQL Server Authenticated User option requires the SQL Server instance hosting the application databases to support both Windows and SQL Server authentication. By default, SQL Server is configured for Windows (Integrated) authentication only, because SQL Server authentication is considered less secure. It is recommended that you employ the SQL Server Authenticated User option only in special circumstances, such as when Windows user accounts cannot be authenticated.

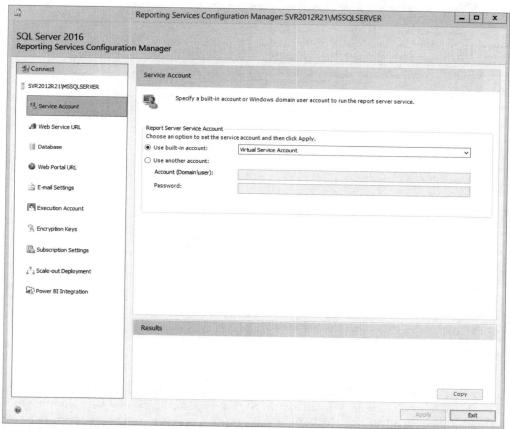

FIGURE 22-1: Configuration Manager Service Account page.

The application database account is set during installation and can be modified later using the Reporting Services Configuration Manager, as shown in Figure 22-2. If you installed using a default configuration, the application database account was automatically set to use the service account.

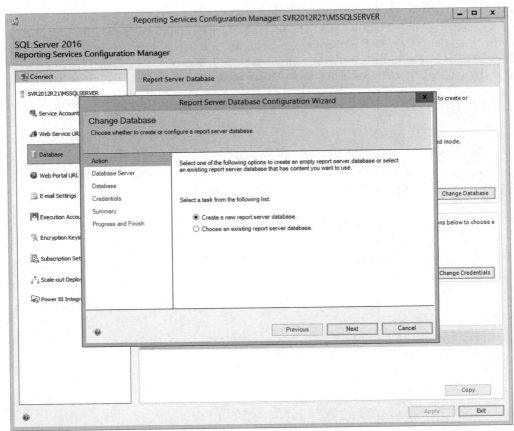

FIGURE 22-2: Report Server Database Configuration Wizard.

If you use the service account or Windows user option, a login is created within SQL Server mapped to this Windows account. (If you use the SQL Server Authenticated User option, you need to create a login in advance.) The login is then granted access to the two Reporting Services application databases as well as the master and msdb system databases. Within each database, the account is mapped to a collection of roles that provides it the rights it needs to handle Reporting Services database operations, including the creation and management of jobs through a SQL Agent. Table 22-2 lists the database roles to which the application database account is mapped.

It is important to note that if you change the application database account used by Reporting Services to connect to its application databases, the Reporting Services Configuration Manager does not remove the previous application database account from the SQL Server instance. Instead, a valid

TABLE 22-2: Databases and Roles

DATABASE	ROLES
Master	public
	RSExecRole
Msdb	public
	RSExecRole
	SQLAgentOperatorRole
	SQLAgentReaderRole
	SQLAgentUserRole
ReportServer	db_owner
	public
	RSExecRole
ReportServerTempDB	db_owner
	public
	RSExecRole

login is left within the instance of SQL Server Database Engine, retaining its membership in the database roles listed in Table 22-2. If you change the application database account, you should follow up by removing the prior login from these roles or from the SQL Server instance.

The Unattended Execution Account

Reports might need to access files on remote servers or data sources that do not require authentication. To access these resources, you can specify that no credentials are required as part of the datasource definition. When you do so, you are instructing Reporting Services to use the credentials it has cached for the *unattended execution account* (also known as the *unattended report processing account* or simply the *execution account*) when accessing the resource.

By default, the unattended execution account is disabled and should remain so unless a specific need is recognized that cannot be addressed by other reasonable means. To enable the account and configure its credentials, access the Execution Account page within the Configuration Manager and provide the required credentials, as shown in Figure 22-3.

System-Level Roles

System-level roles give members the rights to perform tasks across the Reporting Services site. Reporting Services comes preconfigured with two system-level roles: System User and System Administrator. The System User role allows users to retrieve information about the site and to execute reports in Report Builder that have not yet been published to the site. The System Administrator role gives administrators the rights required to manage the site, including the rights to create additional roles. Table 22-3 describes the specific system-level tasks assigned to these roles.

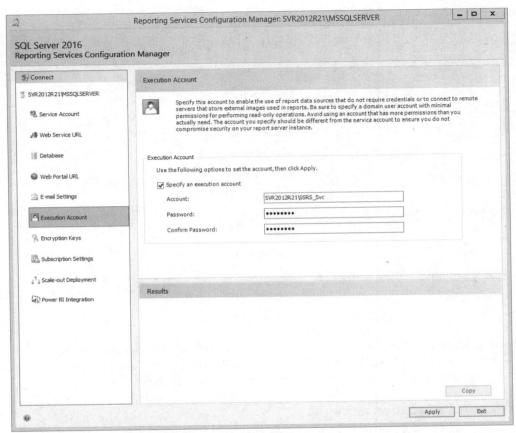

FIGURE 22-3: Configuration Execution Account page.

TABLE 22-3: System Roles and Task Permissions

TASK	DESCRIPTION	SYSTEM ADMINISTRATOR	SYSTEM USER
Execute report definitions	Start execution from the report definition without publishing it to the Report Server	Yes	Yes
Generate events	Lets an application generate events within the Report Server namespace	No	No
Manage jobs	View and cancel running jobs	Yes	No

TASK	DESCRIPTION	SYSTEM ADMINISTRATOR	SYSTEM USER
Manage Report Server properties	View and modify properties that apply to the Report Server and to items managed by the Report Server	Yes	No
Manage roles	Create, view, modify, and delete role definitions	Yes	No
Manage shared schedules	Create, view, modify, and delete shared schedules used to run reports or refresh a report	Yes	No
Manage Report Server security	View and modify system-wide role assignments	Yes	No
View Report Server properties	View properties that apply to the Report Server	No	Yes
View shared schedules	View a predefined schedule that has been made available for general use	No	Yes

You can create additional site-level roles using SQL Server Management Studio. Doing so allows you to permit site-level tasks to be performed by others without granting them System Administrator rights. The process of creating these roles, assigning tasks, and granting membership is nearly identical to the creation of item-level roles. The only difference is that system-level roles are created through the `System Roles` folder instead of the `Roles` folder within SQL Server Management Studio, as shown in Figure 22-4.

By default, the BUILTIN\Administrators group is assigned to both the System Administrator system-level role and the Content Manager item-level role within the `Home` folder. You are encouraged to alter this so that a more appropriate user account or group is assigned these permissions. If you decide to leave the BUILTIN\Administrators group in these roles, carefully consider who is allowed administrative rights on your servers.

Surface Area Management

A feature that is not enabled is one that cannot be exploited. This is the general principle behind *surface area management.*

Reporting Services comes with several features disabled. These include the execution account, e-mail delivery, and My Reports. Still other features are enabled by default but are not necessarily required within your Reporting Services environment. These include Report Builder, Web Portal, the use of Windows Integrated security to access report data sources, and scheduling and delivery functionality. Carefully consider which Reporting Services features are truly required, and disable any that are not needed. Books Online provides documentation on disabling each of these features.

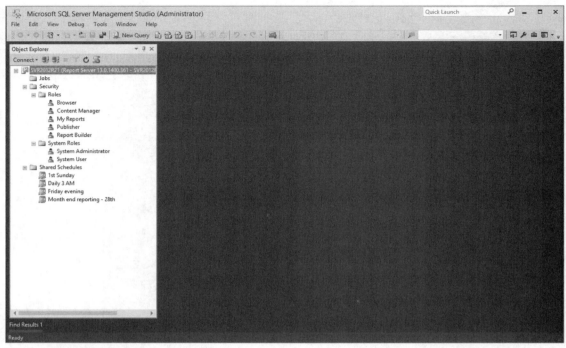

FIGURE 22-4: SSMS Report Server Roles.

BACKUP AND RECOVERY

Although redundant hardware solutions offer considerable protection against many types of failure, they do not shield you from every eventuality. Regular backups of the critical components of your Reporting Services environment are required to better ensure its recoverability.

Of course, simply making backups is not enough. Your backups must be properly managed to ensure their availability following a failure event. This typically involves secured, off-site storage and the development of retention schedules so that you have the option to recover to various points in time.

In addition, those responsible for recovery should have experience with the recovery techniques. They should also be well versed in the procedures for accessing the backup media. It's not much fun to attempt a recovery when you do not know how to locate and use the recovery media.

Finally, you should establish policies regarding how communications and decision making will be handled during a recovery event. You want to ensure that all those potentially involved understand these policies. This will help minimize confusion during what can be an already stressful situation.

This section of the chapter reviews the backup and recovery of the following critical components of a Reporting Services environment:

- ➤ Application databases
- ➤ Encryption keys
- ➤ Configuration files
- ➤ Other items

Application Databases

Reporting Services uses two application databases. The primary database, ReportServer, houses content, whereas the secondary database, ReportServerTempDB, houses cached data. These default names are offered by the Configuration Manager, but can be changed.

> **NOTE** *Although the names of the application databases can vary, the secondary application database must always be named the same as the primary, with TempDB appended. For example, if the primary application database is named MyRS, the secondary database associated with it must be named MyRSTempDB. The names of these databases should not be altered after they are created, and the two databases must always exist within the same SQL Server instance.*

The primary application database, ReportServer, should be backed up on a regular basis and following any significant content changes. This database operates under the Full recovery model, which allows both data and log backups to be performed. If properly managed, the combination of data and log backups allows for point-in-time recovery of the ReportServer database.

The secondary application database, ReportServerTempDB, does not actually require a backup. If you need to recover it, you can create a new database appropriately named within the SQL Server instance housing the ReportServer database. Within this new database, execute the `CatalogTempDB.sql` script found within the *drive:*`\Program Files\Microsoft SQL Server\ MSRS13.`*instancename*`\Reporting Services\ReportServer` folder. The script re-creates the database objects required by Reporting Services. Be sure to run this from within the ReportServerTempDB database you just created.

If you decide to back up ReportServerTempDB, it is important to note that it operates under the Simple recovery model. This model allows for data backups but not log backups. Ideally, both databases should be backed up and restored as a set to maintain server consistency. However, a current backup of this database is not always critical, because it manages only temporary cached report execution information.

> **NOTE** *Books Online includes a script for the backup and recovery of the ReportServer and ReportServerTempDB databases to another server. This script uses the* COPY_ONLY *backup option and modifies the recovery model used with ReportServerTempDB. It is important to note that this script is provided in the context of performing a database migration, not a standard backup-and-recovery operation. Be sure to work with your database administrators to develop a backup-and-recovery plan that is tailored to the needs of your environment and that you have tested prior to promoting an environment to production status.*

If you recover a backup of ReportServerTempDB, be sure to purge its contents following recovery. You can use the following statement to perform this task. After the database is purged, it is recommended that you restart the Reporting Services service.

```
exec ReportServerTempDB.sys.sp_MSforeachtable
    @command1='truncate table #',
    @replacechar='#'
```

If you need to recover your application databases to another SQL Server instance, it is important to preserve the databases' original names. If Reporting Services uses a SQL Server authenticated account to connect to its application databases, you need to re-create that login in the new SQL Server instance. Following the restoration of the databases, you need to reassociate the user account in your application databases with the re-created login. This script demonstrates one technique for performing this task:

```
exec ReportServer.dbo.sp_change_users_login
    @Action = ' Update_One',
    @UserNamePattern = 'MyDbAccount',
    @LoginName = 'MyDbAccount'

exec ReportServerTempDB.dbo.sp_change_users_login
    @Action = 'Update_One',
    @UserNamePattern = 'MyDbAccount',
    @LoginName = 'MyDbAccount'
```

> **NOTE** *Without getting too deep into the trappings of SQL Server user and login management, it is important to understand that you cannot move a database. The user/login mappings are not preserved by default, resulting in a scenario called "orphaned users." This is because users are internally identified using unique system IDs rather than user name. The* sp_change_users_login *command described in this section may be used to resolve this common issue.*

As soon as the database user and login are properly associated, launch the Reporting Services Configuration Manager against your Reporting Services instance, and locate the Database page, as shown in Figure 22-5.

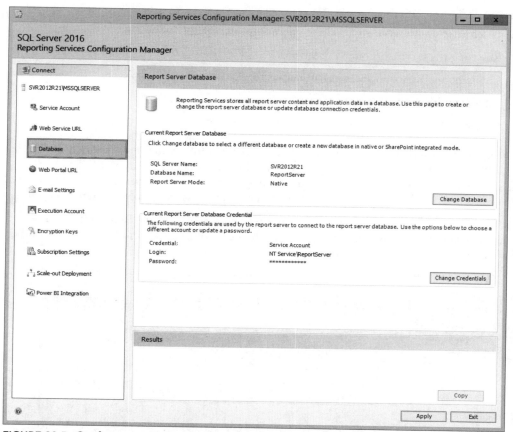

FIGURE 22-5: Configuration Manager Database page.

From this page, click the Change Database button. In the resulting dialog, enter the information required to connect to the primary application database at its new location. Restarting Reporting Services from the Reporting Service Configuration Manager completes the process.

Encryption Keys

Reporting Services protects the sensitive information it stores through encryption based on a *symmetric key* generated during initialization. The symmetric key, per its definition, is used in both encryption and decryption operations. To prevent unauthorized decryption of sensitive data, the symmetric key itself must be protected. This is accomplished by encrypting the symmetric key using an asymmetric key pair generated by the operating system.

Although this protects the symmetric key, also called the *encryption key*, it increases the system's administrative complexity. Certain operations invalidate the asymmetric key pair. Unless handled properly, these operations cause Reporting Services to lose its ability to decrypt the symmetric key, leaving its sensitive data inaccessible. These operations include the following:

➤ Resetting the service account's password

➤ Changing the Reporting Services Windows service account

➤ Changing the server's name

➤ Changing the name of the Reporting Services instance

If you need to perform these operations, it is critical that you follow the steps outlined in this chapter and in Books Online. If the precise steps required by these operations are not followed, the symmetric key can no longer be decrypted. Your options then are to either recover the key from a backup or delete it. Deleting the key, as described in a moment, is extremely disruptive to your site.

To back up the encryption key, use either the Encryption Keys page of the Reporting Services Configuration Manager, shown in Figure 22-6, or the rskeymgmt command-line utility with the -e parameter:

```
rskeymgmt.exe -e -i MSSQLSERVER -f c:\backups\rs_2012_11_04.snk -p p@ssw0rd
```

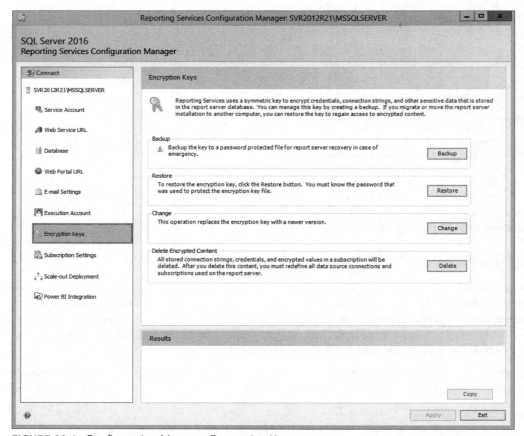

FIGURE 22-6: Configuration Manager Encryption Keys page.

With either approach, you need to provide a name for the backup file, along with a password to protect its contents.

> **NOTE** *The* -i *parameter is used to specify the name of the Reporting Services instance on the local system. The default instance is identified with the* MSSQLSERVER *keyword.*

It is recommended that you back up the encryption key when the server is first initialized, when the service account is changed, or whenever the key is deleted or re-created. Although it is password-protected, the backup file should be secured to prevent unauthorized access to sensitive information.

If you suspect that the encryption key has been compromised, you can re-create it using the Reporting Services Configuration Manager or the rskeymgmt command-line utility with the -s parameter:

```
rskeymgmt.exe -s -i MSSQLSERVER
```

This operation can be time-consuming, so you might want to restrict user access to the Reporting Services instance until you're finished.

> **NOTE** *If your Reporting Services instance is part of a scale-out deployment, you need to reinitialize the other instances in the environment with the newly created key per the instructions provided in Books Online.*

To recover the encryption key, use either the Reporting Services Configuration Manager or the rskeymgmt command-line utility with the -a parameter. Both approaches require you to identify the backup file and supply its password:

```
rskeymgmt.exe -a -i MSSQLSERVER -f c:\backups\rs_2012_11_04.snk -p p@ssw0rd
```

Deleting the encryption key is considered an operation of last resort. After doing so, you need to re-create all shared and report-specific connection strings containing it and reactivate all subscriptions. As before, you can perform this operation using the Reporting Services Configuration Manager or the rskeymgmt command-line utility, this time with the -d parameter:

```
rskeymgmt.exe -d -i MSSQLSERVER
```

> **NOTE** *If your Reporting Services instance is part of a scale-out deployment, you need to delete the key on each instance in the environment. Refer to Books Online for instructions on completing this operation.*

Configuration Files

Several configuration files affect Reporting Services. To fully recover your installation, you need backups of these files. Reporting Services itself does not provide a mechanism for this. However, you can use any number of file backup techniques to safeguard these files. Table 22-4 describes the configuration files you will want to back up and their default locations.

TABLE 22-4: Configuration Files

CONFIGURATION FILE	DEFAULT LOCATION
`ReportingServicesService.exe.config`	`drive:\Program Files\Microsoft SQL Server\MSRS13.`*instancename*`\Reporting Services\ReportServer\Bin`
`RSReportServer.config`	`drive:\Program Files\Microsoft SQL Server\MSRS13.`*instancename*`\Reporting Services\ReportServer`
`RSSrvPolicy.config`	`drive:\Program Files\Microsoft SQL Server\MSRS13.`*instancename*`\Reporting Services\ReportServer`
`RSMgrPolicy.config`	`drive:\Program Files\Microsoft SQL Server\MSRS13.`*instancename*`\Reporting Services\ReportManager`
`Web.config`	`drive:\Program Files\Microsoft SQL Server\MSRS13.`*instancename*`\Reporting Services\ReportServer`
`Microsoft.ReportingServices.Portal.WebHost.exe.config`	`drive:\Program Files\Microsoft SQL Server\MSRS13.MSSQLSERVER\Reporting Services\RSWebApp`
`Machine.config`	`drive:\Windows\Microsoft.NET\Framework\`*version*`\CONFIG`

Other Items

Your backup-and-recovery plan should consider any custom scripts or components in use by your installation. In addition, you will want to make sure that purchased components, installation media, service packs, and hotfixes are available during a recovery event. If you have created a database to house execution log data (discussed later), you may want to back this up as well.

MONITORING

Effective monitoring should allow you to quickly identify or even anticipate problems within your environment. Reporting Services provides various features to support this activity. You can use Reporting Services as a tool to present this data to administrators in an easier-to-consume manner.

This section explores the use of:

➤ Setup logs

➤ Windows application event logs

➤ Trace logs

➤ Execution log

➤ Performance counters

➤ Server management reports

Setup Logs

During installation, the setup application creates a series of text-based log files that record messages and statistics generated as part of the process. By default, these are located in subfolders of the *drive*:\Program Files\Microsoft SQL Server\130\Setup Bootstrap\LOG folder. These subfolders are named using the convention *YYYYMMDD_nnnnnn*, where *YYYY*, *MM*, and *DD* represent the year, month, and day of the installation. The *nnnn* portion of the name represents an incrementing four-digit number, the highest value of which identifies the most recent installation attempt.

The contents of these folders are a bit overwhelming but worth exploring if you experience errors during an installation attempt. To review the summary status of the most recent installation attempt, simply direct your attention to the Summary.txt file within the *drive*:\Program Files\ Microsoft SQL Server\130\Setup Bootstrap\LOG folder.

Windows Application Event Logs

Reporting Services writes critical error, warning, and informational messages to the *Windows application event log*. These messages are identified as originating from the Report Server, Web Portal, and Scheduling and Delivery Processor event sources.

The complete list of Reporting Services event log messages is documented in Books Online. Administrators will want to familiarize themselves with this list and periodically review the Windows Application event log for these and other critical messages. You can view the Windows event logs using the operating system's Event Viewer applet.

Trace Logs

The *trace logs* are a great source of information about activity taking place within the Reporting Services Windows service. You can locate these files in the *drive*:\Program Files\Microsoft SQL Server\MSRS13.*instancename*\Reporting Services\LogFiles folder. The logs are by default named *ReportServerService__MM_DD_YYYY_hh_mm_ss*, where *MM*, *DD*, *YYYY*, *hh*, *mm*, and *ss* represent the month, day, year, hour, minute, and second, respectively, that the file was created. You can view each of these files using a simple text editor.

By default, Reporting Services is configured to write exceptions, warnings, restart, and status messages to the trace log files. Log files are retained for a configurable number of days. A new log file is created at the beginning of the day, when the Reporting Services Windows service is started, or when the file reaches a configurable maximum size. The configuration settings affecting the trace logs are found within the RStrace section of the ReportingServicesService.exe.config file, typically located in the *drive*:\Program Files\Microsoft SQL Server\MSRS13.*instancename*\Reporting Services\ReportServer\Bin folder. The RStrace settings are described in Table 22-5, along with their defaults.

TABLE 22-5: Log Configuration Settings

SETTING	DEFAULT	DESCRIPTION
FileName	ReportServerService_	The first part of the filename. A string indicating the date and time the file was created, along with a .log extension, is appended to produce the full filename.
FileSizeLimitMb	32	The maximum size of the trace file in megabytes (MB). A value *less than or equal to* 0 is treated as 1.
KeepFilesForDays	14	The number of days to retain a trace file. A value *less than or equal to* 0 is treated as 1.
Prefix	tid,time	A generated value that distinguishes the log instance for which a time stamp value is applied. *Do not modify.*
TraceListeners	debugwindow,file	A comma-delimited list of one or more trace log output targets. Valid values within the list include debugwindow, file, and stdout.
TraceFileMode	Unique (default)	A value indicating that each trace file should contain data for a single day. Do not modify this setting.

SETTING	DEFAULT	DESCRIPTION
`DefaultTraceSwitch`	3	The default trace level for any component identified in the `Components` setting but for which no trace switch is provided. Here are the values: 0—Disabled 1—Exceptions and restarts 2—Exceptions, restarts, and warnings 3—Exceptions, restarts, warnings, and status messages 4—Verbose mode
`Components`	`All:3`	A comma-delimited list of components and their associated trace levels determining the information to be included in the trace. These components represent activities that can produce trace messages. Here are the valid components: `RunningJobs`—Report and subscription execution `SemanticQueryEngine`—Report model usage `SemanticModelGenerator`—Report model generation `All`—Any of the components, except `http`, not otherwise specified `http`—HTTP requests received by Reporting Services The type of message written for each specified component is controlled by a trace level. The levels are as follows: 0—Disabled 1—Exceptions and restarts 2—Exceptions, restarts, and warnings 3—Exceptions, restarts, warnings, and status messages 4—Verbose mode

The `http` component identified in this table was introduced in SQL Server 2008 Reporting Services. It remains unchanged in the current product version. It instructs Reporting Services to record HTTP requests to a separate trace log file in the traditional W3C extended log format.

The `http` component is not covered by the `All` component. Therefore, the default `Components` setting of `All:3` leaves HTTP logging disabled. To enable HTTP logging, append the `http` component to the `Components` list with a trace level of 4. Any other trace level for the `http` component leaves it disabled.

The HTTP trace log files are stored in the same folder as the traditional trace files. Trace configuration settings such as `FileSizeLimitMb` and `KeepFilesForDays` serve double duty, affecting the management of both the traditional and HTTP trace log files.

Two HTTP trace log–specific settings, `HttpTraceFileName` and `HttpTraceSwitches`, are manually added to the `ReportingServicesService.exe.config` file to override the default HTTP trace log filename and data format, respectively. If the `HttpTraceSwitches` setting is not specified, the fields identified as defaults in Table 22-6 are recorded to the HTTP trace logs.

TABLE 22-6: Trace Log Fields

FIELD	DESCRIPTION	DEFAULT
HttpTraceFileName	Optional. Default: `ReportServerServiceHTTP`. *Used to customize the file trace file name.*	Yes
HttpTraceSwitches	Optional. Comma-delimited list of fields used in the log file.	No
Date	The date of the event	No
Time	The time of the event	No
ClientIp	The IP address of the client accessing the Report Server	Yes
UserName	The name of the user who accessed the Report Server	No
ServerPort	The port number used for the connection	No
Host	The content of the host header	No
Method	The action or SOAP method called from the client	Yes
UriStem	The resource accessed	Yes
UriQuery	The query used to access the resource	No
ProtocolStatus	The HTTP status code	Yes
BytesReceived	The number of bytes received by the server	No
TimeTaken	The time (in milliseconds) from the instant that `HTTP.SYS` returns request data until the server finishes the last send, excluding network transmission time	No
ProtocolVersion	The protocol version used by the client	No

FIELD	DESCRIPTION	DEFAULT
UserAgent	The browser type used by the client	No
CookieReceived	The content of the cookie received by the server	No
CookieSent	The content of the cookie sent by the server	No
Referrer	The previous site visited by the client	No

The following sample shows the RSTrace section of the ReportingServicesService.exe
.config file with both traditional and HTTP logging enabled and the HttpTraceFileName and
HttpTraceSwitches settings explicitly configured. Note the Components setting with the http component specified with a trace level of 4:

```
<RStrace>
    <add name="FileName" value="ReportServerService_" />
    <add name="FileSizeLimitMb" value="32" />
    <add name="KeepFilesForDays" value="14" />
    <add name="Prefix" value="tid, time" />
    <add name="TraceListeners" value="debugwindow, file" />
    <add name="TraceFileMode" value="unique" />
    <add name="HttpTraceFileName" value="RS_HTTP_" />
    <add name="HttpTraceSwitches" value="Date,Time,ActivityID,
        SourceActivityID,ClientIp,UserName,Method,
        UriStem,UriQuery,ProtocolStatus,BytesSent,
        BytesReceived,TimeTaken" />
    <add name="Components" value="runningjobs:3,all:2,http:4" />
</RStrace>
```

> **NOTE** *When you modify the configuration file, it is important to make a backup
> in case a problem arises with your changes. Also, be aware that setting names are
> case-sensitive, although the values do not appear to be.*

Execution Logs

Reporting Services stores quite a bit of data about the execution of reports in a collection of tables
in the ReportServer database. Log information is stored in the ExecutionLogStorage table and can
be queried by using the ExecutionLog, ExecutionLog2, and ExecutionLog3 views.

The volume of data associated with the execution logs can get quite large. Reporting Services is
configured by default to retain execution log data for 60 days. You can alter this setting through
SQL Server Management Studio by connecting to the Reporting Services instance, right-clicking
the instance object, and selecting Properties from the context menu. In the Server Properties dialog,
shown in Figure 22-7, navigate to the Logging page. Here you can change the number of days that
the data is retained or disable execution logging.

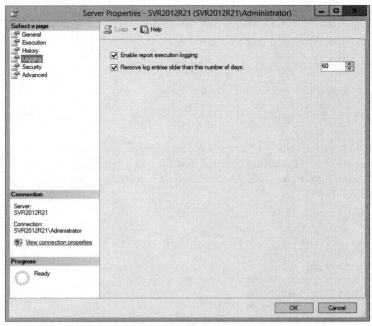

FIGURE 22-7: Server Properties Logging page.

Performance Counters

Windows performance counters provide insight into system utilization and stability. Administrators have long used these to monitor a system's overall health, identify trends that may lead to problems, and verify the effect of changes on various system components. To support this activity, Reporting Services provides three performance objects: SQL Server 2016 Web Service, SQL Server 2016 Windows Service, and ReportServer Service. There are alternative versions of the web service and Windows service counters for SharePoint Integrated mode.

The SQL Server 2016 Web Service object presents counters related to report processing. The SQL Server 2016 Windows Service object presents counters related to scheduled operations, such as subscription execution and delivery and snapshot execution. The ReportServer Service object presents counters related to HTTP- and memory-related events. Although focused on different subject areas, many of the counters presented by these objects are named and defined identically. Table 22-7 lists the counters and the objects with which they are associated.

> **TIP** *The number of performance counters related to Reporting Services can be a bit overwhelming. In my experience, you can typically find what you are looking for by observing a just a few key counters after briefly examining the behavior of several. Keep it simple and don't overdo it. With a little observation you should be able to spot the counters that will be most useful, depending on what you are looking for and the issue you are trying to resolve.*

TABLE 22-7: Reporting Services Performance Counters

COUNTER	DESCRIPTION	SQL SERVER 2016 WEB SERVICE	SQL SERVER 2016 WINDOWS SERVICE	REPORT SERVER SERVICE
Active Connections	Number of connections active against the server	No	Yes	Yes
Active Sessions	Number of active sessions	Yes	Yes	No
Bytes Received/Sec	Rate of bytes received per second	No	Yes	Yes
Bytes Received Total	Number of bytes received	No	Yes	Yes
Bytes Sent/Sec	Rate of bytes sent per second	No	No	Yes
Bytes Sent Total	Number of bytes sent	No	No	Yes
Cache Hits/Sec	Number of Report Server cache hits per second	Yes	Yes	No
Cache Hits/Sec (semantic models)	Number of times per second that models can be retrieved from the cache	Yes	Yes	No
Cache Misses/Sec	Number of times per second that reports cannot be retrieved from the cache	Yes	Yes	No
Cache Misses/Sec (semantic models)	Number of times per second that models cannot be retrieved from the cache	Yes	Yes	No
Errors/Sec	Number of errors that occur during the execution of HTTP requests (error codes 400s and 500s) per second	No	No	Yes
Errors Total	Total number of errors that occur during the execution of HTTP requests (error codes 400s and 500s)	No	No	Yes
First Session Requests/Sec	Number of new user sessions that are started per second	Yes	Yes	No

continues

TABLE 22-7 *(continued)*

COUNTER	DESCRIPTION	SQL SERVER 2016 WEB SERVICE	SQL SERVER 2016 WINDOWS SERVICE	REPORT SERVER SERVICE
Logon Attempts/ Sec	Rate of logon attempts	No	No	Yes
Logon Attempts Total	Number of logon attempts for RSWindows authentication types	No	No	Yes
Logon Successes/ Sec	Rate of successful logons	No	No	Yes
Logon Successes Total	Number of successful logons for RSWindows authentication types	No	No	Yes
Memory Cache Hits/ Sec	Number of times per second that reports can be retrieved from the in-memory cache	Yes	Yes	No
Memory Cache Miss/Sec	Number of times per second that reports cannot be retrieved from the in-memory cache	Yes	Yes	No
Memory Pressure State	A number from 1 to 5 indicating the server's current memory state: 1—No pressure 2—Low pressure 3—Medium pressure 4—High pressure 5—Exceeded pressure	No	No	Yes
Memory Shrink Amount	Number of bytes the server asked to shrink	No	No	Yes
Memory Shrink Notifications/Sec	Number of shrink notifications the server issued in the last second	No	No	Yes

COUNTER	DESCRIPTION	SQL SERVER 2016 WEB SERVICE	SQL SERVER 2016 WINDOWS SERVICE	REPORT SERVER SERVICE
Next Session Requests/Sec	Number of requests per second for reports that are open in an existing session	Yes	Yes	No
Report Requests	Number of active report requests	Yes	Yes	No
Reports Executed/Sec	Number of reports executed per second	Yes	Yes	No
Requests Disconnected	Number of requests that have been disconnected because of a communication failure	No	Yes	Yes
Requests Executing	Number of requests currently executing	No	No	Yes
Requests Not Authorized	Number of requests failing with HTTP 401 error code	No	Yes	Yes
Requests Rejected	Total number of requests not executed because of insufficient server resources	No	Yes	Yes
Requests/Sec	Number of requests per second	Yes	Yes	Yes
Requests Total	The total number of requests received by the Report Server service since service startup	No	No	Yes
Tasks Queued	Represents the number of tasks that are waiting for a thread to become available for processing	No	Yes	Yes
Total Cache Hits	Total number of Report Server cache hits	Yes	Yes	No
Total Cache Hits (semantic models)	Total number of cache hits made in the model cache	Yes	Yes	No

continues

TABLE 22-7 *(continued)*

COUNTER	DESCRIPTION	SQL SERVER 2016 WEB SERVICE	SQL SERVER 2016 WINDOWS SERVICE	REPORT SERVER SERVICE
Total Cache Misses	Total number of cache misses	Yes	Yes	No
Total Cache Misses (semantic models)	Total number of cache misses made in the model cache	Yes	Yes	No
Total Memory Cache Hits	Total number of cache hits made in the in-memory cache	Yes	Yes	No
Total Memory Cache Misses	Total number of cache misses made in the in-memory cache	Yes	Yes	No
Total Processing Failures	Total number of processing failures	Yes	Yes	No
Total Rejected Threads	Total number of rejected threads as a result of thread pressure	Yes	Yes	No
Total Reports Executed	Total number of reports executed	Yes	Yes	No
Total Requests	Total number of requests being processed	Yes	Yes	No

Together, these three objects present 72 counters with which you can monitor an installation. It is not advised that you monitor each one. Instead, consider using high-level statistics such as Active Sessions, Requests/Sec, Reports Executed/Sec, and First Session Requests/Sec for your day-to-day monitoring. As specific needs arise, you will want to incorporate additional counters until those needs are addressed.

In addition to the Reporting Services performance counters, you might consider monitoring the Reporting Services Windows service from the operating system's perspective. Windows provides a Process performance object through which a number of performance counters are provided. Table 22-8 describes a few of the more commonly monitored counters under this object.

Finally, you will want to keep tabs on a few counters that indicate the overall health of the systems on which Reporting Services resides. Commonly monitored performance counters in this category include those listed in Table 22-9.

TABLE 22-8: Reporting Services Windows Service Counters

COUNTER	DESCRIPTION
% Processor Time	The percentage of elapsed time that all process threads used the processor to execute instructions
Page Faults/sec	The rate at which page faults by the threads executing in this process are occurring
Virtual Bytes	The current size, in bytes, of the virtual address space the process is using

TABLE 22-9: Recommended Windows System Counters

OBJECT	COUNTER	DESCRIPTION
Processor	% Processor Time	The primary indicator of processor activity. Displays the average percentage of busy time observed during the sample interval.
System	Processor Queue Length	The number of threads in the processor queue.
Memory	Pages/sec	The rate at which pages are read from or written to disk to resolve hard page faults. This counter is a primary indicator of the kinds of faults that cause system-wide delays.
Logical Disk	% Free Space	The percentage of total usable free space on the selected logical disk drive.
Physical Disk	Avg. Disk Queue Length	The average number of both read and write requests that were queued for the selected disk during the sample interval.
Network Interface	Current Bandwidth	An estimate of the current bandwidth of the network interface in bits per second (BPS). For interfaces that do not vary in bandwidth or for those where no accurate estimation can be made, this value is the nominal bandwidth.
Network Interface	Bytes Total/sec	The rate at which bytes are sent and received over each network adapter, including framing characters. Network Interface\Bytes Total/sec is a sum of Network Interface\Bytes Received/sec and Network Interface\Bytes Sent/sec.

Server Management Reports

As previously mentioned, the Reporting Services samples come with three reports for reviewing the extracted execution log data. Two other sample reports are provided with the Reporting Services tasks to give administrators insight into database structures. Collectively, these are known as the *server management reports*.

The server management reports are not intended to address all your administrative needs. Instead, they illustrate how Reporting Services can be used as a tool supporting its own administration and management. It is not hard to imagine a number of additional administrative reports providing deeper insight into the execution log data. With a bit of effort, data sources such as the performance counters, trace logs, and Windows Application event logs can also be integrated and made accessible for reporting.

The possibilities for server management reporting are endless. With some up-front investment to consolidate data sources, you can leverage Reporting Services functionality to reduce your environment's overall administrative burden.

CONFIGURATION

Reporting Services supports several configurable features and options to meet your organization's precise needs. Books Online documents many of these, and still others can be identified with a little exploration. The following sections explore a few of the more frequently configured Reporting Services elements:

➤ Memory management

➤ URL reservations

➤ E-mail delivery

➤ Rendering extensions

➤ My Reports

Memory Management

The following four settings in the `RSReportServer.config` configuration file, typically located in the `drive:\Program Files\Microsoft SQL Server\MSRS13.instancename\Reporting Services\ReportServer` folder, determine how Reporting Services manages its memory:

➤ `WorkingSetMinimum`

➤ `WorkingSetMaximum`

➤ `MemorySafetyMargin`

➤ `MemoryThreshold`

The `WorkingSetMinimum` and `WorkingSetMaximum` settings determine the range of memory that Reporting Services may use. By default, these settings are not recorded in the configuration file. Instead, Reporting Services assumes values of 60 percent and 100 percent of the system's physical memory, respectively.

To override these defaults, you can add the settings to the configuration file under the same parent as `MemorySafetyMargin` and `MemoryThreshold`. The values associated with the `WorkingSetMinimum` and `WorkingSetMaximum` settings represent absolute kilobytes of memory. If you are running multiple memory-intensive applications on your Reporting Services server, you should consider implementing these settings to avoid memory contention.

Within the range of memory available to it, Reporting Services implements a state-based memory management model. The `MemorySafetyMargin` setting, defaulted to 80 percent of the `WorkingSetMaximum`, defines the boundary between the low and medium memory pressure states. The `MemoryThreshold` setting, defaulted to 90 percent of the `WorkingSetMaximum`, defines the boundary between the medium and high memory pressure states.

Within each memory pressure state, Reporting Services grants and takes back memory for report requests differently. For systems experiencing consistent loads, operating in the low and medium states is ideal. The default settings for `MemorySafetyMargin` and `MemoryThreshold` favor these states.

For systems experiencing spikes in memory utilization, such as might occur if several large reports are processed simultaneously, the medium and even high memory states may allow for greater concurrency, although reports may be rendered a bit more slowly. If this better matches your system's usage pattern, you might want to lower the `MemorySafetyMargin` and `MemoryThreshold` settings to more quickly move into these memory states.

URL Reservations

If you performed a Files Only installation of Reporting Services, you must configure URL reservations for the Reporting Services Web service and Web Portal. *URL reservations* tell the operating system's HTTP.SYS driver where to direct requests intended for Reporting Services. URL reservations minimally consist of a virtual directory, an IP address, and a TCP port.

> **NOTE** *Advanced configuration options enable you to associate an SSL certificate with the URL reservation. This is addressed in Books Online.*

The virtual directory identifies the application to which communications will be targeted. Web Portal typically uses the `reports` virtual directory, whereas the Web service typically uses the `reportserver` virtual directory.

> **NOTE** *Named instances typically use the* `reports_instancename` *and* `reportserver_instancename` *virtual directories for Web Portal and the Web service, respectively.*

The URL reservation's IP address identifies which IP addresses in use by the server the Reporting Services application will be associated with. The URL reservation typically is configured to be associated with all IP addresses in use on the server. But you can configure it to be associated with a specific IP address, including the loopback address, or to work with any IP addresses not explicitly reserved by other applications. This latter option is not recommended in most situations.

Finally, the URL reservation is tied to a TCP port. Typically, HTTP communications take place over TCP port 80. You may have multiple applications on a given server listening on the same TCP port, so long as the overall URL reservation is unique on the server. If you specify a TCP port other than 80 (or 433 if you are using HTTPS communications), you need to include the port number in the URL whenever you communicate with Web Portal or the Web service.

> **NOTE** *If you are running Reporting Services on 32-bit Windows XP (SP2), TCP ports cannot be shared between URL reservations. Therefore, it is suggested that you use TCP port 8080 on this system for HTTP communications with Reporting Services. For more information on this topic, see Books Online.*

To configure a URL reservation for the Reporting Services Web service, access the Web Service URL page of the Reporting Services Configuration Manager, as shown in Figure 22-8. On this page, enter the virtual directory, IP address, and TCP port for the Web service's URL reservation. After the changes are applied, you are presented with the Web services URL, which you can click to test.

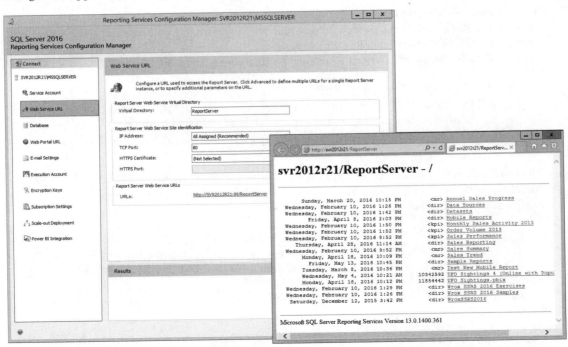

FIGURE 22-8: Web Service URL and the ReportServer web page.

To configure a URL reservation for the Web Portal application, access the Web Portal URL page of the Reporting Services Configuration Manager, as shown in Figure 22-9. The Web Portal URL reservation leverages the IP address and TCP port settings of the Web service's reservation. Enter the Web Portal's virtual directory, apply the changes, and click the provided URL to test the changes.

> **NOTE** *The Web Portal, which is typically accessed using the "Reports" virtual folder on the report server, replaces Report Manager in previous versions of Reporting Services.*

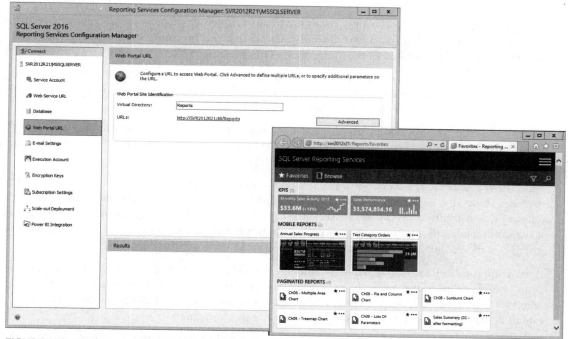

FIGURE 22-9: Web Portal URL page and the web portal

This has been a high-level discussion of URL reservations. Advanced options are available that require deeper knowledge of networking concepts. If you're familiar with these topics, you should have no problem understanding the interfaces and configuring Reporting Services appropriately. If you need to configure the Reporting Services URL reservations differently from what is discussed here, it is recommended that you engage your network support staff to explore your options.

E-mail Delivery

The e-mail subscription and data-driven features for Reporting Services rely on the e-mail delivery configuration for the report server.

> **NOTE** *The recommended method for e-mail delivery from Reporting Services is to use an existing Exchange Server or company e-mail service via SMTP. Prior versions of Reporting Services worked only with an SMTP service without authentication, like the old service that installed with Internet Information Services (IIS). The IIS mail service is no longer a supported option in Windows Server and Reporting Services will now work with standard mail servers that require authentication.*
>
> *You can find detailed instructions for configuring SSRS 2016 to send e-mail at* `https://msdn.microsoft.com/en-us/library/ms189342.aspx`.

To enable e-mail delivery, you simply configure the e-mail delivery extension, and provide server and message delivery information. Books Online documents variations on its configuration, but most systems use what is described as the "minimum configuration."

The *minimum configuration* requires the name or IP address of a remote SMTP server (or gateway) and a valid e-mail account on the SMTP server. This information is entered into the E-mail Settings page of the Reporting Services Configuration Manager.

Communication with the SMTP server occurs through the Reporting Services service account. The service account requires SendAs rights with the SMTP server to send e-mail through the configured e-mail account.

Mail delivery errors are accessible in the Windows application event log, as well as in the status message associated with e-mail–based subscriptions in Web Portal. However, problems with e-mail delivery downstream from the SMTP server are not reflected in Reporting Services. For this reason, it is recommended that you test your e-mail configuration by setting up a test subscription to a monitored e-mail account and verify end-to-end delivery of the subscription message.

After configuration, users assigned the "Manage individual subscriptions" or "Manage all subscriptions" tasks are given the option to use e-mail delivery (and any other enabled delivery options) when setting up subscriptions. Reporting Services does not provide a mechanism to secure the e-mail delivery option separately from other delivery mechanisms.

After it is enabled, you can disable e-mail delivery by simply removing the settings recorded in the Reporting Services Configuration Manager. Be aware that although this disables e-mail delivery, subscriptions already configured to use this delivery mechanism will continue to run as is and fail until they are disabled or reconfigured to use another delivery mechanism. For this reason, it is suggested that you disable e-mail delivery in phases.

In the first phase, prevent the creation of new e-mail–based subscriptions by commenting out the appropriate Extension entry within the `DeliveryUI` section of the `RSReportServer.config` file. This removes e-mail delivery as an option in Web Portal. The following code sample illustrates this modification:

```
<DeliveryUI>
    <!-- Extension Name="Report Server Email"
```

```
                Type="Microsoft.ReportingServices.EmailDeliveryProvider
                    .EmailDeliveryProviderControl,
                    ReportingServicesEmailDeliveryProvider">
                    <Configuration>
                        <RSEmailDPConfiguration>
                            <DefaultRenderingExtension>MHTML</DefaultRenderingExtension>
                        </RSEmailDPConfiguration>
                    </Configuration>
                </Extension -->
                <Extension Name="Report Server FileShare"
              Type="Microsoft.ReportingServices.FileShareDeliveryProvider.FileShareUIControl,
                    ReportingServicesFileShareDeliveryProvider">
                        <DefaultDeliveryExtension>True</DefaultDeliveryExtension>
                </Extension>
            </DeliveryUI>
```

It is important to note that although this removes e-mail delivery as an option in Web Portal, it does not prevent applications from creating new e-mail–based subscriptions through the Web services interface. If applications use this interface to create subscriptions, work with the application owners to disable this feature.

The second phase of disabling e-mail delivery involves reconfiguring any subscriptions that use e-mail delivery. Work with content owners to determine appropriate alternatives as part of this work. When migration is completed, you can then safely proceed with disabling e-mail delivery.

Rendering Extensions

Reporting Services comes preconfigured to render reports to a number of formats. The formats available are determined by the rendering extensions installed on the server and configured in the `Render` section of the `RSReportServer.config` file. Here is a sample entry for the Image rendering extension:

```
<Extension Name="IMAGE"
Type="Microsoft.ReportingServices.Rendering.ImageRenderer.ImageRenderer,
    Microsoft.ReportingServices.ImageRendering"/>
```

Each rendering extension entry minimally consists of name and type attributes. These identify the extension within the configuration file. The value associated with the `Name` attribute serves as a unique identifier for the extension within the configuration file. The `Type` attribute associates the entry with a particular rendering extension.

The name of the extension displayed to end users is the rendering extension's default display name, unless an `OverrideNames` setting is entered into the configuration file. The `OverrideNames` setting is recorded with the extension:

```
<Extension Name="IMAGE"
Type="Microsoft.ReportingServices.Rendering.ImageRenderer.ImageRenderer,
    Microsoft.ReportingServices.ImageRendering">
    <OverrideNames>
        <Name Language="en-US">TIFF</Name>
    </OverrideNames>
</Extension>
```

In this example, the default name of the Image rendering extension, `TIFF File`, is overridden with the shortened name of `TIFF`.

It is important to note that the `Language` attribute associated with the `OverrideNames` setting should match the language settings of the Reporting Services server. If the wrong or no language is specified, the `OverrideNames` entry is ignored, and the rendering extension's default name is used.

As mentioned previously, rendering extensions can support various formats. In addition, aspects of how each extension renders to a particular format are configurable. To override the default rendering settings of a particular rendering extension, you can add `DeviceInfo` settings to an extension's entry in the configuration file. In addition, more than one entry for a rendering extension, typically with a different set of `DeviceInfo` settings, can be recorded in the configuration file so long as each extension entry is identified with a unique name attribute.

The following example illustrates this using the Image rendering extension. In this example, the Image rendering extension is registered twice. In the first entry, the Image rendering extension is configured for its default settings, allowing TIFF images to be produced. In the second entry, the Image rendering extension is configured to produce BMP images.

```
<Extension Name="IMAGE"
Type="Microsoft.ReportingServices.Rendering.ImageRenderer.ImageRenderer,
    Microsoft.ReportingServices.ImageRendering"/>
<Extension Name="BMP"
Type="Microsoft.ReportingServices.Rendering.ImageRenderer.ImageRenderer,
    Microsoft.ReportingServices.ImageRendering">
    <OverrideNames>
        <Name Language="en-US">BMP</Name>
    </OverrideNames>
    <Configuration>
        <DeviceInfo>
            <OutputFormat>BMP</OutputFormat>
            <PageHeight>11in</PageHeight>
            <PageWidth>8.5in</PageWidth>
        </DeviceInfo>
    </Configuration>
</Extension>
```

`DeviceInfo` settings are rendering-extension–specific. Books Online documents these settings for each of the default rendering extensions. It is important to note that without configuring device info settings in the `RSReportServer.config` file, you can still supply device info settings when accessing a report through URL access or Web services calls to control report rendering for a specific request. In addition, URL access is the only mechanism allowing device info settings for the CSV rendering extension to be set, resulting in a tab-delimited file.

Finally, you should disable the `Extension` entry for any rendering extensions you do not intend to use by commenting it out in the `RSReportServer.config` file. However, if you simply want to prevent a file format from being used with a particular subscription delivery option, you should add its name to the `ExcludedRenderFormats` section under the appropriate delivery extension within the `RSReportServer.config` file. In the following example, the extensions with `Name` attributes set to `HTMLOWC`, `NULL`, `RGDI`, and `IMAGE` are excluded from use with File Share delivery:

```
<Extensions>
    <Delivery>
        <Extension Name="Report Server FileShare"
```

```
Type="Microsoft.ReportingServices.FileShareDeliveryProvider.FileShareProvider,
    ReportingServicesFileShareDeliveryProvider">
        <MaxRetries>3</MaxRetries>
        <SecondsBeforeRetry>900</SecondsBeforeRetry>
        <Configuration>
            <FileShareConfiguration>
                <ExcludedRenderFormats>
                    <RenderingExtension>HTMLOWC</RenderingExtension>
                    <RenderingExtension>NULL</RenderingExtension>
                    <RenderingExtension>RGDI</RenderingExtension>
                    <RenderingExtension>IMAGE</RenderingExtension>
                </ExcludedRenderFormats>
            </FileShareConfiguration>
        </Configuration>
    </Extension>
    ...
    </Delivery>

    ...
    </Extensions>
```

Each extension is visible by default, which means that it will appear as an option in the user interface. Every applicable extension can be hidden from view by adding the `Visible="false"` attribute. You will see examples of this setting in the file for legacy rendering formats such as `"WORD"` and `"EXCEL"`, which have been replaced by newer rendering extensions. Any hidden extension can still be used through the web services or URL parameters.

My Reports

> **NOTE** *SQL Server 2016 Reporting Services introduces the concept of Favorites, which has some functional duplication with the My Reports feature. The My Reports feature is still offered for backward-compatibility but it might confuse users to enable both without some guidance. Personally, I'm not a fan of the My Reports feature but it may have utility in very specific report management scenarios.*

The My Reports feature gives users a personal folder in Reporting Services within which they can manage and view their own content. This is a powerful feature for users, but it can quickly get out of hand. The critical concern is that users are, by default, assigned elevated rights within their My Reports folder. These rights allow them to store content on the site with no mechanism to restrict the type or size of that content.

By default, the My Reports feature is disabled. If it is enabled, a `My Reports` folder is presented to each user in his or her home directory. This folder is actually a link to a user-specific folder created by Reporting Services within the `Users Folders` folder. Only System Administrators have direct access to the `Users Folders` folder.

Within his or her `My Reports` folder, a user is a member of a preset role. By default, this is the My Reports role, which has the following tasks assigned to it:

➤ Create linked reports

➤ View reports

➤ Manage reports

➤ View resources

➤ View folders

➤ Manage folders

➤ Manage report history

➤ Manage individual subscriptions

➤ View data resources

➤ Manage data sources

These tasks, discussed in the preceding chapter, provide elevated rights within this space. You might consider removing some of these tasks from the My Reports role or creating an alternative role with lesser privileges. Then you can use that as the default role assignment for the My Reports feature.

To enable the My Reports feature, open SQL Server Management Studio, and connect to the Reporting Services instance. Right-click the instance object and select Properties to launch the Server Properties dialog. Within the default General page of this dialog, shown in Figure 22-10, use the checkbox next to the "Enable a My Reports folder for each user" option to toggle this feature on and off. If this is enabled, you can assign a role to each user within his or her My Reports folder through the drop-down just below the checkbox.

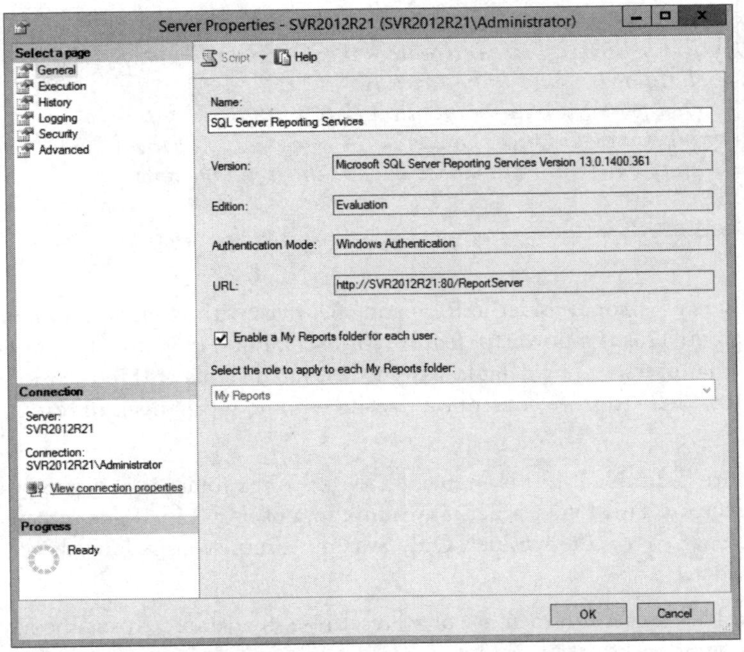

FIGURE 22-10: Server Properties dialog.

If you decide to enable this feature, closely monitor the consumption of space by users, and work with them to understand the feature's appropriate use. If you decide to disable the feature after having made it available, users will no longer be able to access their My Reports folder. However, the content of these folders remains within the system. Any subscriptions and snapshots associated with reports in these folders continue to run. To properly clean up the My Reports folders, you need to work with your users to migrate or drop their content.

SUMMARY

In this chapter, you have explored elements of Reporting Services with the goal of developing a comprehensive administrative program. Although there are recommended best practices, there is no one right approach. It is important to understand your options and then work with your users, developers, and administrators to develop a program tailored to your specific needs. After it is in place, it is important to follow through on the actions specified, and to be on the lookout for threats and changes in needs that may require adjustments to your routines and practices.

INDEX

Symbols and Numerals

% Free Space counter, 741
% Processor Time counter, 741
* character, 556
3-D charts, 224

A

\<A> tag (HTML), 189
account management, for server administration, 717–721
actions
  limitations, 434
  and navigation, 385–392
Active Connections counter, 737
Active Sessions counter, 737, 740
ActiveSubscriptions database table, 81
ActiveX control, 31
Add method, for IDataParameter interface, 547
Add New dialog, 142
Add New Item dialog, 159, 215, 511
Add Table dialog, Views tab, 159
Add Web Reference dialog, 480, 482
ADO.NET object model, 528
Adventure Works Cycles data warehouse database, 56
Adventure Works Multidimensional database, shared data source for, 438
aggregate function, 433
aggregation, 116
  cube management of, 309
  detail row summaries, 167–168
  functions for, 155, 200–203
  of numeric columns, 149
alert colors, threshold, 219
alias, 123
All component, 734
Analysis Services. See SQL Server Analysis Services (SSAS)

analytical reports, 224
analytics solutions, 10–11
Angry Koala Analytics reports, 322–324, 341, 362–363
Anonymous Access, 502
application database account, 718–721
application databases, backup and recovery, 725–727
application domain management, 71
application shortcuts, 8
applications, integration with reports, 7–10
area charts, 226, 229
ASP.NET applications, 70–71
  creating, 502–508
    web.config file modification, 502–503
  deployment, 502
ASP.NET Web Forms applications, 510
AsyncRender parameter, for SharePoint URL, 470
Atom Feed feature, 581
Atom rendering extension, 77
attribute hierarchy, 286–287
authentication, 69, 502
  types, 70
authentication element, in web.config file, 503
authoring phase, of reporting life cycle, 63
authorization, 69, 502
Auto Detect feature, and corresponding joins, 117, 118
auto-hide feature
  preventing, 159
  in Report Designer, 144
automation in content management, 710–714
  RS utility, 710–712
Avg. Disk Queue Length counter, 741
AVG() function, 201
axis labels for charts, changing, 243–244
axis titles for charts, 241–242

B

\<B\> tag (HTML), 190
background color
  for displaying relative number, 454
  of heading row, 107
  of KPI tile, 624
  for selected item, 162
BackGroundColor property, 219
  for Cube Browser report, 353
  of current row in cub, 320
  of textbox, 188
BackGroundImage property, of textbox, 188
backup and recovery, for server administration, 724–730
  application databases, 725–727
  of configuration files, 730
  encryption keys, 727–729
backups
  copy/paste method for creating, 146
  for experimenting, 146
bar charts, 226
  vs. doughnut charts, 231
  DynamicHeight property, 232
  for mobile devices, 591
Basic authentication, 70
BeginTransaction method, of DataSetConnection object, 538–539
best practices, for shared datasets, 402
BI Semantic Model (BISM), 422
BIDS. *See* Business Intelligence Development Studio (BIDS)
BIDS (Business Intellligence Development Studio), 16, 24, 140
bin directory, for extensions, 566
Binary Interchange File Format (BIFF), 522
BindingFieldPairs property, 455
Bing Maps, Internet connection for, 450
blank pages, preventing, 178
BMP rendering extension, 77
bold text, 212
  HTML tag for, 190
bookmark, navigating to, 380
Books Online, 723
  script for backup and recovery of databases, 726
Border ribbon group, 107
BorderColor property, of textbox, 188
borders, images as, 434
BorderStyle property, of textbox, 188
BorderWidth property, of textbox, 188
\<BR\> tag (HTML), 190
branding, 420–421, 707–709

example elements, 710
bridge table, script to add, 674–677
Browse view, in Web Portal, 681–682
Bruckner, Robert, *SQL Server Reporting Services Recipes*, 581
bubble charts, 227, 233
bubble map, 592
build errors, checking for, 410
built-in fields, 367
  on page header, 183
BUILTIN\Administrators group, 723
business intelligence, 10–11
Business Intelligence Development Studio (BIDS), 16, 24, 140
business managers, 6
Business Objects, 280
business rules, in cube design, 302, 309
byte array
  for final report, 495
  for Render method, 497–498
  from ReportExecutionService object, 505
Bytes Received Total counter, 737
Bytes Received/Sec counter, 737
Bytes Sent Total counter, 737
Bytes Sent/Sec counter, 737
Bytes Total/sec counter, 741

C

C#, vs. VB.NET, interface method declarations, 524
Cache Hits/Sec counter, 737
Cache Misses/Sec counter, 737
cached copy, 75
caching, 120
  of dataset, 413
  for Mobile Reports, 582–583
  report execution, 75
  report session, 75
Caching page for report, 693
calculated fields, in expressions, 369–371
candlestick chart, 227
cascading parameters, 257–259
  in MDX queries, 309
case-sensitivity
  of parameter names, 448
  of trace log names, 735
Catalog database table, 81
CatalogItem objects, 487
CatalogTempDB.sql script, 725
category chart
  data properties for, 613
  vs. Totals chart, 591

Category Group Properties dialog, 447
Category Sales chart, 600
CDATE() function (Visual Basic), 375
CDEC() function (Visual Basic), 375
cells, embedded content, and dimensions, 196
chart area
  controlling position, 249
  properties for, 239
Chart Area object, 235
Chart Area Properties dialog, 240
chart data grid, 593–594, 653–662
  chart properties, 658–660
  datasets
    creating, 654–655
    importing, 655–656
  field properties, 658
  fitting for phone layout, 660–662
  properties for selection list controls, 656–658
  rearranging columns, 661
  visual properties, 665
Chart Data window, 446
  ToolTip property, 244, 245
Chart object, 235
  hierarchy of, 236
Chart Properties dialog, Filters page, 448
charts
  3-D, 224
  advantages, 222–224
  anatomy of, 235–237
  axis text placement and rotation, 248
  controlling number of items displayed on axis, 248
  creating and styling, 240–244
    axis titles and formatting, 241–242
  dynamically increasing size, 249
  field expression with Sum function for series, 246
  interactive sparkline and, 443–450
  in mobile reports, 589–591, 604
  multi-series, creating, 245–248
  perspective and skewing, 224–225
  properties, 236
    for styles, 223
    visual, 640
  repeating, matrix report with, 197
  in Reporting Services, 32–33
  series, axes, and areas, 237–238
  simplicity as goal, 222–223
  types, 225–233
    area, 226, 229
    bar, 226
    bubble, 227, 233
    column, 225, 228–229
    doughnut, 226, 229–232

    line, 226, 229
    pie, 226, 229–232
    polar (radar), 228
    range (Gantt), 227
    scatter, 227
    shape, 227
    stock, 227, 233
    Sunburst chart, 233–235
    Tree map, 233–234
  visual storytelling, 224
  width and gap between columns or bars, 249
check-out/check-in policies, in version control, 409
Choose Color dialog, 162
CHOOSE() function (Visual Basic), 375
ChunkData database table, 81, 82
CINT() function (Visual Basic), 375
ClickOnce application, 96
Client Tools, 41
Close method, of DataSetConnection
  object, 540
closing window, 144
Code Editor window, 376
code variables, 434
color. See also background color
  of chart series line, 248
  for fonts, for Cube Browser report,
    353
  of geographic shapes, 453–454
  for mobile reports, 613–616
  for navigation action, 386
  for threshold alerts, 219
color palette, for mobile report, 642–646
Color property
  conditional logic for, 372
  of textbox, 188
color.json file, 708
ColorRule property, 455
column charts, 225, 228–229
  for mobile devices, 591
column selectors, 104
columns in cube
  changing hierarchy, 357
  restricting, 353–354
columns in tables
  aggregation of numeric, 149
  selecting, 108
    in Query Designer, 117
  for ungrouped detail cells, 182
Command object, 528
Command parameter, for URL access, 471–472
command-line utilities, 65
CommandText method, 558

CommandText property, of DataSetCommand class, 552–559

CommandTimeout property, of DataSetCommand class, 560

CommandType property, of DataSetCommand class, 560–561

comma-separated values (CSV)-rendering extension, 78

Comparison charts, 590

ComponentArt, 578

Components setting, for log configuration, 733

composite reports, and embedded content, 187

conditional expressions, 371–372, 433

conditional logic, 264–266

configuration files, backup and recovery, 730

configuration for server administration, 742–751
  e-mail delivery, 745–747
  memory management, 742–743
  My Reports, 749–751
  rendering extensions, 747–749
  URL reservations, 743–745

ConfigurationInfo database table, 81

"Connect to Server" dialog, 121

connecting
  to report server, 609
  server access, and live mobile, 647–650
  users to databases, standards for, 421

Connection object, 528

Connection Properties dialog, 100–101, 283

ConnectionString property, of DataSetConnection object, 540–542

ConnectionTimeout property, of DataSetConnection object, 542

consolidation, of new reports, 426

content management, 63, 679–714
  activities, 683–698
    folders, 684–685
    report resources, 694–695
    reports, 688–694
    shared data sources, 685–688
    shared schedules, 695–696
  automation, 710–714
    RS utility, 710–712
  in native mode, 412–413
  Reporting Services scripts, 710–712
  security, 696–706
    item-level security, 697–706
    site security, 697
  in SharePoint, 413–414
  site branding, 707–709
  synchronization, 409–410

Web Portal for, 680–683

controls, 95

copy and paste, for creating backups, 146

core processing, 73

COUNT() function, 201

COUNTDISTINCT() function, 201

COUNTROWS() function, 201

Country Selection list, 604, 644
  Data properties, 639

CreateCommand method, of DataSetConnection object, 539

CreateParameter method, of DataSetCommand class, 561

credentials
  for connections to data sources, 75
  management, 717

CSTR() function (Visual Basic), 375

CSV rendering extension, 77, 78, 523

Cube Browser Metadata report, 356

Cube Browser reports, 313, 341, 342–363
  anatomy of, 342–346
  cube restricting rows, 326–332
    pRowCount parameter, 327–328
    restricting row count in MDX query, 329–330
  details, 346–351
  dynamic rows report anatomy, 313–322
    datasets, 314–317
    design surface modifications, 325–326
    dynamic number formatting, 321
    expanded, 324–326
    highlighting current row, 320–321
    matrix content, 318
    parameters, 313
    summary, 322–324
  footer information, 360–362
  formatting row label, 318–319
  hierarchy display, 344
  key navigation paths, 345
  main report, 344–345
  MDX queries for, 347–351
  Member report, 346
  Metadata report, 345–346
  Profit and loss report, 343
  Query Parameters dialog, 317
  query results, 317
  report body setup, 351–353
  restricting rows and columns, 353–354
  Sales report, 343
  swap actions, 354–355
  titles, 355–356

cube data, 278
Cube Dynamics Rows report, 346
cube metadata, 332–341
  adding, 336–341
        dimensions dataset, 340
        Hierarchies dataset, 338, 340
        Levels dataset, 338, 341
        MeasureGroupDimensions dataset, 338
        measures dataset, 337–340
    MeasureGroups dataset, 334–336
cubes, 279
  business rules in design, 302
  dynamic expressions, for modifying properties, 306
  dynamic rows, 312–324
  filtering data from, 288–289
  formatting, and MDX properties, 305–306
  keys and unique identifiers in, 307
  slicing, 289–290
  WHERE clause for slicing, 297–298
currency, formatting column for, 108
Current Bandwidth counter, 741
custom application
  integrating reports into, 509–519
  slider in report, 514
  URLs to embed Reporting Services reports, 468
custom code, 375–380
  use in report, 376–377
custom data processing extension, 76
custom layouts, for mobile report, 642–646
custom maps, shape and data files for, 642
Customer US Map report, 456

D

dashboard, 7, 8
  components, 222
  data sources and datasets, 582–583
  mobile solution, 29
  pinned report visuals on, 36
  report design, trial-and-error for, 582
  sketch, 406
data, visualization of, 223–224
data access, 9
  Analysis Services to simplify, 422
  through view, 421
data aggregation, 19
Data Analysis Expressions (DAX), 278
data analysts, 5
Data Connections library, 419
data consumers, 4
data filters, parameters for Cube Browser, 346–347

data flow, 150
data grids, in mobile reports, 593–594
data mart, 15
data model, learning details of, 407
data presentation, Reporting Services
    limitations, 432
data processing extensions (DPEs), 75–76, 522,
    527–529
  creating custom, 529–572
        DataSetCommand class, 547–561
        DataSetConnection object, 533–542
        DataSetParameter class, 542–543
        DataSetParameterCollection class,
        545–547
        implementing IDataParameter interface,
        543–545
        project creation and setup, 530–533
        scenario, 530
data properties
  Keys and Labels properties, selection lists for, 657
  for number gauges, 612–613
  for Time navigator, 610–611
Data properties panel, 611
  for Time navigator, 638
data regions, 92–95
  datasets for multiple, embedding, 199
  lists, 94–95
  matrix, 93–94
  repeating, 196–200
        drill-through navigation, 200
        as master/detail container, 198–199
  tables, 93
Data Source Configuration Wizard, 510
Data Source Properties dialog, 98–99, 687–688
  Credentials page, 570
  with DATASET type selected, 569
  Windows authentication setting, 570
data source queries, 113
data sources, 89–90
  access, and security, 419
  changing name, 284
  creating, 98–99
  for dashboard, 582–583
  embedded and shared, 115–119
  management, 115–119
  for MDX queries, creating, 281–284
  report, 18–19
  shared, 401–402
  for URL requests, 465–467
Data Sources folder, on report server, 419
Data Sources Properties page, 693

data tables, adding to mobile report, 607–610
data types
  changing text to integer, 131–134
  for Report Data window, 253
data warehouse system, 19
DataAdapter object, 528
database credentials, parameter prefixes to send,
  469–470
Database Engine and Reporting Services, instance
  name for, 49–50
database projects, creating, 398–399
data-driven subscriptions, in Reporting Services, 67
DataReader object, 528
Dataset Properties dialog, 101, 103, 124, 135, 334
  adding new item to Fields collection, 370
  adding query script, 168
  Available Values page, 168, 169
  Default Value page, 168
  for naming query parameters, 272
  Parameters page, 252–253, 274
  with query, 127
  query command, 571
DataSetCommand class, 547–561
  Cancel method, 550–551
  CommandText property, 552–559
  CommandTimeout property, 560
  CommandType property, 560–561
  constructors, 549–550
  CreateParameter method, 561
  ExecuteReader method, 551–552
  IDbCommand interface, 550
  Parameters property, 561
  variable declarations, 548–549
DataSetConnection object, 533–542
  BeginTransaction method, 538–539
  Close method, 540
  ConnectionString property, 540–542
  ConnectionTimeout property, 542
  constructors, 534–535
  CreateCommand method, 539
  IDbConnectionExtension, 535
  Impersonate property, 535–536
  implementing IDbConnection interface, 537–538
  IntegratedSecurity property, 536
  Open method, 539–540
  UserName and Password properties, 536–537
  variable declarations, 534
DataSetDataExtension extension, testing,
  569–572
DataSetDataProcessing extension

installation, 566–569
  server, 566–567
  server security configuration, 567–568
  workstation, 568
  workstation security configuration, 568–569
DataSetDataReader object, 562–566
  declarations, 562
  FieldCount property, 565–566
  GetFieldType method, 563–564
  GetName method, 564
  GetValue method, 564–565
  implementing IDataReader, 562–563
  Read method, 565
  returning, 551–552
DataSetName property, 196, 455
DataSetParameter class, 542–543
DataSetParameterCollection class,
  545–547, 561
datasets, 18, 92, 119–137
  calculated members in fields collection, 301
  for chart data grid, 654–655
    importing, 655–656
  creating, for Cube Browser report, 328
  creating embedded, 116
  for dashboard, 582–583
  embedded and shared, 120
  master/detail relationship to correlate two, 653
  MDX Query Designer for building, 284–288
  for mobile report, 602–604
  for multiple, embedded data regions, 199
  for populat6ing parameter lists, 257–258
  query design, 158–160
  scope of, groups and, 200
  shared, 120
    in mobile reports, 604–605
  special-use row function, 201
Datasets folder, in SSDT, 606
DataSource database table, 81
Datazen, 578
  Dashboard Publisher, 583
Date hierarchy, recording and reporting
  metrics, 631
date member, in Cube Browser, changing, 358–360
date picker calendar control, 271
date value ranges in MDX queries, 271–275
  range expression as set, 273–275
  range of members, 271–273
DateFrom parameter, 271
DateTo parameter, 271
dBase data file (.dbf)

for maps, 592
    opening, 641–642
declarations, in Windows Forms class code, 483
default instance, 58–60
default mobile report layout, 645
default parameter value, 137
default path, for project file, 140
default slicer, 290
default TempDB, 52
Default value, for textbox border properties, 188
default view, reports in, 170
default Web Portal, 462
DefaultTraceSwitch setting, for log
    configuration, 733
Define Query Parameters dialog, 125
deleting encryption keys, 728, 729
delivery extensions, 80, 522
delivery phase, of reporting life cycle, 64
deployment folder, TargetFolder property, 400
deployment of reports
    checking location, 411
    excluding report from, 410
    single, or suite, 410
desktop reporting tool, vs. SQL Server Reporting
    Services, 17
detail cells
    adding field reference to, 161
    tablix headers and, 182
detail report, navigating to, 390
detail row, in tables, 93
Developer Edition of SQL Server, 42, 58
    vs. Enterprise edition, 40
development sandbox environment, 399
device information settings, 77, 473–474
DeviceInfo settings, for extension entry in
    configuration file, 748
diagramming tool, for Reporting Services, 405
dimensional modeling, simplicity as goal, 279
Disabled property, 193
<DIV> tag (HTML), 190
DocMapAreaWidth parameter, for SharePoint
    URL, 470
document map, 209–210
doughnut charts, 226, 229–232
    vs. bar charts, 231
drill-down effect, 163–167, 312–313
drill-through actions
    navigation for repeating data regions, 200
    navigation in mobile reports, 581
    navigation with thumbnail map, 450–456

    adding spatial point markers, 454–456
    geographic shape colors, 453–454
    Related content property for KPI action, 629
    in Sales Summary report, 386–392
    self-calling, 321–322, 354
drill-through reports, 378–380
    adding pRowCount to self-calling, 331
    for MDX datasets, 280
    mobile, 662–675
        opening and updating, 668–670
        pagination and, 666–670
    in SSAS, 307–308
drop-down lists
    code to populate for file formats, 484
    IntelliSense Auto List Members to provide, 368
dsp prefix, for Reporting Services parameters,
    469–470
dsu prefix, for Reporting Services parameters,
    469–470
Dundas Software, .NET charting components, 223
dynamic cube browser, with SSRS, 312
dynamic expressions
    creating report from template with, 215–219
    in cube design, for modifying properties, 306
dynamic filters, parameters for Cube Browser,
    346–347
dynamic management views (DMVs), 332–336
    getting full list, 333
dynamic memory, 42
dynamic reports, 10
DynamicWidth property, of chart, 249

E

Edge Browser, HTML Viewer and, 66
e-mail delivery
    configuration, 745–747
    for subscriptions, 690–691
embedded content, composite reports and, 187
embedded data sources, 115–119
embedded datasets, 120
    creating, 116
embedded formatting, for textbox, 189–195
embedded sparkline, 443–450
EMF rendering extension, 77
employee hierarchy, visualizing, 383
employee/manager relationship, 381
encryption keys
    backup and recovery, 727–729
    recovering, 729

recreating, 729
endpoints, 482
　web services, 711
end-user authors, 63
enterprise data, storage location, 418
Enterprise Edition of SQL Server, 58
　deployment, 57–62
　vs. Developer edition, 40
enterprise scale, 19
Environmental Systems Research Institute
　　(ESRI), 592
environments, multiple, for reports, 399–400
#Error, 185
Errors Total counter, 737
Errors/Sec counter, 737
Event database table, 81
event logs, for Reporting Services, 731
Excel, 5
　export, 431–435
　　　　limitations, 433, 434
　report rendered to, 31, 195
Excel extension, 77, 79, 522
EXCEL format, 501, 508
Excel Office Open XML format (XLSX), 79
Excel PivotTables, 581
Excel Workbook files, managing through web
　　portal, 684
EXCELOPENXML format, for reports, 508
ExecuteReader method, 551–552
execution account, 721
execution logs, for monitoring server administration,
　　735–736
execution time. See performance
Execution Time field, 183
ExecutionCache database table, 82
ExecutionLogStorage database table, 81, 735
ExecutionTime, for report, 361
expectations, 20
Express Edition of SQL Server, 58
Expression Builder dialog, 255, 366,
　　367–368
Expression Editor, 154, 164–165, 169
　for month abbreviations, 243
　multi-value parameter added, 390
expressions
　basics, 154–155, 365–367
　in calculated fields, 369–371
　conditional, 371–372
　for conditional formatting, 433
　custom code, 375–380
　dynamic, creating report from template with,
　　215–219

filter for chart, 447
IIF() function, 372–375
links and drill-through reports, 378–380
as placeholder in report design, 200–201
placeholders, 154
　in textbox, 185
extensions, 74, 521–572. See also data processing
　　extensions (DPEs)
　data processing, 75–76
　location for, 566
　Reporting Services types, 522–523
　through interfaces, 524–529

F

failover cluster, Reporting Services
　　databases on, 61
Favorites view, in Web Portal, 680–681
Few, Stephen, 223
field properties, for chart data grid, 658
FieldCount property, of DataSetDataReader
　　object, 565–566
fields, 119–137
　adding reference to detail cell, 161
　calculated, in expressions, 369–371
　validating names, 555–556
fields in table, adding, 104
fieldSplit regular expression, 556
file formats
　code to populate drop-down lists for, 484
　for reports, 18
FileName setting, for log configuration, 732
files, rendering report to, 495–501
files only installation, 62
FileSizeLimitMb setting, for
　　log configuration, 732
filesystem folders, for multiple instances of SQL
　　Server, 58–59
FillColor expression, 443
Filter cell, parameters for, 149
Filter Expression
　for chart, 447
　defining for MDX query, 289
filters, 117
　changing hierarchy in Cube Browser, 357
　controls for, 587
　in Cube Browser report, 344
　testing for enabled, 558
　text in Query Designer, 160
Finlan, Chris, 30
FireEvent method, 80
firewall, 647

Internet connection through, 618
FIRST() function, 183–184, 201
First Session Requests/Sec counter, 737, 740
fit, and design, 222
fixed role permissions, 699–700
flow control, 176–178
FlowingData.com, 223
folders
    accessing for URL requests, 464
    in content management, 684–685
    creating, 97
    inheritance cascade through hierarchy, 706
    managing, 420
    multiple, for reports, 400–401
Font property, of textbox, 188
<FONT> tag (HTML), 189
fonts
    color, 321
            for Cube Browser report, 353
    embedding in PDF rendering extension, 79
    for textbox, 161
footers, 154, 178–187
    in Cube Browser report, 360–362
    group, adding category value to, 164
    page number in, 366
form, in design, 222
Form_Load event
    for ReportViewer control, 515–519
    for setting credentials, 483–484
Format class, 496
FORMAT() function (Visual Basic), 374
Format parameter, for URL access, 471, 472–473
Format property, of Number group, 162
formatting
    conditional, 371–372
    Cube Browser report, row label, 318–319
    embedded, for textbox, 189–195
    Reporting Services limitations, 433
    T-SQL vs. MDX queries, 305–306
formatting properties, 107–109
    for axis values, 248
    for charts, 241–242
function, and design, 222
functions
    for aggregation, 200–203
    writing, 375–380
funnel chart, 227

G

Gantt (range) charts, 227
Gauge Data window, 442

    for KPIs, 291–292
gauges, 441–443
    data properties for, 612–613
    in Mobile Report Publisher, properties, 634
    in mobile reports, 588–589, 604
geographic shape colors, 453–454
geospatial point value, 455
GetFieldType method, 563–564
GetItemParameterAsync method, 491–492
GetItemParameters method, of
        ReportingService2010 object, 491
GetName method, of DataSetDataReader
        object, 564
GetReportExecutionParameters function, 497
GetResourceContents command, 467
GetValue method, of DataSetDataReader object,
        564–565
GitHub, 16, 66, 407
Google Chrome, HTML Viewer and, 66
governance rules, for information, 417
gradient heat map, 592
graphical Query Designer, 146–147
graphical reports, 173
Grid control, 588
grid size, for mobile layout, 585
gripper space, for printers, 177
Gross Profit Margin KPI, 438
GROUP BY clause, 123, 149
group expressions, 111
Group Properties dialog, 111, 151, 454
    Advanced page, 383
    Document map property, 209
    field expression in, 367
    General page, 382
    Page Breaks page, 151–152
    Recursive parent property, 381
    for Row Groups pane, 318
    Sorting page, 157, 318
    Visibility page, 166
group total, 93
grouped column headers, 433
grouping data, 110–113
Grouping window
    Advanced Mode, 186–187
    in Report Designer, 143
groups. *See also* report groups
    adding category value to footer, 164
    assigning roles to, 698
    and dataset scope, 200
    numeric measures and, 116–117
    for report users, 421
    separation lines on table, 188

H

HangingIndent property, for text, 188, 189
HeaderArea parameter, for SharePoint URL, 470
headers, 154, 178–187
   designing, 182–187
   repeating, 186–187
headers and footers
   content in rectangle, 192
   on report template, 211–212
         adding title and logo to header, 212–214
heading row in table
   background color, 107
   selecting, 107
Help icon, for Web Portal, 683
hex color values, modifying, 708
hiding window, 144
hierarchy
   attribute, 286–287
   of Chart object, 236
   in Cube Browser, changing, 357
   display in Cube Browser reports, 344
   recursive, 381
   for Time navigator, 587
   user, 286–287
highlighting current row, in Cube Browser report,
      320–321
History database table, 81
History snapshots page, 694
<Hn> tag (HTML), 190
Home page, folders list, 684
Home ribbon, Number group, dollar sign icon, 108
Horizontal Axis Properties dialog, 242–243
HTML, 431
   embedded formatting, 189–191
   rendering limitations, 434
   version 5 standards, 33
HTML extension, 522
HTML rendering engine, 26
HTML rendering extension, 77, 78
HTML Viewer, 66
http component, trace messages from, 733–734
HTTP interfaces, 68
HTTP listener, 69
HTTPS, URL request of, 470
HTTP.SYS driver, 69
HttpTraceFileName setting, 734
HttpTraceSwitches setting, 734
Hyperion Essbase, 76, 280
hyperlinks, 8
Hyper-V role, 42

I

<I> tag (HTML), 190
IBM Cognos, 280
IBM DB2, 18
IDataParameter interface, 529, 543–545
   ParameterName property, 544
   Value property, 544–545
IDataParameterCollection interface, 529, 545
   implementing, 546–547
IDataReader interface, 529, 562
   implementing, 562–563
IDataReaderExtension interface, 529
IDbCommand interface, 529, 550
IDbCommandAnalysis interface, 529
IDbConnection interface, 529
   CreateCommand method, 552
IDbConnectionExtension interface, 529, 535
IDbTransaction interface, 529
IDbTransactionExtension interface, 529
IExtension interface, 529, 537–538
IIF() function, 372–375
Image extension, 523
IMAGE format, 473–474
Image Properties dialog, 213
   navigation properties in, 378–379
Image rendering extension, 78, 748
images
   as borders, 434
   files as report resources, 694–695
<img> tag, src attribute, 467
Impersonate property, of DataSetConnection
      object, 535–536
impersonation, 503
importing datasets, 655
Imports statement, 483
IN function (T-SQL), comma-separated values
      list, 135
indenting, in textbox, 188
indicator data grid, 593
Indicator Properties dialog, 291
information, governance rules for, 417
information workers, 5
   and analysis services, 279
inheritance, 706
inner joins, 149
inserting columns in tables, 105
installing SQL Server, local instance, 39
instance name, 59
   for Database Engine and Reporting Services, 49–50
instances, default and named, 58–60

`INSTR()` function (Visual Basic), 375
integer, changing text to, 131–134
`IntegratedSecurity` property, of
 `DataSetConnection` object, 536
IntelliSense Auto List Members feature, 368
interactive sizing mode, for reports, 176
interactive sparkline, 443–450
`InteractiveSize` property, for reports, 176
Interface AutoComplete, 525, 547
interfaces
 basics, 524
 extensions through, 524–529
 language differences, 524–527
Internet connection, for Bing Maps, 450
Internet Explorer, HTML Viewer and, 66
Internet Information Server (IIS), 69
Internet Sales Dashboard report, 468
 passing parameters to, 475
 query string for rendering, 507–508
IP address
 for URL reservation, 744
 for Web Portal address, 649
iPad, mobile report on, 14, 578–579
`IPCONFIG`, 647
iPhone
 Power BI app for, 12
 web portal on, 13
`ISNOTHING()` function (Visual Basic), 375

J

JavaScript function, for pop-up window, 380
`JOIN` function (VB.NET), 255–256
joins, 149–150
 changing type, 150
JPEG rendering extension, 77

K

`KeepFilesForDays` setting, for
 log configuration, 732
Kerberos, 70
key performance indicators (KPIs), 13, 30–31, 280,
 623–632
 aggregating states, 292
 and business decisionrs, 630
 creating, 625–626
 elements, 624
 and goals, 630–631
 properties, 291–292
 for report design, 285

 scorecard, 437–441
 table in report designer, 439
 time-series calculations and time grain, 631–632
 visualizing, 290–293
 in Web Portal, 629
Keys database table, 81
key/value pairs, for binding polygon to data,
 453–454
`keywordSplit` regular expression, 553
KPI scorecard, 582

L

Label field property, 255
 vs. Value field property, 255
labels, for report version, 409
`LAST()` function, 183–184, 201
layouts
 custom, for mobile report, 642–646
 for mobile reports, 613–616
 for report, designing, 102–106
`LEFT()` function (Visual Basic), 374
`Left Padding` property, 383
`LeftIndent` property, for text, 188, 189
`LEVEL` function, 201, 383
`<LI>` tag (HTML), 190
libraries, managing, 420
licensing requirements, multiple instances and, 60
line charts, 226, 229
links, 378–380
list data region, Tablix object vs. table for, 192
`ListChildren` method, 485–486, 487–489, 502
`ListChildrenAsync` method, 487–489
lists, 94–95
`LoadParametersGroupBox` method, 492–494
`LoadReportsBox` method, 489–490
local Administrators group membership, 42
local development environment, copying `.rdl` file
 to, 406
Local mode, 17
 for `ReportViewer` control, 511
Local Processing mode, for Report Viewer
 control, 66
local service account, 717
local system account, 717
`LocalHost`, 283
`LocalHost` alias, 100
location, for mobile report, 596–597
logical drive, SQL Server setup DVD image mounted
 as, 43
logical folders, multiple, for reports, 400–401

logo, adding to header, 213–214
Logon Attempts Total counter, 738
Logon Attempts/Sec counter, 738
Logon Successes Total counter, 738
Logon Successes/Sec counter, 738
logs
    execution, 735–736
    setup, 731
    trace, 732–735
    Windows application event, 731
LOOKUP function, 196
LOOKUPSET function, 196

M

Machine.config file, 730
mail delivery errors, Windows application event log
    for, 746
maintenance, of report process, 426
management phase, of reporting life cycle, 63
Management Studio. See SQL Server Management
    Studio (SSMS)
map gallery, 451
Map Layers window, 453
Map report item, 450
MapBindingFieldPair Collection Editor, 454
maps
    adding as control, 593
    in mobile reports, 591–593, 671–675
    properties, 641–642
    reports with all available, 671
margins, 177
"mark of approval" logo, 420
MarkerRule property, 455
markers, spatial point, 454–456
MarkupType property, for text placeholder, 190
master/detail reports, 195–203, 653
    repeating data regions, 196–200
        drill-through navigation, 200
        list data region as container, 198–199
        matrix as container, 197
        subreport, 199
        table as container, 196–197
    matrix, 93–94
        adding totals to report, 153–154
        creating report from template, 215–218
        data region, 217–218
        inserting, 128–129
        as master/detail container, 197
MAX() function, 201
MaximumValue property, for gauge scale, 442–443

MDX queries
    adding calculated members to, 296–300
    Analysis Services and, 279
    cascading parameters in, 309
    for Cube Browser, 347–351
    cube design, measure formatting, 305–306
    for cube dynamic rows report, 314–316
    date value ranges, 271–275
        range expression as set, 273–275
        range of members, 271–273
    and filters, 289–290
    modifying, 293–302, 324–325
    multi-valued parameters in, 270–271
    and parameters, 266–275
        single-valued, 270
        as text, 272
    properties, and cube formatting, 305–306
    restricting number of rows, 329–330
    SSMS for, 267
    style preferences, 295
    table bound to, 206
MDX Query Designer, 281–293, 439
    advanced MDX and, 293
    building dataset query, 284–288
    building query with, 293–302
    creating data source, 281–284
    Cube metadata pane
        KPIs node, 285–286
        slicing cube, 289–290
    filled in, 288
    hidden datasets for parameters, 292
    Parameter drop-down, 292
    parameterized queries, 288–289
    for sparkline chart, 444–445
    switching to text query view, 294
MDX studio, for reformatting MDX query script,
    295
measure
    in Cube Browser, 346
    dynamic formatting for value, 321
    for row member properties, 316
MeasureGroups dataset, for cube metadata,
    334–336
memory, 40
    dynamic, 42
    minimum system requirements, 42
Memory Cache Hits/Sec counter, 738
memory management, 71
    configuration, 742–743
Memory Pressure State counter, 738
Memory Shrink Amount counter, 738

Memory Shrink Notifications/Sec counter, 738
MemorySafetyMargin setting, for memory management, 743
MemoryThreshold setting, for memory management, 743
metadata objects, in Analysis Services, 287
methods, wrappers for, 547
Microsoft, Datazen acquisition, 28
Microsoft .NET Framework, 43
Microsoft Office 2016, standards, 25
Microsoft SQL Server, 17
Microsoft Team Foundation Server, 16, 407
Microsoft.ReportingServices.DataProcessing namespace, 531, 532
Microsoft.ReportingServices.Interfaces namespace, 531
Microsoft.ReportingServices.Portal.WebHost.exe.config file, 730
MID() function (Visual Basic), 374
migration error message, 503
migration of Reporting Services instance, 60
migration strategies, for reports, 425–426
MIN() function, 201
mobile device reporting, 11–13
mobile phone, report on, 580
mobile report design patterns, 623–651
    key performance indicators (KPIs), 623–632
        and business decisions, 630
        creating, 625–626
        elements, 624
        and goals, 630–631
        time-series calculations and time grain, 631–632
        in Web Portal, 629
    Time series, 632–650
        layout with design-first development, 633–635
Mobile Report Publisher, 12, 17, 583–586
    adding tables from shared datasets, 609
    Dashboard Settings page, 585
    Data page, 584, 588, 610
        Add Data, 635–636
    for drill-through report, 663
    Layout page, 584, 586, 597–598
    opening, 594–595
    Preview page, 585–586
    Settings page, 595–596
    visual controls, 586–594
        charts, 589–591
        data grids, 593–594
        gauges, 588–589

    maps, 591–593
    navigators, 587–588
mobile reports, 28–30, 398, 577
    adding data, 602–613
        data properties for category chart, 613
        data properties for number gauges, 612–613
        data properties for selection list, 611–612
        data tables, 607–610
        datasets, 602–604
        shared datasets and report tables, 604–605
    cached and on-demand, 582–583
    chart data grid, 653–662
        chart properties, 658–660
        datasets creation, 654–655
        field properties, 658
        fitting for phone layout, 660–662
        importing datasets, 655–656
        properties for selection list controls, 656–658
    creating, from Web Portal, 594
    data preparation for, 582
    default layout, 645
    design-first development, 593–620
    drill-through navigation, 581, 662–675
        opening and updating, 668–670
        pagination and, 666–670
    experience and business case, 578–583
    layouts and color styling, 613–616
    location for, 596–597
    maps, 671–675
    pagination and, 582
    previewing, 601–602
    saving, 636–638
    saving copies, 585
    shared datasets for, 145
    testing
        on phone or tablet, 598
        from server, 616–620
    visual controls, 598–600
    when to use, 581–583
    WiFi access for connecting to, 618
mockup, 406
"modern," 583
monitoring server administration, 731–742
    execution logs, 735–736
    performance counters, 736–741
    server management reports, 741–742
    setup logs, 731
    trace logs, 732–735
    Windows application event logs, 731
MonthList dataset, query for, 264
months, sorting, 309

`MSReportServer_ConfigurationSetting` class, 72–73
`MSReportServer_Instance` class, 72–73
`MSSQLSERVER` keyword, 729
Multidimensional Expressions (MDX) language, 278, 280–302. *See also* MDX queries
  simple or complex, 280–281
multi-select report parameter, 253–254
multi-series chart, creating, 245–248
My Reports, configuration, 749–751
MySQL, 18, 115

N

Name property, in `ReportItem` class, 491
name reference, fully-qualified, 268
named instance, 58–60
  of SQL Server, connecting to, 121
  URL for, 96
names
  for application databases, 725
  for instance, 50
  for project, 142
  for report parts, 424–425
  for reports, 401
      from web service, 505
  validating for tables and fields, 555–556
namespaces, 545–546
  aliases, 532–533
Native mode
  content management in, 412–413, 679
  for Reporting Services, 41, 61, 68
      default configuration option, 62
  scale-out topology in, 61
navigating
  and actions, 385–392
  to bookmark, 380
  reports, 208–210
  to URL, 379–380
navigation links, 9
navigators, in mobile reports, 587–588
Negotiate authentication type, 70
nested `IIF()` function, 372
.NET assembly, 375
.NET Framework, 522
.NET Windows Forms, 510
network service account, 718
New Linked Report page, 691–692
New Map Layer dialog, 451–452
New Project dialog, 509
    Business Intelligence, Reporting Services, 141, 399
New Report or Dataset dialog (Report Builder), 606

New Role Assignment page, 705–706
Next Session Requests/Sec counter, 739
node, 61
`NON EMPTY` directive, 309
Notifications database table, 81
`NotSupported` exception, 560
NT Lan Manager (NTLM), 70
NULL values, 445
  as 0s, 433
  for parameters, 475
`NullReference` exceptions, 373
number control, 589
number formatting
  dynamic, 321
  with zero decimals, 162
Number gauge controls, 604
  in Mobile Report Publisher
      Data properties, 639
      properties, 634
Number group, Format property, 162
numeric columns, aggregation, 149
numeric measures, 116

O

Object Explorer, 121–122, 144
objects, properties, 150
ODS. *See* operational data stores (ODS)
offline report cache, synchronization, 13
`<OL>` tag (HTML), 190
OLAP cubes, 19
on-demand results, for Mobile Reports, 582–583
OneDrive, 140
online analytical processing (OLAP), 11
Open File dialog, 144
Open method, of `DataSetConnection` object, 539–540
Open XML Office format (XLSX), 522
operational data stores (ODS), 18, 403
optimizing performance, 19–20
Oracle, 18
orphaned users, 726
outer joins, 149
output folder, for reports, 501
output format, device-information settings based on, 469
`OverrideNames` setting, for report formats, 747–748
`OverwriteDatasets` setting, 411
`OverwriteDataSources` setting, 411, 412
ownership of report, defining for self-service reporting, 417–418

P

<P> tag (HTML), 190
padding properties, 383
  of textbox, 188
page breaks, 151–152, 581
  forcing, 192
  setting in rectangle properties, 193
Page Header Properties dialog, 181, 212
page number, in report footer, 366
Page_Load event, for rendering reports, 506–507
PageBreak Disabled property, setting with
  expression, 194
pages
  headers and footers, 178–179
      built-in fields, 183
      designing headers, 182–187
      footers, 183
      long parameter text in, 194
  rectangle report item container and flow
      management, 193
  total number of, 110
PageSize property, for reports, 176
Pages/sec counter, 741
paginated reports, 176–178, 398, 688–694
parameter bar, grid arrangement, 266
parameter layout control, 26
Parameter Properties dialog, 125–126, 132–133, 693
parameterized queries, 288–289
ParameterLanguage parameter, for Web service
  URL, 471
parameters
  arranging in parameter bar, 259
  cascading, 257–259
      in MDX queries, 309
  collection of objects, 545
  default value, 137, 663
  enhancing, 131–134
  for Filter cell, 149
  interacting with, 331
  list creation, 168–171
  managing long lists, 259–261
  in MDX queries
      multi-valued, 270–271
      single-valued, 270
  prefixes, 469–470
  for report
      retrieving, 490–494, 496–497
      using, 368
  server-side, 479
  using multiple values, 134–137
  values, and running report, 137

Parameters property, of DataSetCommand
  class, 561
parent of group, 153
password
  for backup file, 729
  for server connection, 619
Password property, of DataSetConnection
  object, 536–537
path
  for Database Engine instance, 52
  for shared components, 49
  for web portal, 96
Path property, in ReportItem class, 491
PDF (Portable Document Format), 78–79
PDF rendering extension, 77, 78–79, 523
PerceptualEdge.com, 223
performance
  Analysis Services and, 279
  long parameter lists and, 260
  optimizing, 19–20
  sorting and, 155
  subreports and, 203
performance counters, for monitoring server
  administration, 736–741
permissions, 697, 717
  fixed role, 699–700
  system roles and, 722
  task-level, 700–702
PersistedStream database table, 82
personal folder, for My Reports feature, 749
perspective, of charts, 224–225
phone number, Visual Basic function to accept,
  376–377
phones
  fitting chart data grid for layout, 660–662
  mobile report on, 29
      alternative layout for, 585
  report layout in, 615–616
pie charts, 226, 229–232
pinnable items, 35
pinning
  Report Data window, 159
  window in Report Designer, 144
Placeholder Properties dialog, 190, 191
placeholders
  in report design, expressions as, 200–201
  in textbox, 185
PL/SQL, 115
PNG rendering extension, 77
point layer, of map port, 453
points, 383
  for padding, 188

`PointTemplate` group, properties, 455
polar (radar) charts, 228
Policies database table, 81
PolicyUserRole database table, 81
polygon layer, of map port, 453
pop-up window, JavaScript function for, 380
Portable Document Format (PDF), 78–79
portrait orientation, for mobile report, 619–620
Portrait phone layout, 645, 646
PostgreSQL, 18
Power BI app, 5, 13, 278, 632
  adding pinning to report toolbar, 34
  cloud service, 33
  dashboard pinning, 33–36
  for iPhone, 12
Power BI Desktop Reports, 684
Power BI Mobile app, 578, 618, 647
  on iPhone, 648–649
Power Pivot, 5, 24, 278, 632
PowerPoint, rendering, 31
PowerPoint rendering extension, 77, 79
PowerShell CmdLets for Reporting Services, 66, 680
PPTX rendering extension, 523
`Prefix` setting, for log configuration, 732
printable sizing mode, for reports, 176
printers, gripper space for, 177
privacy statement, 47
Processor Queue Length counter, 741
processors, 73–80
Product Details report, 378
Product Inventory report, conditional formatting in, 371–372
`ProductList` dataset, 252
profit margin, textbox for calculating, 369
programmatic rendering
  common scenarios, 478–479
  through Windows, 479–501
    application interface, 479–480
    rendering report to file, 495–501
    retrieving information, 485–490
    retrieving parameters for report, 490–494
    web services set up, 480–485
projects
  names for, 142
  requirements, 401
  storage location for files, 140
properties
  for chart area, 239
  for chart styles, 223
  of objects, 150
Properties window
  for charts, 235

Number group, Format property, 162
  in Report Designer, 143
  Size properties group, 178
prototype, 406
prototyping tool, for Reporting Services, 405
pRowCount parameter, 327–328
  adding to self-calling drill-through report action, 331
Publish Report Parts dialog, 423–424
pull method, of report delivery, 64
push method, of report delivery, 64
pyramid chart, 227

Q

queries, 9. *See also* data source queries; MDX queries
  adding to report dataset, 124–128
  authoring with SQL Server Management Studio, 120–124
  dataset, design, 158–160
  in Dataset Properties dialog, 127
  `GROUP BY` clause, 149
  parameterized, 288–289
  pasting into Query Designer, 125
  for product inventory, 371–372
  for rendering Internet Sales KPI Dashboard report, 507–508
  for Sales Summary report, 387
  sorting records in, 155
  as SSRS shared datasets, 29
  `WHERE` clause, 135, 136
Query Designer, 116, 125, 216
  for creating parameters, 309
  filter text in, 160
  graphical, 146–147
  selecting columns in, 117
  tables added, 148
query joins, 149–150
query parameter, 127
<Query> element, in RDL schema, 511
Quick Access toolbar
  floppy disk icon, 109
  Redo button, 128
  Undo button, 128

R

radar (polar) charts, 228
range (Gantt) charts, 227
range stop map, 592
rc prefix, for Reporting Services parameters, 469
RDL file

updated specification, 27
  XML snippet in, 366
RDL schema, `<Query>` element in, 511
RDLC extension, for report definition file, 17
`Read` method, of `DataSetDataReader` object, 565
readme files, for reports, 467
recovery. *See* backup and recovery
rectangle, as text container, 192–195
recursive relationships, 381–385
reference table of map shape names, 593
Registry by Reporting Services, 69
regular expressions
  `fieldSplit`, 556
  `keywordSplit`, 553
  to validate string format, 541–542
Related content property, for drill-through action for
  KPI, 629
relational data warehouse, vs. relational database,
  278–279
relational databases, 10, 278
  basics, 114–115
relationships, recursive, 381–385
Remote mode, for `ReportViewer` control, 511, 513
remote procedure call (RPC) interface, 73
Remote Processing mode, for Report Viewer
  scontrol, 66
`Render.aspx` ASP.NET page, 503–508
rendering extensions, 77–79, 522
  configuration, 747–749
  limitations, 434
Rendering Object Model (ROM), 78
rendering reports from Reporting Services, 462–520
  programmatic. *See* programmatic rendering
  `ReportViewer` control for, 509–519
    embedding server-side report in Windows
      application, 512–519
  URL access, 462–477
    accessing Reporting Services objects,
      463–469
    limitations, 478, 479
    passing information through URL, 474–477
    URL parameters, 469–474
    URL syntax, 463
  to Web, 502–508
    Integrated Windows authentication for, 502
    rendering to Response object, 503–508
    Report Execution Web Service, 503
    `web.config` file modification, 502–503
`RenderReport` method, 498–500
`ReorderPoint` value, 371
repeating chart, matrix report with, 197
repeating headers, 186–187

Report Builder, 15, 16, 64, 88–89, 400
  creating shared dataset with, 605–607
  enhancements, 25–26
  exercises, 95–113
  Getting Started page, 98
  Home ribbon, 106
    View Report icon, 130
  Insert ribbon, 92, 103
    Matrix button, 128–129
  optimizing user experience, 420
  Options dialog, 423–424
  Query Designer dialog, 101–102, 116–119
  Run ribbon, Navigation, Last icon, 110
  and self-service reporting strategies, 414–415
  and semantic model history, 415
  vs. SSDT design tools, 414–415
  title bar, 109
Report Creation Wizard, 511
report data sources, 18–19
Report Data window
  datasets, Add Calculated Field, 369–370
  dragging items from, 366
  in Report Designer, 143
report dataset, adding query to, 124–128
report definition customization extensions, 523
report design, 87–88
  alternating row shading, 219
  of body, 128–131
  composite, and embedded content, 187
  data building blocks, 89–93
    data regions, 92–95
    data sources, 89–90
    datasets, 92
    report items, 95
  for different information for different users, 430
  formatting properties, 107–109
  interdependencies between elements, 430
  layout, 102–106
  previewing, 109
  reviewing, 106
  sample, 156
  summary totals and drill-down, 163–167
  threshold alert colors, 219
  tools, 88–89
  validating, 110–113
Report Designer, 64
  MDX-based dataset for, 280
  window panes, 142–144
Report Designer grid, 26
report developers, 4
Report elements pane, for mobile layout, 645
report execution caching, 75

Report Execution Web Service, 503
  parameters, 495
  setting up, 503
Report Explorer 2.0, 65
Report Formatting toolbars
  Bold type, 212
  in Report Designer, 142
report groups, 150–158
  adding totals to table or matrix report, 153–154
  aggregate functions and totals, 155
  sorting, 155–157
report items, 95
  BookMark property, 380
report parameter, 127
  adding, 118
Report Parameter Properties dialog, 131–134, 217
  Available Values page, 328
  Default Value page, 269
  General page, 445
  for multiple values, 135
report parts, 437
  designing and deploying, 422
  names for, 424–425
  using, 422–425
Report Portal, viewing report in, 113
report preview pane, 410
report processing extensions, 523
Report Processor, 74–75
Report Properties dialog, 211, 376
  Page Setup page, 177
report recipe concept, 429–430, 581–602
Report Requests counter, 739
report resources, in content management, 694–695
report server
  connecting to, 485–490, 609
  default virtual directory, 480
  navigating directly to, 56
  navigating to content on phone app, 649, 650
  shared datasets as named objects on, 120
Report server page, 465
report session caching, 75
report template
  creating, 210–214
    adding title and logo to header, 212–213
    header setup, 211–212
    report body setup, 210–211
  creating report from, 215–219
report title, 103
Report tool
  choices, 14–19

enterprise scale, 19
IT-designed reports, 16
server-based reports, 17–18
simple report design, 15
user-defined reports, 16–17
report users, 4
Report Viewer 2.0 web parts, 65
Report Viewer control, 66–67
  Remote Processing mode for, 66
Report Viewer web part, 64–65
Report Wizard, 510
ReportData window, for Sales Summary report, 388, 389
ReportDate dataset, 252
reportdefinition namespace, xmns attribute, 27
ReportExecution2005 endpoint, 67
ReportExecutionService object, 504
  byte array from, 505
reporting extensions. See extensions
reporting life cycle, 63–64
Reporting Service Rendering application, 501
Reporting Services (SSRS), 4
  with Analysis Services data, 279–280
  application databases, 80–82
  architecture, strengths and limitations, 431, 432–435
  basic installation, 41–57
  branding page, 708
  charts and visual enhancements, 32–33
  configuration files, 71–72
  configuring to send e-mail, 746
  creating, 398–399
  disabled features, 723
  dynamic cube browser built with, 312
  evolution, 24
  Favorites, 749
  installing, 42–56
    configuration options, 61–62
    samples, exercises, and SQL Server databases, 56–57
  interfaces in Visual Studio, 525
  modes for, 61
  new features, 23–37
  nonadditive measures, 302
    aggregate function, 304–305
  printing capability, 31
  processors and extensions, 73–80
    data processing extensions, 75–76
    rendering extensions, 77–79
    Report Processor, 74–75

query object properties use, 306
report items, 76
report server, 19
scenarios, 398
scripts, 710–712
Site settings, 697
tools, 64–68
users, 4–7
    business managers and leaders, 6
    information consumers, 6
    information workers and data analysts, 5
    software developers, 6–7
    system administrators, 7
Windows service, 68–69
    core processing, 71
    HTTP.SYS and HTTP listener, 69
    security sublayer, 69–70
    service management, 71
    in standard topology, 61
    web portal and web service, 70–71
    WMI and RPC interface, 72–73
Reporting Services Configuration Manager, 33–34, 65, 716, 719–720
    Database page, 726–727
    Encryption Keys page, 728
    Execution Account page, 721, 722
    recreating encryption key, 729
    Service Account page, 718, 719
    Web Service URL page, 744
Reporting Services databases, installing with SQL local instance, 42
Reporting Services SOAP API, 711
Reporting Services Web Service, 67–68
    configuring URL reservation for, 744
Reporting Services Windows service, monitoring, 740, 741
reporting specialists, authoring by, 63
ReportingService2010 object, GetItemParameters method of, 491
ReportingServicesService.exe.config file, 72, 730
    trace logs within, 732
ReportItem class, 488–489, 496
    Name and Path property, 491
ReportParameter object, using/Imports statement for, 516–518
reports, 7. See also master/detail reports; mobile reports; super reports
    adding subreport, 205
    aggregate detail row summaries, 167–168
    with all available maps, 671
    in content management, 688–694
    custom code use in, 376–377
    in default view, 170
    formats for rendering, 747
    graphical, 173
    headers and footers, 178–179, 180
    maintenance process, 426
    managing, 413
    migration strategies, 425–426
    multiple environments, 399–400
    naming conventions, 401
    navigating, 208–210
        with document map, 209–210
    pagination and flow control, 176–178
    parameters, 475–476
    saving, 109
    specifications, 402–406
    URL access for, 467–468
Reports Executed/Sec counter, 739, 740
reports virtual directory, in Web Portal, 743
ReportSchedule database table, 81
ReportServer database, 80–81
    backup and recovery, 725
ReportServer Service object, 736
reportserver virtual directory, for Web service, 743
ReportServerTempDB database, 82
    backup and recovery, 725
ReportService2005.asmx endpoint, 482
ReportService2006.asmx endpoint, 482
ReportService2010 endpoint, 67
ReportServiceAuthentication endpoint, 67
ReportViewer control, 9, 509–519
    embedding server-side report in Windows application, 512–519
    Form_Load event for, 515–519
    report execution scenarios, 511
ReportViewerTasks smart tag panel, 513
Requests Disconnected counter, 739
Requests Executing counter, 739
Requests Not Authorized counter, 739
Requests Rejected counter, 739
Requests Total counter, 739
Requests/Sec counter, 739, 740
requirements, gathering, 406
resources, URLs to access, 467
Response object, rendering to, 503–508
RIGHT() function (Visual Basic), 374
RightIndent property, for text, 188

right-justified text, 212
role-based security, 280
  permissions, 685
roles
  assigning to user or group, 698
  assigning users to, 704–706
  item-level, 703–704
  and SQL databases, 721
  system-level, 721–723
Roles database table, 81
rotation of text, for chart axis, 248
row group, adding totals to, 153
Row group header boundary, 182
Row Groups list, 151, 166
  dragging field into, 161
  fields as groups, 182
row selectors, 104
ROWNUMBER() function, 201
rows in cube
  changing hierarchy, 357
  dynamic, 312–324
  highlighting current, 320–321
  restricting, 353–354
rows in table
  alternating shading, 219
  empty, in MDX Query Designer, 309
rs prefix, for Reporting Services parameters,
    469, 471
RS utility, 710–712
  parameter switches, 712
Rsconfig.exe utility, 65
Rs.exe utility, 65
Rskeymgmt.exe utility, 65, 729
RSMgrPolicy.config file, 72, 730
rspreviewpolicy.config file, 568–569
RSReportDesigner.config file, 568
RSReportServer.config file, 72, 77, 566,
    730, 742
  DeliveryUI section, 746
  Extension entry for unused extensions, 748–749
  Render section, 747
RSSrvPolicy.config file, 72, 567, 730
RunningJobs component, trace messages from, 733
RunningJobs database table, 81
RUNNINGVALUE() function, 201
rv prefix, for Reporting Services parameters,
    469, 470

S

<S> tag (HTML), 190
Sales Summary report

action to navigate, 392, 393
  in Design view, 391
  drill-through actions, 386–392
  ReportData window for, 388, 389
sample reports projects, 144–150
  opening, 147–148
SAP NetWeaver BI, 76
saving
  mobile reports, 636–638, 662
    copies, 585
  reports, 109
scale-out topology, in Native mode, 61
scatter charts, 227
Schedule database table, 81
schedules, shared, in content management, 695–696
Scheduling and Delivery Processor, 80
scope, of dataset, groups and, 200
scorecard, 7
  for KPIs, 437–441
scorecard grid, 587
script injection attacks, preventing, 308
scripts, for content management, 713–714
Secondary Vertical Axis Properties dialog, 247
secondary window, opening drill-through report
    in, 379
Secure Sockets Layer (SSL) certificate, 70, 470
security
  confirming breaking inheritance, 705
  in content management
      item-level security, 697–706
      site security, 697
  Reporting Services and, 478–479
  self-service reporting and, 419
  for server administration, 716–724
      account management, 717–721
      surface area management, 723
      system-level roles, 721–723
  for web portal connection, 686
security extension, 69–70, 523
Select All option, for multi-select parameters, 260
Select Chart Type dialog, 246
Select Country control, filter options for
    properties, 611
Select English QUEry Language (SEQUEL), 115
Select Gauge Type dialog, 442
Select Indicator Type dialog, 440–441
Select Sparkline Type dialog, 446
SELECT statement, multiple, 262
selecting object vs. object name, 147
selection list, 587
  data properties for, 611–612
Selection list control, 588, 604

in Mobile Report Publisher, properties, 633
properties for chart data grid, 656–658
Selector Indicator Type dialog, 301
self-calling drill-through action, 321–322
  invoking, 354
self-service analysts, 5
self-service reporting, 4, 398
  data source and query options, 421–425
    shared data sources, 421–422
  environment planning, 416–425
    data governance, 418–419
    data source access and security, 419
    defining ownership, 417–418
    design approaches and usage scenarios, 416–417
    user education, 419–421
  strategies, and Report Builder, 414–415
semantic data model, 278
SemanticModelGenerator component, trace messages from, 733
SemanticQueryEngine component, trace messages from, 733
sequel, 114–115
series in charts, 237–238
Series Properties dialog, 238, 390, 391
  Axis and Chart Area page, 246, 247
  bubble chart properties, 233, 234
server. *See also* report server; SQL Server
  access, and live mobile connectivity, 647–650
  adding connection, 618–619
  content management, 410–414
    checking deployment location, 411
  installation, 566–567
    security configuration, 567–568
  Property Pages for, 411
  testing mobile report from, 616–620
server administration, 715–751
  backup and recovery, 724–730
    application databases, 725–727
    of configuration files, 730
    encryption keys, 727–729
  configuration, 742–751
    e-mail delivery, 745–747
    memory management, 742–743
    My Reports, 749–751
    rendering extensions, 747–749
    URL reservations, 743–745
  monitoring, 731–742
    execution logs, 735–736
    performance counters, 736–741
    server management reports, 741–742
    setup logs, 731

    trace logs, 732–735
    Windows application event logs, 731
  security, 716–724
    account management, 717–721
    surface area management, 723
    system-level roles, 721–723
Server Properties dialog
  General page, 750
  Logging page, 735–736
server roles, 697
server-side parameters, 479
server-side report, embedding in Windows application, 512–519
service account, 717–718
Service Reference Settings dialog box, 480, 481
SessionData database table, 82
SessionLock database table, 82
Set drillthrough URL dialog, 668
  Available parameters list, 669
setup logs, for monitoring server administration, 731
Setup Wizard, Feature Selection page, Client Tools, 41
shape charts, 227
shape files (.shp) for maps, 592, 671
  opening, 641–642
Shared Data Source Properties dialog, 282
shared data sources, 115–119
  advantages, 145
  in content management, 685–688
  credentials for, 419
  managing, 412
Shared Dataset Properties dialog, Parameters page, 663–664
shared datasets, 120, 401–402, 425
  best practices for, 402
  managing, 413
  for mobile reports, 583, 604–605
  Report Builder for creating, 605–607
  for self-service reports, 421–422
  SSDT for creating, 607
  viewing in web portal, 608
shared schedules, in content management, 695–696
SharePoint
  endpoint parameter, 470
  integration with reports, 10
  managing content in, 413–414
  SSRS integration with, 716
SharePoint Integrated mode, 400, 718
  administrative components, 62
  for Reporting Services, 41, 61, 68
  Reporting Services storage of content and settings, 80

SharePoint libraries, 64–65
SharePoint lists, 18
.shp file. *See* shape files (.shp) for maps
simple data grid, 593
simulated data, for report preview, 601
site branding, 707–709
SizeRule property, 455
sizing, Time navigator, 598
sizing modes for reports, 176
skewing, of charts, 224–225
SL Server 2016 Windows Service object, 736
slicing cubes, 289–290
   WHERE clause for, 297–298
slider, in custom application report, 514
sliding window separator, in Report Designer, 144
SMTP, 746
SnapshotData database table, 81, 82
snapshots, 75
   rendering history, 476–477
Social Security number (SSN), Visual Basic function
   to accept, 376–377
software developers, 6–7
Solution Explorer window, 144
   in Report Designer, 143
   shared datasets in, 401
   Wrox SSRS 2016 Exercises project, 158
Solution name, 142
solutions, 398–407
   project structure and development phases, 399–401
   scope, 403
sorting
   months, 309
   report groups, 155–157
   testing for enabled, 558
source report product textbox, Action expression
   settings, 307–308
sp_change_users_login command, 726
<SPAN> tag (HTML), 190
sparkline, embedded, 443–450
spatial point markers, 454–456
SpatialField property, in SpatialLocation
   field, 455
specialized data management systems, 278
specification document for reports
   formality and detail, 405–406
   reports, 402–406
spreadsheets, 5
SQL, 115
   vs. MDX, 281
   variations, 115
SQL databases, and roles, 721
SQL Server

Developer vs. Enterprise edition, 40
editions, 58
installing local instance, 39
named instance of, connecting to, 121
SQL Server 2000, Reporting Services as add-in tool,
   24
SQL Server 2008 R2, visual elements, 24
SQL Server 2012, in-memory implementation of
   Analysis Services, 11
SQL Server 2016
   changes, 41
   Web Service object, 736
SQL Server Agent job, scheduling, 35
SQL Server Analysis Services (SSAS), 10, 277,
   278–279, 632
   advantages, 302
   best practices for report design, 308–309
   creating, 398–399
   data for Reporting Services, 279–280
   drill-through reports, 307–308
   metadata objects, 287
   moving through hierarchies, 312
   nonadditive measures, 302–305
   parameters, safety precautions, 308
   sample databases, 57
   sample report review, 290
   for simplifying data access, 422
SQL Server Authenticated User option, 719
   creating login for, 720
SQL Server Data Tools (SSDT), 5, 16, 64, 140–150
   opening, 140–141
   Report Designer, 114
   shared data source in, 605, 607
   solutions and projects, 398–407
      key success factors, 402–403
      project structure and development phases,
      399–401
      shared datasets and data sources, 401–402
      templates, 406–407
   Visual Studio downloadable add-in for, 25
SQL Server Database Engine, configuring instance
   of, 51–52
SQL Server Installation Center, 43, 44
SQL Server Integration Services, creating, 398–399
SQL Server Management Studio (SSMS), 41, 65,
   116, 294
   authoring query with, 120–124
   creating site-level roles, 723
   for MDX queries, 267, 281
   New Query button, 294
   Query window, 295
   role permission mapping in, 698

schedule properties in, 696
SQL Server Mobile Report Publisher, 29
SQL Server Pro Magazine, 29
SQL Server Reporting Services Recipes
    (Bruckner), 581
SQL Server Reporting Services (SSRS), 4, 398. *See
    also* Reporting Services (SSRS)
SQL Server setup DVD image, mounted as logical
    drive, 43
SQL Server Setup Wizard, 43
    Collation page, 51
    Database Engine Configuration page, 51, 53
    Disk Space Requirements page, 51
    Feature Configuration Rules page, 53
    Feature Selection page, 48–49
    Global Rules page, 44–45, 46
    Install Setup Files page, 47
    installation page, 44
    Installation Progress page, 53–54
    Instance Configuration pae, 49
    License Terms page, 46
    Product Key page, 46
    Ready to Install page, 53, 54
    Server Configuration page, 51
    Setup Role page, 48
SSAS. *See* SQL Server Analysis Services (SSAS)
SSDT. *See* SQL Server Data Tools (SSDT)
SSMS. *See* SQL Server Management Studio (SSMS)
SSRS. *See also* Reporting Services (SSRS)
SSRS subscription architecture, 35
stacked charts, 228–229
stakeholders
    and report design, 405
    and report requirements, 598
standalone installation, 42
Standard Edition of SQL Server, 40, 58
standard subscriptions, in Reporting Services, 67
Status element for KPI, 624
STDEV() function, 201
STDEVP() function, 201
stock charts, 227, 233
storage space, minimum system requirements, 42
stored procedure, for reports, 421
STRTOMEMBER() function (MDX), 206, 270
    with CONSTRAINED argument flag, 308
STRTOSET function, 270–271, 273
    with CONSTRAINED argument flag, 308
Sub Main code block, in script, 713
Subreport Properties dialog, 207
subreports, 199
    designing, 203–208
    dimensions at design time, 207

federating data with, 205–208
    limitations to content, 204
    uses, 204
subscriptions, 67–68, 689–691
Subscriptions database table, 81
SubString method, 243
subtotal break, creating, 154
Subversion, 407
suite of reports, deployment, 410
SUM function, 112, 123, 155, 201
summarized data, 93
summary report, 8
    aggregate detail row, 167–168
summary totals, 163–167
Sunburst charts, 32–33, 227, 233–235
super reports, 430–435
    Excel export, 431–435
    gauges, 441–443
    interactive sparkline and chart, 443–450
    KPI scorecard, 437–441
    Reporting Services architecture, strengths and
        limitations, 431
surface area management, for server
    administration, 723
swap actions, for Cube Browser report, 354–355
SWITCH function, 374, 443
SyBase, 18
symmetric key, for encryption and decryption, 727
synchronization, of report content, 409–410
System Administrator role, 721–723
system administrators, 7
System Configuration Check Report, 45
system performance, 19–20. *See also* performance
System User role, 721–723
System.Collections.Generic namespace, 545
System.Data namespace, 532
System.IDisposable interface, 524–527
system-level roles, 721–723
    for server administration, 721–723

T

Tableau Desktop, 5
tables, 93, 102
    adding from shared datasets, 609
    adding to mobile report definition, 636
    adding totals to report, 153–154
    design and lay out report, 160–163
    groups in, 151
    headers and footers, repeating headers, 186–187
    heading row, selecting, 107
    inserting, 103–104

inserting columns, 105
interactive sorting, 155
as master/detail container, 196–197
in mobile reports, 604–605
validating name, 555–556
tablets
    alternative layout for, 585
    mobile report for, 28
    screen rotation for, 619–620
tablix
    creating, 325–326
    headers and detail cells, 182
    visualization tweaks, 326
Tablix object, vs. table, for list data region, 192
Tablix Properties dialog, 186
Tablix report, 153
TablixSwap, 354–355
Tagged Image File Format (TIFF), 78
TargetDatasetFolder setting, 411
TargetDataSourceFolder object type, 411
TargetDataSourceFolder property,
    of project, 685
TargetFolder property, of deployment folder, 400
TargetReportFolder object type, 411
TargetReportFolder property, 688
TargetReportPartFolder object type, 411
task-level permissions, 700–702
Tasks Queued counter, 739
TCP port, URL reservation tied to, 744
Team Foundation Services, 142
templates
    for reports, 406–407
    for requirements document, 403–406
Teradata, 18
    extensions, 76
testing
    mobile report navigation, 666
    reports, 426
testing/quality assurance (QA) environment, 400
text
    changing to integer, 131–134
    for chart axis, placement and rotation, 248
    rectangle as container, 192–195
Text Box Properties dialog, 336, 354
    Action page, 379, 388, 390, 392, 393, 449
    Alignment page, 384
text placeholder, MarkupType property for, 190
Text Properties dialog, 190, 323
    Alignment, 318–319
    navigation properties in, 378–379
text query views, switching to, 294
text runs, 366

textbox, 104
    for calculating profit margin, 369
    composite values in, 366
    embedded formatting, 189–195
    expressions and placeholders, 185
    fonts for, 161
    padding and indenting, 188
    unlocking, 187–195
TextboxColHierarchyName, in Cube
    Browser, 357
TextboxDateLabel, 358–360
TextBoxRowHierarchyName, in Cube Browser,
    357
textrun object, 185
threshold alert colors, 219
thumbnail map, with drill-through navigation,
    450–456
TIFF (Tagged Image File Format), 78, 473
TIFF rendering extension, 77
tile layer, of map port, 453
Time chart, in Mobile Report Publisher,
    properties, 635
Time navigator, 587
    data properties for, 610–611
    Data properties panel for, 638
    in mobile report, 598–599, 604
    in Mobile Report Publisher, properties, 633, 634
timeout
    for connection, 542
    for dataset response, 413
time-series calculations, and KPIs, 631–632
title
    adding to header, 212–213
    in Cube Browser report, 355–356
    in footer, 360–362
Titles table, Measure to display, 356
Toolbar parameter, for SharePoint URL, 470
ToolTip property, in Chart Data window, 244, 245
tooltips, for chart value, 248–249
TOPCOUNT function, 326, 329, 354
topology, 60–61
Total Cache Hits counter, 739
Total Cache Misses counter, 740
Total Memory Cache Hits counter, 740
Total Memory Cache Misses counter, 740
total number of pages, 110
Total Processing Failures counter, 740
Total Rejected Threads counter, 740
Total Reports Executed counter, 740
Total Requests counter, 740
totals
    adding to table or matrix report, 153–154

in report groups, 155
Totals chart, 590
touch screen interface, simulation, 601
trace logs, for monitoring server administration, 732–735
    fields, 734–735
TraceFileMode setting, for log configuration, 732
TraceListeners setting, for log configuration, 732
training, for Report Builder, 420
Transact-SQL (T-SQL), 115
    All Value selection, 261–264
    arranging parameters in parameter bar, 259–261
    cascading parameters, 257–259
    conditional logic, 264–266
    generating query, 119
    for KPI dataset, 624–625
    vs. MDX queries, 281
    OR operator, 263
    parameter lists and multi-select, 252–256
    queries
            performance, 20
            result set contents, 305
    UNION statement, WHERE clause, 262–264
Tree map, 227, 233–234
    control, 591
Treemap chart, 32–33
Trend set element, for KPIs, 628
trial-and-error design, for dashboard, 582
trusted subsystem, 479

U

<U> tag (HTML), 190
<UL> tag (HTML), 190
Unattended Execution Account, 686, 721
unattended report processing account, 721
UniqueName property, 307
unlocking textbox, 187–195
URI (Uniform Resource Identifier), 380
URL
    for drill-through report, 379
    navigating to, 379–380
    reservations, 69
    validating, 380
URL access, 462–477
    accessing Reporting Services objects, 463–469
    hard limit on size for HTTP GET request, 475
    passing information through URL, 474–477
    URL parameters, 469–474
    URL syntax, 463
URL parameters
    Command parameter, 471–472

device information settings, 473–474
    Format parameter, 472–473
    prefixes
        rs, 471
        rv, 470
URL reservations
    configuration, 743–745
    for web portal, 680
URLEscapeFragment function, 308
user hierarchy, 286–287
user interaction, 8–9
user interface, creating for parameters, 492
User Role Properties dialog, 704
user-designed reports, reviewing, 425–426
UserID field, 183
username, for server connection, 619
UserName property, of DataSetConnection object, 536–537
users
    accounts, 718
    assigning roles to, 698
    assigning to role, 704–706
    education for self-service reporting, 419–421
    item-level roles, 703–704
    report design for different, 430
    report run by, 361
Users database table, 81
using statement, 482–483

V

ValidateCommandText method, 552–555
ValidateFieldNames method, 556–558
ValidateFiltering method, 558–559
ValidateSorting method, 559
ValidateTableName method, 555–556
validating
    report design, 110–113
    URL, 380
Value field property, 255
    vs. Label field property, 255
VAR() function, 201
VARP() function, 201
VB.NET, vs. C#, interface method declarations, 524
VBScript, 374
version control, 142, 146, 407–409
    getting most recent, 408
    restoring previous version, 409
    setting up, 408
    viewing report history, 409
Vertical Axis Properties dialog, 241–242
view, data access through, 421

View menu, 144
virtual machine, configuration, 42
Visual Basic class library, 374
visual controls for mobile reports, 586–594,
    598–600, 603–604
  charts, 589–591
  data grids, 593–594
  dragging and dropping to layout, 597
  gauges, 588–589
  maps, 591–593
  navigators, 587–588
visual properties, for charts, 640
visual reports. *See also* charts
  design principles, 222–224
Visual Studio, 41. *See also* SQL Server Setup Wizard
  Configuration Manager, 400
  generation of wrapper methods, 525
  interfaces in Class Designer, 533
  for IT-designed reports, 16
  Report Designer add-in, 116
  Reporting Services interfaces in, 525
  SQL Server Data Tools (SSDT) for, 5
  for testing extension project, 572
Visual Studio 2015, 141
Visual Studio Report Designer, 88
Visual Studio SSDT designer, 282
visualization, of data, 223–224
vSalesSummaryYearProduct view, 110

W

Washington State Department of Corrections, 630
Web, rendering reports to, 502–508
  Integrated Windows authentication for, 502
  rendering to Response object, 503–508
  Report Execution Web Service, 503
  web.config file modification, 502–503
web application, incorporating reports into, 8
web browser
  mobile report displayed in, 579
  rendering, 26
  standardiZed rendering, 33
Web edition of SQL Server, 58
web parts, 64–65
Web Portal, 11–12, 41, 55, 64, 70–71
  application downloads, 683
  Browse view, 681–682
  configuring URL reservation for, 745
  for content management, 680–683
  content menu in, 32
  default, 462
  Favorites view, 680–681

Home folder, setting options, 682
  improvements, 31
  IP address for, 649
  on iPhone, 13
  KPIs in, 629
  menu bar, 684
  mobile report creation from, 594
  mobile report name in tiles view, 665
  path for, 96
  Report Properties page, 689
  reports virtual directory in, 743
  shared datasets viewed in, 608
Web portal KPI Designer, 17
web reference, creating, 486
Web Service Description Language (WSDL), 711
Web Services, 70–71
  endpoints, 711
  setting up, 480–485
Web technologies, 7
web.config file, 730
  modification, 502–503
WHERE clause, 135, 136
  dynamic replacment of parameter, 267
  for MonthList dataset, 265–266
  for slicing cubes, 297–298
  to test query parameter, 264
whisker graphs, 227
white space, 188
  in charts, 249
  in visual design, 223
width, of chart series line, 248
WiFi network, for connecting to mobile report, 618
window, pop-up, JavaScript function for, 380
Window Management Instrumentation (WMI),
    72–73
Windows, programmatic rendering through,
    479–501
  application interface, 479–480
  rendering report to file, 495–501
  retrieving information, 485–490
  retrieving parameters for report, 490–494
  web services set up, 480–485
Windows application event logs, for monitoring
    server administration, 731
Windows Authentication, 100, 280
Windows domain user accounts, 717
Windows form, for application interface, 479–480
Windows Forms applications
  controls for, 66
  project template, 513
Windows Installer, 43
Windows Integrated Authentication, 479, 502, 570